ISBN 978-1-334-36466-2
PIBN 10732746

1 MONTH OF
FREE
READING

at

www.ForgottenBooks.com

By purchasing this book you are eligible for one month membership to ForgottenBooks.com, giving you unlimited access to our entire collection of over 1,000,000 titles via our web site and mobile apps.

To claim your free month visit: www.forgottenbooks.com/free732746

English
Français
Deutsche
Italiano
Español
Português

www.forgottenbooks.com

Mythology Photography **Fiction**
Fishing Christianity **Art** Cooking
Essays Buddhism Freemasonry
Medicine **Biology** Music **Ancient**
Egypt Evolution Carpentry Physics
Dance Geology **Mathematics** Fitness
Shakespeare **Folklore** Yoga Marketing
Confidence Immortality Biographies
Poetry **Psychology** Witchcraft
Electronics Chemistry History **Law**
Accounting **Philosophy** Anthropology
Alchemy Drama Quantum Mechanics
Atheism Sexual Health **Ancient History**
Entrepreneurship Languages Sport
Paleontology Needlework Islam
Metaphysics Investment Archaeology
Parenting Statistics Criminology
Motivational

FAMILY EDITION.

THE

POETICAL WORKS AND LETTERS

OF

ROBERT BURNS,

WITH COPIOUS MARGINAL EXPLANATIONS OF
THE SCOTCH WORDS,

AND LIFE.

𝕰𝖎𝖌𝖍𝖙 𝕰𝖓𝖌𝖗𝖆𝖇𝖎𝖓𝖌𝖘 𝖔𝖓 𝕾𝖙𝖊𝖊𝖑.

𝕰𝖉𝖎𝖓𝖇𝖚𝖗𝖌𝖍:
GALL & INGLIS, 6 GEORGE STREET.

1859

LIFE OF ROBERT BURNS.

ROBERT BURNS was born on the 25th of January 1759, in a small roadside cottage, which still stands, about a mile and a-half inland from the county-town and bay of Ayr, on the south-western Scottish coast. His father was from the north, the son of a small farmer, but after various independent struggles to get on in other places, had at least gained by experience, and settled down as working-gardener to a gentleman who showed him the kindness of a patron. He was still a poor man, occupying the rank of a peasant, in a thatched hut, built by his own hands; though with all the intelligence and more than the ordinary integrity of his class, still hopeful of raising himself. The mother belonged to the same station, being a farmer's daughter from the neighbour-hood, homely, placid, careful, and of the average education for her degree; looking up to her husband as, what he really was, strong in character, shrewd from knowledge of the world and its trials, an industrious, thoughtful, devout man. In William Burness and Agnes Brown, their first son had at all events the advantage of parents who were models of excellence for their condition in life; and if his childhood was literally that of a peasant, born to toil, there were, as has been well remarked by his last and most adequate biographer, "fortunate circumstances in his position." What part these fortunate circumstances must have had in raising him to conspicuousness above every other peasant who has yet lived,—and what part in his lot was unpropitious,—it may be a main object of the following sketch to suggest, while as much as possible separating both these considerations from the merit and the fault which were his own.

The father's wish to procure, for all his children, the best education which his means allowed, was characteristic even beyond the usual Scottish desire. Robert was sent in his sixth year to a small school at Alloway Mill, about a mile off; but the anxiety for his instruction was not easily satisfied, and William Burness soon took the chief part in bringing to the immediate vicinity a young man whom he knew, to teach his own along with the neighbours' children, at once more ably, and, doubtless, more under hints from parental notice. Burness himself was a thinking, reading man, with views of his own even on points of orthodoxy : he ruled his family with a firm hand, attentive to every detail of their conduct; nor need it be specially inferred from the household priesthood of the " Cottar's Saturday Night," how their progress in the Shorter Catechism and Bible knowledge was directly seen to, at leisure hours or stated intervals.

But the early tutor of Burns and of his next brother, Gilbert, deserves particular mention, as having contributed no slight share among the favourable influences, mental if not moral, which were then profited by. John Murdoch was no common pedagogue, having already, at the age of eighteen, begun to apply improved methods of teaching, afterwards developed by him in publication. He saw the germs of solid ability in the elder of the two boys, making him a favourite pupil, though fancying Gilbert the livelier. He was careful to impress the precise meaning of every word, and, to prevent mere learning by rote, made them frequently turn passages of verse into natural prose order. Among his branches of education was that of vocal psalmody; with regard to which Robert was peculiarly dull, and his attempts tuneless. Murdoch, for his own improvement, subsequently began to learn French, and imparted the benefit of his proficiency to young Burns ; he became afterwards, also, the instigator to his acquiring some Latin : in the former of which accomplishments the poet somewhat plumed himself in later life.

The positive amount of imparted and regular scholarly learning he possessed in the end was not great, indeed, as distinguished from knowledge acquired at random, by unguided effort; yet Shakspeare had scarcely greater, allowing a good deal for a darker age, which was in reality more alive to classical influence. The chief difference seems to have lain in the Scotch peasant's self-educating disadvantages, his poorer country, and the less generous time on which he was cast; under impulses less sustained by common sympathy, less tending to direct emolument, and less accustomed to indulgence or balanced by a view to success in the world. Conceivable ambition of that kind was not very high near Ayr, before steam-engines worked, or profitable books were common, where the drama had never flourished ; and such ambition did not so much as enter into the minds of William Burness and John Murdoch, whose teaching combined but two objects,—present fitness to take up a farm, or perhaps enter the parochial ministry, and future welfare in another world. Nor can the merit be added to Murdoch's side, that he even insisted on blending the two harmoniously: his intellectual creed might quite agree with that of his humble patron, yet most undoubtedly his practice did not. Having obtained a better situation, and come to spend his farewell night, he brought, among other parting gifts—what the father would infallibly have forbidden had he known more of general literature—the *Titus Andronicus* of Shakspeare, which Murdoch began to read aloud. It is curious that Robert was then the chief objector to this work of an earlier prodigy; soon stubbornly threatening, if it were left, to burn it for the savage element of tragedy it displayed ; whereupon the tutor, declaring that he liked such sensibility, defended his pupil from all charge of ingratitude, and left a French comedy, the *School for Love*, instead.

Mr Murdoch not long afterwards resumed his preceptorship, when elected English teacher at Ayr, whither Robert was sent for a short period, between times of field-work; though the former was eventually obliged to resign his place, from the consequences of disrespectful language on his part when " one evening overtaken in liquor," about the parish minister. But the father himself took up the educational duty when otherwise unfulfilled ; even mingling it with the joint labour required by a small farm, now entered on through assistance from his kind employer. This change was still with a view to keep his children under his own eye, until, to use the son's own words, " they could decern between good and evil;" and in order that, continuing in their peasant station, they might not be " marched off to be among the little underlings about a farm-house." The lease of a farm on the master's estate had been ventured on, to justify which needed every effort from them all; while, as they accompanied him at work, he " was at great pains to lead the conversation to such subjects as might tend to increase our knowledge, or confirm us in virtuous habits." Books were borrowed by him for their behoof, chiefly containing scientific information. From Stackhouse's *History of the Bible,* taken in by parts, " Robert collected," says his brother, " a competent knowledge of ancient history ; for no book was so voluminous as to slacken his industry, or so antiquated as to damp his researches." And let one notable trait be included in the picture of the father, to whom, above all, was owing, probably, what was most ethereal and heaven-born in the mingled product of Burns's genius : taking it from the authority of that more worldly source, Mr Murdoch, whose respect for William Burness seems to have approached affection. " I think I never saw him angry but twice ; the one time it was with the foreman of the band for not reaping the field as he was desired ; and the other time it was with an old man for using smutty inuendoes and *double entendres*. Were every foul-mouthed old man to receive a seasonable check in this way, it would be to the advantage of the rising generation. * * * I shall only add, that he carefully practised every known duty, and avoided everything that was criminal; or, in the apostle's words, *Herein did he exercise himself, in living a life void of offence towards God and towards men.* Oh for a world of men of such dispositions !"

Robert Burns had other teachers, too; teachers of that secret and congenial kind who have most to do with the poetic training. The facts above given, indeed, with a few irregular ekings-out at odd times, comprehend the whole of his formal schooling; which was both small and short, compared with the average in Scotland for his own rank. But in his infant and boyish days, as he has told us, he "owed much to an old woman who resided in the family, remarkable for her ignorance, credulity, and superstition; she had, I suppose, the largest collection in the country of tales and songs concerning devils, ghosts, fairies, brownies, witches, warlocks, spunkies, kelpies, elf-candles, dead-lights, wraiths, apparitions, cantraips, giants, enchanted towers, dragons, and other trumpery. This cultivated the latent seeds of poetry, but had so strong an effect on my imagination, that to this hour, in my nocturnal rambles, I sometimes keep a sharp look-out in suspicious places; and though nobody can be more sceptical than I am in such matters, yet it often takes an effort of philosophy to shake off these idle terrors.". From this catalogue of legendary wonders and terrors—enumerated so superciliously, with such a superior air of eighteenth-century knowledge and of contempt for the humble instrument, poor Betty Davidson, whose mirthful temperament made her a great favourite with the children—there is plainly obvious a defect of the constructive instinct as well as of the reverent spirit, aggravated by the period he lived in, and characteristic of his works on the whole; though not incompatible with lingering side-glances of association or humour, as admirably exemplified in "Tam O'Shanter." He seldom attempted any composition depending for its interest on the story, or upon the historical basis. His preference of the lyric to the ballad, and his subjection to single strong impulses, rather than his mastery of varied tendencies; with the slighting opinion he has critically expressed as to fine relics of the old Border minstrelsy, now admired; all bear out the view which his life impresses,—that if Burns's self-education had less over-balanced the authoritative training he received, or could that age have remedied the want by any one prevalent idea, he would in all likelihood have been a more perfect poet, and a steadier, happier, better man. Even political excitement came too late for him. The great Revolutionary movement could not yet influence his earlier time of youth, to form him, as it almost certainly would have done, into the truest and most ardent of poets for the people—the only inspired voice to herald Radicalism wisely and gradually, or save its martyrs from being wasted; and his gifts were destined to be scattered on innumerable stray objects, his fine ecstasy to be lavished without proportion to the cause, his fiery energy to be spent, squandered, and made a curiosity, with artificial revivals and refreshments of it that were yet more pitiable.

The first book he read in private, besides the few school-manuals, was *The Life of Hannibal*, lent him by his young teacher; the next, *The History of Sir William Wallace*, borrowed from a neigh-bouring blacksmith. Both " gave him more pleasure than any two books he ever read after ;" the first arousing martial enthu-siasm ;" the second " poured a Scottish prejudice into my veins, which will boil along there till the flood-gates of life shut in eternal rest." Addison soon became a favourite author ; so, among others, borrowed from various sources, did Pope, Homer in trans-lation, and Allan Ramsay. An odd volume of English history, a collection of Letters, Locke's celebrated *Essay*, Taylor *On Original Sin, The Ready Reckoner*, Hervey's *Meditations among the Tombs*, the *Spectator*, and a " Select Collection of English Songs—*The Lark*," were the chief works in that little medley which opened the world of letters to Robert Burns's early life. He made *The Lark* his *vade mecum* which " he pored over, driving his cart, or walking to labour—song by song, verse by verse—carefully noting (what he thought) the true, tender, or sublime, (as distinguished) from affectation and fustian."

Then there was still another extra-academical teacher, most important of all. For the same blacksmith who lent the *Life of Wallace* possessed also a daughter of fourteen, who, coming to help the harvest of the Burnesses hard by, when the eldest son was " in my fifteenth autumn," became his partner on the corn-rig. Nelly Kilpatrick by name, a " *bonnie, sweet, sonsie* lass," unwittingly to herself initiated him, he has said, in that delicious passion he was to feel so often, and so to raise above its objects, and to have so dangerous a power of communicating. She sang a song, made by a country laird's son on one of his father's maids, and its air caught upon the tuneless ear which Mr Murdoch had found so dull ; for the voice was sweet among the banded reapers, with their sounding hooks, before the rustling fall of corn ; so that he saw no reason for not rhyming too, to the same tune, about a different subject ; and he strung his first song in honour of Nelly's charms. Afterwards he thought it " very puerile and silly ;" but his heart never failed on that account " to melt, and his blood to sally at the remembrance of the cause itself. To others, at times, he " was not a popular character,"—a "rude and clownish *solitaire*,"—obliged to share the hardship and toil incurred by the father for his family's sake ; doing the work of a man, though a boy in years ; his naturally robust frame having no generous diet to nourish it, his shoulders beginning to stoop already, a

nervous disorder to affect his heart, the unsocial habits required
by economy bringing moodiness on his brow.

With the song and the harvest seem to have ended all care for
the simple blacksmith's daughter; and the embryo time itself
was ended, with almost all the teaching he was to receive from
other instructors than Nature and his own experience. In oppo-
sition even to his father's wishes, however, "he gave his manners
a brush" at a country dancing-school: the elder Burns was strong in
his antipathies, and sometimes in his anger, against which the son
had nevertheless in this case persevered. This he deeply repented
in later years; afterwards tracing, to a sort of dislike to himself for
that disobedience, a main cause of "the dissipation which marked
my succeeding years." The vicinity to Ayr soon furnished a social
attraction, or allowed of easy resort for juvenile debating. He
spent the evenings in the way after his own heart; adding, to
rustic courtships of his own, a confidantship in "half the loves
of the parish of Tarbolton." "Early ingrained piety and virtue
kept" him for several years, however, "within the line of inno-
cence." "The great misfortune of my life was to want an aim.
I had felt early some stirrings of ambition, but they were the blind
gropings of Homer's Cyclops round the walls of his cave."

The farm had been so unproductive as to involve the whole
family in distress; and although William Burness succeeded in
obtaining another, with better expectations of the result, at Loch-
lea, near Tarbolton, yet the speculation turned out in the end still
more disastrous. The change for Robert was at least advanta-
geous, so far as regarded an alteration of local scenery, wilder and
more marked in character; as well as new neighbours, and fresh
opportunities of gaining knowledge, or comparing it with that of
others in the same circumstances. During this period he acquired
some of the elements of mathematics, and associated with a young
men's club at Tarbolton, where he ultimately became a Free-
Mason. His understanding and power of argument were deve-
loped as vigorously as his fancy or sentiment, and by more rapid
degrees. When roused to emotion on a subject, he could over-
whelm an antagonist by a voluble force of language which aston-
ished the hearers; while at the same time, occasional effusions in
verse were handed about, from his growing practice with the pen,
and produced a considerable reputation in the district. Elegant
letter-writing began to be a favourite branch of his leisure pur-
suits—on the model of Queen Anne's reign—to regular corre-
spondents whose replies he encouraged, that he might keep them
beside copies of his own epistles, for careful comparison or improve-
ment; and he "carried this whim so far, that though I had not
three farthings' worth of business in the world, yet almost every
post brought me as many letters as if I had been a broad plodding
son of day-book and ledger." Thus life passed till his twenty-

third year, which he calls an important era; as at that time he tried actual business for himself as a flax-dresser, in partnership with another. The attempt failed, apparently from misconduct of his partner, followed by a fire in the shop at a New-Year carousal. Misfortune was pressing his father to the earth at Lochlea; and the death of the good old man, by a slow decline, after so many years of trouble without success, removed him, at all events, from the evil to come; for the family affairs were now involved in utter ruin, so far as the Lochlea farm was concerned.

On his father's death, Robert Burns joined his brother Gilbert in taking the farm of Mossgiel, mainly in order to provide for their widowed mother and the orphan family of five younger children. On this honourable enterprise Robert entered with resolute purpose to be wise; reading agricultural books, calculating crops, and attending markets. Mossgiel will ever be, indeed, illustrious ground to the classic memories of Scotland, intimately associated as it is with the most brilliant period of poetic development in him who there

> " Walked in glory and in joy,
> Following his plough upon the mountain-side.

At Mossgiel were rapidly produced a large proportion of those genuine native strains by which his fame was earned, and in which is specially unfolded the most original trait of his genius— a feature almost new to poetry in general, that has especially influenced our literature through Wordsworth and his school. We mean, above all, its sympathetic tenderness for dumb life or obscure beauty in nature and the lower creatures, as sharers and companions in human emotion. Common enough now, and apparently easy, this is, of all Burns' characteristics, the most his own. It could scarce have occurred, even to him, but as the feeling of a peasant-farmer struggling against difficulty, holding his own plough, and occupying that doubtful place between master and servant. The elegy on " Poor Mailie " alone, of all these memorable productions referred to, had been previously composed at Lochlea, while his father lived. It was at Mossgiel he spared the "Field-Mouse," turned up the "Daisy," wrote the "Twa Dogs," saluted his "Auld Mare Maggie" in verse, and hit off various other kindred felicities in that track, from the comic or satirical to the deepest pathos. The vein lay unaffectedly deep in him, capable of the most unexpected application; as when it became touchingly patriotic beside a weed in his refractory soil, the national thistle that helped to roughen his career:—

> " I turned the weeder-clips aside,
> And spared the symbol dear."

Here also were written many of his best-known love songs and more elaborate attempts, accumulating beside him without defined purpose to use them further; while other events took their course, so as to complicate the family misfortunes with his own. Polemical divinity in the neighbourhood was embittered by contests between the more zealous Presbyterianism of old time, and the softened latitudinarian doctrine of that day. The clerical adherents of the latter party, often of good family if not of learned pursuits, were characterized by liberal opinions and by social good-breeding, with still more social habits. They partook of contemporary taste, with its supposed philosophical views and elegant manners. In Ayr-shire, however, this moderatism, as it has been called, was not content with negatives; it put forth a counter-zeal of its own, in favour of what became known as the " New Light," a milder form of orthodoxy, combined with subdued continental rationalism. To this, at least in the theological branch of it, old Burness, the father of the poet, had so far leant, through a natural kindness at heart, as to embody it in a private doctrinal manual for domestic use : nor was it wonderful, otherwise, that Robert Burns, when beginning to gain reputation in argument as well as for a poetical turn, at once sided actively with the best-lettered party, thereby drawing prejudice against himself from the devouter one. To this step, with the consequent attacks and retaliations, might be traced not merely the after dislike of sincere piety to his works as a whole, but much of the unhappiness in his own later life and lot, which deepened that evangelical odium. In reality, being afterwards left behind by profound national tendencies, the " Mo-derates " proved but a broken reed for his help, if not a positive injury to his self-development and final culture. A worldly light, shed in great measure from them and their *dilettante* circle, now obsolete, has too long deterred many readers, in all classes from acquaintance with his poems, or from assuming but a tacit and broken enjoyment of them.

One secret, personal reason there was, no doubt, additional to all else, why he came to favour the less rigid and easier party in re-ligion ; unless their looser system of ethics had already exercised a *previous* influence upon him. *New Light* indulgence, perhaps, may have led earlier still to his estrangement from those who pro-fessed the morals of the New Testament ; so as to have directly in-clined him to the conduct, which would *afterwards*, no doubt, still more identify him with the less pious school. While at Mossgiel, he had privately formed an irregular connection with a young woman named Jean Armour, daughter of a Mauchline mason; the marriage laws of Scotland having been, however, formally proceeded upon in writing between them. The consequences could no longer be concealed ; yet the father's decision was, to have the acknowledged contract made void, apparently because of Burns's doubtful pro-spects. Yielding to this stubborn resolution, he nevertheless felt the utmost distress ; and in that mood, despairing of all other expectations, gave up his part in the farm to his brother Gilbert, a coadjutor of steadier impulse and no ordinary practical intelligence. His intention was to leave his native country for the West Indies, where fortune might be kinder than at home. Destitute of money for the passage, he was now advised to raise it by having his stock of verses printed for subscribers, who came forward so far as to ensure a sale of about 350 copies ; and the small volume of " Poems, chiefly Scottish," accordingly appeared at Kilmarnock in 1786, when the author was twenty-seven. His poverty had stood his friend for once. The success of the publication was so great as to prevent further thoughts of exile ; and Burns remained to gain greater glory, and to err and suffer longer, till the close.

From this stage of a strange story must not be omitted one singular episode belonging to Mossgiel, which shows its complex woof of light and shade more curiously yet, nay, with still deeper significance. Before and along with his warm passion for Jean Armour, his future wife,—whose choice denotes the coarser grain in his composition,—he had carried on a gentler affection, evidently less intense at the time, for another young woman in even humbler rank, a maid-servant at a gentleman's house adjacent—Mary Campbell, from the Celtic shire of Argyle. " Highland Mary" may be regarded, from all that seems to have passed, as both the purer in her instincts and the truer in her love of the two ; for Jean Armour gave him up, despite of all that had happened, and, until then, the other appears but a casual affair, no further carried than his pledges to a rival might allow. When fixed on his voyage, he turned, in his desertion, to Mary Campbell, who agreed to share his forsaken and solitary fortunes. Probably knowing the substance of Jean Armour's case, indeed, but trusting him for her own part, when he was clear from other obligations, she yet clung to Highland faith and superstition. She stood first apart from him, beyond a running stream, over which they pledged their troth together, a Bible clasped in the hands of each, before she went home across the water to Campbelton, to tell her friends and prepare her marriage things ; but taking fever on the way, at Greenock, died unseen by him. In his monument at Brig of Doon, the two small volumes of that Bible are showr yet, in a glass case, with her name in his faded hand-writing, the sacred text grown fainter, while a tress of her golden hair lies pale yet unchanged beside it. Jean Armour soon became his lawful wife, faithful to him, commemorated in more than one melodious lyric ; tending his sad death-hours, and surviving him, the mother of his children. To her he continued the lower part of his regard, amidst many deviations : but if Mary had lived to marry him, it is possible that her influence might have been better. At all events, she possessed his memory for ever, in a way more ethereal and like angelic pleading, than as a mere phantasm of sentiment. His purest sense of guileless love was in the song named from her ; and one evening

after work, far off at Ellisland, when the exciseman's office had
been added to his farming toil, when the uproarious contest for
" the Whistle" had been decided and celebrated, the anniversary
of that parting found his remembrance. Jean missed him at the
supper-board, and came out to seek him about the harvest stacks.
He lay upon a mass of straw, silently eying the evening-star, with
thoughts he did not tell to her. It was to " Mary in Heaven"
that his thoughts had tended, downcast, dissatisfied, full of anguish
and gathered-up regret ; nor might the few natural tears shed by
his wife, when she read them, be free from some secret bitterness.
For the stamp of the women whom Burns knew, or had opportunity
to love, had undoubtedly a main effect on his license and his
fickleness. It was in that, as much as in anything, that the dis-
advantage of his origin lay ; seeing how low in rural Scotland,
under that particular age, with its low unspiritual training, had
sunk feminine self-respect and moral or intellectual culture. It
may well be maintained, too, that the tendency of his poetry on
the whole was, however unconsciously, to neutralize and cure such
an evil, by elevating his fancied charmers, when he sang of them,
at least : so that if he himself could not have Beatrices, Imogens,
even Clarindas,-to inspire awe amidst the admiration they attract-
ed, he would yet teach his fellow-countrywomen afterwards to de-
serve his praises, adding one charm to their list, whencesoever
to be derived—the charm of virtue.

Burns' introduction to society and its honours in Edinburgh,
especially while superintending a second edition, brought him
fresh temptations ; from which, indeed, praise, curiosity, invita-
tions, conviviality, and attempted patronage, did not prevent his
emerging with renewed independence of spirit, and a sturdy disdain
for artificial influences. Yet some natural inflation, as well as in-
fection by the fashionable tone, with its relaxed private principles,
was undoubtedly the result. Expectations of material benefit,
such as some permament post of easy duties might have supplied,
without demeaning or exposing him to moral danger, were excited
merely to be unfulfilled.

A second edition, with additions and improvements, was now
issued with increased success ; from Edinburgh itself, with all its
literary influence to back him. After paying all expenses of repub-
lication, he found himself master of nearly £500 ; with which, hav-
ing made a short tour southward to extend his knowledge of the
country, he then took a farm at Ellisland, near Dumfries ; besides
advancing almost half his money to aid his brother Gilbert, still
struggling at Mossgiel. He now took up house, as a married man,
with a family already growing; and he set to for another endeavour
in life, by no means ill-furnished for it, when conscious of fresh
sources in his own mind and pen. Yet it may be easily conceived
how the local circle at Dumfries were inclined to caress and asso-

ciate with him, inducing the resumption of habits that had a fair chance of breaking off, if at all. A yet more unhappy chance was his want of confidence in those very gifts which had raised him; leading to an application for the post of district exciseman, as a help to the farm. The two occupations were, in truth, essentially incompatible; either for pecuniary success in the one, or for rising, by full attention in the other, to a higher office. Field-labour was often left to servants alone, while Burns, as country *gauger*, too glad to rove about, or meet with incident and odd character, pursued the defaulters of revenue throughout Nithsdale. Even when solicited to aid in a " Select Collection of Original Scottish Airs for the Voice," projected by Mr George Thomson in Edinburgh, and consenting to the work, he disdained remuneration with the loftiness of one who would not sell his art; afterwards contributing also to another similar publication, on terms of the same ill-judged superiority to prudence, which were congenial to the elegant literary notions of his day.

Burns *did* now deliberately form resolutions against dissipation, with a matured consciousness of what was right and prudent. Yet intemperance of the kind to which middle age is most prone became now increasingly the same bane to him, as during his youth had been recklessness of another kind. As in the one error there had been a germ of better action, seldom aided by corresponding strength in other persons; so in this, his disposition to excess was neither a morbid craving nor a mere sensual indulgence. Society, as then constituted, made itself fatal to him, in greater proportion than to common men; for in society—in human intercourse and the contact of wit or feeling—Burns found his chief delight. It grew to be the very stimulus to his flagging fancy, or to his lack of subject, when love had ceased to have the old charm; but it is worth noting, that he at least could not be contented with the gross nature of bacchanalian enjoyment, nor be dragged down to its vulgarities. In his prime he had a vigour and glow of intellect which almost transformed this indulgence into something better; till, as it told on his own strength and purpose, its worst issue was to show him striving for the former light and the recollected force through its adventitious help. That, if time had remained to Burns, he must ultimately have sunk into the more pitiable condition of a sot, dependent even in solitude on such stimulants for any lucid interval, is undoubted; but the fire burned too fast within to delay his fate. At more than one drinking-bout for the prize of strongest toper, it was dimly noticed by his yielding rivals that he ceased to drink in proportion as the dialogue ceased, and when the excitement of intercourse was at an end, the spell for him had gone. He sometimes departed like the scornful leader of inferior natures, who were unable to follow him longer; and, once, with a clear recollection of everything, sitting by impartial, even un-

participating, he turned the whole into a wild but masterly pæan
of superiority to his associates or his tempters, a thing which
would help to shame after-generations into common-sense. His
power of self-control for an object seems thus to have been great.
In the presence of a refined or dignified person he was able to
refrain, showing himself equal to the most cultivated discourse ;
and although his blame is in one aspect deeper, the more is it to
be lamented that he had not companions nearer the level of his
own mind. It must not be forgotten, neither, that the earlier
drinking-songs and anacreontics which were supplanted by his
brilliant outbursts, like the old love-ditties superseded by his
strains of living passion, had little before, but their music, to raise
them above our contempt. He could still retire within himself, to
endure sharper self-reproach, more bitter remorse for wasted or
misdirected powers, than cool criticism can now advance against
him ; and was not so forsaken by his better angel, but that, lifting
an upward eye of confession and humiliation, he now deplored
that taint of licence and unfaithfulness in the chief lyrical suc-
cesses he had before accomplished ; for Dante himself never bowed
more awfully before his sainted vision of one illustrious on earth,
than when Burns groaned forth melodious agony to a mere
memory of simple worth and faith,—in her who had best proved
her love to him, and least yielded up its virtue, whom he could
think of as then before their God—the subject of those exquisite
lines, then written, " To Mary in Heaven."

Here, at Ellisland, he still threw off many of his most vigorous
poems, among which the most remarkable is " Tam o' Shanter,"
a work almost perfect of its kind, gathering within brief limits a
whole mythology of native superstition, with a social and domestic
moral, on no broader foundation than " the dull lie of a drunkard
dotard." This was something truly unique in literature, with
more than the Saxon household humour of Cowper's " John Gil-
pin," and all the Scandinavian wildness of Bürger's "Leonore,"
added to homely Scottish pawkiness. It was one quickly-shifting
flight of the most genuine imagination, half-real, half-dreamlike,
rendered artfully plausible by the drunken consciousness ; while,
over-arched by the true poetic wisdom, which fails not, amidst its
most hideous midnight conjuring, to let down a sky-gleam of pity
and morality—

> " Ah! little kenned thy reverend grannie,
> That sark she coft for her wee Nanny,
> Wi' twa Scots punds ('twas a' her riches),
> Wad ever graced a dance o' witches!"

Different, indeed, from the wild remembrances of the " Cottar's
Saturday Night," with its humble goodness, somewhat heavily
and awkwardly rendered up, by a genius less matured at Mossgiel.
Yet " Alloway's auld haunted kirk," near the paternal cottage,

and the tributary monument at Brig of Doon, remains lifted
beyond the seeming profanation, when no longer used for direct
service, by its significance in the hazy brain of home-riding
gossips, who may thus mount the earlier for a vivid thought of

" The lang Scots miles,
The mosses, waters, slaps, and stiles,
That lie between us and our hame,"—

with that distinct picture of the solitary sitter there—

" Our sulky, sullen dame,
Gathering her brows like gathering storm,
Nursing her wrath to keep it warm."

His gifts had, indeed, been what he once represented them, him-
self, to be,—a Muse from above, higher-born and higher-tending
than many things in his personal life: as has been more or less the
case with all genius, in some form or another. It was at this period
that he caught some influence from political ideas, then circulated
by revolutionary zeal; and although known before, and naturally
enough, as a Jacobite, Burns quite as naturally partook now of
the enthusiasm for liberty and rights of man. A fresh vein in his
poetical instinct discovered itself as the result; which has since
been often put to use by later writers for the people, without giving
such offence in higher quarters; though to no one could it have
been so genuine an effect of experience and temper, as with him,
to express first and most forcibly a sense of manhood as the
proudest title to respect, of self-reliance as the surest human
strength, free speech and independent action as a common right.
Toil and trial had enabled him at once to see beyond current
excitement, not only to the dignity of labour, but to the truth
that freedom is the best bond of classes: he could sing even then—

" For a' that, and a' that,
It's coming yet for a' that,
That man to man, the warld o'er,
Shall brothers be for a' that !"

Yet in ordinary talk among his neighbours he uttered opinions
which were thought dangerous; and information being given to
his superiors, the Board of Excise, an inquiry was instituted.
The result was rather favourable on the whole, but not such as
to reinstate him in the good opinion of the Commissioners; interest
was necessary even to retain him in his office; and his promotion,
being deferred, had to depend on future behaviour. The adequate
and secure competency of a collectorship receded into remoter
distance from his hopes, till something like irritability seems to
have mingled with the gloom of undermined health and prolonged
struggle.

Little has been said here of his continued fondness for letter-
writing, enhanced by correspondence with persons in higher sta-
tion; especially with several of those superior women, ladies by

birth and in education, whom his maturer standard of female excellence prompted him to celebrate or address. Friendship began to substitute itself, perhaps, for a warmer feeling in his heart; and his numerous letters are full of this calmer, more satisfactory, and permanent enjoyment. In these are to be found, however, the detached traces of his singular relation to "Clarinda," Mrs M'Lehose, a woman of considerable intellect, and at the same time much sensibility; which bears an interest half romantic, partly Platonic, as connected with one who might possibly have been a fit partner for the poet. Known to him before his final union to Jean Armour, " Clarinda" then corresponded with him in an ardent style, which yet did not prevent his becoming the husband of the former. The letters were of that high-flown character, to a great extent, which " sometimes does not so much reveal passion as mask indifference ;" and they were afterwards occasionally added to. The truth may have been, that in such directions did Burns attempt to compensate to his superior nature for the disadvantage it had suffered by a position in life, such as society could never allow him to overpass. His epistolary compositions have the mark, so seldom visible in his genuine addresses, of being a work of elaboration and calculated effect · the styles of other writers, the circumstances of a different class, are too often before him in producing them ; and he had there greater room for the would-be elegances, the smart affectations, the supposed concealments of pedantry or rusticity, which a poet, whose glory was in his truth to experience and nature, could never hide upon a drawing-room carpet, when neither doing his appointed work nor following his chosen art. Nevertheless, they display great " merit as the effusions of a very uncommon mind, enriched with knowledge far beyond what could have been reasonably expected in his situation ; for he appears to have cultivated English prose with care, and certainly wrote it with a sprightly fluency."

His career had no further stage to develop. In the month of June, 1796, he had to try the effects of sea-bathing on the coast near Dumfries; a remedy which at first seemed to relieve a rheumatic affection of the limbs. After his return home, however, a fever succeeded, attended with delirium and debility ; under the effects of which, sedulously tended by Mrs Burns, he expired on the 21st July, in his thirty-eighth year. The funeral was accompanied with military honours, on the ground of loyal connection with a local volunteer force, to the churchyard of Dumfries, where his remains were interred. He left a widow and four sons, for whose benefit subscriptions were required at the time, and were extended to England; although the subsequent profits of his own works, with the excellent Life by Dr Currie, assisted the surviving members of his family to ultimate independence and professional honour.

CONTENTS.

SONGS.

INDEX OF FIRST LINES.

THE COTTER'S SATURDAY NIGHT.

INSCRIBED TO ROBERT AIKEN, ESQ

Let not ambition mock their useful toil,
Their homely joys and destiny obscure;
Nor grandeur hear, with a disdainful smile,
The short and simple annals of the poor.—GRAY.

My loved, my honoured, much respected friend!
No mercenary bard his homage pays;
With honest pride, I scorn each selfish end:
My dearest meed, a friend's esteem and praise.
To you I sing, in simple Scottish lays,
The lowly train in life's sequester'd scene;
The native feelings strong, the guileless ways;
What Aiken in a cottage would have been;
Ah! though his worth unknown, far happier there, I ween!

November chill blaws loud wi' angry sugh;   whistle
The short'ning winter-day is near a close;
The miry beasts retreating frae the pleugh;
The black'ning trains o' craws to their repose: crows
The toil-worn cotter frae his labour goes,
This night his weekly moil is at an end,
Collects his spades, his mattocks, and his hoes,
Hoping the morn in ease and rest to spend,
And weary o'er the moor, his course does hameward bend.

At length his lonely cot appears in view,
Beneath the shelter of an aged tree;
Th' expectant wee things, toddlin', stacher through   stagger
To meet their dad, wi' flichterin' noise and glee.   father, flut-
His wee bit ingle, blinking bonnily,   fire   [tering
His clean hearthstane, his thriftie wifie's smile,
The lisping infant prattling on his knee,
Does a' his weary kiaugh and care beguile,   anxiety
And makes him quite forget his labour and his toil.

Belyve, the elder bairns come drapping in,   by-and-by
At service out, amang the farmers roun':
Some ca' the pleugh, some herd, some tentie rin   plough, watchful

A cannie errand to a neibor town :   easy
    Their eldest hope, their Jenny, woman grown,
In youthfu' bloom, love sparkling in her e'e,
    Comes hame, perhaps to show a braw new gown,
    Or deposit her sair won penny-fee,   hard won wages
To help her parents dear, if they in hardship be.

With joy unfeigned, brothers and sisters meet,
    And each for other's welfare kindly spiers :   inquires
The social hours, swift-winged, unnoticed fleet ;
    Each tells the uncos that he sees or hears ;   news
    The parents, partial, eye their hopeful years ;
Anticipation forward points the view.
    The mother, wi' her needle and her shears,
Gars auld claes look amaist as weel's the new—   makes, clothes,
The father mixes a' wi' admonition due.   [almost

Their master's and their mistress's command,
    The younkers a' are warnèd to obey ;
And mind their labours wi' an eydent hand,   diligent
    And ne'er, though out o' sight, to jauk or play :   dally
    "And oh ! be sure to fear the Lord alway !
And mind your duty, duly, morn and night !
    Lest in temptation's path ye gang astray,   go
Implore His counsel and assisting might :
They never sought in vain that sought the Lord aright !"

But, hark ! a rap comes gently to the door ;
    Jenny, wha kens the meaning o' the same,   who knows
Tells how a neibor lad cam' o'er the moor   neighbour
    To do some errands, and convoy her hame.   home
    The wily mother sees the conscious flame
Sparkle in Jenny's e'e, and flush her cheek,
    With heart-struck anxious care, inquires his name,
While Jenny hafflins is afraid to speak ;   half
Weel pleased the mother hears it's nae wild, worthless rake.

Wi' kindly welcome, Jenny brings him ben ;   in
    A strappin' youth ; he taks the mother's eye ;
Blythe Jenny sees the visit's no ill ta'en ;
    The father cracks of horses, pleughs, and kye.   cows
    The youngster's artless heart o'erflows wi' joy,
But blate and lathefu', scarce can weel behave ;   bashful, hesi-
    The mother, wi' a woman's wiles, can spy   [tating
What makes the youth sae bashfu' and sae grave :
Weel pleased to think her bairn's respected like the lave. other people

Oh happy love !—where love like this is found !
    Oh heartfelt raptures !—bliss beyond compare !
I've pacèd much this weary, mortal round,
    And sage experience bids me this declare—
    "If Heaven a draught of heavenly pleasure spare,
One cordial in this melancholy vale,
    'Tis when a youthful, loving, modest pair,
In other's arms breathe out the tender tale,
Beneath the milk-white thorn that scents the evening gale."

Is there, in human form, that bears a heart,
   A wretch! a villain! lost to love and truth!
That can, with studied, sly, ensnaring art,
   Betray sweet Jenny's unsuspecting youth?
   Curse on his perjur'd arts! dissembling smooth!
Are honour, virtue, conscience, all exiled?
   Is there no pity, no relenting ruth,
Points to the parents fondling o'er their child?
Then paints the ruined maid, and their distraction wild?

But now the supper crowns their simple board,
   The halesome parritch, chief of Scotia's food;   *porridge*
The soupe their only hawkie does afford,   *cow*
   That 'yont the hallan snugly chows her cood: *inner wall, chews*
   The dame brings forth, in complimental mood,
To grace the lad, her weel-hained kebbuck, fell,   *well-saved cheese,*
   And aft he's prest, and aft he ca's it gude;   *oft [spicy*
   The frugal wifie, garrulous, will tell,
How 'twas a towmond auld, sin' lint was i' the bell.   *twelvemonth,*
                                 [in flower

The cheerfu' supper done, wi' serious face,
   They, round the ingle, form a circle wide;   *fire*
The sire turns o'er, with patriarchal grace,
   The big ha'-bible, ance his father's pride;   *once*
   His bonnet rev'rently is laid aside,
His lyart haffets wearing thin and bare;   *gray cheeks*
   Those strains that once did sweet in Zion glide,
He wales a portion with judicious care;   *selects*
And "Let us worship God!" he says, with solemn air.

They chant their artless notes in simple guise;
   They tune their hearts, by far the noblest aim:
Perhaps Dundee's wild-warbling measures rise;
   Or plaintive Martyrs, worthy of the name,
   Or noble Elgin beets the heavenward flame,   *adds fuel to*
The sweetest far of Scotia's holy lays:
   Compared with these, Italian trills are tame;
The tickled ear no heartfelt raptures raise;
Nae unison ha'e they with our Creator's praise.

The priest-like father reads the sacred page—
   How Abram was the friend of GOD on high;
Or, Moses bade eternal warfare wage
   With Amalek's ungracious progeny;
   Or how the royal bard did groaning lie
Beneath the stroke of Heaven's avenging ire;
   Or Job's pathetic plaint, and wailing cry;
Or rapt Isaiah's wild, seraphic fire;
Or other holy seers that tune the sacred lyre.

Perhaps the Christian volume is the theme—
   How guiltless blood for guilty man was shed;
How HE, who bore in heaven the second name,
   Had not on earth whereon to lay his head:
   How his first followers and servants sped,
The precepts sage they wrote to many a land:

How he, who lone in Patmos banishèd,
  Saw in the sun a mighty angel stand ;
And heard great Bab'lon's doom pronounced by Heaven's command.

Then, kneeling down to HEAVEN'S ETERNAL KING,
  The saint, the father, and the husband prays :
Hope " springs exulting on triumphant wing,"*
  That thus they all shall meet in future days
  There ever bask in uncreated rays,
No more to sigh, or shed the bitter tear,
  Together hymning their Creator's praise,
In such society, yet still more dear ;
While circling time moves round in an eternal sphere.

Compared with this, how poor Religion's pride,
  In all the pomp of method, and of art,
When men display to congregations wide,
  Devotion's every grace, except the heart !
  The Power, incens'd, the pageant will desert,
The pompous strain, the sacerdotal stole ;
  But, haply, in some cottage far apart,
May hear, well pleased, the language of the soul ;
And in His book of life the inmates poor enrol.

Then homeward all take off their several way ;
  The youngling cottagers retire to rest :
The parent-pair their secret homage pay,
  And proffer up to Heaven the warm request,
  That HE, who stills the raven's clamorous nest,
And decks the lily fair in flowery pride,
  Would, in the way his wisdom sees the best,
For them and for their little ones provide ;
But, chiefly, in their hearts with grace divine preside.

From scenes like these old Scotia's grandeur springs,
  That makes her loved at-home, revered abroad :
Princes and lords are but the breath of kings,
  " An honest man's the noblest work of God ;"
  And certes, in fair virtue's heavenly road,
The cottage leaves the palace far behind ;
  What is a lordling's pomp ? a cumbrous load,
Disguising oft the wretch of human kind,
Studied in arts of hell, in wickedness refined !

Oh Scotia ! my dear, my native soil !
  For whom my warmest wish to Heaven is sent !
Long may thy hardy sons of rustic toil
  Be blest with health, and peace, and sweet content !
  And oh ! may Heaven their simple lives prevent
From luxury's contagion, weak and vi'e !
  Then, howe'er crowns and coronets be rent,
A virtuous populace may rise the while,
And stand a wall of fire around their much-loved isle.

        * Pope's *Windsor Forest.—B*

Oh Thou ! who poured the patriotic tide
   That streamed through Wallace's undaunted heart,
Who dared to nobly stem tyrannic pride,
   Or nobly die, the second glorious part,
   (The patriot's God, peculiarly thou art,
His friend, inspirer, guardian, and reward !)
   Oh never, never, Scotia's realm desert ;
But still the patriot, and the patriot bard,
In bright succession raise, her ornament and guard !

A FRAGMENT.

My heart melts at human wretchedness ;
And with sincere, though unavailing sighs,
I view the helpless children of distress.
With tears indignant I behold the oppressor
Rejoicing in the honest man's destruction,
Whose unsubmitting heart was all his crime.
Even you, ye helpless crew, I pity you ;
Ye whom the seeming good think sin to pity ;
Ye poor, despised, abandoned vagabonds,
Whom vice, as usual, has turned o'er to ruin.
—Oh, but for kind, though ill-requited friends,
I had been driven forth like you forlorn,
The most detested, worthless wretch among you !

WINTER, A DIRGE.

The wintry west extends his blast,
   And hail and rain does blaw ;   blow
Or, the stormy north sends driving forth
   The blinding sleet and snaw :   snow
While, tumbling brown, the burn comes down, brook
   And roars frae bank to brae ;   from, hill
And bird and beast in covert rest,
   And pass the heartless day.

" The sweeping blast, the sky o'ercast,"
   The joyless winter day,
Let others fear, to me more dear
   Than all the pride of May :
The tempest's howl, it soothes my soul,
   My griefs it seems to join ;
The leafless trees my fancy please,
   Their fate resembles mine !

Thou Power Supreme, whose mighty scheme
   These woes of mine fulfil,
Here, firm, I rest, they must be best,
   Because they are thy will !

Then all I want (oh, do thou grant
   This one request of mine!)
Since to enjoy thou dost deny,
   Assist me to resign.

A PRAYER,

WRITTEN UNDER THE PRESSURE OF VIOLENT ANGUISH.

OH Thou great Being! what Thou art
   Surpasses me to know:
Yet sure I am, that known to Thee
   Are all thy works below.

Thy creature here before Thee stands,
   All wretched and distrest;
Yet sure those ills that wring my soul
   Obey thy high behest.

Sure Thou, Almighty, canst not act
   From cruelty or wrath!
Oh free my weary eyes from tears,
   Or close them fast in death!

But if I must afflicted be,
   To suit some wise design;
Then man my soul with firm resolves,
   To bear, and not repine!

THE DEATH AND DYING WORDS OF POOR MAILIE,
THE AUTHOR'S ONLY PET YOWE:

AN UNCO MOURNFU' TALE.

	very
As Mailie and her lambs thegither,	together
Were ae day nibbling on the tether,	one, halter
Upon her cloot she coost a hitch,	foot, caught, loop
And owre she warsled in the ditch:	over, struggled
There, groaning, dying, she did lie,	
When Hughoc* he cam' doytin by.	walking stupidly
Wi' glowering een and lifted hands,	staring eyes
Poor Hughoc like a statue stands;	
He saw her days were near-hand ended,	nearly
But, waes my heart! he could na mend it.	alas
He gapèd wide, but naething spak—	
At length poor Mailie silence brak.	

  ' Oh thou, whose lamentable face
Appears to mourn my woefu' case!

* A neighbour herd lad.—B

My dying words attentive hear,
And bear them to my master dear.

" Tell him, if e'er again he keep
As muckle gear as buy a sheep,   *much money*
Oh, bid him never tie them mair   *more*
Wi' wicked strings o' hemp or hair!
But ca' them out to park or hill,   *drive*
And let them wander at their will ;
So may his flock increase, and grow
To scores o' lambs, and packs o' woo'!   *wool*

" Tell him he was a master kin',
And aye was guid to me and mine;   *always, good*
And now my dying charge I gie him—   *give*
My helpless lambs I trust them wi' him.

" Oh, bid him save their harmless lives
Frae dogs, and tods, and butchers' knives!   *from, foxes*
But gie them guid cow-milk their fill,
Till they be fit to fend themsel ;   *provide for*
And tent them duly, e'en and morn,   *tend*
Wi' teats o' hay, and ripps o' corn.   *portions, handfuls*

" And may they never learn the gaets   *ways*
Of other vile, wanrestfu' pets ;   *restless*
To slink through slaps, and reave and steal   *gaps*
At stacks o' peas, or stocks o' kail.   *stem, cabbage*
So may they, like their great forbears,   *ancestors*
For mony a year come through the shears :   *many*
So wives will gie them bits o' breid,   *bread*
And bairns greet for them when they're deid.   *weep*

" My poor toop-lamb, my son and heir,   *tup*
Oh, bid him breed him up wi' care ;
And if he live to be a beast,
To pit some havins in his breast!   *manners*

" And warn him, what 1 winna name,
To stay content wi' yowes at hame ;   *ewes*
And no to rin and wear his cloots,   *hoofs*
Like ither menseless, graceless brutes.   *other senseless*

" And neist my yowie, silly thing,   *next, ewe*
Oh, keep thee frae a tether string ;   *from*
Oh, may thou ne'er forgather up   *encounter*
Wi' ony blastit, moorland toop,   *any, tup*
But aye keep mind to moop and mell   *mump, associate*
Wi' sheep o' credit like thysel'.

" And now, my bairns, wi' my last breath   *children*
I lea'e my blessin' wi' you baith :   *both*
And when you think upo' your mither,
Mind to be kin' to ane anither.   *one another*

" Now, honest Hughoc, dinna fail   *do not*
To tell my master a' my tale."
This said, poor Mailie turned her heid,   *head*
And closed her een amang the deid.   *eyes, dead*

POOR MAILIE'S ELEGY.

Lament in rhyme, lament in prose,
Wi' saut tears tricklin' down your nose;   salt
Our bardie's fate is at a close,   bard
    Past a' remead;   remedy
The last sad cape-stane of his woes—   cope-stone
    Poor Mailie's deid!

It's no the loss o' warl's gear,   world's wealth
That could sae bitter draw the tear,   so
Or mak' our bardie, dowie, wear   sorrowful
    The mourning weed:
He's lost a friend and neibor dear,   neighbour
    In Mailie deid.

Through a' the toun she trotted by him;   town
A lang half-mile she could descry him;   long
Wi' kindly bleat, when she did spy him,   espy
    She ran wi' speed:
A friend mair faithfu' ne'er cam nigh him   more
    Than Mailie deid.

I wat she was a sheep o' sense,   ween
And could behave hersel wi' mense: discretion
I'll say't, she never brak a fence   broke
    Through thievish greed.
Our bardie, lanely, keeps the spence   lonely, inner room
    Sin' Mailie's deid.   since

Or, if he wanders up the howe,   valley
Her living image in her yowe,   ewe
Comes bleating to him, owre the knowe,   over, hillock
    For bits o' breid;
And down the briny pearls rowe   roll
    For Mailie deid.

She was nae get o' moorland tips,   rams
Wi' tawted ket and hairy hips,   matted fleece
For her forbears were brought in ships   ancestors
    Frae yont the Tweed: from beyond
A bonnier fleesh ne'er crossed the clips   fleece
    Than Mailie deid.

Wae worth the man wha first did shape   woe
That vile, wanchancie thing—a rape!   dangerous, rope
It makes guid fellows girn and gape,   grin
    Wi' chokin dreid;
And Robin's bonnet wave wi crape,
    For Mailie deid.

Oh a' ye bards on bonnie Doon!
And wha on Ayr your chanters tune   who, pipes
Come, join the melancholious croon   moan
    O' Robin's reed!
His heart will never get aboon—   above
    His Mailie's deid!

A PRAYER IN THE PROSPECT OF DEATH.

OH thou unknown, Almighty Cause
   Of all my hope and fear!
In whose dread presence, ere an hour,
   Perhaps I must appear!

If I have wandered in those paths
   Of life I ought to shun;
As something, loudly, in my breast,
   Remonstrates I have done;

Thou know'st that Thou hast formed me
   With passions wild and strong;
And listening to their witching voice
   Has often led me wrong.

Where human weakness has come short,
   Or frailty stept aside,
Do Thou, All-good! for such thou art,
   In shades of darkness hide.

Where with intention I have err'd,
   No other plea I have,
But, Thou art good; and goodness still
   Delighteth to forgive.

STANZAS

ON THE SAME OCCASION.

WHY am I loth to leave this earthly scene?
   Have I so found it full of pleasing charms?
Some drops of joy with draughts of ill between:
   Some gleams of sunshine 'mid renewing storms:
Is it departing pangs my soul alarms?
   Or death's unlovely, dreary, dark abode?
For guilt, for guilt, my terrors are in arms;
   I tremble to approach an angry God,
And justly smart beneath his sin-avenging rod.

Fain would I say, "Forgive my foul offence!"
   Fain promise never more to disobey;
But should my Author health again dispense,
   Again I might desert fair virtue's way:
Again in folly's path might go astray;
   Again exalt the brute, and sink the man;
Then how should I for heavenly mercy pray,
   Who act so counter heavenly mercy's plan?
Who sin so oft have mourned, yet to temptation ran?

Oh Thou, great Governor of all below!
  If I may dare a lifted eye to' Thee,
Thy nod can make the tempest cease to blow,
  Or still the tumult of the raging sea:
With that controlling power assist even me
  Those headlong furious passions to confine;
For all unfit I feel my powers to be,
  To rule their torrent in the allowed line;
Oh, aid me with Thy help, Omnipotence Divine!

OH why —— should I repine,
  And be an ill foreboder?
I'm twenty-three, and five feet nine—
  I'll go and be a sodger!

I gat some gear wi' mickle care,   *wealth*
  I held it weel thegither;   *well together*
But now it's gane, and something mair— *gone, more*
  I'll go and be a sodger!

OH leave novels, ye Mauchline belles,
  Ye're safer at your spinning-wheel;
Such witching books are baited hooks
  For rakish rooks like Rob Mossgiel. . . .

Beware a tongue that's smoothly hung,
  A heart that warmly seems to feel;
That feeling heart but acts a part,
  'Tis rakish art in Rob Mossgiel. . . . .

THE FIRST PSALM.

THE man, in life wherever placed,
  Hath happiness in store,
Who walks not in the wicked's way,
  Nor learns their guilty lore!

Nor from the seat of scornful pride
  Casts forth his eyes abroad,
But with humility and awe
  Still walks before his God.

That man shall flourish like the trees
  Which by the streamlets grow;
The fruitful top is spread on high,
  And firm the root below.

But he whose blossom buds in guilt,
  Shall to the ground be cast,

And, like the rootless stubble, tost
Before the sweeping blast.

For why ? that God the good adore
Hath given them peace and rest,
But hath decreed that wicked men
Shall ne'er be truly blest.

THE FIRST SIX VERSES OF THE NINETIETH PSALM.

OH Thou, the first, the greatest friend
Of all the human race !
Whose strong right hand has ever been
Their stay and dwelling-place !

Before the mountains heaved their heads
Beneath Thy forming hand,
Before this ponderous globe itself
Arose at Thy command ;

That Power which raised and still upholds
This universal frame,
From countless, unbeginning time,
Was ever still the same.

Those mighty periods of years
Which seem to us so vast,
Appear no more before Thy sight
Than yesterday that's past.

Thou giv'st the word : Thy creature, man,
Is to existence brought ;
Again Thou say'st, " Ye sons of men,
Return ye into nought !"

Thou layest them with all their cares
In everlasting sleep ;
As with a flood Thou tak'st them off
With overwhelming sweep.

They flourish like the morning flower,
In beauty's pride arrayed ;
But long ere night, cut down, it lies
All withered and decayed.

EPISTLE TO JOHN RANKINE.

I'VE sent you here some rhyming ware,
A' that I bargained for, and mair ;
Sae, when ye hae an hour to spare,
I will expect
Yon sang, ye'll sen 't wi' canny care,
And no neglect.

more
so, when

song, thoughtful

Though, faith, sma' heart hae I to sing!
My Muse dow scarcely spread her wing;   *can*
I've played mysel a bonnie spring,   *tune*
     And danced my fill;
I'd better gaen and sair't the king   *gone, served*
     At Bunker's Hill.

'Twas ae night lately, in my fun,   *one*
I gaed a roving wi' the gun,   *went*
And brought a paitrick to the grun',   *partridge, ground*
     A bonnie hen,
And as the twilight was begun,
     Thought nane wad ken.   *none would know*

The poor wee thing was little hurt;
I straikit it a wee for sport,   *stroked, short time*
Ne'er thinking they wad fash me for't;   *would, trouble*
     But NOCHT I CARE;
Somebody tells the poacher-court
     The hale affair.   *whole*

Some auld used hands had taen a note   *old, taken*
That sic a hen had got a shot;   *such*
I was suspected for the plot,
     I scorned to le;   *lie*
So gat the whistle o' my groat,   *played a losing game*
     And pay't the fee. . .

As soon's the clocking time is by,   *breeding*
And the wee pouts begun to cry,   *poults*
THEN, I'se hae sportin' by and by,
     For my gowd guinea,   *gold*
Though I should hunt the buckskin kye   *buffaloes*
     For't in Virginia. . . .

It puts me aye as mad's a hare;
So I can rhyme and write nae mair,
But pennyworths again is fair,
     When time's expedient:
Meanwhile I am, respected sir,
     Your most obedient.

ELEGY ON THE DEATH OF ROBERT RUISSEAUX.

Now Robin lies in his last lair,
He'll gabble rhyme nor sing nae mair,   *no more*
Cauld poverty, wi' hungry stare,   *cold*
     Nae mair shall fear him;
Nor anxious fear, nor cankert care,   *ill-natured*
     E'er mair come near him.

To tell the truth, they seldom fash't him,   *troubled*
Except the moment that they crush't him;

For sune as chance or fate had hush't em,   soon
   Though e'er sae short,
Then wi' a rhyme or sang he lash't 'em,
   And thought it sport.

Though he was bred to kintra wark,   country work
And counted was baith wight and stark,   athletic, strong
Yet that was never Robin's mark
   To mak a man;
But tell him, he was learned and clark,   ready with pen
   Ye roosed him than!   praised

THE BELLES OF MAUCHLINE.

IN Mauchline there dwells six proper young belles,
   The pride of the place and its neighbourhood a',
Their carriage and dress, a stranger would guess,
   In Lon'on or Paris, they'd gotten it a'.
Miss Miller is fine, Miss Markland's divine,
   Miss Smith she has wit, and Miss Betty is braw,
There's beauty and fortune to get wi' Miss Morton;
   But Armour's the jewel for me o' them a'.

AN EPISTLE TO DAVIE,

A BROTHER POET.

January —

WHILE winds frae aff Ben Lomond blaw,   blow
And bar the doors wi' driving snaw,   snow
   And hing us owre the ingle,   hang, over, fire
I set me down to pass the time,
And spin a verse or two o' rhyme,
   In hamely westlin jingle.   homely, western
While frosty winds blaw in the drift,
   Ben to the chimla lug,   in, chimney nook
I grudge a wee the great folk's gift,   little
   That live sae bien and snug: so comfortably
     I tent less, and want less   notice
     Their roomy fireside;
     But hanker and canker
     To see their HORRID pride.

It's hardly in a body's power
To keep, at times, frae being sour,   from
   To see how things are shared;
How best o' chiels are whiles in want,   fellows, sometimes
While coofs on countless thousands rant,   fools
   And ken na how to war't;   know not, spend
But, Davie, lad, ne'er fash your head,   trouble
   Though we hae little gear   wealth
We're fit to win our daily bread,
   As lang's we're hale and fier: long, sound

" Mair speir na, nor fear na,"*   more ask not
  Auld age ne'er mind a feg,   old, fig
The last o't, the warst o't,   worst
  Is only but to beg.

To lie in kilns and barns at e'en
When banes are crazed, and bluid is thin,   bones, blood
  Is doubtless great distress !
Yet then content could make us blest ;
Even then, sometimes we'd snatch a taste
  Of truest happiness.
The honest heart that's free frae a'   from
  Intended fraud or guile,
However fortune kick the ba',
  Has aye some cause to smile :
    And mind still, you'll find still,
      A comfort this nae sma' ;   not small
    Nae mair then, we'll care then,   no
      Nae farther we can fa'.   fall

What though, like commoners of air,
We wander out we know not where,
  But either house or hal'?   without
Yet Nature's charms, the hills and woods,
The sweeping vales, and foaming floods,
  Are free alike to all.
In days when daisies deck the ground,
  And blackbirds whistle clear,
With honest joy our hearts will bound
  To see the coming year :
    On braes when we please, then,   hillocks
      We'll sit and sowth a tune ;   try
    Syne rhyme till't, we'll time till't,   then
      And sing't when we hae dune.   have done

It's no in titles nor in rank ;
It's no in wealth like Lon'on bank,
  To purchase peace and rest ;
It's no in making muckle *mair ;*   much
It's no in books, it's no in lair,   learning
  To mak us truly blest ;
If happiness hae not her seat
  And centre in the breast,
We may be wise, or rich, or great,
  But never can be blest :
    Nae treasures nor pleasures
      Could make us happy lang ;
    The heart aye's the part aye
      That makes us right or wrang.   wrong

Think ye, that sic as you and I,   such
Wha drudge and drive through wet and dry, who
  Wi' never-ceasing toil ;
Think ye, we are less blest than they,
Wha scarcely tent us in their way,   notice

* Ramsay.

As hardly worth their while?
Alas!·how aft, in haughty mood,   *oft*
God's creatures they oppress!
Or else, neglecting a' that's guid,   *good*
They riot in excess!
  Baith careless and fearless   *both*
    Of either heaven or hell!
  Esteeming and deeming
    It's a' an idle tale!

Then let us cheerfu' acquiesce;
Nor make our scanty pleasures less,
  By pining at our state;
And even should misfortunes come,
I, here wha sit, hae met wi' some,
  An's thankfu' for them yet.
They gie the wit of age to youth;   *give*
  They let us ken oursel';   *know*
They make us see the naked truth,
  The real guid and ill.
  Though losses and crosses
    Be lessons right severe,
  There's wit there, ye'll get there,
    Ye'll find nae other where.

But tent me, Davie, ace o' hearts!   *attend to*
(To say aught less wad wrang the cartes, *would wrong*
  And flatt'ry I detest),
This life has joys for you and I;
And joys that riches ne'er could buy:
  And joys the very best.
There's a' the pleasures o' the heart,
  The lover and the frien';
Ye hae your Meg, your dearest part,
  And I my darling Jean!
  It warms me, it charms me,
    To mention but her name:
  It heats me, it beets me,   *adds fuel*
    And sets me a' on flame!

Oh all ye Powers who rule above!
Oh Thou whose very self art love!
  Thou know'st my words sincere!
The life-blood streaming through my heart,
Or my more dear immortal part,
  Is not more fondly dear!
When heart-corroding care and grief
  Deprive my soul of rest,
Her dear idea brings relief
  And solace to my breast.
  Thou Being, all-seeing,
    Oh hear my fervent prayer!
  Still take her, and make her
    Thy most peculiar care!

All hail, ye tender feelings dear !
The smile of love, the friendly tear,
   The sympathetic glow !
Long since, this world's thorny ways
Had numbered out my weary days,
   Had it not been for you !
Fate still has blest me with a friend,
   In every care and ill ;
And oft a more endearing band,
   A tie more tender still.
     It lightens, it brightens
      The tenebrific scene,   *dark*
     To meet with, and greet with
      My Davie or my Jean !

Oh how that name inspires my style !
The words come skelpin', rank and file, *hastening*
   Amaist before I ken !   *almost, know*
The ready measure rins as fine   *runs*
As Phœbus and the famous Nine
   Were glowrin' owre my pen.   *staring over*
My spaviet Pegasus will limp,   *spavin'd*
   Till ance he's fairly het ;   *warm*
And then he'll hilch, and stilt, and jimp, *hobble*
   And rin an unco fit :   *at a good pace*
     But lest then, the beast then
      Should rue this hasty ride,
     I'll light now, and dight now,   *wipe*
      His sweaty, wizened hide.   *withered*

DEATH AND DR HORNBOOK.

A TRUE STORY.

SOME books are lies frae end to end,   *from*
And some great lies were never penn'd :
Ev'n ministers they hae been kenn'd,   *known*
   In holy rapture,
A rousing whid at times to vend,   *fib*
   And nail't wi' Scripture.

The clachan yill had made me canty— *village ale, merry*
I was na fou, but just had plenty ;   *drunk*
I stachered whyles, but yet took tent aye *staggered, heed*
   To free the ditches ;   *avoid*
And hillocks, stanes, and bushes kenn'd aye *stones, knew*
   Frae ghaists and witches.   *ghosts*

The rising moon began to glow'r   *stare*
The distant Cumnock hills out-owre : *out-over*
To count her horns, wi' a' my power,
   I set mysel ;
But whether she had three or four,
   I could na tell.

I was come round about the hill,
And todlin' down on Willie's mill,   *tottering*
Setting my staff wi' a' my skill,
        To keep me sicker ;   *secure*
Though leeward whyles, against my will,   *sometimes*
        I took a bicker.   *short run*

I there wi' Something did forgather,   *meet with*
That put me in an eerie swither ;   *dismal hesitation*
An awfu' scythe, out-owre ae shouther,   *over one shoulder*
        Clear-dangling, hang ;
A three-taed leister on the ither   *pronged fish-spear, other*
        Lay, large and lang.   *long*

Its stature seemed lang Scotch ells twa,   *two*
The queerest shape that e'er I saw,
For NOT a wame it had ava ;   *belly, at all*
        And then, its shanks,   *legs*
They were as thin, as sharp and sma',
        As cheeks o' branks.*
                                           [*mowing*
" Guid e'en," quo' I; " Friend, hae ye been mawin, *good even,*
When ither folks are busy sawin' ?"   *sowing*
It seemed to mak a kind o' stan',
        But naething spak ;
At length says I, " Friend, whare ye gaun— *where, going*
        Will ye go back ?"

It spak right howe—" My name is Death,   *hollow*
But be na fley'd." Quoth I, " Guid faith, *frightened*
Ye're maybe come to stap my breath ;   *stop*
        But tent me, billie—   *observe, my lad*
I rede ye weel tak care o' scaith,   *advise, well, harm*
        See, there's a gully !"   *clasp-knife*

" Guidman," quo' he, " put up your whittle, *weapon*
I'm no designed to try its mettle ;
But if I did, I wad be kittle   *difficult*
        To be mislear'd ;   *so baulked*
I wadna mind it, no that spittle
        Out-owre my beard."

" Weel, weel !" says I, " a bargain be't ;
Come, gie's your hand, and sae we're gree't ; *agreed*
We'll ease our shanks and tak a seat—
        Come, gie's your news ;
This while ye hae been mony a gate,   *some time, road*
        At mony a house."   *many*

" Ay, ay !" quo' he, and shook his head,
" It's e'en a lang lang time indeed   *long*
Sin' I began to nick the thread,   *cut*
        And choke the breath :
Folk maun do something for their bread,   *must*
        And sae maun Death.   *so*

* A wooden frame, forming, with a rope, a bridle for troublesome cows and horses

B

" Sax thousand years are near hand fled   *six, nearly*
Sin' I was to the butching bred,   *killing*
And mony a scheme in vain's been laid,
      To stap or scaur me ;   *stop, scare*
Till ane Hornbook's ta'en up the trade,   *taken*
      And faith he'll waur me.   *worst*

" Ye ken Jock Hornbook i' the clachan,   *know, village*
I WISH his king's-hood in a spleuchan !   *tobacco-pouch*
He's grown sae weel acquant wi' Buchan*   *acquainted*
      And ither chaps,   *other*
The weans haud out their fingers laughin',   *children hold*
      And pouk my hips.   *poke*

" See, here's a scythe, and there's a dart,
They hae pierced mony a gallant heart ;   *have*
But Doctor Hornbook wi' his art
      And WELL-TRIED skill,
Has made them baith no worth A SCART,   *both, scratch*
      NAE haet they'll kill.   *nothing*

" 'Twas but yestreen, nae further gaen,   *yesterday, past*
I threw a noble throw at ane ;   *one*
Wi' less, I'm sure, I've hundreds slain ;
      But SPITE my care,
It just play'd dirl on the bane,   *quivered, bone*
      But did nae mair.   *more*

" Hornbook was by wi' ready art,
And had sae fortified the part,
That when I looked to my dart,
      It was sae blunt,   *so*
NAE haet o't wad hae pierced the heart
      O' a kail runt.   *cabbage-stem*

" I drew my scythe in sic a fury,   *such*
I nearhand cowpit wi' my hurry,   *nearly tumbled*
But yet the bauld apothecary   *bold*
      Withstood the shock ;
I might as weel hae tried a quarry   *well*
      O' hard whin rock.

" And then a' doctor's saws and whittles,   *knives*
Of a' dimensions, shapes, and metals,
A' kinds o' boxes, mugs, and bottles,
      He's sure to hae ;
Their Latin names as fast he rattles
      As A B C.

" Calces o' fossils, earths, and trees ;
True sal-marinum o' the seas ;
The farina of beans and peas,
      He has't in plenty ;
Aqua fontis, what you please,
      He can content ye."

* Buchan's *Domestic Medicine*.

" Waes me for Johnny Ged's* hole now,"   alas
Quo' I ; " If that thae news be true,   these
His braw calf-ward† where gowans grew,   fine, daisies
    Sae white and bonnie.
Nae doubt they'll rive it wi' the pleugh ;   tear
    They'll ruin Johnny !"

The creature grained an eldritch laugh,   groaned, unearthly
And says, " Ye need na yoke the pleugh,   plough
Kirkyards will soon be tilled eneugh,   enough
    Tak ye nae fear:
They'll a' be trenched wi' mony a sheugh   furrow
    In twa-three year.

" Whare I killed ane a fair strae death,   where, in bed
By loss o' blood or want o' breath,
This night, I'm free to tak my aith,   oath
    That Hornbook's skill
Has clad a score i' their last claith,   clothes
    By drap and pill.   drop

" An honest wabster to his trade,   weaver
Whase wife's twa nieves were scarce weel-bred,   two fists
Gat tippence-worth to mend her head,   got twopence
    When it was sair ;   sore
The wife slade cannie to her bed,   slid gently
    But ne'er spak mair.   spoke more

" That's just a swatch o' Hornbook's way ;   specimen
Thus goes he on from day to day,
Thus does he poison, kill, and slay,
    An's weel paid for't;
Yet stops me o' my lawfu' prey
    Wi' his PILL dirt :

" But hark ! I'll tell you of a plot,
Though dinna ye be speaking o't ;
I'll nail the self-conceited sot
    As dead's a' herrin':
Neist time we meet, I'll wad a groat,   next, wager
    He get's his fairin' !"   drubbing

But just as he began to tell,
The auld kirk-hammer strak the bell
Some wee short hour ayont the twal,   beyond, twelve
    Which raised us baith :   both
I took the way that pleased mysel',
    And sae did Death.

---

* The gravedigger.   † Pasturage of the churchyard.

FIRST EPISTLE TO J. LAPRAIK,

AN OLD SCOTTISH BARD.

April 1, 1785.

WHILE briers and woodbines budding green,
And paitricks scraichin' loud at e'en,   partridges screaming
And morning poussie whiddin seen,   hare scudding
    Inspire my muse,
This freedom in an unknown frien'
    I pray excuse.

On Fasten-e'en we had a rockin',   shrovetide, meeting
To ca' the crack and weave our stockin';   chat
And there was muckle fun and jokin',   much
    Ye need na doubt;
At length we had a hearty yokin'
    At sang about.   song

There was ae sang, amang the rest,   one
Aboon them a' it pleased me best,   above
That some kind husband had addrest
    To some sweet wife:
It thirled the heart-strings through the breast,   enthrall'd
    A' to the life.

I've scarce heard ought described sae weel
What generous manly bosoms feel;
Thought I, " Can this be Pope, or Steele,
    Or Beattie's wark?"
They tauld me 'twas an odd kind chiel   told, fellow
    About Muirkirk.

It pat me fidgin-fain to hear't,   put, excitedly eager
And sae about him there I spier't,   inquired
Then a' that ken't him round declared   knew
    He had ingine,   genius
That nane excelled it, few cam near't,   none
    It was sae fine.

That, set him to a pint of ale,
And either douce or merry tale,   grave
Or rhymes and sangs he'd made himsel,
    Or witty catches,
'Tween Inverness and Teviotdale,
    He had few matches.

Then up I gat, and swore an aith,   got, oath
Though I should pawn my pleugh and graith,   harness
Or die a cadger pownie's death   pedlar poney's
    At some dyke back,   wall
A pint and gill I'd gie them baith   both
    To hear your crack.   chat

But, first and foremost, I should tell,
Amaist as soon as I could spell,   almost

I to the crambo-jingle fell,   *doggerel verses*
 Though rude and rough,
Yet crooning to a body's sell,   *humming*
 Does weel eneugh.   *enough*

I am nae poet, in a sense,   *no*
But just a rhymer, like, by chance,
And hae to learning nae pretence,   *have*
 Yet, what the matter!
Whene'er my Muse does on me glance,
 I jingle at her.

Your critic folk may cock their nose,
And say, "How can you e'er propose,
You, wha ken hardly verse frae prose,   *who know*
 To mak a sang?"
But, by your leaves, my learned foes,
 Ye're maybe wrang.

What's a' your jargon o' your schools
Your Latin names for horns and stool
If honest nature made you fools,
 What sairs your gramms   *serves*
Ye'd better taen up spades and shools,   *taken, shovels*
 Or knappin-hammers.   *stone-hammers*

A set o' dull conceited hashes,   *stupid fellows*
Confuse their brains in college classes!
They gang in stirks, and come out asses, *young bullocks*
 Plain truth to speak;
And syne they think to climb Parnassus   *then*
 By dint o' Greek!

Gie me ae spark o' Nature's fire!   *give*
That's a' the learning I desire;
Then though I drudge through dub and mire
 At pleugh or cart,   *plough*
My Muse, though hamely in attire,   *homely*
 May touch the heart.

Oh for a spunk o' Allan's glee,   *spark*
Or Fergusson's, the bauld and slee,   *bold, sly*
Or bright Lapraik's, my friend to be,
 If I can hit it!
That would be lear eneugh for me,   *learning*
 If I could get it!

Now, sir, if ye hae friends enow,   *enough*
Though real friends I b'lieve are few,
Yet, if your catalogue be fou,   *full*
 I'se no insist,
But gif ye want ae friend that's true.   *if*
 I'm on your list.

I winna blaw about mysel;   *boast*
As ill I like my fauts to tell;   *faults*

But friends and folk that wish me well,
      They sometimes roose me ;   *praise*
Though I maun own, as monie still   *must, many*
      As far abuse me.

But Mauchline race, or Mauchline fair,
I should be proud to meet you there ;
We'se gie ae night's discharge to care,   *give one*
      If we forgather,   *meet together*
And hae a swap o' rhymin'-ware   *exchange*
      Wi' ane anither.   *one another*

The four-gill-chap, we'se gar him clatter,   *make*
And kirsen him wi' reekin' water ;   *christen*
Syne we'll sit down and tak our whitter,   *then, draught*
      To cheer our heart ;
And, faith, we'se be acquainted better
      Before we part.

Awa' ye selfish war'ly race,   *worldly*
Wha think that havins, sense, and grace,   *manners*
Even love and friendship should give place
      To catch the plack !   *small coin*
I dinna like to see your face,
      Nor hear your crack.   *conversation*

But ye whom social pleasure charms,
Whose hearts the tide of kindness warms,
Who hold your being on the terms,
      " Each aid the others,"
Come to my bowl, come to my arms,
      My friends, my brothers !

But, to conclude my lang epistle,   *long*
As my auld pen's worn to the grissle ;   *stump*
Twa lines frae you wad gar me fissle,   *would, fidget*
      Who am, most fervent,
While I can either sing or whissle,   *whistle*
      Your friend and servant.

SECOND EPISTLE TO J. LAPRAIK.

April 21, 1785.

WHILE new-ca'd kye rowte at the stake,   *new-driven, low*
And pownies reek in pleugh or braik,   *ponies smoke, plough.*
This hour on e'enin's edge I take,   *evenings* [harrow
      To own I'm debtor,
To honest-hearted auld Lapraik,   *old*
      For his kind letter.

Forjesket sair, wi' weary legs,   *jaded sore*
Rattlin' the corn out-owre the rigs,   *over*
Or dealing through amang the naigs   *nags*
      Their ten-hours' bite,

My awkwart Muse sair pleads and begs   awkward, sore
     I would na write.

The tapetless ramfeezl'd hizzie,   heedless fatigued lass
She's saft at best, and something lazy,   soft
Quo' she, " Ye ken, we've been sae busy   know, so
     This month and mair,   more
That trouth, my head is grown right dizzie,   indeed
     And something sair."

Her dowff excuses pat me mad: stupid, put
" Conscience," says I, " ye thowless jaud!   feeble creature
I'll write, and that a hearty blaud,   effusion
     This very night;
Sae dinna ye affront your trade,   do not
     But rhyme it right.

" Shall bauld Lapraik, the king o' hearts,   bold
Though mankind were a pack o' cartes,   cards
Roose you sae weel for your deserts,   praise
     In terms sae friendly,
Yet ye'll neglect to shaw your parts,   show
     And thank him kindly ?"

Sae I gat paper in a blink,   twinkling
And down gaed stumpie in the ink: went the pen
Quoth I, " Before I sleep a wink,
     I vow I'll close it;
And if ye winna mak it clink,   will not
     By Jove I'll prose it!"

Sae I've begun to scrawl, but whether
In rhyme, or prose, or baith thegither,   both together
Or some hotch-potch that's rightly neither,   medley
     Let time mak proof;
But I shall scribble down some blether,   nonsense
     Just clean aff-loof.   off-hand

My worthy friend, ne'er grudge and carp,
Though fortune use you hard and sharp;
Come, kittle up your moorland-harp   tickle
     Wi' gleesome touch;
Ne'er mind how Fortune waft and warp—
     She's but a WITCH.

She's gien me monie a jirt and fleg,   many, jerk, kick
Sin' I could striddle owre a rig;   since, over
But, SURE'S I'M HERE, though I should beg
     Wi' lyart pow,   gray head
I'll laugh, and sing, and shake my leg,
     As lang's I dow!   can

Now comes the sax-and-twentieth simmer,   summer
I've seen the bud upo' the timmer,   timber
Still persecuted by the limmer,
     Frae year to year;

But yet, despite the kittle kimmer,   skittish gossip
    I, Rob, am here.

Do ye envy the city gent,
Behint a kist to lie and sklent,   chest, deceive
Or purse-proud, big wi' cent. per cent.
    And muckle wame,   big belly
In some bit brugh to represent   burgh
    A bailie's name?

Or is't the paughty, feudal Thane,   haughty
Wi' ruffled sark and glancing cane,   shirt
Wha thinks himsel nae sheep-shank bane,   bone
    But lordly stalks,
While caps and bonnets aff are taen,   off, taken
    As by he walks?

Oh Thou wha gies us each guid gift!   gives, good
Gie me o' wit and sense a lift,
Then turn me, if Thou please, adrift,
    Through Scotland wide;
Wi' cits nor lairds I wadna shift,
    In a' their pride!

Were this the charter of our state,
" On pain o' hell be rich and great,"
Damnation then would be our fate,
    Beyond remede;   remedy
But, thanks to Heaven, that's no the gate   way
    We learn our creed.

For thus the royal mandate ran,
When first the human race began,
" The social, friendly, honest man,
    Whate'er he be,
'Tis he fulfils great Nature's plan,
    And none but he!"

Oh mandate glorious and divine!
The followers o' the ragged Nine,
Poor thoughtless FELLOWS   yet may shine
    In glorious light,
While sordid sons o' Mammon's line
    Are dark as night.

Though here they scrape, and squeeze, and growl,
Their worthless nievefu' of a soul   handful
May in some future carcase howl,
    The forest's fright;
Or in some day-detesting owl
    May shun the light.

Then may Lapraik and Burns arise,
To reach their native kindred skies,
And sing their pleasures, hopes, and joys,
    In some mild sphere,
Still closer knit in friendship's ties,
    Each passing year!

EPISTLE TO JOHN GOUDIE OF KILMARNOCK,

ON THE PUBLICATION OF HIS ESSAYS.

Oh, Goudie! terror of the Whigs,
Dread of black coats and reverend wigs.
Sour Bigotry, on her last legs,
 Girnin', looks back,   *grinning*
Wishin' the ten Egyptian plagues
 Wad seize you quick.   *would*

Poor gapin', glowerin' Superstition,
Waes me! she's in a sad condition; *alas*
Fie! bring Black Jock, her state physician,
 To see her,
Alas! there's ground o' great suspicion
 She'll ne'er get better.

Auld Orthodoxy lang did grapple, *long*
But now she's got an unco ripple; *great shake*
Haste, gie her name up i' the chapel, *(to be prayed for)*
 Nigh unto death;
See, how she fetches at the thrapple, *strains, windpipe*
 And gasps for breath.

Enthusiasm's past redemption,
Gane in a galloping consumption, *gone*
Not a' the quacks, wi' a' their gumption, *cleverness*
 Will ever mend her.
Her feeble pulse gies strong presumption *gives*
 Death soon will end her.

'Tis you and Taylor are the chief
Wha are to blame for this mischief,
But gin the KIRK's ain fouk gat leave, *if, own folk*
 A toom tar barrel   *empty*
And twa red peats wad send relief,
 And end the quarrel.

THE TWA HERDS, OR THE HOLY TULZIE.

Oh a' ye pious godly flocks,
Weel fed on pastures orthodox, *well*
Wha now will keep ye frae the fox, *who, from*
 Or worrying tykes,   *dogs*
Or wha will tent the waifs and crocks, *stragglers, old ewes*
 About the dykes?   *stone fences*

The twa best herds in a' the wast, *two, west*
That e'er gae gospel horn a blast, *gave*
These five-and-twenty simmers past,
 Oh dool to tell,   *grief*
Hae had a bitter black out-cast *have, quarrel*
 Atween themsel.   *between*

Oh, Moodie, man, and wordy Russell,   worthy
How could you raise so vile a bustle,
Ye'll see how New-Light herds will whistle,
    And think it fine :
The KIRK'S cause ne'er got sic a twistle   twist
    Sin' I hae min'.

O, sirs ! whae'er wad hae expeckit,   have expected
Your duty ye wad sae negleckit,   would so
Ye wha were ne'er by lairds respeckit,   respected
    To wear the plaid,
But by the brutes themselves eleckit,   elected
    To be their guide.

What flock wi' Moodie's flock could rank,
Sae hale and hearty every shank !
Nae poisoned sour Arminian stank
    He let them taste,
Frae Calvin's well, aye clear, they drank—
    Oh sic a feast !   such

The thummart, wil'-cat, brock, and tod,   pole-cat, badger, fox
Weel kenn'd his voice through a' the wood,   well knew
He smelt their ilka hole and road   every
    Baith out and in,   both
And weel he liked to shed their bluid,   blood
    And sell their skin.

What herd like Russell tell'd his tale,
His voice was heard through muir and dale,
He kenn'd the KIRK'S sheep, ilka tail,
    O'er a' the height,
And saw gin they were sick or hale,   if
    At the first sight.

He fine a mangy sheep could scrub,   well
Or nobly fling the gospel club,
And New-Light herds could nicely drub,

   *   *   *   *   *

Sic twa—Oh do I live to see't,   such two
Sic famous twa should disagreet,   disagreed
And names like villain, hypocrite,
    Ilk ither gi'en,   each other given
While New-Light herds, wi' laughin' spite,
    Say neither's licin' !   lying

A' ye wha tent the gospel fauld,   tend, fold
There's Duncan deep, and Peebles shaul,   shallow
But chiefly thou, apostle Auld,
    We trust in thee,
That thou wilt work them, het and cauld,   hot, cold
    Till they agree.

Consider, sirs, how we're beset ;
There's scarce a new herd that we get
But comes frae 'mang that HORRID set
    I winna name.

  *   *   *   *   *

Dalrymple has been lang our fae,   *foe*
M'Gill has wrought us meikle wae,   *much woe*
And that FELL rascal ca'd M'Quhae,
    And baith the Shaws,   *both*
That aft hae made us black and blae,   *oft, blue*
    Wi' vengefu' paws.

Auld Wodrow lang has hatched mischief,
We thought aye death wad bring relief,
But he has gotten, to our grief,
    Ane to succeed him,   *one*
A chield wha'll soundly buff our beef;   *fellow, thrash*
    I meikle dread him.

And mony a ane that I could tell,   *many*
Wha fain would openly rebel,
Forby turn-coats amang oursel;   *besides*
    There's Smith for ane,
I doubt he's but a grey-nick quill,   *unmasculine*
    And that ye'll fin'.

Oh a' ye flocks o'er a' the hills,
By mosses, meadows, moors, and fells,
Come, join your counsel and your skills,
    To cowe the lairds,
And get the brutes the powers themsels
    To choose their herds.

Then Orthodoxy yet may prance,
And Learning in a woody dance,   *halter*
And that fell cur ca'd Common Sense,
    That bites sae sair,   *so sore*
Be banished o'er the sea to France:
    Let him bark there.

Then Shaw's and D'rymple's eloquence,
M'Gill's close nervous excellence,
M'Quhae's pathetic manly sense,
    And guid M'Math,   *good*
Wi' Smith, wha through the heart can glance,
    May a' pack aff.   *off*

TO WILLIAM SIMPSON,

OCHILTREE.

May 1785.

I GAT your letter, winsome Willie;   *got*
Wi' gratefu' heart I thank you brawly;   *heartily*
Though I maun say't, I wad be silly,   *must, would*
    And unco vain,   *very*
Should I believe, my coaxin' billie,   *fellow*
    Your flatterin' strain.

But I'se believe ye kindly meant it,
I sud be laith to think ye hinted   *should, loath*

Ironic satire, sidelins sklented   *sidelong directed*
     On my poor Musie ;
Though in sic phrasin' terms ye've penned it,   *cajoling*
     I scarce excuse ye.

My senses wad be in a creel,   *basket*
Should I but dare a hope to speel,   *climb*
Wi' Allan or wi' Gilbertfield,
     The braes o' fame ;
Or Fergusson, the writer chiel,   *youth*
     A deathless name.

(Oh, Fergusson ! thy glorious parts
     Ill suited law's dry musty arts !
My BAN upon your whunstane hearts,   *whinstone*
     Ye E'nbrugh gentry ;   *Edinburgh*
The tythe o' what ye waste at cartes   *cards*
     Wad stowed his pantry !)   *filled*

Yet when a tale comes i' my head,
Or lasses gie my heart a screed,   *give, rive*
As whiles they're like to be my deid,   *death*
     (Oh sad disease !)
I kittle up my rustic reed ;   *excite*
     It gies me ease.

Auld Coila now may fidge fu' fain,   *Kyle in Ayrshire*
She's gotten poets o' her ain,   *own*
Chiels wha their chanters winna hain,   *youths, pipes, spare*
     But tune their lays,
Till echoes a' resound again
     Her weel-sung praise.

Nae poet thought her worth his while,
To set her name in measured style ;
She lay like some unkenn'd-of isle   *unknown*
     Beside New Holland,
Or whare wild-meeting oceans boil
     Besouth Magellan.   *to southward of*

Ramsay and famous Fergusson
Gied Forth and Tay a lift aboon   *gave, upwards*
Yarrow and Tweed, to monie a tune,   *many*
     Owre Scotland rings,   *over*
While Irwin, Lugar, Ayr, and Doon,
     Naebody sings.

Th' Illissus, Tiber, Thames, and Seine,
Glide sweet in monie a tunefu' line ;
But, Willie, set your fit to mine,   *foot*
     And cock your crest,
We'll gar our streams and burnies shine   *make rivulets*
     Up wi' the best !

We'll sing auld Coila's plains and fells,   *hills*
Her moors red-brown wi' heather bells,

Her banks and braes, her dens and dells,
　　Where glorious Wallace
Aft bure the gree, as story tell,　　　　　　bore the bell
　　Frae southron billies.　　　　　　　　　fellows

At Wallace' name what Scottish blood
But boils up in spring-tide flood!
Oft have our fearless fathers strode
　　By Wallace' side,
Still pressing onward, red-wat shod,　　walking in blood
　　Or glorious died!

O sweet are Coila's haughs and woods　　meadows
When lintwhites chant amang the buds,　linnets
And jinkin' hares, in amorous whids,*
　　Their loves enjoy;
While through the braes the cushat croods　dove coos
　　With wailfu' cry!

Even winter bleak has charms to me
When winds rave through the naked tree;
Or frosts on hills of Ochiltree
　　Are hoary gray:
Or blinding drifts wild furious flee,
　　Darkening the day!

O Nature! a' thy shows and forms
To feeling, pensive hearts hae charms!
Whether the summer kindly warms,
　　Wi' life and light,
Or winter howls, in gusty storms,
　　The lang, dark night!

The Muse, nae poet ever fand her,　　no, found
Till by himsel he learned to wander,
Adown some trotting burn's meander,
　　And no think lang;
O sweet to stray, and pensive ponder
　　A heart-felt sang!

The war'ly race may drudge and drive,　worldly
Hog-shouther, jundie, stretch, and strive　jostle, push
Let me fair Nature's face descrive,　　describe
　　And I, wi' pleasure,
Shall let the busy grumbling hive
　　Bum owre their treasure.　　　　　　buzz over

Fareweel, "my rhyme-composing brither!"　brother
We've been owre lang unkenn'd to ither:　too, unknown, each
Now let us lay our heads thegither,　　　[other
　　In love fraternal;
May Envy wallop in a tether,　　　　　　quiver, halter
　　Black fiend internal!

* Nimble frisking movements of the hare.

While Highlandmen hate tolls and taxes;
While moorlan' herds like guid fat braxies,   dead sheep
While terra firma on her axis
        Diurnal turns,
Count on a friend in faith and practice,
        In Robert Burns.

POSTCRIPT.

My memory's no worth a preen;   pin
I had amaist forgotten clean,   almost, quite
Ye bade me write you what they mean
    ,   By this New Light,
'Bout which our herds sae aft hae been   so oft have
        Maist like to fight.   almost

In days when mankind were but callans   boys
At grammar, logic, and sic talents,   such
They took nae pains their speech to balance,
        Or rules to gie,   give
But spak their thoughts in plain braid lallans, lowland speech
        Like you or me.

In thae auld times, they thought the moon,   these
Just like a sark, or pair o' shoon,   shirt, shoes
Wore by degrees, till her last roon   paring
        Gaed past their viewing,   went
And shortly after she was done,
        They gat a new one.   got

This passed for certain—undisputed;
It ne'er cam i' their heads to doubt it,
Till chiels gat up, and wad confute it   fellows, would
        And ca'd it wrang;
And muckle din there was about it,   much
        Baith loud and lang.   both

Some herds, well learned upo' the beuk,   book
Wad threap auld folk the thing misteuk;   assert, mistook
For 'twas the auld moon turned a neuk,   corner
        And out o' sight,
And backlins-comin', to the leuk   backwards, look
        She grew mair bright.

This was denied—it was affirmed;
The herds and hirsels were alarmed,   flocks
The reverend gray-beards raved and stormed
        That beardless laddies
Should think they better were informed
        Then their auld daddies.   fathers

Frae less to mair, it gaed to sticks;   from, more
Frae words and aiths to clours and nicks, oaths, dints and cuts
And mony a fallow gat his licks,   beating
        Wi' hearty crunt;   blows
And some, to learn them for their tricks,
        Were hanged and brunt.   burned

This game was played in monie lands,
And Auld-Light caddies bure sic hands,   *porters bore*
That, faith, the youngsters took the sands
     Wi' nimble shanks,   *legs*
Till lairds forbade, by strict commands,
     Sic bluidy pranks.   *such bloody*

But New-Light herds gat sic a cowe,
Folk thought them ruined stick-and-stowe,   *completely*
Till now amaist on every knowe   *almost, hillock*
     Ye'll find ane placed ;
And some their New-Light fair avow,
     Just quite barefaced.

Nae doubt the Auld-Light flocks are bleatin';
Their zealous herds are vexed and sweatin';
Mysel' I've even seen them greetin'   *crying*
     Wi' girnin' spite,   *grinning*
To hear the moon sae sadly lied on
     By word and write.

But shortly they will cowe the loons !
Some Auld-Light herds in neebor touns   *neighbour*
Are mind't in things they ca' balloons
     To tak a flight,
And stay ae month among the moons,   *one*
     And see them right.

Guid observation they will gie them ;
And when the auld moon's gaun to lea'e them,   *going*
The hindmost shaird, they'll fetch it wi' them,   *fragment*
     Just i' their pouch,
And when the New-Light billies see them,   *fellows*
     I think they'll crouch !

Sae, ye observe that a' this clatter
Is naething but a " moonshine matter ;"   *nothing*
But though dull prose-folk Latin splatter
     In logic tulzie,   *contention*
I hope we bardies ken some better
     Than mind sic brulzie.   *such broil*

THIRD EPISTLE TO JOHN LAPRAIK.

September 13, 1785.

GUIDspeed and furder to you, Johnny,   *prosperity*
Guid health, hale han's, and weather bonny ;
Now when ye're niekan down fu' canny   *cutting*
     The staff o' bread,
May ye ne'er want a stoup o' bran'y   *flagon*
     To clear your head.

May Boreas never thrash your rigs,
Nor kick your rickles aff their legs,   *ricks*

Sendin' the stuff o'er muirs and haggs,   *morasses*
     Like drivin' wrack ;   *sea-weed*
But may the tapmast grain that wags   *topmost*
     Come to the sack.

I'm bizzie too, and skelpin' at it,   *busy, active*
But bitter, daudin' showers hae wat it,   *beating, wet*
Sae my auld stumpie pen I gat it   *got*
     Wi' muckle wark,   *much trouble*
And took my jocteleg and whatt it,   *knife, mended*
     Like ony clark.   *any*

It's now twa month that I'm your debtor,
For your braw, nameless, dateless letter,
Abusin' me for harsh ill nature
     On holy men,
While NOT a hair yoursel' ye're better,
     But mair profane.

But let the kirk-folk ring their bells,
Let's sing about our noble sel's ;   *selves*
We'll cry nae jads frae heathen hills   *jades*
     To help, or roose us,   *praise*
But browster wives and whisky stills,   *brewer*
     They are the Muses.

Your friendship, sir, I winna quat it,   *quit*
And if ye mak objections at it,
Then han' in nieve some day we'll knot it,   *fist*
     And witness take,
Aud when wi' usquebae we've wat it,   *whisky*
     It winna break.

But if the beast and branks be spared   *curb*
Till kye be gaun without the herd,   *cows, going*
And a' the vittel in the yard,   *victuals*
     And theekit right,   *thatched*
I mean your ingle-side to guard   *fireside*
     Ae winter night.   *one*

Then muse-inspirin' aqua vitæ
Shall make us baith sae blythe and witty,   *both*
Till ye forget ye're auld and gutty,   *gouty*
     And be as canty   *cheerful*
As ye were nine year less than thretty,
     Sweet ane and twenty !

But stooks are cowpet wi' the blast,   *shocks, overturned*
And now the sinn keeks in the west,   *sun peeps*
Then I maun rin among the rest,   *run*
     And quat my chanter ;   *quit, pipes*
Sae I subscribe myself in haste,
     Your's, Rab the Ranter.

EPISTLE TO THE REV. JOHN M'MATH.

September 17, 1785.

WHILE t the stook the shearers cower	shock, reapers
To shun the bitter blaudin' shower,	beating
Or in gulravage rinnin' scower	confusion
To pass the time,	
To you I dedicate the hour	
In idle rhyme.	

My Musie, tired wi' mony a sonnet	
On gown, and ban', and douce black bonnet,	sober
Is grown richt eerie now she's done it,	fearful
Lest they should blame her,	
And rouse their holy thunder on it,	
And anathem her.	

I own t'was rash, and rather hardy,	
That I, a simple, country bardie,	bard
Should meddle wi' a pack sae sturdy,	
Wha, if they ken me,	knew
Can easy, wi' a single wordie,	
Lowse KIRKS upon me.	loose

But I gae mad at their grimaces,	
Their sighin', cantin', grace-proud faces,	
Their three-mile prayers, and hauf-mile graces,	half
Their raxin' conscience,	stretching
Whase greed, revenge, and pride disgraces	whose
Waur nor their nonsense.	worse than

There's Gawn,* misea't waur than a beast,	blamed
Wha has mair honour in his breast	
Than mony scores as guid's the priest	
Wha sae abus't him ;	
And may a bard no crack his jest	
What way they've nse't him ?	

See him, the poor man's friend in need,	
The gentleman in word and deed,	
And shall his fame and honour bleed	
By worthless skellums,	wretches
And not a Muse erect her head	
To cowe the blellums ?	talkative fellows

Oh, Pope, had I thy satire's darts	
To gie the rascals their deserts,	give
I'd rip their rotten, hollow hearts,	
And tell aloud	
Their jugglin' hocus-pocus arts	
To cheat the crowd.	

A' KEN I'm no the thing I should be,
Nor am I even he thing I could be,

* Gavin Hamilton.

C

But twenty times I rather would be
      An atheist clean,
Than under gospel colours hid be
      Just for a screen.

An honest man may like a glass,
An honest man may like a lass,
But mean revenge, and malice fause   *false*
      He'll still disdain,
And then cry zeal for gospel laws,
      Like some we ken.

They take religion in their mouth ;
They talk o' mercy, grace, and truth,
For what ? to gie their malice skouth   *scope*
      On some puir wight,   *poor*
And hunt him down o'er right and ruth,
      To ruin straight.

All hail, Religion ! maid divine !
Pardon a Muse sae mean as mine,
Who in her rough imperfect line,
      Thus daurs to name thee ;   *dares*
To stigmatize false friends of thine
      Can ne'er defame thee.

Though blotch't and foul wi' mony a stain
And far unworthy of thy train,
With trembling voice I tune my strain
      To join with those
Who boldly daur thy cause maintain
      In spite o' foes :

In spite o' crowds, in spite o' mobs,
In spite o' undermining jobs,
In spite o' dark banditti stabs
      At worth and merit,
By scoundrels, even wi' holy robes,
      But WICKED spirit.

O Ayr ! my dear, my native ground,
Within thy presbyterial bound
A candid liberal band is found
      Of public teachers,
As men, as Christians too, renowned,
      And manly preachers.

Sir, in that circle you are named ;
Sir, in that circle you are famed ;
And some, by whom your doctrine's blamed
      (Which gies you honour),
Even, sir, by them your heart's esteemed,
      And winning manner.

Pardon this freedom I have ta'en,
And if impertinent I've been,

Impute it not, good sir, in ane   *one*
    Whase heart ne'er wrang'd ye,   *whose*
But to his utmost would befriend
    Ought that belang'd ye.   *belonged to*

TO A MOUSE,

ON TURNING UP HER NEST WITH THE PLOUGH, NOVEMBER 1785.

WEE, sleekit, cow'rin', tim'rous beastie,
Oh what a panic's in thy breastie !
Thou need na start awa sae hasty,
    Wi' bickering brattle !   *hasty clatter*
I wad be laith to rin and chase thee,   *loath*
    Wi' murd'ring pattle !   *ploughstaff*

I'm truly sorry man's dominion
Has broken nature's social union,
And justifies that ill opinion,
    Which makes thee startle
At me, thy poor earth-born companion,
    And fellow mortal !

I doubt na, whyles, but thou may thieve ;   *sometimes*
What then ? poor beastie, thou maun live !   *must*
A daimen icker in a thrave   *ear of corn, 24 sheaves*
    'S a sma request :   *small*
I'll get a blessin' wi' the laive,   *rest*
    And never miss't !

Thy wee bit housie, too, in ruin !   *little*
Its silly wa's the win's are strewin' !   *weak walls, winds*
And naething now to big a new ane   *build*
    O' foggage green,   *rank grass*
And bleak December's winds ensuin',
    Baith snell and keen !   *both sharp*

Thou saw the fields laid bare and waste,
And weary winter comin' fast,
And cozie here, beneath the blast,   *comfortable*
    Thou thought to dwell,
Till, crash ! the cruel coulter passed   *ploughshare*
    Out through thy cell.

That wee bit heap o' leaves and stibble,   *stubble*
Has cost thee mony a weary nibble !   *many*
Now thou's turned out for a' thy trouble,
    But house or hald,   *without, hold*
To thole the winter's sleety dribble,   *endure, drizzle*
    And cranreuch cauld !   *hoar-frost*

But, Mousie, thou art no thy lane,   *alone*
In proving foresight may be vain :

The best-laid schemes o' mice and men,
    Gang aft a-gley,   *go oft wrong*
And lea'e us nought but grief and pain,
    For promised joy.

Still thou art blest, compared wi' me !
The present only toucheth thee :
But, och ! I backward cast my ee,   *eye*
    On prospects drear !
And forward, though I canna see,
    I guess and fear.

HALLOWE'EN.*

The following poem will, by many readers, be well enough understood; but for the sake of those who are unacquainted with the manners and traditions of the country where the scene is cast, notes are added, to give some account of the principal charms and spells of that night, so big with prophecy to the peasantry in the west of Scotland. The passion of prying into futurity makes a striking part of the history of human nature in its rude state, in all ages and nations; and it may be some entertainment to a philosophic mind, if any such should honour the author with a perusal, to see the remains of it among the more unenlightened in our own.

    " Yes ! let the rich deride, the proud disdain,
    The simple pleasures of the lowly train ; -
    To me more dear, congenial to my heart,
    One native charm, than all the gloss of art."
                    GOLDSMITH.—*B.*

UPON that night, when fairies light,
    On Cassilis Downans† dance,
Or owre the lays, in splendid blaze,   *over,* fields
    On sprightly coursers prance ;
Or for Colean the route is ta'en,
    Beneath the moon's pale beams ;
There, up the Cove‡ to stray and rove
    Amang the rocks and streams
        To sport that night.

Amang the bonny, winding banks,
    Where Doon rins, wimplin', clear,   *meandering*
Where Bruce§ ance ruled the martial ranks,   *once*
    And shook his Carrick spear,
Some merry, friendly, country folks
    Together did convene,
To burn their nits, and pou their stocks,   *nuts,* pull
    And haud their Hallowe'en   *hold*
        Fu' blythe that night.

* Hallowe'en or All Hallow Eve is thought to be a night when witches, devils, and other mischief-making beings are all abroad on their baneful midnight errands ; particularly those aërial people, the fairies, are said on that night to hold a grand anniversary.—*B.*
† Certain little romantic, rocky, green hills, in the neighbourhood of the ancient seat of the Earls of Cassilis.—*B.*
‡ A noted cavern near Colean House, called the Cove of Colean ; which, as well as Casilis Downans, is famed in country story for being a favourite haunt of fairies.—*B.*
§ The famous family of that name, the ancestors of Robert, the great deliverer of his country, were Earls of Carrick.—*B.*

Then first and foremost, through the kail,
  Their stocks maun a' be sought ance;
They steek their een, and grap, and wale,
  For muckle anes and straught anes

Hallowe'en p 39

The lasses feat, and cleanly neat, — trim
Mair braw than when they're fine;
Their faces blythe, fu' sweetly kythe, — show
Hearts leal, and warm, and kin': — true
The lads sae trig, wi' wooer-babs — spruce, knots
Weel knotted on their garten, — garter
Some unco blate, and some wi' gabs — very bashful, tongues
Gar lasses' hearts gang startin' — make, go
Whiles fast at night. — sometimes

Then, first and foremost, through the kail, — cabbage
Their stocks* maun a' be sought ance; — [choose
They steek their een, and graip, and wale, — close, eyes, grope,
For muckle anes and straught anes. — big, straight ones
Poor hav'rel Will fell aff the drift, — fool
And wandered through the bow-kail. — cabbage
And pou't, for want o' better shift, — pulled
A runt was like a sow-tail, — stem
Sae bow't that night. — so crooked

Then, straught or crooked, yird or nane, — earth
They roar and cry a' throu'ther;
The very wee things, todlin', rin — tottering
Wi' stocks out-owre their shouther: — over, shoulder
And gif the custoc's sweet or sour, — if, pith
Wi' joctelegs they taste them; — knives
Syne coziely aboon the door, — then comfortably above
Wi' cannie care they've placed them — gentle
To lie that night.

The auld guidwife's weel-hoordet nits† — well-hoarded
Are round and round divided,
And mony lads' and lasses' fates
Are there that night decided:
Some kindle, couthie, side by side, — kindly
And burn thegither trimly; — together
Some start awa wi' saucy pride, — away
And jump out-owre the chimlie — over, chimney
Fu' high that night.

Jean slips in twa wi' tentie ee; — two, watchful
Wha 'twas, she wadna tell;
But this is Jock, and this is me,
She says in to hersel':

* The first ceremony of Hallowe'en is pulling each a stock or plant of cabbage. They must go out, hand in hand, with eyes shut, and pull the first they meet with; its being big or little, straight or crooked, is prophetic of the size and shape of the grand object of all their spells—the husband or wife. If any yird, or earth, stick to the root, that is tocher, or fortune; and the taste of the custoc, that is, the heart of the stem, is indicative of the natural temper and disposition. Lastly, the stems, or, to give them their ordinary appellation, the runts, are placed somewhere above the head of the door, and the Christian names of people whom chance brings into the house are, according to the priority of placing the runts, the names in question.—B.
† Burning the nuts is a famous charm. They name the lad and lass to each particular nut as they lay them in the fire, and accordingly as they burn quietly together, or start from beside one another, the course and issue of the courtship will be.—B.

He bleezed owre her, and she owre him,
  As they wad never mair part :
Till, fuff ! he started up the lum,   *chimney*
  And Jean had e'en a sair heart,   *sore*
      To see't that night.

Poor Willie, wi' his bow kail-runt,
  Was brunt wi' primsie Mallie ;   *burnt, demure*
And Mary, nae doubt, took the drunt,   *pet*
  To be compared to Willie.
Mall's nit lap out wi' pridefu' fling,   *leapt*
  And her ain fit it brunt it ;   *own foot*
While Willie lap, and swore, by jing,
  'Twas just the way he wanted
      To be that night.

Nell had the fause-house in her min',
  She pits hersel' and Rob in ;   *puts*
In loving bleeze they sweetly join,   *blaze*
  Till white in ase they're sobbin'.   *ashes*
Nell's heart was dancin' at the view,
  She whispered Rob to leuk for't :   *observe*
Rob, stowlins, prie'd her bonny mou,   *stealthily kissed*
  Fu' cozie in the neuk for't,   *snugly, nook*
      Unseen that night.

But Merran sat behint their backs,
  Her thoughts on Andrew Bell ;
She lea'es them gashin' at their cracks, *conversing*
  And slips out by hersel :
She through the yard the nearest taks,
  And to the kiln she goes then, .
And darklins graipit for the bauks,   *groped, cross-beams*
  And in the blue-clue* throws then,
      Right fear't that night.

And aye she win't, and aye she swat, *winded, perspired*
  I wat she made nae jaukin' ;   *know, dallying*
Till something held within the pat,   *pot*
  AND THEN ! but she was quakin' !
But whether 'twas the deil himsel,
  Or whether 'twas a bauk-en',   *beam-end*
Or whether it was Andrew Bell,
  She did na wait on talkin'
      To spier that night.   *inquire*

Wee Jenny to her granny says,
  " Will ye go wi' me, granny ?
I'll eat the apple† at the glass
  I gat frae uncle Johnny :"

---

* Whoever would, with success, try this spell, must observe these directions:— Steal out, all alone, to the kiln, and, darkling, throw into the pot a clue of blue yarn ; wind it in a clue off the old one, and, towards the latter end, something will hold the thread ; demand " wha hauds?" that is, who holds ? An answer will be returned from the kiln-pot, by naming the Christian and surname of your future spouse.—B.

† Take a candle, and go alone to a looking-glass ; eat an apple before it, and comb your hair all the time ; the face of your conjugal companion, to be, will be seen in the glass, as if peeping over your shoulder.—B.

She fuff't her pipe wi' sic a lunt,   blew, smoke
  In wrath she was sae vap'rin',   so
She notic't na, an aizle brunt   cinder burnt
  Her braw new worset apron   worsted
    Out through that night.

" Ye little skelpie-limmer's face !   wild girl
  I daur you try sic sportin',   dare
As seek the foul thief ony place,   any
  For him to spae your fortune :   tell
Nae doubt but ye may get a sight !
  Great cause ye hae to fear it ;
For mony a ane has gotten a fright,   many one
  And lived and died deleeret   delirious
    On sic a night.

" Ae hairst afore the Sherra-muir—   one harvest
  I mind't as weel's yestreen,   well, yesterday
I was a gilpey then, I'm sure   young girl
  I was na past fifteen :
The simmer had been cauld and wat,   summer, cold, wet
  And stuff was unco green ;   very
And aye a rantin' kirn we gat   noisy harvest-home
  And just on Hallowe'en
    It fell that night."

  *   *   *   *   *   *

Then up gat fechtin' Jamie Fleck,   fighting
  And he swore by his conscience,
That he could saw* hemp-seed a peck ;   sow
  For it was a' but nonsense.
The auld guidman raught down the pock,   reached
  And out a handfu' gied him ;   gave
Syne bad him slip frae 'mang the folk,   then
  Some time when nae ane see'd him,   saw
    And try't that night.

He marches through amang the stacks,
  Though he was something sturtin ;   timorous
The graip he for a harrow taks,   dung-fork
  And haurls at his curpin ;   drags, rear
And every now and then he says,
  " Hemp-seed, I saw thee,
And her that is to be my lass,
  Come after me, and draw thee,
    As fast this night."

He whistled up Lord Lennox' march,
  To keep his courage cheerie ;
Although his hair began to arch,
  He was sae fley'd and eerie :   frightened

* Steal out, unperceived, and sow a handful of hemp-seed, harrowing it with anything you can conveniently draw after you. Repeat, now and then, " Hemp-seed I saw thee, hemp-seed I saw thee ; and him (or her) that is to be my true love, come after me and pou thee." Look over your left shoulder, and you will see the appearance of the person invoked, in the attitude of pulling hemp. Some traditions say, " Come after me, and shaw thee," that is, show thyself; in which case it simply appears. Others omit the harrowing, and say, " Come after me, and harrow thee."—*B.*

Till presently he hears a squeak,
And then a grane and gruntle;   groan, grunt
He by his shouther ga'e a keek,   peep
And tumbled wi' a wintle   stagger
    Out-owre that night.

He roared a horrid murder-shout,
In dreadfu' desperation !
And young and auld cam rinnin' out
And hear the sad narration :
He swore 'twas hilchin Jean M'Craw,   halting
Or crouchie Merran Humphie,   crook-backed
Till, stop—she trotted through them a'—
And wha was it but Grumphie   the pig
    Asteer that night !   astir

Meg fain wad to the barn hae gaen,   would, gone
To win three wechts o' naething ;*   corn-baskets
But for to meet the deil her lane,
She pat but little faith in :   put
She gies the Herd a pickle nits,   few nuts
And twa red-checkit apples,
To watch, while for the barn she sets,
In hopes to see Tam Kipples
    That very night.

She turns the key wi' canny thraw,   gentle
And owre the threshold ventures ;   over
But first on Sawny gies a ca',
Syne bauldly in she enters :   then boldly
A ratton rattled up the wa',   rat
And she cried out, " Preserve her !"
And ran through midden hole and a',
And prayed wi' zeal and fervour,
    Fu' fast that night.

They hoy't out Will, wi' sair advice ;   urged, strong
They hecht him some fine braw ane ;   promised, one
It chanced, the stack he faddom't thrice,†   measured
Was timmer-propt for thrawin' ;   timber, twisting
He taks a swirly auld moss oak   twisted
For some black, grousome carlin ;   odious-looking fellow
And loot a winze and drew a stroke,   let, oath
Till skin in blypes cam haurlin'   shreds, dragging
    Aff's nieves that night.   off his hands

A wanton widow Leezie was,
As canty as a kittlin ;   merry, kitten

* This charm must likewise be performed unperceived, and alone. You go to the barn, and open both doors, taking them off the hinges if possible; for there is danger that the being about to appear may shut the doors, and do you some mischief. Then take that instrument used in winnowing the corn which, in our country dialect, we call a wecht, and go through all the attitudes of letting down corn against the wind. Repeat it three times; and the third time an apparition will pass through the barn, in at the window door, and out at the other, having both the figure in question, and the appearance or retinue, marking the employment or station in life.—B.
† Take an opportunity of going, unnoticed, to a bean-stack, and fathom it three times round. The last fathom of the last time you will catch in your arms the appearance of your future conjugal yoke-fellow.—B.

But, och! that night, amang the shaws,   *woods*
  She got a fearfu' settlin'!   *[stones*
She through the whins, and by the cairn,   *gorse, heap of*
  And owre the hill gaed scrievin,   *went swiftly*
Where three lairds' lands meet at a burn,*
  To dip her left sark-sleeve in,   *shift*
      Was bent that night.

Whyles owre a linn the burnie plays,   *sometimes, cascade*
  As through the glen it wimpl't;   *meandered*
Whyles round a rocky scaur it strays;   *cliff*
  Whyles in a wiel it dimpl't;   *eddy*
Whyles glittered to the nightly rays,
  Wi' bickering, dancing dazzle;   *racing*
Whyles cookit underneath the braes,   *appear and disappear*
  Below the spreading hazel,
      Unseen that night.

Amang the brackens, on the brae,   *fern*
  Between her and the moon,
The deil, or else an outler quey,   *unhoused*
  Gat up and gae a croon: *moan*
Poor Leezy's heart maist lap the hool;   *almost, leapt, sheath*
  Near lav'rock-height she jumpit,   *lark*
But mist a fit, and in the pool   *missed, foot*
  Out-owre the lugs she plumpit,   *ears*
      Wi' a plunge that night.

In order, on the clean hearth-stane,
  The luggies three are ranged.   *dishes*
And every time great care is ta'en
  To see them duly changed:
Auld uncle John, wha wedlock's joys
  Sin' Mar's year† did desire,
Because he gat the toom dish thrice   *empty*
  He heaved them on the fire
      In wrath that night.

Wi' merry sangs, and friendly cracks,
  I wat they did na weary;   *know*
And unco tales and funny jokes,   *strange*
  Their sports were cheap and cheery;
Till butter'd so'ns,‡ wi' fragrant lunt,   *smoke*
  Set a' their gabs a-steerin;   *mouths*
Syne, wi' a social glass o' strunt,   *then, spirits*
  They parted aff careerin'
      Fu' blythe that night.§

---

* You go out, one or more, for this is a social spell, to a south running spring or rivulet, where "three lairds' lands meet," and dip your left shirt-sleeve. Go to bed in sight of a fire, and hang your wet sleeve before it to dry. Lie awake: and some time near midnight, an apparition, having the exact figure of the grand object in question, will come and turn the sleeve, as if to dry the other side of it.—B.
† The year 1715, when the Earl of Mar raised an insurrection in Scotland.
‡ Sowens, with butter instead of milk to them, is the Hallowe'en supper.—B.
§ Most of these superstitious ceremonies have fallen into disuse.

SECOND EPISTLE TO DAVIE,

A BROTHER POET.

AULD NEIBOR,

    I'M three times doubly o'er your debtor,
For your auld-farrant, frien'ly letter ;   **sen**sible
Though I maun say't,·I doubt ye flatter,   must
    Ye speak sae fair,
For my puir, silly, rhymin' clatter   poor
    Some less maun sair.   serve

Hale be your heart, hale be your fiddle ;
Lang may your elbock jink and diddle,   elbow
To cheer you through the weary widdle   bustle
    O' war'ly cares,   worldly
Till bairns' bairns kindly cuddle   caress
    Your auld gray hairs.

But, Davie lad, I'm red ye're glaikit;   guess, foolish
I'm tauld the Muse ye hae negleckit ;   told
And gif it's sae, you sud be licket,   if so, should, beaten
    Until ye fyke ;   be restless
Sic hauns as you sud ne'er be faiket,   hands, wanted
    Be hain't wha like.   spared

For me, I'm on Parnassus' brink,
Rivin' the words to gar them clink ;   tearing, make
Whyles daez't wi' love, whyles daez't wi' drink, stupified
    Wi' jads or masons ;
And whyles, but aye owre late, I think,   sometimes, too
    Braw sober lessons.

Of a' the thoughtless son's o' man,
Commen' me to the bardie clan ;   poet
Except it be some idle plan
    O' rhymin' clink,
NAE NEED INDEED that I sud ban,   should
    They ever think.

Nae thought, nae view, nae scheme o' livin',
Nae cares to gie us joy or grievin ;'
But just the pouchie put the nieve in,   pocket, fist
    And while ought's there,
Then hiltie skiltie, we gae scrievin',   gleesomely
    And fash nae mair.   trouble

Leeze me on rhyme ! it's aye a treasure, blessings on
My chief, amaist my only pleasure,   almost
At hame, a-fiel', at wark, or leisure ; in field, work
    The Muse, poor hizzie !   lass
Though rough and raploch be her measure, coarse
    She's seldom lazy.

Haud to the Muse, my dainty Davie :   keep
The warl' may play you monie a shavie ; prank

But for the Muse, she'll never leave ye,
  Though e'er sae puir,   poor
Na, even though limpin' wi' the spavie
  Frae door to door.

MAN WAS MADE TO MOURN.

A DIRGE.

WHEN chill November's surly blast
  Made fields and forests bare,
One evening, as I wandered forth
  Along the banks of Ayr,
I spied a man whose aged step
  Seemed weary, worn with care;
His face was furrowed o'er with years,
  And hoary was his hair,

"Young stranger, whither wanderest thou?"
  Began the reverend sage:
"Does thirst of wealth thy step constrain,
  Or youthful pleasure's rage?
Or haply, prest with cares and woes,
  Too soon thou hast began
To wander forth, with me, to mourn
  The miseries of man.

"The sun that overhangs yon moors,
  Outspreading far and wide,
Where hundreds labour to support
  A haughty lordling's pride:
I've seen yon weary winter sun
  Twice forty times return,
And every time has added proofs
  That man was made to mourn.

"Oh, man! while in thy early years,
  How prodigal of time;
Misspending all thy precious hours,
  Thy glorious youthful prime!
Alternate follies take the sway;
  Licentious passions burn;
Which tenfold force gives Nature's law,
  That man was made to mourn.

"Look not alone on youthful prime,
  Or manhood's active might;
Man then is useful to his kind,
  Supported is his right:
But see him on the edge of life,
  With cares and sorrows worn;
Then age and want—oh ill-matched pair!—
  Show man was made to mourn.

" A few seem favourites of fate,
    In pleasure's lap carest;
Yet think not all the rich and great
    Are likewise truly blest.
But, oh ! what crowds in every land,
    All wretched and forlorn !
Through weary life this lesson learn---
    That man was made to mourn.

" Many and sharp the numerous ills
    Inwoven with our frame !
More pointed still we make ourselves
    Regret, remorse, and shame ;
And man, whose heaven-erected face
    The smiles of love adorn,
Man's inhumanity to man
    Makes countless thousands mourn !.

" See yonder poor, o'erlaboured wight,
    So abject, mean, and vile,
Who begs a brother of the earth
    To give him leave to toil ;
And see his lordly fellow-worm
    The poor petition spurn,
Unmindful, though a weeping wife
    And helpless offspring mourn.

" If I'm designed yon lordling's slave--
    By Nature's law designed—
Why was an independent wish
    E'er planted in my mind ?
If not, why am I subject to
    His cruelty or scorn ?
Or why has man the will and power
    To make his fellow mourn ?

" Yet let not this too much, my son,
    Disturb thy youthful breast ;
This partial view of human kind
    Is surely not the last !
The poor, oppressed, honest man
    Had never, sure, been born,
Had there not been some recompense
    To comfort those that mourn !

" Oh, Death ! the poor man's dearest friend --
    The kindest and the best !
Welcome the hour my aged limbs
    Are laid with thee at rest !
The great, the wealthy, fear thy blow,
    From pomp and pleasure torn !
But, oh ! a blest relief to those
    That, weary-laden, mourn !"

ADDRESS TO THE DEIL.

Oh Prince! oh chief of many throned powers,
That led the embattled seraphim to war.—MILTON.

GREAT is thy power, and great thy fame;
Far ken'd and noted is thy name;   known
And though yon lowin' heugh's thy hame,   flaming hollow
    Thou travels far;
And, faith! thou's neither lag nor lame,   slow
    Nor blate nor scaur.   bashful, easily scared

Whyles, ranging like a roaring lion,   sometimes
For prey a' holes and corners tryin';
Whyles on the strong-winged tempest flyin',
    Tirlin' the kirks;   uncovering
Whyles in the human bosom pryin',
    Unseen thou lurks.

I've heard my reverend grannie say,
In lanely glens ye like to stray;
Or where auld ruined castles, gray,
    Nod to the moon,
Ye fright the nightly wanderer's way
    Wi' eldritch croon.   hideous moan

When twilight did my grannie summon,
To say her prayers, douce, honest woman!   grave
Aft yont the dike she's heard you bummin',   wall, buzzing
    Wi' eerie drone;   dreary
Or, rustlin', through the boortries comin',   elder-trees
    Wi' heavy groan.

Ae dreary, windy, winter night,   one
The stars shot down wi' sklentin' light,   glancing
Wi' you, mysel, I gat a fright
    Ayont the loch,
Ye, like a rash-bush, stood in sight,   rush
    Wi' waving sough.   sound

The cudgel in my nieve did shake,   fist
Each bristled hair stood like a stake,
When wi' an eldritch, stoor quaick—quaick,   frightful, hoarse
    Amang the springs,
Awa ye squattered, like a drake,   fluttered
    On whistling wings.

Let warlocks grim, and withered hags,
Tell how wi' you, on ragweed nags,   ragwort
They skim the muirs and dizzy crags,
    Wi' wicked speed;
And in kirkyards renew their leagues
    Owre howkit dead.   over excavated

Thence countra wives, wi' toil and pain,   country
May plunge and plunge the kirn in vain;   churn
For, oh! the yellow treasure's taen   taken
    By witching skill

And dawtit, twal-pint Hawkie's gaen   petted, twelve, become
     As yell's the bill.   *   *   *   milkless, bull

When thowes dissolve the snawy hoord,   thaws
And float the jinglin' icy boord,
Then water-kelpies haunt the foord,   water-spirits
     By your direction ;
And 'nighted travellers are allured
     To their destruction.

And aft your moss-traversing spunkies   Will o' the Wisp
Decoy the wight that late and drunk is :
The bleezin', WILD, mischevious monkeys   blazing
     Delude his eyes,
Till in some miry slough he sunk is,
     Ne'er mair to rise.   more

When mason's mystic word and grip,
In storms and tempests raise you up,
Some cock or cat your rage maun stop,
     Or, strange to tell !
The youngest brother ye wad whip
     Aff straught YOURSEL.

Langsyne, in Eden's bonny yard,
When youthfu' lovers first were paired,
And all the soul of love they shared,
     The raptured hour,
Sweet on the fragrant flowery swaird,   sward
     In shady bower.

Then you, ye auld sneck-drawing dog !   old stealthy
Ye came to Paradise incog.,
And played on man a cursed brogue,   trick
     (Black be your fa !)
And gied the infant warld a shog,   gave, shake
     'Maist ruined a'.

D'ye mind that day, when in a bizz,   [hair
Wi' reekit duds, and reestit gizz,   smoked clothes, withered
Ye did present your smootie phiz   dirty
     'Mang better folk,
And sklented on the man of Uzz   glanced
     Your spitefu' joke ?

And how ye gat him i' your thrall,
And brak him out o' house and hall,
While scabs and blotches did him gall,
     Wi' bitter claw,
And lows'd his ill-tongued, wicked scawl,   scolding wife
     Was warst ava ?   worst of all

But a' your doings to rehearse,
Your wily snares and fechtin' fierce,   fighting
Sin' that day Michael did you pierce,
     Down to this time,

Wad ding a Lallan tongue, or Erse,   beat, Lowland,
    In prose or rhyme.   [Highland

And now, auld Cloots, I ken ye're thinkin',   know
A certain' bardie's rantin', drinkin',
Some luckless hour will send him linkin'
    To your black pit ;
But, faith ! he'll turn a corner jinkin',   suddenly
    And cheat you yet.

But fare-you-weel, auld Nickie-ben !
O wad ye tak a thought and men' !
Ye aiblins might—I dinna ken—   perhaps
    Still hae a stake—
I'm wae to think upo' yon den,
    Even for your sake !

TO JAMES SMITH.

" Friendship ! mysterious cement of the soul !
Sweet'ner of life, and solder of society !
I owe thee much !"—BLAIR.

DEAR Smith, the slee'est, paukie thief,   sly, wheedling
That e'er attempted stealth or rief,   robbery
Ye surely hae some warlock-breef   spell
    Owre human hearts ;
For ne'er a bosom yet was prief   proof
    Against your arts.

For me, I swear by sun and moon,
And every star that blinks aboon,   twinkles
Ye've cost me twenty pair o' shoon   shoes
    Just gaun to see you ;   going
And every ither pair that's done,   other
    Mair ta'en I'm wi' you.   more taken

That auld capricious carlin, Nature,   woman
To mak amends for scrimpit stature,   stinted
She's turned you aff, a human creature
    On her first plan ;
And in her freaks, on every feature
    She's wrote, the Man.

Just now I've ta'en the fit o' rhyme,
My barmie noddle's working prime,   yeasty
My fancy yerkit up sublime   fermented
    Wi' hasty summon :
Hae ye a leisure-moment's time
    To hear what's comin' ?

Some rhyme a neighbour's name to lash ;
Some rhyme (vain thought !) for needfu' cash ;
Some rhyme to court the country clash,   gossip
    And raise a din ;

For me, an aim I never fash—   trouble
  I rhyme for fun.

The star that rules my luckless lot,
Has fated me the russet coat,
CONDEMNED my fortune to the groat; fourpence
  But in requit,
Has blest me wi' a random shot
  O' country wit.

This while my notion's ta'en a sklent, bent
To try my fate in guid black prent; print
But still the mair I'm that way bent,
  Something cries "Hoolie! gently
I red you, honest man, tak tent! warn, care
  Ye'll shaw your folly. show

" There's ither poets much your betters,
Far seen in Greek, deep men o' letters,
Hae thought they had insured their debtors
  A' future ages;
Now moths deform in shapeless tatters
  Their unknown pages."

Then farewell hopes o' laurel-boughs
To garland my poetic brows!
Henceforth I'll rove where busy ploughs
  Are whistling thrang, busy
And teach the lanely heights and howes lonely, hollows
  My rustic sang.

I'll wander on, with tentless heed careless
How never-halting moments speed,
Till fate shall snap the brittle thread;
  Then, all unknown,
I'll lay me with the inglorious dead,
  Forgot and gone!

But why o' death begin a tale?
Just now we're living sound and hale,
Then top and maintop crowd the sail,
  Heave care o'er side!
And large before enjoyment's gale,
  Let's tak the tide.

This life, sae far's I understand,
Is a' enchanted fairy land,
Where pleasure is the magic wand,
  That, wielded right,
Maks hours like minutes, hand-in-hand,
  Dance by fu' light.

The magic wand then let us wield;
For, ance that five-and-forty's speel'd, once, climbed
See, crazy, weary, joyless eild, age
  Wi' wrinkled face,

Comes hostin', hirplin' owre the field,   coughing, limping
      Wi' creepin' pace.   [o'er

When ance life's day draws near the gloamin',   twilight
Then fareweel vacant careless.roamin';
And fareweel cheerfu' tankards foamin',
      And social noise;
And fareweel dear, deluding woman!
      The joy of joys!

Oh, Life! how pleasant in thy morning,
Young Fancy's rays the hills adorning!
Cold-pausing Caution's lesson scorning,
      We frisk away,
Like schoolboys, at the expected warning,
      To joy and play.

We wander there, we wander here,
We eye the rose upon the brier,
Unmindful that the thorn is near,
      Among the leaves!
And though the puny wound appear,
      Short while it grieves.

Some, lucky, find a flowery spot,
For which they never toiled or swat;
They drink the sweet and eat the fat,
      But care or pain;   without
And, haply, eye the barren hut
      With high disdain.

With steady aim some Fortune chase;
Keen Hope does every sinew brace;
Through fair, through foul, they urge the race,
      And seize the prey:
Then cannie, in some cozie place,   quietly, snug
      They close the day.

And others, like your humble servan',
Poor wights! nae rules nor roads observin';
To right or left, eternal swervin',
      They zig-zag on;
Till, curst with age, obscure and starvin',
      They aften groan.   oft

Alas! what bitter toil and straining—
But truce with peevish, poor complaining!
Is Fortune's fickle Luna waning?
      E'en let her gang!   go
Beneath what light she has remaining,
      Let's sing our sang.

My pen I here fling to the door,
And kneel, "Ye Powers," and warm implore,
"Though I should wander Terra o'er,
      In all her climes,
Grant me but this, I ask no more,
      Aye rowth o' rhymes.   abundance

"Gie dreeping roasts to country lairds,   *dripping*
Till icicles hing frae their beards;
Gie fine braw claes to fine life-guards,   *clothes*
          And maids of honour!
And yill and whisky gie to cairds,   *ale, tinkers*
          Until they sconner.   *are nauseated*

"A title, Dempster merits it;
A garter gie to Willie Pitt;
Gie wealth to some be-ledgered cit,   *give*
          In cent. per cent.;
But give me real, sterling wit,
          And I'm content.

"While ye are pleased to keep me hale,   *healthy*
I'll sit down o'er my scanty meal,
Be't water-brose, or muslin kail,   *broth*
          Wi' cheerfu' face,
As lang's the Muses dinna fail
          To say the grace."

An anxious ee I never throws   *eye*
Behint my lug or by my nose;   *ear*
I jouk beneath Misfortune's blows   *shy away*
          As weel's I may;
Sworn foe to sorrow, care, and prose,
          I rhyme away.

Oh ye douce folk, that live by rule,   *sober*
Grave, tideless-blooded, calm and cool,
Compared wi' you—oh fool! fool! fool!
          How much unlike;
Your hearts are just a standing pool,
          Your lives a dike!   *wall*

Nae hairbrained, sentimental traces,
In your unlettered nameless faces!
In arioso trills and graces
          Ye never stray,
But gravissimo, solemn basses
          Ye hum away.

Ye are sae grave, nae doubt ye're wise;
Nae ferly though ye do despise   *wonder*
The hairum-scairum, ram-stam boys,   *hairbrained, forward*
          The rattling squad:
I see you upward cast your eyes—
          —Ye ken the road.

Whilst I—but I shall haud me there—
Wi' you I'll scarce gang onywhere—
Then, Jamie, I shall say nae mair,
          But quat my sang,   *quit*
Content with you to mak a pair,
          Whare'er I gang.

THE VISION.

DUAN FIRST.*

THE sun had closed the winter day,
The curlers† quat their roaring play,   quit
And hunger'd maukin ta'en her way   hare
        To kail-yards green,   cabbage
While faithless snaws ilk step betray   snows, each
        Whare she has been.

The thrasher's weary flingin' tree   flail
The lee-lang day had tirèd me;   live-long
And when the day had closed his ee,   eye
        Far i' the west,
Ben i' the spence, right pensivelie,   inner-room
        I gaed to rest.   went

There, lanely by the ingle-cheek,   lonely, fireside
I sat and eyed the spewing reek,   smoke
That filled wi' hoast-provoking smeek   cough, smoke
        The auld clay biggin';   house
And heard the restless rattons squeak   rats
        About the riggin'.

All in this mottie, misty clime,   full of motes
I backward mused on wasted time,
How I had spent my youthfu' prime,
        And done nae thing,
But stringin' blethers up in rhyme,   nonsense
        For fools to sing.

Had I to guid advice but harkit,   hearkened
I might, by this, hae led a market,   ere
Or strutted in a bank, and clarkit   clerked
        My cash-account:
While here, half-mad, half-fed, half-sarkit, shirted
        Is a' the amount.

I started, muttering, blockhead! coof!   fool
And heaved on high my waukit loof,   hardened palm
To swear by a' yon starry roof,
        Or some rash aith,   oath
That I henceforth would be rhyme-proof,
        Till my last breath—

When, click! the string the snick did draw; latch
And, jee! the door gaed to the wa';   went
And by my ingle-lowe I saw,   fire-flame
        Now bleezin' bright.   blazing
A tight, outlandish hizzie, braw,   woman
        Come full in sight.

---

* *Duan*, a term of Ossian's for the different divisions of a digressive poem. See his "Cath-Loda," vol. ii. of M'Pherson's translation.—*B.*
† A game on the ice nearly resembling bowls; large stones, smooth on the bottom. are hurled along the ice instead of bowls.

Ye needna doubt I held my whist;   tongue
The infant aith, half-formèd was crusht;
I glowr'd as eerie's I'd been dusht   stared, struck down
     In some wild glen;
When sweet, like modest Worth, she blusht,
     And steppèd ben.   in

Green, slender, leaf-clad holly-boughs
Were twisted gracefu' round her brows;
I took her for some Scottish Muse,
     By that same token,
And come to stop those reckless vows,
     Would soon been broken.

A "hairbrained, sentimental trace"
Was strongly markèd in her face;
A wildly-witty, rustic grace
     Shone full upon her;
Her eye, even turned on empty space,
     Beam'd keen with honour.

Down flowed her robe, a tartan sheen,
Till half a leg was scrimply seen;
And such a leg! my bonny Jean
     Could only peer it;
Sae straught, sae taper, tight and clean,   straight, neat
     Nane else cam near it.   none

Her mantle large, of greenish hue,
My gazing wonder chiefly drew;
Deep lights and shades, bold-mingling, threw
     A lustre grand;
And seemed to my astonished view
     A well-known land.

Here, rivers in the sea were lost;
There, mountains to the skies were tost:
Here, tumbling billows mark'd the coast
     With surging foam;
There, distant shone Art's lofty boast—
     The lordly dome.

Here Doon pour'd down his far-fetched floods;
There, well-fed Irwine stately thuds: sounds
Auld hermit Ayr staw through his woods,   stole
     On to the shore,
And many a lesser torrent scuds   runs quickly
     With seeming roar.

Low in a sandy valley spread,
An ancient borough reared her head   (Ayr)
Still, as in Scottish story read,
     She boasts a race,
To every nobler virtue bred,
     And polished grace.

By stately tower or palace fair,
Or ruins pendant in the air,

Bold stems of heroes, here and there,
    I could discern;
Some seemed to muse, some seemed to dare,
    With feature stern.

My heart did glowing transport feel,
  To see a race heroic wheel,   (the Wallaces)
And brandish round the deep-dyed steel
    In sturdy blows;
While back-recoiling seemed to reel
    Their suthron foes.   southern

His country's saviour, mark him well!   (Wm. Wallace)
Bold Richardton's heroic swell;
The chief on Sark who glorious fell   (Wallace of Craigie)
    In high command;
And he whom ruthless fates expel
    His native land.

There, where a sceptered Pictish shade*
Stalked round his ashes lowly laid,
I mark'd a martial race, portrayed
    In colours strong;
Bold, soldier-featured, undismayed
    They strode along.   (the Montgomeries)

Through many a wild romantic grove,   (Barskimming)
Near many a hermit-fancied cove
(Fit haunts for friendship or for love),
    In musing mood,
An aged judge, I saw him rove,
    Dispensing good.

With deep-struck reverential awe,
The learned sire and son I saw,†
To Nature's God and Nature's law
    They gave their lore,
This, all its source and end to draw;
    That, to adore.

Brydone's brave ward I well could spy,   (Col. Fullerton)
Beneath old Scotia's smiling eye;
Who called on Fame, low standing by,
    To hand him on,
Where many a patriot-name on high,
    And hero shone

DUAN SECOND.

With musing-deep, astonished stare,
I viewed the heavenly-seeming fair;
A whispering throb did witness bear
    Of kindred sweet,

* Coilus, king of the Picts, from whom the district of Kyle is said to take its name, lies buried, as tradition says, near the family seat of the Montgomeries of Coilsfield, where his burial-place is still shown.—B.
† The Rev. Dr Matthew Stewart, the celebrated mathematician, and his son, Professor Dugald Stewart.

When with an elder sister's air
　　　She did me greet,

" All hail! my own inspirèd bard!
In me thy native Muse regard!
Nor longer mourn thy fate is hard,
　　　Thus poorly low
I come to give thee such reward
　　　As we bestow.

" Know, the great genius of this land
Has many a light, aërial band,
Who, all beneath his high command,
　　　Harmoniously,
As arts or arms they understand,
　　　Their labours ply.

" They Scotia's race among them share;
Some fire the soldier on to dare;
Some rouse the patriot up to bear
　　　Corruption's heart:
Some teach the bard, a darling care,
　　　The tuneful art.

" 'Mong swelling floods of reeking gore,
They, ardent, kindling spirits, pour;
Or, 'mid the venal senate's roar,
　　　They, sightless, stand,
To mend the honest patriot-lore,
　　　And grace the hand.

" And when the bard, or hoary sage,
Charm or instruct the future age,
They bind the wild, poetic rage
　　　In energy,
Or point the inconclusive page
　　　Full on the eye.

" Hence Fullarton, the brave and young;
Hence Dempster's zeal-inspired tongue;
Hence sweet harmonious Beattie sung
　　　His ' Minstrel lays;'
Or tore, with noble ardour stung,
　　　The sceptic's bays.

" To lower orders are assigned
The humbler ranks of humankind,
The rustic bard, the labouring hind,
　　　The artizan;
All choose, as various they're inclined,
　　　The various man.

" When yellow waves the heavy grain,
The threatening storm some, strongly, rein;
Some teach to meliorate the plain,
　　　With tillage skill;
And some instruct the shepherd-train,
　　　Blithe o'er the hill.

"Some hint the lover's harmless wile;
Some grace the maiden's artless smile;
Some soothe the labourer's weary toil,
For humble gains,
And make his cottage-scenes beguile
His cares and pains.

"Some, bounded to a district-space,
Explore at large man's infant race,
To mark the embryotic trace
Of rustic bard;
And careful note each opening grace,
A guide and guard.

"Of these am I—Coila my name;
And this district as mine I claim,
Where once the Campbells, chiefs of fame,
Held ruling power:
I marked thy embryo tuneful flame,
Thy natal hour.

"With future hope, I oft would gaze,
Fond, on thy little early ways,
Thy rudely-carrolled, chiming phrase,
In uncouth rhymes,
Fired at the simple, artless lays,
Of other times.

"I saw thee seek the sounding shore,
Delighted with the dashing roar;
Or when the north his fleecy store
Drove through the sky,
I saw grim Nature's visage hoar
Struck thy young eye.

"Or when the deep green-mantled earth
Warm cherished every floweret's birth,
And joy and music pouring forth
In every grove,
I saw thee eye the general mirth
With boundless love.

"When ripened fields, and azure skies,
Called forth the reaper's rustling noise,
I saw thee leave their evening joys,
And lonely stalk,
To vent thy bosom's swelling rise
In pensive walk.

"When youthful love, warm-blushing, strong,
Keen-shivering shot thy nerves along,
Those accents, grateful to thy tongue,
Th' adored Name,
I taught thee how to pour in song,
To soothe thy flame.

"I saw thy pulse's maddening play,
Wild send thee Pleasure's devious way,

Misled by Fancy's meteor-ray,
      By Passion driven;
But yet the light that led astray
      Was light from Heaven.

" I taught thy manners painting strains,
The loves, the wants of simple swains,
Till now, o'er all my wide domains
      Thy fame extends;
And some, the pride of Coila's plains,
      Become thy friends.

" Thou canst not learn, nor can I show,
To paint with Thomson's landscape glow;
Or wake the bosom-melting throe,
      With Shenstone's art;
Or pour, with Gray, the moving flow
      Warm on the heart.

" Yet, all beneath the unrivalled rose,
The lowly daisy sweetly blows;
Though large the forest's monarch throws
      His army shade,
Yet green the juicy hawthorn grows
      Adown the glade.

" Then never murmur nor repine;
Strive in thy humble sphere to shine;
And, trust me, not Potosi's mine,
      Nor king's regard,
Can give a bliss o'ermatching thine,
      A rustic bard.

" To give my counsels all in one—
Thy tuneful flame still careful fan;
Preserve the dignity of man,
      With soul erect;
And trust, the universal plan
      Will all protect.

" And wear thou this "—she solemn said,
And bound the holly round my head.
The polished leaves, and berries red,
      Did rustling play;
And, like a passing thought, she fled
      In light away.

ADDITIONAL STANZAS OF " THE VISION."

A manuscript in Burns' handwriting, containing additional stanzas of " The Vision," is now in the possession of Mr John Dick, bookseller, Ayr; it seems to be the manuscript sent by Burns to Mrs Stewart of Stair, when contemplating his West-Indian voyage.
By Mr Dick's kind permission we are enabled to give the additional stanzas here.

AFTER 18th stanza of printed copies :
    With secret throes I marked that earth,
    That cottage, witness of my birth;

And near 1 saw, bold issuing forth
  In youthful pride,
A Lindsay, race of noble worth,
  Famed far and vide.

Where, hid behind a spreading wood,
An ancient Pict-built mansion stood,
I spied, among an angel brood,
  A female pair;
Sweet shone their high maternal blood   (Sundrum)
  And father's air.

An ancient tower to memory brought   (Stair)
How Dettingen's bold hero fought;
Still far from sinking into nought,
  It owns a lord
Who " far in western"* climates fought,
  With trusty sword.

There, where a sceptred Pictish shade
Stalked round his ashes lowly laid,
I saw a martial race portrayed   (the Montgomeries)
  In colours strong;
Bold, sodger-featured, undismayed,
  They stalked along.

Among the rest I well could spy
One gallant, graceful, martial boy,
The sodger sparkled in his eye,
  A diamond water;
I blest that noble badge with joy
  That owned me *frater*.†

After the 20th stanza:

Near by arose a mansion fine,   (Auchinleck)
The seat of many a Muse divine;
Not rustic Muses such as mine,
  With holly crowned,
But th' ancient, tuneful, laurelled Nine,
  From classic ground.

I mourned the card that Fortune dealt,
To see where bonny Whitefoords dwelt; (Ballochmyle)
But other prospects made me melt,
  That village near;   (Mauchline)
There Nature, Friendship, Love I felt,
  Fond mingling dear.

Hail! Nature's pang, more strong than death!
Warm Friendship's glow, like kindling wrath!
Love, dearer than the parting breath
  Of dying friend!

* These words are written over the original in another hand.
† Captain James Montgomery, Master of St James's Lodge, Tarbolton, to which the author has the honour to belong.—B.

"Not even"* with life's wild devious path,
   Your force shall end!
The power that gave the soft alarms,
In blooming Whitefoord's rosy charms,
Still threats the tiny-feathered arms,
   The barbèd dart;
While lovely Wilhelmina warms
   The coldest heart.†

After the 21st—

Where Lugar leaves his moorland plaid, (Cumnock)
Where lately Want was idly laid
I markèd, busy, bustling Trade,
   In fervid flame,
Beneath a patroness's aid,
   Of noble name;

While countless hills I could survey,
And countless flocks as well as they;
But other scenes did charms display,
   That better please,
Where polished manners dwelt with Gray (Mrs F. Gray)
   In rural ease.

Where Cessnock pours with gurgling sound, (Auchinskieth)
And Irwine, marking out the bound,
Enamoured of the scenes around,
   Slow runs his race,
A name I doubly honoured found, (Caprington)
   With knightly grace.

Brydone's brave ward, I saw him stand, (Col. Fullarton)
Fame humbly offering her hand;
And near his kinsman's rustic band, (Dr Fullarton)
   With one accord,
Lamenting their late blessed land
   Must change its lord.

The owner of a pleasant spot,
Near sandy wilds I did him note; (Orangefield)
A heart too warm, a pulse too hot,
   At times o'erran;
But large in every feature wrote,
   Appeared the man.

---

* Originally written "only."
† Miss Wilhelmina Alexander, the "Bonny Lass of Ballochmyle"

SCOTCH DRINK.

" Gie him strong drink, until he wink,
 That's sinking in despair;
And liquor guid to fire his bluid,
 That's prest wi' grief and care;
There let him boose and deep carouse,
 Wi' bumpers flowing o'er,
Till he forgets his loves or debts,
 And minds his griefs no more."

LET other poets raise a fracas
'Bout vines, and wines, and drucken Bacchus,
And crabbit names and stories wrack us,   crabbed, vex
   And grate our lug,   ear
I sing the juice Scotch beare can mak us,   barley
   In glass or jug.

O thou, my Muse! guid auld Scotch drink;
Whether through wimplin' worms thou jink,   twisting, turn
Or, richly brown, ream o'er the brink,   cream
   In glorious faem,   foam
Inspire me, till I lisp and wink,
   To sing thy name!

Let husky wheat the haughs adorn,   valleys
And aits set up their awnie horn,   oats, bearded
And peas and beans, at e en or morn,
   Perfume the plain,
Leeze me on thee, John Barleycorn,   blessings on
   Thou king o' grain!

On thee aft Scotland chows her cood,   chews, cud
In souple scones, the wale o' food!   supple cakes, choice
Or tumbling in the boilin' flood
   Wi' kail and beef;   cabbage
But when thou pours thy strong heart's blood,
   There thou shine's chief.

Food fills the wame, and keeps us livin'   belly
Though life's a gift no worth receivin',
When heavy dragg'd wi' pine and grievin';   pain
   But, oiled by thee,
The wheels o' life gae down-hill scrievin',   swiftly
   Wi' rattling glee.

Thou clears the head o' doited Lear;   stupid, learning
Thou cheers the heart o' drooping Care;
Thou strings the nerves o' Labour sair,   sore
   At's weary toil;
Thou even brightens dark Despair
   Wi' gloomy smile.

Aft clad in massy siller weed,   in silver mugs
Wi' gentles thou erects thy head;
Yet humbly kind in time o' need,   (beer)
   The poor man's wine,
His wee drap parritch, or his bread,
   Thou kitchens fine.   givest relish to

Thou art the life o' public haunts ;
But thee, what were our fairs and rants ?   *without*
Even godly meetings o' the saunts,   *saints*
    By thee inspired,
When gaping they besiege the tents,
    Are doubly fired.

That merry night we got the corn in,
O sweetly then thou reams the horn in !   *froths*
Or reekin' on a New-year morning   *smoking*
    In cog or bicker,   *wooden vessels*
And just a wee drap sp'ritual burn in.   *spirits*
    And gusty sucker !   *savoury sugar*

When Vulcan gies his bellows breath.
And ploughmen gather wi' their graith,   *implements*
Oh rare! to see thee fizz and freath,   *froth*
    I' the lugget caup !   *eared cup*
Then Burnewin comes on like death   *blacksmith*
    At every chap.   *blow*

Nae mercy, then, for airn or steel ;   *iron*
The brawnie, bainie, ploughman chiel,   *bony*
Brings hard owerhip, wi' sturdy wheel,
    The strong forehammer,
Till block and studdie ring and reel   *anvil*
    Wi' dinsome clamour.

When neebors anger at a plea,
And just as wud as wud can be,   *mad*
How easy can the barley-bree   *juice*
    Cement the quarrel !
Its aye the cheapest lawyer's fee
    To taste the barrel.

Alake ! that e'er my Muse has reason
To wyte her countrymen wi' treason !   *blame*
But monie daily weet their weason   *many, wet, throat*
    Wi' liquors nice,
And hardly, in a winter's season,
    E'er spier her price.   *ask*

Wae worth that brandy, burning trash !   *woe*
Fell source o' monie a pain and brash !   *sickness*
Twins monie a poor, doylt, drucken hash,   *deprives, stupid,*
    O' half his days ;   [*fool*
And sends, beside, auld Scotland's cash
    To her warst faes.   *foes*

Ye Scots, wha wish auld Scotland well,
Ye chief, to you my tale I tell,
Poor plackless FELLOWS like mysel',   *moneyless*
    It sets you ill,
Wi' bitter, dearthfu' wines to mell,   *high-priced, meddle*
    Or foreign gill.

Thee, Ferintosh! oh sadly lost!
Scotland lament frae coast to coast!
Now colic grips, and barkin' hoast,   *cough*
    May kill us a';
For loyal Forbes' chartered boast
    Is ta'en awa!*

Fortune! if thou'll but gie me still
Hale breeks, a scone, and whisky gill,   *whole breeches, cake*
And rowth o' rhyme to rave at will,   *abundance*
    Tak a' the rest,
And deal't about as thy blind skill
    Directs thee best.

THE AUTHOR'S EARNEST CRY AND PRAYER

TO THE SCOTCH REPRESENTATIVES IN THE HOUSE OF COMMONS.

" Dearest of distillation! last and best!
How thou art lost!"—PARODY ON MILTON.

YE Irish lords, ye knights and squires,
Wha represent our brughs and shires,   *who, burghs*
And doucely manage our affairs   *soberly*
    In parliament,
To you a simple Bardie's prayers
    Are humbly sent.

Alas! my roopit Muse is hearse!   *hoarse*
Your honour's heart wi' grief 'twad pierce,
To see her sittin',
    Low i' the dust,
And screechin' out prosaic verse,   *screaming*
    And like to burst!

Tell them wha hae the chief direction,   *have*
Scotland and me's in great affliction,
E'er sin' they laid that FELL restriction
    On aqua vitæ;
And rouse them up to strong conviction,
    And move their pity.

Stand forth, and tell yon Premier youth,   *(Pitt)*
The honest, open, naked truth:
Tell him o' mine and Scotland's drouth,   *thirst*
    His servants humble:
MAY EVERY BREEZE BUT blaw ye south,
    If ye dissemble.

Does ony great man glunch and gloom?   *frown*
Speak out, and never fash your thoom!   *trouble, thumb*
Let posts and pensions sink or soom   *swim*
    Wi' them wha grant 'em:

* Alluding to the privilege possessed by the Ferintosh Distillery of distilling whisky free of duty; the privilege was abolished in 1755.

If honestly they canna come,
Far better want 'em.

In gath'rin' votes you were na slack;
Now stand as tightly by your tack;   hold
Ne'er claw your lug, and fidge your back, scratch, ear, fidget
And hum and haw;
But raise your arm, and tell your crack,   speech
Before them a'.

Paint Scotland greetin' ower her thrissle, weeping, thistle
Her mutchkin stoup as toom's a whistle; empty
And ᴇᴀᴄʜ exciseman in a bussle,   bustle
Seizin' a stell,   still
Triumphant crushin't like a mussel
Or lampit shell.   shell-fish

Then on the tither hand present her,   other
A blackguard smuggler, right behint her
And cheek-for-chow a chuffie vintner, fat-faced
Colleaguing join,
Picking her pouch as bare as winter
Of a' kind coin.

Is there, that bears the name o' Scot,
But feels his heart's bluid rising hot,
To see his poor auld mither's pot
Thus dung in staves,   knocked
And plundered o' her hindmost groat
By gallows knaves?

Alas! I'm but a nameless wight,
Trod i' the mire out o' sight!
But could I like Montgomeries fight,
Or gab like Boswell,   talk
There's some sark-necks I wad draw tight, shirt
And tie some hose well.

Bᴜᴛ bless your honours, can you see't,
The kind, auld, cantie carlin greet, cheerful old wife
And no get warmly to your feet,
And gar them hear it, make
And tell them with a patriot heat,
Ye winna bear it?

Some o' you nicely ken the laws,
To round the period and pause,
And wi' rhetoric clause on clause
To mak harangues;
Then echo through Saint Stephen's wa's walls
Auld Scotland's wrangs.

Dempster, a true blue Scot I'se warran';
Thee, aith-detesting, chaste Kilkerran; oath
And that glib-gabbet Highland baron, ready-tongued
The Laird o' Graham;

And ane, a chap that's REAL auldfarran,   sagacious
    Dundas his name.

Erskine, a spunkie Norland billie ;   spirited fellow
True Campbells, Frederick and Ilay ;
And Livingstone, the bauld Sir Willie ;   bold
    And mony ithers,   others
Whom auld Demosthenes or Tully
    Might own for brithers.   brothers

See, sodger Hugh, my watchman stented,   appointed
If bardies e'er are represented ;
I ken if that your sword were wanted,   know
    Ye'd lend a hand,
But when there's ought to say anent it,   regarding it
    Ye're at a stand.

Arouse, my boys ! exert your mettle,
To get auld Scotland back her kettle ;
Or faith ! I'll wad my new plough-pettle,   pledge, ploughstick
    Ye'll see't or lang,   ere
She'll teach you wi' a reekin' whittle,   knife
    Anither sang.

This while she's been in crankous mood,   fretful
Her lost militia fired her bluid ;
(I wuss they never mair do guid,   wish
    Played her that pliskie !)   trick
And now she's like to rin red-wud   run mad
    About her whisky.

BESIDES ! if ance they pit her till't,   put, to it
Her tartan petticoat she'll kilt,   tuck up
And durk and pistol at her belt,
    She'll tak the streets,
And rin her whittle to the hilt   knife
    I' th' first she meets !

FOR ONY SAKE then speak her fair,
And straik her cannie wi' the hair,   stroke, gently
And to the muckle house repair,   big
    Wi' instant speed,
And strive, wi' a' your wit and lear,   learning
    To get remead.   remedy

Yon ill-tongued tinkler, Charlie Fox,   tinker
May taunt you wi' his jeers and mocks ;
But gie him't het, my hearty cocks !   hot
    E'en cow the cadie !   fellow
And send him to his dicing box
    And CANKERED lady.   ill-natured

Tell yon guid bluid o' auld Boconnock's,*   good blood
I'll be his debt twa mashlum bannocks,   mixed grain, cakes
And drink his health in auld Nanse Tinnock's
    Nine times a week,

* Pitt's grandfather was Robert Pitt of Boconnock.

If he some scheme, like tea and winnocks,   *windows*
    Wad kindly seek.

Could he some commutation broach,
I'll pledge my aith in guid braid Scotch,   *oath*
He need na fear their foul reproach,
    Nor erudition,
Yon mixtie-maxtie queer hotch-potch,   *mixture, broth*
    The Coalition.

Auld Scotland has a raucle tongue;   *rash*
She's just A RANDY wi' a rung;   *bludgeon*
And if she promise auld or young
    To tak their part,
Though by the neck she should be strung,
    She'll no desert.

And now, ye chosen Five-and-Forty,
May still your mither's heart support ye;
Then, though a minister grow dorty,   *sulky*
    And kick your place,
Ye'll snap your fingers poor and hearty,
    Before his face.

God bless your honours a' your days,
Wi' sowps o' kail and brats o' claise,   *food and clothes*
In spite o' a' the thievish kaes   *jackdaws*
    That haunt St Jamie's!
Your humble Poet sings and prays,
    While Rab his name is.

POSTSCRIPT.

Let half-starved slaves in warmer skies
See future wines, rich clust'ring, rise;
Their lot auld Scotland ne'er envies,
    But blythe and frisky,
She eyes her freeborn, martial boys
    Tak aff their whisky.

What though their Phœbus kinder warms,
While fragrance blooms and beauty charms!
When wretches range in famished swarms,
    The scented groves,
Or hounded forth, dishonour arms
    In hungry droves.

Their gun's a burden on their shouther;   *shoulder*
They downa bide the stink o' powther;   *cannot, powder*
Their bauldest thought's a hank'ring swither   *uncertainty*
    To stan' or rin,
Till skelp—a shot—they're aff, a' throwther,   *in confusion*
    To save their skin.

But bring a Scotchman frae his hill,
Clap in his cheek a Highland gill,

Say such is royal George's will,
            And there's the foe,
He has nae thought but how to kill
            Twa at a blow.

Nae cauld, faint-hearted doubtings tease him ;
Death comes—wi' fearless eye he sees him ;
Wi' bluidy han' a welcome gies him ;
            And when he fa's,
His latest draught o' breathin' lea'es him
            In faint huzzas!

Sages their solemn een may steek,   *eyes, shut*
And raise a philosophic reek,
And physically causes seek,
            In clime and season ;
But tell me whisky's name in Greek,
            I'll tell the reason.

Scotland, my auld, respected mither !
Though whiles ye moistify your leather, *sometimes, moisten*
Till whare ye sit, on craps o' heather   *crops*
            Ye tine your dam ;   *lose*
Freedom and whisky gang thegither :—
            Tak aff your dram !

THE AULD FARMER'S NEW-YEAR MORNING SALU-
TATION TO HIS AULD MARE MAGGIE,

ON GIVING HER THE ACCUSTOMED RIPP OF CORN TO HANSEL
IN THE NEW YEAR.

A GUID New-year I wish thee, Maggie !
Hae, there's a ripp to thy auld baggie :   *handful*
Though thou's howe-backit now, and knaggie, *hollow, show-*
            I've seen the day   [*ing the bones*
Thou could hae gaen like ony staggie   *colt*
            Out-owre the lay.   *over, field*

Though now thou's dowie, stiff, and crazy,   *melancholy*
And thy auld hide's as white's a daisy,
I've seen thee dappl't, sleek, and glaizie,   *glossy*
            A bonny gray :
He should been tight that daur't to raize thee *prepared,excite*
            Ance in a day.   *once*

Thou ance was i' the foremost rank,
A filly buirdly, steeve, and swank,   *stately, firm, agile*
And set weel down a shapely shank
            As e'er tread yird ;   *earth*
And could hae flown out-owre a stank   *stagnant ditch*
            Like ony bird.

It's now some nine-and-twenty year,
Sin' thou was my guid-father's meare ;   *mare*

E

He gied me thee, o' tocher clear   gave, dowry
  And fifty mark;
Though it was sma', 'twas weel-won gear,   goods
  And thou was stark.   strong

When first I gaed to woo my Jenny,   went
Ye then was trottin' wi' your minnie: mother
Though ye was trickie, slee, and funnie,   sly
  Ye ne'er was donsie;   restive
But hamely, tawie, quiet, and cannie,   quiet to handle, gentle
  And unco sonsie.   very, engaging

That day ye pranced wi' muckle pride,   much
When you bure hame my bonny bride: bore
And sweet and gracefu' she did ride,
  Wi' maiden air!
Kyle Stewart I could braggèd wide,
  For sic a pair.

Though now ye dow but hoyte and hobble,   can, limp
And wintle like a saumont-coble,   stagger, salmon-boat
That day ye was a jinker noble,   runner
  For heels and win'!
And ran them till they a' did wauble   reel
  Far, far behin'!

When thou and I were young and skeigh,   high-mettled
And stable-meals at fairs were dreigh,   tedious
How thou would prance, and snore, and skreigh,   scream
  And tak' the road!
Town's bodies ran, and stood abeigh,   aloof
  And ca't thee mad.

When thou was corn't, and I was mellow,
We took the road aye like a swallow:
At brooses thou had ne'er a fellow   race at a marriage
  For pith and speed;
But every tail thou pay't them hollow,
  Whare'er thou gaed.

The sma' droop-rumpl't, hunter cattle,   [short race
Might aiblins waur't thee for a brattle;   perhaps, worst,
But sax Scotch miles thou try't their mettle,   six
  And gar't them whaizle: made, wheeze
Nae whip nor spur, but just a wattle   wand
  O' saugh or hazle.   willow

Thou was a noble fittie-lan',*
As e'er in tug or tow was drawn!   harness
Aft thee and I, in aught hours' gaun,   eight, going
  In guid March weather,
Hae turned sax rood beside our han'
  For days thegither.   together

Thou never braindg't, and fetch't, and fliskit,†
But thy auld tail thou wad hae whisket,   whisked

---

* The right-hand horse in the plough.
† Ran rashly, capered, pulled irregularly.

And spread abreed thy weel-filled brisket, abroad, breast
  Wi' pith and power,
Till spritty knowes wad rair't and risket,*
   And slypet owre.   turned over

When frosts lay lang, and snaws were deep,
And threatened labour back to keep,
I gied thy cog a wee bit heap   wooden dish
  Aboon the timmer;   above, edge
I kenn'd my Maggie wadna sleep   knew
  For that, or simmer.   ere

In cart or car thou never reestit;   stopt
The steyest brae thou wad hae face'd it; steepest
Thou never lap, and sten't and breastit, leapt, strained, sprung
   Then stood to blaw;   breathe [forward
But just thy step a wee thing hastit,   hasted
  Thou snoov't awa.   went smoothly on

My pleugh is now thy bairn-time a';
Four gallant brutes as e'er did draw;
Forbye sax mae I've sell't awa,   besides, more
  That thou hast nurst:
They drew me thretteen pund and twa, fifteen
  The very warst.   worst

Monie a sair daurk we twa hae wrought, sore day's work
And wi' the weary warl' fought!   world
And monie an anxious day I thought   many
  We wad be beat!   would
Yet here to crazy age we're brought,
  Wi' something yet.

And think na, my auld trusty servan',
That now perhaps thou's less deservin',
And thy auld days may end in starvin',
  For my last fow,   heap of corn
A heapit stimpart, I'll reserve ane eighth of bushel
  Laid by for you.

We've worn to crazy years thegither;
We'll toyte about wi' ane anither;   totter
Wi' tentie care I'll flit thy tether, observant, move, halter
  To some bain'd rig,   spared ridge
Where ye may nobly rax you leather, stretch
  Wi' sma' fatigue.

THE TWA DOGS.

A TALE.

'Twas in that place o' Scotland's isle
That bears the name o' Auld King Coil, (Kyle in Ayrshire)
Upon a bonnie day in June,
When wearing through the afternoon,

  * Rushy hillocks, would, roared, rasped.

Twa dogs that were na thrang at hame,   busy
Forgathered ance upon a time.   .   met

The first I'll name, they ca'd him Cæsar,
Was keepit for his honour's pleasure ;
His hair, his size, his mouth, his lugs,   ears
Showed he was nane o' Scotland's dogs,
But whalpit some place far abroad,   whelped
Whare sailors gang to fish for cod.   where, go

His lockèd, lettered, braw brass collar,   fine
Showed him the gentleman and scholar ;
But though he was o' high degree,
NAE HAET CONCEIT—nae pride had he ;   none
But wad hae spent a hour caressin',   would
E'en wi' a tinkler-gipsy's messan.   cur
At kirk or market, mill or smiddie,   smithy
Nae tawted tyke, though e'er sae duddie,   shaggy, ragged
But he wad stan't, as glad to see him,
And FRISK OWRE stanes and hillocks wi' him.

The tither was a ploughman's collie,   other
A rhyming, ranting, roving billie,   blade
Wha for his friend and comrade had him,
And in his freaks had Luath ca'd him,
After some dog in Highland sang,   (Ossian)
Was made langsyne—nane kens how lang.

He was a gash and faithful tyke,   sagacious
As ever lap a sheugh or dyke.   jumped, ditch
His honest, sonsie, baws'nt face,   plump, brindled
Aye gat him friends in ilka place.   always got, each
His breast was white, his touzie back   shaggy
Weel clad wi' coat o' glossy black ;
His gaucie tail, wi' upward curl,   stately
Hung o'er his hurdies wi' a swirl.   hips, swirling motion

Nae doubt but they were fain o' ither,   fond
And unco pack and thick thegither ;   very intimate [ted
Wi' social nose whyles snuff'd and snowkit, sometimes scen-
Whyles mice and moudieworts they howkit ;   moles, dug
Whyles scoured awa in lang excursion,   away
And worried ither in diversion ;   each other
Until wi' daffin' weary grown,   sporting
Upon a knowe they sat them down,   hillock
And there began a lang digression   long
About the lords o' the creation.

CÆSAR.

I've aften wondered, honest Luath,
What sort o' life poor dogs like you have ;
And when the gentry's life I saw,
What way poor bodies lived ava.   at all

Our laird gets in his racked rents,   [ments
His coals, his kain, and a' his stents ;   rent in kind, assess-

He rises when he likes himsel;
His flunkies answer at the bell;
He ca's his coach, he ca's his horse;
He draws a bonnie silken purse
As lang's my tail, whare, through the steeks, *stitches*
The yellow lettered Geordie keeks. *peeps*

Frae morn to e'en it's nought but toiling,
At baking, roasting, frying, boiling;
And though the gentry first are stechin, *stuffing*
Yet e'en the ha' folk fill their pechan *kitchen-people, stomach*
Wi' sauce, ragouts, and sic-like trashtrie,
That's little short o' downright wastrie. *waste*
Our whipper-in, wee STUPID wonner,*
Poor worthless elf, it eats a dinner
Better than ony tenant man
Better honour has i' a' the lan';
And what poor cot-folk pit their painch in, *put, stomach*
I own it's past my comprehension.

LUATH.

Trowth, Cæsar, whyles they're fash't enough; *troubled*
A cotter howkin' in a sheugh, *digging, trench*
Wi' dirty stanes biggin' a dyke, *building, wall*
Barring a quarry, and sic-like: *fencing*
Himself, a wife, he thus sustains,
A smytrie o' wee duddie weans, *number, ragged children*
And nought but his han' darg, to keep *day's work*
Them right and tight in thack and rape. *daily wants*

And when they meet wi' sair disasters, *sore*
Like loss o' health, or want o' masters,
Ye maist wad think, a wee touch langer, *almost, longer*
And they maun starve o' cauld and hunger; *must*
But, how it comes, I never kenn'd yet, *knew*
They're maistly wonderfu' contented:
And buirdly chiels, and clever hizzies, *stalwart fellows, girls*
Are bred in sic a way as this is.

CÆSAR.

But then to see how ye're negleckit,
How huffed, and cuffed, and disrespeckit!
DEED, man, our gentry care as little
For delvers, ditchers, and sic cattle; *such*
They gang as saucy by poor folk, *go*
As I wad by a stinkin' brock. *badger*
I've noticed, on our Laird's court-day,
And mony a time my heart's been wae, *grieved*
Poor tenant bodies, scant o' cash,
How they maun thole a factor's snash: *bear with, abuse*
He'll stamp and threaten, curse and swear,
He'll apprehend them, poind their gear; *distrain, goods*
While they maun stan', wi aspect humble, *must*
And hear it a', and fear and tremble!

* A person residing in the place.

I see how folk live that hae riches ;
But surely poor folk maun be wretches !

LUATH.

They're no sae wretched's ane wad think   *so, one*
Though constantly on poortith's brink :   *poverty*
They're sae accustomed wi' the sight,
The view o't gies them little fright.
Then chance and fortune are sae guided,
They're aye in less or mair provided ;
And though fatigued wi' close employment,
A blink o' rest's a sweet enjoyment.

The dearest comfort o' their lives,
Their grushie weans and faithfu' wives ;   *thriving children*
The prattling things are just their pride,
That sweetens a' their fireside ;
And whyles twalpenny worth* o' nappy   *ale*
Can mak' the bodies unco happy ;   *very*
They lay aside their private cares,
To mind the Kirk and State affairs :
They'll talk o' patronage and priests,
Wi' kindling fury in their breasts,
Or tell what new taxation's comin',
And ferlie at the folk in Lon'on.   *wonder*

As bleak-faced Hallowmas returns,   *All-Hallow*
They get the jovial, rantin kirns,   *harvest-homes*
When rural life o' every station
Unite in common recreation ;
Love blinks, Wit slaps, and social Mirth
Forgets there's Care upo' the earth.

That merry day the year begins,
They bar the door on frosty win's ;
The nappy reeks wi' mantling ream,   *ale, froth*
And sheds a heart-inspiring steam ;
The luntin pipe, and sneeshin-mill,   *smoking, snuff-box*
Are handed round wi' right guidwill ;
The cantie auld folks crackin' crouse,   *cheerful, talking briskly*
The young anes rantin' through the house—   *ones*
My heart has been sae fain to see them,
That I for joy hae barkit wi' them.

Still it's owre true that ye hae said,
Sic game is now owre aften played.   *such, too*
There's monie a creditable stock
O' decent, honest, fawsont fo'k   *seemly*
Are riven out baith root and branch,
Some rascal's pridefu' greed to quench,
Wha thinks to knit himsel the faster
In favour wi' some gentle master,
Wha aiblins thrang a parliamentin',   *perhaps busy*
For Britain's guid his saul indentin'——.   *soul*

* Twelve pence Scotch is equal to one penny sterling.

CÆSAR.

Haith, lad, ye little ken about it;
For Britain's guid! guid faith, I doubt it.
Say rather, gaun as Premiers lead him,   going
And saying Ay or No's they bid him:
At operas and plays parading,
Mortgaging, gambling, masquerading;
Or maybe, in a frolic daft,   merry
To Hague or Calais takes a waft,
To mak a tour and tak a whirl,
To learn *bon ton,* and see the worl'.

There, at Vienna or Versailles,
He rives his father's auld entails;   tears
Or by Madrid he takes the route,
To thrum guitars, and fecht wi' nowte;   bullocks
Then bouses drumly German water,   drinks muddy
To mak himsel' look fair and fatter.

For Britain's guid!—for her destruction!
Wi' dissipation, feud, and faction.

LUATH.

Hech man! dear sirs! is that the gate   way
They waste sae mony a braw estate!   many, fine
Are we sae foughten and harrassed   exhausted
For gear to gang that gate at last!   money

Oh would they stay aback frae courts,   from
And please themsels wi' country sports,
It wad for every ane be better,   would, one
The Laird, the Tenant, and the Cotter!
For thae frank, rantin', rambling' billies,   those, fellows
NAE haet o' them's ill-hearted fellows;   none
EXCEPT FOR shootin' hare or moor-cock,
The ne'er a bit they're ill to poor folk.

But will ye tell me, Master Cæsar,
Sure great folk's life's a life o' pleasure?
Nae cauld or hunger e'er can steer them,   cold, stir
The very thought o't need na fear them.

CÆSAR.

Man, were ye but whyles whare I am,   sometimes
The gentles ye wad ne'er envy 'em.
It's true they needna starve or sweat,
Through winter's cauld, or simmer's heat;
They've nae sair wark to craze their banes   sore, bones
And fill auld age wi' grips and granes;   gripes, groans
But human bodies are sic fools,   such
For a' their colleges and schools,
That when nae real ills perplex them,
They make anow themsels to vex them;
And aye the less they hae to sturt them,   molest
In like proportion less will hurt them.

A country fellow at the pleugh   plough
His acres tilled, he's right eneugh ;
A country girl at her wheel,
Her dizzen's done, she's unco weel: dozen, very well
But Gentlemen, and Ladies warst,   worst
Wi' even-down want o' wark are curst.   work
They loiter, lounging, lank, and lazy ;
Though NAE haet ails them, yet uneasy ;   nothing
Their days insipid, dull, and tasteless ;
Their nights unquiet, lang, and restless.

And e'en their sports, their balls and races,
Their galloping through public places,
There's sic parade, sic pomp, and art,
The joy can scarcely reach the heart.

The men cast out in party matches   quarrel
Then sowther a' in deep debauches ;   solder
Ae night they're mad wi' drink PROCURING,
Niest day their life is past enduring.   next

The Ladies arm-in-arm in clusters,
As great and gracious a' as sisters ;
But hear their absent thoughts o' ither,   each other
They're a' run WILD and jads thegither,
Whyles o'er the wee bit cup and platie,
They sip the scandal potion pretty ;
Or lee-lang nights, wi' crabbit leuks,   livelong, looks
Pore ower the devil's pictured beuks ;   cards
Stake on a chance a farmer's stackyard,
And cheat like ony unhanged blackguard.   any

There's some exception, man and woman ;
But this is Gentry's life in common.

By this, the sun was out o' sight,
And darker gloaming brought the night: twilight
The bum-clock humm'd wi' lazy drone ;   beetle
The kye stood rowtin' i' the loan ;   cows, bellowing
When up they gat, and shook their lugs,   ears
Rejoiced they were na men, but dogs ;
And each took aff his several way,   off
Resolved to meet some ither day.   other

TO A LOUSE,

ON SEEING ONE ON A LADY'S BONNET AT CHURCH.

HA ! where ye gaun, ye crawlin' ferlie ?   going, wonder
Your impudence protects you sairly :   very much
I canna say but ye strunt rarely   strut
         Owre gauze and lace ;
Though faith I fear ye dine but sparely
         On sic a place.   such

Ye ugly, creepin', nasty wonner,
Detested, shunn'd, by saunt and sinner,
How dare you set your fit upon her,   foot
    Sae fine a lady?
Gae somewhere else, and seek your dinner   go
    On some poor body.

                        [sprawl
Swith, in some beggar's haffet squattle ;   quick, cheek,
There ye may creep, and sprawl, and sprattle   scramble
Wi' ither kindred, jumping cattle,
    In shoals and nations ;
Whare horn nor bane ne'er daur unsettle   dare
    Your thick plantations.

Now haud you there, ye're out o' sight,   remain
Below the fatt'rel's, snug and tight ;   ribbon-ends
Na, faith ye yet ! ye'll no be right
    Till ye've got on it,
The very tapmost, towering height
    O' Miss's bonnet.

My sooth ! right bauld ye set your nose out,   bold
As plump and gray as ony grozet ;   gooseberry
Oh for some rank, mercurial rozet,   rosin
    Or fell, red smeddum,   powder
I'd gie you sic a hearty doze o't
    Wad dress your droddum !   breech

I wad na been surprised to spy   would not
You on an auld wife's flannen toy ;   flannel cap
Or aiblins some bit duddie boy,   perhaps, ragged
    On's wyliecoat ;   under vest
But Miss's fine Lunardi ! fie !
    How daur ye do't ?

Oh, Jenny, dinna toss your head,   do not
And set your beauties a' abroad !   abroad
Ye little ken what FEARFU' speed   know
    The beastie's makin' ?
Thae winks and finger-ends, I dread,   those
    Are notice takin' !

Oh wad some power the giftie gie us   would, gift
To see oursels as others see us !
It wad frae mony a blunder free us,   from many
    And foolish notion :
What airs in dress and gait wad lea'e us,
    And even devotion !

AN ADDRESS TO THE UNCO GUID, OR THE RIGIDLY RIGHTEOUS.

My son, these maxims make a rule,
  And lump them aye thegither:
The Rigid Righteous is a fool,
  The Rigid Wise anither:
The cleanest corn that e'er was dight
  May hae some pyles o' caff in;
So ne'er a fellow-creature slight
  For random fits o' daffin.

OH ye wha are sae guid yoursel',   good
  Sae pious and sae holy,   so
Ye've nought to do but mark and tell
  Your neebour's fauts and folly!   neighbour's faults
Whase life is like a weel-gaun mill,   whose, well-going
  Supplied wi' store o' water,
The heapèd happer's ebbing still,   hopper
  And still the clap plays clatter.

Hear me, ye venerable core,   company
  As counsel for poor mortals,
That frequent pass douce Wisdom's door   grave
  For glaiket Folly's portals;   idle
I, for their thoughtless, careless sakes,
  Would here propone defences,
Their donsie tricks, their black mistakes,   unlucky
  Their failings and mischances.

Ye see your state wi' theirs compared,
  And shudder at the niffer,
But cast a moment's fair regard,   exchange
  What maks the mighty differ?
Discount what scant occasion gave
  That purity ye pride in,
And (what's aft mair than a' the lave)   oft, more, rest
  Your better art o' hiding.

Think, when your castigated pulse
  Gies now and then a wallop,   quick motion
What ragings must his veins convulse,
  That still eternal gallop;
Wi' wind and tide fair i' your tail,
  Right on ye scud your sea-way;
But in the teeth o' baith to sail,
  It makes an unco lee-way.   great

        *   *   *   *

Then gently scan your brother man,
  Still gentler sister woman;
Though they may gang a kennin' wrang,   go, trifle
  To step aside is human:
One point must still be greatly dark,
  The moving why they do it:
And just as lamely can ye mark
  How far perhaps they rue it.

Who made the heart, 'tis He alone
Decidedly can try us,
He knows each chord—its various tone,
Each spring—its various bias:
Then at the balance let's be mute,
We never can adjust it;
What's done we partly may compute,
But know not what's resisted.

THE INVENTORY.

IN ANSWER TO A MANDATE BY THE SURVEYOR OF THE TAXES.

SIR, as your mandate did request,
I send you here a faithfu' list
O' gudes and gear, and a' my graith,   riches, harness
To which I'm clear to gie my aith.   oath

Imprimis, then, for carriage cattle,
I have four brutes o' gallant mettle,
As ever drew afore a pettle.   plough-stick
My han' afore's* a gude auld has-been,
And wight and wilfu' a' his days been.   stout
My han' ahin's† a weel-gaun filly,
That aft has borne me hame frae Killie,   Kilmarnock
And your auld burro' mony a time,
In days when riding was nae crime—
But ance, whan in my wooing pride,   once
I like a blockhead boost to ride,   behoved
I played my filly sic a shavie.   trick
She's a MADE USELESS wi' the spavie.
My fur ahin's a wordy beast,   right horse behind, worthy
As e'er in tug or tow was traced.   plough, harnessed
The fourth's a Highland Donald hastie,
A DAFT red wud Kilburnie beastie!   wild
Forbye a cowte o' cowtes the wale,   besides, colt, choice
As ever ran afore a tail,
If he be spared to be a beast,
He'll draw me fifteen pun' at least—   pounds
Wheel carriages I hae but few,
Three carts, and twa are feckly new;   nearly
Ae auld wheelbarrow, mair for token   one
Ae leg and baith the trams are broken;   both, shafts
I made a poker o' the spin'le,
And my auld mither brunt the trin'le.   burnt, wheel

For men I've three mischievous boys,
Run WILD for rantin' and for noise;
A gaudsman ane, a thrasher t'other,   ploughman one
Wee Davock hauds the nowt in fother.   keeps, cattle, fodder
I rule them, as I ought, discreetly,
And aften labour them completely;   belabour
And aye on Sundays duly, nightly,   alway
I on the Questions targe them tightly;   examine

* Left horse in front of plough.   † Left horse behind.

Till, faith, wee Davock's turned sae gleg,   *quick*
Though scarcely langer than your leg,   *taller*
He'll screed you aff Effectual Calling,   *repeat, off*
As fast as ony in the dwalling.,
Wi' weans I'm mair than weel contented,   *children*
Heaven sent me ane mae than I wanted.   **one** *more*
My sonsie, smirking, dear-bought Bess, **stout,** *good-natured*
She stares the daddy in her face,
Enough of ought ye like but grace ;
But her, my bonny sweet wee lady,
I've paid enough for her already.

   And now, remember, Mr Aiken,
Nae kind of license out I'm takin';
My travel, a' on foot I'll shank it,   *walk*
I've sturdy bearers, praise be thankit.
Sae dinna put me in your buke,   *book*
Nor for my ten white shillings luke.   *look*

   This list wi' my ain hand I've wrote it,
The day and date as under noted ;
Then know all ye whom it concerns,
Subscripsi huic,   ROBERT BURNS.
MOSSGIEL, *February* 22, 1786.

THOU flattering mark of friendship kind,
Still may thy pages call to mind
   The dear, the beauteous Donor :
Though sweetly female every part,
Yet such a head, and more the heart,
   Does both the sexes honour.
She showed her taste refined and just
   When she selected thee,
Yet deviating own I must,
   In sae approving me ;
     But kind still, I'll mind still
     The Giver in the gift—
     I'll bless her, and wiss her   *wish*
     A friend aboon the lift.   *above, sky*

TO A MOUNTAIN DAISY,
ON TURNING ONE DOWN WITH THE PLOUGH IN APRIL 1786.

WEE, modest, crimson-tippèd flower,
Thou's met me in an evil hour ;
For I maun crush amang the stoure   *must, dust*
   Thy slender stem :
To spare thee now is past my power,
   Thou bonnie gem.

Alas ! it's no thy neibor sweet,
The bonnie lark, companion meet,

Bending thee 'mang the dewy weet !   wet
    Wi' speckled breast,
When upward-springing, blithe, to greet
    The purpling east.

Cauld blew the bitter-biting north   cold
Upon thy early, humble birth ;
Yet cheerfully thou glinted forth   glanced
    Amid the storm,
Scarce reared above the parent earth
    Thy tender form.

The flaunting flowers our gardens yield,
High sheltering woods and wa's maun shield : walls must
But thou, beneath the random bield   shelter
    O' clod or stane,   stone
Adorns the histie stibble-field,   dry stubble
    Unseen, alane.   alone

There, in thy scanty mantle clad,
Thy snawie bosom sunward spread,   snowy
Thou lifts thy unassuming head
    In humble guise ;
But now the share uptears thy bed,
    And low thou lies !

Such is the fate of artless maid,
Sweet floweret of the rural shade !
By love's simplicity betrayed,
    And guileless trust,
Till she, like thee, all soiled, is laid
    Low i' the dust.

Such is the fate of simple bard,
On life's rough ocean luckless starr'd !
Unskilful he to note the card
    Of prudent lore,
Till billows rage, and gales blow hard,
    And whelm him o'er !

Such fate to suffering worth is given,
Who long with wants and woes has striven,
By human pride or cunning driven
    To misery's brink,
Till wrenched of every stay but Heaven,
    He, ruined, sink !

Even thou who mourn'st the Daisy's fate,
That fate is thine—no distant date ;
Stern Ruin's ploughshare drives, elate,
    Full on thy bloom,
Till crushed beneath the furrow's weight,
    Shall be thy doom.

LAMENT.

*"Alas! how oft does goodness wound itself,
And sweet affection prove the spring of woe!"—*HOME.

OH thou pale orb, that silent shines,
  While care-untroubled mortals sleep !
Thou seest a wretch who inly pines,
  And wanders here to wail and weep !
With woe I nightly vigils keep
  Beneath thy wan, unwarming beam ;
And mourn, in lamentation deep,
  How life and love are all a dream.

I joyless view thy rays adorn
  The faintly-marked distant hill :
I joyless view thy trembling horn
  Reflected in the gurgling rill :
My fondly-fluttering heart be still !
  Thou busy power, remembrance, cease
Ah ! must the agonizing thrill
  For ever bar returning peace !

No idly-feigned poetic pains
  My sad, love-lorn lamentings claim ;
No shepherd's pipe—Arcadian strains ;
  No fabled tortures, quaint and tame :
The plighted faith ; the mutual flame ;
  The oft-attested Powers above ;
The promised father's tender name ;
  These were the pledges of my love!

Encircled in her clasping arms,
  How have the raptured moments flown !
How have I wished for fortune's charms,
  For her dear sake, and her's alone !
And must I think it !—is she gone,
  My secret heart's exulting boast ?
And does she heedless hear my groan ?
  And is she ever, ever lost ?

Oh can she bear so base a heart,
  So lost to honour, lost to truth,
As from the fondest lover part,
  The plighted husband of her youth !
Alas ! life's path may be unsmooth !
  Her way may lie through rough distress !
Then who her pangs and pains will soothe,
  Her sorrows share, and make them less ?

Ye wingèd hours that o'er us passed,
  Enraptured more, the more enjoyed,
Your dear remembrance in my breast,
  My fondly-treasured thoughts employed.
That breast, how dreary now, and void,
  For her too scanty once of room !

Even every ray of hope destroyed,
And not a wish to gild the gloom!

The morn that warms th' approaching day,
Awakes me up to toil and woe:
I see the hours in long array,
That I must suffer, lingering, slow.
Full many a pang, and many a throe,
Keen recollection's direful train,
Must wring my soul ere Phœbus, low,
Shall kiss the distant, western main.

And when my nightly couch I try,
Sore harassed out with care and grief,
My toil-beat nerves, and tear-worn eye
Keep watchings with the nightly thief:
Or if I slumber, fancy, chief,
Reigns haggard-wild in sore affright:
Even day, all bitter, brings relief
From such a horror-breathing night.

Oh thou bright queen, who o'er the expanse,
Now highest reign'st, with boundless sway!
Oft has thy silent-marking glance
Observed us, fondly-wandering, stray!
The time, unheeded, sped away,
While love's luxurious pulse beat high,
Beneath thy silver-gleaming ray,
To mark the mutual kindling eye.

Oh scenes in strong remembrance set!
Scenes never, never to return!
Scenes, if in stupor I forget,
Again I feel, again I burn!
From every joy and pleasure torn,
Life's weary vale I'll wander through;
And hopeless, comfortless, I'll mourn
A faithless woman's broken vow.

DESPONDENCY.

AN ODE.

Oppressed with grief, oppressed with care,
A burden more than I can bear,
I set me down and sigh:
Oh life! thou art a galling load,
Along a rough, a weary road,
To wretches such as I!
Dim-backward as I cast my view,
What sickening scenes appear!
What sorrows yet may pierce me through.
Too justly I may fear!

Still caring, despairing,
Must be my bitter doom ;
My woes here shall close ne'er
But with the closing tomb !

Happy, ye sons of busy life,
Who, equal to the bustling strife,
No other view regard !
Even when the wishèd end's denied,
Yet while the busy means are plied,
They bring their own reward :
Whilst I, a hope-abandoned wight,
Unfitted with an aim,
Meet every sad returning night
And joyless morn the same ;
You, bustling, and justling,
Forget each grief and pain ;
I, listless, yet restless,
Find every prospect vain.

How blest the solitary's lot,
Who, all-forgetting, all-forgot,
Within his humble cell,
The cavern wild with tangling-roots,
Sits o'er his newly-gathered fruits,
Beside his crystal well !
Or haply to his evening thought,
By unfrequented stream,
The ways of men are distant brought,
A faint collected dream ;
While praising, and raising
His thoughts to heaven on high,
As wand'ring, meand'ring,
He views the solemn sky.

Than I, no lonely hermit placed,
Where never human footstep traced,
Less fit to play the part ;
The lucky moment to improve,
And just to stop, and just to move,
With self-respecting art :
But ah ! those pleasures, loves, and joys,
Which I too keenly taste,
The solitary can despise,
Can want, and yet be blest !
He needs not, he heeds not,
Or human love or hate,
Whilst I here, must cry here
At perfidy ingrate !

Oh enviable, early days,
When dancing thoughtless pleasure's maze,
To care, to guilt unknown !
How ill exchanged for riper times,
To feel the follies, or the crimes,
Of others, or my own !

Ye tiny elves that guiltless sport,
  Like linnets in the bush,
Ye little know the ills ye court,
  When manhood is your wish!
    The losses, the crosses,
      That active man engage!
    The fears all, the tears all,
      Of dim declining age.

TO RUIN.

ALL hail! inexorable lord!
At whose destruction-breathing word
  The mightiest empires fall!
Thy cruel, wo-delighted train,
The ministers of grief and pain,
  A sullen welcome, all!
With stern-resolved, despairing eye,
  I see each aimèd dart;
For one has cut my dearest tie,
  And quivers in my heart.
    Then lowering and pouring,
      The storm no more I dread;
    Though thick'ning and black'ning
      Round my devoted head.

And thou grim power, by life abhorred,
While life a pleasure can afford,
  Oh hear a wretch's prayer!
No more I shrink appalled, afraid;
I court, I beg thy friendly aid,
  To close this scene of care!
When shall my soul in silent peace,
  Resign life's joyless day;
My weary heart its throbbings cease,
  Cold mouldering in the clay?
    No fear more, no tear more,
      To stain my lifeless face;
    Enclaspèd and graspèd
      Within thy cold embrace!

TO GAVIN HAMILTON.

MOSSGIEL, *May* 8, 1783.

I HOLD it, sir, my bounden duty,
To warn you how that Master Tootie,
  Alias, Laird M'Gaun,
Was here to hire yon lad away
'Bout whom ye spak the tither day,   spoke, other
  And wad hae done't aff han':   would, instantly

F

But lest he learn the callan tricks,   boy
  As, faith, I muckle doubt him,
Like scrapin' out auld Crummie's nicks, (on cow's horn)
  And tellin' lies about them ;
    As lieve then, I'd have then,   content
     Your clerkship he should sair,   serve
    If sae be ye may be   so
    Nor fitted other where.   elsewhere

Although I say't, he's gleg enough,   sharp
And 'bout a house that's rude and rough,
  The boy might learn to swear ;
But then wi' you he'll be sae taught,
And get sic fair example straught,   straight
  I havena ony fear   have not any
Ye'll catechise him every quirk,
  AND WHEN YE HEAR THE BELL,
YE'LL gar him follow to the kirk—
  —Aye when ye gang yoursel.
    If ye, then, maun be, then,
     Frae hame this comin' Friday ;   from home
    Then please sir, to lea'e, sir,
     The orders wi' your leddy.   lady

My word of honour I hae gi'en,   given
In Paisley John's, that night at e'en,
  To meet the warld's worm ;*
To try to get the twa to gree,   agree
And name the airles and the fee,   earnest money
  In legal mode and form :
I ken he weel a sneck can draw,   know, is crafty
  When simple bodies let him.
    *   *   *   *   *   *
    To phrase you, and praise you,
     Ye ken your Laureat scorns :
    The prayer still, you share still,
     Of grateful MINSTREL BURNS.

EPISTLE TO A YOUNG FRIEND.

(ANDREW AIKEN.)

                May 1786.
I LANG hae thought, my youthfu' friend,   long have
  A something to have sent you,
Though it should serve nae other end   no
  Than just a kind memento ;
But how the subject-theme may gang,   go
  Let time and chance determine ;
Perhaps it may turn out a sang,   song
  Perhaps turn out a sermon.

Ye'll try the world fu' soon, my lad,   full
  And, Andrew dear, believe me,

* A mean avaricious character.

Ye'll find mankind an unco squad,   *strange*
  And muckle they may grieve ye :
For care and trouble set your thought,
  Even when your end's attained ;
And a' your views may come to nought,
  Where every nerve is strained.

I'll no say men are villains a' ;
  The real, hardened wicked,
Wha hae nae check but human law,   *who*
 . Are to a few restricked ;
But, och! mankind are unco weak,   *very*
  And little to be trusted ;
If self the wavering balance shake,
  It's rarely right adjusted !

Yet they wha fa' in fortune's strife,   *fall*
  Their fate we should na censure,   *not*
For still th' important end of life
  They equally may answer ;
A man may hae an honest heart,   *have*
  Though poortith hourly stare him ;   *poverty*
A man may tak a neibor's part,   *neighbour's*
  Yet hae nae cash to spare him.

Aye free, aff han' your story tell,   *always, off hand*
  When wi' a bosom crony ;   *companion*
But still keep something to yoursel
  Ye scarcely tell to ony.   *any*
Conceal yoursel as weel's ye can
  Frae critical dissection,
But keek through every other man,   *look*
  Wi sharpened, sly inspection.

The secret lowe o' weel-placed love,   *flame*
  Luxuriantly indulge it ;
But never tempt th' illicit rove,
  Though naething should divulge it :   *nothing*
I waive the quantum o' the sin,
  The hazard of concealing ;
But, och ! it hardens a' within,
  And petrifies the feeling !

To catch dame Fortune's golden smile,
  Assiduous wait upon her ;
And gather gear by every wile   *wealth*
  That's justified by honour ;
Not for to hide it in a hedge,
  Nor for a train-attendant,
But for the glorious privilege
  Of being independent.

The fear o' hell's a hangman's whip,
  To haud the wretch in order ;   *keep*
But where you feel your honour grip,
  Let that aye be your border

Its slightest touches, instant pause—
  Debar a' side pretences;
And resolutely keep its laws,
  Uncaring consequences.

The great Creator to revere
  Must sure become the creature;
But still the preaching cant forbear,
  And even the rigid feature:
Yet ne'er with wits profane to range,
  Be complaisance extended
An Athiest laugh's a poor exchange
  For Deity offended !

When ranting round in pleasure's ring,
  Religion may be blinded;
Or if she gi'e a random sting,   *give*
  It may be little minded;
But when on life we're tempest driven,
  A conscience but a canker,
A correspondence fixed wi' Heaven,
  Is sure a noble anchor !

Adieu, dear, amiable youth !
  Your heart can ne'er be wanting !
May prudence, fortitude, and truth,
  Erect your brow undaunting !
In ploughman phrase, " God send you speed,"
  Still daily to grow wiser:
And may you better reck the rede   *heed, counsel*
  Than ever did th' adviser !

A DREAM.

" Thoughts, words, and deeds, the statute blames with reason !
  But surely dreams were ne'er indicted treason."

On reading, in the public papers, the " Laureate's Ode," with the other parade of
June 4, 1786, the author was no sooner dropt asleep, than he imagined himself tran-
sported to the birthday levee; and in his dreaming fancy made the following
" Address: "—

GUID-MORNIN' to your Majesty !
  May Heaven augment your blesses,
On every new birthday, ye see,
  A humble poet wishes !
My bardship here, at your levee,
  On sic a day as this is,   *such*
Is sure an uncouth sight to see,
  Amang thae birthday dresses   *these*
      Sae fine this day.   *so*

I see ye're complimented thrang,   *busily*
  By many a lord and lady;
" God save the king !" 's a cuckoo sang
  That's unco easy said aye;   *very*

The poets, too, a venal gang,
  Wi' rhymes weel-turned and ready,
Wad gar ye trow ye ne'er do wrang,   would make
  But aye unerring steady,
      On sic a day.

For me! before a monarch's face
  Even there I winna flatter;   will not
For neither pension, post, nor place,
  Am I your humble debtor:
So, nae reflection on your grace,   no
  Your kingship to bespatter;
There's mony waur been o' the race,   worse
  And aiblins ane been better   perhaps one
      Than you this day.

'Tis very true, my sovereign king,
  My skill may weel be doubted: well
But facts are chiels that winna ding, fellows, be beaten
  And downa be disputed: cannot
Your royal nest, beneath your wing,
  Is e'en right reft and clouted,   broken, patched
And now the third part of the string, (American colonies)
  And less, will gang about it   go
      Than did ae day.   one

Far be't frae me that I aspire   from
  To blame your legislation,
Or say ye wisdom want, or fire,
  To rule this mighty nation!
But faith! I muckle doubt, my sire,   much
  Ye've trusted ministration
To chaps, wha, in a barn or byre,   who
  Wad better filled their station   would have
      Than courts yon day.

And now ye've gien auld Britain peace; given old
  Her broken shins to plaister;
Your sair taxation does her fleece,   sore
  Till she has scarce a tester;
For me, thank HEAVEN, my life's a lease,
  Nae bargain wearing faster,
Or, faith! I fear, that, wi' the geese,
  I shortly boost to pasture   behoved
      I' the craft some day.   field

I'm no mistrusting Willie Pitt,
  When taxes he enlarges,
(And Will's a true guid fallow's get, good fellow's child
  A name not envy spairges),   asperses
That he intends to pay your debt,
  And lessen a' your charges;
But, DEAR SAKE! let nae saving fit
  Abridge your bonny barges   navy
      And boats this day.

Adieu, my liege! may Freedom geck   sport
  Beneath your high protection;
And may you rax Corruption's neck,   stretch
  And gie her for dissection.   give
But since I'm here, I'll no neglect,
  In loyal, true affection,
To pay your Queen, with due respect,
  My fealty and subjection
            This great birthday.

Hail Majesty Most Excellent!
  While nobles strive to please ye,
Will ye accept a compliment
  A simple poet gies ye?
Thae bonnie bairn-time, Heaven has lent, those children
  Still higher may they heeze ye   raise
In bliss, till fate some day is sent,
  For ever to release ye
            Frae care that day!   from

For you, young potentate o' Wales,
  I tell your Highness fairly,
Down pleasure's stream, wi' swelling sails,
  I'm tauld ye're driving rarely;   told
But some day ye may gnaw your nails,
  And curse your folly sairly,   sorely
That e'er ye brak Diana's pales,
  Or rattled dice wi' Charlie,
            By night or day.

Yet aft a ragged cowte's been known,   oft, colt
  To mak a noble aiver;   cart-horse
So, ye may doucely fill a throne,   soberly
  For a' their clish-ma-claver: tall
There, him at Agincourt wha shone,
  Few better were or braver;
And yet, wi' funny queer Sir John,
  He was an unco shaver,   wag
            For monie a day.   many

For you, right reverend Osnaburg,   (Duke of York)
  Nane sets the lawn-sleeve sweeter,   none
Although a ribbon at your lug   ear
  Wad been a dress completer: would
As ye disown yon paughty dog   proud
  That bears the keys of Peter,
Then, swith! and get a wife AT ANCE,   quick
  Or, trouth! ye'll stain the mitre
            Some luckless day.

Ye, lastly, bonnie blossoms a';
  Ye royal lasses dainty,
Heaven mak ye guid as weel as braw,   good
  And gie you lads a-plenty:
But sneer na British boys awa',   not
  For kings are unco scant aye;   very

And German gentles are but sma',
They're better just than want aye
   On ony day.

Now bless you a'! consider now,
   Ye're unco muckle dautet;   much caressed
But ere the course o' life be through,
   It may be bitter sautet: salted
And I hae seen their coggie fou,   bowl full
   That yet hae tarrow't at it;   lingered
But or the day was done, I trow,   ere
   The laggen they hae clautet   corners, scraped
      Fu' clean that day.

ON A SCOTCH BARD,

GONE TO THE WEST INDIES.

A' YE wha live by sowps o' drink,   quantities
A' ye wha live by crambo-clink,   versifying
A' ye wha live and never think,
   Come, mourn wi' me!
Our billie's gien us a' a jink,   brother, the slip
   And owre the sea.   over

Lament him a' ye rantin' core,   noisy folks
Wha dearly like a random-splore,   who, frolic
Nae mair he'll join the merry roar   no more
   In social key;
For now he's ta'en anither shore,
   And owre the sea l

Auld cantie Kyle may weepers wear,   cheerful
And stain them wi' the saut, saut tear;   salt
'Twill mak her poor auld heart, I fear,
   In flinders flee;   splinters
He was her laureat mony a year,
   That's owre the sea.

He saw misfortune's cauld nor-west
Lang mustering up a bitter blast;
A jillet brak his heart at last,   jilt
   Ill may she be!
So, took a berth afore the mast,
   And owre the sea.

To tremble under fortune's cummock,   rod
On scarce a bellyfu' o' drummock,   meal and water
Wi' his proud, independent stomach,
   Could ill agree;
So row't his hurdies in a hammock,   wrapped himself
   And owre the sea.

He ne'er was gien to great misguiding,   given
Yet coin his pouches wad na bide in;   would not

Wi' him it ne'er was under hiding—
    He dealt it free :
The Muse was a' that he took pride in,
    That's owre the sea.

Jamaica bodies, use him weel,
And hap him in a cozie biel: *wrap, snug shelter*
Ye'll find him aye a dainty chiel,   *fellow*
    And fou o' glee ;   *full*
He wad na wranged the very deil,
    That's owre the sea.

Fareweel, my rhyme-composing billie !   *brother*
Your native soil was right ill-willie ;   *ill-natured*
But may ye flourish like a lily,
    Now bonnilie !
I'll toast ye in my hindmost gillie,   *gill*
    Though owre the sea !   *over*

A BARD'S EPITAPH.

Is there a whim-inspirèd fool,
Owre fast for thought, owre hot for rule,   *too*
Owre blate to seek, owre proud to snool, *bashful, succumb*
    Let him draw near ;
And owre this grassy heap sing dool,   *o'er, sorrow*
    And drap a tear.   *drop*

Is there a bard of rustic song,
Who, noteless, steals the crowds among,
That weekly this area throng,
    Oh, pass not by !
But, with a frater-feeling strong,
    Here, heave a sigh.

Is there a man, whose judgment clear,
Can others teach the course to steer,
Yet runs himself life's mad career,
    Wild as the wave ;
Here pause—and, through the starting tear,
    Survey this grave.

The poor inhabitant below,
Was quick to learn, and wise to know,
And keenly felt the friendly glow,
    And softer flame ;
But thoughtless follies laid him low,
    And stained his name !

Reader, attend—whether thy soul
Soars fancy's flights beyond the pole,
Or darkling grubs this earthly hole,
    In low pursuit ;
Know, prudent, cautious self-control
    Is wisdom's root.

A DEDICATION TO GAVIN HAMILTON, ESQ.

Expect na. sir, in this narration,   *not*
A fleechin, flethr'in dedication,   *wheedling, flattering*
To roose you up, and ca' you guid,   *praise, call, good*
And sprung o' great and noble bluid,   *blood*
Because ye're surnamed like his Grace ;   *(Duke of Hamilton)*
Perhaps related to the race ;
Then when I'm tired, and sae are ye,   *so*
Wi' mony a fulsome, sinfu' lie,
Set up a face, how I stop short,
For fear your modesty be hurt.

This may do—maun do, sir, wi' them who   *must*
Maun please the great folk for a wamefou ;   *bellyfull*
For me ! sae laigh I needna bow,   *low*
For, I am thankfu' I can plough ;
And when I downa yoke a naig,   *cannot, nag*
Then, I'll be thankfu' I can beg ;
Sae I shall sae, and that's nae flatterin',
It's just sic poet, and sic patron.   *such*

The Poet, some guid angel help him,
Or else, I fear some ill ane skelp him,   *strike*
He may do weel for a' he's done yet,   *well*
But only he's no just begun yet.

The Patron (sir, ye maun forgie me,
I winna lie, come what will o' me),   *wont*
On every hand it will allowed be,
He's just—nae better than he should be.   *no*

I readily and freely grant,
He downa see a poor man want ;   *will not*
What's no his ain he winna tak it,   *not, own, will not*
What ance he says he winna break it ;   *once*
Ought he can lend he'll no refus't
Till aft his gudeness is abused ;   *often*
And rascals whiles that do him wrang,   *sometimes*
Even that, he does na mind it lang :   *long*
As master, landlord, husband, father,
He does na fail his part in either.

But then nae thanks to him for a that,
Nae godly symptom ye can ca' that ;
It's naething but a milder feature
Of our poor sinfu', corrupt nature :
Ye'll get the best o' moral works,
'Mang black Gentoos and pagan Turks,
Or hunters wild on Ponotaxi,
Wha never heard of orthodoxy.   *who*
That he's the poor man's friend in need,
The gentleman in word and deed.

Morality, thou deadly bane,
Thy tens o' thousands thou hast slain !

Vain is his hope whose stay and trust is
In moral mercy, truth, and justice!

No—stretch a point to catch a plack ;   *coin*
Abuse a brother to his back ;
Be to the poor like ony whunstane,   *any whinstone*
And haud their noses to the grunstane,   *hold, grindstone*
Ply every art o' legal thieving ;
No matter—stick to sound believing!

Learn three-mile prayers, and half-mile graces,
Wi' weel-spread looves, and lang wry faces ;   *palms, long*
Grunt up a solemn, lengthened groan,
CONDEMN a' parties but your own ;
I'll warrant, then, ye're nae deceiver—
A steady, sturdy, stanch believer.

Oh ye wha leave the springs o' Calvin,
For gumlie dubs of your ain delvin'!   *muddy*
Ye sons of heresy and error,
Ye'll some day squeel in quaking terror!
When Vengeance draws the sword in wrath,
And in the fire throws the sheath ;
When Ruin, with his sweeping besom,
Just frets, till Heaven commission gies him :
While o'er the harp pale Misery moans,
And strikes the ever-deepening tones,
Still louder shrieks, and heavier groans!

Your pardon, Sir, for this digression,
I maist forgot my dedication ;   *almost*
But when divinity comes cross me,
My readers still are sure to lose me.

So, sir, ye see 'twas nae daft vapour,   *foolish*
But I maturely thought it proper,
When a' my works I did review,
To dedicate them, sir, to you :
Because (ye need na tak it ill)
I thought them something like yoursel.

Then patronise them wi' your favour,
And your petitioner shall ever——
I had amaist said, ever pray,   *almost*
But that's a word I need na say :
For prayin' I hae little skill o't ;
I'm baith dead sweer, and wretched ill o't ;   *both, unwilling*
But I'se repeat each poor man's prayer
That kens or hears about you, sir—   *knows*

" May ne'er misfortune's gowling bark   *galling*
Howl through the dwelling o' the Clerk !   *(Mr Hamilton)*
May ne'er his generous, honest heart,
For that same generous spirit smart !
May Kennedy's far-honoured name
Lang beet his hymeneal flame,
Till Hamiltons, at least a dizen,   *dozen*
Are by their canty fireside risen :   *comfortable*

Five bonnie lassies round their table,
And seven braw fellows, stout and able,
To serve their king and country weel,   *well*
By word, or pen, or pointed steel!
May health and peace, with mutual rays,
Shine on the evening o' his days,
Till his wee curlie John's ier-oe,   *great-grandchild*
When ebbing life nae mair shall flow,   *no more*
The last, sad, mournful rites bestow."

I will not wind a lang conclusion
With complimentary effusion:
But whilst your wishes and endeavours
Are blest with fortune's smiles and favours,
I am, dear sir, with zeal most fervent,
Your much indebted, humble servant.

But if (which powers above prevent!)
That iron-hearted carl, Want,
Attended in his grim advances
By sad mistakes and black mischances,
While hopes, and joys, and pleasures fly him,
Make you as poor a dog as I am,
Your humble servant then no more;
For who would humbly serve the poor?
But by a poor man's hopes in Heaven!
While recollection's power is given,
If, in the vale of humble life,
The victim sad of fortune's strife,
I, through the tender-gushing tear,
Should recognize my master dear,
If friendless, low, we meet together,
Then, sir, your hand—my friend and brother.

TO MR M'KENZIE.

FRIDAY first's the day appointed
By the Right Worshipful anointed,
  To hold our grand procession;
To get a blad o' Johnie's morals,   *piece*
And taste a swatch o' Manson's barrels   *sample*
  I' the way of our profession.
The Master and the Brotherhood
  Would a' be glad to see you;
For me I would be mair than proud   *more*
  To share the mercies wi' you.   *entertainment*
    If Death, then, wi' skaith, then,   *hurt*
      Some mortal heart is hechtin',   *threatening*
    Inform him, and storm him,
      That Saturday you'll fecht him.   *fight*

              ROBERT BURNS.

MOSSGIEL, *An. M.* 5790.

THE FAREWELL.

"The vallant, in himself, what can he suffer ?
Or what does he regard his single woes ?
But when, alas! he multiplies himself,
To dearer selves, to the loved tender fair,
To those whose bliss, whose being hangs upon him,
To helpless children !—then, oh then! he feels
The point of misery festering in his heart,
And weakly weeps his fortune like a coward.
Such, such am I! undone!"

THOMSON'S *Edward and Eleanora.*

FAREWELL, old Scotia's bleak domains,
Far dearer than the torrid plains
   Where rich ananas blow !
Farewell, a mother's blessing dear !
A brother's sigh ! a sister's tear !
   My Jean's heart-rending throe !
Farewell, my Bess ! though thou'rt bereft
   Of my parental care,
A faithful brother I have left,
   My part in him thou'lt share !
     Adieu too, to you too,
      My Smith, my bosom frien' ;
     When kindly you mind me,
      Oh then befriend my Jean !

What bursting anguish tears my heart !
From thee, my Jeany, must I part !
   Thou, weeping, answ'rest "No !"
Alas ! misfortune stares my face,
And points to ruin and disgrace,
   I for thy sake must go !
Thee, Hamilton, and Aiken dear,
   A grateful, warm adieu !
I, with a much-indebted tear,
   Shall still remember you !
     All-hail then, the gale then,
      Wafts me from thee, dear shore !
     It rustles, and whistles—
      I'll never see thee more !

LINES WRITTEN ON A BANK NOTE.

WAE worth thy power, provoking leaf,   woe
Fell source o' a' my woe and grief :
For lack o' thee I've lost my lass,
For lack o' thee I scrimp my glass ;   stint
I see the children of affliction
Unaided, through thy sole restriction.
I've seen the oppressor's cruel smile
Amid his hapless victim's spoil,
And, for thy potence, vainly wished
To crush the villain in the dust.

For lack o' thee I leave this much-loved shore,
Never perhaps to greet old Scotland more.

R. B.—*Kyle.*

WRITTEN

ON A BLANK LEAF OF A COPY OF THE POEMS, PRESENTED TO AN OLD SWEETHEART, THEN MARRIED.

ONCE fondly loved and still remembered dear :
Sweet early object of my youthful vows !
Accept this mark of friendship, warm, sincere—
Friendship ! 'tis all cold duty now allows.

And when you read the simple artless rhymes,
One friendly sigh for him—he asks no more,
Who distant burns in flaming torrid climes,
Or haply lies beneath th' Atlantic's roar.

VERSES WRITTEN UNDER VIOLENT GRIEF.

ACCEPT the gift a friend sincere
Wad on thy worth be pressin';   would
Remembrance oft may start a tear,
But oh ! that tenderness forbear,
Though 'twad my sorrows lessen.

My morning raise sae clear and fair,   so
I thought sair storms wad never   sore
Bedew the scene ; but grief and care
In wildest fury hae made bare   have
My peace, my hope, for ever !

You think I'm glad ; oh, I pay weel
For a' the joy I borrow,
In solitude—then, then I feel
I canna to mysel' conceal   cannot
My deeply-ranklin' sorrow.

Farewell ! within thy bosom free
A sigh may whyles awaken ;   sometimes
A tear may wet thy laughin' ee,   eye
For Scotia's son,—ance gay like thee—   once
Now hopeless, comfortless, forsaken !

THE CALF.

TO THE REV. MR JAMES STEVEN.

RIGHT, sir ! your text I'll prove it true,
Though Heretics may laugh ;

For instance, there's yoursel' just now,
  A' ᴋᴇɴ, an unco calf!   know, great

And should some patron be so kind,
  As bless you wi' a kirk,
I doubt nae, sir, but then we'll find
  Ye're still as great a stirk.

And in your lug, most reverend James,   ear
  To hear you roar and rowte,   bellow
Few men o' sense will doubt your claims
  To rank among the nowte.   cattle

And when ye're numbered wi' the dead,
  Below a grassy hillock,
Wi' justice they may mark your head—
  " Here lies a famous bullock l"

WILLIE CHALMERS.

Wɪ' braw new branks in mickle pride,   bridle, much
  And eke a braw new brechan,   also, collar
My Pegasus I'm got astride,
  And up Parnassus pechin;   panting
Whiles owre a bush wi' downward crush, sometimes, over
  The doited beastie stammers;   stupid
Then up he gets, and off he sets
  For sake of Willie Chalmers.

I doubt na, lass, that well-kenned name not, well-known
  May cost a pair o' blushes;
I am na stranger to your fame,   no
  Nor his warm urgèd wishes.
Your bonnie face sae mild and sweet,   sc
  His honest heart enamours,
And faith ye'll no be lost a whit,
  Though waired on Willie Chalmers.   spent

Auld truth hersel' might swear ye're fair,
  And honour safely back her,
And modesty assume your air,
  And ne'er à ane mistak' her: one
And sic twa love-inspiring een   such two, eyes
  Might fire even holy palmers;
Nae wonder then they've fatal been   no
  To honest Willie Chalmers.

I doubt na fortune may you shore   offer
  Some mim-mou'd pouther'd priestie, prim, powdered
Fu' lifted up wi' Hebrew lore,
  And band upon his breastie
But oh l what signifies to you
  His lexicons and grammars;

The feeling heart's·the royal blue,
And that's wi' Willie Chalmers.

Some gapin' glowerin' country laird   *staring*
  May warsle for your favour;   *wrestle*
May claw his lug, and straik his beard,   *scratch, ear, stroke*
  And hoast up some palaver.   *cough*
My bonnie maid, before ye wed
  Sic clumsy-witted hammers,
Seek Heaven for help, and barefit skelp   *barefoot run*
  Awa' wi' Willie Chalmers.

Forgive the Bard! my fond regard
  For ane that shares my bosom,
Inspires my muse to gie'm his dues,
  For NOT a hair I roose him   *flatter*
May powers aboon unite you soon,   *above*
  TIME BUT THE MORE ENAMOURS,
And every year come in mair dear   *more*
  To you and Willie Chalmers.

TAM SAMSON'S ELEGY.

"An honest man's the noblest work of God."—POPE.

HAS auld Kilmarnock seen the deil?
Or great M'Kinlay thrawn his heel?   *(a preacher)*
Or Robertson again grown weel
    To preach and read?
"Na, war than a'! cries ilka chiel—   *worse, every one*
    Tam Samson's deid!   *dead*

Kilmarnock lang may grunt and grane,   *groan*
And sigh, and sob, and greet her lane,   *weep, alone*
And cleed her bairns, man, wife, and wean,   *clothe, child*
    In mourning weed;
To death she's dearly paid the kane—   *tribute*
    Tam Samson's deid!

The brethren o' the mystic level   *(masons)*
May hing their head in woefu' bevel,   *hang, posture*
While by their nose the tears will revel,
    Like ony bead;   *any*
Death's gi'en the lodge an unco devel--   *blow*
    Tam Samson's deid!

When Winter muffles up his cloak,
And binds the mire like a rock;
When to the loch the curlers* flock   *lake*
    Wi' gleesome speed,
Wha will they station at the cock?—   *who, mark*
    Tam Samson's deid!

He was the king o' a' the core,   *company*
  To guard,† or draw,‡ or wick a bore,§

---

* See note, p. 53.   ‡ Go straight to the mark.
† Guard stones at the mark   § Go between flanking stones.

Or up the rink like Jehu roar   course
    In time o' need ;
But now he lags on death's hog-score—*
    Tam Samson's deid !

Now safe the stately sawmont sail,   salmon
And trouts be-dropp'd wi' crimson hail,   spotted
And eels weel kenn'd for souple tail.   well known, supple
    And geds for greed,   pikes
Since dark in death's fish-creel we wail
    Tam Samson deid !

Rejoice, ye birring paitricks a' ;   whirring partridges
Ye cootie moorcocks, crousely craw ;†
Ye maukins, cock your fud fu' braw,   hares
    Withouten dread ;
Your mortal fae is now awa'—   foe
    Tam Samson's dead

That woefu' morn be ever mourn'd
Saw him in shootin' graith adorn'd,   dress
While pointers round impatient burn'd,
    Frae couples freed ;   from
But, och ! he gaed, and ne'er return'd !—   went
    Tam Samson's deid !

In vain auld age his body batters ;
In vain the gout his ankles fetters ;
In vain the burns cam' down like waters
    An acre braid !   broad
Now every auld wife, greetin', clatters   weeping
    Tam Samson's dead !

Owre many a weary hag he limpit,   over, moss-ditch
And aye the tither shot he thumpit,   still, other
Till coward Death behind him jumpit,   jumped
    Wi' deadly feide ;   enmity
Now he proclaims, wi' tout o' trumpet,   blast
    Tam Samson's deid !

When at his heart he felt the dagger,
He reel'd his wonted bottle-swagger,
But yet he drew the mortal trigger
    Wi' weel-aimed heed ;
" IT's five !" he cried, and owre did stagger—
    Tam Samson's deid !

Ilk hoary hunter mourn'd a brither ;   each, brother
Ilk sportsman youth bemoan'd a father ;
Yon auld gray stane, amang the heather,   stone
    Marks out his head,
Where Burns has wrote in rhyming blether,   nonsense
    Tam Samson's dead !

There low he lies, in lasting rest ;
Perhaps upon his mouldering breast

* Stones not reaching this line are removed.   † Feathery legged, bravely crow

Some spitefu' muirfowl bigs her nest,   builds
   To hatch and breed ;
Alas ! nae mair he'll them molest !—   no more
        Tam Samson's deid !

When August winds the heather wave,
And sportsmen wander by yon grave,
Three volleys let his memory crave
        O' pouther and lead,   powder
Till echo answer frae her cave,   from
        Tam Samson's deid !

Heaven rest his saul, whare'er he be !   soul
Is th' wish o' mony mae than me ;   more
He had twa fauts, or maybe three,   two, faults
        Yet what remead ?   remedy
Ae social, honest man want we :   one
        Tam Samson's deid !

EPITAPH.

Tam Samson's weel-worn clay here lies,   well
   Ye canting zealots spare him !
If honest worth in heaven rise,
   Ye'll mend or ye win near him.   get

PER CONTRA.

Go, Fame, and canter like a filly
Through a' the streets and neuks o' Killie, (Kilmarnock)
Tell every social, honest billie   fellow
   To cease his grievin',
For yet, unskaithed by Death's gleg gullie, sharp knife
       Tam Samson's leevin' !   living

TO MR M'ADAM OF CRAIGENGILLAN.

Sir, o'er a gill I gat your card,
   I trow it made me proud ;
" See wha taks notice o' the Bard !"   who takes
   I lap and cried fu' loud.   leapt

Wha cares a bit about their jaw,
   The senseless, gawky million :
I'll cock my nose aboon them a'—   above
   I'm roosed by Craigengillan !   praised

'Twas noble, sir ; 'twas like yoursel',
   To grant your high protection :
A great man's smile, ye ken fu' well,   know
   Is aye a blest infection ;—

Though, by his banes who in a tub bones (Diogenes)
   Matched Macedonian Sandy !   Alexander
On my ain legs through dirt and dub,   own
   I independent stand aye.

And when those legs to guid, warm kail,   broth
  Wi' welcome canna bear me ;
A lee dyke-side, a sybow-tail,   wall, leek
  And barley-scone, shall cheer me.   cake

Heaven spare you lang to kiss the breath
  O' many flowery simmers !   summers
And bless your bonny lasses baith—   both
  I'm tauld they're lo'esome kimmers !   told, lovesome girls

And God bless young Dunaskin's laird,
  The blossom of our gentry !
And may he wear an auld man's beard,
  A credit to his country.

VERSES

LEFT IN THE ROOM WHERE HE SLEPT.

OH thou dread Power, who reign'st above
  I know thou wilt me hear,
When for this scene of peace and love,
  I make my prayer sincere !

The hoary sire—the mortal stroke,
  Long, long be pleased to spare,
To bliss his filial little flock,
  And show what good men are.

She, who her lovely offspring eyes
  With tender hopes and fears,
Oh bless her with a mother's joys,
  But spare a mother's tears !

Their hope, their stay, their darling youth,
  In manhood's dawning blush—
Bless him, thou God of love and truth,
  Up to a parent's wish !

The beautous, seraph sister-band,
  With earnest tears I pray;
Thou knowest the snares on every hand—
  Guide thou their steps alway.

When soon or late they reach that coast,
  O'er life's rough ocean driven,
May they rejoice, no wanderer lost,
  A family in heaven !

THE BRIGS OF AYR.

INSCRIBED TO JOHN BALLANTYNE, ESQ., AYR.

THE simple Bard, rough at the rustic plough,
Learning his tuneful trade from every bough ;
The chanting linnet, or the mellow thrush,
Hailing the setting sun, sweet, in the green thorn bush ;

The soaring-lark, the perching red-breast shrill,
Or deep-toned plovers, gray, wild-whistling o'er the hill ;
Shall he, nurst in the peasant's lowly shed,
To hardy independence bravely bred,
By early poverty to hardship steeled,
And trained to arms in stern misfortune's field—
Shall he be guilty of their hireling crimes,
The servile, mercenary Swiss of rhymes ?
Or labour hard the panegyric close,
With all the venal soul of dedicating prose ?
No! though his artless strains he rudely sings,
And throws his hand uncouthly o'er the strings,.
He glows with all the spirit of the Bard,
Fame, honest fame, his great, his dear reward!
Still, if some patron's generous care he trace,
Skilled in the secret to bestow with grace ;
When Ballantyne befriends his humble name,
And hands the rustic stranger up to fame,
With heartfelt throes his grateful bosom swells,
The godlike bliss, to give, alone excels.

'Twas when the stacks get on their winter hap,   covering
And thack and rape secure the toil-won crap; thatch, rope, crop
Potatoe bings are snuggèd up frae skaith   heaps, danger
Of coming Winter's biting, frosty breath ;
The bees, rejoicing o'er their summer toils,
Unnumbered buds and flowers' delicious spoils,
Sealed up with frugal care in massive waxen piles,
Are doomed by man, that tyrant o'er the weak,
The death TO SUFFER, smoored wi' brimstone reek: smothered,
The thundering guns are heard on every side,   [smoke
The wounded coveys, reeling, scatter wide ;
The feathered field-mates, bound by nature's tie,
Sires, mothers, children, in one carnage lie :
(What warm, poetic heart, but inly bleeds,
And execrates man's savage, ruthless deeds !)
Nae mair the flower in field or meadow springs ; no more
Nae mair the grove with airy concert rings,
Except, perhaps, the robin's whistling glee,
Proud o' the height o' some bit half-lang tree . short
The hoary morns precede the sunny days,
Mild, calm, serene, wide spreads the noon-tide blaze,
While thick the gossamer waves wanton in the rays.

'Twas in that season, when a simple Bard,
Unknown and poor, simplicity's reward.
Ae night, within the ancient brugh of Ayr, one, burgh
By whim inspired, or haply prest wi' care,
He left his bed, and took his wayward route, •
And down by Simpson's wheeled the left about : (a tavern)
(Whether impelled by all-directing Fate,
To witness what I after shall narrate ;
Or whether, rapt in meditation high,
He wandered out he knew not where or why)

The drowsy Dungeon-clock had numbered two,
And Wallace Tower had sworn the fact was true:
The tide-swoln Firth, with sullen sounding roar,
Through the still night dashed hoarse along the shore.
All else was hushed as Nature's closed e'e: eye
The silent moon shone high o'er tower and tree:

The chilly frost, beneath the silver beam,
Crept, gently-crusting, o'er the glittering stream.
When lo! on either hand the listening Bard,
The clanging sough of whistling wings is heard; sound
Two dusky forms dart through the midnight air,
Swift as the gos drives on the wheeling hare: falcon

Ane on the Auld Brig his airy shape uprears,   one
The ither flutters o'er the rising piers: other
Our warlock Rhymer instantly descried
The Sprites that owre the Brigs of Ayr preside. o'er
(That Bards are second-sighted is nae joke,
And ken the lingo of the sp'ritual folk;   know
Fays, Spunkies, Kelpies,* a', they can explain them,
And even the very deils they brawly ken them.) well
Auld Brig appeared of ancient Pictish race,
The very wringles Gothic in his face:
He seemed as he wi' Time had warstl'd lang, wrestled
Yet, teughly doure, he bade an unco bang.‡
New Brig was buskit in a braw new coat,   dressed
That he at Lon'on, frae ane Adams, got;
In's hand five taper staves as smooth's a bead,
Wi' virls and whirlygigums at the head. rings, ornaments
The Goth was stalking round with anxious search,
Spying the time-worn flaws in every arch;
It chanced his new-come neebour took his ee, neighbour
And e'en a vexed and angry heart had he!
Wi' thieveless sneer to see his modish mien, spited
He, down the water, gies him his guid-e'en:— good evening

AULD BRIG.

I doubt na, frien', ye'll think ye're nae sheepshank,†
Ance ye were streekit o'er frae bank to bank, once, stretched
But gin ye be a brig as auld as me—   when
Though, faith, that day I doubt ye'll never see;
There'll be, if that date come, I'll wad a boddle, bet a doit
Some fewer whigmaleeries in your noddle. fancies, head

NEW BRIG.

Auld Vandal, ye but show your little mense civility
Just much about it wi' your scanty sense;
Will your poor, narrow footpath of a street—
Whare twa wheelbarrows tremble when they meet- where two
Your ruined, formless bulk o' stane and lime,
Compare wi' bonnie Brigs o' modern time?

---

* Fairies, ignis fatuis, water sprites.   † No contemptible one.
‡ Toughly obdurate, endured a severe stroke.

There's men o' taste would tak the Ducat Stream,   (a ford)
Though they should cast the very sark and swim,   shirt
Ere they would grate their feelings wi' the view
Of sic an ugly Gothic hulk as you.   such

AULD BRIG.

Conceited gowk, puff'd up wi' windy pride !   fool
This mony a year I've stood the flood and tide ;
And though wi' crazy eild I'm sair forfairn,   age, sore enfeebled
I'll be a Brig when ye're a shapeless cairn !
As yet ye little ken about the matter,   know
But twa-three winters will inform ye better.   two or three
When heavy, dark, continued a'-day rains,
Wi' deepening deluges o'erflow the plains ;
When from the hills where springs the brawling Coil,
Or stately Lugar's mossy fountains boil,
Or where the Greenock winds his moorland course,
Or haunted Garpal draws his feeble source,
Aroused by blustering winds and spotting thowes,   thaws
In mony a torrent down his snaw-broo rowes ;   water, rolls
While crashing ice, borne on the roaring speat,   flood
Sweeps dams, and mills, and brigs a' to the gate ;   away
And from Glenbuck* down to the Ratton-key†
Auld Ayr is just one lengthened tumbling sea—
Then down ye'll hurl, AND MAY ye never rise !
And dash the gumlie jaups up to the pouring skies. muddy drops
A lesson sadly teaching, to your cost,
That Architecture's noble art is lost !

NEW BRIG.

Fine Architecture, trowth, I needs must say't o't !   indeed
WE ARE SAE thankfu' that we've tint the gate o't !   lost, way
Gaunt, ghastly, ghaist-alluring edifices,   ghost
Hanging with threatening jut, like precipices ;
O'er-arching, mouldy, gloom-inspiring coves,
Supporting roofs fantastic, stony groves :
Windows, and doors in nameless sculpture drest,
With order, symmetry, or taste unblest ;
Forms like some bedlam statuary's dream,
The crazed creations of misguided whim ;
Forms might be worshipp'd on the bended knee,
And still the second dread command be free,
Their likeness is not found on earth, in air, or sea.
Mansions that would disgrace the building taste
Of any mason reptile, bird, or beast ;
Fit only for a doited monkish race,   foolish
Or cuifs of latter times, wha held the notion   fools
That sullen gloom was sterling true devotion ;
Fancies that our good Brugh denies protection !   burgh
And soon may they expire, unblest with resurrection !

* The source of the River Ayr.—*B.*
† A small landing-place above the large key.—

AULD BRIG.

Oh ye, my dear remember'd ancient yealings, coevals
Were ye but here to share my wounded feelings !
Ye worthy Proveses, and mony a Bailie, Provosts, many
Wha in the paths o' righteousness did toil aye ;
Ye dainty Deacons and ye douce Conveeners, sober
To whom our moderns are but causey-cleaners ; scavengers
Ye godly Councils wha hae blest this town ;
Ye godly brethren o' the sacred gown,
Wha meekly gie your hurdies to the smiters ;
And (what would now be strange) ye godly writers ;
A' ye douce folk I've borne aboon the broo, above, water
Were ye but here, what would ye say or do !
How would your spirits groan in deep vexation,
To see each melancholy alteration ;
And agonizing, curse the time and place
When ye begat the base degenerate race !
Nae langer reverend men, their country's glory, no longer
In plain braid Scots hold forth a plain braid story ! broad
Nae langer thrifty citizens and douce,
Meet owre a pint, or in the council-house ; [giddy
But staumrel, corky-headed, graceless gentry, half-witted,
The herryment and ruin of the country ; plunderers
Men three parts made by tailors and by barbers,
Wha waste your weel-bain'd gear on THAE well-saved money
  new Brigs and Harbours !

NEW BRIG.

Now haud you there, for faith you've said enough, hold
An muckle mair than ye can make to through ; make good
As for your Priesthood I shall say but little,
Corbies and Clergy are a shot right kittle : crows, ticklish
But, under favour o' your langer beard, longer
Abuse o' magistrates might weel be spared : well
To liken them to your auld warld squad, old-world
I must needs say comparisons are odd.
In Ayr, wag-wits nae mair can hae a handle no more, have
To mouth " a citizen," a term o' scandal ;
Nae mair the Council waddles down the street,
In all the pomp of ignorant conceit ;
Men wha grew wise priggin' owre hops and rasins, bargaining
Or gathered liberal views in bonds and seisins,
If haply Knowledge, on a random tramp,
Had shor'd them with a glimmer of his lamp, offered
And would to Common-sense for once betrayed them,
Plain, dull Stupidity stept kindly in to aid them.

———

What further clish-ma-claver might been said, palaver
What bloody wars, if Sprites had blood to shed,
No man can tell ; but all before their sight,
A fairy train appeared in order bright ;

Adown the glittering stream they featly danced ;   spracely
Bright to the moon their various dresses glanced :
They footed o'er the watery glass so neat,
The infant ice scarce bent beneath their feet :
While arts of minstrelsy among them rung,
And soul-ennobling bards heroic ditties sung.
Oh had M'Lachlan, thairm-inspiring sage,   cat-gut
Been there to hear this heavenly band engage,
When through his dear strathspeys they bore with
   Highland rage ;
Or when they struck old Scotia's melting airs,
The lover's raptured joys or bleeding cares ;
How would his Highland lug been nobler fired,   ear
And even his matchless hand with finer touch inspired !
No guess could tell what instrument appeared,
But all the soul of Music's self was heard ;
Harmonious concert rung in every part,
While simple melody poured moving on the heart.

   The Genius of the stream in front appears,
A venerable chief advanced in years ;
His hoary head with water-lilies crowned,
His manly leg with garter tangle bound.
Next came the lovelist pair in all the ring,
Sweet Female Beauty hand-in-hand with Spring ;
Then, crowned with flowery hay, came Rural Joy,
And Summer, with his fervid-beaming eye :
All cheering Plenty, with her flowing horn,
Led yellow Autumn, wreathed with nodding corn ;
Then winter's time-bleached locks did hoary show,
By Hospitality with cloudless brow.
Next followed Courage, with his martial stride,
From where the Feal wild woody coverts hide ;*
Benevolence, with mild, benigant air,
A female form, came from the towers of Stair :
Learning and Worth in equal measures trode,†
From simple Catrine, their long-loved abode :
Last, white-robed Peace, crowned with a hazel wreath,
To rustic Agriculture did bequeath
The broken iron instruments of death ;
At sight of whom our Sprites forgat their kindling wrath.

LINES ON MEETING WITH BASIL, LORD DAER.

THIS wot ye all whom it concerns,
I, Rhymer Robin, alias Burns,
     October twenty-third,
A ne'er-to-be-forgotten day,
Sae far I sprachled up the brae,   so, clambered
    I dinner'd wi' a Lord.

I've been at drucken writers' feasts,   drunken
Nay, been BLIN' fou 'mang godly priests,   drunk
    Wi' reverence be it spoken ;

  * Coilsfield.   † Dugald Stewart.

I've even joined the honour'd jorum,   drinking-vessel
When mighty squireships of the quorum
        Their hydra drouth did sloken.   thirst, slake

But wi' a Lord!—stand out my shin,
A Lord—a Peer—an Earl's son!
        Up higher yet my bonnet!
And sic a Lord!—lang Scotch ells twa,   such
Our Peerage he o'erlooks them a',
        As I look o'er my sonnet.

But oh for Hogarth's magic power!
To show Sir Bardie's willyart glower,   bewildered look
        And how he star'd and stammer'd,
When goavan, as if led wi' branks,   moving stupidly, bridle
And stumpin' on his ploughman shanks,   legs
        He in the parlour hammer'd.

I sidling shelter'd in a nook,
And at his Lordship steal't a look,
        Like some portentous omen;
Except good sense and social glee,
And (what surprised me) modesty,
        I markéd nought uncommon.

I watch'd the symptoms o' the great,
The gentle pride, the lordly state,
        The arrogant assuming;
BUT NOUGHT o' pride, nae pride had he,
Nor sauce, nor state, that I could see,
        Mair than an honest ploughman.

Then from his Lordship I shall learn
Henceforth to meet with unconcern
        One rank as weel's another;
Nae honest worthy man need care
To meet with noble youthful Daer,
        For he but meets a brother.

EPISTLE TO MAJOR LOGAN.

HAIL, thairm-inspirin', rattlin' Willie!   fiddle-string
Though Fortune's road be rough and hilly
To every fiddling, rhyming billie,   fellow
        We never heed,
But take it like the unbacked filly,
        Proud o' her speed.
                                            [sometimes
When idly goavan whyles we saunter,   moving stupidly
Yirr, Fancy barks, awa we canter   snarl
Up hill, down brae, till some mishanter,   accident
        Some black bog-hole,
Arrests us, then the scaith and banter   harm
        We're forced to thole.   bear

Hale be your heart !—hale be your fiddle !
Lang may your elbock jink and diddle   *elbow move nimbly*
To cheer you through the weary widdle,   *wriggle*
       O' this wild warl',   *world*
Until you on a crummock driddle   *staff, saunter*
       A gray-haired carle.

Come wealth, come poortith, late or soon,   *poverty*
Heaven send your heart-strings aye in tune,
And screw your temper-pins aboon   *above*
       A fifth or mair,   *more*
The melancholious, lazy croon,   *murmur*
       O' cankrie care.   *peevish*

May still your life from day to day
Nae " lente largo " in the play,
But " allegretto forte " gay
       Harmonious flow
A sweeping, kindling, bauld strathspey—   *bold*
       Encore ! bravo !

A blessing on the cheery gang
Wha dearly like a jig or sang,
And never think o' right and wrang
       By square and rule,
But as the clegs o' feeling stang,   *gad-flies, sting*
       Are wise or fool.

My hand-waled BAN keep hard in chase   *chosen*
The harpy, hoodock, purse-proud race,   *miserly*
Wha count on poortith as disgrace—   *poverty*
       Their tuneless hearts !
May fireside discords jar a bass
       To a' their parts !

But come, your hand, my careless brither,   *brother*
I' th' ither warl', if there's anither—   *other*
And that there is I've little swither   *doubt*
       About the matter—
We cheek for chow shall jog thegither ;   *cheek by jole*
       I'se ne'er bid better.   *expect*

We've faults and failings—granted clearly,
We're frail backsliding mortals merely,
Eve's bonnie squad, priest wyte them sheerly   *blame, entirely*
       For our grand fa' ;
But still, but still—I like them dearly—
       BLESS ! bless them a' !

Ochon for poor Castalian drinkers,
When they fa' foul o' earthly jinkers,   *sprightly girls*
The witching, DEAR, delicious blinkers   *eyes*
       Hae put me hyte,   *mad*
And gart me weet my waukrife winkers   *made, wet, sleepless*
       Wi' girnin' spite.   *grinning*

But by yon moon !—and that's high swearin'—
And every star within my hearin' !

And by her een wha was a dear ane!   eyes who
  I'll ne'er forget;
I hope to gie the jads a clearin'   lasses
  In fair-play yet.

My loss I mourn, but not repent it,
I'll seek my pursie whare I tint it,.   purse, where, lost
Ance to the Indies I were wonted,   when, arrived
  Some cantrip hour,   witching
By some sweet elf I'll yet be dinted,
  Then, *vive l'amour!*

Faites mes baise mains respectueuses,
To sentimental sister Susie,
And honest Lucky; no to roose you,   not, praise
  Ye may be proud,
That sic a couple fate allows ye   such
  To grace your blood.

Nae mair at present can I measure,   no more
And trowth, my rhymin' ware's nae treasure;   indeed
But when in Ayr, some half-hour's leisure,
  Be't light, be't dark,
Sir Bard will do himself the pleasure
  To call at Park.

ROBERT BURNS.

MOSSGIEL, *October* 30, 1786.

ADDRESS TO EDINBURGH.

EDINA! Scotia's darling seat!
  All hail thy palaces and towers,
Where once beneath a monarch's feet
  Sat Legislation's sovereign powers!
From marking wildly-scattered flowers,
  As on the banks of Ayr I strayed,
And singing, lone, the lingering hours,
  I sheltered in thy honoured shade.

Here wealth still swells the golden tide,
  As busy Trade his labour plies;
There Architecture's noble pride
  Bids elegance and splendour rise;
Here Justice, from her native skies,
  High wields her balance and her rod;
There Learning, with his eagle eyes,
  Seeks Science in her coy abode.

Thy sons, Edina! social, kind,
  With open arms the stranger hail;
Their views enlarged, their liberal mind,
  Above the narrow, rural vale;
Attentive still to sorrow's wail,
  Or modest merit's silent claim:

And never may their sources fail!
And never envy blot their name!

Thy daughters bright thy walks adorn,
  Gay as the guilded summer sky,
Sweet as the dewy milk-white thorn,
  Dear as the raptured thrill of joy!
Fair Burnet strikes th' adoring eye,
  Heaven's beauties on my fancy shine;
I see the Sire of Love on high,
  And own his work indeed divine!

There, watching high the least alarms,
  Thy rough, rude fortress gleams afar;
Like some bold veteran, gray in arms,
  And mark'd with many a seamy scar;
The ponderous wall and massy bar,
  Grim-rising o'er the rugged rock;
Have oft withstood assailing war,
  And oft repelled the invader's shock.

With awe-struck thought, and pitying tears,
  I view that noble, stately dome,
Where Scotia's kings of other years,
  Famed heroes! had their royal home:
Alas, how changed the times to come!
  Their royal name low in the dust!
Their hapless race wild-wandering roam,
  Though rigid law cries out, 'twas just!

Wild beats my heart to trace your steps,
  Whose ancestors, in days of yore,
Through hostile ranks and ruined gaps,
  Old Scotia's bloody lion bore:
Even I who sing in rustic lore,
  Haply, my sires have left their shed,
And faced grim danger's loudest roar,
  Bold-following where your fathers led!

Edina! Scotia's darling seat!
  All hail thy palaces and towers,
Where once beneath a monarch's feet
  Sat Legislation's sovereign powers!
From marking wildly scattered flowers,
  As on the banks of Ayr I strayed,
And singing, lone, the lingering hours,
  I shelter in thy honoured shade.

ON CHARLES EDWARD'S BIRTH-DAY.

FALSE flatterer, Hope, away!
Nor think to lure us as in days of yore;
  We solemnize this sorrowing natal-day
To prove our loyal truth; we can no more;

And owning Heaven's mysterious sway,
Submissive low adore.

Ye honoured mighty dead!
Who nobly perished in the glorious cause,
Your king, your country, and her laws!
From great Dundee who smiling Victory led,
And fell a martyr in her arms
(What breast of northern ice but warms?)
To bold Balmerino's undying name,
Whose soul of fire, lighted at Heaven's high flame,
Deserves the proudest wreath departed heroes claim.

Nor unavenged your fate shall be,
It only lags the fatal hour;
Your blood shall with incessant cry
Awake at last th' unsparing power;
As from the cliff, with thundering course,
The snowy ruin smokes along,
With doubling speed and gathering force,
Till deep it crashing whelms the cottage in the vale

TO MISS LOGAN, WITH BEATTIE'S POEMS,

AS A NEW-YEAR'S GIFT.

January 1, 1787.

AGAIN the silent wheels of time
Their annual round have driven,
And you, though scarce in maiden prime,
Are so much nearer heaven.

No gifts have I from Indian coasts
The infant year to hail;
I send you more than India boasts
In Edwin's simple tale.

Our sex with guile and faithless love
Is charged, perhaps, too true;
But may, dear maid, each lover prove
An Edwin still to you!

BURNS TO THE GUDEWIFE OF WAUCHOPE HOUSE.

I MIND it weel in early date,   well
When I was beardless, young, and blate,   bashful
And first could thrash the barn;
Or haud a yoking at the pleugh;   hold, team, plough
And though forfoughten sair eneugh,   fatigued sore
Yet unco proud to learn: very
When first among the yellow corn
A man I reckon'd was.

And wi' the lave ilk merry morn   *rest each*
  Could rank my rig and lass,
    Still shearing, and clearing,
      The tither stookèd raw,   *other, row*
    Wi' claivers and haivers,   *talk, nonsense*
      Wearing the day awa.

E'en then, a wish, I mind its power—
A wish that to my latest hour
  Shall strongly heave my breast—
That I, for poor auld Scotland's sake,
Some usefu' plan or beuk could make,   *book*
  Or sing a sang at least.
The rough burr-thrissle, spreading wide   *Scotch thistle*
  Amang the bearded bere,   *barley*
I turned the weeder-clips aside,   *weeding-iron*
  And spared the symbol dear :
    No nation, no station,
      My envy e'er could raise,
    A Scot still, but blot still,
      I knew nae higher praise.

But still the elements o' sang
In formless jumble, right and wrang,
  Wild floated in my brain ;
Till on that har'st I said before,   *harvest*
My partner in the merry core,   *company*
  She roused the forming strain ;
I see her yet, the sonsie quean,   *stout & good-natured*
  That lighted up her jingle,
Her witching smile, her pauky een   *sly eyes*
  That gart my heart-strings tingle :   *made*
    I firèd, inspirèd,
      At every kindling keek,   *glance*
    But bashing and dashing,
      I fearèd aye to speak.

Health to the sex, ilk guid chiel says,   *each good fellow*
Wi' merry dance in winter days,
  And we to share in common :
The gust o' joy, the balm of woe,
The saul o' life, the heaven below,   *soul*
  Is rapture-giving woman.
Ye surly sumphs, who hate the name,   *fools*
  Be mindfu' o' your mither ;
She, honest woman, may think shame
  That ye're connected with her.
    Ye're wae men, ye're nae men,   *poor, not*
      That slight the lovely dears ;
    To shame ye, disclaim ye,
      Ilk honest birkie swears.   *each, fellow*

For you, no bred to barn and byre,
Wha sweetly tune the Scottish lyre,   *who*
  Thanks to you for your line :

The marled plaid ye kindly spare,   chequered
  By me should gratefully be ware;   worn
  'Twad please me to the Nine.
I'd be mair vauntie o' my hap,   proud, covering
  Douce hinging owre my curple,   sober, back
Than ony ermine ever lap,   any, leapt
  Or proud imperial purple.
  Fareweel then, lang heal then,
    And plenty be your fa',   fate
  May losses and crosses
    Ne'er at your hallan ca'!   inner door

ON WILLIE SMELLIE.*

WILLIE SMELLIE to Crochallan came,
The old cocked hat, the gray surtout, the same;
His bristling beard just rising in its might;
'Twas four long nights and days till shaving night;
His uncombed grizzly locks, wild staring, thatched
A head for thought profound and clear unmatched;
Yet though his caustic wit was biting rude,
His heart was warm, benevolent, and good.

ON WILLIE DUNBAR.

As I cam by Crochallan,
  I cannilie keekit ben;   gently looked in
Rattlin', roarin' Willie
  Was sitting at yon boord-en';   board-end
Sitting at yon boord-en',
  And amang gude companie;
Rattlin', roarin' Willie,
  Ye're welcome hame to me!

TO MRS DAVID WILSON.

My blessings on ye, honest wife,
  I ne'er was here before;
Ye've wealth o' gear for spoon and knife—
  Heart could not wish for more.

Heaven keep you clear of sturt and strife,   trouble
  Till far ayont four score,   beyond
And if I keep my health and life,
  I'll ne'er gae by your door!   go

* The printer of his poems.

VERSES UNDER THE PORTRAIT OF FERGUSSON.

SHAME on ungrateful man, that can be pleased,
And yet can starve the author of the pleasure !
Oh thou, my elder brother in misfortune,
By far my elder brother in the Muses,
With tears I pity thy unhappy fate !
Why is the Bard unpitied by the world,
Yet has so keen a relish of its pleasures ?

TO A HAGGIS.

FAIR fa' your honest, sonsie face,	good luck, plump
Great chieftain o' the puddin'-race !	
Aboon them a' ye tak your place,	above
Painch, tripe, or thairm :	
Weel are ye wordy of a grace	worthy
As lang's my arm.	long

The groaning trencher there ye fill,
Your hurdies like a distant hill,
Your pin wad help to mend a mill
In time o' need,
While through your pores the dews distil
Like amber bead.

His knife see rustic labour dight,	clean
And cut you up wi' ready slight,	
Trenching your gushing entrails bright	
Like ony ditch ;	any
And then, oh what a glorious sight,	
Warm-reekin', rich !	smoking

Then horn for horn they stretch and strive,	
SHAME ON the hindmost, on they drive,	
Till a' their weel-swall'd kytes belyve	stomachs, by and by
Are bent like drums ;	
Then auld guid man, maist like to rive,	burst
"Bethankit" hums.	returns thanks

Is there that o'er his French ragout,	
Or olio that wad staw a sow,	would nauseate
Or fricassee wad mak her spew	
Wi' perfect scunner,	disgust
Looks down wi' sneerin', scornfu' view	
On sic a dinner !	

Poor FELLOW ! see him owre his trash,	over
As feckless as a withered rash,	feeble
His spindle shank a good whip-lash,	thin legs, good
His nieve a nit ;	fist, nut
Through bloody flood or field to has	
Oh how unfit !	

But mark the rustic, haggis-fed,
The trembling earth resounds his tread,
Clap in his walie nieve a blade,   put, lusty fist
     He'll mak it whissle ;   whiz
And legs, and arms, and heads will sned,   shear
     Like taps o' thrissle.   tops of thistles

Ye powers wha mak mankind your care,   who make
And dish them out their bill o' fare,
Auld Scotland wants nae skinkin ware   thin stuff
     That jaups in luggies ;   splashes in bowls
But, if ye wish her gratefu' pray'r,
     Gie her a Haggis !   give

EXTEMPORE IN THE COURT OF SESSION.

TUNE—*Killiecrankie.*

LORD ADVOCATE.

HE clenched his pamphlets in his fist,
     He quoted and he hinted,
Till in a declamation-mist,
     His argument he tint it :   lost
He gapèd for't, he graipèd for't,   groped
     He fand it was awa', man ;   found, away
But what his common-sense came short,
     He ekèd out wi' law, man.

MR ERSKINE.

Collected Harry stood a wee,
     Then opened out his arm, man :
His lordship sat wi' ruefu' e'e,   eye
     And eyed the gathering storm, man ;
Like wind-driven hail, it did assail,
     Or torrents owre a linn, man ;   cascade
The Bench sae wise lift up their eyes,   so
     Half-wauken'd wi' the din, man.   awakened

PROLOGUE, SPOKEN BY MR WOODS ON HIS BENEFIT NIGHT.

Monday, April 16, 1787.

WHEN by a generous Public's kind acclaim,
That dearest meed is granted—honest fame ;
When here your favour is the actor's lot,
Nor even the man in private life forgot ;
What breast so dead to heavenly Virtue's glow,
But heaves impassioned with the grateful throe.

Poor is the task to please a barbarous throng,
It needs no Siddons' powers in Southern's song;
But here an ancient nation famed afar,
For genius, learning high, as great in war—
Hail, CALEDONIA, name for ever dear!
Before whose son's I'm honoured to appear!
Where every science—every nobler art—
That can inform the mind, or mend the heart,
Is known; as grateful nations oft have found
Far as the rude barbarian marks the bound.
Philosophy, no idle pedant dream,
Here holds her search by heaven-taught Reason's beam;
Here History paints with elegance and force
The tide of Empire's fluctuating course;
Here Douglas forms wild Shakspeare into plan,
And Harley* rouses all the god in man,
When well-formed Taste and sparkling Wit unite
With manly Lore, or female Beauty bright
(Beauty, where faultless symmetry and grace,
Can only charm us in the second place),
Witness my heart, how oft with panting fear,
As on this night, I've met these judges here!
But still the hope Experience taught to live,
Equal to judge—you're candid to forgive.
No hundred-headed Riot here we meet,
With Decency and Law beneath his feet;
Nor Insolence assumes fair Freedom's name;
Like CALEDONIANS, you applaud or blame.

Oh thou dread Power! whose empire-giving hand
Has oft been stretched to shield the honoured land!
Strong may she glow with all her ancient fire!
May every son be worthy of his sire!
Firm may she rise with generous disdain
At Tyranny's or direr Pleasure's chain!
Still self-dependent in her native shore,
Bold may she brave grim Danger's loudest roar,
Till Fate the curtain drops on worlds to be no more.

WILLIE'S AWA.

AULD chuckie Reekie's† sair distrest,	sore
Down droops her ance weel-burnished crest,	once
Nae joy her bonny buskit nest	no, decorated
Can yield ava,	at all
Her darling bird that she lo'es best—	
Willie's awa!	

Oh Willie was a witty wight,	wise
And had o' things an unco slight;	was clever-handed
Auld Reekie aye he keepit tight,	
And trig and braw:	neat

* The "Man of Feeling.'   † A familiar *sobriquet* for Edinburgh.

But now they'll busk her like a fright—   dress
    Willie's awa!

The stiffest o' them a he bowed;
The bauldest o' them a' he cowed;   boldest
They durst nae mair than he allowed,   more
    That was a law:
We've lost a birkie weel worth gowd—   fellow, gold
    Willie's awa!

Now gawkies, tawpies, gowks, and fools,   simpleton, slut, silly
Frae colleges and boarding-schools,
May sprout like simmer puddock-stools   (a fungus)
    In glen or shaw;   wood
He wha could brush them down to mools,   dust
    Willie's awa!

The brethren o' the Commerce-Chaumer   chamber
May mourn their loss wi' doolfu' clamour;   sorrowful
He was a dictionar and grammar
    Amang them a';
I fear they'll now mak mony a stammer—
    Willie's awa!

Nae mair we see his levee door
Philosophers and poets pour,
And toothy critics by the score,
    In bloody raw!   row
The adjutant o' a' the core,   company
    Willie's awa!

Now worthy Gregory's* Latin face,
Tytler's†·and Greenfield's‡ modest grace;
Mackenzie§, Stewart,‖ sic a brace   such
    As Rome ne'er saw;
They a' maun meet some ither place,   must, other
    Willie's awa!

Poor Burns—e'en Scotch drink canna quicken,   cannot
He cheeps like some bewilder'd chicken,   chirps
Scar'd frae its minnie and the clecken,   mother, brood
    By hoodie-craw;   hooded-crow
Grief's gien his heart an unco kickin'—   given, great
    Willie's awa!

    [talker
Now every sour-mou'd girnin' blellum,   mouthed grinning.
And Calvin's folk, are fit to fell him;
And self-conceited critic skellum   worthless fellow
    His quill may draw;
He wha could brawlie ward their bellum   well, force
    Willie's awa!

Up wimpling stately Tweed I've sped,   winding
And Eden scenes on crystal Jed,

---

* Dr James Gregory.   § Author of "Man of Feeling."
† Lord Woodhouslee.   Professor Dugald Stewart.
‡ Professor Greenfield.

And Ettrick banks now roaring red,
  While tempests blaw ;   *blaw*
But every joy and pleasure's fled—
  Willie's awa !

May I be slander's common speech ;
A text for infamy to preach ;
And lastly, streekit out to bleach *stretched*
  In winter snaw ;   *snow*
When I forget thee, Willie Creach,
  Though far awa !

May never wicked Fortune touzle him *handle roughly*
May never wicked men bamboozle him
Until a pow as auld's Methusalem   *head*
  He canty claw !   *cheerful, scratch*
Then to the blessed New Jerusalem,
  Fleet wing away !

TO SIMON GRAY.

DEAR SYMON GRAY,
     The other day,
  When you sent me some rhyme,
1 could not then just ascertain
  Its worth, for want of time.
But now to-day, good Mr Gray,
  I've read it o'er and o'er,
Tried all my skill, but find I'm still
  Just where I was before.

COMPOSED

ON LEAVING A PLACE IN THE HIGHLANDS WHERE HE HAD
BEEN KINDLY ENTERTAINED.

WHEN death's dark stream I ferry o'er—
  A time that surely shall come—
In heaven itself I'll ask no more
  Than just a Highland welcome !

ON READING IN A NEWSPAPER

THE DEATH OF JOHN M'LEOD, ESQ.,

BROTHER TO A YOUNG LADY, A PARTICULAR FRIEND OF THE
AUTHOR'S.

SAD thy tale, thou idle page,
  And rueful thy alarms—
Death tears the brother of her love
  From Isabella's arms.

Sweetly decked with pearly dew
   The morning rose may blow,
But cold successive noontide blasts
   May lay its beauties low.

Fair on Isabella's morn
   The sun propitious smiled,
But, long ere noon, succeeding clouds
   Succeeding hopes beguiled.

Fate oft tears the bosom cords
   That nature finest strung;
So Isabella's heart was formed,
   And so that heart was wrung.

Were it in the poet's power,
   Strong as he shares the grief
That pierces Isabella's heart,
   To give that heart relief!

Dread Omnipotence, alone,
   Can heal the wound he gave—
Can point the brimful grief-worn eyes
   To scenes beyond the grave.

Virtue's blossoms there shall blow,
   And fear no withering blast;
There Isabella's spotless worth
   Shall happy be at last.

ON THE DEATH OF SIR JAMES HUNTER BLAIR.

THE lamp of day, with ill-presaging glare,
   Dim, cloudy, sank beneath the western wave;
The inconstant blast howled through the darkening air,
   And hollow whistled in the rocky cave.

Lone as I wandered by each cliff and dell,
   Once the loved haunts of Scotia's royal train;*
Or mused where limpid streams once hallowed well,†
   Or mouldering ruins marked the sacred fane. ‡

The increasing blast roared round the beetling rocks,
   The clouds, swift-winged, flew o'er the starry sky,
The groaning trees untimely shed their locks,
   And shooting meteors caught the startled eye.

The paly moon rose in the livid east,
   And 'mong the cliffs disclosed a stately form,
In weeds of woe that frantic beat her breast,
   And mixed her wailings with the raving storm.

Wild to my heart the filial pulses glow,
   'Twas Caledonia's trophied shield I viewed:
Her form majestic drooped in pensive woe,
   The lightning of her eye in tears imbued.

---

* Park, Holyrood.   † St Anthony's Well.   ‡ St Anthony's Chapel.

Reversed that spear, redoubtable in war,
    Reclined that banner, erst in fields unfurled,
That like a deathful meteor gleamed afar,
    And braved the mighty monarchs of the world.

" My patriot son fills an untimely grave !"
    With accents wild and lifted arms—she cried
" Low lies the hand that oft was stretched to save,
    Low lies the heart that swelled with honest pride.

" A weeping country joins a widow's tear ;
    The helpless poor mix with the orphan's cry ;
The drooping Arts surround their patron's bier ;
    And grateful Science heaves the heartfelt sigh !

" I saw my sons resume their ancient fire ;
    I saw fair Freedom's blossoms richly blow :
But ah ! how Hope is born but to expire !
    Relentless Fate has laid their guardian low.

" My patriot falls, but shall he lie unsung,
    While empty greatness saves a worthless name ?
No : every Muse shall join her tuneful tongue,
    And future ages hear his growing fame.

" And I will join a mother's tender cares,
    Through future times to make his virtue last ;
That distant years may boast of other Blairs !"
    She said, and vanished with the sweeping blast.

TO MISS FERRIER,

ENCLOSING THE FOREGOING ELEGY ON SIR J. H. BLAIR.

NAE heathen name shall I prefix
    Frae Pindus or Parnassus ;
Auld Reekie dings them a' to sticks,   (Edinburgh) beats
    For rhyme-inspiring lasses.

Jove's tunefu' dochters three times three   daughters
    Made Homer deep their debtor ;
But, gi'en the body half an e'e,   eye
    Nine Ferriers wad done better !   would

Last day my mind was in a bog,
    Down George's Street I stoited ;   tottered
A creeping cauld prosaic fog   cold
    My very senses doited.   stupified

Do what I dought to set her free,   could
    My saul lay in the mire ;   soul
Ye turned a neuk—I saw your e'e—   corner, eye
    She took the wing like fire !

The mournfu' sang I here enclose,   song
  In gratitude I send you ;
And [wish and] pray in rhyme sincere,
  A' gude things may attend you !   good

LINES ON STIRLING.

HERE Stuarts once in triumph reigned,
And laws for Scotland's weal ordained ;
But now unroofed their palace stands,
Their sceptre's fallen to other hands.
The injured Stuarts' line are gone,
A race outlandish fill their throne—
An idiot race to honour lost :
Who know them best, despise them most.—BURNS.

On some one reproving him for writing these lines, Burns added,—

" Rash mortal, and slanderous poet, thy name
Shall no longer appear in the records of fame ;
Dost not know that old Mansfield, who writes like the Bible,
Says the more 'tis a truth, sir, the more 'tis a libel ? "

WRITTEN

WITH A PENCIL OVER THE CHIMNEY-PIECE IN THE PARLOUR OF
THE INN AT KENMORE, TAYMOUTH.

ADMIRING Nature in her wildest grace,
These northern scenes with weary feet I trace ;
O'er many a winding dale and painful steep,
The abodes of covied grouse and timid sheep,
My savage journey, curious, I pursue,
Till famed Breadalbane opens to my view.
The meeting cliffs each deep-sunk glen divides,
The woods, well scattered, clothe their ample sides ;
The outstretching lake, embosomed 'mong the hills,
The eye with wonder and amazement fills ;
The Tay, meandering sweet in infant pride,
The palace, rising on its verdant side ;
The lawns, wood-fringed in Nature's native taste ;
The hillocks, dropt in Nature's careless haste ;
The arches, striding o'er the new-born stream ;
The village, glittering in the noontide beam—
     *   *   *   *   *
Poetic ardours in my bosom swell,
Lone wandering by the hermit's mossy cell :
The sweeping theatre of hanging woods ;
Th' incessant roar of headlong tumbling floods—
     *   *   *   *   *
Here Poesy might wake her heaven-taught lyre,
And look through Nature with creative fire :

Here to the wrongs of fate half reconciled,
Misfortune's lightened steps might wander wild ;
And Disappointment, in these lonely bounds,
Find balm to soothe her bitter rankling wounds :
Here, heartstruck Grief might heavenward stretch her scan,
And injured Worth forget and pardon man.

* * * * *

THE HUMBLE PETITION OF BRUAR WATER TO THE NOBLE DUKE OF ATHOLE.

My lord, I know your noble ear
  Woe ne'er assails in vain ;
Emboldened thus, I beg you'll hear
  Your humble slave complain,
How saucy Phœbus' scorching beams,
  In flaming summer-pride,
Dry-withering, waste my foamy streams,
  And drink my crystal tide.

The lightly-jumpin' glowerin trouts,   *staring*
  That through my waters play,
If, in their random, wanton spouts,
  They near the margin stray ;
If, hapless chance ! they linger lang,   *long*
  I'm scorching up so shallow,
They're left the whitening stanes amang,   *among*
  In gasping death to wallow.

Last day I grat wi' spite and teen,   *wept, vexation*
  As Poet Burns came by,
That to a bard I should be seen
  Wi' half my channel dry :
A panegyric rhyme, I ween,
  Even as I was he shored me ;   *promised*
But had I in my glory been,
  He, kneeling, wad adored me.   *would have*

Here, foaming down the shelvy rocks,
  In twisting strength I rin ;
There, high my boiling torrent smokes,
  Wild roaring o'er a linn :   *cascade*
Enjoying large each spring and well,
  As Nature gave them me,
I am, although I say't mysel,
  Worth gaun a mile to see.   *going*

Would, then, my noble master please
  To grant my highest wishes,
He'll shade my banks wi' towering trees,
  And bonnie spreading bushes.
Delighted doubly, then, my lord,
  You'll wander on my banks,
And listen mony a grateful bird
  Return you tuneful thanks.

The sober laverock, warbling wild,　　　　　lark
　　Shall to the skies aspire ;
The gowdspink, Music's gayest child,　　　　goldfinch
　　Shall sweetly join the choir :
The blackbird strong, the lintwhite clear,　　linnet
　　The mavis mild and mellow;　　　　　　thrush
The robin pensive autumn cheer,
　　In all her locks of yellow.

This, too, a covert shall insure
　　To shield them from the storm ;
And coward maukin sleep secure,　　　　　　hare
　　Low in her grassy form :
Here shall the shepherd make his seat,
　　To weave his crown of flowers ;
Or find a sheltering safe retreat
　　From prone descending showers.

And here, by sweet endearing stealth,
　　Shall meet the loving pair,
Despising worlds with all their wealth
　　As empty idle care.
The flowers shall vie in all their charms
　　The hour of heaven to grace,
And birks extend their fragrant arms　　　　birches
　　To screen the dear embrace.

Here haply too, at vernal dawn,
　　Some musing bard may stray,
And eye the smoking, dewy lawn,
　　And misty mountain gray ;
Or, by the reaper's nightly beam,
　　Mild-chequering through the trees,
Rave to my darkly-dashing stream,
　　Hoarse swelling on the breeze.

Let lofty firs, and ashes cool,
　　My lowly banks o'erspread,
And view, deep-bending in the pool,
　　Their shadow's watery bed !
Let fragrant birks in woodbines drest
　　My craggy cliffs adorn ;
And, for the little songster's nest,
　　The close embowering thorn.

So may old Scotia's darling hope,
　　Your little angel band,
Spring, like their fathers, up to prop
　　Their honoured native land !
So may, through Albion's farthest ken,
　　To social-flowing glasses,
The grace be—" Athole's honest men,
　　And Athole's bonnie lasses !"

WRITTEN

WHILE STANDING BY THE FALL OF FYERS, NEAR LOCH NESS

AMONG the heathy hills and ragged woods,
The foaming Fyers pours his mossy floods;
Till full he dashes on the rocky mounds,
Where, through a shapeless breach, his stream resounds.
As high in air the bursting torrents flow,
As deep recoiling surges foam below;
Prone down the rock the whitening sheet descends,
And viewless Echo's ear, astonished, rends.
Dim seen, through rising mists and ceasless showers,
The hoary cavern, wide surrounding, lowers;
Still through the gap the struggling river toils,
And still below, the horrid caldron boils –
*　　*　　*　　*

CASTLE-GORDON.

TUNE—*Moray.*

STREAMS that glide in orient plains,
Never bound by Winter's chains;
　Glowing here on golden sands,
There commixed with foulest stains
　From tyranny's empurpled band;
These, their richly-gleaming waves,
I leave to tyrants and their slaves;
Give me the stream that sweetly laves
　　The banks by Castle-Gordon.

Spicy forests, ever gay,
Shading from the burning ray
　Helpless wretches sold to toil,
Or the ruthless native's way,
　Bent on slaughter, blood, and spoil:
Woods that ever verdant wave,
I leave the tyrant and the slave;
Give me the groves that lofty brave
　　The storms by Castle-Gordon.

Wildly here, without control,
Nature reigns and rules the whole;
　In that sober, pensive mood,
Dearest to the feeling soul,
　She plants the forest, pours the flood;
Life's poor day I'll musing rave,
And find at night a sheltering cave,
Where waters flow and wild woods wave,
　　By bonnie Castle-Gordon.

ON SCARING SOME WATER-FOWL IN LOCH TURIT.

WHY, ye tenants of the lake,
For me your watery haunt forsake ?
Tell me, fellow-creatures, why
At my presence thus you fly ?
Why disturb your social joys,
Parent, filial, kindred ties ?—
Common friend to you and me,
Nature's gifts to all are free :
Peaceful keep your dimpling wave,
Busy feed, or wanton lave ;
Or, beneath the sheltering rock,
Bide the surging billow's shock.

Conscious, blushing for our race,
Soon, too soon, your fears I trace.
Man, your proud usurping foe,
Would be lord of all below :
Plumes himself in Freedom's pride,
Tyrant stern to all beside.
The eagle, from the cliffy brow,
Marking you his prey below,
In his breast no pity dwells,
Strong necessity compels :
But man, to whom alone is given
A ray direct from pitying Heaven.
Glories in his heart humane—
And creatures for his pleasure slain.
In these savage, liquid plains,
Only known to wandering swains,
Where the mossy riv'let strays,
Far from human haunts and ways,
All on Nature you depend,
And life's poor season peaceful spend

Or, if man's superior might
Dare invade your native right,
On the lofty ether borne,
Man with all his powers you scorn
Swiftly seek, on clanging wings,
Other lakes and other springs ;
And the foe you cannot brave,
Scorn at least to be his slave.

TO MISS CRUIKSHANK, A VERY YOUNG LADY.

WRITTEN ON THE BLANK LEAF OF A BOOK PRESENTED TO HER BY THE AUTHOR.

BEAUTEOUS rose-bud, young and gay,
Blooming in thy early May,
Never may'st thou, lovely flower,
Chilly shrink in sleety shower

Never Boreas' hoary path,
Never Eurus' poisonous breath,
Never baleful stellar lights,
Taint thee with untimely blights!
Never, never reptile thief
Riot on thy virgin leaf!
Nor even Sol too fiercely view
Thy bosom blushing still with dew!

May'st thou long, sweet crimson gem,
Richly deck thy native stem:
'Till some evening, sober, calm,
Dropping dews and breathing balm,
While all around the woodland rings,
And every bird thy requiem sings;
Thou, amid the dirgeful sound,
Shed thy dying honours round,
And resign to parent earth
The loveliest form she e'er gave birth.

ADDRESS TO MR WILLIAM TYTLER.

REVERED defender of beauteous Stuart,   (Mary. Queen of Scots
  Of Stuart, a name once respected—
A name which to love was the mark of a true heart,
  But now 'tis despised and neglected.

Though something like moisture conglobes in my eye,
  Let no one misdeem me disloyal;
A poor friendless wand'rer may well claim a sigh,
  Still more if that wand'rer were royal.

My fathers that name have revered on a throne
  My fathers have fallen to right it;
Those fathers would spurn their degenerate son,
  That name should he scoffingly slight it.

Still in prayers for King George I most heartily join,
  The Queen, and the rest of the gentry;
Be they wise, be they foolish, is nothing of mine,
  Their title's avowed by my country.

But why of that epocha make such a fuss,
  That gave us the Hanover stem;
If bringing them over was lucky for us,
  I'm sure 'twas as lucky for them.

But loyalty, truce! we're on dangerous ground,
  Who knows how the fashions may alter?
The doctrine, to-day, that is loyalty sound,
  To-morrow may bring us a halter!

I send you a trifle, a head of a bard,
  A trifle scarce worthy your care;
But accept it, good sir, as a mark of regard,
  Sincere as a saint's dying prayer.

Now life's chilly evening dim shades on your eye,
  And ushers the long dreary night;
But you, like the star that athwart gilds the sky,
  Your course to the latest is bright.

ELEGY ON THE DEATH OF LORD PRESIDENT DUNDAS.

LONE on the bleaky hills the straying flocks
Shun the fierce storms among the sheltering rocks;
Down from the rivulets, red with dashing rains,
The gathering floods burst o'er the distant plains
Beneath the blasts the leafless forests groan;
The hollow caves return a sullen moan.

Ye hills, ye plains, ye forests, and ye caves,
Ye howling winds, and wintry swelling waves!
Unheard, unseen, by human ear or eye,
Sad to your sympathetic scenes I fly;
Where to the whistling blast and waters' roar
Pale Scotia's recent wound I may deplore.
Oh heavy loss, thy country ill could bear!
A loss these evil days can ne'er repair!
Justice, the high vicegerent of her God,
Her doubtful balance eyed, and swayed her rod;
Hearing the tidings of the fatal blow,
She sank, abandoned to the wildest wo.

Wrongs, injuries, from many a darksome den,
Now gay in hope explore the paths of men:
See from his cavern grim Oppression rise,
And throw on Poverty his cruel eyes;
Keen on the helpless victim see him fly,
And stifle, dark, the feebly-bursting cry.

Mark ruffian Violence, distained with crimes,
Rousing elate in these degenerate times;
View unsuspecting Innocence a prey,
As guileful Fraud points out the erring way:
While subtile Litigation's pliant tongue
The life-blood equal sucks of Right and Wrong:
Hark, injured Want recounts th' unlistened tale,
And much-wronged Misery pours th' unpitied wail

Ye dark waste hills, and brown unsightly plains
To you I sing my grief-inspirèd strains:
Ye tempests, rage! ye turbid torrents, roll!
Ye suit the joyless tenor of my soul.
Life's social haunts and pleasures I resign,
Be nameless wilds and lonely wanderings mine,
To mourn the woes my country must endure,
That wound degenerate ages cannot cure.

ELPHINSTONE'S TRANSLATION OF MARTIAL'S EPIGRAMS.

OH thou, whom poesy abhors !
Whom prose has turned out of doors !
Heard'st thou yon groan ? proceed no further !
'Twas laurel'd Martial roaring murther !

A FAREWELL TO CLARINDA,

ON LEAVING EDINBURGH.

CLARINDA, mistress of my soul,
  The measured time is run !
The wretch beneath the dreary pole
  So marks his latest sun.

To what dark cave of frozen night
  Shall poor Sylvander hie ;
Deprived of thee, his life and light,
  The sun of all his joy ?

We part—but, by these precious drops
  That fill thy lovely eyes !
No other light shall guide my steps
  Till thy bright beams arise.

She, the fair sun of all her sex,
  Has blest my glorious day ;
And shall a glimmering planet fix
  My worship to its ray ?

TO CLARINDA :

WITH A PRESENT OF A PAIR OF DRINKING-GLASSES

FAIR Empress of the Poet's soul,
  And Queen of Poetesses ;
Clarinda, take this little boon,
  This humble pair of glasses.

And fill them high with generous juice,
  As generous as your mind ;
And pledge me in the generous toast—
  " The whole of human kind ! "

" To those who love us ! "—second fill ;
  But not to those whom we love ;
Lest we love those who love not us !—
  A third—" To thee and me, love "

EPISTLE TO HUGH PARKER.

IN this strange land, this uncouth clime,	
A land unknown to prose or rhyme;	
Where words ne'er crost the muse's heckles,*	
Nor limpet in poetic shackles;	limped
A land that Prose did never view it,	
Except when drunk he stacher't through it;	staggered
Here, ambush'd by the chimla cheek,	chimney
Hid in an atmosphere of reek,	smoke
I hear a wheel thrum i' the neuk,	sound, corner
I hear it—for in vain I leuk.	look
The red peat gleams, a fiery kernel,	
Enhusked by a fog internal:	
Here, for my wonted rhyming raptures,	
I sit and count my sins by chapters;	
For life and spunk like ither Christians,	spirit, other
I'm dwindled down to mere existence—	
Wi' nae converse but Gallowa' bodies,	no
Wi' nae kenn'd face but Jenny Geddes.	known (his mare)
Jenny, my Pegasean pride!	
Dowie she saunters down Nithside,	sad
And aye a westlin leuk she throws,	westward look
While tears hap o'er her auld brown nose l	cover
Was it for this, wi' canny care,	gentle
Thou bure the Bard through many a shire?	bore
At howes or hillocks never stumbled,	hollows
And late or early never grumbled?	
Oh, had I power like inclination,	
I'd heeze thee up a constellation,	raise
To canter with the Sagitarre,	
Or loup the ecliptic like a bar;	jump
Or turn the pole like any arrow;	
Or, when auld Phœbus bids good-morrow,	
Down the zodiac urge the race,	
And cast dirt on his godship's face;	
For I could lay my bread and kail	dinner
He'd ne'er cast saut upo' thy tail.	salt
Wi' a' this care and a' this grief,	
And sma', sma' prospect of relief,	small
And nought but peat-reek i' my head,	peat smoke
How can I write what ye can read?	
Torbolton, twenty-fourth o' June,	
Ye'll find me in a better tune;	
But till we meet and weet our whistle,	wet, throats
Tak this excuse for nae epistle.	no

ROBERT BURNS.

* An instrument for dressing flax.

THE FETE CHAMPETRE.

Tune—*Killicrankie.*

Oh wha will to Saint Stephen's House,   *who*
  To do our errands there, man ?
Oh wha will to Saint Stephen's House,
  O' th' merry lads o' Ayr, man ?
Or will ye send a man-o'-law ?
  Or will ye send a sodger ?
Or him wha led o'er Scotland a'
  The meikle Ursa-Major ?   *big*

Come, will ye court a noble lord,
  Or buy a score o' lairds, man ?
For worth and honour pawn their word,
  Their vote shall be Glencaird's, man.
Ane gies them coin, ane gies them wine,   *one gives*
  Anither gies them clatter ;
Anbank, wha guessed the ladies' taste,
  He gies a Fête Champêtre.

When Love and Beauty heard the news,
  The gay greenwoods amang, man,   *among*
Where, gathering flowers and busking bowers,   *dressing*
  They heard the blackbird's sang, man :
A vow, they scal'd it with a kiss,
  Sir Politics to fetter,
As theirs alone, the patent-bliss,
  To hold a Fête Champêtre.

Then mounted Mirth, on gleesome wing,
  Ower hill and dale she flew, man ;   *over*
Ilk whimpling burn, ilk crystal spring,   *each meandering*
  Ilk glen and shaw she knew, man :   *wood*
She summoned every social sprite,
  That sports by wood and water,
On th' bonnie banks o' Ayr to meet,
  And keep this Fête Champêtre.

Cauld Boreas, wi' his boisterous crew,
  Were bound to stakes like kye, man ;   *cows*
And Cynthia's car, o' silver fu',
  Clamb up the starry sky, man :
Reflected beams dwell in the streams,
  Or down the current shatter ;
The western breeze steals through the trees
  To view this Fête Champêtre.

How many a robe sae gaily floats !   *so*
  What sparking jewels glance, man !
To Harmony's enchanting notes,
  As moves the mazy dance, man.
The echoing wood, the winding flood,
  Like Paradise did glitter,
When angels met, at Adam's yett,   *gate*
  To hold their Fête Champêtre,

When Politics came there, to mix
  And make his ether-stane, man !   *adder-stone*
He circled round the magic ground,
  But entrance found he nane, man :   *none*
He blushed for shame, he quat his name,   *quitted*
  Forswore it, every letter,
Wi' humble prayer to join and share
  This festive Fête Champêtre.

FIRST EPISTLE TO MR GRAHAM OF FINTRY.

WHEN Nature her great masterpiece designed,
And framed her last, best work, the human mind,
Her eye intent on all the mazy plan,
She formed of various parts the various man.

Then first she calls the useful many forth ;
Plain plodding industry, and sober worth :
Thence peasants, farmers, native sons of earth,
And merchandise' whole genus take their birth :
Each prudent cit a warm existence finds,
And all mechanics' many-apron'd kinds.
Some other rarer sorts are wanted yet,
The lead and buoy are needful to the net ;
The *caput mortuum* of gross desires
Makes a material for mere knights and squires ;
The martial phosphorus is taught to flow ;
She kneads the lumpish philosophic dough,
Then marks the unyielding mass with grave designs
Law, physic, politics, and deep divines ;
Last, she sublimes the Aurora of the poles,
The flashing elements of female souls.
The order'd system fair before her stood,
Nature, well-pleased, pronounced it very good ;
But e'er she gave creating labour o'er,
Half-jest, she tried one curious labour more.
Some spumy, fiery, *ignis fatuus* matter,
Such as the slightest breath of air might scatter
With arch alacrity and conscious glee
(Nature may have her whim as well as we,
Her Hogarth-art perhaps she meant to show it)
She forms the thing, and christens it—a poet,
Creature, though oft the prey of care and sorrow
When blest to-day, unmindful of to-morrow.
A being formed t' amuse his graver friends,
Admired and praised—and there the homage ends ;—
A mortal quite unfit for fortune's strife,
Yet oft the sport of all the ills of life ;
Prone to enjoy each pleasure riches give,
Yet haply wanting wherewithal to live ;
Longing to wipe each tear, to heal each groan,
Yet frequent all unheeded in his own.

But honest Nature is not quite a Turk,
She laughed at first, then felt for her poor work.
Pitying the propless climber of mankind,
She cast about a standard tree to find ;
And, to support his helpless woodbine state,
Attached him to the generous truly great,
A title, and the only one I claim,
To lay strong hold for help on bounteous Graham.

Pity the tuneful Muses' hapless train,
Weak, timid landsmen on life's stormy main !
Their hearts no selfish stern absorbent stuff,
That never gives—though humbly takes enough ;
The little fate allows, they share as soon,
Unlike sage proverb'd wisdom's hard-wrung boon.
The world were blest did bliss on them depend,
Ah, that " the friendly e'er should want a friend !"
Let prudence number o'er each sturdy son,
Who life and wisdom at one race begun,
Who feel by reason and who give by rule
(Instinct's a brute and sentiment a fool !)—
Who make poor *will do* wait upon *I should*—
We own they're prudent, but who feels they're good ?
Ye wise ones, hence ! ye hurt the social eye !
God's image rudely etched on base alloy !
But come, ye who the godlike pleasure know,
Heaven's attribute distinguished—to bestow !
Whose arms of love would grasp the human race :
Come thou who giv'st with all a courtier's grace ;
Friend of my life, true patron of my rhymes !
Prop of my dearest hopes for future times.
Why shrinks my soul half-blushing, half-afraid,
Backward, abashed, to ask thy friendly aid ?
I know my need, I know thy giving hand,
I crave thy friendship at thy kind command ;
But there are such who court the tuneful Nine—
Heavens ! should the branded character be mine !
Whose verse in manhood's pride sublimely flows,
Yet vilest reptiles in their begging prose.
Mark, how their lofty independent spirit
Soars on the spurning wing of injured merit !
Seek not the proofs in private life to find ;
Pity the best of words should be but wind !
So to heaven's gate the lark's shrill song ascends,
But grovelling on the earth the carol ends.
In all the clam'rous cry of starving want,
They dun benevolence with shameless front ;
Oblige them, patronise their tinsel lays,
They persecute you all your future days !
Ere my poor soul such condemnation stain,
My horny fist assume the plough again ;
The piebald jacket let me patch once more ;
On eighteenpence a week I've lived before.
Though, thanks to Heaven, I dare even that last shift !

I trust, meantime, my boon is in thy gift :
That, placed by thee upon the wished-for height,
Where, man and nature fairer in her sight,
My Muse may imp her wing for some sublime flight.

SECOND EPISTLE TO MR GRAHAM OF FINTRY.

FINTRY, my stay in worldly strife,
Friend o my Muse, friend o' my life,
    Are ye as idle's I am ?
Come then, wi' uncouth, kintra fleg,   country fling
O'er Pegasus I'll fling my leg,
    And ye shall see me try him.

I'll sing the zeal Drumlanrig bears,   (Duke of Queensberry)
Who left the all-important cares
    Of princes and their darlings ;
And, bent on winning borough towns,
Came shaking hands wi' wabster loons,   weaver
    And kissing barefit carlins.   barefoot, old women

Combustion through our boroughs rode,
Whistling his roaring pack abroad,
    Of mad, unmuzzled lions ;
As Queensberry buff and blue unfurled,   (Fox's colours)
And Westerha' and Hopetoun hurled
    To every Whig defiance.

But Queensberry, cautious, left the war,
The unmannered dust might soil his star,
    Besides, he hated bleeding ;
But left behind him heroes bright,
Heroes in Cæsarean fight
    Or Ciceronian pleading.

O for a throat like huge Mons-Meg,   (a large cannon)
To muster o'er each ardent Whig
    Beneath Drumlanrig's banner ;
Heroes and heroines commix
All in the field of politics,
    To win immortal honours.

M'Murdo and his lovely spouse   (the chamberlain)
(Th' enamoured laurels kiss her brows)
    Led on the Loves and Graces ;
She won each gaping burgess' heart,
While he, all-conquering, played his part,
    Among their wives and lasses.

Craigdarroch led a light-armed corps ;
Tropes, metaphors, and figures pour,
    Like Hecla streaming thunder ;
Glenriddel, skilled in rusty coins,
Blew up each Tory's dark designs,
    And bared the treason under.

In either wing two champions fought,
Redoubted Staig, who set at nought   (Provost of Dumfries)
 The wildest savage Tory,
And Welsh, who ne'er yet flinched his ground,   (the Sheriff)
High waved his magnum bonum round
 With Cyclopean fury.

Miller brought up the artillery ranks,   (of Dalswinton)
The many-pounders of the Banks,
 Resistless desolation ;
While Maxwelton, that baron bold,   (Sir R. Lawrie, M.P.)
Mid Lawson's port entrenched his hold,
 THREATENING EXTERMINATION.

To these, what Tory hosts opposed ;
With these, what Tory warriors closed,
 Surpasses my descriving :   describing
Squadrons extended long and large,
With furious speed rushed to the charge,
 Like raging MONSTERS driving.

What verse can sing, what prose narrate,
The butcher deeds of bloody fate
 Amid this mighty tulzie ?   conflict
Grim Horror grinned ; pale Terror roared,
As Murther at his thrapple shored,   throat threatened
 And WILD mixed in the brulzie !   broil

As Highland crags, by thunder cleft,
When lightnings fire the stormy lift,   firmament
 Hurl down wi' crashing rattle ;
As flames amang a hundred woods ;
As headlong foam a hundred floods ;
 Such is the rage of battle.

The stubborn Tories dare to die ;
As soon the rooted oaks would fly,
 Before th' approaching fellers ;
The Whigs come on like Ocean's roar,
When all his wintry billows pour
 Against the Buchan Bullers.   (rocks at Peterhead)

Lo, from the shades of Death's deep night,
Departed Whigs enjoy the fight,
 And think on former daring !
The muffled murtherer of Charles   (Charles I.)
The Magna-Charta flag unfurls,
 All deadly gules its bearing.

Nor wanting ghosts of Tory fame ;
Bold Scrimgeour follows gallant Grahame—
 Auld Covenanters shiver—
(Forgive, forgive, much-wronged Montrose !
While death AT LAST engulfs thy foes,
 Thou liv'st on high for ever !)

Still o'er the field the combat burns ;
The Tories, Whigs, give way by turns :

But fate the word has spoken—
For woman's wit, or strength of man,
Alas! can do but what they can—
The Tory ranks are broken.

O that my een were flowing burns!   eyes, rivulets
My voice a lioness that mourns
Her darling cub's undoing!
That I might greet, that I might cry,   weep
While Tories fall, while Tories fly,
And furious Whigs pursuing!

What Whig but wails the good Sir James;
Dear to his country by the names
Friend, Patron, Benefactor?
Not Pulteney's wealth can Pulteney save!
And Hopetoun falls, the generous, brave!
And Stuart bold as Hector!

Thou, Pitt, shall rue this overthrow,
And Thurlow growl a curse of wo,
And Melville melt in wailing!
Now Fox and Sheridan, rejoice!
And Burke shall sing: " O prince, arise!
Thy power is all-prevailing!"

For your poor friend, the Bard afar,
He hears, and only hears the war,
A cool spectator purely;
So when the storm the forest rends,
The robin in the hedge descends,
And sober chirps securely.

THIRD EPISTLE TO MR GRAHAM OF FINTRY, 1791.

LATE crippled of an arm, and now a leg,
About to beg a pass for leave to beg:
Dull, listless, teased, dejected, and deprest,
(Nature is adverse to a cripple's rest);
Will generous Graham list to his Poet's wail?
(It soothes poor misery, hearkening to her tale),
And hear him BAN the light he first surveyed,
And doubly BAN the luckless rhyming trade?

Thou, Nature, partial Nature! I arraign;
Of thy caprice maternal I complain.
The lion and the bull thy care have found,
One shakes the forests, and one spurns the ground:
Thou giv'st the ass his hide, the snail his shell,
Th' envenomed wasp, victorious, guards his cell;
Thy minions, kings, defend, control, devour,
In all th' omnipotence of rule and power;
Foxes and statesmen, subtile wiles insure:
The cit and polecat stink, and are secure:

Toads with their poison, doctors with their drug,
The priest and hedgehog in their robes are snug ;
Ev'n silly woman has her warlike arts,
Her tongue and eyes, her dreaded spear and darts;—
But, oh ! thou bitter stepmother and hard,
To thy poor, fenceless, naked child—the Bard !
A thing unteachable in world's skill,
And half an idiot, too, more helpless still :
No heels to bear him from the opening dun ;
No claws to dig, his hated sight to shun ;
No nerves olfactory, Mammon's trusty cur,
Clad in rich dulness' comfortable fur ;—
In naked feeling, and in aching pride,
He bears the unbroken blast from every side :
Vampyre booksellers drain him to the heart,
And scorpion critics cureless venom dart.

Critics !—appalled I venture on the name,
Those cut-throat bandits in the paths of fame :
Bloody dissectors, worse that ten Monroes !
He hacks to teach, they mangle to expose.

His heart by causeless wanton malice wrung,
By blockheads' daring into madness stung ;
His well-won bays, than life itself more dear,
By miscreants torn, who ne'er one sprig must wear :
Foiled, bleeding, tortured, in the unequal strife,
The hapless poet flounders on through life ;
Till fled each hope that once his bosom fired,
And fled each muse that glorious once inspired,
Low sunk in squalid, unprotected age,
Dead, even resentment, for his injured page,
He heeds or feels no more the ruthless critic's rage !

So, by some hedge, the generous steed deceased,
For half-starved snarling curs a dainty feast :
By toil and famine wore to skin and bone,
Lies senseless, AND THEIR RAVENING UNKNOWN.

O dulness ! portion of the truly blest !
Calm sheltered haven of eternal rest !
Thy sons ne'er madden in the fierce extremes
Of fortune's polar frost, or torrid beams.
If mantling high she fills the golden cup,
With sober selfish ease they sip it up :
Conscious the bounteous meed they well deserve,
They only wonder " some folks " do not starve.
The grave sage hern that easy picks his frog,   heron
And thinks the mallard a sad worthless dog.   wild drake
When disappointment snaps the clue of hope,
And through disastrous night they darkling grope,
With deaf endurance sluggishly they bear,
And just conclude that " fools are fortune's care."
So, heavy, passive to the tempest's shocks,
Strong on the sign-post stands the stupid ox.

Not so the idle Muses' mad-cap train,
Not such the workings of their moon-struck brain.

I dread thee, fate, relentless and severe,
With all a poet's, husband's, father's fear!
Already one strong hold of hope is lost,
Glencairn, the truly noble, lies in dust;
(Fled, like the sun eclipsed as noon appears,
And left us darkling in a world of tears:)
O hear my ardent, grateful, selfish prayer!—
Fintry, my other stay, long bless and spare!
Through a long life his hopes and wishes crown
And bright in cloudless skies his sun go down!
May bliss domestic smooth his private path,
Give energy to life, and soothe his latest breath,
With many a filial tear circling the bed of death!

LAMENTATION

FOR THE DEATH OF MRS FERGUSSON OF CRAIGDARROCH'S SON
—AN UNCOMMONLY PROMISING YOUTH OF EIGHTEEN OR
NINETEEN YEARS OF AGE.

FATE gave the word, the arrow sped,
  And pierc'd my darling's heart;
And with him all the joys are fled
  Life can to me impart.
By cruel hands the sapling drops,
  In dust dishonour'd laid:
So fell the pride of all my hopes,
  My age's future shade.

The mother linnet in the brake
  Bewails her ravish'd young;
So I, for my lost darling's sake,
  Lament the live-day long.
Death! oft I've feared thy fatal blow,
  Now, fond I bare my breast;
Oh, do thou kindly lay me low
  With him I love, at rest!

LINES WRITTEN IN FRIARS' CARSE HERMITAGE, NITHSIDE.

THOU whom chance may hither lead,
Be thou clad in russet weed,
Be thou deckt in silken stole,
Grave these counsels on thy soul.

Life is but a day at most,
Sprung from night, in darkness lost;
Hope not sunshine every hour,
Fear not clouds will always lower.

As youth and love with sprightly dance,
Beneath thy morning star advance,
Pleasure with her siren air
May delude the thoughtless pair ;
Let Prudence bless Enjoyment's cup,
Then raptured sip, and sip it up.

As thy day grows warm and high,
Life's meridian flaming nigh,
Dost thou spurn the humble vale ?
Life's proud summits would'st thou scale ?
Check thy climbing step, elate,
Evils lurk in felon wait :
Dangers eagle-pinioned, bold,
Soar around each cliffy hold,
While cheerful Peace, with linnet song,
Chants the lowly dells among.

As the shades of ev'ning close,
Beck'ning thee to long repose ;
As life itself becomes disease,
Seek the chimney-nook of ease ;
There ruminate with sober thought,
On all thou'st seen, and heard, and wrought,
And teach the sportive younkers round,
Saws of experience, sage and sound.
Say, man's true, genuine estimate,
The grand criterion of his fate,
Is not—Art thou high or low ?
Did thy fortune ebb or flow ?

Did many talents gild thy span ?
Or frugal Nature grudge thee one ?
Tell them, and press it on their mind,
As thou thyself must shortly find,
The smile or frown of awful Heav'n
To virtue or to vice is given.
Say, to be just, and kind, and wise,
There solid self-enjoyment lies ;
That foolish, selfish, faithless ways
Lead to be wretched, vile, and base.

Thus resigned and quiet, creep
To the bed of lasting sleep ;
Sleep, whence thou shalt ne'er awake,
Night, where dawn shall never break,
Till future life, future no more,
To light and joy the good restore,
To light and joy unknown before.

Stranger, go ! Heav'n be thy guide !
Quod the Bedesman of Nithside !

ELEGY ON THE YEAR 1788.

Jan. 1, 1789.

FOR Lords or Kings I dinna mourn,   do not
E'en let them die—for that they're born :
But oh ! prodigious to reflec' !
A towmont, sirs, is gane to wreck !   twelvemonth, gone
Oh Eighty-eight, in thy sma' space
What dire events ha'e taken place !
Of what enjoyments thou hast reft us !
In what a pickle thou hast left us !

The Spanish empire's tint a head,   lost, (Charles III.)
And my auld teethless Bawtie's dead ;   (his dog)
The tulzie's sair 'tween Pitt and Fox,   fight, sore
And our guidwife's wee birdie cocks ;
Ye ministers, come mount the pu'pit,
And cry till ye be hearse and roopit,   hoarse, croup
For Eighty-eight he wished you weel,   well
And gied ye a' baith gear and meal;   gave, both money
E'en mony a plack, and mony a peck,   many, coin
Ye ken yoursels, for little feck ! . . .   know, consideration

Observe the very nowte and sheep,   cattle
How dowf and dowie now they creep :   lethargic, dull
Nay, even the yirth itsel' does cry,   earth
For Embro' wells are grutten dry.   Edinburgh, wept

Oh Eighty-nine, thou's but a bairn,
And no owre auld, I hope, to learn !   not too old
Thou beardless boy, I pray tak care,   (Prince Regent)
Thou now has got thy daddy's chair,   (George III.)
Nae hand-cuffed, muzzled, hap-shackled Regent   foot-tied
But, like himsel', a full free agent.
Be sure ye follow out the plan
Nae waur than he did, honest man !   no worse
As muckle better as you can.   much

A SKETCH.

A LITTLE, upright, pert, tart, tripping wight,
And still his precious self his dear delight ;
Who loves his own smart shadow in the streets,
Better than e'er the fairest she he meets.
A man of fashion too, he made his tour,
Learned *vive la bagatelle, et vive l'amour ;*
So travelled-monkeys their grimace improve,
Polish their grin, nay, sigh for ladie's love.
Much specious lore, but little understood ;
Veneering oft outshines the solid wood :
His solid sense—by inches you must tell,
But mete his cunning by the old Scotch ell
His meddling vanity, a busy fiend,
Still making work his selfish craft must mend.

EXTEMPORE TO CAPTAIN RIDDEL,

ON RETURNING A NEWSPAPER.

ELLISLAND, *Monday Evening.*

YOUR news and review, sir, I've read through and through, sir,
  With little admiring or blaming ;
The papers are barren of home news or foreign,
  No murders AT ALL worth the naming.

Our friends, the reviewers, those chippers and hewers,
  Are judges of mortar and stone, sir ;
But of *meet* or *unmeet*, in a *fabric complete*,
  I'll boldly pronounce they are none, sir.

My goose-quill too rude is to tell all your goodness
  Bestowed on your servant the poet ;
Would I ONLY had one, like a beam of the sun,
  And then all the world, sir, should know it !

ODE,

SACRED TO THE MEMORY OF MRS OSWALD.

DWELLER in yon dungeon dark,
Hangman of creation, mark !
Who in widow weeds appears,
Laden with unhonoured years,
Noosing with care a bursting purse,
Baited with many a deadly curse !

STROPHE.

View the withered beldam's face—
Can thy keen inspection trace
Aught of Humanity's sweet melting grace ?
Note that eye, 'tis rheum o'erflows,
Pity's flood there never rose.
See these hands, ne'er stretched to save,
Hands that took—but never gave.
Keeper of Mammon's iron chest,
Lo, there she goes, unpitied and unblest.

          *   *   *   *   *

EPODE.

And are they of no more avail,
Ten thousand glittering pounds a year ?
In other words, can Mammon fail,
Omnipotent as he is here ?
O bitter mockery of the pompous bier,
While down the wretched vital part is driv'n !
The cave-lodged beggar, with a conscience clear,
Expires in rags, unknown, and goes to heav'n.

TO JOHN TAYLOR.

WITH Pegasus upon a day,
  Apollo weary flying,
Through frosty hills the journey lay,
  On foot the way was plying.

Poor slip-shod giddy Pegasus
  Was but a sorry walker;
To Vulcan then Apollo goes,
  To get a frosty calker.

Obliging Vulcan fell to work,
  Threw by his coat and bonnet,
And did Sol's business in a crack;
  Sol paid him with a sonnet.

Ye Vulcan's sons of Wanlockhead,
  Pity my sad disaster;
My Pegasus is poorly shod—
  I'll pay you like my master.
RAMAGE'S, 3 *o'clock.*

SKETCH.

INSCRIBED TO CHARLES JAMES FOX.

How Wisdom and Folly meet, mix, and unite;
How Virtue and Vice blend their black and their white;
How Genius, the illustrious father of Fiction,
Confounds rule and law, reconciles contradiction—
I sing: if these mortals, the critics, should bustle,
I care not, not I, let the critics go whistle.

But now for a Patron, whose name and whose glory
At once may illustrate and honour my story.

Thou first of our orators, first of our wits,
Yet whose parts and acquirements seem mere lucky hits;
With knowledge so vast, and with judgment so strong,
No man with the half of 'em e'er went far wrong;
With passions so potent, and fancies so bright,
No man with the half of 'em e'er went quite right:
A sorry, poor misbegot son of the Muses,
For using thy name offers fifty excuses.

On his one ruling passion Sir Pope hugely labours,
That, like th' old Hebrew walking switch, eats up its
    neighbours:
Mankind are his show-box—a friend, would you know him!
Pull the string, ruling passion the picture will show him.
What pity, in rearing so beauteous a system,
One trifling particular, truth, should have miss'd him;
For, spite of his fine theoretic positions,
Mankind is a science defies definitions.

Some sort all our qualities each to its tribe,
And think human nature they truly describe ;
Have you found this, or t'other ! there's more in the wind,
As by one drunken fellow his comrades you'll find.
But such is the flaw, or the depth of the plan,
In the make of that wonderful creature call'd man,
No two virtues, whatever relation they claim,
Nor even two different shades of the same,
Though like as was ever twin-brother to brother,
Possessing the one shall imply you've the other.

But truce with abstraction and truce with the Muse,
Whose rhymes you'll perhaps, sir, ne'er deign to peruse :
Will you leave your justings, your jars, and your quarrels,
Contending with Billy for proud-nodding laurels.   (Pitt)
My much-honoured Patron, believe your poor Poet,
Your courage much more than your prudence you shew it :
In vain with Squire Billy for laurels you struggle,
He'll have them by fair trade, if not he will smuggle ;
Not cabinets even of kings would conceal 'em,
He'd up the back-stairs and BE CERTAIN TO steal 'em !
Then feats like Squire Billy's you ne'er can achieve 'em,
It is not, outdo him—the task is, out-thieve him !

DELIA.

FAIR the face of orient day,
    Fair the tints of op'ning rose ;
But fairer still my Delia dawns,
    More lovely far her beauty shews.

Sweet the lark's wild warbled lay,
    Sweet the tinkling rill to hear ;
But, Delia, more delightful still,
    Steal thine accents on mine ear.

The flower-enamoured busy bee
    The rosy banquet loves to sip ;
Sweet the streamlet's limpid lapse
    To the sun-browned Arab's lip.

But, Delia, on thy balmy lips
    Let me, no fragrant insect, rove ;
O let me steal one liquid kiss,
    For, oh ! my soul is parched with love !

ON SEEING A WOUNDED HARE LIMP BY ME,

WHICH A FELLOW HAD JUST SHOT.

INHUMAN man ! curse on thy barb'rous art,
    And blasted be thy murder-aiming eye ;
May never pity soothe thee with a sigh,
    Nor ever pleasure glad thy cruel heart !

Go live, poor wanderer of the wood and field!
  The bitter little that of life remains :
  No more the thickening brakes and verdant plains
To thee shall home, or food, or pastime yield.

Seek, mangled wretch, some place of wonted rest,
  No more of rest, but now thy dying bed!
  The sheltering rushes whistling o'er thy head,
The cold earth with thy bloody bosom prest.

Oft as by winding Nith I, musing, wait
  The sober eve, or hail the cheerful dawn,
  I'll miss thee sporting o'er the dewy lawn,
And curse the ruffian's aim, and mourn thy hapless fate.

LETTER TO JAMES TENNANT OF GLENCONNER.

AULD comrade dear, and brither sinner,	old, brother
How's a' the folk about Glenconner?	
How do you, this blae eastlin wind,	chilly eastern
That's like to blaw a body blind?	blow
For me, my faculties are frozen,	
And ilka member nearly dozen'd.	each, stupified
I've sent you here, by Johnnie Simpson,	
Twa sage philosophers to glimpse on;	
Smith, wi' his sympathetic feeling,	
And Reid, to common-sense appealing.	
Philosophers have fought and wrangled,	
And meikle Greek and Latin mangled,	much
Till, wi' their logic jargon tir'd,	
And in the depths of science mir'd,	
To common-sense they now appeal,	
What wives and wabsters see and feel.	weavers
But, hark ye, friend! I charge you strictly,	
Peruse them, and return them quickly,	
For now I'm grown sae VERA douce,	very quiet
I pray and ponder butt the house;	inside
My shins, my lane, I there sit roastin',	alone
Perusing Bunyan, Brown, and Boston;	
Till, by and by, if I haud on,	hold
I'll grunt a real gospel groan:	
Already I begin to try it,	
To cast my e'en up like a pyet	magpie
When by the gun she tumbles o'er,	
Flutt'ring and gasping in her gore:	
Sae shortly you shall see me bright,	
A burning and a shining light.	

My heart-warm love to guid auld Glen,	
The ace and wale o' honest men:	choice
When bending down wi' auld grey hairs,	
Beneath the load of years and cares,	
May He who made him still support him,	
And views beyond the grave comfort him:	

His worthy fam'ly far and near,
God bless them a' wi' grace and gear !   wealth

My auld schoolfellow, preacher Willie,
The manly tar, my mason Billie,
And Auchinbay, I wish him joy ,
If he's a parent—lass, or boy—
May he be dad, and Meg the mither,   father
Just five-and-forty years thegither !
And no forgetting wabster Charlie,
I'm told he offers very fairly.
And AYE remember singing Sannock,
Wi' hale breeks, saxpence, and a bannock ;   cake
And next my auld acquaintance Nancy,
Since she is fitted to her fancy ;
And her kind stars hae airted till her   directed to
A good chiel wi' a pickle siller.   fellow, some money
My kindest, best respects I sen' it,
To cousin Kate, and sister Janet ;
Tell them, frae me, wi' chiels be cautious,   lads
For, faith, they'll aiblins fin them fashious.   possibly
And lastly, Jamie, for yoursel',   [troublesome
    *   *   *   *   *

May ye get mony a merry story ;
Mony a laugh, and mony a drink,   many
And aye eneugh o' needfu' clink.   money

Now fare-you-weel, and joy be wi' you ;
For my sake this I beg it o' you,
Assist poor Simson a' ye can,
Ye'll fin' him just an honest man :
Sae I conclude, and quat my chanter,   quit, pipes
Yours, saint or sinner, ROB THE RANTER.

ADDRESS TO THE TOOTHACHE.

MY ban upon thy venom'd stang,   sting
That shoots my tortur'd gums alang ;   along
And through my lugs gies mony a twang,   ears, gives
          Wi' gnawing vengeance ;
Tearing my nerves wi' bitter pang,
          Like racking engines !

When fevers burn, or ague freezes,
Rheumatics gnaw, or cholic squeezes ;
Our neighbour's sympathy may ease us,
          Wi' pitying moan ;
But thee—thou worst o' a' diseases,
          Aye mocks our groan !

O! a' the num'rous human dools,   sorrows
Ill har'sts, daft bargains, cutty-stools,   harvests, foolish
Or worthy friends rak'd i' the mools,   clods
          Sad sight to see !

The tricks o' knaves, or fash o' fools—   trouble
    Thou bear'st the gree.   superiority

O thou grim mischief-making chiel,   fellow
That gars the notes of discord squeel,   makes
Till daft mankind aft dance a reel
    In gore a shoe-thick !—
Gie a the faes o' Scotland's weal   give, foes, welfare
    A towmond's toothache !   year's

THE KIRK'S ALARM.

ORTHODOX, orthodox,
  Wha believe in John Knox,   who
Let me sound an alarm to your conscience ;
    There's a heretic blast
    Has been blawn in the wast,   blown
That what is not sense must be nonsense.

  Dr Mac, Dr Mac,   (Rev. Dr M'Gill)
    You should stretch on a rack,
To strike evil doers wi' terror ;
    To join faith and sense
    Upon any pretence
Is heretic HORRIBLE error.

  Town of Ayr, town of Ayr,
    It was mad, I declare,
To meddle wi' mischief a-brewing ;
    Provost John is still deaf
    To the church's relief,
And orator Bob is its ruin.   (Robert Aiken)

  Singet Sawney, Singet Sawney,   (Rev. Alex. Moodie)
    Are ye huirding the penny,   hoarding
Unconscious what evils await ;
    Wi' a jump, yell, and howl,
    Alarm every soul,
For the foul thief is just at your gate.

  Daddy Auld, Daddy Auld,   (Rev. Mr Auld)
    There's a tod in the fauld,   fox, fold
A tod meikle waur than the clerk ;   much worse
    Though ye downa do skaith,   cannot harm
    Ye'll be in at the death,
And if ye canna bite, ye may bark.

  Davie Bluster, Davie Bluster,   (Mr Grant, Ochiltree)
    For a saint if ye muster,
The corps is no nice of recruits ;
    Yet to worth lets be just,
    Royal blood ye might boast,
If the ass was the king of the brutes.

  Jamy Goose, Jamy Goose,   (Mr Young, Cumnock)
    Ye hae made but toom roose,   empty praise

In hunting the wicked lieutenant;
But the Doctor's your mark,
For the Kirk's haly ark,   holy
He has cooper'd and cawt a wrong pin in't.   driven

Andro Gouk, Andro Gouk,   (Rev. Dr Mitchell, Monkton)
Ye may slander the book,
And the book not the waur, let me tell ye;   worse
Ye are rich, and look big,
But lay by hat and wig,
And ye'll hae a calf's head o' sma' value.

Barr Steenie, Barr Steenie,   (Rev. Mr Young, Barr)
What mean ye—what mean ye?
If ye'll meddle nae mair wi' the matter,   more
Ye may hae some pretence
To havins and sense,   manners
Wi' people wha ken ye nae better.   know, no

Irvine-side, Irvine-side,   (Rev. Mr Smith, Galston)
Wi' your turkey-cock pride,
Of manhood but sma' is your share;
Ye've the figure, 'tis true,
Even your faes will allow,   foes
And your friends they dare grant you nae mair.   more

Muirland Jock, Muirland Jock,   (Rev. Mr Shepherd,
Whom HIS PRIDE made a rock   [Muirkirk)
To crush Common Sense for her sins,
If ill manners were wit,
There's no mortal so fit
To confound the poor Doctor at ance.   once

Holy Will, Holy Will,
There was wit i' your skull,
When ye pilfered the alms o' the poor;
The timmer is scant,   timber
When ye're ta'en for a saunt,   saint
Wha should swing in a rape for an hour.   rope

Calvin's sons, Calvin's sons,
Seize your spir'tual guns,
Ammunition you never can need;
Your hearts are the stuff,
Will be powther enough,   powder
And your skulls are storehouses o' lead.

Poet Burns, Poet Burns,
Wi' your priest-skelping turns,
Why desert ye your auld native shire?
Though your Muse is a gipsy,
Yet were she e'en tipsy,
She could ca' us nae waur than we are.   call, worse

THE WHISTLE.

I SING of a whistle, a whistle of worth,
I sing of a whistle, the pride of the North,
Was brought to the court of our good Scottish king,
And long with this whistle all Scotland shall ring.

Old Loda, still rueing the arm of Fingal,   (see Ossian
The god of the bottle sends down from his hall—
" This whistle's your challenge—to Scotland get o'er,
And drink them DEAD DRUNK, sir ! or ne'er see me more !"

Old poets have sung, and old chronicles tell,
What champions ventured, what champions fell ;
The son of great Loda was conqueror still,
And blew on the whistle his requiem shrill.

Till Robert, the lord of the Cairn and the Skarr,
Unmatched at the bottle, unconquered in war,
He drank his poor godship as deep as the sea—
No tide of the Baltic e'er drunker than he.

Thus Robert, victorious, the trophy has gained,
Which now in his house has for ages remained ;
Till three noble chieftains, and all of his blood,
The jovial contest again have renewed.

Three joyous good fellows, with hearts clear of flaw :
Craigdarroch, so famous for wit, worth, and law ;
And trusty Glenriddel, so skilled in old coins ;
And gallant Sir Robert, deep-read in old wines.

Craigdarroch began, with a tongue smooth as oil,
Desiring Glenriddel to yield up the spoil ;
Or else he would muster the heads of the clan,
And once more, in claret, try which was the man.

" By the gods of the ancients !" Glenriddel replies,
" Before I surrender so glorious a prize,
I'll conjure the ghost of the great Rorie More,
And bumper his horn with him twenty times o'er."

Sir Robert, a soldier, no speech would pretend,
But he ne'er turned his back on his foe—or his friend,
Said, Toss down the whistle, the prize of the field,
And knee-deep in claret, he'd die, or he'd yield.

To the board of Glenriddel our heroes repair,
So noted for drowning of sorrow and care ;
But for wine and for welcome not more known to fame
Than the sense, wit, and taste of a sweet lovely dame.

A bard was selected to witness the fray,
And tell future ages the feats of the day ;
A bard who detested all sadness and spleen,
And wished that Parnassus a vineyard had been.

The dinner being over, the claret they ply,
And every new cork is a new spring of joy;
In the bands of old friendship and kindred so set,
And the bands grew the tighter the more they were wet.

Gay Pleasure ran riot as bumpers ran o'er;
Bright Phœbus ne'er witnessed so joyous a core,
And vowed that to leave them he was quite forlorn,
Till Cynthia hinted he'd see them next morn.

Six bottles a piece had well wore out the night,
When gallant Sir Robert, to finish the fight,
Turn'd o'er in one bumper a bottle of red,
And swore 'twas the way that their ancestors did.

Then worthy Glenriddel, so cautious and sage,
No longer the warfare, ungodly, would wage;
A high ruling elder to wallow in wine!
He left the foul business to folks less divine.

The gallant Sir Robert fought hard to the end;
But who can with fate and quart-bumpers contend?
Though fate said—a hero shall perish in light;
So up rose bright Phœbus—and down fell the knight.

Next up rose our bard, like a prophet in drink :—
" Craigdarroch, thou'lt soar when creation shall sink ;
But if thou would flourish immortal in rhyme,
Come—one bottle more—and have at the sublime!

" Thy line, that have struggled for freedom with Bruce,
Shall heroes and patriots ever produce :
So thine be the laurel, and mine be the bay ;
The field thou hast won, by yon bright god of day !"

TO MARY IN HEAVEN.

THOU ling'ring star, with less'ning ray,
  That lov'st to greet the early morn,
Again thou usher'st in the day
  My Mary from my soul was torn.
O Mary! dear departed shade!
  Where is thy place of blissful rest?
See'st thou thy lover lowly laid?
  Hear'st thou the groans that rend his breast?

That sacred hour can I forget,
  Can I forget the hallowed grove,
Where by the winding Ayr we met,
  To live one day of parting love!
Eternity will not efface
  Those records dear of transports past;
Thy image at our last embrace,
  Ah! little thought we 'twas our last!

Ayr, gurgling, kissed his pebbled shore,
    O'erhung with wild woods, thick'ning green ;
The fragrant birch, and hawthorn hoar,
    Twined am'rous round the raptured scene ;
The flowers sprang wanton to be prest,
    The birds sang love on every spray—
Till too, too soon, the glowing west
    Proclaim'd the speed of winged day.

Still o'er these scenes my mem'ry wakes,
    And fondly broods with miser care !
Time but th' impression stronger makes,
    As streams their channels deeper wear.
My Mary ! dear departed shade !
    Where is thy place of blissful rest ?
See'st thou thy lover lowly laid ?
    Hear'st thou the groans that rend his breast ?

TO DR BLACKLOCK.

ELLISLAND, *Oct.* 21, 1789.

Wow, but your letter made me vauntie !	elated
And are ye hale, and weel, and cantie ?	well, merry
I kenned it still your wee bit jauntie,	knew, short, jaunt
Wad bring ye to :	would
COME you aye BACK as weel's I want ye,	
And then ye'll do.	

But what d'ye think, my trusty fier,   companion
I'm turned a gauger—Peace be here !   exciseman
Parnassian queans, I fear, I fear,
    Ye'll now disdain me !
And then my fifty pounds a year
    Will little gain me.

Ye glaiket, gleesome, dainty damies,   giddy, dames
Wha, by Castalia's wimplin' streamies,   winding
Loup, sing, and lave your pretty limbies,   leap
    Ye ken, ye ken,   know
That strang necessity supreme is
    'Mang sons 'o men.

I hae a wife and twa wee laddies,   have, two, boys
They maun hae brose and brats o' duddies;   must, food, clothes
Ye ken yoursels my heart right proud is—
    I need na vaunt,   not
But I'll sned besoms—thraw saugh woodies,*   cut
    Before they want.

OH help me through this warld o' care !
I'm weary sick o't late and air !   early
Not but I hae a richer share   have
    Than mony ithers ;   many others

* Twist willow wands.

But why should ae man better fare,   *one*
    And a' men brithers ?   *brothers*

Come, firm Resolve, take thou the van,
Thou stalk o' earl-hemp in man !   *seed-hemp*
And let us mind, faint heart ne'er wan   *won*
    A lady fair :
Wha does the utmost that he can,   *who*
    Will whyles do mair.   *sometimes, more*

But to conclude my silly rhyme
(I'm scant o' verse, and scant o' time),
To make a happy fireside clime
    To weans and wife,   *children*
That's the true pathos and sublime
    Of human life.

My compliments to sister Beckie ;
And eke the same to honest Lucky,   *also*
I wat she is a dainty chuckie,   *know, chick*
    As e'er tread clay !
And gratefully, my guid auld cockie,
    I'm yours for aye.
          ROBERT BURNS.

ON CAPTAIN GROSE'S PEREGINATIONS THROUGH SCOTLAND,

COLLECTING THE ANTIQUITIES OF THAT KINGDOM.

Here, land o' Cakes, and brither Scots,   *brother*
Frae Maidenkirk* to Johnny Groat's ;
If there's a hole in a' your coats,
    I rede you tent it :   *warn, observe*
A chiel's amang you taking notes,   *fellow, among*
    And, faith, he'll prent it.   *print*

If in your bounds ye chance to light
Upon a fine, fat, fodgel wight   *plump fellow*
O' stature short, but genius bright,
    That's he, mark weel—   *well*
And wow ! he has an unco slight   *great cleverness*
    O' cauk and keel.   *chalk, red crayon*

By some auld houlet-haunted biggin,   *owl, building*
Or kirk deserted by its riggin,   *roof*
Its ten to ane you'll find him snug in   *one*
    Some eldritch part,   *fearful*
Wi' WARLOCKS, SP'RITES, AND IMPS colleaguin'
    At some black art.

Ilk ghaist that haunts auld ha' or chaumer, *each ghost, chamber*
Ye gipsy-gang that deal in glamour,   *necromancy*

* An inversion of the name of Kirkmaiden, in Wigtonshire, the most *southerly* parish in Scotland. John O' Groats is the most *northerly* dwelling in Scotland.

And you deep-read in a' black grammar,
    Warlocks and witches;   *wizards*
Ye'll quake at his conjuring hammer,
    Ye midnight WRETCHES.

It's tauld he was a sodger bred,   *told, soldier*
And ane wad rather fa'n than fled;   *one, would, fallen*
But now he's quat the spurtle blade,   *quitted, thin sword*
    And dog-skin wallet,
And ta'en the—Antiquarian trade,
    I think they call it.

He has a fouth o' auld nick-nackets,   *abundance, old*
Rusty airn caps and jinglin' jackets,   *iron*
Wad haud the Lothians three in tackets, *keep, shoe-nails*
    A towmont guid;   *twelvemonth full*
And parritch-pats, and auld saut-backets *porridge-pot,*
    Before the Flood.   *[salt-box*

Forbye, he'll shape you aff, fu' gleg, *besides, off quickly*
The cut of Adam's philabeg;   *dress*
The knife that nicket Abel's craig,   *neck*
    He'll prove you fully,
It was a faulding jocteleg,   *clasp-knife*
    Or lang-kail gully.   *large knife*

But wad ye see him in his glee,   *would*
For meikle glee and fun has he,   *much*
Then set him down, and twa or three
    Guid fellows wi' him;   *good*
And port, O port! shine thou a wee,   *little*
    And then ye'll see him!

Now, by the powers o' verse and prose!
Thou art a dainty chiel, O Grose!—   *fellow*
Whae'er o' thee shall ill suppose,
    They sair misca' thee,   *much asperse*
I'd take the rascal by the nose,
    Wad say, shame fa' thee.   *would*

THE FIVE CARLINES.

THERE were five carlines in the south, *old women*
    They fell upon a scheme,
To send a lad to Lon'on town,
    To bring them tidings hame.   *home*

Nor only bring them tidings hame,
    But do their errands there,
And aiblins gowd and honour baith *possibly, gold, both*
    Might be that laddie's share.

There was Maggy by the banks o' Nith,
    A dame wi' pride eneugh,   *enough*
And Marjory o' the Mony Lochs,
    A carline auld and teugh.   *woman, tough*

And Blinkin' Bess o' Annandale,
  That dwelt near Solwayside,
And Whisky Jean, that took her gill,
  In Galloway sae wide.   so

And Black Joan frae Crichton Peel,   from
  O' gipsy kith and kin—
Five wighter carlines werna foun'   handsomer, were not
  The south contra within.   country

To send a lad to Lon'on town,
  They met upon a day,
And mony a knight and mony a laird   many
  Their errand fain would gae.   go

O mony a knight and mony a laird
  This errand fain would gae ;
But nae ane could their fancy please,   no one
  O ne'er a ane but twae.   two

The first he was a belted knight,   (Sir James Johnston)
  Bred o' a Border clan,
And he wad gae to Lon'on town,
  Might'nae man him withstan'.

And he wad do their errands weel,   well
  And meikle he wad say,   much, would
And ilka ane at Lon'on court,   each one
  Would bid to him guid-day.   good-day

Then next came in a sodger youth,   (Captain Miller)
  And spak wi' modest grace,
And he wad gae to Lon'on town,
  If sae their pleasure was.

He wadna hecht them courtly gifts,   wouldn't promise
  Nor meikle speech pretend,
But he wad hecht an honest heart   would
  Wad ne'er desert a friend.

Now, wham to choose, and wham refuse,   whom
  At strife thir carlines fell ;   these
For some had gentle folks to please,
  And some wad please themsel.

Then out spak mim-mou'ed Meg o' Nith,   prim-mouthed
  And she spak up wi' pride,
And she wad send the sodger youth,
  Whatever might betide.

For the auld guidman o' Lon'on court   (The King)
  She didna care a pin ;
But she wad send the sodger youth
  To greet his eldest son.   (Prince of Wales)

Then up sprang Bess o' Annandale,
  And a deadly aith she's ta'en,
That she wad vote the Border knight,   oath
  Though she should vote her lane.   alone

For far-aff fowls hae feathers fair,   have
  And fools o' change are fain;
But I hae tried the Border knight,
  And I'll try him yet again.

Says Black Joan frae Crichton Peel,
  A carline stoor and grim,   austere
The auld guidman, and the young guidman,
  For me may sink or swim;

For fools will freit o' right or wrang,   talk superstitiously
  While knaves laugh them to scorn;
But the sodger's friends hae blawn the best,   blown
  So he shall bear the horn.

Then Whisky Jean spak owre her drink,   over
  Ye weel ken, kimmers a',   well know, gossips
The auld guidman o' Lon'on court
  His back's been at the wa';   wall

And mony a friend that kiss'd his cup
  Is now a fremit wight: estranged
But it's ne'er be said o' Whisky Jean—
  I'll send the Border knight.

Then slow raise Marjory o' the Loch's,   arose
  And wrinkled was her brow,
Her ancient weed was russest gray,
  Her auld Scots bluid was true;   blood

There's some great folks set light by me—
  I set as light by them;
But I will send to Lon'on town
  Wham I like best at hame.   whom

Sae how this weighty plea may end   so
  Nae mortal wight can tell: no
Grant THAT the king and ilka man   every
  May look weel to himsel.   well

SKETCH—NEW-YEAR'S DAY, 1790.

TO MRS DUNLOP.

THIS day, Time winds th' exhausted chain,
To run the twelvemonth's length again:
I see the old, bald-pated fellow,
With ardent eyes, complexion sallow,
Adjust the unimpaired machine,
To wheel the equal, dull routine.

The absent lover, minor heir,
In vain assail him with their prayer;
Deaf as my friend, he sees them press,
Nor makes the hour one moment less.
Will you (the Major's with the hounds
The happy tenants share his rounds:

Coila's fair Rachel's care to-day,
And blooming Keith's engaged with Gray)
From housewife cares a minute borrow—
—That grandchild's cap will do to-morrow—
And join with me a-moralising,
This day's propitious to be wise in.
First, what did yesternight deliver?
" Another year is gone for ever."
And what is this day's strong suggestion?
" The passing moment's all we rest on!"
Rest on—for what? what do we here?
Or why regard the passing year?
Will time, amused with proverbed lore,
Add to our date one minute more?
A few days may—a few years must—
Repose us in the silent dust.
Then is it wise to damp our bliss?
Yes—all such reasonings are amiss!
The voice of Nature loudly cries,
And many a message from the skies,
That something in us never dies:
That on this frail, uncertain state,
Hang matters of eternal weight:
That future life in worlds unknown
Must take its hue from this alone;
Whether as heavenly glory bright,
Or dark as misery's woeful night.
Since, then, my honoured, first of friends,
On this poor being all depends,
Let us th' important *now* employ,
And live as those who never die.
Though you, with days and honours crowned,
Witness that filial circle round
(A sight, life's sorrows to repulse,
A sight, pale envy to convulse),
Others now claim your chief regard;
Yourself, you wait your bright reward.

PROLOGUE,

SPOKEN AT THE THEATRE, DUMFRIES, ON NEW-YEAR'S-DAY
EVENING, 1790.

No song nor dance I bring from yon great city
That queens it o'er our taste—the more's the pity
Though, by the by, abroad why will you roam?
Good sense and taste are natives here at home:
But not for panegyric I appear,
I come to wish you all a good new-year!
Old Father Time deputes me here before ye,
Not for to preach, but tell his simple story:
The sage grave ancient coughed, and bade me say
" You're one year older this important day."

If wiser, too—he hinted some suggestion,
But 'twould be rude, you know, to ask the question;
And with a would-be roguish leer and wink,
He bade me on you press this one word—" think ! "

Ye sprightly youths, quite flushed with hope and spirit,
Who think to storm the world by dint of merit,
To you the dotard has a deal to say,
In his sly, dry, sententious, proverb way :
He bids you mind, amid your thoughtless rattle,
That the first blow is ever half the battle ;
That though some by the skirt may try to snatch him,
Yet by the forelock is the hold to catch him ;
That whether doing, suffering, or forbearing,
You may do miracles by persevering.

Last, though not least in love, ye youthful fair,
Angelic forms, high Heaven's peculiar care !
To you old Bald-pate smooths his wrinkled brow,
And humbly begs you'll mind the important now !
To crown your happiness he asks your leave,
And offers bliss to give and to receive.

For our sincere, though haply weak endeavours,
With grateful pride we own your many favours ;
And howsoe'er our tongues may ill reveal it,
Believe our glowing bosoms truly feel it.

PROLOGUE FOR MR SUTHERLAND'S BENEFIT NIGHT, DUMFRIES.

WHAT need's this din about the town o' Lon'on,
How this new play and that new sang is comin' ?   song
Why is outlandish stuff sae meikle courted ?   so much
Does nonsense mend like whisky, when imported ?
Is there nae poet, burning keen for fame,   no
Will try to gie us songs and plays at hame ?   give, home
For comedy abroad he needna toil,   need not
A fool and knave are plants of every soil ;
Nor need he hunt as far as Rome and Greece
To gather matter for a serious piece ;
There's themes enough in Caledonian story,
Would show the tragic Muse in a' her glory.

Is there no daring bard will rise, and tell
How glorious Wallace stood, how hapless fell ?
Where are the Muses fled that could produce
A drama worthy o' the name o' Bruce ;
Now here, even here, he first unsheathed the sword
Gainst mighty England and her guilty lord ;
And after mony a bloody, deathless doing,   many
Wrenched his dear country from the jaws of ruin ?
O for a Shakspeare or an Otway scene,
To draw the lovely, hapless Scottish Queen !

Vain all the omnipotence of female charms
'Gainst headlong, ruthless, mad rebellion's arms.
She fell, but fell with spirit truly Roman,
To glut the vengeance of a rival woman:
A woman—though the phrase may seem uncivil—
As able and as cruel as the devil!
One Douglas lives in Home's immortal page,
But Douglasses were heroes every age:
And though your fathers, prodigal of life,
A Douglas followed to the martial strife,
Perhaps if bowl's row right, and Right succeeds,
Ye yet may follow where a Douglas leads!
As ye hae generous done, if a' the land   *have*
Would take the Muses' servants by the hand;
Not only hear, but patronise, befriend them,
And where ye justly can commend, commend them;
And aiblins when they winna stand the test,   *perhaps, wont*
Wink hard, and say the folks hae done their best! ·
Would a' the land do this, then I'll be caution
Ye'll soon hae poets o' the Scottish nation,
Will gar Fame blaw until her trumpet crack,   *make, blow*
And warsle Time, and lay him on his back!   *strive with*
For us and for our stage should ony spier,   *any ask*
" Wha's aught thae chiels maks a' this bustle here?"   *who are,*
My best leg foremost, I'll set up my brow,   *[fellows*
We have the honour to belong to you!
We're your ain bairns, e'en guide us as you like,
But like gude mithers, shore before you strike.   *mothers,*
And gratefu' still I hope ye'll ever find us,   *[threaten*
For a' the patronage and meikle kindness   *much*
We've got frae a' professions, sets, and ranks: *from*
WE'VE NOCHT TO GIE! we're poor—ye'se get but thanks.   *nothing,*
    [give

PEG NICHOLSON.

PEG Nicholson was a good bay mare,
   As ever trod on airn;   *iron*
But now she's floating down the Nith,
   And past the mouth o' Cairn.

Peg Nicholson was a good bay mare,
   And rode through thick and thin;
But now she's floating down the Nith,
   And wanting even the skin.

Peg Nicholson was a good bay mare,
   And ance she bore a priest;   *once*
But now she's floating down the Nith,
   For Solway fish a feast.

Peg Nicholson was a good bay mare,
   And the priest he rode her sair;   *sore*
And much oppressed and bruised she was,
   As priest-rid cattle are.

WRITTEN

TO A GENTLEMAN WHO HAD SENT THE POET A NEWSPAPER,
AND OFFERED TO CONTINUE IT FREE OF EXPENSE.

KIND Sir, I've read your paper through,
And, faith, to me 'twas really new!
How guessed ye, sir, what maist I wanted?   most
This mony a day I've graned and gaunted,   groan, yawned
To ken what French mischief was brewin',   know
Or what the drumlie Dutch were doin';   muddy
Or how the collieshangie works   contention
Atween the Russians and the Turks;
Or if the Swede, before he halt,   (Gustavus III.)
Would play anither Charles the Twalt: twelfth
If Denmark, anybody spak o't;
Or Poland, wha had now the tack o't;   lease
If Spaniard, Portuguese, or Swiss,
Were sayin' or takin' aught amiss:
Or how our merry lads at hame,   home
In Britian's court kept up the game:
How Royal George, AND THEM AROUND HIM,
Was managing St Stephen's quorum;
If sleekit Chatham Will was livin',   smooth
Or glaikit Charlie got his nieve in;   thoughtless, fist
How Daddie Burke the plea was cookin',
If Warren Hasting's neck was yeukin';   uneasy
A' this and mair I never heard of,
And but for you I might despaired of.
So gratefu', back your news I send you,
And pray, a' guid things may attend you!   good

ELLISLAND, *Monday morning*, 1790.

ON CAPTAIN MATTHEW HENDERSON.

" Should the poor be flattered?"—SHAKSPEARE.

But now his radiant course is run,
For Matthews course was bright:
His soul was like the glorious sun,
A matchless, heavenly light!

HE'S gane! he's gane! he's frae us torn,   gone, from
The ae best fellow e'er was born!   one
Thee, Matthew, Nature's sel' shall mourn   self
        By wood and wild,
Where, haply, Pity strays forlorn,
        Frae man exiled!

Ye hills! near neibors o' the starns,   neighbours, stars
That proudly cock your cresting cairns!
Ye cliffs, the haunts of sailing yearns,   eagles
        Where echo slumbers!
Come join, ye Nature's sturdiest bairns,   children
        My wailing numbers!

Mourn, ilka grove the cushat kens !   *each, wood-pigeon knows*
Ye hazelly shaws and briery dens !   *hollows, dingles*
Ye burnies, wimplin' down your glens,   *meandering*
     Wi' toddlin' din,   *purling*
Or foaming strang, wi' hasty stens,   *strong, leaps*
     Frae lin to lin !   *cascade*

Mourn, little harebells o'er the lea ;
Ye stately foxgloves fair to see ;
Ye woodbines, hanging bonnilie,
     In scented bowers ;
Ye roses on your thorny tree,
     The first o' flowers.

At dawn, when every grassy blade
Droops with a diamond at its head,
At even, when beams their fragrance shed,
     I' th' rustling gale,
Ye maukins whiddin through the glade,   *hares, scudding*
     Come join my wail.

Mourn, ye wee songsters o' the wood ;
Ye grouse that crap the heather bud ;   *crop*
Ye curlews calling through a clud ;   *cloud*
     Ye whistling plover ;
And mourn, ye whirring paitrick brood !—   *partridge*
     He's gane for ever !

Mourn, sooty coots, and speckled teals,
Ye fisher herons, watching eels ;
Ye duck and drake, wi' airy wheels
     Circling the lake ;
Ye bitterns, till the quagmire reels,
     Rair for his sake.   *roar*

Mourn, clam'ring craiks at close o' day,   *land-rails*
'Mang fields o' flowering clover gay ;
And when ye wing your annual way
     Frae our cauld shore,   *cold*
Tell thae far warlds, wha lies in clay   *these, worlds, who*
     Wham we deplore.   *whom*

Ye houlets, frae your ivy bower,   *owls*
In some auld tree or eldritch tower,   *dismal*
What time the moon, wi' silent glower   *stare*
     Sets up her horn,
Wail through the dreary midnight hour
     Till waukrife morn.   *wakeful*

O rivers, forests, hills, and plains !
Oft have ye heard my canty strains :   *cheerful*
But now, what else for me remains
     But tales of wo ?
And frae my een the drapping rains   *eyes*
     Maun ever flow.   *must*

Mourn, Spring, thou darling of the year !
Ilk cowslip cup shall kep a tear :   *each, catch*

Thou, Simmer, while each corny spear   summer
    Shoots up its head,
Thy gay, green, flowery tresses shear
    For him that's dead.

Thou, Autumn, wi' thy yellow hair,
In grief thy sallow mantle tear!
Thou, Winter, hurling through the air
    The roaring blast,
Wide o'er the naked world declare
    The worth we've lost!

Mourn him, thou Sun, great source of light
Mourn, empress of the silent night!
And you, ye twinkling starnies bright,   stars
    My Matthew mourn!
For through your orbs he's ta'en his flight,
    Ne'er to return.

O Henderson! the man—the brother!
And art thou gone, and gone for ever?
And hast thou crossed that unknown river,
    Life's dreary bound?
Like thee, where shall I find another,
    The world around?

Go to your sculptured tombs ye great,
In a' the tinsel trash o' state!
But by thy honest turf I'll wait,
    Thou man of worth;
And weep the ae best fellow's fate   one
    E're lay in earth.

THE EPITAPH.

STOP, passenger! my story's brief,
    And truth I shall relate, man;
I tell nae common tale o' grief—   no
    For Matthew was a great man.

If thou uncommon merit hast,
    Yet spurned at Fortune's door, man,
A look of pity hither cast—
    For Matthew was a poor man.

If thou a noble sodger art,
    That passest by this grave, man,
There moulders here a gallant heart—
    For Matthew was a brave man.

If thou on men, their works and ways,
    Canst throw uncommon light, man,
Here lies wha weel had won thy praise—   who well
    For Matthew was a bright man.

If thou at friendship's sacred ca',   call
    Wad life itself resign, man,   would
Thy sympathetic tear maun fa'—
    For Matthew was a kind man.

If thou art stanch without a stain,
  Like the unchanging blue, man,
This was a kinsman o' thy ain—   *own*
  For Matthew was a true man.

If thou hast wit, and fun, and fire,
  And ne'er guid wine did fear, man,   *good*
This was thy billie, dam, and sire— *brother*
  For Matthew was a queer man.

If ony whiggish whingin' sot,   *any, peevish*
  To blame poor Matthew dare, man,
May dool and sorrow be his lot !   *grief*
  For Matthew was a rare man.

TAM O' SHANTER:

A TALE.

" Of brownyis and of bogilis full is this buke."
             GAWIN DOUGLAS.

WHEN chapman billies leave the street, *fellows*
And drouthy neibors, neibors meet, *thirsty neighbours*
As market-days are wearing late,
And folk begin to tak the gate ;   *road*
While we sit bousing at the nappy, *drinking ale*
And gettin' fou and unco happy, *tipsy, very*
We think na on the lang Scots miles, *not*
The mosses, waters, slaps, and stiles, *gaps*
That lie between us and our hame, *home*
Where sits our sulky sullen dame,
Gathering her brows like gathering storm,
Nursing her wrath to keep it warm.

This truth fand honest Tam o' Shanter, *found*
As he frae Ayr ae night did canter, *from, one*
(Auld Ayr, wham ne'er a town surpasses *whom*
For honest men and bonnie lasses.)

O Tam ! hadst thou but been sae wise, *so*
As ta'en thy ain wife Kate's advice ! *own*
She tauld thee weel thou was a skellum, *told, worthless one*
A blethering, blustering, drunken blellum ; *idle talker*
That frae November till October,
Ae market day thou was na sober ;
That ilka melder, wi' the miller, *each corn-grinding*
Thou sat as lang as thou had siller ; *long*
That every naig was ca'd a shoe on, *nag, nailed*
The smith and thee gat roaring fou on ; *got, drunk*
That at the Lord's house, even on Sunday,
Thou drank AT Kirkton Jeans till Monday.
She prophesied, that, late or soon,
Thou would be found deep drowned in Doon,
Or catched wi' warlocks in the mirk, *darkness*
By Alloway's auld haunted kirk.

Ah, gentle dames ! it gars me greet,   makes, weep
To think how mony counsels sweet,   many
How mony lengthened sage advices,
The husband frae the wife despises !   from

But to our tale :—Ae market-night,   one
Tam had got planted unco right,   very
Fast by an ingle bleezing finely,   fire, blazing
Wi' reaming swats, that drank divinely ;   frothing new ale
And at his elbow, Souter Johnny,   shoemaker
His ancient, trusty, drouthy crony ;   thirsty companion
Tam lo'ed him like a vera brither—   very brother
They had been fou' for weeks thegither !   together
The night drave on wi' sangs and clatter,   drove, songs
And aye the ale was growing better :   still
The landlady and Tam grew gracious,
Wi' favours secret, sweet, and precious ;
The Souter tauld his queerest stories,   told
The landlord's laugh was ready chorus :
The storm without might rair and rustle—   roar
Tam didna mind the storm a whistle.   did not

Care, mad to see a man sae happy,
E'en drowned himself amang the nappy !   ale
As bees flee hame wi' lades o' treasure,   home, loads
The minutes winged their way wi' pleasure :
Kings may be blest, but Tam was glorious,
O'er a' the ills o' life victorious.

But pleasures are like poppies spread,
You seize the flower, its bloom is shed ;
Or like the snowfall in the river,
A moment white—then melts for ever ;
Or like the borealis race,
That flit ere you can point their place ;
Or like the rainbow's lovely form
Evanishing amid the storm.
Nae man can tether time or tide,   no, bind
The hour approaches, Tam maun ride ;   must
That hour, o' night's black arch the key-stane,   stone
That dreary hour he mounts his beast in ;
And sic a night he taks the road in   such
As ne'er poor sinner was abroad in.

The wind blew as 'twad blawn its last;   'twould blown
The rattling showers rose on the blast ;
The speedy gleams the darkness swallowed,
Loud, deep, and lang the thunder bellowed :   long
That night, a child might understand,
The Deil had business on his hand.

Weel mounted on his gray mare, Meg,   well
A better never lifted leg,
Tam skelpit on through dub and mire,   dashed
Despising wind, and rain, and fire ;
Whiles holding fast his guid blue bonnet,   sometimes, good
Whiles crooning o'er some auld Scots sonnet;   humming

Whiles glowering round wi' prudent cares,   *staring*
Lest bogles catch him unawares.   *spirits*
Kirk-Alloway was drawing nigh,
Where gaists and houlets nightly cry.   *ghosts, owls*

By this time he was cross the ford,
Where in the snaw the chapman smoored;   *snow, smothered*
And past the birks and meikle stane,   *birches, big*
Where drunken Charlie brak's neck-bane;   *bone*
And through the whins, and by the cairn,   *gorse*
Where hunters fand the murdered bairn;   *found*
And near the thorn, aboon the well,   *above*
Where Mungo's mither hanged hersel.   *mother*
Before him Doon pours all his floods;
The doubling storm roars through the woods;
The lightnings flash from pole to pole,
Near and more near the thunders roll;
When, glimmering through the groaning trees,
Kirk-Alloway seemed in a bleeze;   *blaze*
Through ilka bore the beams were glancing,   *every crevice*
And loud resounded mirth and dancing.

Inspiring bold John Barleycorn!
What dangers thou canst make us scorn!
Wi' tippenny we fear nae evil;   *two-penny ale*
Wi' usquebae we'll face the devil!—   *whisky*
The swats sae reamed in Tammie's noddle,   *ale so worked, head*
Fair play, he cared na deils a boddle.   *small copper coin*
But Maggie stood right sair astonished,   *sore*
Till, by the heel and hand admonished,
She ventured forward on the light;
And, wow! Tam saw an unco sight!   *strange*
Warlocks and witches in a dance;   *wizards*
Nae cotillon brent new frae France,   *no, brought*
But hornpipes, jigs, strathspeys, and reels,
Put life and mettle in their heels:
A winnock-bunker in the east,   *window-seat*
There sat auld Nick, in shape o' beast;
A towzie tyke, black, grim, and large,   *shaggy dog*
To gie them music was his charge;   *giv*
He screwed the pipes and gart them skirl,   *made, scream*
Till roof and rafters a' did dirl.   *vibrate*
Coffins stood round, like open presses,
That shawed the dead in their last dresses   *shewed*
And by some devilish cantrip slight   *trick*
Each in its cauld hand held a light—   *cold*
By which heroic Tam was able
To note upon the haly table,   *holy*
A murderer's banes in gibbet airns;   *bones, irons*
Twa span-lang, wee unchristened bairns;   *two, long*
A thief, new-cutted frae a rape,   *from, rope*
Wi' his last gasp his gab did gape;   *mouth*
Five tomahawks, wi' bluid red-rusted;   *blood*
Five scimitars, wi' murder crusted;

A garter which a babe had strangled ;
A knife, a father's throat had mangled,
Whom his ain son o' life bereft,　　　　　　　own
The gray hairs yet stack to the heft :　　　stuck, haft
Wi' mair o' horrible and awfu',　　　　　　more
Which even to name wad be unlawfu'.　　　would

As Tammie glowred, amazed and curious,　　stared
The mirth and fun grew fast and furious :
The piper loud and louder blew ;
The dancers quick and quicker flew ;
They reeled, they set, they crossed, they cleekit,　　linked
Till ilka carline swat and reekit,　　each, sweated, smoked
And coost her duddies to the wark,　　cast, clothes, work
And linket at it in her sark !　　tripped, shift

Now Tam, O Tam ! had thae been queans,　　these
A' plump and strappin' in their teens ;
Their sarks, instead o' creeshie flannen,　　greasy flannel
Been snaw-white seventeen-hunder linen !　　(fine linen)
Thir breeks o' mine, my only pair,　　these trews
That ance were plush, o' guid blue hair,　　once, good
I wad hae gi'en them off my hurdies,
For ae blink o' the bonnie burdies !
But withered beldams, auld and droll,　　old
Rigwoodie hags, wad spean a foal,　　would, wean
Louping and flinging on a cummock,　　stick
I wonder didna turn thy stomach.

But Tam kenned what was what fu' brawlie ;　　knew, well
There was ae winsome wench and walie,　　one, goodly
That night enlisted in the core,　　company
(Lang after kenned on Carrick shore ;　　known
For mony a beast to dead she shot,　　many, to death
And perished mony a bonnie boat,
And shook baith meikle corn and bear,　　both, much, barley
And kept the country-side in fear.)
Her cutty-sark, o' Paisley harn,　　short shift, coarse tow
That while a lassie she had worn,
In longitude though sorely scanty,
It was her best, and she was vauntie—　　boastful
Ah ! little kenned thy reverend grannie　　knew
That sark she coft for her wee Nannie,　　bought
Wi' twa pund Scots ('twas a' her riches),
Wad ever graced a dance o' witches !

But here my Muse her wing maun cour,　　must cower
Sic flights are far beyond her power ;　　such
To sing how Nannie lap and flang,　　leapt
(A souple jad she was and strang,)　　agile, strong
And how Tam stood like ane bewitched,　　one
And thought his very een enriched ;　　eyes
Even Satan glowred and fidged fu' fain,　　stared, fidgeted
And hotched and blew mi' might and main :　　moved
Till first ae caper, syne anither,　　then
Tam tint his reason a' thegither,　　lost, together

Ae spring brought off her master hale,
But left behind her ain gray tail.

p. 163

And roars out, " Weel done, Cutty-sark !"   well
And in an instant all was dark :
And scarcely had he Maggie rallied,
When out the hellish legion sallied.
As bees bizz out wi' angry fyke,   fret
When plundering herds assail their byke ;   nest
As open pussie's mortal foes,   the hare
When, pop ! she starts before their nose ;
As eager runs the market-crowd,
When " Catch the thief !" resounds aloud ;
So Maggie runs, the witches follow,
Wi' mony an eldritch screech and hollow.   frightful scream

Ah, Tam ! ah, Tam ! thou'll get thy fairin' !
For now they'll roast thee like a herrin' !
In vain thy Kate awaits thy comin' !
Kate soon will be a woefu' woman !
Now, do thy speedy utmost, Meg,
And win the keystane* o' the brig ;
There at them thou thy tail may toss,
A running stream they darena cross !   dare not
But ere the keystane she could make,
Nae haet a tail she had to shake !
For Nannie, far before the rest,
Hard upon noble Maggie prest,
And flew at Tam wi' furious ettle,   endeavour
But little wist she Maggie's mettle—
Ae spring brought off her master hale,
But left behind her ain gray tail :   own
The carline claught her by the rump,   laid hold
And left poor Maggie scarce a stump.

Now, wha this tale o' truth shall read,   who
Ilk man and mother's son take heed :   each
Whene'er to drink you are inclined,
Or cutty-sarks run in your mind,
Think ! ye may buy the joys ower dear—   too
Remember Tam o' Shanter's mare.

STANZAS

ON THE BIRTH OF A POSTHUMOUS CHILD, BORN UNDER PECULIAR
CIRCUMSTANCES OF FAMILY DISTRESS.

Sweet floweret, pledge o' meikle love,   much
  And ward o' mony a prayer,
What heart o' stane wad thou na move,   stone would, not
  Sae helpless, sweet, and fair !   so

* It is a well-known fact that witches, or any evil spirits, have no power to follow
a poor wight any farther than the middle of the next running stream. It may be
proper likewise to mention to the benighted traveller, that when he falls in with
bogles, whatever danger may be in his going forward, there is much more hazard
in turning back.—B.

November hirples o'er the lea   limps
  Chill on thy lovely form ;
And gane, alas ! the sheltering tree   gone
  Should shield thee frae the storm.

May He who gives the rain to pour,
  And wings the blast to blaw,
Protect thee frae the driving shower,   from
  The bitter frost and snaw !

May He, the friend of wo and want,
  Who heals life's various stounds,   pangs
Protect and guard the mother-plant,
  And heal her cruel wounds !

But late she flourished, rooted fast,
  Fair on the summer morn ;
Now, feebly bends she in the blast,
  Unsheltered and forlorn.

Blest be thy bloom, thou lovely gem,
  Unscathed by ruffian hand !
And from thee many a parent stem
  Arise to deck our land !

ELEGY ON THE LATE MISS BURNET OF MONBODDO.

LIFE ne'er exulted in so rich a prize
As Burnet, lovely from her native skies ;
Nor envious death so triumphed in a blow,
As that which laid th' accomplished Burnet low.

Thy form and mind, sweet maid, can I forget ?
In richest ore the brightest jewel set !
In thee, high Heaven above was truest shown,
As by his noblest work the Godhead best is known.

In vain ye flaunt in summer's pride, ye groves ;
  Thou crystal streamlet with thy flowery shore,
Ye woodland choir that chant your idle loves,
  Ye cease to charm—Eliza is no more !

Ye heathy wastes, immixed with reedy fens ;
  Ye mossy streams, with sedge and rushes stored
Ye rugged cliffs, o'erhanging dreary glens,
  To you I fly, ye with my soul accord.

Princes, whose cumbrous pride was all their worth,
  Shall venal lays their pompous exit hail ?
And thou, sweet excellence ! forsake our earth,
  And not a Muse in honest grief bewail ?

We saw thee shine in youth and beauty's pride,
  And virtue's light, that beams beyond the spheres ;
But, like the sun eclipsed at morning-tide,
  Thou left'st us darkling in a world of tears.

The parent's heart that nestled fond in thee,
 That heart how sunk, a prey to grief and care;
So decked the woodbine sweet yon aged tree;
 So from it ravished, leaves it bleak and bare.

LAMENT

OF MARY QUEEN OF SCOTS ON THE APPROACH OF SPRING.

Now Nature hangs her mantle green
 On every blooming tree,
And spreads her sheets o' daisies white
 Out o'er the grassy lea:
Now Phœbus cheers the crystal streams,
 And glads the azure skies;
But nought can glad the weary wight.
 That fast in durance lies.

Now lav'rocks wake the merry morn,
 Aloft on dewy wing;
The merle, in his noontide bower,   blackbird
 Makes woodland echoes ring;
The mavis wild wi' mony a note,   thrush, many
 Sings drowsy day to rest:
In love and freedom they rejoice,
 Wi' care nor thrall opprest.

Now blooms the lily by the bank,
 The primrose down the brae;
The hawthorn's budding in the glen,
 And milk-white is the slae;   sloe
The meanest hind in fair Scotland   peasant
 May rove their sweets amang;
But I, the queen of a' Scotland,
 Maun lie in prison strang!   must, strong

I was the queen o' bonnie France,
 Where happy I hae been;   have
Fu' lightly rase I in the morn,   rose
 As blithe lay down at e'en:
And I'm the sovereign of Scotland.
 And mony a traitor there;   many
Yet here I lie in foreign bands,
 And never-ending care.

But as for thee, thou false woman!
 My sister and my fae,   foe
Grim vengeance yet shall whet a sword
 That through thy soul shall gae!   go
The weeping blood in woman's breast
 Was never known to thee;
Nor th' balm that draps on wounds of wo   drops
 Frae woman's pitying ee.   from

My son! my son! may kinder stars
 Upon thy fortune shine!

And may those pleasures gild thy reign,
  That ne'er wad blink on mine!   would
God keep thee frae thy mother's faes,
  Or turn their hearts to thee:
And where thou meet'st thy mother's friend,
  Remember him for me!

O soon, to me, may summer suns
  Nae mair light up the morn!   no more
Nae mair, to me, the autumn winds
  Wave o'er the yellow corn!
And in the narrow house o' death
  Let winter round me rave;
And the next flowers that deck the spring
  Bloom on my peaceful grave!

LAMENT

FOR JAMES, EARL OF GLENCAIRN.

THE wind blew hollow frae the hills,   from
  By fits the sun's departing beam
Looked on the fading yellow woods
  That waved o'er Lugar's winding stream:
Beneath a craigy steep, a Bard,   rocky
  Laden with years and meikle pain,   much
In loud lament bewailed his lord,
  Whom death had all untimely ta'en.   taken

He leaned him to an ancient aik,   oak
  Whose trunk was mouldering down with years
His locks were bleachèd white with time,
  His hoary cheek was wet wi' tears;
And as he touched his trembling harp,
  And as he tuned his doleful sang,   song
The winds, lamenting through their caves,
  To echo bore the notes alang: along

" Ye scattered birds that faintly sing,
  The reliques of the vernal quire!
Ye woods that shed on a' the winds
  The honours of the aged year!
A few short months, and glad and gay,
  Again ye'll charm the ear and ee;   eye
But nocht in all revolving time   nought
  Can gladness bring again to me.

" I am a bending, aged tree,
  That long has stood the wind and rain;
But now has come a cruel blast,
  And my last hold of earth is gane: gone
Nae leaf o'mine shall greet the spring,   no
  Nae simmer sun exalt my bloom;
But I maun lie before the storm,   must
  And ithers plant them in my room.   others

"I've seen sae mony changefu' years,   30
  On earth I am a stranger grown ;
I wander in the ways of men,
  Alike unknowing and unknown :
Unheard, unpitied, unrelieved,
  I bear alane my lade o' care,   alone, load
For silent, low, on beds of dust,
  Lie a' that would my sorrows share.

" And last (the sum of a' my griefs !)
  My noble master lies in clay ;
The flower amang our barons bold,
  His country's pride ! his country's stay—
In weary being now I pine,
  For a' the life of life is dead,
And hope has left my aged ken,
  On forward wing for ever fled.

" Awake thy last sad voice, my harp !
  The voice of wo and wild despair ;
Awake ! resound thy latest lay—
  Then sleep in silence evermair !   evermore
And thou, my last, best, only friend,
  That fillest an untimely tomb,
Accept this tribute from the bard,
  Thou brought from fortune's mirkiest gloom   darkest

" In poverty's low barren vale
  Thick mists, obscure, involved me round ;
Though oft I turn'd the wistful eye,
  Nae ray of fame was to be found :
Thou found'st me, like the morning sun.
  That melts the fogs in limpid air,
The friendless bard and rustic song
  Became alike thy fostering care.

" O why has worth so short a date ?
  While villains ripen gray with time ;
Must thou, the noble, generous, great,
  Fall in bold manhood's hardy prime !
Why did I live to see that day ?
  A day to me so full of wo !—
Oh had I met the mortal shaft
  Which laid my benefactor low !

" The bridegroom may forget the bride,
  Was made his wedded wife yestreen ;
The monarch may forget the crown
  That on his head an hour has been ;
The mother may forget the child
  That smiles sae sweetly on her knee ;   50
But I'll remember thee, Glencairn,
  And a' that thou hast done for me !"

LINES

SENT TO SIR JOHN WHITEFOORD, BART. OF WHITEFOORD, WITH
THE FOREGOING POEM.

THOU, who thy honour as thy God rever'st,
Who, save thy mind's reproach, naught earthly fear'st,
To thee this votive offering I impart,
The tearful tribute of a broken heart.
The friend thou valued'st, I the patron loved ;
His worth, his honour, all the world approved.
We'll mourn till we too go as he has gone,
And tread the dreary path to that dark world unknown.

ADDRESS TO THE SHADE OF THOMSON,

ON CROWNING HIS BUST AT EDNAM, ROXBURGHSHIRE WITH
BAYS.

WHILE virgin Spring, by Eden's flood,
Unfolds her tender mantle green,
Or pranks the sod in frolic mood,
Or tunes Æolian strains between :

While Summer with a matron grace
Retreats to Dryburgh's cooling shade,
Yet oft, delighted, stops to trace
The progress of the spiky blade :

While Autumn, benefactor kind,
By Tweed erects his aged head,
And sees, with self-approving mind,
Each creature on his bounty fed :

While maniac Winter rages o'er
The hills whence classic Yarrow flows,
Rousing the turbid torrent's roar,
Or sweeping, wild, a waste of snows :

So long, sweet poet of the year !
Shall bloom that wreath thou well hast won ;
While Scotia, with exulting tear,
Proclaims that Thomson was her son.

TO MR MAXWELL OF TERRAUGHTY, ON HIS BIRTH-DAY.

HEALTH to the Maxwells' veteran chief !
Health, aye unsoured by care or grief   always
Inspired, I turned Fate's sybil leaf
This natal morn ;
I see thy life is stuff o' prief,   proof
Scarce quite half worn.

This day thou metes threescore eleven,
And I can tell, that bounteous Heaven
(The second-sight, ye ken, is given   know
    To ilka Poet)   each
On thee a tack o' seven times seven   lease
    Will yet bestow it.

If envious buckies view wi' sorrow   perverse fellows
Thy lengthened days on this blest morrow,
May desolation's lang-teethed harrow,
    Nine miles an hour,
Rake them like Sodom and Gomorrah,
    In brunstane stoure!

But for thy friends, and they are mony,   many
Baith honest men and lasses bonnie,   both
May couthie Fortune, kind and cannie,   kindly, gentle
    In social glee,
Wi' mornings blythe, and e'enings funny,
    Bless them and thee!

Farewell, auld birkie! GRACE be near ye,   fellow
And then NAE EVIL daurs TO steer ye: dares, move
Your friends aye love, your faes aye fear ye;   foes
    For me, shame fa' me,   fall
If neist my heart I dinna wear ye   next, do not
    While BURNS they ca' me!   call

FOURTH EPISTLE TO MR GRAHAM OF FINTRY.

I CALL no goddess to inspire my strains,
A fabled Muse may suit a bard that feigns;
Friend of my life! my ardent spirit burns,
And all the tribute of my heart returns,
For boons accorded, goodness ever new,
The gift still dearer, as the giver, you.

Thou orb of day! thou other paler light!
And all ye many sparkling stars of night;
If aught that giver from my mind efface,
If I that giver's bounty e'er disgrace;
Then roll to me, along your wandering spheres,
Only to number out a villain's years!

SWEET Sensibility, how charming,
    Thou, my friend, canst truly tell;
But how Distress, with horrors arming,
    Thou, alas! hast known too well!

Fairest Flower, behold the lily,
    Blooming in the sunny ray;
Let the blast sweep o'er the valley,
    See it prostrate on the clay.

Hear the wood-lark charm the forest,
   Telling o'er his little joys ;
But, alas ! a prey the surest
   To each pirate of the skies.

Dearly bought the hidden treasure
   Finer feelings can bestow :
Cords that vibrate sweetest pleasure
   Thrill the deepest notes of wo.

THE RIGHTS OF WOMAN,

AN OCCASIONAL ADDRESS SPOKEN BY MISS FONTENELLE ON HER
BENEFIT NIGHT, NOV. 26, 1792.

WHILE Europe's eye is fixed on mighty things,
The fate of empires and the fall of kings ;
While quacks of state must each produce his plan
And even children lisp the Rights of Man ;
Amid this mighty fuss just let me mention,
The Rights of Woman merit some attention.

First, in the sexes' intermixed connection,
One sacred Right of Woman is--Protection.
The tender flower that lifts its head, elate,
Helpless, must fall before the blasts of fate,
Sunk on the earth, defaced its lovely form,
Unless your shelter ward th' impending storm.

Our second Right—but needless here is caution,
To keep that Right inviolate's the fashion,
Each man of sense has it so full before him,
He'd die before he'd wrong it--'tis Decorum.
There was, indeed, in far less polished days,
A time when rough rude man had naughty ways ;
Would swagger, swear, get drunk, kick up a riot,
Nay, even thus invade a lady's quiet.
Now, thank our stars ! these Gothic times are fled ;
Now, well-bred men—and you are all well-bred—
Most justly think (and we are much the gainers)
Such conduct neither spirit, wit, nor manners.

For Right the third, our last, our best, our dearest,
That right to fluttering female hearts the nearest,
Which even the Rights of Kings in low prostration
Most humbly own—'tis dear, dear Admiration !
In that blest sphere alone we live and move ;
There taste that life of life—immortal love.
Smiles, glances, sighs, tears, fits, flirtatious, airs,
'Gainst such an host what flinty savage dares—
When awful Beauty joins with all her charms,
Who is so rash as rise in rebel arms ?
But truce with kings and truce with constitutions,
With bloody armaments and revolutions,
Let majesty your first attention summon,
Ah ! *ça ira !* THE MAJESTY OF WOMAN !

TO MISS FONTENELLE,

ON SEEING HER IN A FAVOURITE CHARACTER.

SWEET naïveté of feature,
  Simple, wild, enchanting elf,
Not to thee, but thanks to Nature,
  Thou art acting but thyself.

Wert thou awkward, stiff, affected,
  Spurning nature, torturing art;
Loves and graces all rejected,
  Then indeed thou'dst act a part.

SONNET,

WRITTEN ON THE 25TH JANUARY 1793, THE BIRTHDAY OF THE
AUTHOR, ON HEARING A THRUSH SING IN A MORNING WALK.

SING on, sweet thrush, upon the leafless bough,
  Sing on, sweet bird, I listen to thy strain;
  See aged Winter, 'mid his surly reign,
At thy blythe carol clears his furrowed brow.

So in lone Poverty's dominion drear,
  Sits meek Content with light unanxious heart;
  Welcomes the rapid moments, bids them part,
Nor asks if they bring ought to hope or fear.

I thank thee, Author of this opening day!
  Thou whose bright sun now gilds yon orient skies!
  Riches denied, thy boon was purer joys,
What wealth could never give nor take away!

Yet come, thou child of poverty and care,
  The mite high Heaven bestowed, that mite with thee I'll share

EPITAPH ON A LAP-DOG.

IN wood and wild, ye warbling throng,
  Your heavy loss deplore!
Now half extinct your powers of song,
  Sweet Echo is no more.

Ye jarring, screeching things around,
  Scream your discordant joys!
Now half your din of tuneless song
  With Echo silent lies.

IMPROMPTU

ON MRS RIDDEL'S BIRTHDAY, 4TH NOVEMBER 1793.

OLD Winter, with his frosty beard,
  Thus once to Jove his prayer preferred:
  "What have I done of all the year,
  To bear this hated doom severe?

My cheerless suns no pleasure know;
Night's horrid car drags, dreary slow;
My dismal months no joys are crowning,
But spleeny English, hanging, drowning.

"Now, Jove, for once be mighty civil,
To counterbalance all this evil;
Give me, and I've no more to say,
Give me Maria's natal-day!
That brilliant gift shall so enrich me,
Spring, summer, autumn, cannot match me.'
" 'Tis done!" says Jove; so ends my story,
And Winter once rejoiced in glory.

MONODY

ON A LADY FAMED FOR HER CAPRICE.

How cold is that bosom which folly once fired,
   How pale is that cheek where the rouge lately glistened
How silent that tongue which the echoes oft tired,
   How dull is that ear which to flattery so listened!

If sorrow and anguish their exit await,
   From friendship and dearest affection removed;
How doubly severer, Eliza, thy fate,
   Thou diedst unwept, as thou livest unloved.

Loves, Graces, and Virtues, I call not on you;
   So shy, grave, and distant, ye shed not a tear:
But come, all ye offspring of Folly so true,
   And flowers let us cull for Eliza's cold bier.

We'll search through the garden for each silly flower,
   We'll roam through the forrest for each idle weed;
But chiefly the nettle, so typical, shower,
   For none e'er approached her but rued the rash deed

We'll sculpture the marble, we'll measure the lay;
   Here Vanity strums on her idiot lyre;
There keen Indignation shall dart on her prey,
   Which spurning Contempt shall redeem from his ire.

THE EPITAPH.

Here lies, now a prey to insulting neglect,
   What once was a butterfly gay in life's beam:
Want only of wisdom denied her respect,
   Want only of goodness denied her esteem.

EPISTLE FROM ESOPUS TO MARIA.

From those drear solitudes and frowsy cells,
Where infamy with sad repentance dwells;
Where turnkeys make the jealous portal fast,
And deal from iron hands the spare repast;

Where truant 'prentices, yet young in sin,
Blush at the curious stranger peeping in ;
Where tiny thieves not destined yet to swing,
Beat hemp for others, riper for the string :
From these dire scenes my wretched lines I date,
To tell Maria her Esopus' fate.

'Alas! I feel I am no actor here!'
'Tis real hangmen, real scourges bear !
Prepare, Maria, for a horrid tale
Will turn thy very rouge to deadly pale ;
Will make thy hair, though erst from gipsy polled,
By barber woven, and by barber sold,
Though twisted smooth with Harry's nicest care,
Like hoary bristles to erect and stare.
The hero of the mimic scene, no more
I start in Hamlet, in Othello roar ;
Or haughty chieftain, 'mid the din of arms,
In Highland bonnet woo Malvina's charms ;
While *sans culottes* stoop up the mountain high,
And steal from me Maria's prying eye.
Blest Highland bonnet ! once my proudest dress,
Now prouder still, Maria's temples press.
I see her wave thy towering plumes afar,
And call each coxcomb to the wordy war ;
I see her face the first of Ireland's sons,
And even out-Irish his Hibernian bronze ;
The crafty colonel leaves the tartaned lines,
For other wars, where he a hero shines ;
The hopeful youth, in Scottish senate bred,
Who owns a Bushby's heart without the head,
Comes 'mid a string of coxcombs to display,
That *veni, vidi, vici*, is his way ;
The shrinking Bard adown an alley skulks,
And dreads a meeting worse than Woolwich hulks ;
Though there, his heresies in church and state
Might well award him Muir and Palmer's fate :
Still she undaunted reels and rattles on,
And dares the public like a noontide sun.
(What scandal called Maria's jaunty stagger,
The rick'et reeling of a crooked swagger ;
Whose spleen e'en worse than Burns's venom when
He dips in gall unmixed his eager pen—
And pours his vengeance in the burning line,
Who christened thus Maria's lyre divine ;
The idiot strum of vanity bemused,
And even th' abuse of poesy abused ;
Who called her verse a parish workhouse, made
For motley, foundling fancies, stolen or strayed ?}

A workhouse ! ah, that sound awakes my woes,
And pillows on the thorn my racked repose !
In durance vile here must I wake and weep,
And all my frowsy couch in sorrow steep !
That straw where many a rogue has lain of yore,

And vermined gipsies littered heretofore.
Why Lonsdale thus, thy wrath on vagrants pour ·
Must earth no rascal save thyself endure?
Thou know'st the Virtues cannot hate thee worse;
The Vices also, must they club their curse?
Or must no tiny sin to others fall,
Because thy guilt's supreme enough for all?

Maria, send me, too, thy griefs and cares;
In all of thee sure thy Esopus shares.
As thou at all mankind the flag unfurls,
Who on my fair one satire's vengeance hurls?
Who calls thee pert, affected, vain coquette,
A wit in folly, and a fool in wit?
Who says that fool alone is not thy due,
And quotes thy treacheries to prove it true?
Our force united ɔn thy foes we'll turn,
And dare the war with all of woman born:
For who can write and speak as thou and I?
My periods that deciphering defy,
And thy still matchless tongue that conquers all reply.

A VISION.

As I stood by yon roofless tower,
　Where the wa'-flower scents the dewy air,
Where th' howlet mourns in her ivy bower,　　　　ɔwl
　And tells the midnight moon her care;

The winds were laid, the air was still,
　The stars they shot along the sky;
The fox was howling on the hill,
　And the distant echoing glens reply.

The stream, adown its hazelly path,
　Was rushing by the ruined wa's,
Hasting to join the sweeping Nith,
　Whose distant roaring swells and fa's.

The cauld blue north was streaming forth　　　cold
　Her lights, wi' hissing eerie din;　　　　　　.dreary
Athort the lift they start and shift,　　　athwart, sky
　Like fortune's favours, tint as win.　　　　　ost

By heedless chance I turned mine eyes,
　And, by the moonbeam, shook to see
A stern and stalwart ghaist arise,　　　　　　ghost
　Attired as minstrels wont to be.

Had I a statue been o stane,　　　　　　　　stone
　His darin' look had daunted me;
And on his bonnet graved was plain,
　The sacred posy—" Libertie !"

And frae his harp sic strains did flow,　　from, such
　Might roused the slumb'ring dead to hear ·

But oh ! it was a tale of wo,
  As ever met a Briton's ear.

He sang wi' joy the former day,
  He weeping wailed his latter times ;
But what he said it was nae play—
  I winna ventur't in my rhymes.

SONNET ON THE DEATH OF GLENRIDDEL.

No more, ye warblers of the wood, no more ;
  Nor pour your descant grating on my soul :
  Thou young-eyed Spring, gay in thy verdant stole—
More welcome were to me grim Winter's wildest roar.

How can ye charm, ye flowers, with all your dyes ?
  Ye blow upon the sod that wraps my friend !
  How can I to the tuneful strain attend ?
That strain flows round th' untimely tomb where Riddel lies.

Yes, pour, ye warblers, pour the notes of wo,
  And soothe the Virtues weeping o'er his bier :
  The Man of Worth, and hath not left his peer,
Is in his narrow house, for ever darkly low.

  Thee, Spring, again with joy shall others greet ;
  Me, memory of my loss will only meet.

Thee, Caledonia, thy wild heaths among,
Thee, famed for martial deed and sacred song,
  To thee I turn with swimming eyes ;
Where is that soul of freedom fled ?
Immingled with the mighty dead,
  Beneath the hallowed turf where Wallace lies
Hear it not, Wallace, in thy bed of death,
  Ye babbling winds, in silence sweep,
  Disturb ye not the hero's sleep,
Nor give the coward secret breath.
Is this the power in freedom's war,
  That wont to bid the battle rage ?
Behold that eye which shot immortal hate,
  Braved usurpation's boldest daring ;
That arm which, nerved with thundering fate,
  Crushed the despot's proudest bearing :
One quenched in darkness like the sinking star,
  And one the palsied arm of tottering, powerless age

VERSES TO MISS GRAHAM OF FINTRY.

Here, where the Scottish Muse immortal lives,
  In sacred strains and tuneful numbers joined,
Accept the gift, though humble he who gives ;
  Rich is the tribute of the grateful mind.

So may no ruffian feeling in thy breast,
  Discordant jar thy bosom-chords among;
But Peace attune thy gentle soul to rest,
  Or Love ecstatic wake his seraph song :

Or Pity's notes, in luxury of tears,
  As modest Want the tale of wo reveals ;
While conscious Virtue all the strain endears,
  And heaven-born Piety her sanction seals.

THE TREE OF LIBERTY.

HEARD ye o' the tree o' France,
  I watna what's the name o't ;   know not
Around it a' the patriots dance,
  Weel Europe kens the fame o't.   well, knows
It stands where ance the Bastile stood,   once
  A prison built by kings, man,
When Superstition's WICKED brood
  Kept France in leading-strings, man.

Upo' this tree there grows sic fruit,   such
  Its virtues a' can tell, man ;
It raises man aboon the brute,   above
  It maks him ken himsel, man.   know
Gif ance the peasant taste a bit,   if once
  He's greater than a lord, man,
And wi' the beggar shares a mite
  O' a' he can afford, man.

This fruit is worth a' Afric's wealth,
  To comfort us 'twas sent, man :
To gie the sweetest blush o' health,
  And mak us a' content, man.
It clears the een, it cheers the heart,   eyes
  Maks high and low gude friends, man ;
And he wha acts the traitor's part,
  It to DESTRUCTION sends, man.

My blessings aye attend the HAN',
  Wha pitied Gallia's slaves, man.   who
And staw a branch, FRAE THAT FAR LAN',   stole
  Frae yont the western waves, man.   from beyond
Fair Virtue watered it wi' care,
  And now she sees wi' pride, man,
How weel it buds and blossoms there,   well
  Its branches spreading wide, man.

But vicious folk aye hate to see
  The works o' Virtue thrive, man ;
The courtly vermin's banned the tree,
  And grat to see it thrive, man ;   wept
King Loui' thought to cut it down,
  When it was unco sma', man ;   very
For this the watchman cracked his crown,
  Cut aff his head and a', man.

A wicked crew syne, on a time,   *then*
  Did tak a solemn aith, man,   *oath*
It ne'er should flourish to its prime,
  I wat they pledged their faith, man.   *know*
Awa they gaed wi' mock parade,   *away, went*
  Like beagles hunting game, man,
But soon grew weary o' the trade,
  And wished they'd been at hame, man.   *home*

For Freedom, standing by the tree,
  Her sons did loudly ca', man ;
She sang a sang o' liberty,
  Which pleased them ane and a', man.   *one*
By her inspired, the new-born race
  Soon drew the avenging steel, man ;
The hirelings ran—her foes gied chase,   *gave*
  And banged the despot weel, man.   *beat*

Let Britain boast her hardy oak,
  Her poplar and her pine, man,
Auld Britain ance could crack her joke,   *once*
  And o'er her neighbours shine, man.
But seek the forest round and round,
  . And soon 'twill be agreed, man,
That sic a tree can not be found
  'Twixt London and the Tweed, man.

Without this tree, alake this life
  Is but a vale o' wo, man ;
A scene o' sorrow mixed wi' strife,
  Nae real joys we know, man.   *no*
We labour soon, we labour late,
  To feed the titled knave, man ;
And a' the comfort we're to get,
  Is that ayont the grave, man.   *beyond*

Wi' plenty o' sic trees, I trow,
  The warld would live in peace, man ;   *world*
The sword would help to mak a plough,
  The din o' war wad cease, man.
Like brethren in a common cause,
  We'd on each other smile, man ;
And equal rights and equal laws
  Wad gladden every isle, man   *would*

Wae worth the loon wha wadna eat   *woe, fellow, wouldn't*
  Sic halesome dainty cheer, man ;   *wholesome*
I'd gie my shoon frae aff my feet,   *give, shoes, off*
  To taste sic fruit, I swear, man.   *such*
Syne let us pray, auld England may   *then*
  Sure plant this far-famed tree, man ;
And blithe we'll sing, and hail the day
  That gave us liberty, man.

TO DR MAXWELL,

ON MISS JESSIE STAIG'S RECOVERY.

MAXWELL, if merit here you crave,
  That merit I deny :
You save fair Jessy from the grave !—
  An angel could not die !

TO CHLORIS.

'TIS Friendship's pledge, my young, fair friend,
  Nor thou the gift refuse,
Nor with unwilling ear attend
  The moralising Muse.

Since thou, in all thy youth and charms,
  Must bid the world adieu,
(A world 'gainst peace in constant arms)
  To join the friendly few :

Since thy gay morn of life o'ercast,
  Chill came the tempest's lower ;
(And ne'er miisfortune's eastern blast
  Did nip a fairer flower :)

Since life's gay scenes must charm no more ;
  Still much is left behind ;
Still nobler wealth hast thou in store—
  The comforts of the mind !

Thine is the self-approving glow,
  On conscious honour's part ;
And, dearest gift of Heaven below,
  Thine friendship's truest heart.

The joys refined of sense and taste,
  With every Muse to rove :
And doubly were the Poet blest,
  These joys could he improve.

TOAST FOR THE 12TH OF APRIL.

INSTEAD of a song, boys, I'll give you a toast—
Here's the memory of those on the twelfth that we lost !—
That we lost, did I say ? nay, IN TRUTH, that we found ;
For their fame it shall last while the world goes round.
The next in succession, I'll give you—the King
Whoe'er would betray him, on high may he swing ;
And here's the grand fabric, our free Constitution,
As built on the base of the great Revolution ;
And longer with politics not to be crammed,
MAY Anarchy PERISH—be Tyrants condemned ;
And who would to Liberty e'er prove disloyal,
May his son be a hangman, and he his first trial !

INSCRIPTION

FOR AN ALTAR TO INDEPENDENCE, AT KERROUGHTREE, THE
SEAT OF MR HERON.

THOU of an independent mind,
With soul resolved, with soul resigned;
Prepared Power's proudest frown to brave,
Who wilt not be, nor have a slave;
Virtue alone who dost revere,
Thy own reproach alone dost fear,
Approach this shrine, and worship here.

VERSES

ON THE DESTRUCTION OF THE WOODS NEAR DRUMLANRIG.

AS on the banks o' wandering Nith,
 Ae smiling simmer-morn I strayed,   *one*
And traced its bonnie howes and haughs,   *vales, uplands*
 Where linties sang and lambkins played,   *linnets*
I sat me down upon a craig,
 And drank my fill o' fancy's dream,
When, from the eddying deep below,
 Uprose the Genius of the stream.]

Dark, like the frowning rock, his brow,
 And troubled, like his wintry wave,
And deep, as sughs the boding wind   *whistles*
 Amang his eaves, the sigh he gave—   *among*
"And came you hear, my son," he cried,
 "To wander in my birken shade?   *birchen*
To muse some favourite Scottish theme,
 Or sing some favourite Scottish maid.

"There was a time, it's nae lang syne,   *not, long ago*
 Ye might hae seen me in my pride,   *have*
When a' my banks sae bravely saw,   *so*
 Their woody pictures in my tide;
When hanging beech and spreading elm
 Shaded my stream sae clear and cool;
And stately oaks their twisted arms
 Threw broad and dark across the pool;

"When, glinting through the trees, appeared
 The wee white cot aboon the mill,   *above*
And peacefu' rose its ingle reek,   *fire, smoke*
 That slowly curled up the hill.
But now the cot is bare and cauld   *cold*
 Its branchy shelter's lost and gane,   *gone*
And scarce a stunted birk is left   *stunted birch*
 To shiver in the blast its lane."   *alone*

"Alas!" said I, what ruefu' chance
 Has twined ye o' your stately trees?   *deprived*

Has laid your rocky bosom bare?
Has stripped the cleeding o' your braes?   clothing
Was it the bitter eastern blast,
    That scatters blight in early spring?
Or was't the wil'fire scorched their boughs,   wild-fire
    Or canker-worm wi' secret sting?"

" Nae eastlin blast," the sp'rite replied;   eastern
    " It blew na here sae fierce and fell,   not so
And on my dry and halesome banks   wholesome
    Nae canker-worms get leave to dwell:
Man! cruel man!" the Genius sighed—
    As through the cliffs he sank him down—
" The worm that gnawed my bonnie trees,
    That reptile wears a ducal crown."

ADDRESS,

SPOKEN BY MISS FONTENELLE ON HER BENEFIT-NIGHT, 1795.

STILL anxious to secure your partial favour,
And not less anxious, sure, this night, than ever,
A Prologue, Epilogue, or some such matter,
'Twould vamp my bill, said I, if nothing better;
So sought a Poet, roosted ne'er the skies,
Told him I came to feast my curious eyes;
Said, nothing like his works was ever printed;
And last, my Prologue-business slily hinted.
" Ma'am, let me tell you," quoth my man of rhymes,
" I know your bent—these are no laughing times:
Can you—but, Miss, I own I have my fears—
Dissolve in pause and sentimental tears,
With laden sighs, and solemn rounded sentence;
Rouse from his sluggish slumbers fell Repentance;
Paint Vengeance as he takes his horrid stand,
Waving on high the desolating brand,
Calling the storms to bear him o'er a guilty land?"

I could no more—askance the creature eyeing,
D'ye think, said I, this face was made for crying?
I'll laugh, that's poz—nay, more, the world shall know it.
And so, your servant! gloomy Master Poet!
Firm as my creed, Sirs, 'tis my fixed belief,
That Misery's another word for Grief;
I also think—so may I be a bride!
That so much laughter, so much life enjoyed.

Thou man of crazy care and ceaseless sigh,
Still under bleak Misfortune's blasting eye;
Doomed to that sorest task of man alive—
To make three guineas do the work of five:
Laugh in Misfortune's face—the beldam witch!
Say, you'll be merry, though you can't be rich.
Thou other man of care, the wretch in love,
Who long with jiltish arts and airs hast strove;

Who, as the boughs all temptingly project,
Measur'st in desperate thought—a rope—thy neck—
Or, where the beetling cliff o'erhangs the deep,
Peerest to meditate the healing leap :
Wouldst thou be cured, thou silly, moping elf !
Laugh at her follies—laugh e'en at thyself :
Learn to despise those frowns now so terrific,
And love a kinder—that's your grand specific.

To sum up all, be merry, I advise ;
And as we're merry, may we still be wise.

TO COLLECTOR MITCHELL.

FRIEND of the Poet, tried and leal,	loyal
Wha, wanting thee, might beg or steal ;	who
Alake, alake, the meikle deil	
Wi' a' his witches	
Are at it, skelpin' jig and reel,	jumping
In my poor pouches !	pockets
I modestly fu' fain wad hint it,	would
That one-pound-one, is sairly want it ;	sorely
If wi' the hizzie down ye sent it,	servant-girl
It would be kind ;	
And while my heart wi' life-blood dunted,	throbbed
I'd bear't in mind.	
So may the auld year gang out moaning	go
To see the new come, laden, groaning,	
Wi' double plenty o'er the loanin	pathway
To thee and thine :	
Domestic peace and comforts crowning	
The hale design.	whole

POSTSCRIPT.

Ye've heard this while how I've been licket,	troubled
And by fell death was nearly nicket ;	seized
Grim loon ! he got me by the fecket,	fellow, waistcoat
And sair me sheuk ;	sore, shook
But by guid luck I lap a wicket,	jumped
And turned a neuk.	nook
But by that health, I've got a share o't,	
And by that life, I'm promised mair o't,	more
My hale and weel I'll tak a care o't,	health, welfare
A tentier way ;	more careful
Then farewell folly, hide and hair o't,	entirely
For ance and aye.	

THE DEAN OF FACULTY.
A BALLAD.

DIRE was the hate at old Harlaw,
  That Scot to Scot did carry;
And dire the discord Langside saw,
  For beauteous hapless Mary:
But Scot with Scot ne'er met so hot,
  Or were more in fury seen, sir,
Than 'twixt Hal and Bob* for the famous job,
  Who should be Faculty's Dean, sir.

This Hal for genius, wit, and lore,
  Among the first was numbered;
But pious Bob, 'mid learning's store,
  Commandment tenth remembered.
Yet simple Bob the victory got,
  And won his heart's desire;
    *   *   *   *

Squire Hal besides had in this case
  Pretensions rather brassy,
For talents to deserve a place
  Are qualifications saucy;
So their worships of the Faculty,
  Quite sick of merit's rudeness,
Chose one who should owe it all, d'ye see,
  To their gratis grace and goodness.

In your heretic sins may you live and die,
  Ye heretic Eight-and-Thirty,
But accept, ye sublime majority,
  My congratulations hearty.
With your Honours and a certain King
  In your servants this is striking,
The more incapacity they bring,
  The more they're to your liking.

THE HERMIT.

WRITTEN ON A MARBLE SIDEBOARD, IN THE HERMITAGE BE-
LONGING TO THE DUKE OF ATHOLE, IN THE WOOD OF ABER-
FELDY.

WHOE'ER thou art, these lines now reading,
Think not, though from the world receding,
I joy my lonely days to lead in
      This desert drear;
That fell remorse a conscience bleeding
      Hath led me here.

No thought of guilt my bosom sours;
Free-will'd I fled from courtly bowers;

---

* Henry Erskine and Robert Dundas. Dundas was chosen by a majority of 123
to 38 **votes.**

For well I saw in halls and towers
    That lust and pride,
The arch-fiend's dearest, darkest powers,
    In state preside.

I saw mankind with vice incrusted;
I saw that honour's sword was rusted;
That few for aught but folly lusted;
That he was still deceived who trusted
    To love or friend;
And hither came, with men disgusted,
    My life to end.

In this lone cave, in garments lowly,
Alike a foe to noisy folly,
And brow-bent gloomy melancholy,
    I wear away
My life, and in my office holy
    Consume the day.

This rock my shield, when storms are blowing,
The limpid streamlet yonder flowing
Supplying drink, the earth bestowing
    My simple food;
But few enjoy the calm I know in
    This desert wood.

Content and comfort bless me more in
This grot, than e'er I felt before in
A palace—and with thoughts still soaring
    To God on high,
Each night and morn with voice imploring,
    This wish I sigh:

"Let me, O Lord! from life retire,
Unknown each guilty worldly fire,
Remorse's throb, or loose desire;
    And when I die,
Let me in this belief expire—
    To God I fly."

Stranger, if full of youth and riot,
And yet no grief has marred thy quiet,
Thou haply throw'st a scornful eye at
    The hermit's prayer—
But if thou hast good cause to sigh at
    Thy fault or care;

If thou hast known false love's vexation,
Or hast been exiled from thy nation,
Or guilt affrights thy contemplation,
    And makes thee pine,
Oh! how must thou lament thy station,
    And envy mine!

THE VOWELS:

A TALE.

'Twas where the birch and sounding thong are plied,
The noisy domicile of pedant pride;
Where Ignorance her darkening vapour throws,
And Cruelty directs the thickening blows;
Upon a time, Sir Abece the great,
In all his pedagogic powers elate,
His awful chair of state resolves to mount,
And call the trembling vowels to account.

First entered A, a grave, broad, solemn wight,
But, ah! deformed, dishonest to the sight!
His twisted head looked backward on his way,
And flagrant from the scourge he grunted, *ai!*

Reluctant, E stalked in; with piteous race
The justling tears ran down his honest face!
That name, that well-worn name, and all his own,
Pale he surrenders at the tyrant's throne!
The pedant stifles keen the Roman sound
Not all his mongrel diphthongs can compound;
And next the title following close behind,
He to the nameless, ghastly wretch assigned.

The cobwebbed Gothic dome resounded, Y!
In sullen vengeance, I, disdained reply:
The pedant swung his felon cudgel round,
And knocked the groaning vowel to the ground!

In rueful apprehension entered O,
The wailing minstrel of despairing wo;
Th' Inquisitor of Spain the most expert,
Might there have learnt new mysteries of his art;
So grim, deformed, with horrors entering, U
His dearest friend and brother scarcely knew!

As trembling U stood staring all aghast,
The pedant in his left hand clutched him fast,
In helpless infants' tears he dipped his right,
Baptised him *eu*, and kicked him from his sight.

ON PASTORAL POETRY.

Hail Poesie! thou Nymph reserved!
In chase o' thee, what crowds hae swerved　　　have
Frae common-sense, or sunk ennerved　　　from
'Mang heaps o' clavers;　　　babblings
And och! ower aft thy joes hae starved,　　too oft, lovers
Mid a' thy favours

Say, Lassie, why thy train amang,
While loud, the trump's heroic clang,

And sock or buskin skelp alang   *dash*
    To death or marriage ;
Scarce ane has tried the shepherd-sang   *one*
    But wi' miscarriage ?

In Homer's craft Jock Milton thrives ;
Eschylus' pen Will Shakspeare drives ;
Wee Pope, the knurlin, 'till him rives   *dwarf*
    Horatian fame ;
In thy sweet sang, Barbauld, survives
    Ev'n Sappho's flame.

But thee, Theocritus, wha matches ?   *who*
They're no herd's ballats, Maro's catches ;   *ballads*
Squire Pope but busks his skinklin patches   *dresses, spark-*
    O' heathen tatters :   [ling
I pass by hunders, nameless wretches,   *hundreds*
    That ape their betters.

In this braw age o' wit and lear,   *learning*
Will nane the Shepherd's whistle mair   *none, mor*
Blaw sweetly in its native air   *blow*
    And rural grace ;
And wi' the far-famed Grecian, share
    A rival place ?

Yes ! there is ane ; a Scottish callan—   *one, lad*
There's ain ; come forrit, honest Allan !   *forward*
Thou need na jouk behint the hallan,   *skulk, door*
    A chiel sae clever ;   *man so*
The teeth o' Time may gnaw Tantallan,
    But thou's for ever !

Thou paints auld Nature to the nines,
In thy sweet Caledonian lines ;
Nae gowden stream through myrtles twines,   *golden*
    Where Philomel,
While nightly breezes sweep the vines,
    Her griefs will tell !

In gowany glens thy burnie strays,   *daisied*
Where bonnie lasses bleach their claes ;   *clothes*
Or trots by hazelly shaws and braes,   *wood*
    Wi' hawthorns grey,
Where blackbirds join the shepherd's lays
    At close o' day.

Thy rural loves are nature's sel' ;   *sel*
Nae bombast spates o' nonsense swell ;   *no, flood*
Nae snap conceits, but that sweet spell
    O' witchin' love ;
That charm that can the strongest quell,
    The sternest move.

TO A KISS.

HUMID seal of soft affections,
  Tend'rest pledge of future bliss,
Dearest tie of young connections,
  Love's first snow-drop, virgin kiss.

Speaking silence, dumb confession,
  Passion's birth, and infant's play,
Dove-like fondness, chaste concession,
  Glowing dawn of brighter day.

Sorrowing joy, adieu's last action,
  When ling'ring lips no more must join;
What words can ever speak affection,
  So thrilling and sincere as thine!

LAMENT,

WRITTEN WHEN THE POET WAS ABOUT TO LEAVE SCOTLAND.

O'ER the mist-shrouded cliffs of the lone mountain straying,
  Where the wild winds of winter incessantly rave,
What woes wring my heart while intently surveying
  The storm's gloomy path on the breast of the wave.

Ye foam-crested billows, allow me to wail,
  Ere ye toss me afar from my lov'd native shore;
Where the flower which bloom'd sweetest in Coila's green vale,
  The pride of my bosom, my Mary's no more.

No more by the banks of the streamlet we'll wander,
  And smile at the moon's rimpled face in the wave;
No more shall my arms cling with fondness around her,
  For the dew-drops of morning fall cold on her grave.

No more shall the soft thrill of love warm my breast,
  I haste with the storm to a far distant shore;
Where unknown, unlamented, my ashes shall rest,
  And joy shall revisit my bosom no more.

AN EXTEMPORE EFFUSION,

ON BEING APPOINTED TO THE EXCISE.

SEARCHING auld wives' barrels,
      Och, hon! the day!
That clarty barm should stain my laurels;   dirty yeast
      But—what'll ye say!
These muvin' things ca'd wives and weans,   moving, children
Wad muve the very hearts o' stanes!   stones

TO MY BED.

THOU bed, in which I first began
To be that various creature—*Man !*
And when again the Fates decree,
The place where I must cease to be ;—
When sickness comes, to whom I fly,
To soothe my pain, or close mine eye ;—
When cares surround me, where I weep,
Or loose them all in balmy sleep ;—
When sore with labour, whom I court,
And to thy downy breast resort—
The centre thou—where grief and pain,
Disease and rest, alternate reign.
Oh, since within thy little space,
So many various scenes take place ;
Lessons as useful shalt thou teach,
As sages dictate—churchmen preach ;
And man, convinced by thee alone,
This great important truth shall own :
" *That thin partitions do divide*
The bounds where good and ill reside ;
That nought is perfect here below ;
But BLISS *still bordering upon* WOE."

LINES

SENT TO A GENTLEMAN WHOM HE HAD OFFENDED.

THE friend whom wild from wisdom's way,
    The fumes of wine infuriate send
(Not moony madness more astray)—
    Who but deplores that hapless friend ?

Mine was th' insensate frenzied part,
    Ah, why should I such scenes outlive !
Scenes so abhorrent to my heart !
    'Tis thine to pity and forgive.

THE RUINED MAID'S LAMENT.

OH, meikle do I rue, fause love,   much, regret, false
    Oh sairly do I rue,
That e'er I heard your flattering tongue,
    That e'er your face I knew.

Oh, I hae tint my rosy cheeks,   lost
    Likewise my waist sae sma' ;
And I hae lost my lightsome heart,
    That little wist a fa'.

Now I maun thole the scornfu' sneer   must bear
    O' mony a saucy quean ;   many, proud

When, gin the truth were a but kent,   If, known
  Her life's been warse than mine.   worse

Whene'er my father thinks on me,
  He stares into the wa';
My mother, she has ta'en the bed   taken
  Wi' thinking on my fa'.

Whene'er I hear my father's foot,
  My heart wad burst wi' pain ;   would
Whene'er I meet my mither's ee,   eye
  My tears rin down like rain.

Alas ! sae sweet a tree as love
  Sic bitter fruit should bear !
Alas ! that e'er a bonnie face
  Should draw a sauty tear !   salt
    *   *   *   *

ON THE DUKE OF QUEENSBERRY.

How shall I sing Drumlanrig's Grace—
Discarded remnant of a race
     Once great in martial story ?
His forbears' virtues all contrasted—   ancestors
The very name of Douglas blasted—
     His that inverted glory.

Hate, envy, oft the Douglas bore ;
But he has superadded more,
     And sunk them in contempt ;
Follies and crimes have stain'd the name,
But, Queensberry, thine the virgin claim,
     From ought that's good exempt.

ON THE DEATH OF A FAVOURITE CHILD.

OH sweet be thy sleep in the land of the grave,
  My dear little angel, for ever ;
For ever—oh no ! let not man be a slave,
  His hopes from existence to sever.

Though cold be the clay where thou pillow'st thy head,
  In the dark silent mansions of sorrow,
The spring shall return to thy low narrow bed,
  Like the beam of the day-star to-morrow.

The flower-stem shall bloom like thy sweet seraph form,
  Ere the spoiler had nipt thee in blossom,
When thou shrunk'st frae the scowl of the loud winter storm,
  And nestled thee close to that bosom.

Oh still I behold thee, all lovely in death,
  Reclined on the lap of thy mother;
When the tear trickled bright, when the short stifled breath,
  Told how dear ye were aye to each other.

My child, thou art gone to the home of thy rest,
  Where suffering no longer can harm ye,
Where the songs of the good, where the hymns of the blest,
  Through an endless existence shall charm thee.

While he, thy fond parent, must sighing sojourn,
  Through the dire desert regions of sorrow,
O'er the hope and misfortune of being to mourn,
  And sigh for this life's latest morrow.

WRITTEN IN A LADY'S POCKET-BOOK.

GRANT me, indulgent Heav'n, that I may live,
To see the miscreants feel the pains they give,
Deal freedom's sacred treasures free as air,
Till slave and despot be but things which were.

FRAGMENT.

  THE black-headed eagle
  As keen as a beagle,
He hunted owre height and owre howe;   hollow
  But fell in a trap
  On the braes o' Gemappe,
E'en let him come out as he dowe.   can

WRITTEN ON A PANE OF GLASS,

ON THE OCCASION OF A NATIONAL THANKSGIVING FOR A
NAVAL VICTORY.

YE hypocrites! are these your pranks?—
To murder men, and gie God thanks!
For shame! gie o'er, proceed no further—
God won't accept your thanks for murther!

THE TRUE LOYAL NATIVES.

YE true "Loyal natives," attend to my song
In uproar and riot rejoice the night long:
From envy and hatred your corps is exempt;
But where is your shield from the darts o' contempt?

ON THE AUTHOR'S FATHER.

OH ye whose cheek the tear of pity stains,
  Draw near with pious rev'rence and attend!
Here lie the loving husband's dear remains,
  The tender father, and the gen'rous friend.
The pitying heart that felt for human woe;
  The dauntless heart that fear'd no human pride;
The friend of man, to vice alone a foe;
  " For ev'n his failings lean'd to virtue's side."

EPITAPH ON THE POET'S DAUGHTER.

HERE lies a rose, a budding rose,
  Blasted before its bloom;
Whose innocence did sweets disclose
  Beyond that flower's perfume.
To those who for her loss are grieved,
  This consolation's given—
She's from a world of woe relieved,
  And blooms a rose in Heaven.

"THOUGH FICKLE FORTUNE."

THOUGH fickle Fortune has deceiv'd me,
  She promis'd fair, and perform'd but ill;
Of mistress, friends, and wealth bereav'd me,
  Yet I bear a heart shall support me still.—

I'll act with prudence as far's I'm able,
  But if success I must never find,
Then come, Misfortune, I bid thee welcome,
  I'll meet thee with an undaunted mind.

TO THE OWL.

SAD Bird of Night, what sorrow calls thee forth,
  To vent thy plaints thus in the midnight hour;
Is it some blast that gathers in the north,
  Threat'ning to nip the verdure of thy bow'r?

Is it, sad Owl, that Autumn strips the shade,
  And leaves thee here, unsheltered and forlorn?
Or fear that Winter will thy nest invade?
  Or friendly Melancholy bids thee mourn?

Shut out, lone bird, from all the feather'd train,
  To tell thy sorrows to th' unheeding gloom;
No friend to pity when thou dost complain,
  Grief all thy thought, and solitude thy home.

Sing on, sad mourner! I will bless thy strain,
  And pleased in sorrow listen to thy song:
Sing on, sad mourner! to the night complain,
  While the lone echo wafts thy notes along.

Is beauty less, when down the glowing cheek
  Sad piteous tears in native sorrows fall?
Less kind the heart, when Sorrow bids it break?
  Less happy he who lists to pity's call?

Ah no, sad Owl! nor is thy voice less sweet,
  That sadness tunes it, and that grief is there;
That Spring's gay notes, unskill'd, thou canst repeat,
  And sorrow bids thee to the gloom repair.

Nor that the treble songsters of the day,
  Are quite estranged, sad Bird of Night! from thee;
Nor that the thrush deserts the evening spray,
  When darkness calls thee from thy reverie.

From some old tower, thy melancholy dome,
  While the grey walls and desert solitudes
Return each note, responsive, to the gloom
  Of ivied coverts, and surrounding woods;

There hooting, I will list more pleased to thee,
  Than ever lover to the nightingale;
Or drooping wretch, oppressed with misery,
  Lending his ear to some condoling tale.

TO THE RUINS OF LINCLUDEN ABBEY

Ye holy walls, that still sublime
Resist the crumbling touch of Time,
How strongly still your form displays
The piety of ancient days.
As through your ruins, hoar and grey—
Ruins, yet beauteous in decay—
The silvery moonbeams trembling fly,
The forms of ages long gone by
Crowd thick on Fancy's wond'ring eye,
And wake the soul to musings high.
Ev'n now, as lost in thought profound,
I view the solemn scene around,
And pensive gaze with wistful eyes,
The past returns, the present flies;
Again the dome, in pristine pride,
Lifts high its roof, and arches wide,
That, knit with curious tracery
Each Gothic ornament display;
The high-arched windows, painted fair
Show many a saint and martyr there;

As on their slender forms I gaze,
Methinks they brighten to a blaze ;
With noiseless step and taper bright,
What are yon forms that meet my sight ?
Slowly they move, while every eye
Is heavenward raised in ecstasy :—
'Tis the fair, spotless, vestal train,
That seeks in prayer the midnight fane.
And hark ! what more than mortal sound
Of music breathes the pile around ?
'Tis the soft chaunted choral song,
Whose tones the echoing aisles prolong :
Till thence return'd they softly stray
O'er Cluden's wave with fond delay ;
Now on the rising gale swell high,
And now in fainting murmurs die :
The boatmen on Nith's gentle stream,
That glistens in the pale moon's beam,
Suspend their dashing oars to hear
The holy anthem, loud and clear ;
Each worldly thought awhile forbear,
And mutter forth a half-formed prayer.
But as I gaze, the vision fails,
Like frost-work touch'd by southern gales ;
The altar sinks, the tapers fade,
And all the splendid scene's decay'd.
In window fair the painted pane
No longer glows with holy stain,
But, through the broken glass, the gale
Blows chilly from the misty vale.
The bird of eve flits sullen by,
Her home, these aisles and arches high :
The choral hymn, that erst so clear
Broke softly sweet on Fancy's ear,
Is drowned amid the mournful scream,
That breaks the magic of my dream :
Roused by the sound, I start and see
The ruin'd, sad reality.

VERSES ADDRESSED TO J. RANKINE.

I AM a keeper of the law
In some sma' points, although not a',
Some people tell me gin I fa',   If
        Ae way or ither,   cne, other
The breaking of ae point, tho' sma',
        Breaks a' thegither.   together
    ❋   ❋   *   *   *   ❋

A WINTER NIGHT.

Poor naked wretches, whereso'er you are,
That bide the pelting of the pitiless storm!
How shall your houseless heads and unfed sides,
Your looped and windowed raggedness, defend you
From seasons such as these?—SHAKSPEARE.

WHEN biting Boreas, fell and doure,   keen, sullen
Sharp shivers through the leafless bower ;
When Phœbus gies a short-lived glower   stare
     Far south the lift,   sky
Dim-darkening through the flaky shower,
     Or whirling drift :

Ae night the storm the steeples rocked,   one
Poor Labour sweet in sleep was locked,
While burns, wi' snawy wreathes up-choked,   rivulets
     Wild eddying swirl,
Or, through the mining outlet bocked,   vomited
     Down headlong hurl.

Listening, the doors and winnocks rattle,   windows
I thought me on the ourie cattle,   drooping
Or silly sheep, wha bide this brattle   rattle
     O' winter war,
And through the drift, deep-lairing, sprattle,   wading, scram-
     Beneath a scaur.   cliff [ble

Ilk happing bird, wee, helpless thing,   each hopping
That, in the merry months o' spring,
Delighted me to hear thee sing,
     What comes o' thee ?
Whare wilt thou cower thy chittering wing,   shivering
     And close thy ee ?   eye

Even you, on murdering errands toiled,
Lone from your savage homes exiled,
The blood-stained roost, and sheep-cot spoiled,
     My heart forgets
While pitiless the tempest wild
     Sore on you beats.

Now Phœbe, in her midnight reign,
Dark muffled, viewed the dreary plain ;
Still crowding thoughts, a pensive train,
     Rose in my soul,
When on my ear this plaintive strain
     Slow, solemn, stole :—

" Blow, blow ye winds with heavier gust !
And freeze, thou bitter-biting frost !
Descend, ye chilly, smothering snows !
Not all your rage, as now united, shows
     More hard unkindness, unrelenting,
     Vengeful malice unrepenting,
Than heaven-illumined man on brother man bestows

" See stern Oppression's iron grip,
Or mad Ambition's gory hand,

Sending, like bloodhounds from the slip,
  Woe, want, and murder o'er a land !
E'en in the peaceful rural vale,
Truth, weeping, tells the mournful tale,
How pampered Luxury, Flattery by her side,
  The parasite empoisoning her ear,
  With all the servile wretches in the rear,
Looks o'er proud Property, extended wide ;
  And eyes the simple rustic hind,
    Whose toil upholds the glittering show,
  A creature of another kind,
  Some coarser substance, unrefined,
Placed for her lordly use thus far, thus vile below

  " Where, where is love's fond, tender throe,
    With lordly Honour's lofty brow,
      The powers you proudly own ?
  Is there, beneath Love's noble name,
  Can harbour dark the selfish aim,
   · To bless himself alone !
  Mark maiden innocence a prey
    To love pretending snares,
  This boasted Honour turns away,
  Shunning soft Pity's rising sway,
Regardless of the tears and unavailing prayers !
  Perhaps this hour, in Misery's squalid nest,
  She strains your infant to her joyless breast,
And with a mother's fears shrinks at the rocking blast

  " Oh ye who, sunk in beds of down,
  Feel not a want but what yourselves create,
  Think for a moment on his wretched fate,
Whom friends and fortune quite disown !
Ill satisfied keen Nature's clamorous call,
  Stretched on his straw he lays himself to sleep,
While through the ragged roof and chinky wall,
  Chill o'er his slumbers piles the drifty heap !
    Think on the dungeon's grim confine,
    Where Guilt and poor Misfortune pine,
    Guilt, erring man, relenting view !
    But shall thy legal rage pursue
    The wretch already crushèd low
    By cruel Fortune's undeservèd blow ?
Affliction's sons are brothers in distress ;
A brother to relieve, how exquisite the bliss !"

  I heard nae mair, for Chanticleer   no moie
    Shook off the pouthery snaw,   powdery, snow
  And hailed the morning with a cheer,
    A cottage-rousing craw.

  But deep this truth impressed my mind—
    Through all his works abroad,
  The heart benevolent and kind
    The most resembles GOD.

GRACES BEFORE MEAT.

SOME hae meat and canna eat,   have, cannot
  And some would eat that want it;
But we hae meat and we can eat,
  Sae let the Lord be thankit.

O THOU, who kindly dost provide
  For every creature's want!
We bless Thee, God of Nature wide,
  For all thy goodness lent:
And, if it please Thee, heavenly guide,
  May never worse be sent;
But whether granted or denied,
  Lord, bless us with content!   *Amen !*

O THOU, in whom we live and move,
  Who mad'st the sea and shore;
Thy goodness constantly we prove,
  And grateful would adore.
And if it please Thee, Power above,
  Still grant us, with such store,
The friend we trust, the fair we love,
  And we desire no more.

WILLIE STEWART.

YOU'RE welcome, Willie Stewart;
  You're welcome, Willie Stewart;
There's ne'er a flower that blooms in May,
  That's half sae welcome's thou art.   so

Come, bumpers high, express your joy,
  The bowl we maun renew it;   must
The tappit-hen, gae bring her ben,   tin-quart, go, in
  To welcome Willie Stewart.

May foes be strang, and friends be slack,   strong
  Ilk action may he rue it;   each
May woman on him turn her back,
  That wrangs thee, Willie Stewart!   wrongs

VERSES TO JOHN M'MURDO, ESQ.:

WITH A PRESENT OF BOOKS.

OH, could I give thee India's wealth,
  As I this trifle send,
Because thy joy in both would be
  To share them with a friend!

But golden sands did never grace
   The Heliconean stream ;
Then take what gold could never buy--
   An honest Bard's esteem.

TO MISS JESSY LEWARS :

WITH A PRESENT OF BOOKS.

THINE be the volumes, Jessy fair,
And with them take the Poet's prayer—
That Fate may in her fairest page,
With every kindliest, best presage
Of future bliss, enrol thy name :
With native worth, and spotless fame,
And wakeful caution still aware
Of ill—but chief, man's felon snare ;
All blameless joys on earth we find,
And all the treasures of the mind—
These be thy guardian and reward ;
So prays thy faithful friend, the Bard.

ON SEEING MRS KEMBLE IN YARICO.

KEMBLE, thou cur'st my unbelief
   Of Moses and his rod ;
At Yarico's sweet notes of grief
   The rock with tears had flowed.

TO MR SYME :

WITH A PRESENT OF A DOZEN OF PORTER.

OH, had the malt thy strength of mind,
   Or hops the flavour of thy wit,
'Twere drink for first of human kind,
   A gift that even for Syme were fit.

TO THE SAME,

ON BEING PRESSED TO STAY AND DRINK MORE.

THERE'S Death in the cup, sae beware—
   Nay, mair, there is danger in touching ;
But wha can avoid the fell snare ?
   The man and his wine's sae bewitching.

TO THE SAME,

DECLINING AN INVITATION TO JOIN A DINNER PARTY.

No more of your guests, be they titled or not,
And cookery the first in the nation ;
Who is proof to thy personal converse and wit,
Is proof to all other temptation.

ON JOHN DOVE,

INNKEEPER, MAUCHLINE.

HERE lies Johnny Pigeon ;
What was his religion ?
Wha e'er desires to ken,
To some other warl'   world
Maun follow the carl,   musf follow
For here Johnny Pigeon had nane !

Strong ale was ablution—
Small beer persecution,
A dram was *memento mori ;*
But a full-flowing bowl
Was the joy of his soul,
And port was celestial glory.

ON MISS LEWARS' INDISPOSITION.

SAY, sages, what's the charm on earth
Can turn Death's dart aside ?
It is not purity and worth,
Else Jessy had not died.

MISS LEWARS RECOVERED A LITTLE

BUT rarely seen since Nature's birth,
The natives of the sky ;
Yet still one seraph's left on earth,
For Jessy did not die.

EPITAPH FOR ROBERT AIKEN, ESQ.

KNOW thou, O stranger to the Fame
Of this much-loved, much-honoured name !
For none that knew him need be told)
A warmer heart death ne'er made cold.

ON WEE JOHNNY.

Hic jacet wee Johnny.

WHOE'ER thou art, O reader, know
That death has murdered Johnny!
And here his body lies fu' low—
For saul he ne'er had ony.   soul

ON THE DEATH OF A HENPECKED COUNTRY SQUIRE.

ONE Queen Artemisia, as old stories tell,
When deprived of her husband she loved so well,
In respect for the love and affection he showed her,
She reduced him to dust, and she drank off the powder.

But Queen Netherplace, of a different complexion,
When called on to order the funeral direction,
Would have ate her dead lord, on a slender pretence,
Not to shew her respect, but—to save the expense!

TAM THE CHAPMAN.

As Tam the Chapman on a day
Wi' Death forgathered by the way,   met
Weel pleased, he greets a wight sae famous,   well, so
And Death was nae less pleased wi' Thamas,   no
Wha cheerfully lays down his pack,   who
And there blaws up a hearty crack;   blows
His social, friendly, honest heart
Sae tickled Death, they couldna part:
Sae, after viewing knives and garters,
Death taks him hame to gie him quarters.   home, give

ON MISS J. SCOTT, OF AYR.

OH, had each SCOT of ancient times,
Been JEANY SCOTT, as thou art;
The bravest heart on English ground,
Had yielded like a coward.

ON A WORM-EATEN EDITION OF SHAKSPEARE IN A NOBLEMAN'S LIBRARY.

THROUGH and through th' inspired leaves,
Ye maggots, make your windings;
But oh! respect his lordship's taste,
And spare the golden bindings.

ON MR W. CRUIKSHANK,

OF THE HIGH SCHOOL, EDINBURGH.

HONEST Will to heaven is gane,   gone
   And mony shall lament him ;   many
His faults they a' in Latin lay,
   In English nane e'er kent them.   none, knew

ON MISS BURNS.

CEASE, ye prudes, your envious railings,
   Lovely Burns has charms, confess :
True it is, she had one failing—
   Had a woman ever less ?

WRITTEN IN A COUNTRY CHURCH.

A CAULD, cauld day December blew,   cold
A cauld, cauld kirk, and in't but few ;
A caulder minister never spak,
Ye'se warmer be ere I come back.

ON A FRIEND.

AN honest man here lies at rest
As e'er God with his image blest !
The friend of man, the friend of truth ;
The friend of age, and guide of youth ;

Few hearts like his, with virtue warmed,
Few heads with knowledge so informed :
If there's another world, he lives in bliss ;
If there is none, he made the best of this.

HOWLET FACE.

How daur ye ca' me howlet-faced.   dare, owl
   Ye ugly, glowering spectre ?   staring
My face was but the keckin' glass,   looking
   An' there ye saw your picture.

THE SOLEMN LEAGUE AND COVENANT.

THE Solemn League and Covenant
Cost Scotland blood—cost Scotland tears;
But it sealed freedom's sacred cause—
If thou'rt a slave, indulge thy sneers.

ON A CERTAIN PARSON'S LOOKS.

THAT there is falsehood in his looks
I must and will deny;
They say their master is a knave—
And sure they do not lie.

ON MR M'MURDO.

INSCRIBED ON A PANE OF GLASS IN HIS HOUSE.

BLEST be M'Murdo to his latest day
No envious cloud o'ercast his evening ray;
No wrinkle furrowed by the hand of care,
Nor ever sorrow add one silver hair!
Oh, may no son the father's honour stain,
Nor ever daughter give the mother pain!

WRITTEN ON A WINDOW OF THE GLOBE TAVERN DUMFRIES.

THE graybeard, old Wisdom, may boast of his treasures,
  Give me with gay Folly to live;
I grant him his calm-blooded, time-settled pleasures,
  But Folly has raptures to give.

EXCISEMEN UNIVERSAL.

WRITTEN ON A WINDOW IN THE KING'S ARMS, DUMFRIES.

YE men of wit and wealth, why all this sneering
'Gainst poor excisemen? give the cause a hearing.
What are your landlords' rent-rolls? teasing ledgers:
What premiers—what? even monarchs' mighty gaugers: excisemen
Nay, what are priests, those seeming godly wise men?
What are they, pray, but spiritual excisemen?

ON A GROTTO IN FRIARS' CARSE GROUNDS.

To Riddel, much-lamented man,
  This ivied cot was dear;
Reader, dost value matchless worth ?
  This ivied cot revere.

ON A NOTED COXCOMB.

LIGHT lay the earth on Billy's breast,
  His chicken heart's so tender;
But build a castle on his head,
  His skull will prop it under.

ON A PERSON

BORING A COMPANY WITH REFERENCES TO THE MANY GREAT
PEOPLE HE HAD BEEN VISITING.

No more of your titled acquaintances boast,
  And in what lordly circles you've been:
An insect is still but an insect at most,
  Though it crawl on the head of a queen.

ON SEEING THE BEAUTIFUL SEAT OF THE EARL OF GALLOWAY.

WHAT dost thou in that mansion fair ?—
  Flit, Galloway, and find
Some narrow, dirty, dungeon cave,
  The picture of thy mind !

ON THE SAME.

No Stewart art thou, Galloway,
  The Stewarts all were brave;
Besides, the Stewarts were but fools,
  Not one of them a knave.

Bright ran thy line, O Galloway,
  Through many a far-famed sire !
So ran the far-famed Roman way,
  So ended in a mire.

TO THE SAME,

ON THE AUTHOR BEING THREATENED WITH HIS RESENTMENT

SPARE me thy vengeance, Galloway;
    In quiet let me live:
I ask no kindness at thy hand,
    For thou hast none to give.

TO MISS JESSY LEWARS:

ON A MENAGERIE OF WILD BEASTS.

TALK not to me of savages
    From Afric's burning sun;
No savage e'er could rend my heart,
    As, Jessy, thou hast done.
But Jessy's lovely hand in mine,
    A mutual faith to plight,
Not even to view the heavenly choir
    Would be so blest a sight.

TOAST,

WRITTEN ON A CRYSTAL GOBLET.

FILL me with the rosy wine,
Call a toast—a toast divine;
Give the poet's darling flame,
Lovely Jessy be the name;
Then thou mayest freely boast
Thou hast given a peerless toast.

SONGS.

HANDSOME NELL.

TUNE—*I am a man unmarried*

OH once I loved a bonnie lass,
  Ay, and I love her still ;
And whilst that honour warms my breast,
  I'll love my handsome Nell.

As bonnie lasses I hae seen,
  And mony full as braw ;
But for a modest, gracefu' mein,
  The like I never saw.

A bonnie lass, I will confess,
  Is pleasant to the ee,
But without some better qualities,
  She's no the lass for me.

But Nelly's looks are blithe and sweet,
  And, what is best of a',
Her reputation is complete,
  And fair without a flaw.

She dresses aye sae clean and neat,
  Both decent and genteel :
And then there's something in her gait
  Gars ony dress look weel.

A gaudy dress and gentle air
  May slightly touch the heart ;
But it's innocence and modesty
  That polishes the dart.

'Tis this in Nelly pleases me,
  'Tis this enchants my soul ;
For absolutely in my breast
  She reigns without control.

[Marginal glosses: yes; have; well dressed; eye; so; makes ony*]*

I DREAMED I LAY.

I DREAMED I lay where flowers were springing
  Gaily in the sunny beam;
Listening to the wild birds singing,
  By a falling, crystal stream:
Straight the sky grew black and daring;
  Through the woods the whirlwinds rave;
Trees with aged arms were warring,
  O'er the swelling drumlie wave.   troubled

Such was my life's deceitful morning,
  Such the pleasure I enjoyed;
But lang or noon, loud tempests storming,   long ere
  A' my flowery bliss destroyed.
Though fickle fortune has deceived me,
  She promised fair, and performed but ill;
Of mony a joy and hope bereaved me,   many
  I bear a heart shall support me still.

MY NANIE, O.

TUNE—*My Nanie, O.*

BEHIND yon hills where Lugar flows,
  'Mang moors and mosses many, O,   among
The wintry sun the day has closed,
  And I'll awa to Nanie, O.   away

The westlin wind blaws loud and shill; westerly, blows, shrill
  The night's baith mirk and rainy, O; both dark
But I'll get my plaid, and out I'll steal,
  And owre the hills to Nanie, O.   over

My Nanie's charming, sweet, and young;
  Nae artfu' wiles to win ye, O: no
May ill befa' the flattering tongue
  That wad beguile my Nanie, O!   would

Her face is fair, her heart is true,
  As spotless as she's bonnie, O:
The opening gowan, wet wi' dew,   daisy
  Nae purer is than Nanie. O.

A country lad is my degree,
  And few there be that ken me, O;   know
But what care I how few they be?
  I'm welcome aye to Nanie, O.

My riches a's my penny-fee,   all is, wages
  And I maun guide it cannie, O; must, carefully
But warl's gear ne'er troubles me, world's wealth
  My thoughts are a'—my Nanie, O.

Our auld guidman delights to view   *old goodman*
  His sheep and kye thrive bonnie, O ;   *cows*
But I'm as blithe that hauds his pleugh,   *holds, plough*
  And has nae care but Nanie, O.

Come weel, come woe, I care na by,   *not although*
  I'll tak what Heaven will send me, O ;
Nae ither care in life have I,   *other*
  But live and love my Nanie, O.

TIBBIE, I HAE SEEN THE DAY.

Tune—*Invercauld's Reel.*

Oh Tibbie, I hae seen the day   *have*
  Ye wad na been sae shy ;   *would not*
For lack o' gear ye lightly me,   *money, slight*
  But, trowth, I care na by.   *indeed, although*

Yestreen I met you on the moor,   *last night*
Ye spak na, but gaed by like stoure;   *spoke, went, dust*
Ye geck at me because I'm poor,   *mock*
  But not a hair care I.

I doubt na, lass, but ye may think,
Because ye hae the name o' clink,   *have, money*
That ye can please me at a wink,
  Whene'er you like to try.

But sorrow tak him that's sae mean,   *so*
Although his pouch o' coin were clean,
Wha follows ony saucy quean,   *who, any wench*
  That looks sae proud and high.

Although a lad were e'er sae smart,
If that he want the yellow dirt,
Ye'll cast your head another airt,   *direction*
  And answer him fu' dry.

But if he hae the name o' gear,   *wealth*
Ye'll fasten to him like a brier,
Though hardly he, for sense or lear,   *learning*
  Be better than the kye.   *cows*

But, Tibbie, lass, tak my advice,
Your daddie's gear maks you sae nice,   *father's*
There's no a ane wad speer your price,   *one, ask*
  Were ye as poor as I.

There lives a lass in yonder park,
I would na gi'e her in her sark,   *give, shift*
For thee, wi' a' thy thousan' mark ;
  Ye need na look sae high.

ON CESSNOCK BANKS.

Tune—If he be a butcher neat and trim.

ON Cessnock Banks there lives a lass ;
  Could I describe her shape and mien,
The graces of her weel-faured face,   well-favoured
  And the glancing of her sparkling een !   eyes

She's fresher than the morning dawn
  When rising Phœbus first is seen,
When dewdrops twinkle o'er the lawn ;
  And she's twa glancing sparkling een.   two

She's stately like yon youthful ash,
  That grows the cowslip braes between,   hillocks
And shoots its head above each bush ;
  And she's twa glancing sparkling een.

She's spotless as the flowering thorn,
  With flowers so white and leaves so green,
When purest in the dewy morn ;
  And she's twa glancing sparkling een.

Her looks are like the sportive lamb,
  When flowery May adorns the scene,
That wantons round its bleating dam ;
  And she's twa glancing sparkling een.

Her hair is like the curling mist
  That shades the mountain-side at e'en,
When flower-reviving rains are past ;
  And she's twa glancing sparkling een.

Her forehead's like the showery bow,
  When shining sunbeams intervene,
And gild the distant mountain's brow ;
  And she's twa glancing sparkling een.

Her voice is like the evening thrush
  That sings in Cessnock Banks unseen,
While his mate sits nestling in the bush ;
  And she's twa glancing sparkling een.

Her lips are like the cherries ripe
  That sunny walls from Boreas screen—
They tempt the taste and charm the sight ;
  And she's twa glancing sparkling een.

Her teeth are like a flock of sheep,
  With fleeces newly washen clean,
That slowly mount the rising steep ;
  And she's twa glancing sparkling een.

Her breath is like the fragrant breeze
  That gently stirs the blossomed bean,
When Phœbus sinks beneath the seas ;
  And she's twa glancing sparkling een.

Her cheeks are like yon crimson gem,
 The pride of all the flowery scene,
Just opening on its thorny stem ;
 And she's twa sparkling rogueish een.

But it's not her air, her form, her face,
 Though matching beauty's fabled queen,
But the mind that shines in every grace,
 And chiefly in her sparkling een.

MY FATHER WAS A FARMER.

Tune—*The Weaver and his Shuttle,* O.

My father was a farmer upon the Carrick border, O,
And carefully he bred me in decency and order, O ;
He bade me act a manly part, though I had ne'er a farthing, O ;
For without an honest manly heart no man was worth regard-
 ing, O.

Then out into the world my course I did determine, O ;
Though to be rich was not my wish, yet to be great was charm-
 ing, O :
My talents they were not the worst, nor yet my education, O ;
Resolved was I, at least to try, to mend my situation, O.

In many a way, and vain essay, I courted Fortune's favour, O ;
Some cause unseen still stept between, to frustrate each en-
 deavour, O.
Sometimes by foes I was o'erpowered, sometimes by friends for-
 saken, O ;
And when my hope was at the top, I still was worst mistaken, O.

Then sore harassed, and tired at last, with Fortune's vain delu-
 sion, O,
I dropt my schemes, like idle dreams, and came to this conclu-
 sion, O—
The past was bad, and the future hid—its good or ill untried, O ;
But the present hour was in my power, and so I would enjoy it, O.

No help, nor hope, nor view had I, nor person to befriend me, O ;
So I must toil, and sweat, and broil, and labour to sustain me, O ;
To plough and sow, to reap, and mow, my father bred me early, O ;
For one, he said, to labour bred, was a match for Fortune fairly, O.

Thus all obscure, unknown, and poor, through life I'm doomed to
 wander, O,
Till down my weary bones I lay, in everlasting slumber, O.
No view nor care, but shun whate'er might breed me pain or
 sorrow, O !
I live to-day as well's I may, regardless of to-morrow, O.

But cheerful still I am as well as a monarch in a palace, O,
Though Fortune's frown still haunts me down with all her wonted
 malice, O :

I make indeed my daily bread, but ne'er can make it farther, O;
But as daily bread is all I need, I do not much regard her. O.

When sometimes by my labour I earn a little money, O,
Some unforseen misfortune comes generally upon me, O:
Mischance, mistake, or by neglect, or my good-natured folly, O:
But come what will, I've sworn it still, I'll ne'er be melancholy, O.

All you who follow wealth and power with unremitting ardour, O,
The more in this you look for bliss, you leave your view the
    farther, O:
Had you the wealth Potosi boasts, or nations to adore you, **O,**
A cheerful honest-hearted clown I will prefer before you, O.

JOHN BARLEYCORN.

A BALLAD.

THERE were three kings into the east,
  Three kings both great and high;
And they hae sworn a solemn oath   have
  John Barleycorn should die.

They took a plough and ploughed him down,
  Put clods upon his head;
And they hae sworn a solemn oath
  John Barleycorn was dead.

But the cheerful Spring came kindly **on,**
  And showers began to fall;
John Barleycorn got up again,
  And sore surprised them all.

The sultry sons of Summer came,
  And he grew thick and strong;
His head weel armed wi' pointed spears,
  That no one should him wrong.

The sober Autumn entered mild,
  When he grew wan and pale;
His bending joints and drooping head
  Showed he began to fail.

His colour sickened more and more,
  He faded into age;
And then his enemies began
  To show their deadly rage.

They've taen a weapon, long and sharp,   taken
  And cut him by the knee;
Then tied him fast upon a cart,
  Like a rogue for forgerie.

They laid him down upon his back,
  And cudgelled him full sore;
They hung him up before the storm,
  And turned him o'er and o'er.

They fillèd up a darksome pit
  With water to the brim;
They heavèd in John Barleycorn,
  There let him sink or swim.

They laid him out upon the floor
  To work him farther wo;
And still, as signs of life appeared,
  They tossed him to and fro.

They wasted o'er a scorching flame
  The marrow of his bones;
But a miller used him worst of all,
  For he crushed him 'tween two stones.

And they hae taen his very heart's blood, taken
  And drunk it round and round;
And still the more and more they drank,
  Their joy did more abound.

John Barleycorn was a hero bold,
  Of noble enterprise;
For if you do but taste his blood,
  'Twill make your courage rise. •

'Twill make a man forget his wo;
  'Twill heighten all his joy:
'Twill make the widow's heart to sing,
  Though the tear were in her eye.

Then let us toast John Barleycorn,
  Each man a glass in hand;
And may his great posterity
  Ne'er fail in old Scotland!

MARY MORRISON.

Oh, Mary, at thy window be,
  It is the wished, the trysted hour!
Those smiles and glances let me see,
  That make the miser's treasure poor:
How blithely wad I bide the stoure, would, dust
  A weary slave frae sun to sun, from
Could I the rich reward secure,
  The lovely Mary Morrison.

Yestreen when to the trembling string, last night
  The dance gaed through the lighted ha', went
To thee my fancy took its wing,
  I sat, but neither heard nor saw.
Though this was fair, and that was braw,
  And yon the toast of a' the town,
I sighed, and said amang them a',
  "Ye are na Mary Morrison." not

Oh, Mary, canst thou wreck his peace,
  Wha for thy sake wad gladly die?   who, would
Or canst thou break that heart of his,
  Whase only faut is loving thee?   whose, fault
If love for love thou wilt na gie,   give
  At least be pity to me shown;
A thought ungentle canna be   cannot
  The thought o' Mary Morrison.

THE RIGS O' BARLEY.

TUNE—*Corn Rigs.*

It was upon a Lammas night,
  When corn rigs are bonnie,   ridges
Beneath the moon's unclouded light,
  I held awa to Annie: away
The time flew by wi' tentless heed,   unnoticed
Till 'tween the late and early,
Wi' sma' persuasion she agreed
  To see me through the barley.

The sky was blue, the wind was still,
  The moon was shining clearly;
I set her down wi' right good will
  Amang the rigs o' barley;   among
I ken't her heart was a' my ain;   knew, own
  I loved her most sincerely;
I kissed her owre and owre again,   over
  Amang the rigs o' barley.

I locked her in my fond embrace;
  Her heart was beating rarely:
My blessings on that happy place,
  Amang the rigs o' barley!
But by the moon and stars so bright
  That shone that hour so clearly!
She aye shall bless that happy night,
  Amang the rigs o' barley.

I hae been blithe wi' comrades dear;
  I hae been merry drinkin';
I hae been joyfu' gath'rin' gear;   money
  I hae been happy thinkin':
But a' the pleasures e'er I saw,
  Though three times doubled fairly,
That happy night was worth them a',
  Amang the rigs o' barley.

CHORUS.

  Corn rigs, and barley rigs,
    And corn rigs are bonnie:
  I'll ne'er forget that happy night
    Amang the rigs wi' Annie.

MONTGOMERY'S PEGGY.

TUNE—*Gala Water.*

ALTHOUGH my bed were in yon muir
    Amang the heather, in my plaidie,   among
Yet happy, happy would I be,
    Had I my dear Montgomery's Peggy.

When o'er the hill beat surly storms,
    And winter nights were dark and rainy ;
I'd seek some dell, and in my arms
    I'd shelter dear Montgomery's Peggy.

Were I a baron proud and high,
    And horse and servants waiting ready,
Then a' 'twad gie o' joy to me,   twould, give
    The sharin't with Montgomery's Peggy.   sharing it

SONG COMPOSED IN AUGUST.

TUNE—*I had a horse, I had nae mair.*

Now westlin winds and slaught'ring guns   western
    Bring Autumn's pleasant weather ;
The moorcock springs, on whirring wings,
    Amang the blooming heather :   among
Now waving grain, wide o'er the plain,
    Delights the weary farmer ;
And the moon shines bright, when I rove at night
    To muse upon my charmer.

The partridge loves the fruitful fells ;
    The plover loves the mountains ;
The woodcock haunts the lonely dells ;
    The soaring hern the fountains :   heron
Through lofty groves the cushat roves.   wood-pigeon
    The path of man to shun it ;
The hazel bush o'erhangs the thrush,
    The spreading thorn the linnet.

Thus every kind their pleasure find,
    The savage and the tender ;
Some social join, and leagues combine ;
    Some solitary wander :
Avaunt, away ! the cruel sway,
    Tyrannic man's dominion ;
The sportsman's joy, the murdering cry,
    The fluttering gory pinion.

But Peggy, dear, the evening's clear,
    Thick flies the skimming swallow ;
The sky is blue, the fields in view,
    All fading-green and yellow :

Come, let us stray our gladsome way,
  And view the charms of nature ;
The rustling corn, the fruited thorn,
  And every happy creature.

We'll gently walk, and sweetly talk,
  Till the silent moon shine clearly ;
I'll grasp thy waist, and fondly prest,
  Swear how I love thee dearly :
Not vernal showers to budding flowers,
  Not Autumn to the farmer,
So dear can be as thou to me,
  My fair, my lovely charmer !

GREEN GROW THE RASHES.

Tune—*Green grow the Rashes.*

THERE'S nought but care on every han',
  In every hour that passes, O :
What signifies the life o' man,
  An 'twere na for the lasses, O.

CHORUS.

Green grow the rashes, O !   rashes
  Green grow the rashes, O !
The sweetest hour that e'er I spend
Are spent among the lasses, O.

The warly race may riches chase,   worldly
  And riches still may fly them, O ;
And though at last they catch them fast,
  Their hearts can ne'er enjoy them, O.

But gie me a canny hour at e'en,   give, happy
  My arms about my dearie, O ;
And warly cares, and warly men,
  May a' gae tapsalteerie, O.   topsy-turvy

For you sae douce, ye sneer at this,   sc grave
  Ye're nought but senseless asses, O :
The wisest man the warl' e'er saw,
  He dearly loved the lasses, O.

Auld Nature swears, the lovely dears
  Her noblest work she classes, O :
Her 'prentice hand she tried on man,
  And then she made the lasses, O.

THE CURE FOR ALL CARE.

Tune—*Prepare, my dear Brethren, to the tavern let's fly.*

No churchman am I for to rail and to write,
No statesman nor soldier to plot or to fight,
No sly man of business contriving a snare—
For a big-bellied bottle's the whole of my care.

The peer I don't envy, I give him his bow;
I scorn not the peasant, though ever so low;
But a club of good fellows, like those that are here,
And a bottle like this, are my glory and care.

Here passes the squire on his brother—his horse;
There centum per centum, the cit with his purse;
But see you The Crown, how it waves in the air!
There a big-bellied bottle still eases my care.

The wife of my bosom, alas! she did die;
For sweet consolation to church I did fly;
I found that old Solomon provèd it fair,
That a big-bellied bottle's a cure for all care.

I once was persuaded a venture to make;
A letter informed me that all was to wreck;—
But the pursy old landlord just waddled up stairs,
With a glorious bottle that ended my cares.

' Life's cares, they are comforts"—a maxim laid down
By the bard, what d'ye call him that wore the black gown;
And, faith, I agree with th' old prig to a hair;
For a big-bellied bottle's a heaven of care.

ADDED IN A MASON LODGE.

Then fill up a bumper, and make it o'erflow,
And honours masonic prepare for to throw;
May every true brother of th' compass and square
Have a big-bellied bottle when harassed with care.

FRAGMENT.

TUNE—*John Anderson, my Jo.*

ONE night as I did wander,
 When corn begins to shoot,
I sat me down to ponder,
 Upon an auld tree-root.   old

Auld Ayr ran by before me,
 And bickered to the seas,   raced
A cushat crooded o'er me,   wood-pigeon, cooing
 That echoed through the braes.

ROBIN.

TUNE—*Dainty Davie.*

THERE was a lad was born in Kyle,
But whatna day o' whatna style,   which
I doubt it's hardly worth my while
 To be sae nice with Robin.   so
  Robin was a rovin' boy,
   Rantin' rovin', rantin' rovin';
  Robin was a rovin' boy,
   Rantin' rovin' Robin!

Our monarch's hindmost year but ane   one
Was five-and-twenty days begun,
'Twas then a blast o' Janwar' win'   January
   Blew handsel in on Robin.   a gift

The gossip keekit in his loof,   peeped, palm
Quo' scho, wha lives will see the proof,   she, who
This waly boy will be nae coof;   goodly, no fool
   I think we'll ca' him Robin.

He'll hae misfortunes great and sma,   have
But aye a heart aboon them a';   above
He'll be a credit till us a'—
   We'll a' be proud o' Robin.

But sure as three times three mak nine,
I see by ilka score and line,   every
This chap will dearly like our kin',   fellow
   So lecze me on thee, Robin.   blessings

A FRAGMENT.

TUNE—*I had a horse, I had nae mair*

WHEN first I came to Stewart Kyle,
   My mind it was na steady,   not
Where'er I gaed, where'er I rade,   went, rode
   A SWEETHEART still I had aye.   always

But when I came roun' by Mauchline toun,   town
   Not dreadin' anybody,
My heart was caught before I thought,
   And by a Mauchline lady.

LUCKLESS FORTUNE.

OH raging fortune's withering blast
   Has laid my leaf full low, O!
Oh raging fortune's withering blast
   Has laid my leaf full low, O!

My stem was fair, my bud was green,
   My blossom sweet did blow, O;
The dew fell fresh, the sun rose mild,
   And made my branches grow, O.

But luckless fortune's northern storms
   Laid a' my blossoms low, O,
But luckless fortune's northern storms
   Laid a' my blossoms low, O.

THE BRAES O' BALLOCHMYLE.*

THE Catrine woods were yellow seen,
   The flowers decayed on Catrine lea,

* Composed on the amiable and excellent family of Whitefoord's leaving Ballochmyle, when Sir John's misfortunes obliged him to sell the estate.—*B.*

Nae lav'rock sang on hillock green,   lark
But Nature sickened on the ee.   eye

Through faded groves Maria sang,
   Hersel in beauty's bloom the while,   herself
And aye the wild-wood echoes rang,
   Fareweel the Braes of Ballochmyle !

Low in your wintry beds, ye flowers,
   Again ye'll flourish fresh and fair ;
Ye birdies dumb, in with'ring bowers,
   Again ye'll charm the vocal air.
But here, alas ! for me nae mair   no more
   Shall birdie charm, or flow'ret smile:
Fareweel the bonnie banks of Ayr,
   Fareweel, fareweel ! sweet Ballochmyle !

I AM A SON OF MARS.

TUNE—*Soldiers' Joy.*

I AM a son of Mars, who have been in many wars,
And show my cuts and scars wherever I come ;
This here was for a wench, and that other in a trench,
When welcoming the French at the sound of the drum.
      Lal de daudle, &c.

My 'prenticeship I past where my leader breathed his last,
When the bloody die was cast on the heights of Abram ;
I served out my trade when the gallant game was played,
And the Morro low was laid at the sound of the drum.
      Lal de daudle, &c.

I lastly was with Curtis, among the floating batteries,
And there I left for witness an arm and a limb;
Yet let my country need me, with Elliot to head me,
I'd clatter on my stumps at the sound of a drum.
      Lal de daudle, &c.

And now though I must beg with a wooden arm and leg,
And many a tatter'd rag hanging over my bum,
I'm as happy with my wallet, my bottle and my callet,
As when I used in scarlet to follow a drum.
      Lal de daudle, &c.

JOHN HIGHLANDMAN.

TUNE—*O an ye were dead Guidman.*

A HIGHLAND lad my love was born,
The Lawland laws he held in scorn,   lowland
But he still was faithfu' to his clan,
My gallant braw John Highlandman.

CHORUS.
Sing, hey my braw John Highlandman !
Sing, ho my braw John Highlandman !

There's not a lad in a' the lan'
Was match for my John Highlandman.

With his philabeg and tartan plaid,   **kilt**
And guid claymore down by his side,   good broad-sword
The ladies' hearts he did trepan,
My gallant braw John Highlandman.
    Sing, hey, &c.

We rangèd a' from Tweed to Spey,
And lived like lords and ladies gay ;
For a Lawland face he fearèd none,
My gallant braw John Highlandman
    Sing, hey, &c.

They banished him beyond the sea,
But ere the bud was on the tree,
Adown my cheeks the pearls ran,
Embracing my John Highlandman.
    Sing, hey, &c.

But, oh ! they catched him at the last,
And bound him in a dungeon fast ;
My BAN upon them every one,
They've hanged my braw John Highlandman.
    Sing, hey, &c.

And now a widow, I must mourn
The pleasures that will ne'er return ;
No comfort but a hearty can,
When I think on John Highlandman.
    Sing, hey, &c.

I AM A FIDDLER.

TUNE—*Whistle o'er the lave o't.*

LET me ryke up to dight that tear,   reach, wipe
And go wi' me and be my dear,
And then your every care and fear
    May whistle owre the lave o't.   over, rest

CHORUS.

I am a fiddler to my trade,
And a' the tunes that e'er I played,
The sweetest still to wife or maid,
    Was whistle o'er the lave o't.

At kirns and weddings we'se be there, harvest homes,we'll
And oh ! sae nicely's we will fare ;   so
We'll bouse about till Daddy Care   drink
    Sings whistle o'er the lave o't.
    I am, &c.

Sae merrily the banes we'll pyke,   bones, pick
And sun oursels about the dike,
And at our leisure, when ye like,
    We'll whistle owre the lave o't.
    I am, &c.

But bless me wi' your heaven o' charms,
And while I kittle hair on thairms,   *scrape on fiddle*
Hunger, cauld, and a' sic harms,   *cold, such*
    May whistle o'er the lave o't.
        I am, &c.

I'VE TA'EN THE GOLD.

TUNE—*Clout the Caudron.*

MY bonny lass, I work in brass,
    A tinkler is my station :   *tinker*
I've travelled round all Christian ground
    In this my occupation :
I've ta'en the gold, I've been enrolled
    In many a noble squadron :
But vain they searched, when off I marched
    To go and clout the caudron.   *patch*
        I've ta'en the gold, &c.

Despise that shrimp, that withered imp,
    Wi' a his noise and cap'rin',
And tak a share wi' those that bear
    The budget and the apron.
And by that stoup, my faith and houp,   *flagon, hope*
    And by that dear Kilbagie,   *whisky*
If e'er you want, or meet wi' scant,
    May I ne'er weet my craigie.   *throat*
        And by that stoup, &c.

I AM A BARD.

TUNE—*For a' that, and a' that.*

1 AM a bard of no regard
    Wi' gentle folks, and a' that ;
But Homer-like, the glowrin' byke,   *staring multitude*
    Frae town to town I draw that.   *from*

CHORUS.

    For a' that, and a' that,
        And twice as muckle's a' that,   *much*
    I've lost but ane, I've twa behin,   *one, two*
    I've wife eneugh for a' that.   *enough*

I never drank the Muse's stank,   *pool*
    Castalia's burn and a' that ;
But there it streams, and richly reams,
    My Helicon I ca' that,
        For a' that, &c.

Great love I bear to a' the fair,
    Their humble slave and a' that ;
But lordly will, I hold it still
    A mortal sin to thraw that.   *oppose*
        For a' that, &c.

Their tricks and craft have put me daft,   *stupid*
    They've ta'en me in, and a' that ;

But clear your decks, and here's the sex ;
I like the jads for a' that.   jades

CHORUS.

For a' that, and a' that,
And twice as muckle's a' that ;
My dearest bluid, to do them guid,   blood, good
They're welcome till't for a' that

YOUNG PEGGY.

TUNE—*Last time I came o'er the muir.*

YOUNG Peggy blooms our bonniest lass
Her blush is like the morning,
The rosy dawn, the springing grass,
    With early gems adorning :
Her eyes outshine the radiant beam.
    That gild the passing shower,
And glitter o'er the crystal streams,
    And cheer each freshening flower.

Her lips, more than the cherries bright,
    A richer dye has graced them ;
They charm th admiring gazer's sight,
    And sweetly tempt to taste them :
Her smile is, as the evening, mild,
    When feathered tribes are courting,
And little lambkins wanton wild,
    In playful bands disporting.

Were Fortune lovely Peggy's foe,
    Such sweetness would relent her,
As blooming Spring unbends the brow
    Of surly, savage Winter.
Detraction's eye no aim can gain,
    Her winning powers to lessen ;
And fretful envy grins in vain
    The poisoned tooth to fasten.

Ye powers of honour, love, and truth,
    From every ill defend her ;
Inspire the highly-favoured youth
    The destinies intend her :
Still fan the sweet connubial flame
    Responsive in each bosom,
And bless the dear parental name
    With many a filial blossom.

SONG.

AGAIN rejoicing Nature sees
    Her robe assume its vernal hues ;
Her leafy locks wave in the breeze,
    All freshly steeped in morning dews

In vain to me the cowslips blaw,   blow
 In vain to me the violets spring;
In vain to me, in glen or shaw,   wood
. The mavis and the lintwhite sing. thrush, linnet

The merry ploughboy cheers his team,
 Wi' joy the tentie seedsman stalks; heedful
But life to me's a weary dream,
 A dream of ane that never wauks. one, wakes

The wanton coot the water skims,
 Amang the reeds the ducklings cry,
The stately swan majestic swims,
 And everything is blest but I.
           [in fold
The shepherd steeks his faulding slap, closes, opening
 And owre the moorland whistles shrill;
Wi' wild, unequal, wandering step,
 I meet him on the dewy hill.

And when the lark, 'tween light and dark,
 Blithe wankens by the daisy's side, awakes
And mounts and sings on flittering wings,
 A woe-worn ghaist I hameward glide. ghost

Come, Winter, with thine angry howl,
 And raging bend the naked tree:
Thy gloom will soothe my cheerless soul,
 When Nature all is sad like me!

THE HIGHLAND LASSIE.

Nae gentle dames, though e'er sae fair, no, highborn
Shall ever be my Muse's care:
Their titles a' are empty show;
Gie me my Highland lassie, O.   give

 Within the glen sae bushy, O,   so
 Aboon the plains sae rushy, O, above
 I set me down wi' right good-will,
 To sing my Highland lassie, O.

Oh were yon hills and valleys mine,
Yon palace and yon gardens fine!
The world then the love should know
I bear my Highland lassie, O.

But fickle fortune frowns on me,
And I maun cross the raging sea; must
But while my crimson currents flow,
I'll love my Highland lassie, O.

Although through foreign climes I range,
I know her heart will never change,
For her bosom burns with honour's glow,
My faithful Highland lassie, O.

For her I'll dare the billows' roar,
For her I'll trace a distant shore,
That Indian wealth may lustre throw
Around my Highland lassie, O.

She has my heart, she has my hand,
By sacred truth and honour's band!
'Till the mortal stroke shall lay me low,
I'm thine, my Highland lassie, O.

Farewell the glen sae bushy, O!
Farewell the plain sae rushy, O!
To other lands I now must go,
To sing my Highland lassie, O

———

MARY.

POWERS celestial! whose protection
Ever guards the virtuous fair,
While in distant climes I wander,
Let my Mary be your care:
Let her form sae fair and faultless,
Fair and faultless as your own,
Let my Mary's kindred spirit
Draw your choicest influence down.

Make the gales you waft around her
Soft and peaceful as her breast;
Breathing in the breeze that fans her,
Soothe her bosom into rest:
Guardian angels! oh protect her
When in distant lands I roam;
To realms unknown while fate exiles me,
Make her bosom still my home.

———

WILL YE GO TO THE INDIES, MY MARY!

WILL ye go to the Indies, my Mary,
And leave auld Scotia's shore?   old
Will ye go to the Indies, my Mary,
Across the Atlantic's roar?

Oh sweet grow the lime and the orange,
And the apple on the pine;
But a' the charms o' the Indies   all
Can never equal thine.

I hae sworn by the Heavens to my Mary,   have
I hae sworn by the Heavens to be true;
And sae may the Heavens forget me
When I forget my vow!

Oh plight me your faith, my Mary,
  And plight me your lily-white hand;
Oh plight me your faith, my Mary,
  Before I leave Scotia's strand.

We hae plighted our troth, my Mary,
  In mutual affection to join;
And curst be the cause that shall part us!
  The hour and the moment o' time!

ELIZA.

TUNE—*Gilderoy.*

FROM thee, Eliza, I must go,
  And from my native shore:
The cruel fates between us throw
  A boundless ocean's roar;
But boundless oceans, roaring wide
  Between my love and me,
They never, never can divide
  My heart and soul from thee.

Farewell, farewell, Eliza dear,
  The maid that I adore!
A boding voice is in my ear,
  We part to meet no more!
But the last throb that leaves my heart,
  While death stands victor by,
That throb, Eliza, is thy part,
  And thine that latest sigh!

THOUGH CRUEL FATE.

TUNE—*The Northern Lass.*

THOUGH cruel fate should bid us part,
  Far as the pole and line;
Her dear idea round my heart
  Should tenderly entwine.

Though mountains rise, and deserts howl,
  And oceans roar between,
Yet dearer than my deathless soul,
  I still would love my Jean.

FAREWELL TO THE BRETHREN OF ST JAMES'S LODGE, TORBOLTON.

TUNE—*Good-night, and joy be wi' you a'.*

ADIEU! a heart-warm, fond adieu!
  Dear brothers of the *mystic tie!*
Ye favoured, ye *enlightened* few,
  Companions of my social joy;

Though I to foreign lands must hie,
  Pursuing Fortune's slidd'ry ba',   slippery ball
With melting heart, and brimful eye
  I'll mind you still, though far awa.

Oft have I met your social band,
  And spent the cheerful, festive night;
Oft, honoured with supreme command,
  Presided o'er the *Sons of Light:*
And by that *hieroglyphic* bright
  Which none but *Craftsman* ever saw
Strong Memory on my heart shall write
  Those happy scenes when far awa.

May Freedom, Harmony, and Love,
  Unite you in the *grand design,*
Beneath the Omniscient Eye above,
  The glorious Architect Divine!
That you may keep th' *unerring line,*
  Still rising by the *plummet's law,*
Till Order bright completely shine,
  Shall be my prayer when far awa.

And *you*, farewell! whose merits claim,
  Justly, that *highest badge* to wear!
Heaven bless your honoured, noble name,
  To *masonry* and *Scotia* dear!
A last request permit me here,
  When yearly ye assemble a',
One *round*—I ask it with a *tear*—
  To him, *the Bard that's far awa.*

THE SONS OF OLD KILLIE.

TUNE—*Shawnboy.*

YE sons of old Killie, assembled by Willie,
  To follow the noble vocation;
Your thrifty old mother has scarce such another
  To sit in that honoured station.
I've little to say, but only to pray,
  As praying's the ton of your fashion;
A prayer from the Muse you well may excuse,
  'Tis seldom her favourite passion.

Ye powers who preside o'er the wind and the tide,
  Who markèd each element's border;
Who formèd this frame with beneficent aim,
  Whose sovereign statute is order;
Within this dear mansion may wayward contention
  Or witherèd envy ne'er enter;
May secrecy round be the mystical bound,
  And brotherly love be the centre.

THE BONNIE LASS O' BALLOCHMYLE.

'TWAS even—the dewy fields were green,
  On every blade the pearls hang!
The Zephyr wantoned round the bean,
  And bore its fragrant sweets alang;
In every glen the mavis sang,
  All Nature listening seemed the while,
Except where greenwood echoes rang,
  Amang the braes o' Ballochmyle.

With careless step I onward strayed,
  My heart rejoiced in Nature's joy,
When, musing in a lonely glade,
  A maiden fair I chanced to spy;
Her look was like the morning's eye,
  Her air like Nature's vernal smile,
Perfection whispered passing by,
  Behold the lass o' Ballochmyle!

Fair is the morn in flowery May,
  And sweet is night in Autumn mild;
When roving through the garden gay,
  Or wandering in the lonely wild:
But woman, Nature's darling child!
  There all her charms she does compile,
Even there her other works are foiled
  By the bonnie lass o' Ballochmyle.

Oh had she been a country maid,
  And I the happy country swain!
Though sheltered in the lowest shed
  That ever rose on Scotland's plain,
Through weary Winter's wind and rain,
  With joy, with rapture, I would toil;
And nightly to my bosom strain
  The bonny lass o' Ballochmyle.

Then pride might climb the slippery steep,
  Where fame and honours lofty shine;
And thirst of gold might tempt the deep
  Or downward seek the Indian mine;
Give me the cot below the pine,
  To tend the flocks, or till the soil,
And every day have joys divine
  With the bonny lass o' Ballochmyle.

along
thrush

THE GLOOMY NIGHT IS GATHERING FAST.

TUNE.—*Roslin Castle.*

THE gloomy night is gathering fast,
Loud roars the wild inconstant blast;
Yon murky cloud is foul with rain,
I see it driving o'er the plain;

The hunter now has left the moor,
The scattered coveys meet secure
While here I wander, pressed with care,
Along the lonely banks of Ayr.

The Autumn mourns her ripening corn,
By early Winter's ravage torn;
Across her placid, azure sky,
She sees the scowling tempest fly;
Chill runs my blood to hear it rave—
I think upon the stormy wave,
Where many a danger I must dare,
Far from the bonny banks of Ayr.

'Tis not the surging billow's roar,
'Tis not that fatal deadly shore;
Though death in every shape appear,
The wretched have no more to fear!
But round my heart the ties are bound,
That heart transpierced with many a wound;
These bleed afresh, those ties I tear,
To leave the bonny banks of Ayr.

Farewell old Coila's hills and dales,
Her heathy moors and winding vales;
The scenes where wretched fancy roves,
Pursuing past, unhappy loves!
Farewell, my friends! farewell, my foes
My peace with these, my love with those—
The bursting tears my heart declare;
Farewell the bonny banks of Ayr!

THE AMERICAN WAR:

A POLITICAL BALLAD.

TUNE—*Killiecrankie.*

WHEN Guildford good our pilot stood,	
And did our helm thraw, man,	turn
Ae night, at tea, began a plea,	one
Within America, man:	
Then up they gat the maskin'-pat,	got, infusing-pot
And in the sea did jaw, man;	dash
And did nae less, in full Congress,	no
Than quite refuse our law, man.	

Then through the lakes Montgomery takes,	
I wat he was na slaw, man;	know, not slow
Down Lowrie's burn he took a turn,	
And Carleton did ca', man;	
But yet, what-reck, he, at Quebec,	
Montgomery-like did fa', man,	fall
Wi' sword in hand, before his band,	
Amang his en'mies a', man.	among

Poor Tammy Gage, within a cage,
  Was kept at Boston ha', man;   hall
Till Willie Howe took o'er the knowe   knoll
  For Philadelphia, man;
Wi' sword and gun he thought a sin
  Guid Christian blood to draw, man: good
But at New York, wi' knife and fork,
  Sir-loin he hackèd sma', man.   small

Burgoyne gaed up, like spur and whip, went
  Till Fraser brave did fa', man;
Then lost his way, ae misty day,
  In Saratoga shaw, man.   wood
Cornwallis fought as lang's he dought, was able
  And did the buckskins claw, man;   scratch
But Clinton's glaive frae rust to save, sword from
  He hung it to the wa', man.   wall

Then Montague, and Guildford too,
  Began to fear a fa', man;
And Sackville dour, wha stood the stoure, obdurate, who, dust
  The German Chief to thraw, man: thwart
For Paddy Burke, like ony Turk,   any
  Nae mercy had at a', man;   all
And Charlie Fox threw by the box,
  And lows'd his tinkler jaw, man. loosed, tinker tongue

Then Rockingham took up the game
  Till death did on him ca', man;   call
When Shelburne meek held up his cheek,
  Conform to gospel law, man;
Saint Stephen's boys, wi' jarring noise,
  They did his measures thraw, man, thwart
For North and Fox united stocks,
  And bore him to the wa', man.

Then clubs and hearts were Charlie's cartes, cards
  He swept the stakes awa', man,
Till the diamond's ace, of Indian race,
  Led him a sair FALSE STEP, man; sore
The Saxon lads, wi' loud placads,   cheers
  On Chatham's boy did ca', man;
And Scotland drew her pipe, and blew,
  "Up, Willie, waur them a, man!" overcome

Behind the throne then Grenville's gone,
  A secret word or twa, man;   two
While slee Dundas aroused the class, sly
  Be-north the Roman wa', man:
And Chatham's wraith, in heavenly graith, ghost, armour
  (Inspirèd Bardies saw, man)
Wi' kindling eyes cried, "Willie, rise!
  Would I hae fear'd them a', man?" have

But, word and blow, North, Fox, and Co.,
  Gowff'd Willie like a ba', man, struck, ball

Till Suthron raise, and coost their claise   threw off, clothes
  Behind him in a raw, man;   row
And Caledon threw by the drone,   bagpipe
  And did her whittle draw, man ;   knife
And swoor fu' rude, through dirt and blood,   swore
  To make it guid in law, man.   good

      *   *   *   *   *   *

THE BIRKS OF ABERFELDY.

TUNE—*The Birks of Abergeldy.*

CHORUS.

BONNIE lassie, will ye go,
Will ye go, will ye go ;
Bonnie lassie, will ye go,
  To the birks of Aberfeldy ?

Now simmer blinks on flowery braes,   glances
And o'er the crystal streamlet plays ;
Come, let us spend the lightsome days
  In the birks of Aberfeldy.

The little birdies blithely sing,
While o'er their heads the hazels hing,   hang
Or lightly flit on wanton wing
  In the birks of Aberfeldy.

The braes ascend, like lofty wa's,   walls
The foamy stream deep-roaring fa's,
O'erhung wi' fragrant spreading shaws,   woods
  The birks of Aberfeldy.

The hoary cliffs are crown'd wi' flowers,
White o'er the linns the burnie pours,   cascades
And rising, weets wi' misty showers   wets
  The birks of Aberfeldy.

Let Fortune's gifts at Random flee,
They ne'er shall draw a wish frae me,   from
Supremely blest wi' love and thee,
  In the birks of Aberfeldy.

BLITHE WAS SHE.

TUNE—*Andro and his Cutty Gun.*

CHORUS.

BLITHE, blithe and merry was she,
  Blithe was she butt and ben :
Blithe by the banks of Earn,
  And blithe in Glenturit Glen

By Auchtertyre grows the aik,   oak
  On Yarrow banks the birken shaw;   birch woods
But Phemie was a bonnier lass
  Than braes o' Yarrow ever saw.

Her looks were like a flower in May,
  Her smile was like a simmer morn;
She tripped by the banks o' Earn,
  As light's a bird upon a thorn.

Her bonnie face it was as meek
  As ony lamb upon a lea;   anv, meadow
The evening sun was ne'er sae sweet   so
  As was the blink o' Phemie's ee.   eye

The Highland hills I've wandered wide,
  And o'er the lowlands I ha'e been;   have
But Phemie was the blithest lass
  That ever trod the dewy green.

THE ROSE-BUD.

TUNE—*The Shepherd's Wife.*

A ROSE-BUD by my early walk,
Adown a corn-enclosèd hawk,   open space
Sae gently bent its thorny stalk,   so
  All on a dewy morning.
Ere twice the shades o' dawn are fled,
In a' its crimson glory spread,
And drooping rich the dewy head,
  It scents the early morning.

Within the bush, her covert nest,
A little linnet fondly prest,
The dew sat chilly on her breast
  Sae early in the morning.
She soon shall see her tender brood,
The pride, the pleasure o' the wood,
Amang the fresh green leaves bedewed,
  Awake the early morning.

So thou, dear bird, young Jenny fair!
On trembling string or vocal air,
Shall sweetly pay the tender care
  That tents thy early morning.   guards
So thou, sweet rose-bud, young and gay,
Shalt beauteous blaze upon the day,
And bless the parent's evening ray
  That watched thy early morning.

BRAVING ANGRY WINTER'S STORMS.

TUNE—*Neil Gow's Lamentation for Abercairny.*

WHERE, braving angry winter's storms,
  The lofty Ochils rise,
Far in their shade my Peggy's charms
  First blest my wondering eyes ;
As one who by some savage stream,
  A lonely gem surveys,
Astonished, doubly marks its beam,
  With art's most polished blaze.

Blest be the wild, sequestered shade,
  And blest the day and hour,
Where Peggy's charms I first surveyed—
  When first I felt their power !
The tyrant death, with grim control,
  May seize my fleeting breath ;
But tearing Peggy from my soul
  Must be a stronger death.

MY PEGGY'S FACE

TUNE—*My Peggy's Face.*

MY Peggy's face, my Peggy's form,
The frost of hermit age might warm ;
My Peggy's worth, my Peggy's mind,
Might charm the first of human kind.
I love my Peggy's angel air,
Her face so truly, heavenly fair,
Her native grace so void of art,
But I adore my Peggy's heart.

The lily's hue, the rose's dye,
The kindling lustre of an eye ;
Who but owns their magic sway !
Who but knows they all decay !
The tender thrill, the pitying tear,
The generous purpose, nobly dear,
The gentle look, that rage disarms—
These are all immortal charms.

ON A YOUNG LADY

RESIDING ON THE BANKS OF THE SMALL RIVER DEVON, IN
CLACKMANNANSHIRE, BUT WHOSE INFANT YEARS WERE
SPENT IN AYRSHIRE.

How pleasant the banks of the clear-winding Devon,
  With green-spreading bushes, and flowers blooming fair;
But the bonniest flower on the banks of the Devon
  Was once a sweet bud on the braes of the Ayr.

Mild be the sun on this sweet-blushing flower,
  In the gay rosy morn as it bathes in the dew!
And gentle the fall of the soft vernal shower,
  That steals on the evening each leaf to renew.

Oh spare the dear blossom, ye orient breezes,
  With chill hoary wing as ye usher the dawn!
And far be thou distant, thou reptile that seizes
  The verdure and pride of the garden and lawn!

Let Bourbon exult in his gay-gilded lilies,
  And England triumphant display her proud rose,
A fairer than either adorns the green valleys
  Where Devon, sweet Devon, meandering flows.

MACPHERSON'S FAREWELL.

TUNE—*M'Pherson's Rant.*

FAREWELL, ye dungeons dark and strong,
  The wretch's destinie!
Macpherson's time will not be long
  On yonder gallows-tree.
    Sae rantingly, sae wantonly,   *so*
    Sae dauntingly gaed he;   *went*
    He played a spring, and danced it round, *a tune*
    Below the gallows-tree.

Oh, what is death but parting breath?
  On many a bloody plain
I've dared his face, and in this place
  I scorn him yet again!

Untie these bands from off my hands,
  And bring to me my sword;
And there's no a man in all Scotland,
  But I'll brave him at a word.

I've lived a life of sturt and strife;   *trouble*
  I die by treacherie:
It burns my heart I must depart,
  And not avenged be.

Now farewell light—thou sunshine bright,
  And all beneath the sky!
May coward shame distain his name,
  The wretch that dares not die!

STAY MY CHARMER.

TUNE—*An Gillie dubh ciar dhubh.*

STAY, my charmer, can you leave me?
Cruel, cruel to deceive me
Well you know how much you grieve me;
  Cruel charmer, can you go?
  Cruel charmer, can you go?

By my love so ill requited,
By the faith you fondly plighted,
By the pangs of lovers slighted,
  Do not, do not leave me so !
  Do not, do not, leave me so !

STRATHALLAN'S LAMENT.

THICKEST night, o'erhang my dwelling !
  Howling tempests, o'er me rave !
Turbid torrents, wintry swelling,
  Still surround my lonely cave !

Crystal streamlets gently flowing,
  Busy haunts of base mankind,
Western breezes softly blowing,
  Suit not my distracted mind.

In the cause of right engagèd,
  Wrongs injurious to redress,
Honour's war we strongly wagèd,
  But the heavens denied success.

Ruin's wheel has driven o'er us,
  Not a hope that dare attend :
The wide world is all before us—
  But a world without a friend !

THE YOUNG HIGHLAND ROVER.

TUNE—*Morag.*

LOUD blaw the frosty breezes,   blow
  The snaws the mountains cover ;   snows
Like winter on me seizes,
  Since my young Highland Rover   (Prince Charlie)
  Far wanders nations over.
Where'er he go, where'er he stray,
  May Heaven be his warden,
Return him safe to fair Strathspey,
  And bonnie Castle-Gordon !

The trees now naked groaning,
  Soon shall wi' leaves be hinging,   hanging
The birdies dowie moaning,   sorrowful
  Shall a' be blithely singing,
  And every flower be springing.
Sae I'll rejoice the lee-lang day,   live-long
  When by his mighty warden
My youth's returned to fair Strathspey
  And bonnie Castle-Gordon.

RAVING WINDS ABOUND HER BLOWING.[*]

TUNE—*Macgregor of Ruara's Lament.*

RAVING winds around her blowing,
Yellow leaves the woodlands strowing,
By a river hoarsely roaring,
Isabella strayed deploring—
" Farewell hours that late did measure
Sunshine days of joy and pleasure ;
Hail, thou gloomy night of sorrow,
Cheerless night that knows no morrow !

" O'er the past too fondly wandering,
On the hopeless future pondering ;
Chilly grief my life-blood freezes,
Fell despair my fancy seizes.
Life, thou soul of every blessing,
Load to misery most distressing,
Gladly how would I resign thee,
And to dark oblivion join thee !"

MUSING ON THE ROARING OCEAN.[†]

TUNE—*Druimion Dubh.*

MUSING on the roaring ocean,
    Which divides my love and me ;
Wearying Heaven in warm devotion,
    For his weal where'er he be.

Hope and fear's alternate billow
    Yielding late to Nature's law,
Whisp'ring spirits round my pillow'
    Talk of him that's far awa.

Ye whom sorrow never wounded,
    Ye who never shed a tear,
Care-untroubled, joy-surrounded,
    Gaudy day to you is dear.

Gentle night, do thou befriend me ;
    Downy sleep, the curtain draw ;
Spirits kind, again attend me,
    Talk of him that's far awa.

[*] I composed these verses on Miss Isabella M'Leod of Raasay, alluding to her feelings on the death of her sister, and the still more melancholy death (1786) of her sister's husband, the late Earl of Loudon, who shot himself out of sheer heart-break at some mortifications he suffered owing to the deranged state of his finances.—*B.*
[†] I composed these verses out of compliment to a Mrs Maclachlan, whose husband is an officer in the East Indies.—*B.*

BONNIE PEGGY ALISON.

TUNE—Braes o' Balquhidder.

CHORUS.

I'LL kiss thee yet, yet,
    And I'll kiss thee o'er again,
And I'll kiss thee yet, yet,
    My bonnie Peggy Alison!

Ilk care and fear, when thou art near,   each
    I ever mair defy them, O!   more
Young kings upon their hansel throne   lucky
Are no sae blest as I am, O!   not so

When in my arms, wi' a' thy charms,
    I clasp my countless treasure, O,
I seek nae mair o' heaven to share   no
    Than sic a moment's pleasure, O!   such

And by thy een, sae bonnie blue,   eyes
    I swear I'm thine for ever, O'—
And on thy lips I seal my vow,
    And break it shall I never, O!

I LOVE MY JEAN.

TUNE—Miss Admiral Gordon's Strathspey

O' A' the airts the wind can blaw,   quarters, blow
    I dearly loe the west,   love
For there the bonnie lassie lives,
    The lass that I loe best:
There wild woods grow, and rivers row,   roll
    Wi' mony a hill between;   many
But day and night my fancy's flight
    Is ever wi' my Jean.

I see her in the dewy flowers,
    Sae lovely sweet and fair: so
I hear her voice in ilka bird,   every
    Wi' music charm the air:
There's not a bonnie flower that springs
    By fountain, shaw, or green;   wood
There's not a bonnie bird that sings,
    But minds me o' my Jean.

OH, WERE I ON PARNASSUS' HILL!

TUNE—My Love is lost to me.

OH, were I on Parnassus' hill!
Or had of Helicon my fill;
That I might catch poetic skill,
    To sing how dear I love thee.

But Nith maun be my Muse's well,   must
My Muse maun be thy bonnie sel';   self
On Corsincon I'll glower and spell,   stare, narrate
    And write how dear I love thee.

Then come, sweet Muse, inspire my lay!
For a' the lee-lang simmer's day   live-long summer
I couldna sing, I couldna say,   could not
    How much, how dear I love thee.
I see thee dancing o'er the green,
Thy waist sae jimp, thy limbs sae clean,   small, neat
Thy tempting lips, thy roguish een—   eyes
    By heaven and earth I love thee!

By night, by day, a-field, at hame,   home
The thoughts of thee my breast inflame;
And aye I muse and sing thy name—   still
    I only live to love thee.
Though I were doomed to wander on
Beyond the sea, beyond the sun,
Till my last weary sand was run;
    Till then—and then I love thee.

THE DAY RETURNS.

TUNE—*Seventh of November.*

THE day returns, my bosom burns,
    The blissful day we twa did meet;   two
Though winter wild in tempest toiled,
    Ne'er summer sun was half sae sweet.   so
Than a' the pride that loads the tide,
    And crosses o'er the sultry line;
Than kingly robes, than crowns and globes,
    Heaven gave me more—it made thee mine!

While day and night can bring delight,
    Or nature aught of pleasure give,
While joys above my mind can move,
    For thee, and thee alone, I live.
When that grim foe of life below
    Comes in between to make us part,
The iron hand that breaks our band,
    It breaks my bliss—it breaks my heart!

THE LAZY MIST.

TUNE—*The Lazy Mist.*

THE lazy mist hangs from the brow of the hill,
Concealing the course of the dark-winding rill;
How languid the scenes, late so sprightly, appear
As autumn to winter resigns the pale year.

The forests are leafless, the meadows are brown,
And all the gay foppery of summer is flown :
Apart let me wander, apart let me muse,
How quick time is flying, how keen fate pursues !

How long I have liv'd—but how much liv'd in vain !
How little of life's scanty span may remain !
What aspects old Time, in his progress, has worn !
What ties cruel fate in my bosom has torn !
How foolish, or worse, till our summit is gained !
And downward, how weaken'd, how darken'd, how pain'd !
This life's not worth having with all it can give—
For something beyond it poor man sure must live.

I HAE A PENNY TO SPEND.

TUNE—*I hae a Wife o' my ain.*

I HAE a penny to spend,	have
There—thanks to naebody ;	nobody
I hae naething to lend,	
I'll borrow frae naebody.	from
I am naebody's lord,	
I'll be slave to naebody ;	
I hae a guid braid sword,	good broad
I'll tak dunts frae naebody.	blows
I'll be merry and free,	
I'll be sad for naebody ;	
If naebody care for me,	
I'll care for naebody.	

AULD LANG SYNE.

SHOULD auld acquaintance be forgot,
And never brought to mind ?
Should auld acquaintance be forgot,
And days o' lang syne.

CHORUS.

For auld lang syne, my dears,
For auld lang syne,
We'll tak a cup o' kindness yet,
For auld lang syne.

We twa hae run about the braes,	two have
And pu'd the gowans fine ;	pulled, daisies
But we've wandered mony a weary foot,	
Sin' auld lang syne.	
We twa hae paidl't i' the burn,	dabbled
Frae morning sun till dine ;	from, noon

We twa hae run about the braes,
And pu'd the gowans fine.

p. 234

But seas between us braid hae roar'd, broad
Sin' auld lang syne.

And here's a hand, my trusty fiere, friend
And gie's a hand o' thine; give
And we'll tak a right guid willie-waught good, draught
For auld lang syne.

And surely ye'll be your pint-stoup, flagon
And surely I'll be mine;
And we'll tak a cup o' kindness yet
For auld lang syne.

MY BONNIE MARY.

Go fetch to me a pint o' wine,
And fill it in a silver tassie; cup
That I may drink before I go,
A service to my bonnie lassie.
The boat rocks at the pier o' Leith,
Fu' loud the wind blaws frae the Ferry; blows from
The ship rides by the Berwick-law,
And I maun leave my bonnie Mary. must

The trumpets sound, the banners fly,
The glittering spears are rankèd ready;
The shouts o' war are heard afar,
The battle closes thick and bloody;
But it's not the roar o' sea or shore
Wad make me langer wish to tarry; would
Nor shouts o' war that's heard afar—
It's leaving thee, my bonnie Mary.

WILLIE BREWED A PECK O' MAUT.

O WILLIE brewed a peck o' maut, malt
And Rob and Allan cam to pree: came, taste
Three blither hearts that lee-lang night, live-long
Ye wad na find in Christendie. would not
We are na fou', we're nae that fou', tipsy
But just a drappie in our ee; drop, eye
The cock may craw, the day may daw, crow, dawn
And aye we'll taste the barley bree.

Here are we met, three merry boys,
Three merry boys, I trow, are we;
And mony a night we've merry been, many
And mony mae we hope to be! more

It is the moon, I ken her horn, know
That's blinkin' in the lift sae hie; sky, so high
She shines sae bright to wile us hame, home
But, by my sooth, she'll wait a wee! while

Wha first shall rise to gang awa',   go
  A FECKLESS coward loon is he!   silly, fellow
Wha last beside his chair shall fa',
  He is the king amang us three!   among

THE LADDIES BY THE BANKS O' NITH.

TUNE—*Up and waur them a'.*

THE laddies by the banks o' Nith,
  Wad trust his Grace wi' a', Jamie,   would
But he'll sair them as he sair'd the king—   serve
  Turn tail and rin awa, Jamie.
    Up and waur them a', Jamie,   baffle
    Up and waur them a';
      The Johnstons hae the guidin' o't,   have
      Ye turncoat Whigs, awa'.

The day he stude his country's friend,   stood
  Or gied her faes a claw, Jamie,   gave, foes
Or frae puir man a blessin' wan,   from poor, won
  That day the Duke ne'er saw, Jamie.

But wha is he, his country's boast?   who
  Like him there is na twa, Jamie;   two
There's no a callant tents the kye,   boy, tends, cows
  But kens o' Westerha', Jamie.   knows

To end the wark, here's Whistlebirck,   work
  Lang may his whistle blaw, Jamie;   long, blow
And Maxwell true o' sterling blue,
  And we'll be Johnstons a', Jamie.

THE BLUE-EYED LASSIE.

I GAED a waefu' gate yestreen,   went, woeful, last night
  A gate, I fear, I'll dearly rue;   road
I gat my death frae twa sweet een,   got, two
  Twa lovely een o' bonnie blue.   eyes
'Twas not her golden ringlets bright;
  Her lips like roses wat wi' dew,   wet
Her heaving bosom, lily-white—
  It was her een sae bonnie blue.   so

She talked, she smiled, my heart she wiled;
  She charmed my soul—I wist na how;
And aye the stound, the deadly wound,   still, pang
  Cam frae her een sae bonnie blue.   from
But, spare to speak, and spare to speed;
  She'll aiblins listen to my vow: perhaps
Should she refuse, I'll lay my dead   death
  To her twa een sae bonnie blue.

SONG.

AIR—*Maggy Lauder.*

WHEN first I saw fair Jeanie's face,
 I couldna tell what ailed me,   could not
My heart went fluttering pit-a-pat,
 My een they almost failed me.   eyes
She's aye sae neat, sae trim, sae tight,   so
 All grace does round her hover,
Ae look deprived me o' my heart,   one
 And I became a lover.
  She's aye, aye sae blithe, sae gay,
   She's aye so blithe and cheerie ;
  She's aye sae bonny, blithe, and gay,
   O gin I were her dearie !   that

Had I Dundas's whole estate,
 Or Hopetoun's wealth to shine in :
Did warlike laurels crown my brow,
 Or humbler bays entwining—
I'd lay them a' at Jeanie's feet,
 Could I but hope to move her,
And prouder than a belted knight,
 I'd be my Jeanie's lover.
  She's aye, aye sae blithe, sae gay, &c.

But sair I fear some happier swain   sore
 Has gained sweet Jeanie's favour :
If so, may every bliss be hers,
 Though I maun never have her.   must
But gang she east, or gang she west,   go
 'Twixt Forth and Tweed all over,
While men have eyes, or ears, or taste,
 She'll always find a lover.
  She's aye, aye sae blithe, sae gay, &c.

MY LOVELY NANCY.

TUNE—*The Quaker's Wife.*

THINE am I, my faithful fair,
 Thine, my lovely Nancy ;
Every pulse along my veins,
 Every roving fancy.

To thy bosom lay my heart,
 There to throb and languish :
Though despair had wrung its core,
 That would heal its anguish.

Take away those rosy lips,
 Rich with balmy treasure ;
Turn away thine eyes of love,
 Lest I die with pleasure.

What is life when wanting love ?
　Night without a morning :
Love's the cloudless summer sun,
　Nature gay adorning.

TIBBIE DUNBAR.

TUNE—*Johnny M'Gill.*

O WILT thou go wi' me, sweet Tibbie Dunbar ?
O wilt thou go wi' me, sweet Tibbie Dunbar ?
Wilt thou ride on a horse or be drawn in a car,
Or walk by my side, sweet Tibbie Dunbar ?

I carena thy daddie, his lands and his money,　　care not for
I carena thy kin, sae high and sae lordly ;　　　　so
But say thou wilt hae me, for better for waur,　　have, worse
And come in thy coatie, sweet Tibbie Dunbar !

THE GARDENER WI' HIS PAIDLE.

TUNE—*The Gardener's March.*

WHEN rosy morn comes in wi' showers,
To deck her gay green birken bowers,　　　　birch
Then busy, busy are his hours,
　　　The gardener wi' his paidle.　　　　　　hoe

The crystal waters gently fa',
The merry birds are lovers a',
The scented breezes round him blaw,　　　　blow
　　　The gardener wi' his paidle.

When purple morning starts the hare,
To steal upon her early fare,
Then through the dews he maun repair,　　　must
　　　The gardener wi' his paidle.

When day, expiring in the west,
The curtain draws of Nature's rest,
He flies to her arms he loes the best,　　　loves
　　　The gardener wi' his paidle.

DAINTY DAVIE.

TUNE—*Dainty Davie.*

NOW rosy May comes in wi' flowers,
To deck her gay, green-spreading bowers ;
And now come in my happy hours,
　　　To wander wi' my Davie.

CHORUS.

Meet me on the warlock knowe,   knoll
  Dainty Davie, dainty Davy;   worthy
There I'll spend the day wi' you,
  My ain dear dainty Davie.   own

The crystal waters round us fa',
The merry birds are lovers a',
The scented breezes round us blaw,   blow
A-wandering wi' my Davie.

When purple morning starts the hare,
To steal upon her early fare,
Then through the dews I will repair,
  To meet my faithfu' Davie.

When day, expiring in the west,
The curtain draws o' Nature's rest,
I flee to his arms I loe best,   love
  And that's my ain dear Davie.

HIGHLAND HARRY.

My Harry was a gallant gay,
  Fu' stately strode he on the plain:
But now he's banished far away;
  I'll never see him back again.
    O for him back again!
    O for him back again!
  I wad gie a' Knockhaspie's land   would give
    For Highland Harry back again.

When a' the lave gae to their bed,   rest go
  I wander dowie up the glen;   sad
I set me down and greet my fill,   cry
  And aye I wish him back again.   always
O were some villains hangit high,   hanged
  And ilka body had their ain!   each, own
Then I might see the joyfu' sight,
  My Highland Harry back again.

BONNIE ANN.

AIR—*Ye Gallants bright*

Ye gallants bright, I rede ye right,   tell
  Beware o' bonnie Ann;
Her comely face sae fu' o' grace,   so
  Your heart she will trepan.
Her een sae bright, like stars by night, eyes
  Her skin is like the swan;
Sae jimply laced her genty waist,   small, neat
  That sweetly ye might span.

Youth, grace, and love attendant move,
  And pleasure leads the van :
In a' their charms and conquering arms
  They wait on bonnie Ann.
The captive bands may chain the hands,
  But love enslaves the man ;
Ye gallants braw, I rede you a',   tell
  Beware o' bonnie Ann !

JOHN ANDERSON.

TUNE—*John Anderson my jo.*

JOHN Anderson my jo, John,
  When we were first acquent,
Your locks were like the raven,
  Your bonnie brow was brent ;   smooth
But now your brow is beld, John,   bald
  Your locks are like the snaw ;
But blessings on your frosty pow,   head
  John Anderson my jo.

John Anderson my jo, John,
  We clamb the hill thegither,   climbed
And mony a canty day, John,   many, happy
  We've had wi' ane anither :   one another
Now we maun totter down, John,   must
  But hand in hand we'll go,
And sleep thegither at the foot,   together
  John Anderson my jo.

THE BATTLE OF SHERIFF-MUIR.

TUNE— *Cameronian Rant.*

" O CAM ye here the fight to shun,   came
  Or herd the sheep wi' me, man ?
Or were ye at the Sherra-muir,
  And did the battle see, man ?"
" I saw the battle, sair and tough,   sore
And reekin' red ran mony a sheugh ;   smoking, channel
My heart, for fear, gaed sough for sough,   gave sigh
To hear the thuds, and see the cluds   knocks, clouds
O' clans frae woods, in tartan duds,   from, clothes
  Wha glaumed at kingdoms three, man.   who grasped

" The red-coat lads, wi' black cockades,
  To meet them were na slaw, man ;   not slow
They rushed and pushed, and bluid outgushed.   blood
  And mony a bouk did fa', man :   many, corpse
The great Argyle led on his files,
I wat they glanced for twenty miles :   believe
They hacked and hashed, while broadswords clashed,
And through they dashed, and hewed, and smashed,
  Till fey men died awa, man.   predestined

"But had you seen the philabegs,   *the kilts*
  And skyrin tartan trews, man; *shining*
When in the teeth they dared our Whigs,
  And covenant true blues, man;
In lines extended lang and large, *long*
When bayonets opposed the targe, *target*
And thousands hastened to the charge,
Wi' Highland wrath they frae the sheath *from*
Drew blades o' death, till, out o' breath,
  They fled like frighted doos, man." *doves*

"O how, MAN, Tam, can that be true?
  The chase gaed frae the North, man; *went*
I saw myself, they did pursue
  The horsemen back to Forth, man;
And at Dunblane, in my ain sight, *own*
They took the brig wi' a' their might,
And straught to Stirling winged their flight; *straight*
But, FEARFU' lot! the gates were shut;
And mony a huntit, poor red-coat, *many, hunted*
  For fear amaist did swarf, man!" *almost, swoon*

"My sister Kate cam up the gate,
  Wi' crowdie unto me, man; *porridge*
She swore she saw some rebels run
  Frae Perth unto Dundee, man:
Their left-hand general had nae skill, *no*
The Angus lads had nae good will
That day their neibors' blood to spill; *neighbours*
For fear, by foes, that they should lose
Their cogs o' brose—all crying woes: *basin*
  And so it goes, you see, man.

"They've lost some gallant gentlemen
  Amang the Highland clans, man:
I fear my Lord Panmure is slain,
  Or fallen in Whiggish hands, man:
Now wad ye sing this double fight, *would*
Some fell for wrang, and some for right; *wrong*
But mony bade the world guid-night;
Then ye may tell, how pell and mell,
By red claymores, and muskets' knell,
Wi' dying yell, the Tories fell,
  And Whigs AWA' did flee, man."

BLOOMING NELLY.

TUNE—*On a Bank of Flowers.*

ON a bank of flowers, in a summer day,
  For summer lightly drest,
The youthful, blooming Nelly lay,
  With love and sleep opprest;

When Willie, wandering through the wood,
   Who for her favour oft had sued,
He gazed, he wished, he feared, he blushed,
   And trembled where he stood.

Her closèd eyes like weapons sheathed,
   Were sealed in soft repose ;
Her lip, still as she fragrant breathed,
   It richer dyed the rose.
The springing lillies sweetly prest,
   Wild-wanton, kissed her rival breast ;
He gazed, he wished, he feared, he blushed—
   His bosom ill at rest.

Her robes light waving in the breeze,
   Her tender limbs embrace ;
Her lovely form, her native ease,
   All harmony and grace :
Tumultuous tides his pulses roll,
   A faltering, ardent kiss he stole ;
He gazed, he wished, he feared, he blushed,
   And sighed his very soul.

As flies the partridge from the brake
   On fear-inspirèd wings,
So Nelly starting, half awake,
   Away affrighted springs :
But Willy followed, as he should ;
   He overtook her in the wood ;
He vowed, he prayed, he found the maid
   Forgiving all and good.

MY HEART'S IN THE HIGHLANDS.

TUNE—*Failte na Miosg.*

My heart's in the Highlands, my heart is not here ;
My heart's in the Highlands a-chasing the deer ;
A-chasing the wild deer, and following the roe—
My heart's in the Highlands wherever I go.

Farewell to the Highlands, farewell to the North,
The birthplace of valour, the country of worth ;
Wherever I wander, wherever I rove,
The hills of the Highlands for ever I love.

Farewell to the mountains high covered with snow ;
Farewell to the straths and green valleys below :
Farewell to the forests and wild-hanging woods ;
Farewell to the torrents and loud-pouring floods.

My heart's in the Highlands, my heart is not her ;
My heart's in the Highlands a-chasing the deer ;
A-chasing the wild deer, and following the roe—
My heart's in the Highlands wherever I go.

THE BANKS OF NITH.

TUNE—*Robie donna Gorach.*

THE Thames flows proudly to the sea,
  Where royal cities stately stand ;
But sweeter flows the Nith, to me,
  Where Cummins ance had high command ;   once
When shall I see that honoured land,
  That winding stream I love so dear !
Must wayward Fortune's adverse hand
  For ever, ever keep me here ?

How lovely, Nith, thy fruitful vales,
  Where spreading hawthorns gaily blooms !
How sweetly wind thy sloping dales,
  Where lambkins wanton through the broom !
Though wandering, now, must be my doom,
  Far from thy bonnie banks and braes,
May there my latest hours consume,
  Amang the friends of early days !

MY HEART IS A-BREAKING, DEAR TITTIE !

MY heart is a-breaking, dear tittie !   sister
  Some counsel unto me come len',
To anger them a' is a pity,
  But what will I do wi' Tam Glen ?

I'm thinking wi' sic a braw fellow   such
  In poortith I might make a fen' ;   poverty, shift
What care I in riches to wallow,
  If I maunna marry Tam Glen ?   must not

There's Lowrie, the Laird o' Drumeller,
  Guid-day to you, brute ! he comes ben ;   good-day, in
He brags and he blaws o' his siller,   boasts
  But when will he dance like Tam Glen ?

My minnie does constantly deave me,   mother, deafen
  And bids me beware o' young men ;
They flatter, she says, to deceive me,
  But wha can think sae o' Tam Glen ?   who, sc

My daddie says, gin I'll forsake him,   if
  He'll gie me guid hunder marks ten :   give, good
But if it's ordained I maun take him,   must
  O wha will I get but Tam Glen ?

Yestreen at the valentines' dealing,   last night
  My heart to my mou gied a sten ;   mouth, gave, bound
For thrice I drew ane without failing,   one
  And thrice it was written—Tam Glen.

The last Halloween I was waukin   watching
  My droukit sark-sleeve, as ye ken ·   wet shift, know

His likeness cam up the house staukin,   stalking
  And the very gray breeks o' Tam Glen!   trews

Come counsel, dear tittie! don't tarry—
  I'll gie you my bonnie black hen,
Gif ye will advise me to marry   if
  The lad I loe dearly—Tam Glen.   love

THERE'LL NEVER BE PEACE TILL JAMIE COMES HAME.

BY yon castle wa', at the close of the day,
I heard a man sing, though his head it was gray;
And as he was singing, the tears fast down came—
There'll never be peace till Jamie comes hame.   home
The church is in ruins, the state is in jars:
Delusions, oppressions, and murderous wars;
We darena weel say't, though we ken wha's to blame,   dare not,
There'll never be peace till Jamie comes hame.   [know

My seven braw sons for Jamie drew sword,
And now I greet round their green beds in the yerd. weep, church-
It brak the sweet heart of my faithfu' auld dame—   [yard
There'll never be peace till Jamie comes hame.
Now life is a burden that bows me down,
Since I tint my bairns, and he tint his crown;   lost
But till my last moments my words are the same—
There'll never be peace till Jamie comes hame!

LOVELY DAVIES.

TUNE—*Miss Muir.*

O HOW shall I, unskilfu', try
  The poet's occupation,
The tunefu' powers, in happy hours,
  That whisper inspiration?
Even they maun dare an effort mair   must, more
  Than aught they ever gave us,
Ere they rehearse, in equal verse,
  The charms o' lovely Davies.

Each eye it cheers, when she appears,
  Like Phœbus in the morning,
When past the shower, and every flower
  The garden is adorning.
As the wretch looks o'er Siberia's shore,
  When winter-bound the wave is;
Sae droops our heart when we maun part   so
  Frae charming, lovely Davies.   from

Her smile's a gift, frae 'boon the lift,   sky
  That maks us mair than princes;   makes
A sceptered hand, a king's command,
  Is in her darting glances:

The man in arms, 'gainst female charms,
    Even he her willing slave is;
He hugs his chain, and owns the reign
    Of conquering, lovely Davies.

My Muse to dream of such a theme,
    Her feeble powers surrender;
The eagle's gaze alone surveys
    The sun's meridian splendour:
I wad in vain essay the strain,   would
    The deed too daring brave is;
I'll drop the lyre, and mute admire
    The charms o' lovely Davies.

THE BONNIE WEE THING.

TUNE—*Bonnie wee Thing.*

BONNIE wee thing, cannie wee thing,   gentle
    Lovely wee thing, wert thou mine,
I wad wear thee in my bosom,   would
    Lest my jewel I should tine!   lose
Wishfully I look and languish
    In that bonnie face o' thine;
And my heart it stounds wi' anguish,   throbs
    Lest my wee thing be na mine.   not

Wit, and grace, and love, and beauty,
    In ae constellation shine;   one
To adore thee is my duty,
    Goddess o' this soul o' mine!
Bonnie wee thing, cannie wee thing,
    Lovely wee thing, wert though mine,
I wad wear thee in my bosom,
    Lest my jewel I should tine!

SONG OF DEATH.

AIR—*Oran an Aoig.*

Scene—A Field of Battle—Time of the day, Evening—The wounded and
lying of the victorious army are supposed to join in the following song:—

FAREWELL, thou fair day, thou green earth, and ye skies,
    Now gay with the bright setting sun;
Farewell loves and friendships, ye dear tender ties—
    Our race of existence is run!

Thou grim King of Terrors, thou life's gloomy foe!
    Go, frighten the coward and slave;
Go, teach them to tremble, fell tyrant! but know
    No terrors hast thou to the brave!

Thou strik'st the dull peasant—he sinks in the dark,
    Nor saves e'en the wreck of a name;

Thou strik'st the young hero—a glorious mark !
He falls in the blaze of his fame !

In the field of proud honour—our swords in our hands,
    Our king and our country to save—
While victory shines on life's last ebbing sands,
    Oh ! who would not die with the brave ?

SONG.

Tune—*Rory Dall's Port.*

Ae fond kiss, and then we sever !   one
Ae fareweel, and then for ever !
Deep in heart-wrung tears I'll pledge thee,
Warring sighs and groans I'll wage thee.

Who shall say that Fortune grieves him,
While the star of hope she leaves him ?
Me, nae cheerful twinkle lights me ;   no
Dark despair around benights me.

I'll ne'er blame my partial fancy,
Naething could resist my Nancy :
But to see her was to love her ;
Love but her, and love for ever.

Had we never loved sae kindly,   so
Had we never loved sae blindly !
Never met—or never parted,
We had ne'er been broken-hearted.

Fare-thee-weel, thou first and fairest !
Fare-thee-weel, thou best and dearest !
Thine be ilka joy and treasure,   every
Peace, Enjoyment, Love, and Pleasure !

Ae fond kiss, and then we sever !
Ae fareweel, alas ! for ever !
Deep in heart-wrung tears I'll pledge thee,
Warring sighs and groans I'll wage thee.

SONG.

To a charming plaintive Scots Air.

Ance mair I hail thee, thou gloomy December !   once more
    Ance mair I hail thee wi' sorrow and care :
Sad was the parting thou mak'st me remember,
    Parting wi' Nancy, oh, ne'er to meet mair !

Fond lover's parting is sweet, painful pleasure,
    Hope beaming mild on the soft parting hour ;
But the dire feeling, oh, farewell for ever !
    Anguish unmingled and agony pure !

Wild as the winter now tearing the forest,
  Till the last leaf o' the summer is flown,
Such is the tempest has shaken my bosom,
  Since my last hope and last comfort is gone!

Still as I hail thee, thou gloomy December,
  Still shall I hail thee wi' sorrow and care;
For sad was the parting thou mak'st me remember,
  Parting wi' Nancy, oh, ne'er to meet mair!

O MAY, THY MORN.

O MAY, thy morn was ne'er so sweet,
  As the mirk night o' December,   *dark*
For sparkling was the rosy wine,
  And secret was the chamber;
And dear was she I darena name,   *dare not*
  But I will aye remember: *always*
And dear was she I darena name,
  But I will aye remember.

And here's to them that like oursel'
  Can push about the jorum;   *jug of drink*
And here's to them that wish us weel,
  May a' that's guid watch o'er them!
And here's to them we darena name,
  The dearest o' the quorum:
And here's to them we darena tell,
  The dearest o' the quorum.

MY NANNIE'S AWA.

Now in her green mantle blithe Nature arrays,
And listens the lambkins that bleat o'er the braes,
While birds warble welcome in ilka green shaw;   *wood*
But to me it's delightless—my Nannie's awa.   *away*

The snawdrap and primrose our woodlands adorn,   *snowdrop*
And violets bathe in the weet o' the morn;   *dew*
They pain my sad bosom, sae sweetly they blaw,   *so, blow*
They mind me o' Nannie—and Nannie's awa.

Thou laverock that springs frae the dews of the lawn,   *lark, from*
The shepherd to warn o' the grey-breaking dawn;
And thou mellow mavis that hails the night fa',   *thrush*
Give over for pity—my Nannie's awa.

Come Autumn, sae pensive, in yellow and gray,
And soothe me with tidings o' Nature's decay:
The dark, dreary winter, and wild driving snaw
Alane can delight me—Now Nannie's awa!   *alone*

BONNIE LESLEY.

O saw ye bonnie Lesley,
  As she gaed ower the Border ?   went, over
She's gane, like Alexander,   gone
  To spread her conquests farther.

To see her is to love her,
  And love but her for ever ;
For Nature made her what she is,
  And never made anither !   another

Thou art a queen, fair Lesley,
  Thy subjects we, before thee;
Thou art divine, fair Lesley,
  The hearts o' men adore thee.

Nae body dares to scaith thee,   harm
  Or aught that wad belang thee ;   would belong
They'd look into thy bonnie face,
  And say, " I canna wrang thee !" cannot, wrong

The powers aboon will tent thee ;   above, tend
  Misfortune sha' na steer thee ;   shall not stir
Thou'rt like themselves sae lovely,   so
  That ill they'll ne'er let near thee.

Return again, fair Lesley,
  Return to Caledonie !
That we may brag, we hae a lass   boast, have
  There's nane again sae bonnie.   none

CRAIGIEBURN WOOD.

Sweet fa's the eve on Craigieburn,
  And blithe awakes the morrow ;
But a' the pride o' Spring's return
  Can yield me nocht but sorrow.   nought

I see the flowers and spreading trees,
  I hear the wild birds singing ;
But what a weary wight can please,
  And care his bosom wringing ?

Fain, fain would I my griefs impart,
  Yet darena for your anger ;   dare not
But secret love will break my heart
  If I conceal it langer.   longer

If thou refuse to pity me,
  If thou shalt love anither,
When yon green leaves fade frae the tree, from
  Around my grave they'll wither.

FRAE THE FRIENDS AND LAND I LOVE.

AIR—*Carron Side.*

FRAE the friends and land I love   from
  Driven by Fortune's felly spite,   fell
Frae my best beloved I rove,
  Never mair to taste delight ;   more
Never mair maun hope to find   must
  Ease frae toil, relief frae care :
When remembrance wracks the mind,   racks
  Pleasures but unveil despair.

Brightest climes shall mirk appear,   dark
  Desert ilka blooming shore,   every
Till the Fates nae mair severe,
  Friendship, love, and peace restore ;
Till Revenge, wi' laurelled head,
  Bring our banished hame again ;   home
And ilk loyal bonnie lad   each
  Cross the seas and win his ain.   own

MEIKLE THINKS MY LOVE.

TUNE—*My Tocher's the Jewel.*

O MEIKLE thinks my luve o' my beauty,   much
  And meikle thinks my luve o' my kin ;
But little thinks my luve I ken brawlie   know well
  My tocher's the jewel has charms for him.   dower
It's a' for the apple he'll nourish the tree ;
  It's a' for the honey he'll cherish the bee ;
My laddie's sae meikle in love wi' the siller,   money
  He canna hae luve to spare for me.   cannot, have

Your proffer o' luve's an arle-penny,   earnest-money
  My tocher's the bargain ye wad buy ;   would
But an ye be crafty, I am cunnin',   if
  Sae ye wi' anither your fortune maun try.   so, must
Ye're like to the timmer o' yon rotten wood,   timber
  Ye're like to the bark o' yon rotten tree,
Ye'll slip frae me like a knotless thread,   from
  And ye'll crack your credit wi mae nor me.   more

WHAT CAN A YOUNG LASSIE ?

TUNE—*What can a Young Lassie do wi' an Auld Man?*

WHAT can a young lassie, what shall a young lassie,
  What can a young lassie do wi' an auld man ?
Bad luck on the penny that tempted my minnie   mother
  To sell her poor Jenny for siller and lan' !   money

He's always compleenin' frae mornin' to e'enin'.
He hoasts and he hirples the weary day lang;   *coughs*
He's doyl't and he's dozin', his bluid it is frozer,   *stupid, blood*
  O dreary's the time wi' a crazy auld man!

He hums and he hankers, he frets and he cankers,
  I never can please him, do a' that I can;
He's peevish and jealous of a' the young fellows:
  O dool on the day I met wi' an auld man!   *sorrow*

My auld auntie Katie upon me takes pity,
  I'll do my endeavour to follow her plan;
I'll cross him, and wrack him, until I heart-break him,   *rack*
  And then his auld brass will buy me a new pan.

HOW CAN I BE BLITHE AND GLAD?

Tune—*The Bonnie Lad that's far awa.*

O HOW can I be blithe and glad,
  Or how can I gang brisk and braw,   *go*
When the bonnie lad that I loe best   *love*
  Is ower the hills and far awa?   *over, away*

It's no the frosty winter wind,
  It's no the driving drift and snaw;
But aye the tear comes in my ee,   *eye*
  To think on him that's far awa.

A pair o' gloves he bought to me,
  And silken snoods he gae me twa   *band for hair, gave,*
And I will wear them for his sake,   [*two*
  The bonnie lad that's far awa.

I DO CONFESS THOU ART SAE FAIR.

I DO confess thou art sae fair,   *so*
  I wad been ower the lugs in love,   *would, ears*
Had I na found the slightest prayer   *not*
  That lips could speak thy heart could move.
I do confess thee sweet, but find
  Thou art sae thriftless o' thy sweets,   *so*
Thy favours are the silly wind,
  That kisses ilka thing it meets.   *every*

See yonder rose-bud, rich in dew,
  Among its native briers sae coy;
How sune it tines its scent and hue   *soon, loses*
  When poned, and worn a common toy!   *pulled*
Sic fate, ere lang, shall thee betide,   *such*
  Though thou may gaily bloom awhile;
Yet sune thou shalt be thrown aside
  Like ony common weed and vile.   *any*

YON WILD MOSSY MOUNTAINS.

TUNE—*Yon wild Mossy Mountains.*

YON wild mossy mountains sae lofty and wide,   sc
That nurse in their bosom the youth o' the Clyde,
Where the grouse lead their coveys through the heather to feed,
And the shepherd tents his flock as he pipes on his reed.

Not Gowrie's rich valleys, nor Forth's sunny shores,
To me hae the charms o' yon wild mossy moors ;   have
For there, by a lanely and sequestered stream,   lonely
Resides a sweet lassie, my thought and my dream.

Amang thae wild mountains shall still be my path,   these
Ilk stream, foaming down its ain green, narrow strath ;   each, own,
For there, wi' my lassie, the day lang I rove,   [valley
While o'er us unheeded flee the swift hours o' love.

She is not the fairest, although she is fair ;
O' nice education but sma' is her share ;
Her parentage humble as humble can be ;
But I loe the dear lassie because she loes me.   love

To beauty what man but maun yield him a prize,   must
In her armour of glances, and blushes, and sighs !
And when wit and refinement hae polished her darts,   have
They dazzle our een, as they flee to our hearts. .   eyes

But kindness, sweet kindness, in the fond sparkling ee,   eye
Has lustre outshining the diamond to me ;
And the heart beating love as I'm clasped in her arms,
Oh, these are my lassie's all-conquering charms !

O' FOR ANE-AND-TWENTY, TAM.

TUNE—*The Moudiewort.*

CHORUS.

AND O for ane-and twenty, Tam,   twenty-one
  And hey, sweet ane-and-twenty, Tam,
I'll learn my kin a rattlin' sang,   song
  An I saw ane-and-twenty, Tam.

They snool me sair, and haud me down,   snub, sore, keep
  And gar me look like bluntie, Tam !   make, stupid
But three short years will soon wheel roun'—
  And then comes ane-and-twenty, Tam.

A gleib o' lan', a claut o' gear,   piece, lot of wealth
  Was left me by my auntie, Tam ;
At kith or kin I needna spier,   ask
  An I saw ane-and-twenty, Tam.   if

They'll hae me wed a wealthy coof,   *fool*
    Though I mysel' hae plenty, Tam;   *have*
But hear'st thou, laddie—there's my loof—   *hand*
    I'm thine at ane-and-twenty, Tam.

BESS AND HER SPINNING-WHEEL.

Tune—*The Sweet Lass that loes me.*

O LEEZE me on my spinning-wheel,   *blessings on*
O leeze me on my rock and reel;
Frae tap to tae that cleeds me bien,   *top to toe, clothes,*
And haps me fiel and warm at e'en!   *wraps, soft* [*well*
I'll set me down and sing and spin,
While laigh descends the simmer sun,   *low, summer*
Blest wi' content, and milk and meal—
O leeze me on my spinning-wheel!

On ilka hand the burnies trot,   *every, run*
And meet below my theekit cot;   *thatched*
The scented birk and hawthorn white,   *birch*
Across the pool their arms unite,
Alike to screen the birdie's nest,
And little fishes' caller rest: *cool*
The sun blinks kindly in the biel',   *shelter*
Where blithe I turn my spinning-wheel.

On lofty aiks the cushats wail,   *oaks, wood-pigeons*
And echo cons the doolfu' tale;   *sorrowful*
The lintwhites in the hazel braes,   *linnets*
Delighted, rival ither's lays: *each others*
The craik amang the clover hay,   *land-rail*
The paitrick whirrin' o'er the ley,   *partridge, grass fields*
The swallow jinkin' round my shiel,   *whirling, hut*
Amuse me at my spinning-wheel.

Wi' sma' to sell, and less to buy,   *little*
Aboon distress, below envy,   *above*
Oh wha wad leave this humble state,   *who would*
For a' the pride of a' the great?
Amid their flaring, idle toys,
Amid their cumbrous, dinsome joys,
Can they the peace and pleasure feel
Of Bessy at her spinning-wheel?

NITHSDALE'S WELCOME HAME.

THE noble Maxwells and their powers
    Are coming o'er the Border,
And they'll gae bigg Terregles towers,   *go build*
    And set them a' in order.
And they declare Terregles fair,
    For their abode they choose it :
There's no a heart in a' the land
    But's lighter at the news o't.

Though stars in skies may disappear,
   And angry tempests gather,
The happy hour may soon be near
   That brings us pleasant weather :
The weary night o' care and grief
   May hae a joyful morrow ;   have
So dawning day has brought relief—
   Fareweel our night o' sorrow !

COUNTRY LASSIE.

TUNE—*The Country Lass*

IN simmer, when the hay was mawn,   mown
   And corn waved green in ilka field,   every
While claver blooms white o'er the lea, clover, field
   And roses blaw in ilka bield ; blow, every shelter
Blithe Bessie in the milking shiel,   hut
   Says : " I'll be wed, come o't what will."
Out spak a dame in wrinkled eild :   age
   " O' guid advisement comes nae ill. good, no

" It's ye hae wooers mony ane,   have, many
   And, lassie, ye're but young, ye ken know
Then wait a wee, and cannie wale little, quietly chose
   A routhie butt, a routhie ben : well-stored house
There's Johnnie o' the Buskie Glen,
   Fu' is his barn, fu' is his byre ;
Tak this frae me, my bonnie hen,   from
   It's plenty beets the luver's fire."   feeds

" For Johnnie o' the Buskie Glen,
   I dinna care a single flie ;
He loes sae weel his craps and kye, well, crops, cows
   He has nae luve to spare for me :   no
But blithe's the blink o' Robbie's ee,   eye
   And, weel I wat, he loes me dear : well, know, loves
Ae blink o' him I wadna gie one, wouldn't give
   For Buskie Glen and a' his gear.   wealth

" O thoughtless lassie, life's a faught ; struggle
   The canniest gate, the strife is sair quietest road, sore
But aye fou han't is fechtin best, full-handed, fighting
   A hungry care's an unco care.   great
But some will spend, and some will spare,
   And wilfu' folk maun hae their will ; must have
Syne as ye brew, my maiden fair,   then
   Keep mind that ye maun drink the yill." ale

" O gear will buy me rigs o' land,   money
   And gear will buy me sheep and kye ; cows
But the tender heart o' leesome luve   happy
   The gowd and siller canna buy. gold, silver

We may be poor—Robbie and I,
  Light is the burden luve lays on ;
Content and luve brings peace and joy—
  What mair hae queens upon a throne ?"   more have

FAIR ELIZA.

Turn again, thou fair Eliza,
  Ae kind blink before we part,   one
Rue on thy despairing lover !   repent
  Canst thou break his faithfu' heart ?
Turn again, thou fair Eliza ;
  If to love thy heart denies,
For pity hide the cruel sentence,
  Under friendship's kind disguise !

Thee, dear maid, hae I offended ?   have
  The offence is loving thee :
Canst thou wreck his peace for ever,
  Wha for thine wad gladly die ?   who would
While the life beats in my bosom,
  Thou shalt mix in ilka throe ;   every
Turn again, thou lovely maiden,
  Ae sweet smile on me bestow.

Not the bee upon the blossom,
  In the pride o' sunny noon ;
Not the little sporting fairy,
  All beneath the simmer moon ;   summer
Not the poet in the moment
  Fancy lightens on his ee,   eye
Kens the pleasure, feels the rapture   knows
  That thy presence gies to me.   gives

O LUVE WILL VENTURE IN.

Tune—*The Posie.*

O luve will venture in where it daurna weel be seen ;   daren't well
O luve will venture in where wisdom ance has been ;   once
But I will down yon river rove, among the woods sae green—   so
  And a' to pu' a posie to my ain dear May.   pull, nosegay

The Primrose I will pu', the firstling o' the year,
And I will pu' the Pink, the emblem o' my dear ;
For she's the pink o' womankind, and blooms without a peer—
  And a' to be a posie to my ain dear May.

I'll pu' the budding Rose, when Phœbus peeps in view,
For it's like a baumy kiss o' her sweet bonnie mou' ;
The Hyacinth for constancy, wi' its unchanging blue—
And   a' to be a posie to my ain dear May.

The Lily it is pure, and the Lily it is fair,
And in her lovely bosom I'll place the Lily there;
The Daisy's for simplicity and unaffected air—
    And a' to be a posie to my ain dear May.

The Hawthorn I will pu' wi' its locks o' siller gray,   silver
Where, like an aged man, it stands at break of day;
But the songster's nest within the bush I winna tak away—   will not
    And a' to be a posie to my ain dear May.

The Woodbine I will pu' when the e'ening star is near,
And the diamond draps o' dew shall be her e'en sae clear;   eyes so
The Violet's for modesty, which weel she fa's to wear—   well, falls
    And a' to be a posie to my ain dear May.

I'll tie the posie round wi' the silken band o' luve,
And I'll place it in her breast, and I'll swear by a' above,
That to my latest draught o' life the band shall ne'er remove—
    And this shall be a posie to my ain dear May.

THE BANKS OF DOON.

TUNE—*Caledonian Hunt's Delight.*

YE banks and braes o' bonnie Doon,
    How can ye bloom sae fresh and fair;   so
How can ye chant, ye little birds,
    And I sae weary fu' o' care!   full
Thou'lt break my heart, thou warbling bird,
    That wantons through the flowering thorn:
Thou minds me o' departed joys,
    Departed—never to return!

Aft hae I roved by bonnie Doon,   oft have
    To see the rose and woodbine twine;
And ilka bird sang o' its luve,   every
    And fondly sae did I o' mine.
Wi'-lightsome heart I pu'd a rose,
    Fu' sweet upon its thorny tree;
And my fause luver stole my rose,   false
    But ah! he left the thorn wi' me.

WILLIE WASTLE.

TUNE—*The Eight Men of Moidart.*

WILLIE WASTLE dwalt on Tweed,   dwelt
    The spot they called it Linkum-doddie;
Willie was a wabster guid,   weaver good
    Could stown a clew wi' ony bodie.   steal, any one
He had a wife was dour and din,   stubborn, dun
    Oh, Tinkler Madgie was her mither—   tinker, mother
Sic a wife as Willie had,   such
    I wadna gie a button for her.   would not give

She has an ee—she has but ane,   *eye, one*
  The cat has twa the very colour ;   *two*
Five rusty teeth, forbye a stump,   *besides*
  A clapper-tongue wad deave a miller :   *would, deafen*
A whiskin' beard about her mou',
  Her nose and chin they threaten ither—   *each other*
Sic a wife as Willie had,
  I wadna gie a button for her.

She's bough-houghed, she's hein-shinned,
  Ae limpin' leg a hand-breed shorter ;   *breadth*
She's twisted right, she's twisted left,
  To balance fair in ilka quarter :   *each*
She has a hump upon her breast,
  The twin o' that upon her shouther—   *shoulder*
Sic a wife as Willie had,
  I wadna gie a button for her.

Auld baudrons by the ingle sits,   *cat, fire*
  And wi' her loof her face a-washin' ;   *palm*
But Willie's wife is na sae trig,   *not so tidy*
  She dights her grunzie wi' a hushion ;   *wipes, mouth, cushion*
Her walie nieves like midden-creels,   *huge fists*
  Her face wad fyle the Logan-Water—   *would dirty*
Sic a wife as Willie had,
  I wadna gie a button for her.

FLOW GENTLY, SWEET AFTON.

Tune—*The Yellow-haired Laddie.*

FLOW gently, sweet Afton, among thy green braes,
Flow gently, I'll sing thee a song in thy praise ;
My Mary's asleep by thy murmuring stream,
Flow gently, sweet Afton, disturb not her dream.

Thou stock-dove whose echo resounds through the glen,
Ye wild whistling blackbirds in yon thorny den,
Thou green-crested lapwing thy screaming forbear,
I charge you disturb not my slumbering fair.

How lofty, sweet Afton, thy neighbouring hills,
Far marked with the courses of clear winding rills ;
There daily I wander as noon rises high,
My flocks and my Mary's sweet cot in my eye.

How pleasant thy banks and green valleys below,
Where wild in the woodlands the primroses blow ;
There oft as mild evening weeps over the lea,   *green fields*
The sweet-scented birk shades my Mary and me.   *birch*

Thy crystal stream, Afton, how lovely it glides,
And winds by the cot where my Mary resides ;
How wanton thy waters her snowy feet lave,
As gathering sweet flowerets she stems thy clear wave.

Flow gently, sweet Afton, among thy green braes,
Flow gently, sweet river, the theme of my lays ;
My Mary's asleep by thy murmuring stream,
Flow gently, sweet Afton, disturb not her dream.

THE SMILING SPRING.

TUNE—*The Bonny Bell.*

THE smiling Spring comes in rejoicing,
　And surly Winter grimly flies ;
Now crystal clear are the falling waters,
　And bonnie blue are the sunny skies.
Fresh o'er the mountains breaks forth the morning,
　The evening gilds the ocean's swell ;
All creatures joy in the sun's returning,
　And I rejoice in my bonnie Bell.

The flowery Spring leads sunny Summer,
　And yellow Autumn presses near,
Then in his turn comes gloomy Winter,
　Till smiling Spring again appear.
Thus seasons dancing, life advancing,
　Old Time and Nature their changes tell,
But never ranging, still unchanging,
　I adore my bonnie Bell.

THE GALLANT WEAVER.

TUNE—*The Weavers' March.*

WHERE Cart rins rowin to the sea,   *rolling*
By mony a flower and spreading tree,   *many*
There lives a lad, the lad for me,
　He is a gallant weaver.

O I had wooers aucht or nine,   *eight*
They gied me rings and ribbons fine ;   *gave*
And I was feared my heart would tine,   *afraid, be lost*
　And I gied it to the weaver.

My daddie signed my tocher-band,   *dowry-bond*
To gie the lad that has the land ;   *give*
But to my heart I'll add my hand,
　And gie it to the weaver.

While birds rejoice in leafy bowers ;
While bees delight in opening flowers ;
While corn grows green in simmer showers,   *summer*
　I'll love my gallant weaver.

SHE'S FAIR AND FAUSE.

TUNE—*She's Fair and Fause.*

SHE'S fair and fause that causes my smart,   false
  I loed her meikle and lang;   loved, much
She's broken her vow, she's broken my heart,
  And I may e'en gae hang.   go

A coof cam in wi' routh o' gear,   fool, abundance, wealth
And I hae tint my dearest dear;   have lost
But woman is but warld's gear,   world's
  Sae let the bonnie lass gang.   go

Whae'er ye be that woman love,
  To this be never blind—
Nae ferlie 'tis though fickle she prove,   wonder
  A woman has't by kind.

O woman, lovely woman fair!
An angel form's fa'n to thy share,
'Twad been ower meikle to gien thee mair—   'twould, too,
  I mean an angel mind.   [given, more

MY WIFE'S A WINSOME WEE THING.

SHE is a winsome wee thing,   winning
She is a handsome wee thing,
She is a bonnie wee thing,
This sweet wee wife o' mine.

I never saw a fairer,
I never loed a dearer;   loved
And neist my heart I'll wear her,   next
For fear my jewel tine.   lose

O leeze me on my wee thing,   blessings
My bonnie blithesome wee thing;
Sae lang's I hae my wee thing,   so long, have
I'll think my lot divine.

Though warld's care we share o't,   world's
And may see meikle mair o't;   much more
Wi' her I'll blithely bear it,
And ne'er a word repine.

HIGHLAND MARY.

TUNE—*Katharine Ogie.*

YE banks, and braes, and streams around
  The castle o' Montgomery,
Green be your woods, and fair your flowers,
  Your waters never drumlie!   muddy

There Simmer first unfauld your robes,   *summer, unfold*
   And there the langest tarry;   *longest*
For there I took the last fareweel
   O' my sweet Highland Mary.

How sweetly bloom'd the gay green birk,   *birch*
   How rich the hawthorn's blossom,
As underneath their fragrant shade,
   I clasp'd her to my bosom!
The golden hours, on angel wings,
   Flew o'er me and my dearie;
For dear to me, as light and life,
   Was my sweet Highland Mary.

Wi' monie a vow, and lock'd embrace,   **many**
   Our parting was fu' tender;
And, pledging aft to meet again,   *oft*
   We tore oursels asunder;
But oh! fell death's untimely frost,
   That nipt my flower sae early!   *so*
Now green's the sod, and cauld's the clay, *cold*
   That wraps my Highland Mary!

O pale, pale now, those rosy lips,
   I aft hae kiss'd sae fondly!   *have*
And closed for aye the sparkling glance,
   That dwelt on me sae kindly!
And mould'ring now in silent dust,
   That heart that lo'ed me dearly!
But still within my bosom's core
   Shall live my Highland Mary.

MY AIN KIND DEARIE.

TUNE—*The Lea-Rig.*

WHEN o'er the hill the eastern star
   Tells bughtin time is near, my jo;   *sheep-folding*
And owsen frae the furrowed field   *oxen from*
   Return sae dowf and weary O: *lethargic*
Down by the burn, where scented birks, *birches*
   Wi' dew are hanging clear, my jo,
I'll meet thee on the lea-rig,   *shelter'd field*
   My ain kind dearie O.   *own*

In mirkest glen, at midnight hour,   *darkest*
   I'd rove, and ne'er be eerie O,   *fearful*
If through that glen I gaed to thee,   *went*
   My ain kind dearie, O.
Although the night were ne'er sae wild, *so*
   And I were ne'er sae wearie O,   **weary**
I'd meet thee on the lea-rig,
   My ain kind dearie O.

R

The hunter loes the morning sun,   loves
  To rouse the mountain deer, my jo :
At.noon the fisher seeks the glen,
  Along the burn to steer, my jo ;   move
Gie me the hour o' gloamin gray,   give, twilight
  It maks my heart sae cheery O,   so
To meet thee on the lea-rig,
  My ain kind dearie O.

AULD ROB MORRIS.

THERE'S auld Rob Morris that wons in yon glen,   dwells
He's the king o' guid fellows and wale o' auld men ;   choice
He has gowd in his coffers, he has owsen and kine,   gold, oxen
And ae bonnie lassie, his darling and mine.   one

She's fresh as the morning, the fairest in May ;
She's sweet as the evening amang the new hay ;
As blithe and as artless as the lambs on the lea,   pasture
And dear to my heart as the light to my ee.   eye

But oh! she's an heiress, auld Robin's a laird,
And my daddie has nought but a cot-house and yard ;
A wooer like me maunna hope to come speed,   must not
The wounds I must hide that will soon be my deid.   death

The day comes to me, but delight brings me nane ;   none
The night comes to me, but my rest it is gane ;   gone
I wander my lane like a night-troubled ghaist,   alone, ghost
And I sigh as my heart it would burst in my breast.   would

O had she but been of a lower degree,
I then might hae hoped she wad smiled upon me !
O how past descriving had then been my bliss,   describing
As now my distraction no words can express !

DUNCAN GRAY.

DUNCAN Gray cam here to woo,   came
  Ha, ha, the wooing o't,
On blithe Yule-night when we were fou',   Christmas
  Ha, ha, the wooing o't.
Maggie coost her head fu' high,   raised
Looked asklent and unco skeigh,   sideways, very disdainful
Gart poor Duncan stand abeigh ;   made, aloof
  Ha, ha, the wooing o't.

Duncan fleeched, and Duncan prayed ;   flattered
  Ha, ha, the wooing o't ;
Meg was deaf as Ailsa Craig,   (a rock in the Clyde)
  Ha, ha, the wooing o't.
Duncan sighed baith out and in,   both
Grat his een baith bleert and blin',   wept, eyes both
Spak o' lowpin' owre a linn ;   jumping
  Ha, ha, the wooing o't.

Duncan fleeched. and Duncan prayed.
Ha. ha. the wooing o't,
Meg was deaf as Ailsa Craig.
Ha. ha. the wooing o't.

p. 260

Time and chance are but a tide,
   Ha, ha, the wooing o't;
Slighted love is sair to bide,   sore, bear
   Ha, ha, the wooing o't.
Shall I, like a fool, quoth he,
For a haughty hizzie die?   jade
She may gae to—France for me !   go
   Ha, ha, the wooing o't.

How it comes let doctors tell,
   Ha, ha, the wooing o't;
Meg grew sick—as he grew hale,   whole
   Ha, ha, the wooing o't.
Something in her bosom wrings,
For relief a sigh she brings ;
And oh, her een, they spak sic things !   spoke, such
   Ha, ha, the wooing o't.

Duncan was a lad o' grace,
   Ha, ha, the wooing o't;
Maggie's was a piteous case,
   Ha, ha, the wooing o't.
Duncan couldna be her death,   could not
Swelling pity smoored his wrath ;   smothered
Now they're crouse and canty baith;   lively, happy both
   Ha, ha, the wooing o't.

HERE'S A HEALTH TO THEM THAT'S AWA.

Tune—Here's a Health to them that's awa.

Here's a health to them that's awa,   away
Here's a health to them that's awa ;
And wha winna wish guid luck to our cause,   who wont, good
May never guid luck be their fa' !   fate
It's guid to be merry and wise,   good
It's guid to be honest and true,
It's guid to support Caledonia's cause,
And bide by the buff and the blue.   (Whig colours)

Here's a health to them that's awa,
Here's a health to them that's awa ;
Here's a health to Charlie, the chief o' the clan,   (Fox)
Although that his band be sma.'
May liberty meet wi' success !
May prudence protect her frae ill !   from
May tyrants and tyranny tine in the mist,   be lost
AND EVER KEEP WANDERING STILL.

Here's a health to them that's awa,
Here's a health to them that's awa ;
Here's a health to Tammie, the Norland laddie,   (Lord Erskine)
That lives at the lug o' the law !

Here's freedom to him that wad read,   would
Here's freedom to him that wad write !
There's nane ever feared that the truth should be heard,
But they wham the truth wad indite.   whom, accuse

Here's a health to them that's awa,
Here's a health to them that's awa ;
Here's Chieftain M'Leod, a chieftain worth gowd,   gold
Though bred among mountains o' snaw !   snow
Here's friends on both sides of the Forth,
And friends on both sides of the Tweed ;
And wha wad betray old Albion's rights,   who would
May they never eat of her bread.

O POORTITH CAULD.
Tune—*Cauld Kail in Aberdeen.*

O POORTITH cauld, and restless love,   poverty, cold
  Ye wreck my peace between ye ;
Yet poortith a' I could forgive,
  An 'twere na for my Jeanie.   not
O why should Fate sic pleasure have,   such
  Life's dearest bands untwining ?
Or why sae sweet a flower as love,   so
  Depend on Fortune's shining ?

This warld's wealth, when I think on   world's
  Its pride, and a' the lave o't ;   rest
Fie, fie on silly coward man
  That he should be the slave o't !
     O why, &c.

Her een sae bonnie blue betray   eyes
  How she repays my passion ;
But prudence is her o'erword, aye   repetition, always
  She talks of rank and fashion.
     O why, &c.

O wha can prudence think upon,   who
  And sic a lassie by him ?
O wha can prudence think upon,
  And sae in love as I am ?
     O why, &c.

How blest the humble cotter's fate !
  He woos his simple dearie ;
The silly bogles, wealth and state,   ghosts
  Can never make them eerie.   timorous
     O why, &c.

GALA WATER.

THERE'S braw, braw lads on Yarrow braes,
  That wander through the blooming heather ;
But Yarrow braes, nor Ettrick shaws,   woods
  Can match the lads o' Gala Water.

But there is ane, a secret ane,   one
  Aboon them a' I loe him better;   above, love
And I'll be his and he'll be mine,
  The bonnie lad o' Gala Water.

Although his daddie was nae laird,   no
  And though I hae na meikle tocher;   have, much dower
Yet rich in kindness, truest love,
  We'll tent our flocks by Gala Water.   tend

It ne'er was wealth, it ne'er was wealth,
  That coft contentment, peace, or pleasure ·   bought
The bands and bliss o' mutual love,
  O that's the chiefest warld's treasure!   world's

LORD GREGORY.

O MIRK, mirk is this midnight hour,   dark
  And loud the tempest's roar;
A waefu' wanderer seeks thy tower,   woeful
  Lord Gregory, ope thy door.

An exile frae her father's ha',   from
  And a' for loving thee;
At least some *pity* on me shaw,   show
  If *love* it may na be.

Lord Gregory, mind'st thou not the grove
  By bonnie Irwine side,
Where first I owned that virgin-love
  I lang, lang had denied?   long

How aften didst thou pledge and vow   often
  Thou wad for aye be mine;   would
And my fond heart, itsel' sae true,   so
  It ne'er mistrusted thine.

Hard is thy heart, Lord Gregory,
  And flinty is thy breast:
Thou dart of heaven that flashest by,
  O wilt thou give me rest!

Ye mustering thunders from above
  Your willing victim see!
But spare and pardon my fause love,   false
  His wrangs to Heaven and me!   wrongs

OPEN THE DOOR TO ME, OH!

" O OPEN the door, some pity to show,
  O open the door to me, oh!
Though thou hast been false, I'll ever prove true,
  O open the door to me, oh

" Cauld is the blast upon my pale cheek,   cold
     But caulder thy love for me, oh !
The frost that freezes the life at my heart,
     Is nought to my pains frae thee, oh !   from

" The wan moon is setting behind the white wave,
     And time is setting with me, oh !
False friends, false love, farewell ! for mair   more
     I'll ne'er trouble them, nor thee, oh ! ".

She has opened the door, she has opened it wide ;
     She see's his pale corse on the plain, oh !
" My true love !" she cried; and sank down by his side,
     Never to rise again, oh !

YOUNG JESSIE.

TUNE—*Bonnie Dundee.*

TRUE-HEARTED was he, the sad swain of the Yarrow,
    And fair are the maids on the banks o' the Ayr,
But by the sweet side o' the Nith's winding river,
    Are lovers as faithful, and maidens as fair :
To equal young Jessie seek Scotland all over ;
    To equal young Jessie you seek it in vain ;
Grace, beauty, and elegance fetter her lover,
    And maidenly modesty fixes the chain.

O fresh is the rose in the gay dewy morning,
    And sweet is the lily at evening close ;
But in the fair presence o' lovely young Jessie
    Unseen is the lily, unheeded the rose.
Love sits in her smile, a wizard ensnaring ;
    Enthroned in her een he delivers his law :   eyes
And still to her charms she alone is a stranger—
    Her modest demeanour's the jewel of a' !

THE SOLDIER'S RETURN.

AIR—*The Mill, Mill O.*

WHEN wild war's deadly blast was blawn,   blown
     And gentle peace returning,
Wi' mony a sweet babe fatherless,
     And mony a widow mourning :   many
I left the lines and tented field,
     Where lang I'd been a lodger,   long
My humble knapsack a' my wealth,
     A poor but honest sodger.   soldier

A leal, light heart was in my breast,   true
     My hand unstained wi' plunder :
And for fair Scotia, hame again,   home
     I cheery on did wander.
I thought upon the banks o' Coil,
     I thought upon my Nancy ;

The wars are o'er, and I'm come hame,
    And find thee still true hearted!
Though poor in gear, we're rich in love,
    And mair we se ne'er be parted.

p. 265

I thought upon the witching smile
  That caught my youthful fancy.

At length I reached the bonnie glen
  Where early life I sported ;
I passed the mill, and trysting thorn,   *meeting*
  Where Nancy aft I courted :
Wha spied I but my ain dear maid   *who saw, own*
  Down by her mother's dwelling !
And turned me round to hide the flood
  That in my een was swelling.   *eyes*

Wi' altered voice, quoth I, " Sweet lass,
  Sweet as yon hawthorn's blossom,
O happy, happy may he be,
  That's dearest to thy bosom !
My purse is light, I've far to gang,   *go*
  And fain would be thy lodger ;
I've served my king and country lang—   *long*
  Take pity on a sodger ! "   *soldier*

Sae wistfully she gazed on me,   *so*
  And lovelier was than ever ;
Quo' she, " A sodger ance I loed,   *once, loved*
  Forget him shall I never :
Our humble cot and hamely fare   *homely*
  Ye freely shall partake o't ;
That gallant badge, the dear cockade,
  Ye're welcome for the sake o't.

She gazed—she reddened like a rose—
  Syne pale like ony lily ;   *then, any*
She sank within my arms, and cried,
  " Art thou my ain dear Willie ? "
" By Him who made yon sun and sky,
  By whom true love's regarded,
I am the man ; and thus may still
  True lovers be rewarded.

" The wars are o'er, and I'm come hame,
  And find thee still true-hearted !
Though poor in gear, we're rich in love,   *money*
  And mair, we'se ne'er be parted."   *more*
Quo' she, " My grandsire left me gowd,   *gold*
  A mailen plenished fairly ;   *farm*
And come, my faithfu' sodger lad,
  Thou'rt welcome to it dearly."

For gold the merchant ploughs the main,
  The farmer ploughs the manor ;
But glory is the sodger's prize,
  The sodger's wealth is honour.
The brave poor sodger ne'er despise,
  Nor count him as a stranger ;
Remember he's his country's stay
  In day and hour of danger.

WANDERING WILLIE.

HERE awa, there awa, wandering Willie,	hither, thither
Here awa, there awa, haud awa hame ;	keep
Come to my bosom, my ain only dearie,	own
Tell me thou bring'st me my Willie the same.	

Winter winds blew loud and cauld at our parting,	cold
Fears for my Willie brought tears in my ee ;	
Welcome now simmer, and welcome my Willie,	summer
The simmer to nature, my Willie to me.	

Rest, ye wild storms, in the cave of your slumbers,	
How your dread howling a lover alarms!	
Wauken, ye breezes! row gently, ye billows!	awaken
And waft my dear laddie ance mair to my arms!	once more

But oh, if he's faithless, and minds na his Nannie,	not
Flow still between us, thou wide-roaring main!	
May I never see it, may I never trow it,	believe
But, dying, believe that my Willie's my ain.	own

MEG O' THE MILL.

AIR—O Bonnie Lass, will you lie in a Barrack ?

O KEN ye what Meg o' the Mill has gotten ?	know
And ken ye what Meg o' the Mill has gotten ?	
She has gotten a coof wi' a claut o' siller,	fool, lot, money
And broken the heart o' the barley Miller.	

The Miller was strappin', the Miller was ruddy ;	
A heart like a lord, and a hue like a lady :	
The Laird was a widdiefu', bleerit knurl ;—	pitiful, dwarf
She's left the guid fellow and taen the churl.	good, taken

The Miller he hecht her a heart leal and loving;	offered, true
The Laird did address her wi' matter more moving,	
A fine pacing horse wi' a clear chainèd bridle,	
A whip by her side, and a bonnie side-saddle.	

O wae on the siller, it is sae prevailing !	woe, so
And wae on the love that is fixed on a mailen !	farm
A tocher's nae word in a true lover's parle,	dower, no
But gie me my love, and a fig for the warl !	give, world

ADDRESS TO DUMOURIER.

TUNE—Robin Adair.

YOU'RE welcome to Despots, Dumourier ;
You're welcome to Despots, Dumourier.
How does Dampierre do ?
Ay, and Beurnonville too ?
Why did they not come along with you,
Dumourier ?

I will fight France with you, Dumourier;
I will fight France with you, Dumourier;
  I will fight France with you,
  I will take my chance with you;
By my soul, I'll dance a dance with you,
      Dumourier.

Then let us fight about, Dumourier;
Then let us fight about, Dumourier;
  Then let us fight about,
  Till freedom's spark is out,
Then we'll be KILLED, no doubt—
      Dumourier.

FAREWELL, THOU STREAM THAT WINDING FLOWS.

FAREWELL, thou stream that winding flows
  Around Eliza's dwelling!
O mem'ry! spare the cruel throes
  Within my bosom swelling.
Condemned to drag a hopeless chain,
  And yet in secret languish,
To feel a fire in every vein,
  Nor dare disclose my anguish.

Love's veriest wretch, unseen, unknown,
  I fain my griefs would cover:
The bursting sigh, the unweeting groan,
  Betray the hapless lover.
I know thou doom'st me to despair,
  Nor wilt, nor canst relieve me;
But, oh! Eliza, hear one prayer,
  For pity's sake forgive me!

The music of thy voice I heard,
  Nor wist while it enslaved me;
I saw thine eyes, yet nothing feared,
  Till fears no more had saved me.
Th' unwary sailor thus aghast,
  The wheeling torrent viewing,
'Mid circling horrors sinks at last
  In overwhelming ruin.

BLITHE HAE I BEEN ON YON HILL.

TUNE—*Liggeram Cosh.*

BLITHE hae I been on yon hill,
  As the lambs before me;
Careless ilka thought and free,
  As the breeze flew o'er me:
Now nae longer sport and play,
  Mirth or sang can please me;
Lesley is sae fair and coy,
  Care and anguish seize me.

Heavy, heavy is the task,
  Hopeless love declaring ;
Trembling, I dow nocht but glower,   can, do nothing,
  Sighing, dumb, despairing !   [stare
If she winna ease the thraws   will not, pangs
  In my bosom swelling,
Underneath the grass-green sod,
  Soon maun be my dwelling.   must

LOGAN BRAES.
Tune—*Logan Water*.

O LOGAN, sweetly didst thou glide,
That day I was my Willie's bride !
And years sinsyne hae o'er us run,   since then hae
Like Logan to the simmer sun.   summe
But now thy flowery banks appear
Like drumlie winter, dark and drear,   gloomy
While my dear lad maun face his faes,* must, foes
Far, far frae me and Logan braes.   from

Again the merry month o' May
Has made our hills and valleys gay ;
The birds rejoice in leafy bowers,
The bees hum round the breathing flowers :
Blithe morning lifts his rosy eye,
And evening's tears are tears of joy :
My soul, delightless, a' surveys,
While Willie's far frae Logan braes.

Within yon milk-white hawthorn bush,
Amang her nestlings sits the thrush ;   among
Her faithfu' mate will share her toil,
Or wi' his songs her cares beguile :
But I wi' my sweet nurslings here,
Nae mate to help, nae mate to cheer,   no
Pass widowed nights and joyless days,
While Willie's far frae Logan braes.

O wae upon you, men o' state,   woe
That brethren rouse to deadly hate !
As ye make many a fond heart mourn,
Sae may it on your heads return !
How can your flinty hearts enjoy
The widow's tear, the orphan's cry ?
But soon may peace bring happy days,
And Willie hame to Logan braes !

OH WERE MY LOVE YON LILAC FAIR.
Tune—*Hughie Graham.*

O WERE my love yon lilac fair,
  Wi' purple blossoms to the spring ;
And I, a bird to shelter there,
  When wearied on my little wing !

How I wad mourn, when it was torn   would
  By Autumn wild, and Winter rude!
But I wad sing on wanton wing
  When youthfu' May its bloom renewed.

O gin my love were yon red rose,   that
  That grows upon the castle wa';
And I mysel' a drap o' dew,   drop
  Into her bonnie breast to fa'!

O there, beyond expression blest,
  I'd feast on beauty a' the night;
Sealed on her silk-saft faulds to rest,   saft folds
  Till fleyed awa by Phœbus' light!   frighted

BONNIE JEAN.

THERE was a lass, and she was fair,
  At kirk and market to be seen;
When a' the fairest maids were met,
  The fairest maid was bonnie Jean.

And aye she wrought her mammie's wark,   work
  And aye she sang sae merrilie: so
The blithest bird upon the bush
  Had ne'er a lighter heart than she.

But hawks will rob the tender joys
  That bless the little lintwhite's nest;   linnets
And frost will blight the fairest flowers,
  And love will break the soundest rest.

Young Robie was the brawest lad,
  The flower and pride of a' the glen;
And he had owsen, sheep, and kye,   oxen, kine
  And wanton naigies nine or ten.   horses

He gaed wi' Jeanie to the tryste,   went, meeting
  He danced wi' Jeanie on the down;
And lang ere witless Jeanie wist,   knew
  Her heart was tint, her peace was stown.   lost, stolen

As in the bosom o' the stream
  The moonbeam dwells at dewy e'en,   even
So trembling, pure, was tender love
  Within the breast o' bonnie Jean.

And now she works her mammie's wark,
  And aye she sighs wi' care and pain;
Yet wist na what her ail might be,   ailment
  Or what wad mak her weel again.   would, well

But did na Jeanie's heart loup light,   jump
  And did na joy blink in her ee,   eye
As Robie tauld a tale o' love   told
  Ae e'enin on the lily lea?   one

The sun was sinking in the west,
    The birds sang sweet in ilka grove ;   every
His cheek to hers he fondly prest,
    And whispered thus his tale o' love :

" O Jeanie fair, I loe thee dear ;
    O canst thou think to fancy me ;
Or wilt thou leave thy mammie's cot,
    And learn to tent the farms wi' me ?   tend

" At barn or byre thou shalt na drudge,   not
    Or naething else to trouble thee ;   nothing
But stray amang the heather-bells,
    And tent the waving corn wi' me."

Now what could artless Jeanie do ?
    She had nae will to say him na ;   no
At length she blushed a sweet consent,
    And love was aye between them twa.   two

PHILLIS THE FAIR.

TUNE—*Robin Adair*

WHILE larks with little wing
    Fanned the pure air,
Tasting the breathing spring,
    Forth I did fare :
Gay the sun's golden eye
Peeped o'er the mountains high ;
Such thy morn ! did I cry,
    Phillis the fair.

In each bird's careless song,
    Glad did I share ;
While yon wild-flowers among,
    Chance led me there :
Sweet to the opening day,
Rosebuds bent the dewy spray ;
Such thy bloom ! did I say,
    Phillis the fair.

Down in a shady walk
    Doves cooing were ;
I marked the cruel hawk
    Caught in a snare :
So kind may fortune be,
Such make his destiny,
He who would injure thee,
    Phillis the fair.

HAD I A CAVE.

TUNE—*Robin Adair.*

HAD I a cave on some wild distant shore,
Where the winds howl to the waves' dashing roar;
    There would I weep my woes,
    There seek my lost repose,
    Till grief my eyes should close,
      Ne'er to wake more!

Falsest of womankind! canst thou declare,
All thy fond-plighted vows—fleeting as air!
    To thy new lover hie,
    Laugh o'er thy perjury;
    Then in thy bosom try
      What peace is there!

BY ALLAN STREAM I CHANCED TO ROVE.

TUNE—*Allan Water.*

BY Allan stream I chanced to rove,
  While Phœbus sank beyond Benledi;
The winds were whispering through the grove,
  The yellow corn was waving ready:
I listened to a lover's sang,   *song*
  And thought on youthfu' pleasures mony;   *many*
And aye the wild-wood echoes rang—
  Oh, dearly do I love thee, Annie!

Oh, happy be the woodbine bower,
  Nae nightly bogle make it eerie;   *ghost, dismal*
Nor ever sorrow stain the hour,
  The place and time I met my dearie!
Her head upon my throbbing breast,
  She, sinking, said, " I'm thine for ever!"
While mony a kiss the seal imprest,
  The sacred vow, we ne'er should sever.

The haunt o' Spring's the primrose brae,
  The Simmer joys the flocks to follow;
How cheery through her shortening day,
  Is Autumn, in her weeds o' yellow!
But can they melt the glowing heart,
  Or chain the soul in speechless pleasure?
Or through each nerve the rapture dart.
  Like meeting her, our bosom's treasure?

WHISTLE, AND I'LL COME TO YOU, MY LAD.

TUNE—*Whistle, and I'll come to you, my Lad*

O WHISTLE, and I'll come to you, my lad,
O whistle, and I'll come to you, my lad;
Though father and mither and a' should gae mad,   *go*
O whistle, and I'll come to you, my lad.

But warily tent, when ye come to court me,   take care
And come na unless the back-yett be a-jee ;   gate, ajar
Syne up the back-stile, and let naebody see,   then
And come as ye were na comin' to me.   not

At kirk, or at market, whene'er you meet me,
Gang by me as though that ye cared nae a flie ;   go, not
But steal me a blink o' your bonnie black ee,   eye
Yet look as ye were na lookin' at me.

Aye vow and protest that ye care na for me,
And whiles ye may lichtlie my beauty a wee ;   slight
But court na anither, though jokin' ye be,
For fear that she wile your fancy frae me.   from

ADOWN WINDING NITH I DID WANDER.

TUNE—*The Mucking o' Geordie's Byre.*

ADOWN winding Nith I did wander,
  To mark the sweet flowers as they spring;
Adown winding Nith I did wander,
  Of Phillis to muse and to sing.

CHORUS.

Awa wi' your belles and your beauties,   away
' They never wi' her can compare :
Whaever has met wi' my Phillis,
  Has met wi' the queen o' the fair.

The daisy amused my fond fancy,
  So artless, so simple, so wild;
Thou emblem, said I, o' my Phillis !
  For she is simplicity's child.

The rose-bud's the blush o' my charmer,
  Her sweet balmy lip when 'tis prest :
How fair and how pure is the lily,
  But fairer and purer her breast.

Yon knot of gay flowers in the arbour,
  They ne'er wi' my Phillis can vie :
Her breath is the breath o' the woodbine,
  Its dew-drop o' diamond her eye.

Her voice is the song of the morning,
  That wakes through the green-spreading grove,
When Phœbus peeps over the mountains,
  On music, and pleasure, and love.

But, beauty, how frail and how flecting—
  The bloom of a fine summer's day !
While worth in the mind o' my Phillis
  Will flourish without a decay.

Bruce, mounted only on a little poney, struck De Bohun with his battle-axe so terrible a blow, that he was hurled dead, to the ground. *Hist of Scotland*)

Lay the proud usurpers low
Tyrants fall in every foe

COME, LET ME TAKE THEE TO MY BREAST.

AIR—*Cauld Kail.*

COME, let me take thee to my breast,
And pledge we ne'er shall sunder;
And I shall spurn as vilest dust
The warld's wealth and grandeur: world's
And do I hear my Jeanie own
That equal transports move her?
I ask for dearest life alone
That I may live to love her.

Thus in my arms, wi' all thy charms,
I clasp my countless treasure;
I'll seek nae mair o' heaven to share,   no more
Than sic a moment's pleasure: such
And by thy een sae bonnie blue,   eyes
I swear I'm thine for ever!
And on thy lips I seal my vow,
And break it shall I never!

BRUCE TO HIS MEN AT BANNOCKBURN.

TUNE—*Hey, tuttie taitie.*

SCOTS, wha hae wi' Wallace bled,   who have
Scots, wham Bruce has aften led,   whom, often
Welcome to your gory bed,
Or to victory!

Now's the day, and now's the hour;
See the front o' battle lour:
See approach, proud Edward's power—
Chains and slavery!

Wha will be a traitor knave?
Wha can fill a coward's grave?
Wha sae base as be a slave?
Let him turn and flee!

Wha for Scotland's king and law
Freedom's sword will strongly draw,
Freeman stand, or freeman fa',   fall
Let him follow me!

By oppression's woes and pains!
By your sons in servile chains!
We will drain our dearest veins,
But they shall be free!

Lay the proud usurpers low!
Tyrants fall in every foe!
Liberty's in every blow!—
Let us do or dee.   die

BEHOLD THE HOUR.

TUNE—*Oran Gaoil.*

BEHOLD the hour, the boat arrive;
  Thou goest, thou darling of my heart
Severed from thee, can I survive?
  But fate has willed, and we must part.
I'll often greet this surging swell,
  Yon distant isle will often hail:
" E'en here I took the last farewell;
  There latest marked her vanished sail."

Along the solitary shore,
  While flitting sea-fowl round me cry,
Across the rolling, dashing roar,
  I'll westward turn my wistful eye:
Happy thou Indian grove, I'll say,
  Where now my Nancy's path may be!
While through thy sweets she loves to stray,
  Oh, tell me, does she muse on me?

DOWN THE BURN, DAVIE.

AS down the burn they took their way,
  And through the flowery dale;
His cheek to hers he aft did lay,   oft
  And love was aye the tale.   always

With " Mary, when shall we return,
  Sic pleasure to renew?"   such
Quoth Mary: " Love, I like the burn,
  And aye shall follow you."

THOU HAST LEFT ME EVER.

TUNE—*Fee him, Father.*

THOU hast left me ever, Jamie! thou hast left me ever;
Thou hast left me ever, Jamie! thou hast left me ever:
Aften hast thou vowed that death only should us sever;   oft
Now thou'st left thy lass for aye—I maun see thee never, Jamie,
    I'll see thee never.

Thou hast me forsaken, Jamie! thou hast me forsaken;
Thou hast me forsaken, Jamie! thou hast me forsaken:
Thou canst love anither jo, while my heart is breaking;   lover
Soon my weary een I'll close—never mair to waken, Jamie, eyes
    Ne'er mair to waken!   more

WHERE ARE THE JOYS?

TUNE—*Saw ye my Father?*

WHERE are the joys I have met in the morning,
  That danced to the lark's early song?
Where is the peace that awaited my wandering.
  At evening the wild-woods among?

No more a-winding the course of yon river,
   And marking sweet flowerets so fair ; ·
No more I trace the light footsteps of pleasure,
   But sorrow and sad sighing care.

Is it that Summer's forsaken our valleys,
   And grim, surly Winter is near ?
No, no ! the bees humming round the gay roses,
. Proclaim it the pride of the year.

Fain would I hide what I fear to discover,
   Yet long, long too well have I known,
All that has causèd this wreck in my bosom
   Is Jenny, fair Jenny alone.

Time cannot aid me, my griefs are immortal,
   Not hope dare a comfort bestow :
Come, then, enamoured and fond of my anguish,
   Enjoyment I'll seek in my wo.

DELUDED SWAIN, THE PLEASURE.

TUNE—*The Collier's Bonnie Lassie.*

DELUDED swain, the pleasure
   The fickle fair can give thee,
Is but a fairy treasure—
   Thy hopes will soon deceive thee.

The billows on the ocean,
   The breezes idly roaming,
The clouds' uncertain motion—
   They are but types of woman.

Oh! art thou not ashamed
   To dote upon a feature ?
If man thou would'st be named,
   Despise the silly creature.

Go, find an honest fellow ;
   Good claret set before thee :
Hold on till thou art mellow,
   And then to bed in glory.

MY SPOUSE NANCY.

TUNE—*My Joe Janet.*

" HUSBAND, husband, cease your strife,
   Nor longer idly rave, sir ;
Though I am your wedded wife,
   Yet I am not your slave, sir."

⁑ One of two must still obey,
   Nancy, Nancy ;

Is it man, or woman, say,
My spouse, Nancy ?"

" If 'tis still the lordly word,
Service and obedience ;
I'll desert my sovereign lord,
And so good-by allegiance !"

" Sad will I be, so bereft,
Nancy, Nancy ;
Yet I'll try to make a shift,
My spouse, Nancy."

" My poor heart then break it must,
My last hour I'm near it :
When you lay me in the dust,
Think, think how you will bear it."

" I will hope and trust in Heaven,
Nancy, Nancy ;
Strength to bear it will be given,
My spouse, Nancy."

" Well, sir, from the silent dead,
Still I'll try to daunt you ;
Ever round your midnight bed
Horrid sp'rites shall haunt you."

" I'll wed another like my dear,
Nancy, Nancy ;
Then THE SP'RITES will fly for fear,
My spouse, Nancy."

THE LOVELY LASS OF INVERNESS.

TUNE—*Lass of Inverness.*

THE lovely lass o' Inverness,	
Nae joy nor pleasure can she see ;	**no**
For e'en and morn she cries, alas !	
And aye the saut tear blin's her ee ;	salt, blinds, eye
Drumossie Moor—Drumossie-day—	
A waeful day it was to me !	woeful
For there I lost my father dear—	
·My father dear, and brethren three.	

Their winding sheet the bluidy clay,	bloody
Their graves are growing green to see ;	
And by them lies the dearest lad	
That ever blest a woman's ee !	eye
Now wae to thee, thou cruel lord,	woe
A bluidy man I trow thou be ;	
For mony a heart thou hast made sair,	many, sore
That ne'er did wrong to thine or thee.	

A RED, RED ROSE.

Tune—Graham's Strathspey.

O MY luve's like a red, red rose,   love
  That's newly sprung in June:
O my luve's like the melodie,
  That's sweetly played in tune.
As fair art thou, my bonnie lass,
  So deep in luve am I:
And I will luve thee still, my dear,
  Till a' the seas gang dry.   go

Till a' the seas gang dry, my dear,
  And the rocks melt wi' the sun;
1 will love thee still, my dear,
  While the sands o' life shall run.
And fare thee weel, my only luve!
  And fare thee weel awhile!
And I will come again, my luve,
  Though it were ten thousand mile.

OUT OVER THE FORTH.

Tune—Charlie Gordon's welcome hame.

OUT over the Forth I look to the north,
  But what is the north and its Highlands to me?
The south nor the east gie ease to my breast,   give
  The far foreign land, or the wild rolling sea.

But I look to the west, when I gae to rest,   go
  That happy my dreams and my slumbers may be;
For far in the west lives he I loe best,
  The lad that is dear to my babie and me.

LOUIS, WHAT RECK I BY THEE?

Tune—Louis, what reck I by thee?

LOUIS, what reck I by thee,
  Or Geordie on his ocean?
Dyvor, beggar loons to me—   bankrupt, fellows
  I reign in Jeanie's bosom.

Let her crown my love her law,
  And in her breast enthrone me:
Kings and nations—swith, awa!   sooth, away
  Reif randies, I disown ye!   thief-beggars

SOMEBODY!

Tune—For the sake of Somebody.

MY heart is sair—I dare na tell—   sore
  My heart is sair for somebody;

I could wake a winter night
    For the sake of somebody.
        Oh-hon ! for somebody !
        Oh-hey ! for somebody !
I could range the world around,
    For the sake o' somebody !

Ye powers that smile on virtuous love,
    O sweetly smile on somebody !
Frae ilka danger keep him free,   from every
    And send me safe my somebody !
        Oh-hon ! for somebody !
        Oh-hey ! for somebody !
I wad do—what wad I not ?   would
    For the sake o' somebody !

WILT THOU BE MY DEARIE ?
AIR—*The Sutor's Dochter.*

WILT thou be my dearie ?
When sorrow wrings thy gentle heart,
Wilt thou let me cheer thee ?
By the treasure of my soul,
That's the love I bear thee !
I swear and vow that only thou
Shall ever be my dearie.
Only thou, I swear and vow,
Shall ever be my dearie.

Lassie, say thou loes me ;   lovest
Or if thou wilt na be my ain,   not, own
Say na thou'lt refuse me :
If it winna, canna be,   will not, cannot
Thou, for thine may choose me,
Let me, lassie, quickly die,
Trusting that thou loes me.
Lassie, let me quickly die,
Trusting that thou loes me.

LOVELY POLLY STEWART.
TUNE—*Ye're welcome, Charlie Stewart.*

O LOVELY Polly Stewart
    O charming Polly Stewart !
There's not a flower that blooms in May
    That's half so fair as thou art.
The flower it blaws, it fades and fa's,   blows, falls
    And art can ne'er renew it ;
But worth and truth eternal youth
    Will give to Polly Stewart.

May he whose arms shall fauld thy charms,   fold
    Possess a leal and true heart ;
To him be given to ken the heaven   know
    He grasps in Polly Stewart.

O lovely Polly Stewart!
O charming Polly Stewart!
There's ne'er a flower that blooms in May
That's half so sweet as thou art.

COULD AUGHT OF SONG.

Tune—*At Setting Day.*

Could aught of song declare my pains,
　Could artful numbers move thee,
The Muse should tell, in laboured strains,
　O Mary, how I love thee!
They who but feign a wounded heart
　May teach the lyre to languish;
But what avails the pride of art,
　When wastes the soul with anguish?

Then let the sudden bursting sigh
　The heart-felt pang discover;
And in the keen, yet tender eye,
　O read th' imploring lover!
For well I know thy gentle mind
　Disdains art's gay disguising;
Beyond what fancy e'er refined,
　The voice of Nature prizing.

WAE IS MY HEART.

Tune—*Wae is my Heart.*

Wae is my heart, and the tear's in my ee;　　woe, eye
Lang, lang, joy's been a stranger to me:　　long
Forsaken and friendless, my burden I bear,
And the sweet voice o' pity ne'er sounds in my ear.

Love, thou hast pleasures, and deep hae I loved;　have
Love, thou hast sorrows, and sair hae I proved;　sore
But this bruisèd heart that now bleeds in my breast,
I can feel its throbbings will soon be at rest.

Oh, if I were happy, where happy I hae been,
Down by yon stream, and yon bonnie castle-green;
For there he is wand'ring, and musing on me,
Wha wad soon dry the tear frae Phillis's ee.　　who would

HERE'S TO THY HEALTH MY BONNIE LASS.

Tune—*Laggan Burn.*

Here's to thy health, my bonnie lass,
　Guid-night, and joy be wi' thee;　　good
I'll come nae mair to thy bower-door,　　no more
　To tell thee that I loe thee.　　love

O dinna think, my pretty pink,   don't
   But I can live without thee :
I vow and swear I dinna care
   How lang ye look about ye.   long

Thou'rt aye sae free informing me   so
   Thou hast nae mind to marry ;
I'll be as free informing thee
   Nae time hae I to tarry.   have
I ken thy friends try ilka means,   know, every
   Frae wedlock to delay thee ;
Depending on some higher chance—
   But fortune may betray thee.

I ken they scorn my low estate,
   But that does never grieve me ;
But I'm as free as any he,
   Sma' siller will relieve me.   wealth
I count my health my greatest wealth,
   Sae long as I'll enjoy it :   so
I'll fear nae scant, I'll bode nae want,   scarcity, forbode
   As lang's I get employment.

But far-off fowls hae feathers fair,
   And aye until ye try them :
Though they seem fair, still have a care,
   They may prove waur thàn I am.   worse
But STILL at night, when the moon shines bright,
   My dear, I'll come and see thee ;
For the man that loes his mistress weel,
   Nae travel makes him weary.

ANNA, THY CHARMS.

TUNE—*Bonnie Mary.*

ANNA, thy charms my bosom fire,
   And waste my soul with care ;
But, ah ! how bootless to admire,
   When fated to despair !
Yet in thy presence, lovely fair,
   To hope may be forgiven ;
For sure 'twere impious to despair,
   So much in sight of heaven.

MY LADY'S DINK.

MY lady's dink, my lady's drest,   trim
The flower and fancy of the west,
But the lassie that a man loes best,
O that's the lass to make him blest.

Out ower yon muir, out ower yon moss,   o'er
Whare gor-cocks through the heather pass, where moorcocks
There wons auld Colin's bonnie lass—   dwells
A lily in a wilderness.

Sae sweetly move her gentle limbs,   so
Like music notes o' lovers' hymns:
The diamond dew is her een sae blue,   eyes
Where laughing love sae wanton swims.

JOCKEY'S TAEN THE PARTING KISS.

TUNE—*Jockey's taen the parting Kiss.*

JOCKEY'S taen the parting kiss,   taken
  O'er the mountains he is gane;   gone
And with him is a' my bliss,
  Nought but griefs with me remain.
Spare my luve, ye winds that blaw,   love, blow
  Plashy sleets and beating rain!
Spare my luve, thou feathery snaw,   snow
  Drifting o'er the frozen plain.

When the shades of evening creep
  O'er the day's fair, gladsome ee,   eye
Sound and safely may he sleep,
  Sweetly blithe his waukening be!   awaking
He will think on her he loves,
  Fondly he'll repeat her name;
For where'er he distant roves,   home
  Jockey's heart is still at hame.

O LAY THY LOOF IN MINE, LASS.

TUNE—*Cordwainers' March.*

O LAY thy loof in mine, lass,   hand
In mine, lass, in mine, lass;
And swear on thy white hand, lass,
  That thou wilt be my ain.   own

A slave to love's unbounded sway,
He aft has wrought me meikle wae;   oft, much woe
But now he is my deadly fae,   foe
  Unless thou be my ain.

There's mony a lass has broke my rest,
That for a blink I hae loed best;   moment, I've loved
But thou art queen within my breast,
  For ever to remain.
    O lay thy loof in mine, lass,
    In mine, lass, in mine, lass;
    And swear on thy white hand, lass,
      That thou wilt be my ain.

O MALLY'S MEEK, MALLY'S SWEET.

O MALLY'S meek, Mally's sweet,
  Mally's modest and discreet,
Mally's rare, Mally's fair,
  Mally's every way complete.

As I was walking up the street,
　A barefit maid I chanced to meet;
But oh, the road was very hard
　For that fair maiden's tender feet.

It were mair meet that those fine feet　　more
　Were weel laced up in silken shoon;　　shoes
And 'twere more fit that she should sit
　Within yon chariot gilt aboon.　　above

Her yellow hair, beyond compare,
　Comes trinkling down her swan-like neck;
And her two eyes, like stars in skies,
　Would keep a sinking ship frae wreck.　　from

THE BANKS OF CREE.

TUNE—*The Banks of Cree.*

HERE is the glen, and here the bower
　All underneath the birchen shade;
The village-bell has tolled the hour,
　O what can stay my lovely maid?

'Tis not Maria's whispering call;
　'Tis but the balmy-breathing gale,
Mixed with some warbler's dying fall,
　The dewy star of eve to hail.

It is Maria's voice I hear!—
　So calls the woodlark in the grove,
His little faithful mate to cheer;
　At once 'tis music and 'tis love.

And art thou come?—and art thou true?
　O welcome, dear, to love and me!
And let us all our vows renew,
　Along the flowery banks of Cree.

ON THE SEAS AND FAR AWAY.

TUNE—*O'er the Hills, &c.*

How can my poor heart be glad,
When absent from my sailor lad?
How can I the thought forego,
He's on the seas to meet the foe?
Let me wander, let me rove,
Still my heart is with my love:
Nightly dreams, and thoughts by day,
Are with him that's far away.

CHORUS.

　On the seas and far away,
　On stormy seas and far away;
　Nightly dreams, and thoughts by day,
　Are aye with him that's far away.

When in Summer's noon I faint,
As weary flocks around me pant,
Haply in the scorching sun
My sailor's thundering at his gun :
Bullets, spare my only joy !
Bullets, spare my darling boy !
Fate, do with me what you may,
Spare but him that's far away !

At the starless midnight hour,
When Winter rules with boundless power ;
As the storms the forest tear,
And thunders rend the howling air,
Listening to the doubling roar,
Surging on the rocky shore,
All I can—I weep and pray,
For his weal that's far away.

Peace, thy olive wand extend,
And bid wild War his ravage end,
Man with brother man to meet,
And as a brother kindly greet ;
Then may Heaven, with prosperous gales,
Fill my sailor's welcome sails,
To my arms their charge convey,
My dear lad that s far away.

CA' THE YOWES TO THE KNOWES.

CHORUS.

Ca' the yowes to the knowes,	call, ewes, knolls
Ca' them where the heather grows,	
Ca' them where the burnie rows,	streamlet, rolls
My bonny dearie !	

Hark ! the mavis' evening-sang	thrush
Sounding Cluden's woods amang ;	among
Then a-faulding let us gang,	sheep-fold
My bonny dearie.	

We'll gae down by Cluden side,	go
Through the hazels spreading wide,	
O'er the waves that sweetly glide	
To the moon sae clearly.	so

Yonder Cluden's silent towers,
Where at moonshine midnight hours,
O'er the dewy bending flowers,
    Fairies dance sae cheery.

Ghaist nor bogle shalt thou fear ;	ghost, spectre
Thou'rt to love and heaven sae dear,	so
Nocht of ill may come thee near,	nought
My bonnie dearie.	

Fair and lovely as thou art,
Thou hast stown my very heart;   *stolen*
I can die—but canna part,   *cannot*
    My bonny dearie.

While waters wimple to the sea;   *meander*
While day blinks in the lift sae hie;   *sky so high*
Till clay-cauld death shall blin' my ee,   *cold, eye*
    Ye shall be my dearie.

ANOTHER VERSION.

Ca' the yowes to the knowes,   *drive, knoll*
Ca' them where the heather grows,
Ca' them where the burnie rows,   *rolls*
    My bonny dearie.

As I gaed down the water-side,   *went*
There I met my shepherd lad,
He rowed me sweetly in his plaid,   *wrapped*
    And he ca'd me his dearie.   *called*

Will ye gang down the water-side,   *go*
And see the waves sae sweetly glide?   *so*
Beneath the hazel spreading wide,
    The moon it shines fu' clearly.

Ye sall get gowns and ribbons meet,   *shall*
Cauf leather shoon upon your feet,   *calf, shoes*
And in my arms ye'se EVER sleep,
    And ye sall be my dearie.

If ye but stand to what ye've said,
I'se gang wi' you, my shepherd lad,   *go*
And ye may row me in your plaid,
    And I sall be your dearie.

While waters wimple to the sea,   *meander*
While day blinks in the lift sae hie,   *sky so high*
Till clay-cauld death shall blin' my ee,   *cold, eye*
    Ye sall be my dearie.

SHE SAYS SHE LOES ME BEST OF A

TUNE—*Onagh's Lock.*

SAE flaxen were her ringlets,   *so*
    Her eyebrows of a darker hue,
Bewitchingly o'er-arching
    Twa laughing een o' bonnie blue.   *two, eyes*
Her smiling, sae wiling,
    Wad make a wretch forget his wo: *would*
What pleasure, what treasure,
    Unto these rosy lips to grow:

Such was my Chloris' bonnie face,
  When first her bonnie face I saw;
And aye my Chloris' dearest charm,
  She says she loes me best of a'.   loves

Like harmony her motion;
  Her pretty ankle is a spy
Betraying fair proportion,
  Wad make a saint forget the sky.   would
Sae warming, sae charming,   so
  Her faultless form and graceful air;
Ilk feature—auld Nature   each
  Declared that she could do nae mair. no more
Hers are the willing chains o' love,
  By conquering beauty's sovereign law;
And aye my Chloris' dearest charm,
  She says she loes me best of a'.   loves

Let others love the city,
  And gaudy show at sunny noon;
Gie me the lonely valley,   give
  The dewy eve, and rising moon
Fair beaming, and streaming,
  Her silver light the boughs amang: among
While falling, recalling,
  The amorous thrush concludes his sang: song
There, dearest Chloris, wilt thou rove
  By wimpling burn and leafy shaw, winding, wood
And hear my vows o' truth and love,
  And say thou loes me best of a'.

SAW YE MY PHELY?

Tune—When she cam ben she bobbit.

Oh, saw ye my dear, my Phely?
Oh, saw ye my dear, my Phely?
She's down i' the grove, she's wi' a new love,
  She winna come hame to her Willy. wont, home

What says she, my dearest, my Phely?
What says she, my dearest, my Phely?
She let's thee to wit, that she has thee forgot, informs
  And for ever disowns thee, her Willy.

Oh, had I ne'er seen thee, my Phely!
Oh, had I ne'er seen thee, my Phely!
As light as the air, and fause as thou's fair, false
  Thou's broken the heart o' thy Willy.

HOW LONG AND DREARY IS THE NIGHT!

Tune—Cauld Kail in Aberdeen.

How long and dreary is the night
  When I am frae my dearie! from
I restless lie frae e'en to morn,
  Though I were ne'er sae weary. so

CHORUS.

For oh, her lanely nights are lang!   lonely
And oh, her dreams are eerie!   glóomy
And oh, her widowed heart is sair,   sore
That's absent frae her dearie!

When I think on the lightsome days
I spent wi' thee, my dearie,
And now what seas between us roar,
How can I be but eerie?

How slow ye move, ye heavy hours!
The joyless day, how dreary!
It was na sae ye glinted by,   not so, glanced
When I was wi' my dearie!

LET NOT WOMAN E'ER COMPLAIN.

TUNE—*Duncan Gray.*

LET not woman e'er complain
Of inconstancy in love;
Let not woman e'er complain
Fickle man is apt to rove.

Look abroad through Nature's range,
Nature's mighty law is change;
Ladies, would it not be strange,
Man should then a monster prove?

Mark the winds, and mark the skies;
Ocean's ebb, and ocean's flow:
Sun and moon but set to rise,
Round and round the seasons go.

Why, then, ask of silly man
To oppose great Nature's plan?
We'll be constant while we can—
You can be no more, you know.

THE LOVER'S MORNING SALUTE TO HIS MISTRESS.

TUNE—*Deil tak the Wars.*

SLEEP'ST thou, or wak'st thou, fairest creature?
Rosy Morn now lifts his eye,
Numbering ilka bud which Nature   each
Waters wi' the tears o' joy:
Now through the leafy woods,
And by the reeking floods,   smoking
Wild Nature's tenants freely, gladly stray;
The lintwhite in his bower   linnet
Chants o'er the breathing flower;
The lav'rock to the sky   lark
Ascends wi' sangs o' joy,   songs
While the sun and thou arise to bless the day.

Phœbus gilding the brow o' morning,
  Banishes ilk darksome shade,
Nature gladd'ning and adorning;
  Such to me my lovely maid.
When absent frae my fair,   *from*
  The murky shades o' care
With starless gloom o'ercast my sullen sky;
  But when in beauty's light,
  She meets my ravished sight,
  When through my very heart
  Her beaming glories dart—
'Tis then I wake to life, to light, and joy!

THE AULD MAN.

But lately seen in gladsome green,
  The woods rejoiced the day;
Through gentle showers the laughing flowers
  In double pride were gay:
But now our joys are fled
  On winter blasts awa!   *away*
Yet maiden May, in rich array,
  Again shall bring them a'.

But my white pow, nae kindly thowe   *head, no, thaw*
  Shall melt the snaws of age;   *snows*
My trunk of eild, but buss or beild, *age, without bush*
  Sinks in Time's wintry rage.   [*shelter*
Oh, age has weary days,
  And nights o' sleepless pain!
Thou golden time o' youthful prime,
  Why com'st thou not again?

MY CHLORIS, MARK HOW GREEN THE GROVES.

Tune—*My Lodging is on the cold Ground.*

My Chloris, mark how green the groves,
  The primrose banks how fair;
The balmy gales awake the flowers,
  And wave thy flaxen hair.

The lav'rock shuns the palace gay,   *lark*
  And o'er the cottage sings:
For Nature smiles as sweet, I ween,
  To shepherds as to kings.

Let minstrels sweep the skilfu' string
  In lordly lighted ha':
The shepherd stops his simple reed,
  Blithe, in the birken shaw.   **birch woods**

The princely revel may survey
  Our rustic dance wi' scorn

But arc their hearts as light as ours
  Beneath the milk-white thorn ?

The shepherd, in the flowery glen,
  In shepherd's phrase will woo :
The courtier tells a finer tale,
  But is his heart as true ?

These wild-wood flowers I've pu'd, to deck
  That spotless breast o' thine :
The courtier's gems may witness love—
  But 'tis na love like mine.   **not**

IT WAS THE CHARMING MONTH OF MAY.

TUNE—*Dainty Davie.*

IT was the charming month of May,
When all the flowers were fresh and gay,
One morning, by the break of day,
  The youthful, charming Chloe ;
From peaceful slumber she arose,
Girt on her mantle and her hose,
And o'er the flowery mead she goes,
  The youthful, charming Chloe.

CHORUS.

Lovely was she by the dawn,
  Youthful Chloe, charming Chloe,
Tripping o'er the pearly lawn,
  The youthful, charming Chloe.

The feathered people, you might see
Perched all around on every tree,
In notes of sweetest melody
  They hail the charming Chloe ;
Till, painting gay the eastern skies,
The glorious sun began to rise,
Out-rivalled by the radiant eyes
  Of youthful, charming Chloe.

LASSIE WI' THE LINT-WHITE LOCKS.

TUNE—*Rothemurchie's Rant.*

CHORUS.

LASSIE wi' the lint-white locks,
  Bonnie lassie, artless lassie,
Wilt thou wi' me tent the flocks,   **tend**
  Wilt thou be my dearie O ?

Now Nature cleeds the flowery lea,   **clothes**
And a' is young and sweet like thee :
Oh, wilt thou share its joys wi' me,
  And say thou'lt be my dearie O ?

And when the welcome simmer shower   summer
Has cheered ilk drooping little flower,   each
We'll to the breathing woodbine bower
    At sultry noon, my dearie O.

When Cynthia lights, wi' silver ray,
The weary shearer's hameward way,   homeward
Through yellow waving fields we'll stray,
    And talk o' love, my dearie O.

And when the howling wintry blast
Disturbs my lassie's midnight rest,
Enclaspèd to my faithful breast,
    I'll comfort thee, my dearie O.

PHILLY AND WILLY.

TUNE—*The Sow's Tail.*

HE.

O PHILLY, happy be that day,
When roving through the gathered hay,
My youthfu' heart was stown away,   stolen
    And by thy charms, my Philly.

SHE.

O Willy, aye I bless the grove
Where first I owned my maiden love,
Whilst thou didst pledge the powers above
    To be my ain dear Willy.

HE.

As songsters of the early year
Are ilka day mair sweet to hear,   every, more
So·ilka day to me mair dear
    And charming is my Philly.

SHE.

As on the brier the budding rose
Still richer breathes and fairer blows,
So in my tender bosom grows
    The love I bear my Willie.

HE.

The milder sun and bluer sky,
That crown my harvest cares wi' joy,
Were ne'er sae welcome to my eye   so
    As is a sight o' Philly.

SHE.

The little swallow's wanton wing,
Though wafting o'er the flowery spring,
Did ne'er to me sic tidings bring,   such
    As meeting o' my Willy.

HE

The bee that through the sunny hour
Sips nectar in the opening flower,
Compared wi' my delight is poor,
　　Upon the lips o' Philly.

SHE.

The woodbine in the dewy weet,　　　　　　weet
When evening shades in silence meet,
Is nocht sae fragrant or sae sweet　　　　nought so
　　As is a kiss o' Willy.

HE.

Let fortune's wheel at random rin,　　　　run
And fools may tyne, and knaves may win ;　lose
My thoughts are a' bound up in ane,　　　 one
　　And that's my ain dear Philly.

SHE.

What's a' the joys that gowd can gie ?　　gold, give
I care na wealth a single flie;　　　　　 not
The lad I love's the lad for me,
And that's my ain dear Willy.

CONTENTED WI' LITTLE.
TUNE—Lumps o' Pudding.

CONTENTED wi' little, and cantie wi' mair,　　merry, more
Whene'er I forgather wi' sorrow and care,　　meet
I gie them a skelp as they're creepin' alang,　give, stroke, along
Wi' a cog o' guid swats, and an auld Scottish sang.　bowl, ale

I whiles claw the elbow o' troublesome thought;　sometimes scratch
But man is a sodger, and life is a faught :　　soldier, fight
My mirth and good-humour are coin in my pouch,　pocket
And my freedom's my lairdship nae monarch dare touch.　no

A towmond o' trouble, should that be my fa',　　year, fate
A night o' guid-fellowship sowthers it a' :　　good, soldiers
When at the blithe end of our journey at last,
What MAN ever thinks o' the road he has past ?

　　　　　　　　　　　　　　　　　　　[totter
Blind Chance, let her snapper and stoyte on her way;　stumble,
Be't to me, be't frae me, e'en let the jade gae:　from, go
Come ease, or come travail; come pleasure, or pain,
My warst word is: "Welcome, and welcome again ! "　worst

CANST THOU LEAVE ME THUS MY KATY ?
TUNE—Roy's Wife.

CHORUS.

CANST thou leave me thus, my Katy ?
Canst thou leave me thus, my Katy ?
Well thou know'st my aching heart,
And canst thou leave me thus for pity ?

Is this thy plighted, fond regard,
  Thus cruelly to part, my Katy?
Is this thy faithful swain's reward—
  An aching, broken heart, my Katy?

Farewell! and ne'er such sorrows tear
  That fickle heart of thine, my Katy!
Thou may'st find those will love thee dear —
  But not a love like mine, my Katy.

FOR A' THAT AND A' THAT.

Is there, for honest poverty,
  That hangs his head, and a' that!
The coward slave we pass him by,
  We dare be poor for a' that!
For a' that, and a' that,
  Our toils obscure, and a' that;
The rank is but the guinea's stamp,
  The man's the gowd for a' that! gold

What though on hamely fare we dine, homely
  Wear hoddin gray, and a' that; coarse cloth
Gie fools their silks, and knaves their wine, give
  A man's a man for a' that!
For a' that, and a' that,
  Their tinsel show, and a' that;
The honest man, though e'er sae poor, so
  Is king o' men for a' that!

Ye see yon birkie, ca'd a lord, young fellow
  Wha struts, and stares, and a' that; who
Though hundreds worship at his word,
  He's but a coof for a' that: fool
For a' that, and a' that,
  His ribbon, star, and a' that;
The man of independent mind,
  He looks and laughs at a' that.

A prince can mak a belted knight,
  A marquis, duke, and a' that;
But an honest man's aboon his might, above
  Guid faith, he maunna fa' that! attempt
For a' that, and a' that,
  Their dignities, and a' that;
The pith o' sense, and pride o' worth,
  Are higher rank than a' that.

Then let us pray that come it may—
  As come it will for a' that—
That sense and worth, o'er a' the earth,
  May bear the gree, and a' that. supremacy
For a' that, and a' that,
  It's coming yet, for a' that,
That man to man, the warld o'e·, world
  Shall brothers be for a' that!

O LASSIE, ART THOU SLEEPING YET!

TUNE—*Let me in this ae Night.*

O LASSIE, art thou sleeping yet?
Or art thou wakin', I would wit?
For love has bound me hand and foot,
    And I would fain be in, jo.

CHORUS.

  O let me in this ae night,   one
    This ae, ae, ae night;
  For pity's sake this ae night,
    O rise and let me in, jo!

Thou hear'st the winter wind and weet,   wet
Nae star blinks through the driving sleet; no
Tak pity on my weary feet,
    And shield me frae the rain, jo.   from

The bitter blast that round me blaws   blows
Unheeded howls, unheeded fa's;   falls
The cauldness o' thy heart's the cause coldness
    Of a' my grief and pain, jo.

Her Answer.

O TELL na me o' wind and rain,   not
Upbraid na me wi' cauld disdain;
Gae back the gait ye cam again—   go, way, came
    I winna let ye in, jo!

CHORUS.

  I tell you now this ae night,
    This ae, ae, ae night;
  And ance for a' this ae night,   once
    I winna let you in, jo!

The snellest blast, at mirkest hours,   darkest
That round the pathless wanderer pours,
Is nocht to what poor she endures,   nought
    That's trusted faithless man, jo.

The sweetest flower that decked the mead,
Now trodden like the vilest weed;
Let simple maid the lesson read,
    The weird may be her ain, jo.   fate, own

The bird that charmed his summer-day,
Is now the cruel fowler's prey;
Let witless, trusting woman say
    How aft her fate's the same, jo!   oft

BALLADS ON MR HERON'S ELECTION, 1795.*

BALLAD FIRST.

WHOM will you send to London town,
  To Parliament and a' that?
Or wha in a' the country round   whc
  The best deserves to fa' that?   try
    For a' that, and a' that,
    Through Galloway, and a' that;
    Where is the laird or belted knight
    That best deserves to fa' that?

Wha sees Kerroughtree's† open yett,   gate
  And wha is't never saw that?
Wha ever wi' Kerroughtree meets,
  And has a doubt of a' that?
    For a' that, and a' that,
    Here's Heron yet for a' that!
    The independent patriot,
    The honest man, and a' that.

Though wit and worth in either sex,
  St Mary's Isle can shaw that   show
Wi' dukes and lords let Selkirk‡ mix,
  And weel does Selkirk fa' that.   well
    For a' that, and a' that,
    Here's Heron yet for a' that!
    The independent commoner
    Shall be the man for a' that.

But why should we to nobles jouk?   bend
  And is't against the law that?
For why, a lord may be a gouk,   fool
  Wi' ribbon, star, and a' that.
    For a' that, and a' that,
    Here's Heron yet for a' that!
    A lord may be a STUPID loun,   fellow
    Wi' ribbon, star, and a' that.

A beardless boy§ comes o'er the hills,
  Wi' uncle's‖ purse and a' that,
But we'll hae ane frae 'mang oursels,   one from
  A man we ken, and a' that.   know
    For a' that, and a' that,
    Here's Heron yet for a' that!
    For we're not to be bought and sold,
    Like naigs, and nowt, and a' that.   horses,cattle

Then let us drink the Stewartry,   (of Kirkcudbright
  Kerroughtree's laird, and a' that,
Our representative to be,
  For weel he's worthy a' that.

---

* For the Stewartry of Kirkcudbright.   § Mr Gordon of Balmaghie, Tory
† Mr Heron, tne Whig candidate.   candidate.
‡ The Earl of Selkirk.   Mr Murray of Broughton.

For a' that, and a' that,
Here's Heron yet for a' that!
A House of Commons such as he,
They would be blest that saw that.

BALLAD SECOND.

Fy, let us a' to Kirkcudbright,
  For there will be bickering there;
For Murray's light horse are to muster,
  And oh, how the heroes will swear!

First, there will be trusty Kerroughtree,
  Whase honour was ever his law;   whose
If the virtues were packed in a parcel,
  His worth might be sample for a'.

And strong and respectfu's his backing,
  The maist o' the lairds wi' him stand;   most
Nae gipsy-like nominal barons,
  Whase property 's paper,* but lands.   whose, without

For there frae the Niddisdale borders,   from
  The Maxwells will gather in droves,
Teugh Jockie,† stanch Geordie,‡ and Wellwood,§   tough
  That griens for the fishes and loaves.   longs

And there will be Heron the Major,‖
  Wha'll ne'er be forgot in the Greys;   who'll
Our flattery we'll keep for some other,
  Him only 'tis justice to praise.

And there will be Maiden Kilkerran,¶
  And also Barskimming's gude knight;**
And there will be roaring Birtwhistle,††
  Wha luckily roars i' the right.

Next there will be wealthy young Richard—‡‡
  Dame Fortune should hing by the neck   hang
For prodigal thriftless bestowing—
  His merit had won him respect.

And there will be rich brother nabobs,§§
  Though nabobs, yet men of the first;
And there will be Collieston's whiskers,‖‖
  And Quintin, o' lads not the warst.¶¶

And there will be stamp-office Johnnie***—
  Take care how ye purchase a dram;

And there will be gay Cassencarrie,*
And there will be gleg Colonel Tam.†   *sharp*

And there will be folk frae St Mary's,
A house of great merit and note ;   *(Selkirk)*
For NAE ane but honours them highly,   *no one*
But THERE's few will gie them a vote.

And there'll be Murray commander,
And Gordon the battle to win ;
Like brothers they'll stand by each other,
Sae knit in alliance and sin.   *so*

And there'll be Kempleton's birkie,‡
A chiel no sae black at the bane ;   *bone*
For as for his fine nabob fortune,
We'll e'en let that subject alane.   *alone*

And there'll be Wigton's new sheriff,§
Dame Justice fu' brawly has sped ;
She's gotten the heart o' a Bushby,
But, what is become o' the head ?

And there is our king's lord-lieutenant,
So famed for his grateful return ;
The birkie is getting his questions,
To say in St Stephen's the morn.

And there will be Douglases doughty,
New-christening towns far and near ;
Abjuring their democrat doings,
By kissing the TAE of a peer,   *toe*

And there'll be lads o' the gospel ;
Muirhead, wha's as guid as he's true ;¶   *who's*
And there'll be Buittle's apostle,**
Wha's mair o' the black than the blue.   *more*

And there'll be Kenmure sae generous,††
Whase honour is proof to the storm ;   *whose*
To save them frae stark reprobation,   *from*
He lent them his name to the firm.

And there'll be Logan M'Dowall,‡‡
Sculduddery and he will be there ;
And also the wild Scot o' Galloway,
Sodgering gunpowder Blair.§§   *soldiering*

But we winna mention Redcastle,‖‖   *will not*
The body, e'en let him escape !
He'd venture the gallows for siller,   *money*
An' 'twere na' the cost o' the rape.   *rope*

---

* Mr Syme of Cassencarrie.   ** Rev. G. Maxwell of Buittle.
† Colonel Goldie of Goldielea.   †† Mr Gordon of Kenmure.
‡ William Bushby of Kempleton.   ‡‡ Captain M'Dowall of Logan.
§ Mr Bushby Maitland.   §§ Mr Blair of Dunskey.
‖ Messrs Douglas of Carlinwark.   ‖‖ Mr Lawrie of Redcastle.
Rev. Mr Muirhead of Urr.

Then hey the chaste interest o' Broughton,
    And hey for the blessings 'twill bring!
It may send Balmaghie to the Commons,
    In PARIS 'twould make him a king.

BALLAD THIRD.

AN EXCELLENT NEW SONG.

TUNE—*Buy Broom Besoms.*

WHA will buy my troggin,
    Fine election ware;
Broken trade o' Broughton,
    A' in high repair.
      Buy braw troggin,
        Frae the banks o' Dee;
      Wha wants troggin
      Let him come to me.
	who, clothes
	
	who

There's a noble earl's *(Galloway)*
    Fame and high renown,
For an auld sang—
    It's thought the gudes were stown. goods, stolen
        Buy braw troggin, &c.

Here's the worth o' Broughton,
    In a needle's ee; eye
Here's a reputation
    Tint by Balmaghie. lost
        Buy braw troggin, &c.

Here's its stuff and lining,
    Cardoness's head; *(Mr Gordon)*
Fine for a sodger, soldier
    A' the wale o' lead. choice
        Buy braw troggin, &c.

Here's a little wadset, mortgage
    Buittle's scrap o' truth,
Pawned in a gin-shop,
    Quenching holy drouth. thirst
        Buy braw troggin, &c.

Here's an honest conscience
    Might a prince adorn;
Frae the downs o' Tinwald— from
    So was never worn.
        Buy braw troggin, &c.

Here's armorial bearings,
    Frae the manse o' Urr;
The crest, a sour crab-apple,
    Rotten at the core.
        Buy braw troggin, &c.

There is Satan's picture,
  Liko a buzzard gled,   kite
Pouncing poor Redcastle,
  Sprawlin' as a taed.   toad
    Buy braw troggin, &c.

Here's the font where Douglas
  Stane and mortar names;   stone
Lately used at C———
  Christening Murray's crimes.
    Buy braw troggin, &c.

Here's the worth and wisdom
  Collieston can boast;
By a thievish midge   gnat
  They had been nearly lost.
    Buy braw troggin, &c.

Here is Murray's fragments
  O' the Ten Commands;
Gifted by Black Jock,
  To get them aff his hands.   off
    Buy braw troggin, &c.

Saw ye e'er sic troggin?
If to buy ye're slack,
Hornie's turning chapman—
  He'll buy a' the pack.
    Buy braw troggin,
      Frae the banks o' Dee;
    Wha wants troggin
    Let him come to me.

BALLAD FOURTH.

JOHN BUSHBY'S LAMENTATION.

TUNE—*The Babes in the Wood.*

'TWAS in the seventeen hunder year
  O' grace and ninety-five,
That year I was the wae'est man saddest
  O' ony man alive.   any

In March the three-and-twentieth morn,
  The sun raise clear and bright;
But oh I was a waefu' man
  Ere to-fa' o' the night.   the close

Yerl Galloway lang did rule this land, Earl, long
  Wi' *equal* right and fame,
And thereto was his kinsman joined
  The Murray's noble name.

Yerl Galloway lang did rule the land,
  Made me the judge o' strife;
But now Yerl Galloway's sceptre's broke,
  And eke my hangman's knife. also

'Twas by the banks o' bonnie Dee,
  Beside Kirkcudbright's towers,
The Stewart and the Murray there
  Did muster a' their powers.

The Murray, on the auld gray yaud,   *mare*
  Wi' *winged spurs* did ride,
That auld gray yaud, yea, Nidsdale rade,   *rode*
  He staw upon Nidside.   *stole*

An' there had na been the yerl himsel',   *not*
  O there had been nae play ;   *no*
But Garlics was to London gane,
  And sae the kye might stray.   *so, kine*

And there was Balmaghie, I ween,
  In front rank he wad shine ;   *would*
But Balmaghie had better been
  Drinking Madeira wine.

Frae the Glenkens came to our aid,
  A chief o' doughty deed ;   *mighty*
In case that worth should wanted be,
  O' Kenmure we had need.

And by our banners marched Muirhead,
  And Buittle was na slack ;
Whase haly priesthood nane can stain,   *holy, none*
  For wha can dye the black ?   *who*

And there sae grave Squire Cardoness,
  Looked on till a' was done ;
Sae, in the tower o' Cardoness,
  A howlet sits at noon.   *owl*

And there led I the Bushby clan,
  My gamesome billie Will ;   *brother*
And my son Maitland, wise as brave,
  My footsteps followed still.

The Douglas and the Heron's name
  We set nought to their score ;
The Douglas and the Heron's name
  Had felt our might before.

But Douglasses o' weight had we,
  The pair o' lusty lairds,
For building cot-houses sae famed,
  And christening kail-yards.   *cabbage*

And there Redcastle drew his sword,
  That ne'er was stained wi' gore,
Save on a wanderer lame and blind,
  To drive him frae his door.   *from*

At last came creeping C——l——n,
  Was mair in fear than wrath ;   *more*
Ae knave was constant in his mind,   *one*
  To keep that knave frae scaith.   *harm*

THE DUMFRIES VOLUNTEERS.

TUNE—*Push about the Jorum.*

DOES haughty Gaul invasion threat ?
  Then let the loons beware, sir ;   fellows
There's wooden walls upon our seas,
  And volunteers on shore, sir.
The Nith shall run to Corsincon,
  And Criffel sink in Solway,
Ere we permit a foreign foe
  On British ground to rally !
    Fall de rall, &c.

Oh, let us not like snarling tykes   dogs
  In wrangling be divided ;
Till, slap, come in an unco loon,.   strange
  And wi' a rung decide it.   bludgeon
Be Britain still to Britain true,
  Among oursels united ;
For never but by British hands
  Maun British wrangs be righted.   must, wrongs
    Fall de rall, &c.

The kettle o' the Kirk and State,
  Perhaps a clout may fail in't ;   mend
But NOT a foreign tinkler loon   tinker
  Shall ever ca' a nail in't.   drive
Our fathers' bluid the kettle bought, blood
  And wha wad dare to spoil it ;   who would
IN TROTH the sacrilegious dog
  Shall fuel be to boil it.
    Fall de rall, &c.

The wretch that wad a tyrant own,   would
  And the wretch his true-born brother,
Who'd set the *mob* aboon the *throne,* above
  LET THEM BE HANGED together !
Who will not sing " God save the King,"
  Shall hang as high's the steeple ;
But while we sing " God save the King,"
  We'll ne'er forget the People.

OH, WAT YE WHA'S IN YON TOWN ?

TUNE—*We'll gang nae mair to yon Town.*

OH, wat ye wha's in yon town,   know, who
  Ye see the e'enin' sun upon ?
The fairest dame's in yon town,
  The e'enin' sun is shining on.

Now haply down yon gay green shaw, wood
  She wanders by yon spreading tree ;
How blest ye flowers that round her blaw, blow
  Ye catch the glances o' her ee l   eye

llow blest ye birds that round her sing,
  And welcome in the blooming year !
And doubly welcome be the spring,
  The season to my Lucy dear.

The sun blinks blithe on yon town,
  And on yon bonnie braes of Ayr ;
But my delight in yon town,
  And dearest bliss, is Lucy fair.

Without my love, not a' the charms
  O' Paradise could yield me joy ;   give
But gie me Lucy in my arms,
  And welcome Lapland's dreary sky !

My cave wad be a lover's bower,
  Though raging Winter rent the air ;
And she a lovely little flower,
  That I would tent and shelter there.   would tend

Oh, sweet is she in yon town,
  Yon sinkin' sun's gane down upon ;   gone
A fairer than's in yon town
  His setting beam ne'er shone upon.

If angry Fate is sworn my foe,
  And suffering I am doomed to bear ;
I careless quit aught else below,
  But spare me—spare me, Lucy dear !

For while life's dearest blood is warm,
  Ae thought frae her shall ne'er depart, one, from
And she—as fairest is her form !
  She has the truest, kindest heart !

ADDRESS TO THE WOODLARK.

TUNE—*Loch Erroch Side.*

O STAY, sweet warbling woodlark, stay !
Nor quit for me the trembling spray ;
A hapless lover courts thy lay,
  Thy soothing, fond complaining.

Again, again that tender part,
That I may catch thy melting art ;
For surely that wad touch her heart   would
  Wha kills me wi' disdaining.   who

Say, was thy little mate unkind,
And heard thee as the careless wind ?
Oh ! nocht but love and sorrow joined,   nought
  Sic notes o' wo could wauken.   such, woe, awake

Thou tells o' never-ending care ;
O' speechless grief, and dark despair :
For pity's sake, sweet bird, nae mair,   no more
  Or my poor heart is broken !

ON CHLORIS BEING ILL.

TUNE—*Aye Wakin O.*

CHORUS.

LONG, long the night,
　Heavy comes the morrow,
While my soul's delight
　Is on her bed of sorrow.

Can I cease to care?
　Can I cease to languish?
While my darling fair
　Is on the couch of anguish?

Every hope is fled,
　Every fear is terror;
Slumber even I dread;
　Every dream is horror.

Hear me, Powers divine!
　Oh, in pity hear me!
Take aught else of mine,
　But my Chloris spare me!

THEIR GROVES O' SWEET MYRTLE.

TUNE—*Humours of Glen.*

THEIR groves o' sweet myrtle let foreign lands reckon,
　Where bright-beaming summers exalt the perfume;
Far dearer to me yon lone glen o' green breckan,　　fern
　Wi' the burn stealing under the lang yellow broom.　long

Far dearer to me are yon humble broom bowers,
　Where the blue-bell and gowan lurk lowly unseen:　daisy
For there, lightly tripping amang the wild-flowers,
　A-listening the linnet, aft wanders my Jean.　　oft

Though rich is the breeze in their gay sunny valleys,
　And cauld Caledonia's blast on the wave;　　cold
Their sweet-scented woodlands that skirt the proud palace,
　What are they?—the haunt of the tyrant and slave!

The slave's spicy forests, and gold-bubbling fountains,
　The brave Caledonian views wi' disdain;
He wanders as free as the winds of his mountains,
　Save love's willing fetters—the chains o' his Jean!

'TWAS NA HER BONNIE BLUE EE WAS MY RUIN.

TUNE—*Laddie be near me.*

'TWAS na her bonnie blue ee was my ruin;　　not, eye
Fair though she be, that was ne'er my undoing:
'Twas the dear smile when naebody did mind us,
'Twas the bewitching, sweet, stown glance o' kindness.　stolen

Sair do I fear that to hope is denied me,   sore
Sair do I fear that despair maun abide me;   must
But though fell fortune should fate us to sever,
Queen shall she be in my bosom for ever!

Mary, I'm thine wi' a passion sincerest,
And thou has plighted me love o' the dearest!
And thou'rt the angel that never can alter,
Sooner the sun in his motion would falter.

HOW CRUEL ARE THE PARENTS!

ALTERED FROM AN OLD ENGLISH SONG.

Tune—*John Anderson my Jo.*

How cruel are the parents,
    Who riches only prize ;
And to the wealthy booby,
    Poor woman sacrifice !
Meanwhile, the hapless daughter
    Has but a choice of strife ;—
To shun a tyrant father's hate,
    Become a wretched wife.

The ravening hawk pursuing,
    The trembling dove thus flies,
To shun impelling ruin
    Awhile her pinions tries :
Till of escape despairing,
    No shelter or retreat,
She trusts the ruthless falconer,
    And drops beneath his feet.

MARK YONDER POMP OF COSTLY FASHION.

Mark yonder pomp of costly fashion,
    Round the wealthy, titled bride :
But when compared with real passion,
    Poor is all that princely pride.
    What are the showy treasures ?
    What are the noisy pleasures ?
The gay gaudy glare of vanity and art :
    The polished jewel's blaze
    May draw the wondering gaze,
    And courtly grandeur bright
    The fancy may delight,
But never, never can come near the heart.

But did you see my dearest Chloris,
    In simplicity's array ;
Lovely as yonder sweet opening flower is,
    Shrinking from the gaze of day.

Oh then, the heart alarming,
And all resistless charming,
In Love's delightful fetters she chains the willing soul!
Ambition would disown
The worlds imperial crown,
Even Avarice would deny
His worshipped deity,
And feel through every vein Love's rapture's roll.

FORLORN, MY LOVE, NO COMFORT NEAR.

TUNE—*Let me in this ae Night.*

FORLORN, my love, no comfort near,
Far, far from thee, I wander here;
Far, far from thee, the fate severe
    At which I most repine, love.

CHORUS.

Oh, wert thou, love, but near me;
But near, near, near me:
How kindly thou wouldst cheer me,
    And mingle sighs with mine, love.

Around me scowls a wintry sky,
That blasts each bud of hope and joy;
And shelter, shade, nor home have I,
    Save in those arms of thine, love.

Cold, altered friendship's cruel part,
To poison Fortune's ruthless dart—
Let me not break thy faithful heart,
    And say that fate is mine, love.

But dreary though the moments fleet,
Oh, let me think we yet shall meet!
That only ray of solace sweet
    Can on thy Chloris shine, love.

LAST MAY A BRAW WOOER.

SCOTTISH BALLAD.

TUNE—*The Lothian Lassie.*

LAST May a braw wooer cam down the lang glen, came, long
    And sair wi' his love he did deave me; sore, deafen
I said there was naething I hated like men— nothing
    O WHAT MADE THE GOMRAL believe me, believe me; fool
    O WHAT MADE THE GOMRAL believe me.

He spak o' the darts o' my bonny black een, spake, eyes
    And vowed for my love he was dying;
I said he might die when he liked for Jean—
    HE'D NEED TO FORGIE ME for lying, for lying; forgive
    HE'D NEED TO FORGIE ME for lying!

A well-stocked mailen—himsel for the laird—   farm
   And marriage aff-hand, were his proffers :
I never loot on that I kenned it, or cared,   noticed, knew
   But thought I might hae waur offers, waur offers ;   worse
   But thought I might hae waur offers.

But what wad ye think ?—in a fortnight or less,   would
   NAE PRAISE TO his taste to gae near her !   no, go
He up the Gateslack to my black cousin Bess,
   Guess ye how, the jad ! I could bear her, could bear her ;
   Guess ye how, the jad ! I could bear her.

But a' the neist week as I fretted wi' care,   next
   I gaed to the tryste o' Dalgarnock,   went, fair
And wha but my fine fickle lover was there !   who
   I glowred as I'd seen a warlock, a warlock !   stared
   I glowred as I'd seen a warlock.

But owre my left shouther I gae him a blink,   o'er, shoulder, gave
   Lest neibors might say I was saucy,   neighbours
My wooer he capered as he'd been in drink,
   And vowed I was his dear lassie, dear lassie ;
   And vowed I was his dear lassie.

I speered for my cousin fu' couthy and sweet,   loving
   Gin she had recovered her hearin',   if
And how my auld shoon fitted her shachl't feet,   shoes, distorted
   BUT HECH ! how he fell a swearin', a swearin' ;
   BUT HECH ! how he fell a swearin'.

He begged for ONYSAKE I'd be his wife,
   Or else I wad kill him wi' sorrow :
So e'en to preserve the poor body in life,
   I think I maun wed him to-morrow, to-morrow ;   must
   I think I maun wed him to-morrow.

FRAGMENT.

TUNE—*The Caledonian Hunt's Delight.*

WHY, why tell thy lover,
   Bliss he never must enjoy ?
Why, why undeceive him,
   And give all his hopes the lie ?

O why, while Fancy, raptured, slumbers,
   Chloris, Chloris all the theme,
Why, why wouldst thou cruel,
   Wake thy lover from his dream ? ·

O THIS IS NO MY AIN LASSIE.

TUNE—*This is no my ain House.*

CHORUS.

O THIS is no my ain lassie,   own
   Fair though the lassie be ;
O weel ken I my ain lassie,   well know
   Kind love is in her ee.   eye

I see a form, I see a face,
Ye weel may wi' the fairest place:
It wants, to me, the witching grace,
   The kind love that's in her ee.

She's bonnie, blooming, straight, and tall,
And lang has had my heart in thrall;   long
And aye it charms my very saul,   soul
   The kind love that's in her ee,

A thief sae pawkie is my Jean,   so sly
To steal a blink, by a' unseen;
But gleg as light are lovers' een,   quick, eyes
   When kind love is in the ee.

It may escape the courtly sparks,
It may escape the learnèd clerks;
But weel the watching lover marks
   The kind love that's in her ee.

NOW SPRING HAS CLAD.

Now Spring has clad the grove in green,
   And strewed the lea wi' flowers:
The furrowed waving corn is seen
   Rejoice in fostering showers;
While ilka thing in nature join   every
   Their sorrows to forego,
O why thus all alone are mine
   The weary steps of wo!

The trout within yon wimpling burn winding
   Glides swift—a silver dart;
And safe beneath the shady thorn
   Defies the angler's art.
My life was ance that careless stream, once
   That wanton trout was I;
But love, wi' unrelenting beam,
   Has scorched my fountains dry.

The little floweret's peaceful lot,
   In yonder cliff that grows,
Which, save the linnet's flight, I wot,
   Nae ruder visit knows,   no
Was mine; till love has o'er me past,
   And blighted a' my bloom,
And now beneath the withering blast
   My youth and joy consume.

The wakened laverock warbling springs, lark
   And climbs the early sky,
Winnowing blithe her dewy wings
   In morning's rosy eye.

As little recked I sorrow's power,
  Until the flowery snare
O' witching love, in luckless hour,
  Made me the thrall o' care.

O had my fate been Greenland snows,
  Or Afric's burning zone,
Wi' man and nature leagued my foes,
  So Peggy ne'er I'd known !
The wretch whase doom is, "hope nae mair,"   whose, no more
  What tongue his woes can tell !
Within whase bosom, save despair,
  Nae kinder spirits dwell.

O BONNIE WAS YON ROSY BRIER.

O BONNIE was yon rosy brier,
  That blooms sae far frae haunt o' man ;   so, from
And bonnie she, and ah ! how dear !
  It shaded frae the e'enin' sun.

Yon rosebuds in the morning dew,
  How pure amang the leaves sae green ;
But purer was the lover's vow
  They witnessed in their shade yestreen.   last night

All in its rude and prickly bower,
  That crimson rose, how sweet and fair ;
But love is far a sweeter flower
  Amid life's thorny path o' care.

The pathless wild and wimpling burn,   winding
  Wi' Chloris in my arms, be mine ;
And I the world, nor wish, nor scorn,
  Its joys and griefs alike resign.

HEY FOR A LASS WI' A TOCHER.

TUNE—*Balinamona ora.*

Awa wi' your witchcraft o' beauty's alarms,   away
The slender bit beauty you grasp in your arms :
O gie me the lass that has acres o' charms,   give
O gie me the lass wi' the weel-stockit farms.   well-stocked

CHORUS.

Then hey for a lass wi' a tocher, then hey for a lass
    wi' a tocher ;   dower
Then hey for a lass wi' a tocher—the nice yellow
    guineas for me.

Your beauty's a flower, in the morning that blows,
And withers the faster, the faster it grows :
But the rapturous charm o' the bonnie green knowes,   knolls
Ilk spring they're new deckit wi' bonnie white yowes.   each, ewes

And e'en when this beauty your bosom has blest,
The brightest o' beauty may cloy, when possest;
But the sweet yellow darlings wi' Geordie imprest,
The langer ye hae them, the mair they're carest.   longer, have,
                                                            [more

---

JESSY.

CHORUS.

HERE's a health to ane I loe dear !   one, love
Here's a health to ane I loe dear !
Thou art sweet as the smile when fond lovers meet,
And soft as their parting tear—Jessy !

Although thou maun never be mine,   must
  Although even hope is denied :
'Tis sweeter for thee despairing,
  Than aught in the world beside—Jessy !

I mourn through the gay, gaudy day,
  As, hopeless, I muse on thy charms ;
But welcome the dream o' sweet slumber,
  For then I am lock't in thy arms—Jessy !

I guess by the dear angel smile,
  I guess by the love-rolling ee ;   eye
But why urge the tender confession,
  'Gainst Fortune's fell cruel decree—Jessy !

OH, WERT THOU IN THE CAULD BLAST.

OH, wert thou in the cauld blast   cold
  On yonder lea, on yonder lea,
My plaidie to the angry airt,   quarter
  I'd shelter thee, I'd shelter thee :
Or did Misfortune's bitter storms
  Around thee blaw, around thee blaw,   blow
Thy bield should be my bosom,   shelter
  To share it a', to share it a'.

Or were I in the wildest waste,
  Sae black and bare, sae black and bare,   so
The desert were a paradise,
  If thou wert there, if thou wert there :
Or were I monarch o' the globe,
  Wi' thee to reign, wi' thee to reign,
The brightest jewel in my crown
  Wad be my queen, wad be my queen.   would

FAIREST MAID ON DEVON BANKS.

TUNE—*Rothemurchie.*

CHORUS.

FAIREST maid on Devon Banks,
Crystal Devon, winding Devon,
Wilt thou lay that frown aside,
And smile as thou were wont to do?

Full well thou know'st I love thee dear,
Couldst thou to malice lend an ear?
Oh, did not love exclaim: " Forbear,
Nor use a faithful lover so!"

Then come, thou fairest of the fair,
Those wonted smiles, oh, let me share!
And by thy beautous self I swear,
No love but thine my heart shall know.

CALEDONIA.

TUNE—*Caledonian Hunt's Delight.*

THERE was once a day—but old Time then was young—
    That brave Caledonia, the chief of her line,
From some of your northern deities sprung
    (Who knows not that brave Caledonia's divine?)
From Tweed to the Orcades was her domain,
    To hunt, or to pasture, or do what she would:
Her heavenly relations there fixèd her reign,
    And pledged her their godheads to warrant it good.

A lambkin in peace, but a lion in war,
    The pride of her kindred the heroine grew:
Her grandsire, old Odin, triumphantly swore,
    " Whoe'er shall provoke thee, th' encounter shall rue!"
With tillage or pasture at times she would sport,
    To feed her fair flocks by her green rustling corn;
But chiefly the woods were her fav'rite resort,
    Her darling amusement the hounds and the horn.

Long quiet she reigned; till thitherward steers
    A flight of bold eagles from Adria's strand:
Repeated, successive, for many long years,
    They darkened the air, and they plundered the land;
Their pounces were murder, and terror their cry,
    They'd conquered and ruined a world beside;
She took to her hills, and her arrows let fly—
    The daring invaders they fled or they died.

The fell harpy-raven took wing from the North,
    The scourge of the seas, and the dread of the shore;
The wild Scandinavian boar issued forth
    To wanton in carnage, and wallow in gore:
O'er countries and kingdoms their fury prevailed,
    No arts could appease them, no arms could repel;
But brave Caledonia in vain they assailed,
    As Largs well can witness, and Loncartie tell.

The Cameleon-savage disturbed her repose,
  With tumult, disquiet, rebellion, and strife ;
Provoked beyond bearing, at last she arose,
  And robbed him at once of his hopes and his life :
The Anglian lion, the terror of France,
  Oft prowling, ensanguined the Tweed's silver flood :
But, taught by the bright Caledonian lance,
  He learned to fear in his own native wood.

Thus bold, independent, unconquered, and free,
  Her bright course of glory for ever shall run :
For brave Caledonia immortal must be ;
  I'll prove it from Euclid as clear as the sun :
Rectangle-triangle the figure we'll choose,
  The upright is Chance, and old Time is the base ;
But brave Caledonia's the hypothenuse ;
  Then ergo, she'll match them, and match them always.

O WHA IS SHE THAT LOES ME ?

TUNE—*Morag.*

O WHA is she that loes me,   who
  And has my heart a keeping ?
O sweet is she that loes me,   loves
  As dews o' simmer weeping,
  In tears the rose-buds steeping l
    O that's the lassie o' my heart,
      My lassie ever dearer ;
    O that's the queen o' womankind,
      And ne'er a ane to peer her.

If thou shalt meet a lassie
  In grace and beauty charming,
That e'en thy chosen lassie,   even
  Erewhile thy breast sae warming, so
  Had ne'er sic powers alarming ; such
    O that's the lassie, &c.

If thou hadst heard her talking,
  And thy attentions plighted,
That ilka body talking,   every
  But her by thee is slighted,
  And thou art all delighted ;
    O that's the lassie, &c.

If thou hast met this fair one ;
  When frae her thou hast parted, from
If every other fair one,
  But her, thou hast deserted,
  And thou art broken-hearted ;
    O that's the lassie o' my heart,
      My lassie ever dearer ;
    O that's the queen o' womankind,
      And ne'er a ane to peer her. one

O WHARE DID YOU GET?

Tune—Bonnie Dundee.

O WHARE did you get that hauver meal bannock ?   where, oat
  O silly blind body, O dinna ye see ?   don't [cake
I gat it frae a brisk young sodger laddie,   got, from
  Between St Johnston and bonnie Dundee.
O gin I saw the laddie that gae me't !   that, gave
  Aft has he doudled me upon his knee ;   dandled
May Heaven protect my bonnie Scots laddie,
  And send him safe hame to his babie and me !   home

My blessin's upon thy sweet wee lippie,   lip
  My blessin's upon thy bonnie ee-bree !   eyebrow
Thy smiles are sae like my blithe sodger laddie,   so
  Thou's aye the dearer and dearer to me !
But I'll big a bower on yon bonnie banks,   build
  Where Tay rins wimplin' by sae clear ;   winding
And I'll cleed thee in the tartan sae fine,   clothe
  And mak thee a man like thy daddie dear.

I AM MY MAMMY'S AE BAIRN.

Tune—I'm owre young to Marry yet.

I AM my mammy's ae bairn,   one
  Wi' unco folk I weary, sir ;   strange
And if I live in your house,
  I'm fley'd 'twill make me eerie, sir.   afraid, gloomy
    I'm owre young to marry yet ;   too
    I'm owre young to marry yet ;
    I'm owre young—'twad be a sin .   'twould
    To tak me frae my mammy yet.   from

Hallowmas is come and gane,   All Hallows, gone
  The nights are lang in winter, sir ;   long
And you and I in wedlock's bands,
  In troth, I dare na venture, sir.   not

Fu' loud and shrill the frosty wind
  Blaws through the leafless timmer, sir ;   blows, timber
But if ye come this gate again,   way
  I'll aulder be gin simmer, sir.   older in summer
    I'm owre young to marry yet ;
    I'm owre young to marry yet ;
    I'm owre young—'twad be a sin
    To tak me frae my mammy yet.

UP IN THE MORNING EARLY.

Tune—Cold blows the Wind.

CAULD blaws the wind frae east to west,   cold blows
  The drift is driving sairly ;   sore
Sae loud and shrill I hear the blast,
  I'm sure it's winter fairly.

CHORUS.

Up in the morning's no for me,
  Up in the morning early;
When a' the hills are covered wi' snaw,   snow
  I'm sure it's winter fairly.

The birds sit chittering in the thorn,   shivering
  A' day they fare but sparely;
And lang's the night frae e'en to morn—   long, from
  I'm sure it's winter fairly.

THERE WAS A LASS.

TUNE—*Duncan Davison.*

THERE was a lass, they ca'd her Meg,   called
  And she held o'er the moors to spin;   went
There was a lad that followed her,
  They ca'd him Duncan Davison.
The moor was dreigh, and Meg was skeigh,   tedious, proud
  Her favour Duncan could na win;
For wi' the rock she wad him knock,   distaff, would
  And aye she shook the temper-pin.*

As o'er the moor they lightly foor,   went
  A burn was clear, a glen was green,
Upon the banks they eased their shanks,   legs
  And aye she set the wheel between:
But Duncan swore a haly aith,   holy oath
  That Meg should be a bride the morn,
Then Meg took up her spinnin' graith,   furniture
  And flang them a' out o'er the burn.   flung

We'll big a house—a wee, wee house,   build
  And we will live like king and queen,
Sae blithe and merry we will be
  When ye set by the wheel at e'en.
A man may drink and no be drunk;
  A man may fight and no be slain;
A man may kiss a bonnie lass,
  And aye be welcome back again.

THE PLOUGHMAN.

THE ploughman he's a bonnie lad,
  His mind is ever true, Jo,
His garters knit below his knee,
  His bonnet it is blue, Jo.
    Then up wi't a', my ploughman lad,
      And hey my merry ploughman;
    Of a' the trades that I do ken,   know
      Commend me to the ploughman.

* A long screw used to tighten the band on the wheel.

I hae been east, I hae been west,   have
  I hae been at St Johnston;
The bonniest sight that e'er I saw,
  Was the ploughman laddie dancin'.
    Up wi't, &c.

Snaw-white stockins on his legs,   snow
  And siller buckles glancin';   silver
A guid blue bonnet on his head,   good
  And oh, but he was handsome.
    Up wi't, &c.

MY HOGGIE.

WHAT will I do gin my hoggie die,   If, young sheep
  My joy, my pride, my hoggie?
My only beast, I had nae mae,   no more
  And oh, but I was vogie.   vain

The lee-lang night we watched the fauld,   livelong, fold
  Me and my faithfu' doggie,
We heard nought but the roaring linn,   cascade
  Amang the braes sae scroggie.   full of stunted bushes

But the howlet cried frae the castle wa',   owl, from
  The blutter frae the boggie,   mire-snipe, bog
The tod replied upon the hill—   fox
  I trembled for my hoggie.

When day did daw and cocks did craw,   dawn, crow
  The morning it was foggie,
An unco tyke lap o'er the dyke,   strange dog, jumped
  And maist has killed my hoggie.   almost [wall

SIMMER'S A PLEASANT TIME.

TUNE—Aye Waukin O.

SIMMER'S a pleasant time,   summer
  Flowers of every colour;
The water rins o'er the heugh,   runs, bank
  And I long for my true lover.
    Aye waukin O,   always waking
      Waukin still and wearie:
    Sleep I can get nane   none
      For thinking on my dearie.

When I sleep I dream,
  When I wauk I'm eerie: watch, timorous
Sleep I can get nane
  For thinking on my dearie.

Lanely night comes on,   lonely
  A' the lave are sleeping;   rest
I think on my bonnie lad,
  And bleer my een wi' greetin'   eyes, weeping

FIRST WHEN MAGGY WAS MY CARE.

TUNE—*Whistle o'er the Lave o't.*

FIRST when Maggy was my care,
Heaven I thought was in her air;
Now we're married—speir na mair—'   ask no more
    Whistle o'er the lave o't.   rest
Meg was meek, and Meg was mild,
Bonnie Meg was Nature's child;
Wiser men than me's beguiled—
    Whistle o'er the lave o't.

How we live, my Meg and me,
How we love, and how we 'gree,   agree
I care na by how few may see—   care not
    Whistle o'er the lave o't.
Wha I wish were maggots' meat,   who
Dished up in her winding-sheet,
I could write—but Meg maun see't—   must
    Whistle o'er the lave o't.

JAMIE, COME TRY ME.

JAMIE, come try me;
   Jamie, come try me;
If thou would win my love,
Jamie, come try me.

If thou should ask my love,
   Could I deny thee?
If thou would win my love,
Jamie, come try me.

If thou should kiss me, love,
   Wha could espy thee?   who
If thou would be my love,
Jamie, come try me.

AWA, WHIGS, AWA!

TUNE—*Awa, Whigs, awa.*

CHORUS.

Awa, Whigs, awa!   away
Awa, Whigs, awa!
Ye're but a pack o' traitor louns,   fellows
Ye'll do nae good at a'.   no

Our thrissles flourished fresh and fair,   thistles
   And bonnie bloomed our roses;
But Whigs came like a frost in June,
   And withered a' our posies.

Our sad decay in Church and State
  Surpasses my descriving ;   *describing*
The Whigs came o'er us for a curse,
  And we hae done wi' thriving.   *have*

Grim vengeance lang has ta'en a nap,   *long*
  But we may see him wauken ;   *awaken*
LANG BE the day when royal heads
  Are hunted like a maukin.   *hare*

WHARE HAE YE BEEN ?

Tune—Killicrankie.

WHARE hae ye been sae braw, lad ?   *where, so*
  Whare hae ye been sae brankie, O ?   *gaudy*
Oh, whare hae ye been sae braw, lad ?
  Cam ye by Killiecrankie, O ?
An ye had been whare I hae been,   *if, have*
  Ye wad na been sae cantic, O ;   *wouldn't, merry*
An ye had seen what I hae seen,
  On the braes of Killiecrankie, O.

I fought at land, I fought at sea ;
  At hame I fought my auntie, O ;   *home*
But, WORST OF A', I met Dundee,
  On the braes o' Killiecrankie, O.
The bauld Pitcur fell in a furr,   *bold, furrow*
  And Clavers got a clankie, O ;   *blow*
Or I had fed an Athole gled,   *kite*
  On the braes o' Killiecrankie, O.

FOR A' THAT, AND A' THAT.

THOUGH women's minds, like winter winds
  May shift and turn, and a' that ;
The noblest breast adores them maist,   *most*
  A consequence I draw that.
    For a' that, and a' that,
      And twice as mickle's a' that,   *much*
    The bonnie lass that I loe best,   *love*
      Shall be my ain for a' that.   *own*

YOUNG JOCKEY.

Tune—Young Jockey

YOUNG Jockey was the blithest lad
  In a' our town or here awa :
Fu' blithe he whistled at the gaud,   *plough*
  Fu' lightly danced he in the ha'

He roosed my een, sae bonnie blue, — praised, eyes
  He roosed my waist, sae genty sma'; — so neatly
And aye my heart came to my mou', — mouth
  When ne'er a body heard or saw.

My Jockey toils upon the plain,
  Through wind and weet, through frost and snaw: — wet
And o'er the lea I leuk fu' fain, — look
  When Jockey's owsen hameward ca'. — oxen
And aye the night comes round again,
  When in his arms he takes me a';
And aye he vows he'll be my ain, — own
  As lang's he has a breath to draw.

THE TITHER MORN.

To a Highland Air.

THE tither morn, when I forlorn — other
  Aneath an aik sat moaning, — beneath, oak
I did na trow, I'd see my jo, — not, believe, lover
  Beside me, gin the gloaming. — by the evening
But he sae trig, lap o'er the rig, — so neat, leapt, ridge
  And dawtingly did cheer me, — endearingly
When I, what reck, did least expec', — heed
  To see my lad so near me.

His bonnet he, a thought ajee, — awry
  Cocked sprush when first he clasped me ; — spruce
And I, I wat, wi' fainness grat, — wot, wept
  While in his grips he pressed me. — gripe
THAT WEARY war ! I late and air, — early
  Hae BANN'D since Jock departed; — have
But now as glad I'm wi' my lad,
  As short syne broken-hearted. — time ago

Fu' aft at e'en wi' dancing keen, — oft
  When a' were blithe and merry,
I cared na by, sae sad was I, — not although
  In absence o' my dearie.
But, NOW I'M blest, my mind's at rest,
  I'm happy wi' my Johnny :
At kirk and fair, I'se aye be there, — I'll always
  And be as canty's ony. — happy

AS I WAS A WANDERING.

TUNE—*Rinn Meudial mo Mhealladh.*

As I was wandering ae midsummer e'enin', — one
  The pipers and youngsters were making their game;
Amang them I spied my faithless fause lover, — false
  Which bled a' the wounds o' my dolour again. — grief

Weel, since he has left me, may pleasure gae wi' him; go
  I may be distressed, but I winna complain ; wont
I flatter my fancy I may get anither, another
  My heart it shall never be broken for ane. one

I couldna get sleeping till dawing for greetin', dawn,
  The tears trickled down like the hail and the rain: [weeping
Had I no got greetin', my heart wad ha' broken, not, would
  For oh! love forsaken's a tormenting pain. [have

Although he has left me for greed o' the siller, money
  I dinna envy him the gains he can win ; dont
I rather wad bear a' the lade o' my sorrow load
  Than ever hae acted sae faithless to him. have, so

THE WEARY PUND O' TOW.

TUNE—*The Weary Pund o' Tow.*

THE weary pund, the weary pund, pound
  The weary pund o' tow ;
I think my wife will end her life
  Before she spin her tow.

I bought my wife a stane o' lint stone, flax
  As guid as e'er did grow ; good
And a' that she has made o' that,
  Is ae poor pund o' tow. one

There sat a bottle in a bole,
  Beyont the ingle lowe, fire flame
And aye she took the tither souk, other suck
  To drouk the stowrie tow. drench, dusty

Quoth I, for shame, ye dirty dame,
  Gae spin your tap o' tow ! go, portion
She took the rock, and wi' a knock
  She brak it o'er my pow. head

At last her feet—I sang to see't—
  Gaed foremost o'er the knowe ; went, knoll
And or I wad anither jad, ere, wed, jade
  I'll wallop in a tow. hang, rope

GANE IS THE DAY.

TUNE—*Guidwife, count the Lawin.*

GANE is the day, and mirk's the night, gone, dark
But we'll ne'er stray for fau't o' light, want
For ale and brandy's stars and moon,
And bluid-red wine's the rising sun.
  Then guidwife, count the lawin, reckoning
   The lawin, the lawin ;
  Then guidwife, count the lawin,
   And bring a coggie mair. cupful more

There's wealth and ease for gentlemen,
And simple folk maun fight and fen ;   must, shift
But here we're a' in ae accord,   one
For ilka man that's drunk's a lord.   every

My coggie is a haly pool,   cup, holy
That heals the wounds o' care and dool ;   sorrow
And pleasure is a wanton trout,
An ye drink but deep ye'll find him out.

IT IS NA, JEAN, THY BONNIE FACE.

Tune—*The Maid's Complaint.*

It is na, Jean, thy bonnie face   not
    Nor shape that I admire,
Although thy beauty and thy grace
    Might weel awake desire.   well
Something, in ilka part o' thee,   every
    To praise, to love, I find ;
But dear as is thy form to me,
    Still dearer is thy mind.

Nae mair ungenerous wish I hae,   no more, have
    Nor stronger in my breast,
Than if I canna mak thee sae,   can't, so
    At least to see thee blest.
Content am I, if Heaven shall give
    But happiness to thee :
And as wi' thee I'd wish to live,
    For thee I'd bear to die.

MY COLLIER LADDIE.

Tune—*The Collier Laddie.*

Where live ye, my bonnie lass ?
    And tell me what they ca' ye ;   call
My name, she says, is Mistress Jean,
    And I follow the Collier Laddie.

See you not yon hills and dales,
    The sun shines on sae brawlie !
They a' are mine, and they shall be thine,
    Gin ye'll leave your Collier Laddie.

Ye shall gang in gay attire,   go
    Weel buskit up sae gaudy ;   dressed so
And ane to wait on every hand,   one
    Gin ye'll leave your Collier Laddie.

Though ye had a' the sun shines on,
    And the earth conceals sae lowly ;
I wad turn my back on you and it a',   would
    And embrace my Collier Laddie.

I can win my five pennies in a day,
And spen't at night fu' brawlie;
And make my bed in the Collier's neuk,   corner
And live wi' my Collier Laddie.

Luve for luve is the bargain for me,
Though the wee cot-house should haud me;   hold
And the world before me to win my bread,
And fair fa' my Collier Laddie.

YE JACOBITES BY NAME.
Tune—*Ye Jacobites by Name.*

Ye Jacobites by name, give an ear, give an ear;
Ye Jacobites by name, give an ear;
  Ye Jacobites by name,
    Your fautes I will proclaim,   faults
    Your doctrines I maun blame—   must
    You shall hear.

What is right and what is wrang, by the law, by the law?
What is right and what is wrang by the law?   wrong
  What is right and what is wrang?
    A short sword and a lang,   long
    A weak arm, and a strang   strong
    For to draw.

What makes heroic strife, famed afar, famed afar?
What makes heroic strife famed afar?
  What makes heroic strife?
    To whet th' assassin's knife,
    Or haunt a parent's life
    Wi' bluidie war.   bloody

Then let your schemes alone, in the state, in the state;
Then let your schemes alone in the state;
  Then let your schemes alone,
    Adore the rising sun,
    And leave a man undone
    To his fate.

LADY MARY ANN.
Tune—*Craigton's Growing.*

Oh, Lady Mary Ann looked o'er the castle wa';   wall
She saw three bonnie boys playing at the ba';   ball
The youngest he was the flower amang them a'—
  My bonnie laddie's young, but he's growin' yet.

O father! O father! an ye think it fit,   if
We'll send him a year to the college yet:
We'll sew a green ribbon round about his hat,
  And that will let them ken he's to marry yet.

Lady Mary Ann was a flower i' the dew,
Sweet was its smell, and bonnie was its hue ;
And the langer it blossomed the sweeter it grew :   longer
   For the lily in the bud will be bonnier yet.

Young Charlie Cochrane was the sprout of an aik ;   oak
Bonnie and bloomin' and straught was its make :   straight
The sun took delight to shine for its sake,
   And it will be the brag o' the forest yet.   boast

The simmer is gane when the leaves they were green,   gone
And the days are awa that we hae seen ;   away
But far better days I trust will come again,
   For my bonnie laddie's young, but he's growin' yet.

KENMURE'S ON AND AWA.
TUNE—*O Kenmure's on and awa, Willie.*

O KENMURE'S on and awa, Willie !   away
   O Kenmure's on and awa !
And Kenmure's lord's the bravest lord
   That ever Galloway saw.

Success to Kenmure's band, Willie !
   Success to Kenmure's band ;
There's no a heart that fears a Whig
   That rides by Kenmure's hand.

Here's Kenmure's health in wine, Willie !
   Here's Kenmure's health in wine ;
There ne'er was a coward o' Kenmure's blude,
   Nor yet o' Gordon's line.

O Kenmure's lads are men, Willie !
   O Kenmure's lads are men ;
Their hearts and swords are metal true—
   And that their faes shall ken.   foes, know

They'll live or die wi' fame, Willie !
   They'll live or die wi' fame ;
But soon, wi' sounding victorie,
   May Kenmure's lord come hame.

Here's him that's far awa, Willie !
   Here's him that's far awa !
And here's the flower that I love best—
   The rose that's like the snaw !   snow

SUCH A PARCEL OF ROGUES IN A NATION.
TUNE—*A Parcel of Rogues in a Nation.*

FAREWELL to a' our Scottish fame,
   Fareweel our ancient glory,
Fareweel even to the Scottish name,
   Sae famed in martial story.   so

Now Sark rins o'er the Solway sands,   *runs*
   And Tweed rins to the ocean,
To mark where England's province stands—
   Such a parcel of rogues in a nation.

What force or guile could not subdue
   Through many warlike ages,
Is wrought now by a coward few,
   For hireling traitors' wages.
The English steel we could disdain,
   Secure in valour's station;
But English gold has been our bane—
   Such a parcel of rogues in a nation.

O would, ere I had seen the day
   That treason thus could fell us,
My auld gray head had lien in clay,   *lain*
   Wi' Bruce and loyal Wallace!
But pith and power, till my last hour,
   I'll make this declaration;
We're bought and sold for English gold—
   Such a parcel of rogues in a nation.

THE CARLES OF DYSART.

TUNE—*Hey, ca' through.*

UP wi' the carles o' Dysart,   *men*
   And the lads o' Buckhaven,
And the kimmers o' Largo,   *gossips*
   And the lasses o' Leven.
   Hey, ca' through, ca' through,
     For we hae mickle ado;   *much*
   Hey, ca' through, ca' through,
     For we hae mickle ado.

We hae tales to tell,   *have*
   And we hae sangs to sing;
We hae pennies to spend,
   And we hae pints to bring.

We'll live a' our days,
   And them that come behin',
Let them do the like,
   And spend the gear they win.   *wealth*

THE SLAVE'S LAMENT.

IT was in Sweet Senegal that my foes did me enthral,
   For the lands of Virginia, O;
Torn from that lovely shore, and must never see it more,
   And alas I am weary, weary, O!

All on that charming coast is no bitter snow or frost,
    Like the lands of Virginia, O ;
There streams for ever flow, and there flowers for ever blow,
    And alas I am weary, weary, O !

The burden I must bear, while the cruel scourge I fear,
    In the lands of Virginia, O ;
And I think on friends most dear, with the bitter, bitter tear,
    And alas I am weary, weary, O !

COMING THROUGH THE RYE.

TUNE—*Coming Through the Rye.*

COMING through the rye, poor body,
    Coming through the rye,
    She draiglet a' her petticoatie,   *draggled*
    Coming through the rye.
        Jenny's a' wat, poor body,   *wet*
        Jenny's seldom dry ;
        She draiglet a' her petticoatie,
        Coming through the rye.

Gin a body meet a body   *if*
    Coming through the rye,
Gin a body kiss a body,
    Need a body cry ?

Gin a body meet a body
    Coming through the glen,
Gin a body kiss a body,
    Need the world ken ?   *know*

YOUNG JAMIE, PRIDE OF A' THE PLAIN.

TUNE—*The Carlin o' the Glen.*

YOUNG Jamie, pride of a' the plain,
Sae gallant and sae gay a swain ;   *so*
Through a' our lasses he did rove,
And reigned resistless king of love :
But now wi' sighs and starting tears,
He strays amang the woods and briers ;
Or in the glens and rocky caves
He sad complaining dowie raves :   *mournful*

I wha sae late did range and rove,   *who so*
And changed with every moon my love,
I little thought the time was near,
Repentance I should buy sae dear.
The slighted maids my torment see,
And laugh at a' the pangs I dree ;   *suffer*
While she, my cruel, scornfu' fair,
Forbids me e'er to see her mair !   *more*

THE LASS OF ECCLEFECHAN.

TUNE—*Jacky Latin.*

GAT ye me, O gat ye me,   got
   O gat ye me wi' naething ;   nothing
Rock and reel, and spinnin' wheel,
   A mickle quarter basin.   large
Bye attour, my gutcher has   besides, grandsire
   A heigh house and a laigh ane,   high, low one
A' forbye my bonnie sel',   besides, self
   The toss of Ecclefechan.   choice

O had your tongue now, Luckie Laing ;   hold
   O haud your tongue and jauner ;   prattle
I held the gate till you I met,   road
   Syne I began to wander :   then
I tint my whistle and my sang,   lost
   I tint my peace and pleasure ;
But your green graff, now, Luckie Laing,   grave
   Wad airt me to my treasure.   would direct

THE CARDIN' O'T.

TUNE—*Salt-fish and Dumplings*

I COFT a stane o' haslock woo',   bought, stone, finest
   To make a coat to Johnny o't ;
For Johnny is my only jo ;
   I loe him best of ony yet.   love, any
     The cardin' o't, the spinnin' o't,
     The warpin' o't, the winnin' o't ;
   When ilka ell cost me a groat,   every
     The tailor staw the lynin' o't.   stole, lining

For though his locks be lyart gray,   mixed
   And though his brow be beld aboon ;   bald, above
Yet I hae seen him on a day,
   The pride of a' the parishen.   parish

THE LASS THAT MADE THE BED TO ME.

TUNE—*The Peacock.*

WHEN winter's wind was blawing cauld,   cold
   As to the north I bent my way,
The mirksome night did me enfauld,   dark, enfold
   I knew na where to lodge till day.   not

A charming girl I chanced to meet,
   Just in the middle o' my care,
And kindly she did me invite
   Her father's humble cot to share.

Her hair was like the gowd sae fine,   *gold so*
  Her teeth were like the ivorie,
Her cheeks like lillies dipt in wine,
  The lass that made the bed to me.

Her bosom was the drifted snaw,
  Her limbs like marble fair to see ;
A finer form nane ever saw   *none*
  Than hers that made the bed to me.

She made the bed baith lang and braid,   *both, broad*
  Wi' twa white hands she spread it down,   *two*
She bade " Guid-night," and smiling said :
  " I hope ye'll sleep baith saft and soun'."   *soft*

Upon the morrow, when I raise,
  I thanked her for her courtesie ;
A blush cam o'er the comely face
  Of her that made the bed for me.

I clasped her waist and kissed her syne ;   *then*
  The tear stude twinkling in her ee ;   *stood, eye*
" O dearest maid, gin ye'll be mine,   *if*
  Ye aye sall mak the bed to me."   *shall*

THE HIGHLAND LADDIE.

TUNE—*If thou'lt play me fair play.*

THE bonniest lad that e'er I saw,
  Bonnie laddie, Highland laddie,
Wore a plaid, and was fu' braw,
  Bonnie Highland laddie.
On his head a bonnet blue,
  Bonnie laddie, Highland laddie ;
His royal heart was firm and true,
  Bonnie Highland laddie.

Trumpets sound, and cannons roar,
  Bonnie lassie, Lowland lassie ;
And a' the hills wi' echoes roar,
  Bonnie Lowland lassie.
Glory, honour, now invite,
  Bonnie lassie, Lowland lassie,
For freedom and my king to fight,
  Bonnie Lowland lassie.

The sun a backward course shall take,
  Bonnie laddie, Highland laddie,
Ere aught thy manly courage shake,
  Bonnie Highland laddie.
Go ! for yourself procure renown,
  Bonnie laddie, Highland laddie ;
And for your lawful king his crown,
  Bonnie Highland laddie.

SAE FAR AWA.

Tune—*Dalkeith Maiden Bridge.*

O SAD and heavy should I part,
  But for her sake sae far awa ;   so, away
Unknowing what my way may thwart,
  My native land sae far awa.
Thou that of a' things Maker art,
  That formed this fair sae far awa,
Gie body strength, and I'll ne'er start   give
  At this my way sae far awa.

How true is love to pure desert,
  So love to her sae far awa ;
And nought can heal my bosom's smart,
  While, oh, she is sae far awa.
Nane other love, nae other dart,   no
  I feel, but hers sae far awa ;
But fairer never touched a heart,
  Than hers, the fair sae far awa.

I'LL AYE CA' IN BY YON TOWN.

I'LL aye ca' in by yon town,   call
  And by yon garden green again ;
I'll aye ca' in by yon town,
  And see my bonnie Jean again.

There's nane sall ken, there's nane sall guess, none, shall
  What brings me back the gate again,   way [know
But she my fairest faithfu' lass,
  And stowlins we sall meet again.   stealthily

She'll wander by the aiken tree,
  When trystin' time draws near again ;   oak
And when her lovely form I see,
  O haith, she's doubly dear again.   indeed

BANNOCKS O' BARLEY.

Tune—*The Killogie.*

BANNOCKS o' bear-meal,   cakes, barley
  Bannocks o' barley ;
Here's to the Highlandman's
  Bannocks o' barley !
Wha in a brulzie   broil
  Will first cry a parley ?
Never the lads wi'
  The bannocks o' barley !

Bannocks o' bear-meal,
 Bannocks o' barley;
Here's to the lads wi'
 The bannocks o' barley !
Wha in his wae-days   who, sad
 Were loyal to Charlie ?—
Wha but the lads wi'
 The bannocks o' barley ?

IT WAS A' FOR OUR RIGHTFU' KING.

TUNE—*It was a' for our rightfu' King.*

IT was a' for our rightfu' king
 We left fair Scotland's strand ;
It was a' for our rightfu' king
 We e'er saw Irish land,
  My dear ;
 We e'er saw Irish land.

Now a' is done that men can do,
 And a' is done in vain ;
My love and native land farewell,
 For I maun cross the main,   must
  My dear ;
 For I maun cross the main.

He turned him right, and round about
 Upon the Irish shore ;
And gae his bridle-reins a shake,   gave
 With adieu for evermore,
  My dear ;
 With adieu for evermore.

The sodger from the wars returns,   soldier
 The sailor frae the main ;   from
But I hae parted frae my love,   have
 Never to meet again,
  My dear ;
 Never to meet again.

When day is gane, and night is come,   gone
 And a' folk bound to sleep ;
I think on him that's far awa',
 The lee-lang night, and weep,   livelong
  My dear ;
 The lee-lang night, and weep.

THE HIGHLAND WIDOW'S LAMENT.

OH, I am come to the low countrie.
 Och-on, och-on, och-rie !
Without a penny in my purse,
 To buy a meal to me.

It was na sae in the Highland hills,   not so
  Och-on, och-on, och-rie !
Nae woman in the country wide   no
  Sae happy was as me.

For then I had a score o' kye,   kine
  Och-on, och-on, och-rie !
Feeding on yon hills so high,
  And giving milk to me.

And there I had threescore o' yowes,   ewes
  Och-on, och-on, och-rie !
Skipping on yon bonnie knowes,   knolls
  And casting woo' to me.   wool

I was the happiest of the clan,
  Sair, sair may I repine ;   sore
For Donald was the brawest lad,
  And Donald he was mine.

Till Charlie Stewart cam at last,
  Sae far to set us free ;   so
My Donald's arm was wanted then,
  For Scotland and for me.

Their waefu' fate what need I tell ?   woeful
  Right to the wrang did yield ;   wrong
My Donald and his country fell
  Upon Culloden's field.

Oh, I am come to the low countrie,
  Och-on, och-on, och-rie !
Nae woman in the world wide
  Sae wretched now as me.

O STEER HER UP.

Tune—*O steer her up, and haud her gaun.*

O STEER her up and haud her gaun—   stir, keep, going
  Her mother's at the mill, jo ;
And gin she winna take a man,   if, won't
  E'en let her tak her will, jo :
First shore her wi' a kindly kiss,   approach
  And ca' another gill, jo ;
And gin she take the thing amiss,   if
  E'en let her flyte her fill, jo.   scold

O steer her up, and be na blate,   bashful
  And gin she take it ill, jo,
Then lea'e the lassie till her fate,
  And time nae langer spill, jo :   no longer
Ne'er break you heart for ae rebute,   one repulse
  But think upon it still, jo ;
Then gin the lassie winna do't,
  Ye'll fin' anither will, jo.   another

WEE WILLIE GRAY.

WEE Willie Gray, and his leather wallet,
Peel a willow-wand, to be him boots and jacket;
The rose upon the brier will be him trouse and doublet,
The rose upon the brier will be him trouse and doublet.

Wee Willie Gray, and his leather wallet,
Twice a lilie flower will be him sark and cravat;   *shirt*
Feathers of a flie wad feather up his bonnet,   *fly*
Feathers of a flie wad feather up his bonnet.

O AYE MY WIFE SHE DANG ME.

TUNE—*My Wife she dang me.*

O AYE my wife she dang me,   *pushed*
  And aft my wife did bang me,   *oft, beat*
If ye gie a woman a' her will,   *give*
  Guid faith, she'll soon o'ergang ye.   *oppress*
On peace and rest my mind was bent,
  And fool I was I married;
But never honest man's intent
  As TERRIBLY miscarried.

O GUID ALE COMES.

O GUID ale comes and guid ale goes,   *good*
Guid ale gars me sell my hose,   *makes*
Sell my hose and pawn my shoon;   *shoes*
Guid ale keeps my heart aboon.   *up*

I had sax owsen in a pleugh,   *six oxen, plough*
They drew a' weel eneugh,   *well enough*
I selt them a' just ane by ane;   *sold, one*
Guid ale keeps my heart aboon.

ROBIN SHURE IN HAIRST.

CHORUS.

ROBIN shure in hairst,   *sheared*
  I shure wi' him;
NOT a heuk had I,   *hook*
  Yet I stack by him.   *stuck*

I gaed up to Dunse,   *went*
  To warp a wab o' plaiden;   *web*
At his daddie's yett,   *gate*
  Wha SPAK me but Robin?   *spoke*

Was na Robin bauld,   *was not, bold*
  Though I was a cotter,
Played me sic a trick,   *such*
  And me the eller's dochter ?   *elder's daughter*

Robin promised me
  A' my winter vittle ;   *provisions*
Nae haet he had but three   *none*
  Goose feathers and a whittle.   *knife*

SWEETEST MAY.

Sweetest May, let Love inspire thee ;
Take a heart which he desires thee ;
As thy constant slave regard it ;
For its faith and truth reward it.

Proof o' shot to birth or money,
Not the wealthy but the bonnie ;
Not high-born, but noble-minded,
In Love's silken band can bind it.

THERE WAS A BONNIE LASS.

There was a bonnie lass, and a bonnie, bonnie lass,
  And she loed her bonnie laddie dear,   *loved*
Till war's loud alarms stole her laddie frae her arms,   *from*
  Wi' monie a sigh and a tear.   *many*

Over sea, over shore, where the cannons loudly roar,
  He still was a stranger to fear ;
And nought could him quail, or his bosom assail,
  But the bonnie lass he loed sae dear.   *so*

CROWDIE.

O that I had ne'er been married,
  I would never had nae care ;   *would, no*
Now I've gotten wife and bairns,
  And they cry crowdie evermair.   *porridge*
    Ance crowdie, twice crowdie,   *once*
      Three times crowdie in a day ;
    Gin ye crowdie ony mair,   *any*
      Ye'll crowdie a' my meal away.

Waefu' want and hunger fley me,   *woeful, fright*
  Glowrin' by the hallan en' ;   *staring, doorway*
Sair I fecht them at the door,   *sore, fight*
  But aye I'm eerie they come ben.   *dismal, in*

Ance crowdie, twice crowdie,
Three times crowdie in a day;
Gin ye crowdie ony mair,
Ye'll crowdie a' my meal away.

THE BLUDE-RED ROSE AT YULE MAY BLAW.

TUNE—*To daunton me.*

THE blude-red rose at Yule may blaw,   blood, Christmas,
The simmer lillies bloom in snaw,   snow   [blow
The frost may freeze the deepest sea ;
But an auld man shall never daunton me.   subdue

To daunton me, and me so young,
Wi' his fause heart and flatt'ring tongue   false
That is the thing you ne'er shall see :
For an auld man shall never daunton me.

For a' his meal and a' his maut,   malt
For a' his fresh beef and his saut,   salt
For a' his gold and white monie,   money
An auld man shall never daunton me.

His gear may buy him kye and yowes,   wealth, cows, ewes
His gear may buy him glens and knowes ;   hills
But me he shall not buy nor fee,
For an auld man shall never daunton me.

He hirples twa-fauld as he dow,   limps, double, can
Wi' his teethless gab and his auld beld pow,   mouth, bald head
And the rain rins down from his red bleer'd ee—   eye
That auld man shall never daunton me.   old

CASSILLIS' BANKS.

Now bank and brae are claith'd in green,   clothed
   And scatter'd cowslips sweetly spring ;
By Girvan's fairy-haunted stream
   The birdies flit on wanton wing.
To Cassillis' banks when e'ening fa's,
   There wi' my Mary let me flee,
There catch her ilka glance of love,   every
   The bonnie blink o' Mary's ee !   eye

The chield wha boasts o' warld's wealth   who, world's
   Is aften laird o' meikle care ;   often, much
But Mary she is a' my ain—   own
   Ah ! Fortune canna gie me mair,   cannot, give, more
Then let me range by Cassillis' banks,
   Wi' her, the lassie dear to me,
And catch her ilka glance o' love,
   The bonnie blink o' Mary's ee '

HUNTING SONG.

TUNE—I red you beware at the Hunting.

THE heather was blooming, the meadows were mawn,   mowed
Our lads gaed a hunting ane day at the dawn,   went, one
Owre moors and owre mosses and mony a glen,   over
At length they discovered a bonny moor-hen.
 I red you beware at the hunting, young men ;   warn
 I red you beware at the hunting, young men ;
 Tak some on the wing, and some as they spring,
  But cannily steal on a bonnie moor-hen.   quietly

Sweet brushing the dew from the brown heather-bells,
Her colours betray'd her on yon mossy fells ;   hills
Her plumage out-lustered the pride o' the spring,
And oh ! as she wantonèd gay on the wing.
 I red you beware, &c.

Auld Phœbus himsel, as he peep'd o'er the hill,
In spite, at her plumage he trièd his skill ;
He levell'd his rays where she bask'd on the brae—
His rays were outshone, and but mark'd where she lay.
 I red you beware, &c.

They hunted the valley, they hunted the hill ;
The best of our lads wi' the best o' their skill ;
But still as the fairest she sat in their sight,
Then, whirr ! she was over a mile at a flight.
 I red you beware, &c.

HEY, THE DUSTY MILLER.

TUNE—The Dusty Miller.

HEY, the dusty miller,
 And his dusty coat ;
He will win a shilling,
 Or he spend a groat.   before
  Dusty was the coat,
  Dusty was the colour,
  Dusty was the kiss
  That I got frae the miller.   from

Hey the dusty miller,
 And his dusty sack ;
Leeze me on the calling   blessings
 Fills the dusty peck—
  Fills the dusty peck,
  Brings the dusty siller ;   money
  I wad gie my coatie   would give
  For the dusty miller.

HER FLOWING LOCKS.

HER flowing locks, the raven's wing,
Adown her neck and bosom hing ;   hang

How sweet unto that breast to cling,
And round that neck entwine her !
Her lips are roses wat wi' dew,   wet
Oh, what a feast her bonnie mou' !   mouth
Her cheeks a mair celestial hue,   more
A crimson still diviner.

RATTLIN' ROARIN' WILLIE.

TUNE—*Rattlin' Roarin' Willie.*

OH, rattlin' roarin' Willie,
  Oh, he held to the fair,   went
And for to sell his fiddle,
  And buy some other ware ;
But parting wi' his fiddle,
  The saut tear blin't his ee ;   salt, eye
And rattlin' roarin' Willie,
  Ye're welcome hame to me !   home

Oh Willie, come sell your fiddle,
  Oh sell your fiddle sae fine ;
Oh Willie, come sell your fiddle,
  And buy a pint o' wine.
If I should sell my fiddle,
  The warl would think I was mad ;   world
For many a rantin' day   many
  My fiddle and I hae had.   have

As I cam by Crochallan,
  I cannily keekit ben—   quietly looked in
Rattlin' roarin' Willie
  Was sitting at yon board en'—
Sitting at yon board en',
  And amang guid companie ;   among good
Rattlin' roarin' Willie,
  Ye're welcome hame to me !

THE CAPTAIN'S LADY.

TUNE—*O Mount and Go.*

WHEN the drums do beat,
  And the cannons rattle,
Thou shalt sit in state,
  And see thy love in battle.

CHORUS.

Oh mount and go,
  Mount and make you ready ;
Oh mount and go,
  And be the captain's lady.

When the vanquish'd foe
  Sues for peace and quiet,
To the shades we'll go,
  And in love enjoy it.

MY LOVE SHE'S BUT A LASSIE YET.

TUNE—*Lady Badinscoth's Reel.*

MY love she's but a lassie yet,
  My love she's but a lassie yet;
We'll let her stand a year or twa,   two
  She'll no be half sae saucy yet.   so
I rue the day I sought her, O,
  I rue the day I sought her, O;
Wha gets her needs na say she's woo'd,   who, not
  But he may say he's bought her, O!

Come draw a drap o' the best o't yet,   drop
  Come draw a drap o' the best o't yet;
Gae seek for pleasure where ye will,   go
  But here I never miss'd it yet.
We're a' dry wi' drinking o't,
  We're a' dry wi' drinking o't;
The minister kiss'd the fiddler's wife,
  And couldna preach for thinking o't.

EPPIE ADAIR.

TUNE—*My Eppie.*

AND oh! my Eppie,
My jewel, my Eppie
Wha wadna he happy   who would not
  Wi' Eppie Adair?
By love, and by beauty,
By law, and by duty,
I swear to be true to
  My Eppie Adair!

And oh! my Eppie,
My jewel, my Eppie,
Wha wadna be happy
  Wi' Eppie Adair?
A' pleasure exile me,
Dishonour defile me,
If e'er I beguile thee
  My Eppie Adair!

THERE'S A YOUTH IN THIS CITY.

To a Gaelic Air.

THERE'S a youth in this city, it were a great pity
  That he frae our lasses should wander awa;   from, away
For he's bonnie and braw, weel-favoured and a',   well
  And his hair has a natural buckle and a'.
His coat is the hue of his bonnet sae blue;   so
  His fecket is white as the new-driven snaw; waistcoat, snow
His hose they are blae, and his shoon like the slae, blue, shoes, sloe
  And his clear siller buckles they dazzle us a'.   silver

For beauty and fortune the laddie's been courtin';   [dower'd
  Weel-featured, weel-tocher'd, weel-mounted, and braw;   well-
But chiefly the siller, that gars him gang till her,   money, makes,
  The penny's the jewel that beautifies a'.   [go
There's Meg wi' the mailen, that fain wad a-haen him ;   farm,
  And Susie, whose daddy was laird o' the ha';   [would, taken
There's lang-tocher'd Nancy maist fetters his fancy—   almost
  But the laddie's dear sel' he loes dearest of a'.   loves

THENIEL MENZIES' BONNIE MARY.

TUNE—*The Ruffian's Rant.*

IN coming by the brig o' Dye,   bridge
  At Darlet we a blink did tarry ;   moment
As day was dawin in the sky,   dawning
  We drank a health to bonnie Mary.
  Theniel Menzies' bonnie Mary ;
  Theniel Menzies' bonnie Mary ;
  Charlie Gregor tint his plaidie,   lost
  Kissin' Theniel's bonnie Mary.

Her een sae bright, her brow sae white,   eyes so
  Her haffet locks as brown's a berry ;   cheek
And aye they dimpl't wi' a smile,
  The rosy cheeks o' bonnie Mary.

We lap and danced the lee-lang day,   leapt, live-long
  Till piper lads were wae and weary,   sorry
But Charlie gat the spring to pay,   got, music
  For kissin' Theniel's bonnie Mary.

COME BOAT ME O'ER TO CHARLIE.

TUNE—*O'er the Water to Charlie.*

COME boat me o'er, come row me o'er,
  Come boat me o'er to Charlie ;
I'll gie John Ross another bawbee,   halfpenny
  To boat me o'er to Charlie.

We'll o'er the water and o'er the sea,
  We'll o'er the water to Charlie ;
Come weal, come woe, we'll gather and go,
  And live or die wi' Charlie.

I loe weel my Charlie's name,   love, well
  Tho' some there be abhor him ;
But oh, to see auld GEORGE gaun hame,   going home
  And Charlie's face before him !

I swear and vow by moon and stars,
  And sun that shines so early,
If I had twenty thousand lives,
  I'd die as aft for Charlie.   oft

ON A PLOUGHMAN.

As I was a-wandering ae morning in spring,   one
I heard a young ploughman sae sweetly to sing;   so
And as he was singing these words, he did say,
There's nae life like the ploughman's in the month of sweet May.   no

The lav'rock in the morning she'll rise frae her nest,   lark, from
And mount the air wi' the dew on her breast,
And wi' the merry ploughman she'll whistle and sing,
And at night she'll return to her nest back again.

EVAN BANKS.

TUNE—*Savourna Delish.*

SLOW spreads the gloom my soul desires,
The sun from India's shore retires:
To Evan banks with temp'rate ray,
Home of youth, he leads the day.

Oh! banks to me for ever dear!
Oh! stream, whose murmurs still I hear!
All, all my hopes of bliss reside
Where Evan mingles with the Clyde.

And she, in simple beauty drest,
Whose image lives within my breast;
Who, trembling, heard my parting sigh,
And long pursued me with her eye:

Does she, with heart unchang'd as mine,
Oft in the vocal bowers recline?
Or, where yon grot o'erhangs the tide,
Muse while the Evan seeks the Clyde?

Ye lofty banks that Evan bound,
Ye lavish woods that wave around,
And o'er the stream your shadows throw
Which sweetly winds so far below;

What secret charm to mem'ry brings
All that on Evan's border springs!
Sweet banks! ye bloom by Mary's side:
Blest stream! she views thee haste to Clyde.

Can all the wealth of India's coast
Atone for years in absence lost!
Return, ye moments of delight,
With richer treasures bless my sight!

Swift from this desert let me part,
And fly to meet a kindred heart!
Nor more may aught my steps divide
From that dear stream which flows to Clyde!

BONNIE PEG.

As I came in by our gate end,
 As day was waxin' weary,
O wha came tripping down the street,   who
 But bonnie Peg, my dearie!

Her air sae sweet, and shape complete.   so
 Wi' nae proportion wanting,   no
The Queen of Love did never move
 Wi' motion mair enchanting.   more

Wi' linked hands, we took the sands
 A-down yon winding river;
And, oh! that hour and broomy bower,
 Can I forget it ever?

HERE'S HIS HEALTH IN WATER.

TUNE—*The Job of Journey-Work.*

ALTHO' my back be at the wa',   wall
 And tho' he be the fautor;   faulty person
Altho' my back be at the wa',
 Yet, here's his health in water!
O! wae gae by his wanton sides,   woe, go
 Sae brawlie he could flatter;   so nicely
Till for his sake I'm slighted sair,   sore
 And dree the kintra clatter.   endure, country
But tho' my back be at the wa',
 And tho' he be the fautor;
But tho' my back be at the wa',
 Yet, here's his health in water.

AH, CHLORIS.

TUNE—*Major Graham.*

AH, Chloris, since it may na be,   not
 That thou of love wilt hear;
If from the lover thou maun flee,   must
 Yet let the friend be dear.

Altho' I love my Chloris mair
 Than ever tongue could tell;
My passion I will ne'er declare,
 I'll say I'll wish thee well:

Tho' a' my daily care thou art,
 And a' my nightly dream,
I'll hide the struggle in my heart,
 And say it is esteem.

[The manuscript of this Song, in Burns' handwriting, is in the possession of Mr John Dick, bookseller, Ayr. By his kind permission we are enabled to give it here.]

SONG,

IN THE CHARACTER OF A RUINED FARMER.

TUNE—*Go from my window, Love, do.*

THE sun he is sunk in the west,
All creatures retirèd to rest,
While here I sit all sore beset
   With sorrow, grief, and wo;
And it's O, fickle Fortune, O!

The prosperous man is asleep,
Nor hears how the whirlwinds sweep;
But misery and I must watch
   The surly tempest blow:
And it's O, fickle Fortune, O!

There lies the dear partner of my breast,
Her cares for a moment at rest:
Must I see thee, my youthful pride,
   Thus brought so very low!
And it's O, fickle Fortune, O!

There lie my sweet babies in her arms,
No anxious fear their little heart alarms
But for their sake my heart doth ache,
   With many a bitter throe:
And it's O, fickle Fortune, O!

I once was by Fortune carest,
I once could relieve the distrest:
Now, life's poor support hardly earned,
   My fate will scarce bestow
And it's O, fickle Fortune, O!

No comfort, no comfort I have!
How welcome to me were the grave!
But then my wife and children dear,
   O whither would they go?
And it's O, fickle Fortune, O!

O whither, O whither shall I turn!
All friendless, forsaken, forlorn!
For in this world rest or peace
   I never more shall know!
And it's O, fickle Fortune, O!

LETTERS.

I.

TO ELLISON BEGBIE.

About 1783.

I **VERILY** believe, my dear E., that the pure genuine feelings of love are as rare in the world as the pure genuine principles of virtue and piety. This, I hope, will account for the uncommon style of all my letters to you. By uncommon, I mean their being written in such a hasty manner, which, to tell you the truth, has made me often afraid lest you should take me for some zealous bigot, who conversed with his mistress as he would converse with his minister. I don't know how it is, my dear, for though, except your company, there is nothing on earth gives me so much pleasure as writing to you, yet it never gives me those giddy raptures so much talked of among lovers. I have often thought that if a well-grounded affection be not really a part of virtue, 'tis something extremely akin to it. Whenever the thought of my E. warms my heart, every feeling of humanity, every principle of generosity, kindles in my breast, it extinguishes every dirty spark of malice and envy which are but too apt to infest me. I grasp every creature in the arms of universal benevolence, and equally participate in the pleasures of the happy, and sympathise with the miseries of the unfortunate. I assure you, my dear, I often look up to the Divine Disposer of events with an eye of gratitude for the blessing which I hope he intends to bestow on me in bestowing you. I sincerely wish that he may bless my endeavours to make your life as comfortable and happy as possible, both in sweetening the rougher parts of my natural temper, and bettering the unkindly circumstances of my fortune. This, my dear, is a passion, at least in my view, worthy of a man, and, I will add, worthy of a Christian. The sordid earthworm may profess love to a woman's person, whilst in reality his affection is centered in her pocket; and the slavish drudge may go a-wooing as he goes to the horse-market, to choose one who is stout and firm, and, as we may say of an old horse, one who will be a good drudge, and draw kindly. I disdain their dirty, puny ideas. I would be heartily out of humour with myself if I thought I were capable of having so poor a notion of the sex, which were designed to crown the pleasures of society. Poor fellows! I don't envy them their happiness who have such notions. For my part, I propose quite other pleasures with my dear partner.   R. B.

II.

TO THE SAME.

MY DEAR E.—I do not remember, in the course of your acquaintance and mine, ever to have heard your opinion on the ordinary way of falling in love amongst people of our station in life. I do not mean the persons who proceed in the way of bargain, but those whose affection is really placed on the person.

Though I be, as you know very well, but a very awkward lover myself, yet as I have some opportunities of observing the conduct of others who are much better skilled in the affair of courtship than I am, I often think it is owing to lucky chance more than to good management that there are not more unhappy marriages than usually are.

It is natural for a young fellow to like the acquaintance of the females, and customary for him to keep them company when occasion serves : some one of them is more agreeable to him than the rest—there is something, he knows not what, pleases him, he knows not how, in her company. This I take to be what is called love with the greater part of us; and I must own, my dear E., it is a hard game such a one as you have to play when you meet with such a lover. You cannot refuse but he is sincere, and yet though you use him ever so favourably, perhaps in a few months, or at farthest in a year or two, the same unaccountable fancy may make him as distractedly fond of another, whilst you are quite forgot. I am aware that perhaps the next time I have the pleasure of seeing you, you may bid me take my own lesson home, and tell me that the passion I have professed for you is perhaps one of those transient flashes I have been describing; but I hope, my dear E., you will do me the justice to believe me, when I assure you that the love I have for you is founded on the sacred principles of virtue and honour, and by consequence, so long as you continue possessed of those amiable qualities which first inspired my passion for you, so long must I continue to love you. Believe me, my dear, it is love like this alone which can render the marriage state happy. People may talk of flames and raptures as long as they please—and a warm fancy, with a flow of youthful spirits, may make them feel something like what they describe ; but sure I am, the nobler faculties of the mind, with kindred feelings of the heart, can only be the foundation of friend-ship, and it has always been my opinion that the married life was only friendship in a more exalted degree. If you will be so good as to grant my wishes, and it should please Providence to spare us to the latest period of life, I can look forward and see that even then, though bent down with wrinkled age—even then, when all other worldly circumstances will be indifferent to me, I will re-gard my E. with the tenderest affection ; and for this plain rea-son, because she is still possessed of those noble qualities, improved to a much higher degree, which first inspired my affection for her.

> " Oh happy state, when souls each other draw,
> When love is liberty, and nature law !"

I know were I to speak in such a style to many a girl, who thinks herself possessed of no small share of sense, she would think it ridiculous ; but the language of the heart is, my dear E., the only courtship I shall ever use to you.

When I look over what I have written, I am sensible it is vastly different from the ordinary style of courtship, but I shall make no apology—I know your good nature will excuse what your good sense may see amiss.   R. B.

III.
TO THE SAME.

I HAVE often thought it a peculiarly unlucky circumstance in love that though, in every other situation in life, telling the truth is not only the safest, but actually by far the easiest way of pro-ceeding, a lover is never under greater difficulty in acting, or more puzzled for expression, than when his passion is sincere, and his intentions are honourable. I do not think that it is very difficult for a person of ordinary capacity to talk of love and fondness which are not felt, and to make vows of constancy and fidelity which are never intended to be performed, if he be villain enough to practise such detestable conduct ; but to a man whose heart glows with the principles of integrity and truth, and who sincerely loves a woman of amiable person, uncommon refinement of senti-ment and purity of manners—to such a one, in such circumstances, I can assure you, my dear, from my own feelings at this present moment, courtship is a task indeed. There is such a number of foreboding fears and distrustful anxieties crowd into my mind when I am in your company, or when I sit down to write to you, that what to speak or what to write I am altogether at a loss.

There is one rule which I have hitherto practised, and which I shall invariably keep with you, and that is, honestly to tell you the plain truth. There is something so mean and unmanly in the arts of dissimulation and falsehood, that I am surprised they can be acted by any one in so noble, so generous a passion as

virtuous love.   No, my dear E., I shall never endeavour to gain
your favour by such detestable practices.   If you will be so good
and so generous as to admit me for your partner, your companion,
your bosom friend through life, there is nothing on this side of
eternity shall give me greater transport; but I shall never think
of purchasing your hand by any arts unworthy of a man, and, I
will add, of a Christian.   There is one thing, my dear, which I
earnestly request of you, and it is this, that you would soon either
put an end to my hopes by a peremptory refusal, or cure me of my
fears by a generous consent.

It would oblige me much if you would send me a line or two
when convenient.   I shall only add further, that if a behaviour
regulated (though perhaps but very imperfectly) by the rules of
honour and virtue, if a heart devoted to love and esteem you, and
an earnest endeavour to promote your happiness—if these are
qualities you would wish in a friend, in a husband, I hope you
shall ever find them in your real friend and sincere lover,   R. B.

IV.
TO THE SAME.

I OUGHT, in good manners, to have acknowledged the receipt of
your letter before this time, but my heart was so shocked with
the contents of it, that I can scarcely yet collect my thoughts so
as to write you on the subject.   I will not attempt to describe
what I felt on receiving your letter.   I read it over and over,
again and again; and though it was in the politest language of
refusal, still it was peremptory : " you were sorry you could not
make me a return, but you wish me"—what, without you, I never
can obtain—" you wish me all kind of happiness."   It would be
weak and unmanly to say, that without you I never can be happy;
but sure I am, that sharing life with you would have given it a
relish that, wanting you, I can never taste.

Your uncommon personal advantages, and your superior good
sense, do not so much strike me ; these, possibly, may be met with
in a few instances in others; but that amiable goodness, that
tender feminine softness, that endearing sweetness of disposition,
with all the charming offspring of a warm, feeling heart—these I
never again expect to meet with, in such a degree, in this world.
All these charming qualities, heightened by an education much
beyond any thing I have ever met in any woman I ever dared to
approach, have made an impression on my heart that I do not
think the world can ever efface.   My imagination has fondly
flattered myself with a wish,—I dare not say it ever reached a
hope,—that possibly I might one day call you mine.   I had formed
the most delightful images, and my fancy fondly brooded over
them ; but now I am wretched for the loss of what I really had

no right to expect. I must now think no more of you as a mistress; still, I presume to ask to be admitted as a friend. As such, I wish to be allowed to wait on you; and as I expect to remove in a few days a little farther off, and you, I suppose, will soon leave this place, I wish to see or hear from you soon: and if an expression should perhaps escape me rather too warm for friendship, I hope you will pardon it in, my dear Miss—(pardon me the dear expression for once) * * * * R. B.

V.
TO HIS FATHER.

IRVINE, *December* 27, 1781

HONOURED SIR,—I have purposely delayed writing in the hope that I should have the pleasure of seeing you on New-Year's Day; but work comes so hard upon us, that I do not choose to be absent on that account, as well as for some other little reasons, which I shall tell you at meeting. My health is nearly the same as when you were here, only my sleep is a little sounder; and, on the whole, I am rather better than otherwise, though I mend by very slow degrees. The weakness of my nerves has so debilitated my mind, that I dare neither review past events nor look forward into futurity: for the least anxiety or perturbation in my breast produces most unhappy effects on my whole frame. Sometimes, indeed, when for an hour or two my spirits are a little lightened, I *glimmer* a little into futurity; but my principal, and indeed my only pleasurable employment, is looking backwards and forwards in a moral and religious way. I am quite transported at the thought that ere long very soon—I shall bid an eternal adieu to all the pains and uneasinesses and disquietudes of this weary life, for I assure you I am heartily tired of it; and if I do not very much deceive myself, I could contentedly and gladly resign it.

" The soul, uneasy and confined at home,
Rests and expatiates in a life to come."

It is for this reason I am more pleased with the 15th, 16th, and 17th verses of the 7th chapter of Revelations than with any ten times as many verses in the whole Bible, and would not exchange the noble enthusiasm with which they inspire me for all that this world has to offer. As for this world, I despair of ever making a figure in it. I am not formed for the bustle of the busy, nor the flutter of the gay. I shall never again be capable of entering into such scenes. Indeed, I am altogether unconcerned at the thoughts of this life. I foresee that poverty and obscurity probably await me: I am in some measure prepared, and daily preparing to meet them. I have but just time and paper to return you my grateful thanks for the lessons of virtue and piety you have given me, which were too much neglected at the time of giving them; but which, I hope, have been remembered ere it is yet too late.   Present my dutiful respects to my mother, and my compliments to Mr and Mrs Muir; and with wishing you a merry New-Year's-Day, I shall conclude.   I am, honoured sir, your dutiful son.

ROBERT BURNS.

P. S.—My meal is nearly out;* but I am going to borrow till I get more.

VI.

TO MR JOHN MURDOCH,

SCHOOLMASTER, STAPLES INN BUILDINGS, LONDON.

LOCHLEA, 15th January 1783.

DEAR SIR,—As I have an opportunity of sending you a letter without putting you to that expense which any production of mine would but ill repay, I embrace it with pleasure to tell you that I have not forgotten, nor ever will forget, the many obligations I lie under to your kindness and friendship.

I do not doubt, sir, but you will wish to know what has been the result of all the pains of an indulgent father and a masterly teacher, and I wish I could gratify your curiosity with such a recital as you would be pleased with; but that is what I am afraid will not be the case.   I have, indeed, kept pretty clear of vicious habits, and in this respect I hope my conduct will not disgrace the education I have gotten ; but as a man of the world I am most miserably deficient.   One would have thought that, bred as I have been under a father who has figured pretty well as *un hommes des affaires*, I might have been what the world calls a pushing, active fellow; but to tell you the truth, sir, there is hardly anything more my reverse.   I seem to be one sent into the world to see and observe, and I very easily compound with the knave who tricks me of my money, if there be anything original about him, which shows me human nature in a different light from anything I have seen before.   In short, the joy of my heart is to "study men, their manners, and their ways;" and for this darling subject I cheerfully sacrifice every other considera-tion.   I am quite indolent about those great concerns that set the bustling busy sons of care agog; and if I have to answer for the present hour, I am very easy with regard to anything fur-ther.   Even the last, worst shift of the unfortunate and the wretched† does not much terrify me : I know that even then my talent for what country folks call a sensible crack,‡ when

---

* It was customary for small farmers, on sending their children to learn a trade, to supply them with oatmeal for their porridge and cakes.

† Mendicancy

‡ Chat.

once it is sanctified by a hoary head, would procure me so much esteem, that even then I would learn to be happy. However, I am under no apprehensions about that; for though indolent, yet so far as an extremely delicate constitution permits, I am not lazy, and in many things, especially in tavern matters, I am a strict economist—not, indeed for the sake of the money, but one of the principal parts in my composition is a kind of pride of stomach; and I scorn to fear the face of any man living: above everything, I abhor the idea of sneaking in a corner to avoid a dun—possibly some pitiful, sordid wretch, who in my heart I despise and detest. 'Tis this, and this alone, that endears economy to me. In the matter of books, indeed, I am very profuse. My favourite authors are of the sentimental kind—such as Shenstone, particularly his *Elegies;* Thomson; *Man of Feeling* —a book I prize next to the Bible; *Man of the World;* Sterne, especially his *Sentimental Journey;* Macpherson's *Ossian,* &c.; these are the glorious models after which I endeavour to form my conduct; and 'tis incongruous, 'tis absurd, to suppose, that the man whose mind glows with sentiments lighted up at their sacred flame—the man whose heart distends with benevolence to all the human race—he "who can soar above this little scene of things"—can he descend to mind the paltry concerns about which the terræfilial race fret, and fume, and vex themselves? Oh how the glorious triumph swells my heart! I forget that I am a poor insignificant fellow, unnoticed and unknown, stalking up and down fairs and markets when I happen to be in them, reading a page or two of mankind, and "catching the manners living as they rise," whilst the men of business jostle me on every side as an idle encumbrance in their way. But I daresay I have by this time tired your patience; so I shall conclude with begging you to give Mrs Murdoch—not my compliments, for that is a mere commonplace story, but my warmest, kindest wishes for her welfare,—and accept of the same for yourself, from, dear sir, yours,

R. B.

See (VI.*), p. 451.

VII.

TO MR BURNESS OF MONTROSE.

LOCHLEA, 17th *February* 1784.

DEAR COUSIN—I would have returned you my thanks for your kind favour of the 13th of December sooner, had it not been that I waited to give you an account of that melancholy event which, for some time past, we have from day to day expected.

On the 13th current I lost the best of fathers. Though, to be sure, we have had long warning of the impending stroke, still the feelings of nature claim their part, and I cannot recollect the tender endearments and parental lessons of the best of friends and ablest of instructors, without feeling what perhaps the calmer dictates of reason would partly condemn.

I hope my father's friends in your country will not let their connection in this place die with him. For my part, I shall ever with pleasure, with pride, acknowledge my connection with those who were allied by the ties of blood and friendship to a man whose memory I shall ever honour and revere.

I expect, therefore, my dear sir, you will not neglect any opportunity of letting me hear from you, which will very much oblige, my dear cousin, yours sincerely, R. B.

VIII.

TO MR JAMES BURNES, MONTROSE.

MOSSGIEL, *August* 1784.

WE have been surprised with one of the most extraordinary phenomena in the moral world which I daresay has happened in the course of this half century. We have had a party of [the] Presbytery [of] Relief, as they call themselves, for some time in this country. A pretty thriving society of them has been in the burgh of Irvine for some years past, till, about two years ago, a Mrs Buchan from Glasgow came, and began to spread some fanatical notions of religion among them, and in a short time made many converts; and among others their preacher, Mr White, who, upon that account, has been suspended and formally deposed by his brethren. He continued, however, to preach in private to his party, and was supported, both he and their spiritual mother, as they affect to call old Buchan, by the contributions of the rest, several of whom were in good circumstances; till, in spring last, the populace rose and mobbed Mrs Buchan, and put her out of the town; on which all her followers voluntarily quitted the place likewise, and with such precipitation, that many of them never shut their doors behind them. One left a washing on the green, another a cow bellowing at the crib without food, or anybody to mind her; and after several stages, they are fixed at present in the neighbourhood of Dumfries. Their tenets are a strange jumble of enthusiastic jargon; among others, she pretends to give them the Holy Ghost by breathing on them, which she does with postures and practices that are scandalously indecent. They have likewise disposed of all their effects, and hold a community of goods, and live nearly an idle life, carrying on a great farce of pretended devotion in barns and woods, where they lodge and lie altogether, and hold likewise a community of women, as it is another of their tenets that they can commit no moral sin. I am personally acquainted with most of them, and I can assure you the above-mentioned are facts.

This, my dear sir, is one of the many instances of the folly of

leaving the guidance of sound reason and common sense in mat-
ters of religion.

Whenever we neglect or despise these sacred monitors, the
whimsical notions of a perturbated brain are taken for the imme-
diate influences of the Deity; and the wildest fanaticism, and the
most inconstant absurdities, will meet with abettors and converts.
Nay, I have often thought that the more out-of-the-way and
ridiculous the fancies are, if once they are sanctified under the
sacred name of religion, the unhappy mistaken votaries are the
more firmly glued to them.   R. B.

IX.

TO MISS MARGARET K——.

1785.

MADAM,—Permit me to present you with the enclosed song
(p. 218), as a small though grateful tribute for the honour of your
acquaintance. I have, in these verses, attempted some faint
sketches of your portrait in the unembellished simple manner of
descriptive TRUTH. Flattery I leave to your LOVERS, whose
exaggerating fancies may make them imagine you still nearer
perfection than you really are.

Poets, madam, of all mankind, feel most forcibly the powers of
BEAUTY; as, if they are really POETS of Nature's making, their
feelings must be finer, and their taste more delicate, than most of
the world. In the cheerful bloom of SPRING, or the pensive mild-
ness of AUTUMN, the grandeur of SUMMER, or the hoary majesty
of WINTER, the poet feels a charm unknown to the rest of his
species. Even the sight of a fine flower, or the company of a fine
woman (by far the finest part of God's works below), have sensa-
tions for the poetic heart that the HERD of men are strangers to.
On this last account, madam, I am, as in many other things, in-
debted to Mr H.'s kindness in introducing me to you. Your
lovers may view you with a wish, I look on you with pleasure:
their hearts, in your presence, may glow with desire, mine rises
with admiration.

That the arrows of misfortune, however they should, as incident
to humanity, glance a slight wound, may never reach your *heart*—
that the snares of villany may never beset you in the road of
life—that INNOCENCE may hand you by the path of HONOUR to
the dwelling of PEACE—is the sincere wish of him who has the
honour to be, &c.   R. B.

X.

TO MR JOHN RICHMOND, EDINBURGH.

MOSSGIEL, *February* 17, 1786.

MY DEAR SIR,—I have not time at present to upbraid you for your silence and neglect; I shall only say I received yours with great pleasure. I have enclosed you a piece of rhyming ware for your perusal. I have been very busy with the Muses since I saw you, and have composed, among several others, The Ordination, a poem on Mr M'Kinlay's being called to Kilmarnock; Scotch Drink, a poem; The Cotter's Saturday Night; An Address to the Devil, &c. I have likewise completed my poem on the Dogs, but have not shown it to the world. My chief patron now is Mr Aiken in Ayr, who is pleased to express great approbation of my works. Be so good as send me Fergusson, by Connel, and I will remit you the money. I have no news to acquaint you with about Mauchline; they are just going on in the old way. I have some very important news with respect to myself, not the most agreeable—news that I am sure you cannot guess, but I shall give you the particulars another time. I am extremely happy with Smith: he is the only friend I have now in Mauchline. I can scarcely forgive your long neglect of me, and I beg you will let me hear from you regularly by Connel. If you would act your part as a friend, I am sure neither good nor bad fortune should strange or alter me. Excuse haste, as I got yours but yesterday. I am, my dear sir, yours,   ROBERT BURNESS.

XI.

TO JOHN BALLANTYNE, ESQ., AYR.

April 1786?

HONOURED SIR,—My proposals came to hand last night, and, knowing that you would wish to have it in your power to do me a service as early as anybody, I enclose you half a sheet of them. I must consult you, first opportunity, on the propriety of sending my quondam friend, Mr Aiken, a copy. If he is now reconciled to my character as an honest man, I would do it with all my soul; but I would not be beholden to the noblest being ever God created, if he imagined me to be a rascal. Apropos, old Mr Armour prevailed with him to mutilate that unlucky paper yesterday. Would you believe it?—though I had not a hope, nor even a wish, to make her mine after her conduct, yet, when he told me the names were all out of the paper, my heart died within me, and he cut my veins with the news. * * *   R. B.

XII.

TO MR M'WHINNIE, WRITER, AYR.

MOSSGIEL, *17th April* 1786.

I⊤ is injuring some hearts, those hearts that elegantly bear the impression of the good Creator, to say to them you give them the trouble of obliging a friend ; for this reason, I only tell you that I gratify my own feelings in requesting your friendly offices with respect to the enclosed (a prospectus of the Poems), because ⌐ know it will gratify yours to assist me in it to the utmost of your power.

I have sent you four copies, as I have no less than eight dozen, which is a great deal more than I shall ever need.

Be sure to remember a poor poet militant in your prayers. He looks forward with fear and trembling to that, to him, important moment which stamps the die with—with—with, perhaps, the eternal disgrace of, my dear sir, your humble, afflicted, tormented,

ROBERT BURNS.

XIII.

TO MR JOHN KENNEDY.

MOSSGIEL, *20th April* 1786.

SIR,—By some neglect in Mr Hamilton, I did not hear of your kind request for a subscription paper till this day. I will not attempt any acknowledgment for this, nor the manner in which I see your name in Mr Hamilton's subscription list. Allow me only to say, sir, I feel the weight of the debt.

I have here likewise enclosed a small piece, the very latest of my productions. I am a good deal pleased with some sentiments myself, as they are just the native querulous feelings of a heart which, as the elegantly melting Gray says, ' melancholy has marked for her own.'

Our race comes on apace—that much expected scene of revelry and mirth ; but to me it brings no joy equal to that meeting with which you last flattered the expectation of, sir, your indebted humble servant, R. B.

XIV.

TO MR DAVID BRICE.

MOSSGIEL, *June* 12, 1786.

DEAR BRICE,—I received your message by G. Paterson, and as I am not very throng [busy] at present, I just write to let you know that there is such a worthless, rhyming reprobate as your

humble servant still in the land of the living, though I can
scarcely say in the place of hope. I have no news to tell you
that will give me any pleasure to mention, or you to hear.

Poor, ill-advised, ungrateful Armour came home on Friday
last. You have heard all the particulars of that affair, and a
black affair it is. What she thinks of her conduct now I don't
know : one thing I do know—she has made me completely miser-
able. Never man loved, or rather adored, a woman more than I
did her; and to confess a truth between you and me, I do still
love her to distraction after all, though I won't tell her so if I were
to see her, which I don't want to do. My poor dear unfortunate
Jean ! how happy have I been in thy arms ! It is not the losing
her that makes me so unhappy, but for her sake I feel most
severely. I foresee she is in the road to, I am afraid, eternal
ruin.

May Almighty God forgive her ingratitude and perjury to me,
as I from my very soul forgive her ; and may His grace be with
her and bless her in all her future life ! I can have no nearer idea
of the place of eternal punishment than what I have felt in my own
breast on her account. I have tried often to forget her ; I have
run into all kinds of dissipation and riots, mason-meetings,
drinking-matches, and other mischief, to drive her out of my
head; but all in vain. And now for a grand cure : the ship is on
her way home that is to take me out to Jamaica ; and then, fare-
well dear old Scotland ! and farewell, dear ungrateful Jean ! for
never, never will I see you more.

You will have heard that I am going to commence poet in
print ; and to-morrow my works go to the press. I expect it will
be a volume of about 200 pages—it is just the last foolish action
I intend to do, and then turn a wise man as fast as possible.
Believe me to be, dear Brice, your friend and well-wisher,

R. B.

XV.

TO JOHN RICHMOND, EDINBURGH.

MOSSGIEL, 9th July 1786.

WITH the sincerest grief I read your letter. You are truly a
son of misfortune. I shall be extremely anxious to hear from you
how your health goes on—if it is anyway re-establishing, or if
Leith promises well—in short, how you feel in the inner man.

I have waited on Armour since her return home ; not from the
least view of reconciliation, but merely to ask for her health, and,
to you I will confess it, from a foolish hankering fondness, very
ill-placed indeed. The mother forbade me the house, nor did

Jean show that penitence that might have been expected. However, the priest, I am informed, will give me a certificate as a single man, if I comply with the rules of the church, which for that very reason I intend to do.

I am going to put on sackcloth and ashes this day. I am indulged so far as to appear in my own seat. *Peccavi, pater; miserere me.* My book will be ready in a fortnight. If you have any subscribers, return them by Connel. The Lord stand with the righteous—Amen, amen l R. B.

XVI.

TO MR DAVID BRICE,

SHOEMAKER, GLASGOW.

Mossgiel, 17*th July* 1786.

I HAVE been so throng [busy] printing my Poems, that I could scarcely find as much time as to write to you. Poor foolish Armour is come back again to Mauchline, and I went to call for her, and her mother forbade me the house; nor did she herself express much sorrow for what she has done. I have already appeared publicly in church, and was indulged in the liberty of standing in my own seat. I do this to get a certificate as a bachelor, which Mr Auld has promised me. I am now fixed to go for the West Indies in October. Jean and her friends insisted much that she should stand along with me in the kirk; but the minister would not allow it, which bred a great trouble, I assure you, and I am blamed as the cause of it, though I am sure I am innocent; but I am very much pleased, for all that, not to have had her company. I have no news to tell you that I remember. I am really happy to hear of your welfare, and that you are so well in Glasgow. I must certainly see you before I leave the country. I shall expect to hear from you soon, and am, dear Brice, yours, R. B.

XVII.

TO MR JOHN RICHMOND.

Old Rome Forest, 30*th July* 1786.

My Dear Richmond,—My hour is now come—you and I will never meet in Britain more. I have orders, within three weeks at farthest, to repair aboard the Nancy, Captain Smith, from Clyde to Jamaica, and to call at Antigua. This, except to our friend Smith, whom God long preserve, is a secret about Mauchline. Would you believe it? Armour has got a warrant to throw

me in jail till I find security for an enormous sum. This they
keep an entire secret, but I got it by a channel they little dream
of; and I am wandering from one friend's house to another, and,
like a true son of the gospel, " have no where to lay my head."
I know you will pour an execration on her head, but spare the
poor, ill-advised girl, for my sake. * * * I write in a moment
of rage, reflecting on my miserable situation—exiled, abandoned,
forlorn. I can write no more : let me hear from you by the
return of coach. I will write you ere I go. I am, dear sir, yours,
here and hereafter, R. B.

XVIII.

TO MONS. JAMES SMITH, MAUCHLINE.

Munday Morning, MOSSGIEL.

MY DEAR SIR,—I went to Dr Douglas yesterday, fully resolved
to take the opportunity of Captain Smith ; but I found the Doctor
with a Mr and Mrs White, both Jamaicans, and they have de-
ranged my plans altogether. They assure him that to send me
from Savannah la Mar to Port Antonio will cost my master,
Charles Douglas, upwards of fifty pounds, besides running the
risk of throwing myself into a pleuritic fever, in consequence of
hard travelling in the sun. On these accounts he refuses sending
me with Smith ; but a vessel sails from Greenock the 1st of Sep-
tember, right for the place of my destination. The captain of
her is an intimate friend of Mr Gavin Hamilton's, and as good a
fellow as heart could wish : with him I am destined to go. Where
I shall shelter I know not, but I hope to weather the storm. * * *
On Thursday morning, if you can muster as much self-denial
as to be out of bed about seven o'clock, I shall see you as I ride
through to Cumnock. After all, Heaven bless the sex ! I feel
there is still happiness for me among them :—

Oh, woman, lovely woman ! Heaven designed you
To temper man!—we had been brutes without you!

R. B.

XIX.

TO MR JOHN KENNEDY.

KILMARNOCK, *August* 1786.

MY DEAR SIR,—Your truly facetious epistle of the 3d instant
gave me much entertainment. I was only sorry I had not the
pleasure of seeing you as I passed your way, but we shall bring
up all our leeway on Wednesday the 16th current, when I hope
to have it in my power to call on you, and take a kind, very pro-
bably a last adieu, before I go for Jamaica ; and I expect orders
to repair to Greenock every day. I have at last made my public

appearance, and am solemnly inaugurated into the numerous class. Could I have got a carrier, you should have had a score of vouchers for my authorship; but, now you have them, let them speak for themselves.·

> Farewell, dear friend! may guid-luck hit you,
> And 'mang her favourites admit you,
> If e'er Detraction shore to smit you,   threaten
> May nane believe him.
>
> R. B.

XX.

TO MR BURNES, MONTROSE.

MOSSGIEL, *September* 26, 1786.

MY DEAR SIR,—I this moment receive yours—receive it with the honest hospitable warmth of a friend's welcome. Whatever comes from you wakens always up the better blood about my heart, which your kind little recollections of my parental friends carries as far as it will go. 'Tis there that man is blest! 'Tis there, my friend, man feels a consciousness of something within him above the trodden clod! The grateful reverence to the hoary (earthly) author of his being—the burning glow when he clasps the woman of his soul to his bosom—the tender yearnings of heart for the little angels to whom he has given existence—these Nature has poured in milky streams about the human heart; and the man who never rouses them to action, by the inspiring influences of their proper objects, loses by far the most pleasurable part of his existence.

' My departure is uncertain, but I do not think it will be till after harvest. I will be on very short allowance of time indeed, if I do not comply with your friendly invitation. When it will be I don't know, but if I can make my wish good, I will endeavour to drop you a line some time before. My best compliments to Mrs ——; I should [be] equally mortified should I drop in when she is abroad; but of that I suppose there is little chance.

What I have wrote Heaven knows; I have not time to review it: so accept of it in the beaten way of friendship. With the ordinary phrase—perhaps rather more than the ordinary sincerity —I am, dear sir, ever yours,   R. B.

XXI.

TO MRS STEWART OF STAIR.

[*August?*] 1786.

MADAM,—The hurry of my preparations for going abroad has hindered me from performing my promise so soon as I intended.

1 have here sent you a parcel of songs, &c., which never made
their appearance, except to a friend or two at most. Perhaps
some of them may be no great entertainment to you, but of that
I am far from being an adequate judge. The song to the tune
of Ettrick Banks [The Bonnie Lass of Ballochmyle, p. 223] you
will easily see the impropriety of exposing much, even in manu-
script. I think myself it has some merit, both as a tolerable de-
scription of one of nature's sweetest scenes, a July evening, and
one of the finest pieces of Nature's workmanship, the finest, indeed,
we know anything of—an amiable, beautiful young woman (Miss
Alexander) ; but I have no common friend to procure me that per-
mission, without which I would not dare to spread the copy.

I am quite aware, madam, what task the world would assign
me in this letter. The obscure bard, when any of the great con-
descend to take notice of him, should heap the altar with the
incense of flattery. Their high ancestry, their own great and
god-like qualities and actions, should be recounted with the most
exaggerated description. This, madam, is a task for which I am
altogether unfit. Besides a certain disqualifying pride of heart,
I know nothing of your connections in life, and have no access to
where your real character is to be found—the company of your
compeers ; and more, I am afraid that even the most refined
adulation is by no means the road to your good opinion.

One feature of your character I shall ever with grateful plea-
sure remember—the reception I got when I had the honour of
waiting on you at Stair. I am little acquainted with politeness,
but I know a good deal of benevolence of temper and goodness of
heart. Surely did those in exalted stations know how happy they
could make some classes of their inferiors by condescension and
affability, they would never stand so high, measuring out with
every look the height of their elevation, but condescend as sweetly
as did Mrs Stewart of Stair.   R. B.

XXII.

TO MR ROBERT AIKEN.

SIR,—I was with Wilson my printer t'other day, and settled
all our bygone matters between us. After I had paid all de-
mands, I made him the offer of the second edition, on the hazard
of being paid out of the first and readiest, which he declines. By
his account, the paper of 1000 copies would cost about twenty-
seven pounds, and the printing about fifteen or sixteen : he offers
to agree to this for the printing if I will advance for the paper,
but this, you know, is out of my power ; so farewell hopes of a
second edition till I grow richer ! an epocha which I think will
arrive at the payment of the British national debt.

There is scarcely anything hurts me so much in being disappointed of my second edition, as not having it in my power to show my gratitude to Mr Ballantine, by publishing my poem ot *The Brigs of Ayr.* I would detest myself as a wretch if I thought I were capable in a very long life of forgetting the honest, warm, and tender delicacy with which he enters into my interests. I am sometimes pleased with myself in my grateful sensations ; but I believe, on the whole, I have very little merit in it, as my gratitude is not a virtue, the consequence of reflection, but sheerly the instinctive emotion of my heart, too inattentive to allow worldly maxims and views to settle into selfish habits.

I have been feeling all the various rotations and movements within respecting the excise. There are many things plead strongly against it ; the uncertainty of getting soon into business the consequences of my follies, which may perhaps make it impracticable for me to stay at home ; and, besides, I have for some time been pining under secret wretchedness, from causes which you pretty well know—the pang of disappointment, the sting of pride, with some wandering stabs of remorse, which never fail to settle on my vitals like vultures, when attention is not called away by the calls of society or the vagaries of the Muse. Even in the hour of social mirth, my gaiety is the madness of an intoxicated criminal under the hands of the executioner. All these reasons urge me to go abroad, and to all these reasons I have only one answer—the feelings of a father. This, in the present mood I am in, overbalances everything that can be laid in the scale against it.

You may perhaps think it an extravagant fancy, but it is a sentiment which strikes home to my very soul ; though sceptical in some points of our current belief, yet I think I have every evidence for the reality of a life beyond the stinted bourne of our present existence ; if so, then how should I, in the presence of that tremendous Being, the Author of existence,—how should I meet the reproaches of those who stand to me in the dear relation of children, whom I deserted in the smiling innocency of helpless infancy ? Oh thou great unknown Power ?—thou Almighty God ! who has lighted up reason in my breast, and blessed me with immortality !—I have frequently wandered from that order and regularity necessary for the perfection of thy works, yet Thou hast never left me nor forsaken me !

Since I wrote the foregoing sheet, I have seen something of the storm of mischief thickening over my folly-devoted head. Should you, my friends, my benefactors, be successful in your applications for me, perhaps it may not be in my power in that way to reap the fruit of your friendly efforts. What I have written in the preceding pages is the settled tenor of my present resolution ; but should inimical circumstances forbid me closing with your kind offer, or enjoying it only threaten to entail further misery——

To tell the truth, I have little reason for complaint, as the world, in general, has been kind to me fully up to my deserts. I was, for some time past, fast getting into the pining, distrustful snarl of the misanthrope. I saw myself alone, unfit for the struggle of life, shrinking at every rising cloud in the chance-directed atmosphere of fortune, while, all defenceless, I looked about in vain for a cover. It never occurred to me, at least never with the force it deserved, that this world is a busy scene, and man a creature destined for a progressive struggle; and that however I might possess a warm heart and inoffensive manners (which last, by the by, was rather more than I could well boast), still, more than these passive qualities, there was something to be done. When all my schoolfellows and youthful compeers (those misguided few excepted who joined, to use a Gentoo phrase, the "hallachores" of the human race) were striking off with eager hope and earnest intent in some one or other of the many paths of busy life, I "was standing idle in the market-place," or only left the chace of the butterfly from flower to flower to hunt fancy from whim to whim.

You see, sir, that if to know one's errors were a probability of mending them, I stand a fair chance; but, according to the reverend Westminster divines, though conviction must precede conversion, it is very far from always implying it. R. B.

XXIII.

TO DR MACKENZIE, MAUCHLINE.

[Enclosing him verses on dining with Lord Daer.]

Wednesday morning, [*October* 25?]

DEAR SIR,--I never spent an afternoon among great folks with half that pleasure as when, in company with you, I had the honour of paying my devoirs to that plain, honest, worthy man the professor [Dugald Stewart]. I would be delighted to see him perform acts of kindness and friendship, though I were not the object; he does it with such a grace. I think his character, divided into ten parts, stands thus—four parts Socrates—four parts Nathaniel—and two parts Shakspeare's Brutus.

The foregoing verses (p. 105) were really extempore, but a little corrected since. They may entertain you a little, with the help of that partiality with which you are so good as to favour the performances of, dear sir, your very humble servant, R. B.

XXIV.
TO MRS DUNLOP OF DUNLOP.

MADAM,—I am truly sorry I was not at home yesterday, when I was so much honoured with your order for my copies, and incomparably more by the handsome compliments you are pleased to pay my poetic abilities. I am fully persuaded there is not any class of mankind so feelingly alive to the titillations of applause as the sons of Parnassus : nor is it easy to conceive how the heart of the poor bard dances with rapture, when those whose character in life gives them a right to be polite judges, honour him with their approbation. Had you been thoroughly acquainted with me, madam, you could not have touched my darling heart-chord more sweetly than by noticing my attempts to celebrate your illustrious ancestor, the saviour of his country.

Great patriot hero! ill-requited chief!

The first book I met with in my earlier years which I perused with pleasure was *The Life of Hannibal*; the next was *The History of Sir William Wallace* ; for several of my earlier years I had few other authors; and many a solitary hour have I stole out, after the laborious vocations of the day, to shed a tear over their glorious but unfortunate stories. In those boyish days I remember in particular being struck with that part of Wallace's story where these lines occur :—

"Syne to the Leglen Wood, when it was late,
To make a silent and a safe retreat."

I chose a fine summer Sunday, the only day my line of life allowed, and walked half-a-dozen of miles to pay my respects to the Leglen Wood, with as much devout enthusiasm as ever pilgrim did to Loretto ; and as I explored every den and dell where I could suppose my heroic countryman to have lodged, I recollect (for even then I was a rhymer) that my heart glowed with a wish to be able to make a song on him in some measure equal to his merits. R. B.

XXV.
TO MR ARCHIBALD LAWRIE.

MOSSGIEL, *November 13th*, 1786.

DEAR SIR,—I have along with this sent two volumes of Ossian, with the remaining volume of the songs.* Ossian I am not in

* Mrs Lawrie had rebuked Burns for some remarks he had made. When the books were opened, a slip of paper containing the following lines dropped out :—

Rusticity's ungainly form
May cloud the highest mind;
But when the heart is nobly warm,
The good excuse will find.

Propriety's cold cautious rules
Warm fervour may o'erlook ;
But spare poor Sensibility
The ungentle, harsh rebuke.

such a hurry about; but I wish the songs, with the volume of the Scotch poets, as soon as they can conveniently be despatched. If they are left at Mr Wilson the bookseller's shop in Kilmarnock, they will easily reach me.

My most respectful compliments to Mr and Mrs Lawrie; and a poet's warmest wishes for their happiness to the young ladies, particularly the fair musician, whom I think much better qualified than ever David was, or could be, to charm an evil spirit out of Saul.

Indeed it needs not the feelings of a poet to be interested in the welfare of one of the sweetest scenes of domestic peace and kindred love that ever I saw; as I think the peaceful unity of St Margaret's Hill can only be excelled by the harmonious concord of the Apocalyptic Zion.   R. B.

XXVI.

TO MISS ALEXANDER OF BALLOCHMYLE.

MOSSGIEL, 18th Nov. 1786.

MADAM,—Poets are such *outré* beings, so much the children of wayward fancy and capricious whim, that I believe the world generally allows them a larger latitude in the laws of propriety than the sober sons of judgment and prudence. I mention this as an apology for the liberties that a nameless stranger has taken with you in the enclosed poem, which he begs leave to present you with. Whether it has poetical merit anyway worthy of the theme, I am not the proper judge; but it is the best my abilities can produce; and, what to a good heart will perhaps be a superior grace, it is equally sincere as fervent.

The scenery was nearly taken from real life, though I daresay, madam, you do not recollect it, as I believe you scarcely noticed the poetic *reveur* as he wandered by you. I had roved out as chance directed, in the favourite haunts of my Muse, on the banks of the Ayr, to view Nature in all the gaiety of the vernal year. The evening sun was flaming over the distant western hills; not a breath stirred the crimson opening blossom, or the verdant spreading leaf. It was a golden moment for a poetic heart. I listened to the feathered warblers, pouring their harmony on every hand, with a congenial kindred regard, and frequently turned out of my path lest I should disturb their little songs, or frighten them to another station. Surely, said I to myself, he must be a wretch indeed who, regardless of your harmonious endeavour to please him, can eye your elusive flights to discover your secret recesses, and to rob you of all the property Nature gives you—your dearest comforts, your helpless nestlings. Even

the hoary hawthorn twig that shot across the way, what heart at
such a time but must have been interested in its welfare, and
wished it preserved from the rudely-browsing cattle, or the wither-
ing eastern blast? Such was the scene, and such the hour, when,
in a corner of my prospect, I spied one of the fairest pieces of
Nature's workmanship that ever crowned a poetic landscape or
met a poet's eye—those visionary bards excepted who hold com-
merce with aërial beings! Had Calumny and Villany taken my
walk, they had at that moment sworn eternal peace with such
an object.

What an hour of inspiration for a poet! It would have raised
plain dull historic prose into metaphor and measure!

The enclosed song was the work of my return home; and per
haps it but poorly answers what might have been expected from
such a scene. * * * I have the honour to be, madam, your
most obedient and very humble servant,   R. B.

XXVII.

TO GAVIN HAMILTON, ESQ., MAUCHLINE.

EDINBURGH, *Dec. 7th*, 1786.

HONOURED SIR,—I have paid every attention to your com-
mands, but can only say, what perhaps you will have heard be-
fore this reach you, that Muirkirklands were bought by a John
Gordon, W.S., but for whom I know not; Mauchlands, Haugh-Mill,
&c., by a Frederick Fotheringham, supposed to be for Ballochmyle
Laird; and Adam-Hill and Shawood were bought for Oswald's
folks. This is so imperfect an account, and will be so late ere it
reach you, that were it not to discharge my conscience, I would
not trouble you with it; but after all my diligence, I could make
it no sooner nor better.

For my own affairs, I am in a fair way of becoming as emi-
nent as Thomas à Kempis or John Bunyan; and you may expect
henceforth to see my birthday inserted among the wonderful events
in the Poor Robin's and Aberdeen Almanacs, along with the
Black Monday and the battle of Bothwell-Bridge. My Lord
Glencairn and the Dean of Faculty, Mr H. Erskine, have taken
me under their wing; and by all probability I shall soon be the
tenth worthy and the eighth wise man of the world. Through
my Lord's influence, it is inserted in the records of the Caledonian
Hunt that they universally, one and all, subscribe for the second
edition. My subscription bills come out to-morrow, and you
shall have some of them next post. I have met in Mr Dalrymple
of Orangefield what Soloman emphatically calls "a friend that
sticketh closer than a brother." The warmth with which he in-

terests himself in my affairs is of the same enthusiastic kind which you, Mr Aiken, and the few patrons that took notice of my earlier poetic days, showed for the poor unlucky devil of a poet.

I always remember Mrs Hamilton and Miss Kennedy in my poetic prayers, but you both in prose and verse.

May cauld ne'er catch you but a hap,   without, coat
Nor hunger but in Plenty's lap!
Amen!   R. B.

XXVIII.

TO JAMES DALRYMPLE, ESQ., OF ORANGEFIELD.

December 10, 1786?

DEAR SIR,—I suppose the devil is so elated with his success with you, that he is determined by a *coup de main* to complete his purposes on you all at once, in making you a poet. I broke open the letter you sent me—hummed over the rhymes—and as I saw they were extempore, said to myself they were very well; but when I saw at the bottom a name that I shall ever value with grateful respect, " I gapit wide, but naething spak." I was nearly as much struck as the friends of Job, of affliction-bearing memory, when they sat down with him seven days and seven nights, and spake not a word.

I am naturally of a superstitious cast; and as soon as my wonder-scared imagination regained its consciousness, and re‹ sumed its functions, I cast about what this mania of yours might portend. My foreboding ideas had the wide stretch of possibility; and several events, great in their magnitude, and important in their consequences, occurred to my fancy. The downfall of the conclave, or the crushing of the cork rumps—a ducal coronet to Lord George Gordon, and the Protestant interest or St Peter's keys to * * * *.

You want to know how I come on. I am just *in statu quo*, or, not to insult a gentleman with my Latin, in " auld use and wont.". The noble Earl of Glencairn took me by the hand to-day, and interested himself in my concerns, with a goodness like that benevolent being whose image he so richly bears. He is a stronger proof of the immortality of the soul than any that philosophy ever produced. A mind like his can never die. Let the worshipful squire H. L., or the Reverend Mass J. M., go into their primitive nothing. At best, they are but ill-digested lumps of chaos—only, one of them strongly tinged with bituminous particles and sulphureous effluvia. But my noble patron, eternal as the heroic swell of magnanimity, and the generous throb of benevolence, shall look on with princely eye at "the war of elements, the wreck of matter, and the crash of worlds." R. B.

XXIX.
TO JOHN BALLANTINE, ESQ., BANKER, AYR.

EDINBURGH, 13th December 1786.

MY HONOURED FRIEND,—I would not write you till I could have it in my power to give you some account of myself and my matters, which, by the by, is often no easy task. I arrived here on Tuesday was se'nnight, and have suffered ever since I came to town with a miserable headache and stomach complaint, but am now a good deal better. I have found a worthy warm friend in Mr Dalrymple of Orangefield, who introduced me to Lord Glencairn, a man whose worth and brotherly kindness to me I shall remember when time shall be no more. By his interest it is passed in the "Caledonian Hunt," and entered in their books, that they are to take each a copy of the second edition, for which they are to pay one guinea. I have been introduced to a good many of the *noblesse*, but my avowed patrons and patronesses are, the Duchess of Gordon—the Countess of Glencairn, with my Lord and Lady Betty*—the Dean of Faculty—Sir John Whitefoord. I have likewise warm friends among the literati; Professors Stewart, Blair, and Mr Mackenzie, the "Man of Feeling." An unknown hand left ten guineas for the Ayrshire bard with Mr Sibbald, which I got. I since have discovered my generous unknown friend to be Patrick Miller, Esq., brother to the Justice-Clerk; and drank a glass of claret with him by invitation at his own house yesternight. I am nearly agreed with Creech to print my book, and I suppose I will begin on Monday. I will send a subscription bill or two next post, when I intend writing my first kind patron, Mr Aiken. I saw his son to-day, and he is very well.

Dugald Stewart, and some of my learned friends, put me in the periodical paper called the *Lounger*, a copy of which I here enclose you. I was, sir, when I was first honoured with your notice, too obscure; now I tremble lest I should be ruined by being dragged too suddenly into the glare of polite and learned observation.

I shall certainly, my ever-honoured patron, write you an account of my every step; and better health and more spirits may enable me to make it something better than this stupid matter-of-fact epistle. I have the honour to be, good sir, your ever grateful, humble servant, R. B.

If any of my friends write me, my direction is, care of Mr Creech, bookseller.

* Lady Betty Cunningham, an unmarried sister of the Earl.

XXX.

TO MR WILLIAM CHALMERS, WRITER, AYR.

EDINBURGH, *December* 27, 1786.

MY DEAR FRIEND,—I confess I have sinned the sin for which there is hardly any forgiveness—ingratitude to friendship—in not writing you sooner ; but of all men living, I had intended to have sent you an entertaining letter ; and by all the plodding, stupid powers, that in nodding, conceited majesty preside over the dull routine of business—a heavily solemn oath this !—I am and have been, ever since I came to Edinburgh, as unfit to write a letter of humour as to write a commentary on the Revelation of St John the Divine, who was banished to the Isle of Patmos by the cruel and bloody Domitian, son to Vespasian, and brother to Titus, both emperors of Rome, and who was himself an emperor, and raised the second or third persecution, I forgot which, against the Christians, and after throwing the said Apostle John, brother to the Apostle James, commonly called James the Greater, to distinguish him from another James, who was on some account or other known by the name of James the Less—after throwing him into a caldron of boiling oil, from which he was miraculously preserved, he banished the poor son of Zebedee to a desert island in the Archipelago, where he was gifted with the second sight, and saw as many wild beasts as I have seen since I came to Edinburgh ; which, a circumstance not very uncommon in story-telling, brings me back to where I set out.

To make you some amends for what, before you reach this paragraph, you will have suffered, I enclose you two poems I have carded and spun since I passed Glenbuck.

One blank in the *Address to Edinburgh*—" Fair B——," is heavenly Miss Burnet, daughter to Lord Monboddo, at whose house I have had the honour to be more than once. There has not been anything nearly like her in all the combinations of beauty, grace and goodness the great Creator has formed, since Milton's Eve on the first day of her existence.

My direction is, care of Andrew Bruce, merchant, Bridge Street.   R. B.

XXXI.

TO THE EARL OF EGLINTOUN.

[EDINBURGH, *January* 11*th*, 1787.]

MY LORD,—As I have but slender pretensions to philosophy, I cannot rise to the exalted ideas of a citizen of the world, but have all those national prejudices which I believe glow peculiarly strong in the breast of a Scotchman. There is scarcely anything to which I am so feelingly alive as the honour and welfare of my country; and as a poet, I have no higher enjoyment than singing her sons and daughters. Fate had cast my station in the veriest shades of life; but never did a heart pant more ardently than mine to be distinguished, though, till very lately, I looked in vain on every side for a ray of light. It is easy, then, to guess how much I was gratified with the countenance and approbation of one of my country's most illustrious sons, when Mr Wauchope called on me yesterday on the part of your Lordship. Your munificence, my Lord, certainly deserves my very grateful acknowledgments; but your patronage is a bounty peculiarly suited to my feelings. I am not master enough of the etiquette of life to know whether there be not some impropriety in troubling your Lordship with my thanks, but my heart whispered me to do it. From the emotions of my inmost soul I do it. Selfish ingratitude, I hope, I am incapable of; and mercenary servility, I trust, I shall ever have so much honest pride as to detest.   R. B.

XXXII.
TO MR MACKENZIE, SURGEON, MAUCHLINE.

EDINBURGH, 11th *January* 1787.

MY DEAR SIR,—Yours gave me something like the pleasure of an old friend's face. I saw *your* friend and *my* honoured patron, Sir John Whitefoord, just after I received your letter, and gave him your respectful compliments. He was pleased to say many handsome things of you, which I heard with the more satisfaction as I knew them to be just.

His son John, who calls very frequently on me, is in a fuss to-day like a coronation. This is the great day—the assembly and ball of the Caledonian Hunt; and John has had the good luck to pre-engage the hand of the beauty-famed and wealth-celebrated Miss M'Adam, our countrywoman. Between friends, John is desperately in for it there, and I am afraid will be desperate indeed.

I am sorry to send you the last speech and dying words of the *Lounger*.

A gentleman waited on me yesterday, and gave me, by Lord Eglintoun's order, ten guineas by way of subscription for a brace of copies of my second edition.

I met with Lord Maitland and a brother of his to-day at breakfast. They are exceedingly easy, accessible, agreeable fellows, and seemingly pretty clever. I am ever, my dear sir, yours,

ROBERT BURNS.

XXXIII.

TO JOHN BALLANTINE, ESQ.

EDINBURGH, *January 14th*, 1787.

MY HONOURED FRIEND,—It gives me a secret comfort to observe in myself that I am not yet so far gone as Willie Gaw's Skate—" past redemption ;" for I have still this favourable symptom of grace, that when my conscience, as in the case of this letter, tells me I am leaving something undone that I ought to do, it teases me eternally till I do it.

I am still " dark as was chaos " in respect to futurity. My generous friend, Mr Patrick Miller, has been talking with me about a lease of some farm or other in an estate called Dalswinton, which he has lately bought near Dumfries. Some life-rented embittering recollections whisper me that I will be happier anywhere than in my old neighbourhood ; but Mr Miller is no judge of land ; and though I daresay he means to favour me, yet he may give me, in his opinion, an advantageous bargain that may ruin me. I am to take a tour by Dumfries as I return, and have promised to meet Mr Miller on his lands some time in May.

I went to a mason-lodge yesternight, where the most Worshipful Grand Master Charteris, and all the Grand Lodge of Scotland, visited. The meeting was numerous and elegant ; all the different lodges about town were present in all their pomp. The Grand Master, who presided with great solemnity and honour to himself as a gentleman and mason, among other general toasts, gave, " Caledonia, and Caledonia's Bard, Brother Burns," which rang through the whole assembly with multiplied honours and repeated acclamations. As I had no idea such a thing would happen, I was downright thunderstruck, and trembling in every nerve, made the best return in my power. Just as I had finished, some of the grand officers said so loud that I could hear, with a most comforting accent, " Very well indeed !" which set me something to rights again.

I have to-day corrected my 152d page. My best good wishes to Mr Aiken. I am ever, dear sir, your much indebted humble servant,   R. B.

XXXIV.

TO MRS DUNLOP.

EDINBURGH, 15*th January* 1787

MADAM,—Yours of the ninth current, which I am this moment honoured with, is a deep reproach to me for ungrateful neglect I will tell you the real truth, for I am miserably awkward at a fib. I wished to have written to Dr Moore before I wrote to you ;

but though, every day since I received yours of December 30th, the idea, the wish to write to him has constantly pressed on my thoughts, yet I could not for my soul set about it. I know his fame and character, and I am one of " the sons of little men." To write him a mere matter-of-fact affair, like a merchant's order, would be disgracing the little character I have; and to write the author of *The View of Society and Manners* a letter of sentiment—I declare every artery runs cold at the thought. I shall try, however, to write to him to-morrow or next day. His kind interposition in my behalf I have already experienced, as a gentleman waited on me the other day, on the part of Lord Eglintoun, with ten guineas, by way of subscription for two copies of my next edition.

The word you object to in the mention I have made of my glorious countryman and your immortal ancestor, is indeed borrowed from Thomson; but it does not strike me as an improper epithet. I distrusted my own judgment on your finding fault with it, and applied for the opinion of some of the literati here, who honour me with their critical strictures, and they all allow it to be proper. The song you ask I cannot recollect, and I have not a copy of it. I have not composed anything on the great Wallace, except what you have seen in print, and the enclosed, which I will print in this edition.* You will see I have mentioned some others of the name. When I composed my *Vision* long ago, I had attempted a description of Kyle, of which the additional stanzas are a part as it originally stood. My heart glows with a wish to be able to do justice to the merits of the " saviour of his country," which, sooner or later, I shall at least attempt.

You are afraid I shall grow intoxicated with my prosperity as a poet. Alas! madam, I know myself and the world too well. I do not mean any airs of affected modesty; I am willing to believe that my abilities deserve some notice; but in a most enlightened, informed age and nation, when poetry is, and has been, the study of men of the first natural genius, aided with all the powers of polite learning, polite books, and polite company—to be dragged forth to the full glare of learned and polite observation, with all my imperfections of awkward rusticity and crude unpolished ideas on my head—I assure you, madam, I do not dissemble when I tell you I tremble for the consequences. The novelty of a poet in my obscure situation, without any of those advantages which are reckoned necessary for that character, at least at this time of day, has raised a partial tide of public notice which has borne me to a height where I am absolutely, feelingly certain, my abilities are inadequate to support me; and too surely do I see that time when the same tide will leave me and recede

---

* Stanzes in *The Vision*, beginning, "By stately tower or palace fair," and ending with the first Duan.

perhaps as far below the mark of truth. I do not say this in the ridiculous affectation of self-abasement and modesty. I have studied myself, and know what ground I occupy ; and however a friend or the world may differ from me in that particular, I stand for my own opinion, in silent resolve, with all the tenaciousness of property. I mention this to you once for all, to disburden my mind, and I do not wish to hear or say more about it. But,

When proud fortune's ebbing tide recedes,

you will bear we witness, that when my bubble of fame was at the highest, I stood unintoxicated, with the inebriating cup in my hand, looking forward with rueful resolve to the hastening time when the blow of calumny should dash it to the ground, with all the eagerness of vengeful triumph.

Your patronizing me, and interesting yourself in my fame and character as a poet, I rejoice in—it exalts me in my own idea ; and whether you can or can not aid me in my subscription, is a trifle. Has a paltry subscription-bill any charms to the heart of a bard, compared with the patronage of the descendant of the immortal Wallace ?   .   R. B.

XXXV.

TO DR MOORE.

EDINBURGH [*January ?*], 1787.

SIR,—Mrs Dunlop has been so kind as to send me extracts of letters she has had from you where you do the rustic bard the honour of noticing him and his works. Those who have felt the anxieties and solicitudes of authorship, can only know what pleasure it gives to be noticed in such a manner by judges of the first character. Your criticisms, sir, I receive with reverence ; only I am sorry they mostly come too late; a peccant passage or two that I would certainly have altered, were gone to the press.

The hope to be admired for ages is, in by far the greatest part of those even who are authors of repute, an unsubstantial dream. For my part, my first ambition was, and still my strongest wish is, to please my compears, the rustic inmates of the hamlet, while ever-changing language and manners shall allow me to be relished and understood. I am very willing to admit that I have some poetical abilities ; and as few, if any writers, either moral or poetical, are intimately acquainted with the classes of mankind among whom I have chiefly mingled, I may have seen men and manners in a different phases from what is common, which may assist originality of thought. Still, I know very well the novelty of my character has by far the greatest share in the learned and polite notice I have lately had ; and in a language where Pope and Churchill have raised the laugh, and Shenstone and Gray

drawn the tear ; where Thomson and Beattie have painted the
landscape, and Lyttleton and Collins described the heart—I am
not vain enough to hope for distinguished poetic fame.   R. B.

XXXVI.
TO JOHN BALLANTINE, ESQ.

[January 1787.]

WHILE here I sit, sad and solitary, by the side of a fire in a
little country inn, and drying my wet clothes, in pops a poor
fellow of a sodger, and tells me he is going to Ayr. ———!
say I to myself, with a tide of good spirits which the magic of
that sound, auld toon o' Ayr, conjured up, I will send my last
song to Mr Ballantine.   Here it is—[*Bonnie Doon*, p. 255].

XXXVII.
TO THE REV. G. LAWRIE.
NEW MILLS, NEAR KILMARNOCK.

EDINBURGH, *February* 5, 1787.

REVEREND AND DEAR SIR,—When I look at the date of your
kind letter, my heart reproaches me severely with ingratitude in
neglecting so long to answer it.   I will not trouble you with any
account, by way of apology, of my hurried life and distracted at-
tention ; do me the justice to believe that my delay by no means
proceeded from want of respect.   I feel, and ever shall feel for you,
the mingled sentiments of esteem for a friend, and reverence for
a father.

I thank you, sir, with all my soul, for your friendly hints,
though I do not need them so much as my friends are apt to
imagine.   You are dazzled with newspaper accounts and distant
reports ; but in reality I have no great temptation to be intoxi-
cated with the cup of prosperity.   Novelty may attract the at-
tention of mankind a while ; to it I owe my present eclat ; but I
see the time not far distant when the popular tide which has
borne me to a height of which I am perhaps unworthy, shall re
cede with silent celerity, and leave me a barren waste of sand, to
descend at my leasure to my former station.   I do not say this in
the affectation of modesty : I see the consequence is unavoidable,
and am prepared for it.   I had been at a good deal of pains to
form a just, impartial estimate of my intellectul powers before I
came here ; I have not added, since I came to Edinburgh, any-
thing to the account ; and I trust I shall take every atom of it
back to my shades, the coverts of my unnoticed early years.

In Dr Blacklock, whom I see very often, I have found what I would have expected in our friend, a clear head and an excellent heart.

By far the most agreeable hours I spend in Edinburgh must be placed to the account of Miss Lawrie and her pianoforte. I cannot help repeating to you and Mrs Lawrie a compliment that Mr Mackenzie, the celebrated " Man of Feeling," paid to Miss Lawrie the other night at the concert. I had come in at the interlude, and sat down by him till I saw Miss Lawrie in a seat not very far distant, and went up to pay my respects to her. On my return to Mr Mackenzie, he asked me who she was: I told him 'twas the daughter of a reverend friend of mine in the west country. He returned, there was something very striking, to his idea, in her appearance. On my desiring to know what it was, he was pleased to say, " She has a great deal of the elegance of a well-bred lady about her, with all the sweet simplicity of a country girl."

My compliments to all the happy inmates of St Margaret's. I am, my dear sir, yours most gratefully,   ROBERT BURNS.

XXXVIII.
TO THE EARL OF BUCHAN.

MY LORD,—The honour your Lordship has done me, by your notice and advice in yours of the 1st instant, I shall ever gratefully remember—

> Praise from thy lips 'tis mine with joy to boast,
> They best can give it who deserve it most.

Your Lordship touches the darling chord of my heart, when you advise me to fire my Muse at Scottish story and Scottish scenes. I wish for nothing more than to make a leisurely pilgrimage through my native country; to sit and muse on those once hard-contended fields, where Caledonia, rejoicing, saw her bloody lion borne through broken ranks to victory and fame; and, catching the inspiration, to pour the deathless names in song, But, my Lord, in the midst of these enthusiastic reveries, a long-visaged, dry, moral-looking phantom, strides across my imagination, and pronounces these emphatic words:—

" I, Wisdom, dwell with Prudence. Friend, I do not come to open the ill-closed wounds of your follies and misfortunes merely to give you pain: I wish through these wounds to imprint a lasting lesson on your heart. I will not mention how many of my salutary advices you have despised; I have given you line upon line, and precept upon precept; and while I was chalking out to you the straight way to wealth and character, with audacious effrontery you have zig-zagged across the path, contemning me to my face. You know the consequences. It is not yet three months since home was so hot for you, that you were on the wing for the western shore of the Atlantic, not to make a fortune, but to hide your misfortune.

" Now that your dear-loved Scotia puts it in your power to return to the situation of your forefathers, will you follow these will-o'-wisp meteors of fancy and whim, till they bring you once more to the brink of ruin ? I grant that the utmost ground you can occupy is but half a step from the veriest poverty ; but still it is half a step from it. If all that I can urge be ineffectual, let her who seldom calls to you in vain, let the call of pride, prevail with you. You know how you feel at the iron gripe of ruthless oppression : you know how you bear the galling sneer of contumelious greatness. I hold you out the conveniences, the comforts of life, independence, and character on the one hand ; I tender you servility, dependence, and wretchedness on the other. I will not insult your understanding by bidding you make a choice."

This, my lord, is unanswerable. I must return to my humble station, and woo my rustic Muse in my wonted way, at the plough-tail. Still, my lord, while the drops of life warm my heart, gratitude to that dear-loved country in which I boast my birth, and gratitude to those her distinguished sons who have honoured me so much with their patronage and approbation, shall, while stealing through my humble shades, ever distend my bosom, and at times, as now, draw forth the swelling tear.

R. B.

XXXIX.

TO DR MOORE.

EDINBURGH, 15th February 1787.

SIR,—Pardon my seeming neglect in delaying so long to acknowledge the honour you have done me in your kind notice of me, January 23d. Not many months ago, I knew no other employment than following the plough, nor could boast anything higher than a distant acquaintance with a country clergyman. Mere greatness never embarasses me ; I have nothing to ask from the great, and I do not fear their judgment; but genius, polished by learning, and at its proper point of elevation in the eye of the world, this of late I frequently meet with, and tremble at its approach. I scorn the affectation of seeming modesty to cover self-conceit. That I have some merit I do not deny ; but I see with frequent wringings of heart that the novelty of my character, and the honest national prejudice of my countrymen, have borne me to a height altogether untenable to my abilities.

For the honour Miss Williams has done me, please sir, return her in my name my most grateful thanks. I have more than once thought of paying her in kind, but have hitherto quitted the idea in hopeless despondency. I had never before heard of her; but the other day I got her poems, which, for several reasons, some belonging to the head, and others the offspring of the heart, give me a great deal of pleasure. I have little pretensions to critic lore: there are, I think, two characteristic features in her poetry — the unfettered wild flight of native genius, and the querulous, sombre tenderness of " time-settled sorrow."

I only know what pleases me, often without being able to tell why.   R. B.

XL.

TO JOHN BALLANTINE, ESQ.

EDINBURGH, *Feb.* 24, 1787.

MY HONOURED FRIEND,—I will soon be with you now, in guid black prent—in a week or ten days at farthest. I am obliged, against my own wish, to print subscribers' names; so if any of my Ayr friends have subscription-bills, they must be sent into Creech directly. I am getting my phiz done by an eminent engraver, and if it can be ready in time, I will appear in my book, looking, like all other *fools,* to my title-page.   R. B.

XLI.

Session-house within the parish of Canongate, the twenty-second day of February, one thousand seven hundred eighty-seven years.

Sederunt of the Managers of the Kirk and Kirkyard Funds of Canongate;

Which day, the treasurer to the said funds produced a letter from Mr Robert Burns, of date the 6th current, which was read and appointed to be engrossed in their sederunt-book, and of which letter the tenor follows :—

"To the Honourable Bailies of Canongate, Edinburgh,—Gentlemen, I am sorry to be told that the remains of Robert Fergusson, the so justly celebrated poet, a man whose talents for ages to come will do honour to our Caledonian name, lie in your churchyard among the ignoble dead, unnoticed and unknown.

" Some memorial to direct the steps of the lovers of Scottish song, when they wish to shed a tear over the " narrow house " of the bard who is no more, is surely a tribute due to Fergusson's memory—a tribute I wish to have the honour of paying.

" I petition you, then, gentlemen, to permit me to lay a simple stone over his revered ashes, to remain an unalienable property to his deathless fame. I have the honour to be, gentlemen, your very humble servant (*sic subscribitur*),

"ROBERT BURNS."

Therefore the said managers, in consideration of the laudable and disinterested motion of Mr Burns, and the propriety of his request, did, and hereby do unanimously, grant power and liberty to the said Robert Burns to erect a headstone at the grave of the said Robert Fergusson, and to keep up and preserve the same to his memory in all time coming.—Extracted forth of the records of the managers, by   WILLIAM SPROT, Clerk.

XLII.
TO ———.

EDINBURGH, 1787.

MY DEAR SIR—You may think, and too justly, that I am a selfish, ungrateful fellow, having received so many repeated instances of kindness from you, and yet never putting pen to paper to say thank you ; but if you knew what a life my conscience has led me on that account, your good heart would think yourself too much avenged. By the by, there is nothing in the whole frame of man which seems to be so unaccountable as that thing called conscience. Had the troublesome yelping cur powers sufficient to prevent a mischief, he might be of use ; but that the beginning of the business, his feeble efforts are to the workings ot passion as the infant frosts of an autumnal morning to the unclouded fervour of the rising sun : and no sooner are the tumultuous doings of the wicked deed over, than amidst the bitter native consequences of folly in the very vortex of our horrors, up starts conscience, and harrows us with the feelings of the damned.

I have enclosed you, by way of expiation, some verses and prose, that, if they merit a place in your truly-entertaining miscellany, you are welcome to. The prose extract is literally as Mr Sprot sent it me.

The inscription on the stone is as follows :—

"HERE LIES ROBERT FERGUSSON, POET.

Born, September 5th, 1751—Died, 16th October 1774

No sculptured marble here, nor pompous lay,
' No storied urn, nor animated bust;'
This simple stone directs pale Scotia's way
To pour her sorrows o'er her poet's dust."

XLIII.
TO THE EARL OF GLENCAIRN.

[EDINBURGH, *February* 1707.]

MY LORD,—I wanted to purchase a profile of your lordship which I was told was to be got in town; but I am truly sorry to see that a blundering painter has spoiled a "human face divine." The enclosed stanzas I intended to have written below a picture or profile of your lordship, could I have been so happy as to procure one with anything of a likeness.

As I will soon return to my shades, I wanted to have something like a material object for my gratitude; I wanted to have it in my power to say to a friend, there is my noble patron, my generous benefactor. Allow me, my lord, to publish these verses. I conjure your lordship, by the honest throe of gratitude, by the generous wish of benevolence, by all the powers and feelings which compose the magnanimous mind, do not deny me this petition. I owe much to your lordship: and, what has not in some other instances always been the case with me, the weight of the obligation is a pleasing load. I trust I have a heart as independent as your lordship's, than which I can say nothing more: and I would not be beholden to favours that would crucify my feelings. Your dignified character in life, and manner of supporting that character, are flattering to my pride; and I would be jealous of the purity of my grateful attachment, where I was under the patronage of one of the much-favoured sons of fortune.

Almost every poet has celebrated his patrons, particularly when they were names dear to fame, and illustrious in their country; allow me, then, my lord, if you think the verses have intrinsic merit, to tell the world how much I have the honour to be, your lordship's highly-indebted, and ever grateful humble servant,   R. B.

XLIV.
TO THE HON. HENRY ERSKINE.

Two o'clock.

SIR,—I showed the enclosed political ballad to my Lord Glencairn, to have his opinion whether I should publish it; as I suspect my political tenets, such as they are, may be rather heretical in the opinion of some of my best friends. I have a few first principles in religion and politics, which, I believe, I would not easily part with; but for all the etiquette of, by whom, in what manner, &c., I would not have a dissocial word about it with any one of God's creatures, particularly an honoured patron or a respected friend. His lordship seems to think the piece may appear in print, but desired me to send you a copy for your suffrage. I am, with the sincerest gratitude for the notice with which you have been pleased to honour the rustic bard, sir, your most devoted humble servant, ROBT. BURNS.

XLV.

TO MR WILLIAM DUNBAR.

LAWNMARKET, *Monday Morning.*

DEAR SIR,—In justice to Spenser, I must acknowledge that there is scarcely a poet in the language could have been a more agreeable present to me ; and in justice to you, allow me to say, sir, that I have not met with a man in Edinburgh to whom I would so willingly have been indebted for the gift. The tattered rhymes I herewith present you, and the handsome volumes of Spenser for which I am so much indebted to your goodness, may perhaps be not in proportion to one another ; but be that as it may, my gift, though far less valuable, is as sincere a mark of esteem as yours.

The time is approaching when I shall return to my shades ; and I am afraid my numerous Edinburgh friendships are of so tender a construction that they will not bear carriage with me. Yours is one of the few that I could wish of a more robust constitution. It is indeed very probable that when I leave this city we part never more to meet in this sublunary sphere ; but I have a strong fancy that in some future eccentric planet, the comet of happier systems than any with which astronomy is yet acquainted, you and I, among the harum-scarum sons of imagination and whim, with a hearty shake of a hand, a metaphor, and a laugh, shall recognise old acquaintance :

> Where Wit may sparkle all its rays,
> Uncurst with Caution's fears;
> That Pleasure, basking in the blaze,
> Rejoice for endless years.

I have the honour to be, with the warmest sincerity, dear sir, &c.
R. B.

XLVI.

TO MR JAMES CANDLISH,*

STUDENT IN PHYSIC, GLASGOW COLLEGE.

EDINBURGH, *March* 21*st*, 1787.

MY EVER DEAR OLD ACQUAINTANCE,—I was equally surprised and pleased at your letter, though I daresay you will think, by

* Father of Rev. Dr Candlish of Edinburgh.

my delaying so long to write to you, that I am so drowned in the intoxication of good fortune as to be indifferent to old and once dear connections. The truth is. I was determined to write a good letter, full of argument, amplification, erudition, and, as Bayes says, *all that.* I thought of it, and thought of it, and by my soul I could not; and, lest you should mistake the cause of my silence, I just sit down to tell you so. Don't give yourself credit, though, that the strength of your logic scares me : the truth is, I never mean to meet you on that ground at all. You have shown me one thing which was to be demonstrated : that strong pride of reasoning, with a little affectation of singularity, may mislead the best of hearts. I likewise, since you and I were first acquainted, in the pride of despising old woman's stories, ventured in " the daring path Spinosa trod ;" but experience of the weakness, not the strength, of human powers, made me glad to grasp at revealed religion.

I am still, in the Apostle Paul's phrase, " The old man with his deeds," as when we were sporting about the " Lady Thorn." I shall be four weeks here yet at least ; and so I shall expect to hear from you : welcome sense, welcome nonsense. I am, with the warmest sincerity,   R. B.

XLVII.

TO MRS DUNLOP.

EDINBURGH, *March* 22, 1787.

MADAM,—I read your letter with watery eyes. A little, very little while ago, I had scarce a friend but the stubborn pride of my own bosom ; now I am distinguished, patronized, befriended by you. Your friendly advices, I will not give them the cold name of criticisms, I receive with reverence. I have made some small alterations in what I before had printed. I have the advice of some very judicious friends among the literati here, but with them I sometimes find it necessary to claim the privilege of thinking for myself. The noble Earl of Glencairn, to whom I owe more than to any man, does me the honour of giving me his strictures : his hints, with respect to impropriety or indelicacy, I follow implicitly.

You kindly interest yourself in my future views and prospects : there I can give you no light. It is all

> " Dark as was chaos ere the infant sun
> Was rolled together, or had tried his beams
> Athwart the gloom profound."

The appellation of a Scottish bard is by far my highest pride to continue to deserve it is my most exalted ambition. Scottish scenes and Scottish story are the themes I could wish to sing. I have no dearer aim than to have it in my power, unplagued with the routine of business—for which, Heaven knows, I am unfit enough—to make leisurely pilgrimages through Caledonia ; to sit on the fields of her battles, to wander on the romantic banks of her rivers, and to muse by the stately towers or venerable ruins, once the honoured abodes of her heroes.

But these are all Utopian thoughts. I have dallied long enough with life ; 'tis time to be in earnest. I have a fond, an aged mother to care for, and some other bosom-ties perhaps equally tender. Where the individual only suffers by the consequences of his own thoughtlessness, indolence, or folly, he may be excusable—nay, shining abilities, and some of the nobler virtues, may half sanctify a heedless character ; but where God and nature have intrusted the welfare of others to his care,— where the trust is sacred and the ties are dear,—that man must be far gone in selfishness, or strangely lost to reflection, whom these connections will not rouse to exertion.

I guess that I shall clear between two and three hundred pounds by my authorship : with that sum I intend, so far as I may be said to have any intention, to return to my old acquaintance, the plough, and if I can meet with a lease by which I can live, to commence farmer. I do not intend to give up poetry ; being bred to labour secures me independence, and the Muses are my chief, sometimes have been my only enjoyment. If my practice second my resolution, I shall have principally at heart the serious business of life ; but while following my plough, or building up my shocks, I shall cast a leisure glance to that dear, that only feature of my character which gave me the notice of my country and the patronage of a Wallace.

Thus, honoured madam, I have given you the bard, his situation and his views, native as they are in his own bosom. R. B.

XLVIII.
TO MRS DUNLOP.

EDINBURGH, 15th April 1787.

MADAM,—There is an affectation of gratitude which I dislike. The periods of Johnson and the pauses of Sterne may hide a selfish heart. For my part, madam, I trust I have too much pride for servility, and too little prudence for selfishness. I have this moment broken open your letter, but

> " Rude am I in speech,
> And therefore little can I grace my cause
> In speaking for myself "—

so I shall not trouble you with any fine speeches and hunted figures. I shall just lay my hand on my heart, and say, I hope I shall ever have the truest, the warmest sense of your goodness.

I come abroad, in print, for certain on Wednesday. Your orders I shall punctually attend to; only, by the way, I must tell you that I was paid before for Dr Moore's and Miss Williams's copies through the medium of Commissioner Cochrane in this place; but that we can settle when I have the honour of waiting on you.

Dr Smith* was just gone to London the morning before I received your letter to him.   R. B.

XLIX.

TO DR MOORE.

EDINBURGH, 23d *April* 1787.

I RECEIVED the books, and sent the one you mentioned to Mrs Dunlop. I am ill skilled in beating the coverts of imagination for metaphors of gratitude. I thank you, sir, for the honour you have done me, and to my latest hour will warmly remember it. To be highly pleased with your book, is what I have in common with the world; but to regard these volumes as a mark of the author's friendly esteem, is a still more supreme gratification.

I leave Edinburgh in the course of ten days or a fortnight, and after a few pilgrimages over some of the classic ground of Caledonia,—Cowden Knowes, Banks of Yarrow, Tweed, &c.,—I shall return to my rural shades, in all likelihood never more to quit them. I have formed many intimacies and friendships here; but I am afraid they are all of too tender a construction to bear carriage a hundred and fifty miles. To the rich, the great, the fashionable, the polite, I have no equivalent to offer; and 1 am afraid my meteor appearance will by no means entitle me to a settled correspondence with any of you, who are the permanent lights of genius and literature.

My most respectful compliments to Miss Williams. If once this tangent flight of mine were over, and I were returned to my wonted leisurely motion in my old circle, I may probably endeavour to return her poetic compliment in kind.   R. B.

L.

TO MRS DUNLOP.

EDINBURGH, 30th *April* 1787.

—— YOUR criticisms, madam, I understand very well, and could have wished to have pleased you better. You are right in your guess that I am not very amenable to counsel. Poets, much my superiors, have so flattered those who possessed the adventitious qualities of wealth and power, that I am determined to flatter no created being, either in prose or verse.

* The author of the *Wealth of Nations*

I set as little by princes, lords, clergy, critics, &c., as all these respective gentry do by my bardship. I know what I may expect from the world by and by—illiberal abuse, and perhaps contemptuous neglect.

I am happy, madam, that some of my own favourite pieces are distinguished by your particular approbation. For my *Dream,* which has unfortunately incurred your loyal displeasure, I hope in four weeks, or less, to have the honour of appearing at Dunlop in its defence in person. R. B.

LI.

TO THE REV. DR HUGH BLAIR.

LAWNMARKET, EDINBURGH, *3d May* 1787.

REV. AND MUCH-RESPECTED SIR,—I leave Edinburgh to-morrow morning, but could not go without troubling you with half a line, sincerely to thank you for the kindness, patronage, and friendship you have shown me. I often felt the embarrassment of my singular situation : drawn forth from the veriest shades of life to the glare of remark, and honoured by the notice of those illustrious names of my country whose works, while they are applauded to the end of time, will ever instruct and mend the heart. However the meteor-like novelty of my appearance in the world might attract notice, and honour me with the acquaintance of the permanent lights of genius and literature, those who are truly benefactors of the immortal nature of man, I knew very well that my utmost merit was far unequal to the task of preserving that character when once the novelty was over : I have made up my mind that abuse, or almost even neglect, will not surprise me in my quarters.

I have sent you a proof-impression of Beugo's work for me, done on Indian paper, as a trifling but sincere testimony with what heart-warm gratitude I am, &c. R. B.

LII.

TO WILLIAM CREECH, ESQ.

SELKIRK, *13th May* 1787.

MY HONOURED FRIEND,—The enclosed (*Willie's Awa,* p. 115) I have just wrote, nearly extempore, in a solitary inn in Selkirk, after a miserably wet day's riding. I have been over most of East Lothian, Berwick, Roxburgh, and Selkirk shires ; and next week I begin a tour through the north of England. Yesterday I dined with Lady Harriet, sister to my noble patron, *Quem Deus conservet !* I would write till I would tire you as much with dull prose, as I daresay by this time you are with wretched verse ; but I am jaded to death ; so, with a grateful farewell, I have the honour to be, good sir, yours sincerely, R. B.

LIII.

TO MR PATTISON, BOOKSELLER, PAISLEY.

BERRYWELL, near DUNSE, *May* 17, 1787.

DEAR SIR,—I am sorry I was out of Edinburgh, making a slight pilgrimage to the classic scenes of this country, when I was favoured with yours of the 11th instant, enclosing an order of the Paisley Banking Company on the Royal Bank for twenty-two pounds seven shillings sterling, payment in full, after carriage deducted, for ninety copies of my book I sent you. According to your motions, I see you will have left Scotland before this reaches you, otherwise I would send you *Holy Willie* with all my heart. I was so hurried, that I absolutely forgot several things I ought to have minded ; among the rest, sending books to Mr Cowan ; but any order of yours will be answered at Creech's shop. You will please remember that non-subscribers pay six shillings—this is Creech's profit ; but those who have subscribed, though their names have been neglected in the printed list, which is very incorrect, are supplied at the subscription price. I was not at Glasgow, nor do I intend for London ; and I think Mrs Fame is very idle to tell so many lies on a poor poet. When you or Mr Cowan write for copies, if you should want any, direct to Mr Hill, at Mr Creech's shop, and I write to Mr Hill by this post to answer either of your orders. Hill is Mr Creech's first clerk, and Creech himself is presently in London. I suppose I shall have the pleasure, against your return to Paisley, of assuring you how much I am, dear sir, your obliged humble servant, R. B.

LIV.

TO MR WILLIAM NICOL,

MASTER OF THE HIGH SCHOOL, EDINBURGH.

CARLISLE, *June* 1, 1787.

KIND, HONEST-HEARTED WILLIE,—I'm sitten' doun here, after seven-and-forty miles' ridin', e'en as forjeskit and forniaw'd as a forfochten cock, to gie you some notion o' my land-lowper-like stravaigin sin' the sorrowfu' hour that I sheuk hands and parted wi' Auld Reekie.

My auld, ga'd gleyde o' a meere has huchyall'd up hill and down brae, in Scotland and England, as teugh and birnie as a very devil wi' me. It's true she's as poor's a sangmaker and as hard's a kirk, and tipper-taipers when she taks the gate, just like a lady's gentlewoman in a minuwae, or a hen on a het girdle ; but she's a yauld, poutherie girran for a' that, and has a stomach like Willie Stalker's meere, that wad hae disgeested tumbler-wheels, for she'll whip me aff her five stimparts o' the best aits at a down-sittin, and ne'er fash her thumb. When ance her ringbanes and spavies, her crucks and cramps, are fairly soupl'd, she beets to, beets to, and aye the hindmost hour the tightest. I could wager her price to a threttie pennies, that for twa or three ooks' ridin' at fifty mile a day, that no a galloper acqueesh Clyde and Whithorn could cast saut on her tail.

I hae dander'd owre a' the kintra frae Dunbar to Selcraig, and hae forgather'd wi' mony a guid fallow, and mony a weel-far'd hizzie. I met wi' twa dink queynes in particular, ane o' them a sonsie, fine, fodgel lass, baith braw and bonnie ; the tither was a clean-shankit, straught, tight, weel-far'd wench, as blythe's a lintwhite on a flowerie thorn, and as sweet and modest's a new-blawn plum-rose in a hazle shaw. They were baith bred to mainers by the beuk, and onie ane o' them had as muckle smed-dum and rumblegumption as the half o' some presbyteries that you and I baith ken. They played me sic a shavie, that I daur say, if my harrigals were turned out, ye wad see twa nicks i' the heart o' me like the mark o' a kail-whittle in a castock.

My best respecks to the guidwife and a' our common friens, especiall Mr and Mrs Cruikshank, and the honest guidman o Jock's Lodge.

I'll be in Dumfries the morn gif the beast be to the fore, and the branks bide hale. Amen!   R. B.

Anglice, thus :—

KIND, HONEST-HEARTED WILLIE,—I have sat down here, after forty-seven miles' hard riding, even as jaded and fatigued as an overfought cock, to give ye some notion of my vagabond-like wandering since the sorrowful hour that I shook hands and parted wi' Auld Reekie [Edinburgh].

My old galled mare has hobbled up hill and down slope in Scotland and England, as tough and lively as a very devil with me. It is true she is as poor as a song-maker, and as hard as a church, and totters when she takes the road just like a lady's gentlewoman in a minuet, or a hen on a hot oven ; but she is an alert, spirited beast notwithstanding; and has a stomach like Willie Stalker's mare, that would have digested cart-wheels, for she'll whip me off five-eighths of a Winchester bushel of the best oats at a time, with no sort of difficulty. When once her ill-assorted joints and spavins, her lameness and cramps, are fairly suppled, she improves by little and little, and always the last hour is her best. I could wager her price against twopence-halfpenny, that for two-three weeks' riding at fifty miles a day, not a gallopper between Clyde and Whithorn could cast salt on her tail.

I have sauntered over the whole country from Dunbar to Selkirk, and have met with many a good fellow aad many a well-favoured maiden. I met with two neat girls, in particular, one of them a fine, plump, comfortable-looking lass, well dressed and pretty; the other a well-limbed, straight, tight, well-favoured wench, as blithe as a linnet on a flowering thorn, and as sweet and modest as a new-blown primrose in a hazel wood. They had both acquired manners from the book, and any one of them had as much smartness and sense as the half of some presbyteries that you and I know of. They played me such a prank, that if my viscera were turned out, you would see two nicks in the heart of me, like the mark of a knife in a cabbage-stalk.

My best respects to your lady and all our common friends, especially Mr and Mrs Cruikshanks, and the honest goodman of Jock's Lodge.

I shall be in Dumfries to-morrow if the beast survive, and the bridle keep whole. Amen!

LV

TO MR JAMES SMITH, LINLITHGOW.

MAUCHLINE, 11th June 1787.

MY DEAR SIR,—I date this from Mauchline, where I arrived on Friday evening last. I slept at John Dow's, and called for my daughter; Mr Hamilton and family; your mother, sister, and brother; my quondam Eliza, &c.—all, all well. If anything had been wanting to disgust me completely at Armour's family, their mean, servile compliance would have done it. Give me a spirit like my favourite hero, Milton's Satan—

> "Hail! horrors, hail!
> Infernal world! and thou profoundest hell
> Receive thy new possessor! one who brings
> A mind not to be changed by *place* or *time!*"

I cannot settle to my mind. Farming—the only thing of which I know anything, and Heaven above knows but little do I understand even of that—I cannot, dare not risk, on farms as they are. If I do not fix, I will go for Jamaica. Should I stay in an unsettled state at home, I would only dissipate my little fortune, and ruin what I intend shall compensate my little ones for the stigma I have brought on their names.   R. B.

LVI.

TO MR WILLIAM NICOL.

MAUCHLINE, *June* 18, 1787

MY DEAR FRIEND,—I am now arrived safe in my native country after a very agreeable jaunt, and have the pleasure to find all my friends well. I breakfasted with your grey-headed, reverend friend, Mr Smith ; and was highly pleased both with the cordial welcome he gave me, and his most excellent appearance and sterling good sense.

I have been with Mr Miller at Dalswinton, and am to meet him again in August. From my view of the lands, and his reception of my bardship, my hopes in that business are rather mended ; but still they are but slender.

I am quite charmed with Dumfries folks—Mr Burnside, the clergyman, in particular, is a man whom I shall ever gratefully remember ; and his wife, guid forgie me ! I had almost broke the tenth commandment on her account ! Simplicity, elegance, good sense, sweetness of disposition, good-humour, kind hospitality, are the constituents of her manner and heart : in short—but if I say one word more about her, I shall be directly in love with her.

I never, my friend, thought mankind very capable of anything generous ; but the stateliness of the patricians in Edinburgh, and the civility of my plebeian brethren (who perhaps formerly eyed me askance) since I returned home, have nearly put me out of conceit altogether with my species. I have bought a pocket Milton, which I carry perpetually about with me, in order to study the sentiments, the dauntless magnanimity, the intrepid, unyielding independence, the desperate daring, and noble defiance of hardship, in that personage, Satan. 'Tis true I have just now a little cash ; but I am afraid the star that hitherto has shed its malignant, purpose-blasting rays full in my zenith ; that noxious planet, so baneful in its influences to the rhyming tribe, I much dread it is not yet beneath my horizon. Misfortune dodges the path of human life ; the poetic mind finds itself miserably deranged in, and unfit for, the walks of business ; add to all, that thoughtless follies and hairbrained whims, like so many *ignes fatui* eternally diverging from the right line of sober discretion, sparkle with step-bewitching blaze in the idly-gazing eyes of the poor heedless bard, till pop, "he falls like Lucifer, never to hope again." God grant this may be an unreal picture with respect to me ! But should it not, 1 have very little dependence on mankind. I will close my letter with this tribute my heart bids me pay you— the many ties of acquaintance and friendship which I have, or think I have, in life, I have felt along the lines, and they are almost all of them of such frail contexture, that I am sure they would not stand the breath of the least adverse breeze of fortune; but from you, my ever dear sir, I look with confidence for the apostolic love that shall wait on me " through good report and bad report"—the love which Solomon emphatically says " is strong as death." My compliments to Mrs Nicol, and all the circle of our common friends.

P.S.—I shall be in Edinburgh about the latter end of July.

R. B.

LVII.

TO MR ROBERT AINSLIE.

ARROCHAR, by LOCH LONG, *June* 28, 1787.

I WRITE you this on my tour through a country where savage streams tumble over savage mountains, thinly overspread with savage flocks, which starvingly support as savage inhabitants. My last stage was Inverary; to-morrow night's stage Dumbarton. I ought sooner to have answered your kind letter, but you know I am a man of many sins.   R. B

LVIII.

TO MR JAMES SMITH.

June 30, 1787.

ON our return, at a Highland gentleman's hospitable mansion, we fell in with a merry party, and danced till the ladies left us, at three in the morning. Our dancing was none of the French or English insipid formal movements; the ladies sang Scotch songs like angels, at intervals; then we flew at " Bab at the Bowster," " Tullochgorum," " Loch Erroch side,"* &c., like midges sporting in the mottie sun, or craws prognosticating a storm in a hairst day. When the dear lasses left us, we ranged round the bowl till the good-fellow hour of six; except a few minutes that we went out to pay our devotions to the glorious lamp of day peering over the towering top of Benlomond. We all kneeled: our worthy landlord's son held the bowl, each man a full glass in his hand; and I, as priest, repeated some rhyming nonsense, like Thomas-a-Rhymer's prophesies I suppose. After a small refreshment of the gifts of Somnus, we proceeded to spend the day on Loch Lomond, and reached Dumbarton in the evening. We dined at another good fellow's house, and consequently pushed the bottle; when we went out to mount our horses, we found ourselves " No vera fou, but gaylie yet." My two friends and I rode soberly down the Loch-side, till by came a Highlandman at the gallop, on a tolerably good horse, but which had never known the ornaments of iron or leather. We scorned to be out-galloped by a Highlandman, so

* Names of Scotch dancing tunes.

off we started, whip and spur. My companions, though seemingly
gaily mounted, fell sadly astern; but my old mare, Jenny Geddes,
one of the Rosinante family, strained past the Highlandman in
spite of all his efforts with the hair-halter. Just as I was passing
him, Donald wheeled his horse, as if to cross before me, to mar
my progress, when down came his horse, and threw his breekless
rider in a clipt hedge; and down came Jenny Geddes over all,
and my bardship between her and the Highlandman's horse.
Jenny Geddes trode over me with such cautious reverence, that
matters were not so bad as might well have been expected; so I
came off with a few cuts and bruises, and a thorough resolution to
be a pattern of sobriety for the future.

I have yet fixed on nothing with respect to the serious business
of life. I am, just as usual, a rhyming, mason-making, raking,
aimless, idle fellow. However, I shall somewhere have a farm
soon. I was going to say a wife too; but that must never be my
blessed lot. I am but a younger son of the house of Parnassus,
and, like other younger sons of great families, I may intrigue, if
I choose to run all risks, but must not marry.

I am afraid I have almost ruined one source, the principal
one, indeed, of my former happiness—that eternal propensity I
always had to fall in love. My heart no more glows with feverish
rapture. I have no paradisical evening interviews stolen from
the restless cares and prying inhabitants of this weary world. 1
have only * * *. This last is one of your distant acquaintances,
has a figure, and elegant manners, and in the train of some great
folks, whom you know, has seen the politest quarters in Europe.
I do like her a good deal; but what piques me is her conduct at
the commencement of our acquaintance. I frequently visited
her when I was in ——— ; and after passing regularly the inter-
mediate degrees between the distant formal bow and the familiar
grasp round the waist, I ventured, in my careless way, to talk of
friendship in rather ambiguous terms; and after her return
to ———, I wrote to her in the same style. Miss, construing my
words farther, I suppose, than even I intended, flew off in a
tangent of female dignity and reserve, like a mounting lark in
an April morning; and wrote me an answer which measured
me out very completely what an immense way I had to travel
before I could reach the climate of her favour. But I am an
old hawk at the sport; and wrote her such a cool, deliberate,
prudent reply, as brought my bird from the aërial towerings pop
down at my foot like Corporal Trim's hat.

As for the rest of my acts, and my wars, and all my wise
sayings, and why my mare was called Jenny Geddes, they shall
be recorded in a few weeks hence, at Linlithgow, in the chronicles
of your memory, by   ROBERT BURNS.

LIX.

TO MISS ———.

MY DEAR COUNTRYWOMAN,—I am so impatient to show you that I am once more at peace with you, that I send you the book I mentioned directly, rather than wait the uncertain time of my seeing you. I am afraid I have mislaid or lost Collins's Poems, which I promised to Miss Irvine. If I can find them, I will forward them by you; if not, you must apologise for me.

: I know you will laugh at it when I tell you that your piano and you together have made mischief somehow about my heart. My breast has been widowed these many months, and I thought myself proof against the fascinating witchcraft; but I am afraid you will "feelingly convince me what I am." I say I am afraid, because I am not sure what is the matter with me. I have one miserable bad symptom: when you whisper or look kindly to another, it gives me a draught of utter misery. I have a kind of wayward wish to be with you ten minutes by yourself, though what I would say, Heaven above knows, for I am sure I know not. I have no formed design in all this, but just, in the nakedness of my heart, write you down a mere matter-of-fact story. You may perhaps give yourself airs of distance on this, and that will completely cure me; but I wish you would not: just let us meet, if you please, in the old beaten way of friendship.

I will not subscribe myself your humble servant, for that is a phrase, I think, at least fifty miles off from the heart; but I will conclude with sincerely wishing that the Great Protector of innocence may shield you from the barbed dart of calumny, and hand you by the covert snare of deceit.   R. B.

LX.

TO MR JOHN RICHMOND.

MOSSGIEL, 7th July 1787. `

MY DEAR RICHMOND,—I am all impatience to hear of your fate since the old confounder of right and wrong has turned you out of place by his journey to answer his indictment at the bar of the other world.* He will find the practice of the court so different from the practice in which he has for so many years been thoroughly hackneyed, that his friends, if he had any connections truly of that kind, which I rather doubt, may well tremble for his sake. His chicane, his left-handed wisdom, which stood so firmly by him, to such good purpose, here, like other accomplices in robbery and plunder, will, now the piratical business is blown, in all probability turn king's evidence.

* Alluding to the recent decease of Richmond's master.

If he has left you any legacy, I beg your pardon for all this; if not, I know you will swear to every word I said about him.

I have lately been rambling over by Dumbarton and Inverary, and running a drunken race on the side of Loch Lomond with a wild Highlandman; his horse, which had never known the ornaments of iron or leather, zig-zagged across before my old spavin'd hunter, whose name is Jenny Geddes, and down came the Highlandman, horse and all, and down came Jenny and my bardship; so I have got such a skinful of bruises and wounds, that I shall be at least four weeks before I dare venture on my journey to Edinburgh.

Not one new thing under the sun has happened in Mauchline since you left it. I hope this will find you as comfortably situated as formerly, or, if Heaven pleases, more so; but, at all events, I trust you will let me know of course how matters stand with you, well or ill. 'Tis but poor consolation to tell the world when matters go wrong; but you know very well your connection and mine stands on a different footing. I am ever, my dear friend, yours,

R. B.

LXI.

TO MR ROBERT AINSLIE.

MAUCHLINE, 23d July 1787.

MY DEAR AINSLIE,—There is one thing for which I set great store by you as a friend, and it is this—that I have not a friend upon earth, besides yourself, to whom I can talk nonsense without forfeiting some degree of his esteem. Now, to one like me, who never cares for speaking anything else but nonsense, such a friend as you is an invaluable treasure. I was never a rogue, but have been a fool all my life; and in spite of all my endeavours, I see now plainly that I shall never be wise. Now, it rejoices my heart to have met with such a fellow as you, who, though you are not just such a hopeless fool as I, yet I trust you will never listen so much to the temptations of the devil as to grow so very wise that you will in the least disrespect an honest fellow because he is a fool. In short, I have set you down as the staff of my old age, when the whole list of my friends will, after a decent share of pity, have forgot me.

> Though in the morn comes sturt and strife,
> Yet joy may come at noon;
> And I hope to live a merry, merry life
> When a' their days are done.

Write me soon, were it but a few lines just to tell me how that good sagacious man your father is—that kind dainty body your mother—that strapping chiel your brother Douglas—and my friend Rachel, who is as far before Rachel of old, as she was before her blear-eyed sister Leah. R. B.

LXII.

TO MR ROBERT AINSLIE, JUNIOR,

BERRYWELL, DUNSE.

EDINBURGH, 23d *August* 1787.

As I gaed up to Dunse,
To warp a pickle yarn, &c.

FROM henceforth, my dear sir, I am determined to set off with
my letters like the periodical writers, namely, prefix a kind of
text, quoted from some classic of undoubted authority, such as the
author of the immortal piece of which my text is a part. What
I have to say on my text is exhausted in the chatter I wrote you
the other day, before I had the pleasure of receiving yours from
Inverleithen; and sure never was anything more lucky, as I have
but the time to write this that Mr Nicol, on the opposite side of
the table, takes to correct a proof-sheet of a thesis. They are
gabbling Latin so loud that I cannot hear what my own soul is
saying in my own skull, so must just give you a matter-of-fact
sentence or two.   *   *   *   *

To-morrow I leave Edinburgh in a chaise: Nicol thinks it more
comfortable than horseback, to which I say, Amen; so Jenny
Geddes [his mare] goes home to Ayrshire, to use a phrase of my
mother's, " wi' her finger in her mouth."

Now for a modest verse of classical authority—

The cats like kitchen,
The dogs like broe;
The lasses like the lads weel,
And th' auld wives too.

And we're a' noddin',
Nid, nid, noddin',
We're a' noddin' fou at e'en.

If this does not please you, let me hear from you; if you write
any time before the first of September, direct to Inverness, to be
left at the post-office till called for; the next week at Aberdeen;
the next at Edinburgh. The sheet is done; and I shall just con-
clude with assuring you that I am, and ever with pride shall be,
my dear sir, yours, &c. R. B.

LXIII.

TO MR ROBERT MUIR, KILMARNOCK.

STIRLING, 26th *August* 1787.

MY DEAR SIR,—I intended to have written you from Edinburgh,
and now write you from Stirling to make an excuse. Here am I,
on my way to Inverness, with a truly original, but very worthy
man, a Mr Nicol, one of the masters of the High School in Edin-

burgh. I left Auld Reekie yesterday morning, and have passed, besides by-excursions, Linlithgow, Borrowstounness, Falkirk, and here am I undoubtedly. This morning I knelt at the tomb of Sir John the Graham, the gallant friend of the immortal Wallace; and two hours ago I said a fervent prayer for old Caledonia over the hole in a blue whinstone, where Robert de Bruce fixed his royal standard on the banks of Bannockburn; and just now, from Stirling Castle, I have seen by the setting sun the glorious prospect of the windings of Forth through the rich carse of Stirling, and skirting the equally rich carse of Falkirk. The crops are very strong, but so very late that there is no harvest except a ridge or two perhaps in ten miles, all the way I have travelled from Edinburgh.

I left Andrew Bruce and family all well. I will be at least three weeks in making my tour, as I shall return by the coast, and have many people to call for.

My best compliments to Charles, our dear kinsman and fellow-saint, and Messrs W. and H. Parkers. I hope Hughoc is going on and prospering with Miss M'Causlin.

If I could think on anything sprightly, I should let you hear every other post; but a dull matter-of-fact business like this scrawl, the less and the seldomer one writes the better.

Among other matters-of-fact, I shall add this—that I am, and ever shall be, my dear sir, your obliged   R. B.

LXIV.

TO GAVIN HAMILTON, ESQ.

STIRLING, 28th August 1787.

MY DEAR SIR,—Here am I on my way to Inverness. I have rambled over the rich, fertile carses of Falkirk and Stirling, and am delighted with their appearance: richly-waving crops of wheat, barley, &c., but no harvest at all yet, except in one or two places an old wife's ridge. Yesterday morning I rode from this town up the meandering Devon's banks, to pay my respects to some Ayrshire folks at Harvieston. After breakfast, we made a party to go and see the famous Caudron Linn, a remarkable cascade in the Devon, about five miles above Harvieston; and after spending one of the most pleasant days I ever had in my life, I returned to Stirling in the evening. They are a family, sir, though I had not had any prior tie—though they had not been the brothers and sisters of a certain generous friend of mine—I would never forget them. I am told you have not seen them these several years, so you can have very little idea of what these young folks are now. Your brother is as tall as you are, but slender rather than otherwise; and I have the satisfaction to inform you, that he is getting the better of those consumptive symptoms which 1 suppose you know were threatening him. His make, and particularly his manner, resemble you, but he will have a still finer face. (I put in the word *still* to please Mrs Hamilton.) Good sense, modesty, and at the same time a just idea of that respect that man owes to man, and has a right in his turn to exact, are striking features in his character ; and, what with me is the Alpha and Omega, he has a heart that might adorn the breast of a poet ! Grace has a good figure and the look of health and cheerfulness, but nothing else remarkable in her person. I scarcely ever saw so striking a likeness as is between her and your little Beenie ; the mouth and chin particularly. She is reserved at first ; but as we grew better acquainted, I was delighted with the native frankness of her manner, and the sterling sense of her observation. Of Charlotte I cannot speak in common terms of admiration : she is not only beautiful, but lovely. Her form is elegant ; her features not regular, but they have the smile of sweetness and the settled complacency of good-nature in the highest degree ; and her complexion, now that she has happily recovered her wonted health, is equal to Miss Burnet's. After the exercise of our riding to the Falls, Charlotte was exactly Dr Donne's mistress :—

> " Her pure and eloquent blood
> Spoke in her cheeks, and so distinctly wrought,
> That one would almost say her body thought."

Her eyes are fascinating ; at once expressive of good sense, tenderness, and a noble mind.

I do not give you all this account, my good sir, to flatter you. I mean it to reproach you. Such relations the first peer in the realm might own with pride ; then why do you not keep up more correspondence with these so amiable young folks ? I had a thousand questions to answer about you. I had to describe the little ones with the minuteness of anatomy. They were highly delighted when I told them that John was so good a boy, and so fine a scholar, and that Willie was going on still very pretty : but I have it in commission to tell her from them that beauty is a poor silly bauble without she be good. Miss Chalmers I had left in Edinburgh, but I had the pleasure of meeting with Mrs Chalmers ; only Lady Mackenzie being rather a little alarmingly ill of a sore throat, somewhat marred our enjoyment.

I shall not be in Ayrshire for four weeks. My most respectful compliments to Mrs Hamilton, Miss Kennedy, and Dr Mackenzie. I shall probably write him from some stage or other. I am ever, sir, yours most gratefully,   R. B.

LXV.

TO MR WALKER, BLAIR OF ATHOLE.

INVERNESS, *5th September* 1787.

MY DEAR SIR,—I have just time to write the foregoing (p. 121), and to tell you that it was (at least most part of it) the effusion of a half-hour I spent at Bruar. I do not mean it was extempore, for I have endeavoured to brush it up as well as Mr Nicol's chat and the jogging of the chaise would allow. It eases my heart a good deal, as rhyme is the coin with which a poet pays his debts of honour or gratitude. What I owe to the noble family of Athole, of the first kind, I shall ever proudly boast—what I owe of the last, so help me, God, in my hour of need! I shall never forget.

The "little angel-band!" I declare I prayed for them very sincerely to-day at the Fall of Eyers. I shall never forget the fine family-piece I saw at Blair: the amiable, the truly noble duchess, with her smiling little seraph in her lap, at the head of the table—the lovely "olive plants," as the Hebrew bard finely says, round the happy mother—the beautiful Mrs Graham; the lovely, sweet Miss Cathcart, &c. I wish I had the powers of Guido to do them justice! My Lord Duke's kind hospitality—markedly kind indeed: Mr Graham of Fintry's charms of conversation: Sir W. Murray's friendship: in short, the recollection of all that polite, agreeable company, raises an honest glow in my bosom.   R. B.

LXVI.

TO MR GILBERT BURNS.

EDINBURGH, *17th September* 1787.

MY DEAR SIR,—I arrived here safe yesterday evening, after a tour of twenty-two days, and travelling near 600 miles, windings included. My farthest stretch was about ten miles beyond Inverness. I went through the heart of the Highlands by Crieff, Taymouth, the famous seat of Lord Breadalbane, down the Tay, among cascades and Druidical circles of stones, to Dunkeld, a seat of the Duke of Athole; thence across Tay, and up one of his tributary streams to Blair of Athole, another of the duke's seats, where I had the honour of spending nearly two days with his Grace and family; thence many miles through a wild country among cliffs gray with eternal snows and gloomy savage glens, till I crossed Spey, and went down the stream through Strathspey, so famous in Scottish music; Badenoch, &c., till I reached Grant Castle, where I spent half a day with Sir James Grant and family; and then crossed the country for Fort-George, but called by the way at Cawdor, the ancient seat of Macbeth; there I saw the identical bed in which tradition says King Duncan was murdered; lastly, from Fort-George to Inverness.

I returned by the coast, through Nairn, Forres, and so on, to Aberdeen, thence to Stonehive (Stonehaven), where James Burnes, from Montrose, met me by appointment. I spent two days among our relations, and found our aunts, Jean and Isabel, still alive, and hale old women. John Caird, though born the same year with our father, walks as vigorously as I can—they have' had several letters from his son in New York. William Brand is likewise a stout old fellow; but further particulars I delay till I see you, which will be in two or three weeks. The rest of my stages are not worth rehearsing: warm as I was from Ossian's country, where I had seen his very grave, what cared I for fishing-towns or fertile carses? I slept at the famous Brodie of Brodie's one night, and dined at Gordon Castle next day, with the duke, duchess, and family. I am thinking to cause my old mare to meet me, by means of John Ronald, at Glasgow; but you shall hear further from me before I leave Edinburgh. My duty and many compliments from the north to my mother; and my brotherly compliments to the rest. I have been trying for a berth for William, but am not likely to be successful. Farewell. R. B.

LXVII.
TO THE REV. JOHN SKINNER.

EDINBURGH, *October* 1787.

REVEREND AND VENERABLE SIR,—Accept, in plain dull prose, my most sincere thanks for the best poetical compliment I ever received. I assure you, sir, as a poet, you have conjured up an airy demon of vanity in my fancy which the best abilities in your other capacity would be ill able to lay. I regret, and while I live I shall regret, that when I was in the north, I had not the pleasure of paying a younger brother's dutiful respect to the author of the best Scotch song ever Scotland saw—" Tullochgorum's my delight!" The world may think slightingly of the craft of song-making, if they please; but, as Job says, " Oh that mine adversary had written a book !"—let them try. There is a certain something in the old Scotch songs, a wild happiness of thought and expression, which peculiarly marks them, not only from English songs, but also from the modern efforts of song-wrights in our native manner and language. The only remains of this enchantment, these spells of the imagination, rest with you. Our true brother, Ross of Lochlee, was likewise " owre cannie"—" a wild warlock"—but now he sings among the " sons of the morning."

I have often wished, and will certainly endeavour, to form a

kind of common acquaintance among all the genuine sons of Cale-
donian song. The world, busy in low prosaic pursuits, may over-
look most of us ; but "reverence thyself." The world is not our
peers, so we challenge the jury. We can lash that world, and find
ourselves a very great source of amusement and happiness inde-
pendent of that world.

There is a work going on in Edinburgh just now which claims
your best assistance. An engraver in this town has set about
collecting and publishing all the Scotch songs, with the music,
that can be found. Songs in the English language, if by Scotch-
men, are admitted, but the music must all be Scotch. Drs Beattie
and Blacklock are lending a hand, and the first musician in town
presides over that department. I have been absolutely crazed
about it, collecting old stanzas, and every information remaining
respecting their origin, authors, &c., &c. This last is but a very
fragment business ; but at the end of his second number—the first
is already published—a small account will be given of the authors,
particularly to preserve those of latter times. Your three songs,
Tullochgorum, John of Badenyon, and *Ewie wi' the Crookit Horn,*
go in this second number. I was determined, before I got your
letter, to write you, begging that you would let me know where
the editions of these pieces may be found, as you would wish them
to continue in future times ; and if you would be so kind to this
undertaking as send any songs, of your own or others, that you
would think proper to publish, your name will be inserted among
the other authors—" Nill ye, will ye." One-half of Scotland
already give your songs to other authors. Paper is done. I beg
to hear from you ; the sooner the better, as I leave Edinburgh in
a fortnight or three weeks. I am, with the warmest sincerity, sir,
your obliged humble servant,   R. B.

LXVIII.

TO MISS CHALMERS.

Sept. 26, 1787.

I SEND Charlotte the first number of the songs ; I would not
wait for the second number; I hate delays in little marks of friend-
ship as I hate dissimulation in the language of the heart. I am
determined to pay Charlotte a poetic compliment, if I could hit
on some glorious old Scotch air, in number second. You will see
a small attempt on a shred of paper in the book ; but though Dr
Blacklock commended it very highly, I am not just satisfied with
it myself. I intend to make it a description of some kind : the
whining cant of love, except in real passion, and by a masterly
hand, is to me as insufferable as the preaching cant of old Father
Smeaton, Whig minister at Kilmaurs. Darts, flames, Cupids

loves, graces, and all that farrago, are just a Mauchline ——— a senseless rabble.

I got an excellent poetic epistle yesternight from the old venerable author of *Tullochgorum, John of Badenyon,* &c. I suppose you know he is a clergyman. It is by far the finest poetic compliment I ever got. I will send you a copy of it.

I go on Thursday or Friday to Dumfries, to wait on Mr Miller about his farms. Do tell that to Lady Mackenzie, that she may give me credit for a little wisdom. " I, Wisdom, dwell with Prudence." What a blessed fireside! How happy should I be to pass a winter evening under their venerable roof, and smoke a pipe of tobacco, or drink water-gruel with them! With solemn, lengthened, laughter-quashing gravity of phiz! What sage remarks on the good-for-nothing sons and daughters of indiscretion and folly! And what frugal lessons, as we straitened the fireside circle, on the uses of the poker and tongs!

Miss Nimmo is very well, and begs to be remembered in the old way to you. I used all my eloquence, all the persuasive flourishes of the hand, and heart-melting modulation of periods in my power, to urge her out to Harvieston; but all in vain. My rhetoric seems quite to have lost its effect on the lovely half of mankind. I have seen the day—but this is a " tale of other years." In my conscience I believe that my heart has been so oft on fire that it is absolutely vitrified. I look on the sex with something like the admiration with which I regard the starry sky in a frosty December night. I admire the beauty of the Creator's workmanship; I am charmed with the wild but graceful cecentricity of their motions; and—wish them good night. I mean this with respect to a certain passion *dont j'ai eu l'honneur d'être un misérable esclave:* as for friendship, you and Charlotte have given me pleasure, permanent pleasure, " which the world cannot give nor take away," I hope, and which will outlast the heavens and the earth.   R. B.

———

LXIX.

TO MR WILLIAM NICOL.

                                    AUCHTERTYRE, *Monday, Oct.* 1787.

MY DEAR SIR,—I find myself very comfortable here, neither oppressed by ceremony nor mortified by neglect. Lady Augusta is a most engaging woman, and very happy in her family, which makes one's outgoings and incomings very agreeable. I called at Mr Ramsay's of Auchtertyre as I came up the country, and am so delighted with him, that I shall certainly accept of his invitation to spend a day or two with him as I return. I leave this place on Wednesday or Thursday.

Make my kind compliments to Mr and Mrs Cruikshank, and Mrs Nicol, if she has returned. I am ever, dear sir, your deeply indebted R. B.

LXX.
TO MR WILLIAM CRUIKSHANK.

AUCHTERTYRE, *Monday, Oct.* 15, 1787.

I HAVE nothing, my dear sir, to write to you, but that I feel myself exceedingly comfortably situated in this good family—just notice enough to make me easy, but not to embarrass me. I was storm-staid two days at the foot of the Ochil Hills, with Mr Tait of Herveyston and Mr Johnston of Alva; but was so well pleased that I shall certainly spend a day on the banks of the Devon as I return. I leave this place I suppose on Wednesday, and shall devote a day to Mr Ramsay at Auchtertyre, near Stirling—a man to whose worth I cannot do justice. My respectful kind compliments to Mrs Cruikshank, and my dear little Jeanie; and if you see Mr Masterton, please remember me to him. I am ever, my dear sir, &c. R. B.

LXXI.
TO MR JAMES HOY, GORDON CASTLE.

EDINBURGH, 20*th October* 1787.

SIR,—I will defend my conduct in giving you this trouble on the best of Christian principles--" Whatsoever ye would that men should do unto you, do ye even so unto them." 1 shall certainly, among my legacies, leave my latest curse to that unlucky predicament which hurried—tore me away from Castle-Gordon. May that obstinate son of Latin prose [Nicol] be curst to Scotch-mile periods, and condemned to seven-league paragraphs; while Declension and Conjugation, Gender, Number, and Tense, under the ragged banners of Dissonance and Disarrangement, eternally rank against him in hostile array!

Allow me, sir, to strengthen the small claim I have to your acquaintance by the following request:—An engraver, James Johnson, in Edinburgh, has, not from mercenary views, but from an honest Scotch enthusiasm, set about collecting all our native songs, and setting them to music, particularly those that have never been set before. Clarke, the well-known musician, presides over the musical arrangement, and Drs Beattie and Blacklock, Mr Tytler of Woodhouselee, and your humble servant to the utmost of his small power, assist in collecting the old poetry, or sometimes, for a fine air, make a stanza when it has no words.

The brats, too tedious to mention, claim a parental pang from my bardship. I suppose it will appear in Johnson's second number— the first was published before my acquaintance with him. My request is—*Cauld Kail in Aberdeen* is one intended for this number, and I beg a copy of his Grace of Gordon's words to it, which you were so kind as to repeat to me. You may be sure we wont prefix the author's name, except you like ; though I look on it as no small merit to this work that the names of so many of the authors of our old Scotch songs—names almost forgotten—will be inserted. I do not well know where to write to you—I rather write at you ; but if you will be so obliging immediately on receipt of this, as to write me a few lines, I shall perhaps pay you in kind, though not in quality. Johnson's terms are :—each number a handsome pocket volume, to consist at least of a hundred Scotch songs, with basses for the harpsichord, &c. The price to subscribers, 5s.; to non-subscribers, 6s. He will have three numbers I conjecture.

My direction for two or three weeks will be at Mr William Cruikshank's, St James' Square, New Town, Edinburgh. I am, sir, yours to command,   R. B.

LXXII.

TO MR JAMES HOY, GORDON CASTLE.

EDINBURGH, *6th November* 1787.

DEAR SIR,—I would have wrote you immediately on receipt of your kind letter ; but a mixed impulse of gratitude and esteem whispered to me that I ought to send you something by way of return. When a poet owes anything, particularly when he is indebted for good offices, the payment that usually recurs to him— the only coin, indeed, in which he is probably conversant—is rhyme. Johnson sends the books by the fly, as directed, and begs me to enclose his most grateful thanks : my return I intended should have been one or two poetic bagatelles which the world have not seen, or perhaps, for obvious reasons, cannot see. These I shall send you before I leave Edinburgh. They may make you laugh a little, which, on the whole, is no bad way of spending one's precious hours, and still more precious breath ; at anyrate, they will be, though a small, yet a very sincere mark of my respectful esteem for a gentleman whose farther acquaintance I should look upon as a peculiar obligation.

The Duke's song, independent totally of his dukeship, charms me. There is I know not what of wild happiness of thought and expression peculiarly beautiful in the old Scottish song style, of which his Grace, old venerable Skinner, the author of *Tullochgorum*, &c., and the late Ross, at Lochlee, of true Scottish poetic memory, are the only modern instances that I recollect, since Ramsay, with his contemporaries, and poor Bob Fergusson, went to the world of deathless existence and truly immortal song. The mob of mankind, that many-headed beast, would laugh at so serious a speech about an old song; but as Job says, " Oh that mine adversary had written a book !" Those who think that composing a Scotch song is a trifling business, let them try.

I wish my Lord Duke would pay a proper attention to the Christian admonition—" Hide not your candle under a bushel," but " let your light shine before men." I could name half-a-dozen dukes that I guess are a great deal worse employed; nay, I question if there are half-a-dozen better; perhaps there are not half that scanty number whom Heaven has favoured with the tuneful, happy, and I will say glorious gift. I am, dear sir, your obliged humble servant, R. B.

LXXIII.
TO MISS CHALMERS.

EDINBURGH, *Nov.* 21, 1787.

I HAVE one vexatious fault to the kindly welcome, well-filled sheet which I owe to your and Charlotte's goodness—it contains too much sense, sentiment, and good spelling. It is impossible that even you two, whom I will give credit for any degree of excellence the sex are capable of attaining—it is impossible you can go on to correspond at that rate; so, like those who, Shenstone says, retire because they have made a good speech, I shall, after a few letters, hear no more of you. I insist that you shall write whatever comes first; what you see, what you read, what you hear, what you admire, what you dislike,—trifles, bagatelles, nonsense: or to fill up a corner, e'en put down a laugh at full length. Now, none of your polite hints about flattery; I leave that to your lovers, if you have or shall have any; though, thank Heaven, I have found at last two girls who can be luxuriantly happy in their own minds and with one another, without that commonly necessary appendage to female bliss—a lover.

Charlotte and you are just two favourite resting-places for my soul in her wanderings through the weary, thorny wilderness of this world. I am ill-fitted for the struggle; I glory in being a poet, and I want to be thought a wise man—I would fondly be generous, and I wish to be rich. After all, I am afraid I am a lost subject. " Some folk ha'e a hantle o' fauts, but I'm but a ne'er-do-weel."

Afternoon.—To close the melancholy reflections at the end of last sheet, I shall just add a piece of devotion, commonly known in Carrick by the title of the " Wabster's grace :"—

"Some say we're thieves, and e'en sae are we,
Some say we lie, and e'en sae do we!"

R. B.

LXXIV.

TO MISS CHALMERS.

MY DEAR MADAM,—I just now have read yours. The poetic compliments I pay cannot be misunderstood. They are neither of them so particular as to point you out to the world at large; and the circle of your acquaintance will allow all I have said. Besides, I have complimented you chiefly, almost solely, on your mental charms. Shall I be plain with you? I will: so look to it. Personal attractions, madam, you have much above par—wit, understanding, and worth, you possess in the first class. This is a very flat way of telling you these truths, but let me hear no more of your sheepish timidity. I know the world a little. I know what they will say of my poems—by second-sight, I suppose —for I am seldom out in my conjectures; and you may believe me, my dear madam, I would not run any risk of hurting you by any ill-judged compliment. I wish to shew to the world the odds between a poet's friends and those of simple prosemen. More for your information—both the pieces go in. One of them—*Where Braving angry Winter's Storms*, is already set—the tune is Neil Gow's *Lamentation for Abercairny*; the other is to be set to an old Highland air in Daniel Dow's collection of ancient Scots music; the name is *Ha a Chaillich air mo Dheith*. My treacherous memory has forgot every circumstance about *Les Incas;* only I think you mentioned them as being in Creech's possession. I shall ask him about it. I am afraid the song of *Somebody* will come too late, as I shall for certain leave town in a week for Ayrshire, and from that to Dumfries; but there my hopes are slender. I leave my direction in town; so anything, wherever I am, will reach me.

I saw yours to ——; it is not too severe, nor did he take it amiss. On the contrary, like a whipt spaniel, he talks of being with you in the Christmas days. Mr —— has given him the invitation, and he is determined to accept of it. Oh selfishness! he owns, in his sober moments, that from his own volatility of inclination, the circumstances in which he is situated, and his knowledge of his father's disposition, the whole affair is chimerical—yet he *will* gratify an idle *penchant* at the enormous, cruel expense of perhaps ruining the peace of the very woman for whom he professes the generous passion of love! He is a gentleman in his mind and manners—*tant pis!* He is a volatile schoolboy—the heir of a man's fortune who well knows the value of two times two!

Ruin seize them and their fortunes before they should make the amiable, the lovely ——, the derided object of their purse-proud contempt!

I am doubly happy to hear of Mrs ——'s recovery, because I really thought all was over with her. There are days of pleasure yet awaiting her :—

> " As I came in by Glemap,
> I met with an aged woman;
> She bade me cheer up my heart,
> For the best o' my days was comin'."

This day will decide my affairs with Creech. Things are, like myself, not what they ought to be; yet better than what they appear to be.

> "Heaven's Sovereign saves all beings but himself—
> That hideous sight—a naked human heart."

Farewell! Remember me to Charlotte.   R. B.

LXXV.

TO MR ROBERT AINSLIE, EDINBURGH.

EDINBURGH, *Sunday Morning, Nov.* 23, 1787

I BEG, my dear sir, you would not make any appointment to take us to Mr Ainslie's to-night. On looking over my engagements, constitution, present state of my health, some little vexatious soul concerns, &c., I find I can't sup abroad to-night. I shall be in to-day till one o'clock, if you have a leisure hour.

You will think it romantic when I tell you, that I find the idea of your friendship almost necessary to my existence. You assume a proper length of face in my bitter hours of blue-devilism, and you laugh fully up to my highest wishes at my good things. I don't know, upon the whole, if you are one of the first fellows in God's world, but you are so to me. I tell you this just now, in the conviction that some inequalities in my temper and manner may perhaps sometimes make you suspect that I am not so warmly as I ought to be your friend,   R. B.

LXXVI.

TO MISS CHALMERS.

I HAVE been at Dumfries, and at one visit more shall be decided about a farm in that county. I am rather hopeless in it; but as my brother is an excellent farmer, and is, besides, an exceedingly prudent, sober man (qualities which are only a younger brother's fortune in our family), I am determined, if my Dumfries business fail me, to remove into partnership with him, and at our leisure take another farm in the neighbourhood.

I assure you I look for high compliments from you and Charlotte
on this very sage instance of my unfathomable, incomprehensible
wisdom. Talking of Charlotte, I must tell her that I have, to the
best of my power, paid her a poetic compliment now completed
[*On a Young Lady*, p. 228]. The air is admirable—true old
Highland. It was the tune of a Gaelic song which an Inverness
lady sang me when I was there; I was so charmed with it, that
I begged her to write me a set of it from her singing, for it had
never been set before. I am fixed that it shall go in Johnson's
next number; so Charlotte and you need not spend your precious
time in contradicting me. I won't say the poetry is first-rate,
though I am convinced it is very well; and what is not always
the case with compliments to ladies—it is not only sincere, but
just.   R. B.

LXXVII.

TO MR GAVIN HAMILTON.

EDINBURGH, *December* 1787.

MY DEAR SIR,—It is indeed with the highest pleasure that I
congratulate you on the return of days of ease and nights of
pleasure after the horrid hours of misery in which I saw you
suffering existence when last in Ayrshire. I seldom pray for any-
body—" I'm baith dead-sweer and wretched ill o't;" but most
fervently do I beseech the Power that directs the world, that you
may live long and be happy, but live no longer than you are
happy. It is needless for me to advise you to have a reverent
care of your health. I know you will make it a point never at
one time to drink more than a pint of wine (I mean an English
pint), and that you will never be witness to more than one bowl
of punch at a time, and that cold drams you will never more
taste; and, above all things, I am convinced, that after drinking
perhaps boiling punch, you will never mount your horse and
gallop home in a chill late hour. Above all things, as I under-
stand you are in the habits of intimacy with that Boanerges of
gospel powers, Father Auld, be earnest with him that he will
wrestle in prayer for you, that you may see the vanity of vanities
in trusting to, or even practising, the carnal moral works of
charity, humanity, generosity, and forgiveness of things, which
you practised so flagrantly that it was evident you delighted in
them, neglecting, or perhaps profanely despising, the wholesome
doctrine of faith without works, the only [means] of salvation.
A hymn of thanksgiving would, in my opinion, be highly becom-
ing from you at present; and in my zeal for your wellbeing, I
earnestly press on you to be diligent in chanting over the two en-
closed pieces of sacred poesy. My best compliments to Mrs
Hamilton and Miss Kennedy. Yours, &c.   R. B.

LXXVIII.

TO MISS MABANE.

Saturday Noon, No. 2 St James's Square,
New Town, Edinburgh.

HERE have I sat, my dear madam, in the stony altitude of per-
plexed study for fifteen vexatious minutes, my head askew, bend-
ing over the intended card; my fixed eye insensible to the very
light of day poured around ; my pendulous goose-feather, loaded
with ink, hanging over the future letter, all for the important
purpose of writing a complimentary card to accompany your
trinket.

Compliment is such a miserable Greenland expression, lies at
such a chilly polar distance from the torrid zone of my constitu-
tion, that I cannot, for the very soul of me, use it to any person
for whom I have the twentieth part of the esteem every one must
have for you who knows you.

As I leave town in three or four days, I can give myself the
pleasure of calling on you only for a minute. Tuesday evening,
some time about seven or after, I shall wait on you for your fare-
well commands.

The hinge of your box I put into the hands of the proper con-
noisseur. The broken glass likewise went under review ; but
deliberative wisdom thought it would too much endanger the
whole fabric. I am, dear madam, with all sincerity of enthusiasm,
your very obedient servant, R. B.

LXXIX.

TO SIR JOHN WHITEFOORD.

EDINBURGH, *December* 1787.

SIR,—Mr Mackenzie, in Mauchline, my very warm and worthy
friend, has informed me how much you are pleased to interest
yourself in my fate as a man, and (what to me is incomparably
dearer) my fame as a poet. I have, sir, in one or two instances,
been patronised by those of your character in life, when I was in-
troduced to their notice by * * * * *, friends to them, and
honoured acquaintances to me ; but you are the first gentleman
in the country whose benevolence and goodness of heart has in-
terested himself for me, unsolicited and unknown. I am not
master enough of the etiquette of these matters to know, nor did
I stay to inquire, whether formal duty bade, or cold propriety
disallowed, my thanking you in this manner, as I am convinced,
from the light in which you kindly view me, that you will do me
the justice to believe this letter is not the manœuvre of the needy,
sharping author, fastening on those in upper life who honour him

with a little notice of him or his works. Indeed, the situation of poets is generally such, to a proverb, as may in some measure palliate that prostitution of heart and talents they have at times been guilty of. I do not think prodigality is, by any means, a necessary concomitant of a poetic turn, but I believe a careless, indolent attention to economy is almost inseparable from it; then there must be in the heart of every bard of Nature's making a certain modest sensibility, mixed with a kind of pride, that will ever keep him out of the way of those windfalls of fortune which frequently light on hardy impudence and foot-licking servility. It is not easy to imagine a more helpless state than his whose poetic fancy unfits him for the world, and whose character as a scholar gives him some pretensions to the *politesse* of life—yet is as poor as I am.

For my part, I thank Heaven my star has been kinder; learning never elevated my ideas above the peasant's shed, and I have an independent fortune at the plough-tail.

I was surprised to hear that any one who pretended in the least to the manners of the gentleman should be so foolish, or worse, as to stoop to traduce the morals of such a one as I am, and so unhumanly cruel, too, as to meddle with that late most unfortunate, unhappy part of my story. With a tear of gratitude, I thank you, sir, for the warmth with which you interposed in behalf of my conduct. I am, I acknowledge, too frequently the sport of whim, caprice, and passion; but reverence to God, and integrity to my fellow-creatures, I hope I shall ever preserve. I have no return sir, to make you for your goodness but one—a return which, I am persuaded, will not be unacceptable—the honest, warm wishes of a grateful heart for your happiness, and every one of that lovely flock who stand to you in a filial relation. If ever calumny aim the poisoned shaft at them, may friendship be by to ward the blow!

R. B.

LXXX.

TO MRS M'LEHOSE (CLARINDA).

Thursday Evening [Dec. 6, 1787].

MADAM,—I had set no small store by my tea-drinking to-night, and have not often been so disappointed. Saturday evening I shall embrace the opportunity with the greatest pleasure. I leave town this day se'nnight, and probably for a couple of twelvemonths; but must ever regret that I so lately got an acquaintance I shall ever highly esteem, and in whose welfare I shall ever be warmly interested.

Our worthy common friend, in her usual pleasant way, rallied me a good deal on my new acquaintance, and in the humour of her ideas I wrote some lines, which I enclose you, as I think they have a good deal of poetic merit; and Miss Nimmo tells me you are not only a critic, but a poetess. Fiction you know is the native region of poetry; and I hope you will pardon my vanity in sending you the bagatelle as a tolerable off-hand *jeu d'esprit*. I have several poetic trifles, which I shall gladly leave with Miss Nimmo or you, if they were worth house-room; as there are scarcely two people on earth by whom it would mortify me more to be forgotten, though at the distance of nine score miles. I am, madam, with the highest respect, your very humble servant,   ROBERT BURNS.

LXXXI.

TO MRS M'LEHOSE.

Saturday Even. [*Dec.* 8.]

I CAN say with truth, madam, that I never met with a person in my life whom I more anxiously wished to meet again than yourself. To-night I was to have had that very great pleasure—I was intoxicated with the idea; but an unlucky fall from a coach has so bruised one of my knees that I can't stir my leg off the cushion. So, if I don't see you again, I shall not rest in my grave for chagrin. I was vexed to the soul I had not seen you sooner. I determined to cultivate your friendship with the enthusiasm of religion; but thus has Fortune ever served me. I cannot bear the idea of leaving Edinburgh without seeing you. I know not how to account for it —I am strangely taken with some people, nor am I often mistaken. You are a stranger to me; but I am an odd being. Some yet unnamed feelings—things, not principles, but better than whims —carry me farther than boasted reason ever did a philosopher.

Farewell! Every happiness be yours.   ROBERT BURNS.

LXXXII.

TO MRS M'LEHOSE.

[*Dec.* 12.]

I STRETCH a point, indeed, my dearest madam, when I answer your card on the rack of my present agony. Your friendship, madam! By heavens, I was never proud before. Your lines, I maintain it, are poetry, and good poetry; mine were indeed partly fiction and partly a friendship which, had I been so blest as to have met with you *in time,* might have led me—none knows where. Time is too short for ceremonies.

I swear solemnly (in all the tenor of my former oath) to remember you in all the pride and warmth of friendship until—I cease to be!

To-morrow, and every day till I see you, you shall hear from me.

Farewell! May you enjoy a better night's repose than I am likely to have.   R. B.

LXXXIII.
TO MRS M'LEHOSE.

[*Dec.* 20.]

YOUR last, my dear madam, had the effect on me that Job's situation had on his friends when " they sat down seven days and seven nights astonied, and spake not a word."—" Pay my addresses to a married woman !" I started as if I had seen the ghost of him I had injured : I recollected my expressions ; some of them indeed were, in the law phrase, " habit and repute," which is being half guilty. I cannot positively say, madam, whether my heart might not have gone astray a little ; but I can declare upon the honour of a poet, that the vagrant has wandered unknown to me. I have a pretty handsome troop of follies of my own ; and, like some other people's retinue, they are but undisciplined blackguards : but the luckless rascals have something of honour in them : they would not do a dishonest thing.

To meet with an unfortunate woman, amiable and young, deserted and widowed by those who were bound by every tie of duty, nature, and gratitude, to protect, comfort, and cherish her ; add to all, when she is perhaps one of the first of lovely forms and noble minds, the mind, too, that hits one's taste as the joys of heaven do a saint—should a vague infant idea, the natural child of imagination, thoughtlessly peep over the fence—were you, my friend, to sit in judgment, and the poor airy straggler brought before you, trembling, self-condemned, with artless eyes, brimful of contrition, looking wistfully on its judge, you could not, my dear madam, condemn the hapless wretch to death " without benefit of clergy ?"

I won't tell you what reply my heart made to your raillery of " seven years ;" but I will give you what a brother of my trade says on the same allusion :—

> " The Patriarch to gain a wife,
> Chaste, beautiful, and young,
> Served fourteen years a painful life
> And never thought it long.
>
> Oh were you to reward such cares,
> And life so long would stay,
> Not fourteen but four hundred years
> Would seem but as one day !"

I have written you this scrawl because I have nothing else to do, and you may sit down and find fault with it, if you have no better way of consuming your time ; but finding fault with the vagaries of a poet's fancy is much such another business as Xerxes chastising the waves of the Hellespont.

My limb now allows me to sit in some peace : to walk I have yet no prospect of, as I can't mark it to the ground.

· I have just now looked over what I have written, and it is such a chaos of nonsense that I daresay you will throw it into the fire, and call me an idle, stupid fellow ; but whatever you think of my brains, believe me to be, with the most sacred respect and heartfelt esteem, my dear madam, your humble servant,

ROBERT BURNS.

LXXXIV.
TO MISS CHALMERS.

EDINBURGH, *Dec.* 12, 1787.

I AM here under the care of a surgeon, with a bruised limb extended on a cushion ; and the tints of my mind vying with the livid horror preceding a midnight thunder-storm. A drunken coachman was the cause of the first, and incomparably the lightest evil ; misfortune, bodily constitution, evil, and myself, have formed a " quadruple alliance " to guarantee the other. I got my fall on Saturday, and am getting slowly better.

I have taken tooth and nail to the Bible, and am got through the five books of Moses, and half-way in Joshua. It is really a glorious book. I sent for my bookbinder to-day, and ordered him to get me an octavo Bible in sheets, the best paper and print in town, and bind it with all the elegance of his craft.

I would give my best song to my worst enemy—I mean the merit of making it—to have you and Charlotte by me. You are angelic creatures, and would pour wine and oil into my wounded spirit.

I enclose you a proof copy of the *Banks of the Devon* (p. 228), which present, with my best wishes, to Charlotte. The *Ochil Hills* (*Where Braving*, p. 228) you shall probably have next week for yourself. None of your fine speeches ! R. B.

LXXXV.
TO CHARLES HAY, ESQ., ADVOCATE.

(*Enclosing verses on the death of the Lord President*, p. 126.)

1787.

SIR,—The enclosed poem was written in consequence of your suggestion last time I had the pleasure of seeing you. It cost me an hour or two of next morning's sleep, but did not please me ; so it lay by an ill-digested effort, till the other day that I gave it a critic brush. These kind of subjects are much hack-neyed ; and, besides, the wailings of the rhyming tribe over the ashes of the great are cursedly suspicious, and out of all character for sincerity. These ideas damped my Muse's fire; however, I have done the best I could; and, at all events, it gives me an opportunity of declaring that I have the honour to be, sir, your obliged humble servant,   R. B.

LXXXVI.

TO MISS CHALMERS.

EDINBURGH, 19*th Dec.* 1787.

I BEGIN this letter in answer to yours of the 17th current, which is not yet cold since I read it. The atmosphere of my soul is vastly clearer than when I wrote you last. For the first time yesterday I crossed the room on crutches. It would do your heart good to see my bardship, not on my poetic, but on my oaken stilts; throwing my best leg with an air! and with as much hilarity in my gait and countenance as a May frog leaping across the newly-harrowed ridge, enjoying the fragrance of the refreshed earth after the long-expected shower!

I can't say I am altogether at my ease when I see anywhere in my path that meagre, squalid, famine-faced spectre— Poverty, attended as he always is by iron-fisted Oppression and leering Contempt; but I have sturdily withstood his buffetings many a hard-laboured day already. and still my motto is—*I dare!* My worst enemy is *moi même.* I lie so miserably open to the inroads and incursions of a mischievous, light-armed, well-mounted banditti, under the banners of Imagination, Whim, Caprice, and Passion; and the heavy-armed veteran regulars of Wisdom, Prudence, and Forethought move so very, very slow, that I am almost in a state of perpetual warfare, and alas! frequent defeat. There are just two creatures I would envy—a horse in his wild state traversing the forests of Asia, or an oyster on some of the desert shores of Europe. The one has not a wish without enjoyment, the other has neither wish nor fear.   R. B.

LXXXVII.

TO CLARINDA.*

Friday Evening [21*st Dec.*]

I BEG your pardon, my dear " Clarinda," for the fragment scrawl I sent you yesterday. I really do not know what I wrote. A gentleman for whose character, abilities, and critical knowledge I have the highest veneration, called in just as I had begun the second sentence, and I would not make the porter wait. I

---

* It was now arranged that for the future Burns and Mrs M'Lehose should sign their epistles respectively as Sylvander and Clarinda.

read to my much-respected friend several of my own bagatelles, and, among others, your lines, which I had copied out. He began some criticisms on them, as on the other pieces, when I informed him they were the work of a young lady in this town, which, I assure you, made him stare. My learned friend seriously protested that he did not believe any young woman in Edinburgh was capable of such lines; and if you know anything of Professor Gregory, you will neither doubt of his abilities nor his sincerity. I do love you, if possible, still better for having so fine a taste and turn for poesy. I have again gone wrong in my usual unguarded way, but you may erase the word, and put esteem, respect, or any other tame Dutch expression you please in its place. I believe there is no holding converse, or carrying on correspondence with an amiable woman, much less a *gloriously amiable fine woman*, without some mixture of that delicious passion whose most devoted slave I have more than once had the honour of being. But why be hurt or offended on that account? Can no honest man have a prepossession for a fine woman, but he must run his head against an intrigue? Take a little of the tender witchcraft of love, and add it to the generous, the honourable sentiments of manly friendship, and I know but *one* more delightful morsel which few, few in any rank ever taste. Such a composition is like adding cream to strawberries: it not only gives the fruit a more elegant richness, but has a peculiar deliciousness of its own.

I enclose you a few lines I composed on a late melancholy occasion. I will not give above five or six copies of it at all, and I would be hurt if any friend should give any copies without my consent.

You cannot imagine, Clarinda (I like the idea of Arcadian names in a commerce of this kind), how much store I have set by the hopes of your future friendship. I do not know if you have a just idea of my character, but I wish you to see me as I am. I am, as most people of my trade are, a strange Will-o'-Wisp being; the victim too frequently of much imprudence and many follies. My great constituent elements are *pride* and *passion*. The first I have endeavoured to humanize into integrity and honour; the last makes me a devotee to the warmest degree of enthusiasm in love, religion, or friendship—either of them, or all together, as I happen to be inspired. 'Tis true I never saw you but once; but how much acquaintance did I form of you in that once! Do not think I flatter you, or have a design upon you, Clarinda: I have too much pride for the one, and too little cold contrivance for the other; but of all God's creatures I ever could approach in the beaten way of my acquaintance, you struck me with the deepest, the strongest, the most permanent impression. I say the most permanent, because I know myself well, and how far I can promise either in my prepossessions or powers. Why are you unhappy? And why are so many of our fellow-creatures —unworthy to belong to the same species with you—blest with all they can wish? You have a hand all benevolent to give : why were you denied the pleasure? You have a heart formed— gloriously formed—for all the most refined luxuries of love : why was that heart ever wrung? Oh Clarinda! shall we not meet in a state, some yet unknown state of being, where the lavish hand of plenty shall minister to the highest wish of benevolence, and where the chill north wind of prudence shall never blow over the flowery fields of enjoyment? If we do not, man was made in vain! I deserved most of the unhappy hours that have lingered over my head; they were the wages of my labour : but what un-provoked demon, malignant as hell, stole upon the confidence of unmistrusting busy fate, and dashed *your* cup of life with unde-served sorrow?

Let me know how long your stay will be out of town; I shall count the hours till you inform me of your return. *Etiquette* for-bids your seeing me just now; and so soon as I can walk I must bid Edinburgh adieu. Why was I born to see misery which I cannot relieve, and to meet with friends whom I cannot enjoy? I look back with the pang of unavailing avarice on my loss in not knowing you sooner: all last winter, these three months past, what luxury of intercourse have I not lost! Perhaps, though, 'twas better for my peace. You see I am either above or inca-pable of dissimulation. I believe it is want of that particular genius. I despise design, because I want either coolness or wis-dom to be capable of it. I am interrupted. Adieu! my dear Clarinda! SYLVANDER.

LXXXVIII.
TO CLARINDA.

MY DEAR CLARINDA,—Your last verses have so delighted me that I have copied them in among some of my own most valued pieces, which I keep sacred for my own use. Do let me have a few now and then.

Did you, madam, know what I feel when you talk of your sor-rows!

ALAS! that one who has so much worth in the sight of heaven, and is so amiable to her fellow-creatures, should be so unhappy. I can't venture out for cold. My limb is vastly better; but I have not any use of it without my crutches. Monday, for the first time, I dine in a neighbour's, next door. As soon as I can go so far, *even in a coach*, my first visit shall be to you. Write me when you leave town, and immediately when you return; and

1 carnestly pray your stay may be short. You can't imagine how miserable you made me when you hinted to me not to write. Farewell, SYLVANDER.

LXXXIX.

TO MR RICHARD BROWN, IRVINE.

EDINBURGH, 30*th Dec.* 1787.

MY DEAR SIR,—I have met with few things in life which have given me more pleasure than Fortune's kindness to you since those days in which we met in the vale of misery; as I can honestly say that I never knew a man who more truly deserved it, or to whom my heart more truly wished it. I have been much indebted since that time to your story and sentiments for steeling my mind against evils, of which I have had a pretty decent share. My Will-o'-Wisp fate you know; do you recollect a Sunday we spent together in Eglinton woods? You told me, on my repeating some verses to you, that you wondered I could resist the temptation of sending verses of such merit to a magazine. It was from this remark I derived that idea of my own pieces which encouraged me to endeavour at the character of a poet. I am happy to hear that you will be two or three months at home. As soon as a bruised limb will permit me, I shall return to Ayrshire, and we shall meet; " and faith I hope we'll not sit dumb, nor yet cast out!"

I have much to tell you " of men, their manners, and their ways;" perhaps a little of the other sex. Apropos, I beg to be remembered to Mrs Brown. There, I doubt not, my dear friend, but you have found substantial happiness. I expect to find you something of an altered, but not a different man; the wild, bold, generous young fellow composed into the steady affectionate husband, and the fond, careful parent. For me, I am just the same Will-o'-Wisp being I used to be. About the first and fourth quarters of the moon I generally set in for the trade wind of Wisdom; but about the full and change I am the luckless victim of mad tornadoes, which blow me into chaos. All-mighty love still reigns and revels in my bosom; and I am at this moment ready to hang myself for a young Edinburgh widow, who has wit and wisdom more murderously fatal than the assassinating stiletto of the Sicilian bandit, or the poisoned arrow of the savage African. My Highland dirk, that used to hang beside my crutches, I have gravely removed into a neighbouring closet, the key of which i cannot command, in case of spring-tide paroxysms. You may guess of her wit by the following verses, which she sent me the other day. * * *

My best compliments to our friend Allan. Adieu! R. B.

XC.

TO CLARINDA.

[After New Year, 1788.]

You are right, my dear Clarinda : a friendly correspondence goes for nothing, except one write their undisguised sentiments. Yours please me for their intrinsic merit, as well as because they are *yours*, which, I assure you, is to me a high recommendation. Your religious sentiments, madam, I revere. If you have, on some suspicious evidence from some lying oracle, learned that I despise or ridicule so sacredly important a matter as real religion, you have, my Clarinda, much misconstrued your friend—" I am not mad, most noble Festus !" Have you ever met a perfect character ? Do we not sometimes rather exchange faults than get rid of them ? For instance, I am perhaps tired with, and shocked at a life too much the prey of giddy inconsistencies and thoughtless follies ; by degrees I grow sober, prudent, and statedly pious —I say statedly, because the most unaffected devotion is not at all inconsistent with my first character—I join the world in congratulating myself on the happy change. But let me pry more narrowly into this affair. Have I, at bottom, anything of a secret pride in these endowments and emendations ? Have I nothing of a Presbyterian sourness, a hypocritical severity, when I survey my less regular neighbours ? In a word, have I missed all those nameless and numberless modifications of indistinct selfishness, which are so near our own eyes that we can scarcely bring them within the sphere of our vision, and which the known spotless cambric of our character hides from the ordinary observer !

My definition of worth is short : truth and humanity respecting our fellow-creatures ; reverence and humility in the presence of that Being, my Creator and Preserver, and who, I have every reason to believe, will one day be my Judge. The first part of my definition is the creature of unbiassed instinct ; the last is the child of after-reflection. Where I found these two essentials, I would gently note, and slightly mention, any attendant flaws— flaws, the marks, the consequences of human nature.

I can easily enter into the sublime pleasures that your strong imagination and keen sensibility must derive from religion, particularly if a little in the shade of misfortune ; but I own I cannot, without a marked grudge, see Heaven totally engross so amiable, so charming a woman, as my friend Clarinda ; and should be very well pleased at *a circumstance* that would put it in the power of somebody (happy somebody !) to divide her attention, with all the delicacy and tenderness of an earthly attachment.

You will not easily persuade me that you have not a grammatical knowledge of the English language. So far from being inaccurate, you are elegant beyond any woman of my acquaintance, except one, whom I wish you knew.

Your last verses to me have so delighted me, that I have got an excellent old Scots air that suits the measure, and you shall see them in print in the *Scots Musical Museum,* a work publishing by a friend of mine in this town. I want four stanzas; you gave me but three, and one of them alluded to an expression in my former letter; so I have taken your two first verses, with a slight alteration in the second, and have added a third; but you must help me to a fourth. Here they are: the latter half of the first stanza would have been worthy of Sappho; I am in raptures with it.

> "Talk not of Love, it gives me pain,
>   For Love has been my foe:
> He bound me with an iron chain,
>   And sunk me deep in woe.
>
> But Friendship's pure and lasting joys
>   My heart was formed to prove :
> There, welcome, win and wear the prize,
>   But never talk of Love."
>
> Your friendship much can make me blest,
>   O why that bless destroy!
>   (only)
> Why urge the odious one request,
>   (will)
>   You know I must deny.

The alteration in the second stanza is no improvement, but there was a slight inaccuracy in your rhyme. The third I only offer to your choice, and have left two words for your determination. The air is "The Banks of Spey," and is most beautiful.

To-morrow evening I intend taking a chair, and paying a visit at Park Place to a much-valued old friend. If I could be sure of finding you at home (and I will send one of the chairmen to call), I would spend from five to six o'clock with you as I go past. I cannot do more at this time, as I have something on my hand that hurries me much. I propose giving you the first call, my old friend the second, and Miss ——, as I return home. Do not break any engagement for me, as I will spend another evening with you at any rate before I leave town.

Do not tell me that you are pleased when your friends inform you of your faults. I am ignorant what they are; but I am sure they must be such evanescent trifles, compared with your personal and mental accomplishments, that I would despise the ungenerous, narrow soul who would notice any shadow of imperfections you may seem to have any other way than in the most delicate agreeable raillery. Coarse minds are not aware how much they injure the keenly-feeling tie of bosom-friendship, when, in their foolish officiousness, they mention what nobody cares for recollecting. People of nice sensibility and generous minds have a certain intrinsic dignity that fires at being trifled with, or lowered, or even too nearly approached.

You need make no apology for long letters: I am even with you. Many happy new-years to you, charming Clarinda! I can't dissemble were it to shun perdition. He who sees you as I have done, and does not love you, deserves to be hanged for his stupidity! He who loves you, and would injure you, deserves to be doubly hanged for his villany! Adieu. SYLVANDER.

XCI.

TO CLARINDA.

SOME days, some nights, nay, some *hours*, like the "ten righteous persons in Sodom," save the rest of the vapid, tiresome, miserable months and years of life. One of these hours my dear Clarinda blest me with yesternight:—

> " One well-spent hour,
> In such a tender circumstance for friends,
> Is better than an age of common time!" THOMSON.

My favourite feature in Milton's Satan is his manly fortitude in supporting what cannot be remedied—in short, the wild, broken fragments of a noble exalted mind in ruins. I meant no more by saying he was a favourite hero of mine.

I mentioned to you my letter to Dr Moore, giving an account of my life: it is truth, every word of it, and will give you the just idea of a man whom you have honoured with your friendship. I am afraid you will hardly be able to make sense of so torn a piece. Your verses I shall muse on, deliciously, as I gaze on your image in my mind's eye, in my heart's core: they will be in time enough for a week to come. I am truly happy your headache is better. —Oh, how can pain or evil be so daringly, unfeelingly, cruelly savage as to wound so noble a mind, so lovely a form!

My little fellow is all my namesake. Write me soon. My every, strongest good wishes attend you, Clarinda!

SYLVANDER.

I know not what I have written—I am pestered with people around me.

XCII.

TO CLARINDA.

Tuesday Night [*Jan.* 8 ?]

I AM delighted, charming Clarinda, with your honest enthusiasm for religion. Those of either sex, but particularly the female, who are lukewarm in that most important of all things, " O my soul, come not thou into their secrets!" I feel myself deeply interested in your good opinion, and will lay before you the outlines of my belief. He who is our Author and Preserver, and will one day be our Judge, must be (not for his sake in the way of duty, but from the native impulse of our hearts) the object of our reverential awe and grateful adoration : He is almighty and all-bounteous, we are weak and dependent ; hence prayer and every other sort of devotion.——" He is not willing that any should perish, but that all should come to everlasting life;" consequently it must be in every one's power to embrace his offer of "everlasting life;" otherwise he could not, in justice, condemn those who did not. A mind pervaded, actuated, and governed by purity, truth, and charity, though it does not *merit* heaven, yet is an absolutely necessary pre-requisite, without which heaven can neither be obtained nor enjoyed ; and, by Divine promise, such a mind shall never fail of attaining " everlasting life :" hence the impure, the deceiving, and the uncharitable extrude themselves from eternal bliss by their unfitness for enjoying it. The Supreme Being has put the immediate administration of all this, for wise and good ends known to himself, into the hands of Jesus Christ—a great personage, whose relation to Him we cannot comprehend, but whose relation to us is [that of] a Guide and Saviour ; and who, except for our own obstinacy and misconduct, will bring us all, through various ways, and by various means, to bliss at last.

These are my tenets, my lovely friend ; and which, I think, cannot be well disputed. My creed is pretty nearly expressed in the last clause of Jamie Deans' grace, an honest weaver in Ayrshire : " Lord, grant that we may lead a gude life ! for a gude life maks a gude end ; at least it helps weel !".

I am flattered by the entertainment you tell me you have found in my packet. You see me as I have been, you know me as I am, and may guess at what I am likely to be. I too may say, " Talk not of love," &c., for indeed he has " plunged me deep in wo !" Not that I ever saw a woman who pleased unexceptionably, as my Clarinda elegantly says, " in the companion, the friend, and the mistress." *One* indeed I could accept—*One*, before passion threw its mists over my discernment, I knew *the* first of women ! Her name is indelibly written in my heart's core—but I dare not look in on it—a degree of agony would be the consequence. Oh ! thou perfidious, cruel, mischief-making demon, who presidest over that frantic passion—thou mayst, thou dost, poison my peace, but thou shalt not taint my honour. I would not, for a single moment, give an asylum to the most distant imagination that would shadow the faintest outline of a selfish gratification, at the expense of her whose happiness is twisted with the threads of my existence.—— May she be as happy as she deserves ! And if my tenderest, faithfulest friendship can add to her bliss, I shall at least have one solid mine of enjoyment in my bosom ! *Don't guess at these ravings !*

I watched at our front window to-day, but was disappointed. It has been a day of disappointments. I am just risen after a two hours' bout after supper with silly or sordid souls, who could relish nothing in common with me but the port.——*One.* 'Tis now " witching time of night;" and whatever is out of joint in the fore-going scrawl impute it to enchantments and spells; for I can't look over it, but will seal it up directly, as I don't care for to-morrow's criticisms on it.

You are by this time fast asleep, Clarinda; may good angels attend and guard you as constantly and faithfully as my good wishes do.

> " Beauty, which, whether waking or asleep,
>   Shot forth peculiar graces."

John Milton, I wish thy soul better rest than I expect on my pillow to-night! Oh for a little of the cart-horse part of human nature! Good-night, my dearest Clarinda!

SYLVANDER.

XCIII.

TO CLARINDA.

Thursday Noon [*Jan.* 10 ?]

I AM certain I saw you, Clarinda; but you don't look to the proper storey for a poet's lodging,

> " Where Speculation roosted near the sky."

I could almost have thrown myself over for very vexation. Why did'nt you look higher? It has spoilt my peace for this day. To be so near my charming Clarinda; to miss her look while it was searching for me. I am sure the soul is capable of disease, for mine has convulsed itself into an inflammatory fever. I am sorry for your little boy: do let me know to-morrow how he is.

You have converted me, Clarinda (I shall love that name while I live: there is heavenly music in it!) Booth and Amelia I know well. Your sentiments on that subject, as they are on every sub-ject, are just and noble. " To be feelingly alive to kindness and to unkindness" is a charming female character.

What I said in my last letter, the powers of fuddling sociality only know for me. By yours I understand my good star has been partly in my horizon when I got wild in my reveries. Had that evil planet, which has almost all my life shed its baleful rays on my devoted head, been as usual in its zenith, I had certainly blabbed something that would have pointed out to you the dear object of my tenderest friendship, and, in spite of me, something more. Had that fatal information escaped me, and it was merely chance or kind stars that it did not, I had been undone! You would never have written me, except, perhaps, *once* more! Oh, I could curse circumstances! and the coarse tie of human laws which keeps fast what common sense would loose, and which bars that happiness itself cannot give—happiness which otherwise love and honour would warrant! But hold—I shall make no more " hairbreadth 'scapes."

My friendship, Clarinda, is a liferent business. My likings are both strong and eternal. I told you I had but one male friend : I have but two female. I should have a third, but she is surrounded by the blandishments of flattery and courtship. Her I register in my heart's core by Peggy Chalmers : Miss Nimmo can tell you how divine she is. She is worthy of a place in the same bosom with my Clarinda. That is the highest compliment I can pay her. Farewell, Clarinda! Remember   SYLVANDER.

XCIV.
TO CLARINDA.

Saturday Morning.

YOUR thoughts on religion, Clarinda, shall be welcome. You may perhaps distrust me when I say 'tis also my favourite topic ; but mine is the religion of the bosom. I hate the very idea of a controversial divinity ; as I firmly believe that every honest, upright man, of whatever sect, will be accepted of the Deity. If your verses, as you seem to hint, contain censure, except you want an occasion to break with me, don't send them. I have a little infirmity in my disposition, that where I fondly love, or highly esteem, I cannot bear reproach.

" Reverence thyself" is a sacred maxim, and I wish to cherish it. I think I told you Lord Bolingbroke's saying to Swift—"Adieu, dear Swift, with all thy faults I love thee entirely ; make an effort to love me with all mine." A glorious sentiment, and without which there can be no friendship! I do highly, very highly esteem you indeed, Clarinda—you merit it all! Perhaps, too, I scorn dissimulation! I could fondly love you : judge, then, what a maddening sting your reproach would be. " Oh! I have sins to *Heaven*, but none to *you!*" With what pleasure would I meet you to-day, but I cannot walk to meet the Fly. I hope to be able to see you on *foot*, about the middle of next week.

I am interrupted—perhaps you are not sorry for it, you will tell me—but I won't anticipate blame. Oh Clarinda! did you know how dear to me is your look of kindness, your smile of approbation! you would not, either in prose or verse, risk a censorious remark.

> " Curst be the verse, how well soe'er it flow,
> That tends to make one worthy man my foe!"

SYLVANDER.

XCV.

TO CLARINDA.

You talk of weeping, Clarinda: some involuntary drops wet your lines as I read them. ·Offend me, my dearest angel! You cannot offend me—you never offended me. If you had ever given me the least shadow of offence, so pardon me my God as I forgive Clarinda. I have read yours again; it has blotted my paper. Though I find your letter has agitated me into a violent headache, I shall take a chair, and be with you about eight. A friend is to be with us at tea, on my account, which hinders me from coming sooner. Forgive, my dearest Clarinda, my unguarded expres-sions! For Heaven's sake, forgive me, or I shall never be able to bear my own mind!—Your unhappy   SYLVANDER.

XCVI.

TO CLARINDA.

Monday Even., ·11 *o'clock.*

WHY have I not heard from you, Clarinda? To-day I expected it; and before supper, when a letter to me was announced, my heart danced with rapture: but behold, 'twas some fool who had taken it into his head to turn poet, and made me an offering of the first-fruits of his nonsense. "It is not poetry, but prose run mad." Did I ever repeat to you an epigram I made on Mr Elphinstone, who has given a translation of Martial, a famous Latin poet? The poetry of Elphinstone can only equal his prose notes. I was sitting in a merchant's shop of my acquaintance, waiting somebody; he put Elphinstone into my hand, and asked my opinion of it; I begged leave to write it on a blank leaf, which I did—

TO MR ELPHINSTONE, &c.

Oh thou, whom Poesy abhors!
Whom Prose has turned out of doors!
Heard'st thou yon groan? proceed no further!
'Twas laurel'd Martial calling murther!

I am determined to see you, if at all possible, on Saturday even-ing. Next week I must sing—

The night is my departing night,
The morn's the day I maun awa;
There's neither friend nor foe o' mine
But wishes that I were awa!

What I hae done for lack o' wit,
I never, never can reca';
I hope ye're a' my friends as yet—
Gude night, and joy be wi' you a'!

If I could see you sooner, I would be so much the happier; but

I would not purchase the dearest gratification on earth, if it must be at your expense in worldly censure, far less inward peace!

I shall certainly be ashamed of thus scrawling whole sheets of incoherence. The only *unity* (a sad word with poets and critics!) in my ideas is CLARINDA. There my heart " reigns and revels!"

" What art thou love? whence are those charms,
  That thus thou bear'st an universal rule?
For thee the soldier quits his arms,
  The king turns slave, the wise man fool.
In vain we chase thee from the field,
  And with cool thoughts resist thy yoke:
Next tide of blood, alas! we yield,
  And all those high resolves are broke!"

I like to have quotations for every occasion. They give one's ideas so pat, and save one the trouble of finding expression adequate to one's feelings. I think it is one of the greatest pleasures attending a poetic genius that we can give our woes, cares, joys, loves, &c., an embodied form in verse, which to me is ever immediate ease. Goldsmith says finely of his Muse—

" Thou source of all my bliss and all my woe;
Thou found'st me poor at first, and keep'st me so."

My limb has been so well to-day that I have gone up and down stairs often without my staff. To-morrow I hope to walk once again on my own legs to dinner. It is only next street. Adieu.

SYLVANDER.

XCVII.

TO CLARINDA.

Tuesday Evening [*Jan.* 15].

THAT you have faults, my Clarinda, I never doubted; but I knew not where they existed, and Saturday night made me more in the dark than ever. Oh Clarinda! why will you wound my soul by hinting that last night must have lessened my opinion of you? True I was " behind the scenes" with you; but what did I see? A bosom glowing with honour and benevolence; a mind ennobled by genius, informed and refined by education and reflection, and exalted by native religion, genuine as in the climes of heaven; a heart formed for all the glorious meltings of friendship, love, and pity. These I saw: I saw the noblest immortal soul creation ever showed me.

I looked long, my dear Clarinda, for your letter; and am vexed that you are complaining. I have not caught you so far wrong as in your idea that the commerce you have with *one* friend hurts you if you cannot tell every tittle of it to *another*. Why have so injurious a suspicion of a good God, Clarinda, as to think that Friendship and Love, on the sacred inviolate principles of Truth Honour, and Religion, can be anything else than an object of His divine approbation?

I have mentioned, in some of my former scrawls, Saturday evening next. Do allow me to wait on you that evening. Oh, my angel! how soon must we part! and when can we meet again? I looked forward on the horrid interval with tearful eyes! What have I lost by not knowing you sooner! I fear, I fear my acquaintance with you is too short to make that *lasting* impression on your heart I could wish.   SYLVANDER.

XCVIII.

TO CLARINDA.

Sunday Night [*Jan.* 20?]

THE impertinence of fools has joined with the return of an old indisposition to make me good for nothing to-day. The paper has lain before me all this evening to write to my dear Clarinda; but

"Fools rushed on fools, as waves succeed to waves."

I cursed them in my soul: they sacrilegiously disturb my meditations on her who holds my heart! What a creature is man! A little alarm last night and to-day that I am mortal has made such a revolution in my spirits! There is no philosophy, no divinity, comes half so home to the mind. I have no idea of courage that braves Heaven. 'Tis the wild ravings of an imaginary hero in Bedlam. I can no more, Clarinda; I can scarce hold up my head; but I am happy you don't know it, you would be so uneasy.

                                        SYLVANDER.

Monday Morning.

I am, my lovely friend, much better this morning, on the whole; but I have a horrid languor on my spirits—

"Sick of the world and all its joy,
My soul in pining sadness mourns;
Dark scenes of wo my mind employ,
The past and present in their turns."

Have you ever met with a saying of the great and likewise good Mr Locke, author of the famous *Essay on the Human Understanding?* He wrote a letter to a friend, directing it " Not to be delivered till after my decease." It ended thus—" I know you loved me when living, and will preserve my memory now I am dead. All the use to be made of it is—that this life affords no solid satisfaction but in the consciousness of having done well, and the hopes of another life. Adieu! I leave my best wishes with you.—J. LOCKE."

Clarinda, may I reckon on your friendship for life? I think I may. Thou Almighty Preserver of men! Thy friendship, which hitherto I have too much neglected, to secure it shall all the

future days and nights of my life be my steady care!—The idea
of my Clarinda follows:—

> "Hide it, my heart, within that close disguise,
> Where, mixed with God's, her loved idea lies."

But I fear inconstancy, the consequent imperfection of human
weakness. Shall I meet with a friendship that defies years of ab-
sence, and the chances and changes of fortune? Perhaps "such
things are." *One* honest man I have great hopes from that way:
but who, except a romance writer, would think on a *love* that could
promise for life, in spite of distance, absence, chance, and change;
and that, too, with slender hopes of fruition? For my own part,
I can say to myself in both requisitions, "Thou art the man!" I
dare, in cool resolve, I dare declare myself that friend and that
lover. If womankind is capable of such things, Clarinda is. I
trust that she is; and feel I shall be miserable if she is not.
There is not one virtue which gives worth, or one sentiment which
does honour to the sex, that she does not possess superior to any
woman I ever saw; her exalted mind, aided a little perhaps by
her situation, is, I think, capable of that nobly-romantic love-
enthusiasm.

May I see you on Wednesday evening, my dear angel? The
next Wednesday again will, I conjecture, be a hated day to us
both. I tremble for censorious remarks for your sake; but in ex-
traordinary cases may not usual and useful precautions be a
little dispensed with? Three evenings, three swift-winged even-
ings, with pinions of down, are all the past—I dare not calculate
the future. I shall call at Miss Nimmo's to-morrow evening;
'twill be a farewell call.

I have written out my last sheet of paper, so I am reduced to
my last half-sheet. What a strange, mysterious faculty is that
thing called imagination! We have no ideas almost at all of
another world; but I have often amused myself with visionary
schemes of what happiness might be enjoyed by small alterations
—alterations that we can fully enter to, in this present state of
existence. For instance, suppose you and I just as we are at pre-
sent, the same reasoning powers, sentiments, and even desires;
the same fond curiosity for knowledge and remarking observation
in our minds—and imagine our bodies free from pain, and the
necessary supplies for the wants of nature at all times and easily
within our reach; imagine further that we were set free from the
laws of gravitation which bind us to this globe, and could at
pleasure fly, without inconvenience, through all the yet uncon-
jectured bounds of creation—what a life of bliss should we lead
in our mutual pursuit of virtue and knowledge, and our mutual
enjoyment of friendship and love!

I see you laughing at my fairy fancies, and calling me a vo-

luptuous Mahometan ; but I am certain I should be a happy crea-
ture, beyond anything we call bliss here below : nay, it would be a
paradise congenial to you too.   Don't you see us hand-in-hand,
making our remarks on Syrius, the nearest of the fixed stars ;
or surveying a comet flaming innoxious by us, as we just now
would mark the passing pomp of a travelling monarch ; while the
most exalted strains of poesy and harmony would be the ready,
spontaneous language of our souls ! Devotion is the favourite em-
ployment of your heart, so is it of mine : what incentives then to,
and powers for reverence, gratitude, faith, and hope, in all the
fervours of adoration and praise to that Being whose unsearch-
able wisdom, power, and goodness so pervaded, so inspired every
sense and feeling ! By this time, I daresay, you will be blessing
the neglect of the maid that leaves me destitute of paper.

                                            SYLVANDER.

XCIX.

TO MISS CHALMERS.

Now for that wayward, unfortunate thing, myself.   I have
broke measures with Creech, and last week I wrote him a frosty,
keen letter.   He replied in terms of chastisement, and promised
me upon his honour that I should have the account on Monday ;
but this is Tuesday, and yet I have not heard a word from him.
God have mercy on me ! a poor, incautious, duped, unfortunate
fool ! The sport, the miserable victim of rebellious pride, hypo-
chondriac imagination, agonising sensibility, and Bedlam passions !
    " I wish that I were dead, but I'm no like to die !"   I had lately
" a hairbreadth 'scape in th' imminent deadly breach" of love too.
Thank my stars, I got off heart-whole, " waur fleyed [worse fright-
ened] than hurt."—Interruption.
    I have this moment got a hint. . . . . I fear I am something
like—undone—but I hope for the best. Come, stubborn pride,
and unshrinking resolution ; accompany me through this, to me,
miserable world! You must not desert me. Your friendship I
think I can count on, though I should date my letters from a
marching regiment. Early in life, and all my life, I reckoned on
a recruiting drum as my forlorn hope. Seriously though, life pre-
sents me with but a melancholy path : but—my limb will soon be
sound, and I shall struggle on.   R. B.

C.

TO MRS DUNLOP.

EDINBURGH, *January* 21, 178.

AFTER six weeks' confinement, I am beginning to walk across the room. They have been six horrible weeks; anguish and low spirits made me unfit to read, write, or think.

I have a hundred times wished that one could resign life as an officer resigns a commission; for I would not take in any poor ignorant wretch, by selling out. Lately I was a sixpenny private, and a miserable soldier enough; now I march to the campaign, a starving cadet—a little more conspicuously wretched.

I am ashamed of all this; for though I do want bravery for the warfare of life, I could wish, like some other soldiers, to have as much fortitude or cunning as to dissemble or conceal my cowardice.

As soon as I can bear the journey, which will be, I suppose, about the middle of next week, I leave Edinburgh; and soon after I shall pay my grateful duty at Dunlop House.   R. B.

CI.

TO ROBERT GRAHAM, ESQ. OF FINTRY

SIR,—When I had the honour of being introduced to you at Athole House, I did not think so soon of asking a favour of you. When Lear, in Shakspeare, asked old Kent why he wished to be in his service, he answers, "Because you have that in your face which I would fain call master." For some such reason, sir, do I now solicit your patronage. You know, I daresay, of an application I lately made to your board to be admitted an officer of Excise. I have, according to form, been examined by a supervisor, and to-day I gave in his certificate, with a request for an order for instructions. In this affair, if I succeed, I am afraid I shall but too much need a patronising friend. Propriety of conduct as a man, and fidelity and attention as an officer, I dare engage for; but with anything like business, except manual labour, I am totally unacquainted.

I had intended to have closed my late appearance on the stage of life in the character of a country farmer; but after discharging some filial and fraternal claims, I find I could only fight for existence in that miserable manner which I have lived to see throw a venerable parent into the jaws of a jail; whence death, the poor man's last and often best friend, rescued him.

I know, sir, that to need your goodness is to have a claim on it; may I therefore beg your patronage to forward me in this

affair, till I be appointed to a division—where, by the help of rigid economy, I will try to support that independence so dear to my soul, but which has been too often so distant from my situa-tior
R. B.

CII.
TO THE EARL OF GLENCAIRN.

My Lord,—I know your lordship will disapprove of my ideas in a request I am going to make to you; but I have weighed, long and seriously weighed, my situation, my hopes, and turn of mind, and am fully fixed to my scheme, if I can possibly effec-tuate it. I wish to get into the Excise; I am told that your lordship's interest will easily procure me the grant from the commissioners; and your lordship's patronage and goodness, which have already rescued me from obscurity, wretchedness, and exile, embolden me to ask that interest. You have likewise put it in my power to save the little tie of home that sheltered an aged mother, two brothers, and three sisters, from destruc-tion. There, my lord, you have bound me over to the highest gratitude.

My brother's farm is but a wretched lease, but I think he will probably weather out the remaining seven years of it; and after the assistance which I have given, and will give him, to keep the family together, I think, by my guess, I shall have rather better than two hundred pounds; and instead of seeking, what is almost impossible at present to find, a farm that I can certainly live by, with so small a stock, I shall lodge this sum in a banking-house, a sacred deposit, excepting only the calls of uncommon distress or necessitous old age.

These, my lord, are my views: I have resolved from the ma-turest deliberation; and now I am fixed, I shall leave no stone unturned to carry my resolve into execution. Your lordship's patronage is the strength of my hopes; nor have I yet applied to anybody else. Indeed, my heart sinks within me at the idea of applying to any other of the great who have honoured me with their countenance, I am ill qualified to dog the heels of greatness with the impertinence of solicitation, and tremble nearly as much at the thought of the cold promise as the cold denial; but to your lordship I have not only the honour, the comfort, but the pleasure of being your lordship's much obliged and deeply-indebted numble servant,
R. B.

CIII.

TO CLARINDA.

Thursday Morning [*January* 24]

" Unlavish Wisdom never works in vain."

I HAVE been tasking my reason, Clarinda, why a woman, who, for native genius, poignant wit, strength of mind, generous sincerity of soul, and the sweetest female tenderness, is without a peer, and whose personal charms have few, very very few, parallels among her sex ; why, or how she should fall to the blessed lot of a poor hairum-scairum poet whom Fortune had kept for her particular use, to wreak her temper on whenever she was in ill-humour. One time I conjectured, that as Fortune is the most capricious jade ever known, she may have taken, not a fit of remorse, but a paroxysm of whim, to raise the poor fellow out of the mire, where he had so often and so conveniently served her as a stepping-stone, and given him the most glorious boon she ever had in her gift, merely for the maggot's sake, to see how his fool head and his fool heart will bear it. At other times I was vain enough to think that Nature, who has a great deal to say with Fortune, had given the coquettish goddess some such hint as, " Here is a paragon of female excellence, whose equal, in all my former compositions, I never was lucky enough to hit on, and despair of ever doing so again ; you have cast her rather in the shades of life ; there is a certain poet of my making ; among your frolics it would not be amiss to attach him to this masterpiece of my hand, to give her that immortality among mankind which no woman, of any age, ever more deserved, and which few rhymsters of this age are better able to confer."

Evening, 9 *o'clock.*

I am here, absolutely unfit to finish my letter—pretty hearty after a bowl, which has been constantly plied since dinner till this moment. I have been with Mr Schetki, the musician, and he has set the song (*Farewell to Clarinda*, p. 127) finely. I have no distinct ideas of anything, but that I have drunk your health twice to-night, and that you are all my soul holds dear in this world. SYLVANDER.

CIV.

TO CLARINDA.

[*Friday, February* 1].

CLARINDA, my life, you have wounded my soul. Can I think of your being unhappy, even though it be not described in your pathetic elegance of language, without being miserable ? Clarinda, can I bear to be told from you that "you will not see me to-morrow night—that you wish the hour of parting were come?" Do not let us impose on ourselves by sounds. * * * * Why, my love, talk to me in such strong terms, every word of which cuts me to the very soul? You know a hint, the slightest signification of your wish, is to me a sacred command.

Be reconciled, my angel, to your God, yourself, and me; and I pledge you Sylvander's honour—an oath, I daresay, you will trust without reserve—that you shall never more have reason to complain of his conduct. Now, my love, do not wound our next meeting with any averted looks. * * * I have marked the line of conduct—a line, I know, exactly to your taste—and which I will inviolably keep; but do not you show the least inclination to make boundaries. Seeming distrust, where you know you may confide, is a cruel sin against sensibility.

" Delicacy, you know, it was which won me to you at once : take care you do not loosen the dearest, most sacred tie that unites us." Clarinda, I would not have stung _your_ soul—I would not have bruised _your_ spirit, as that harsh, crucifying "Take care," did _mine_; no not to have gained heaven! Let me again appeal to your dear self, if Sylvander, even when he seemingly half transgressed the laws of decorum, if he did not show more chastised, trembling, faltering delicacy, than the many of the world do in keeping these laws?

Oh Love and Sensibility, ye have conspired against my Peace! I love to madness, and I feel to torture! Clarinda, how can I forgive myself, that I have ever touched a single chord in your bosom with pain! Would I do it willingly? Would any consideration, any gratification, make me do so? Oh, did you love like me, you would not, you could not, deny or put off a meeting with the man who adores you; who would die a thousand deaths before he would injure you; and who must soon bid you a long farewell!

I had proposed bringing my bosom friend, Mr Ainslie, to-morrow evening, at his strong request, to see you; as he has only time to stay with us about ten minutes, for an engagement. But I shall hear from you : this afternoon, for mercy's sake!—for, till I hear from you, I am wretched. Oh Clarinda, the tie that binds me to thee is intwisted, incorporated with my dearest threads of life !

SYLVANDER.

CV.

TO CLARINDA.

I WAS on the way, my love, to meet you (I never do things by halves) when I got your card. Mr Ainslie goes out of town to-morrow morning to see a brother of his, who is newly arrived from France. I am determined that he and I shall call on you together. So look you, lest I should never see to-morrow, we will call on you to-night. Mary and you may put off tea till about seven, at which time, in the Galloway phrase, " an the beast be to the fore, and the branke bide hale," expect the humblest of your humble servants, and his dearest friend. We only propose staying half an hour—" for ought we ken." I could suffer the lash of misery eleven months in the year, were the twelfth to be composed of hours like yesternight. You are the soul of my enjoyment—all else is of the stuff of stocks and stones !

SYLVANDER.

CVI.

TO CLARINDA.

Sunday Noon.

I HAVE almost given up the Excise idea. I have been just now to wait on a great person, Miss ——'s friend, ——. Why will great people not only deafen us with the din of their equipage, and dazzle us with their fastidious pomp, but they must also be so very dictatorially wise ? I have been questioned like a child about my matters, and blamed and schooled for my inscription on the Stirling window. Come, Clarinda !—" Come, curse me, Jacob ; come, defy me, Israel !"

Sunday Night.

I have been with Miss Nimmo. She is indeed " a good soul," as my Clarinda finely says. She has reconciled me, in a good measure, to the world with her friendly prattle.

Schetki has sent me the song, set to a fine air of his composing. I have called the song Clarinda : I have carried it about in my pocket, and hummed it over all day.

Monday Morning.

If my prayers have any weight in Heaven, this morning looks in on you and finds you in the arms of peace, except where it is charmingly interrupted by the ardours of devotion. I find so much serenity of mind, so much positive pleasure, so much fearless daring toward the world, when I warm in devotion, or feel the glorious sensation—a consciousness of Almighty friendship—that I am sure I shall soon be an honest enthusiast.

> "How are thy servants blest, O Lord!
> How sure is their defence!
> Eternal wisdom is their guide,
> Their help Omnipotence."

I am, my dear madam, yours

SYLVANDER.

CVII.

TO CLARINDA.

Sunday Morning

I HAVE just been before the throne of my God, Clarinda; according to my association of ideas, my sentiments of love and friendship, I next devote myself to you. Yesternight I was happy—happiness that the world cannot give. I kindle at the recollection; but it is a flame where innocence looks smiling on, and honour stands by, a sacred guard. Your heart, your fondest wishes, your dearest thoughts, these are yours to bestow: your person is unapproachable by the laws of your country; and he loves not as I do who would make you miserable.

You are an angel, Clarinda; you are surely no mortal that " the earth owns." To kiss your hand, to live on your smile, is to me far more exquisite bliss than the dearest favours that the fairest of the sex, yourself excepted, can bestow.

Sunday Evening.

You are the constant companion of my thoughts. How wretched is the condition of one who is haunted with conscious guilt, and trembling under the idea of dreaded vengeance! and what a placid calm, what a charming secret enjoyment it gives, to bosom the kind feeling of friendship and the fond throes of love! Out upon the tempest of anger, the acrimonious gall of fretful impatience, the sullen frost of louring resentment, or the corroding poison of withered envy! They eat up the immortal part of man! If they spent their fury only on the unfortunate objects of them, it would be something in their favour; but these miserable passions, like traitor Iscariot, betray their lord and master.

Thou Almighty Author of peace, and goodness, and love! do thou give me the social heart that kindly tastes of every man's cup! Is it a draught of joy?—warm and open my heart to share it with cordial unenvying rejoicing! Is it the bitter portion of sorrow?—melt my heart with sincerely sympathetic woe!—above all, do thou give me the manly mind, that resolutely exemplifies, in life and manners, those sentiments which I would wish to be thought to possess! The friend of my soul; there, may I never deviate from the firmest fidelity and most active kindness! Clarinda, the dear object of my fondest love; there, may the most sacred inviolate honour, the most faithful kindling constancy, ever watch and animate my every thought and imagination!

Did you ever meet with the following lines spoken of religion—your darling topic ?—

" ' *Tis this*, my friend, that streaks our morning bright;
Tis this that gilds the horrors of our night;
When wealth forsakes us, and when friends are few,
When friends are faithless, or when foes pursue;

'Tis this that wards the blow, or stills the smart,
Disarms affliction, or repels its dart:
Within the breast bids purest rapture rise,
Bids smiling Conscience spread her cloudless skies.'

I met with these verses very early in life, and was so delighted with them that I have them by me, copied at school.

Good night, and sound rest, my dearest Clarinda!

SYLVANDER.

CVIII.

TO CLARINDA.

Thursday Night.

I CANNOT be easy, my Clarinda, while any sentiment respecting me in your bosom gives me pain. If there is no man on earth to whom your heart and affections are justly due, it may savour of imprudence, but never of criminality, to bestow that heart and those affections where you please. The God of love meant and made those delicious attachments to be bestowed on somebody; and even all the imprudence lies in bestowing them on an unworthy object. If this reasoning is conclusive, as it certainly is, I must be allowed to " talk of Love."

It is, perhaps, rather wrong to speak highly to a friend of his letter: it is apt to lay one under a little restraint in their future letters, and restraint is the death of a friendly epistle; but there is one passage in your last charming letter, Thomson or Shenstone never exceeded it, nor often came up to it. I shall certainly steal it, and set it in some future poetic production, and get immortal fame by it. 'Tis when you bid the scenes of nature remind me of Clarinda. Can I forget you, Clarinda? I would detest myself as a tasteless, unfeeling, insipid, infamous blockhead! I have loved woman of ordinary merit, whom I could have loved·for ever. You are the first, the only unexceptionable individual of the beauteous sex that I ever met with; and never woman more entirely possessed my soul! I know myself, and how far I can depend on passion's swell. It has been my peculiar study.

I thank you for going to Miers. Urge him, for necessity calls, to have it done by the middle of next week,—Wednesday the latest day. I want it for a breast-pin, to wear next my heart. I propose to keep sacred set times, to wander in the woods and wilds for meditation on you. Then, and only then, your lovely image shall be produced to the day, with a reverence akin to devotion.

＊　　＊　　＊　　＊　　＊

To-morrow night shall not be the last. Good night! I am perfectly stupid, as I supped late yesternight. SYLVANDER.

CIX.

TO CLARINDA.

Saturday Morning.

THERE is no time, my Clarinda, when the conscious thrilling chords of love and friendship give such delight as in the pensive hours of what our favourite Thomson calls " philosophic melancholy." The sportive insects who bask in the sunshine of prosperity, or the worms that luxuriant crawl amid their ample wealth of earth, they need no Clarinda — they would despise Sylvander, if they dared. The family of Misfortune—a numerous group of brothers and sisters !—they need a resting-place to their souls. Unnoticed, often condemned by the world,—in some degree, perhaps, condemned by themselves,—they feel the full enjoyment of ardent love, delicate, tender endearments, mutual esteem, and mutual reliance.

In this light I have often admired religion. In proportion as we are wrung with grief or distracted with anxiety, the ideas of a compassionate Deity, an Almighty Protector, are doubly dear.

> " 'Tis this, my friend, that streaks our morning bright;
> 'Tis this that gilds the horrors of our night."

I have been this morning taking a peep through, as Young finely says, " the dark postern of time long elapsed ;" and you will easily guess 'twas a rueful prospect. What a tissue of thoughtlessness, weakness, and folly ! My life reminded me of a ruined temple : what strength, what proportion in some parts !—what unsightly gaps, what prostrate ruins in others ! I kneeled down before the Father of Mercies, and said, " Father, I have sinned against Heaven, and in thy sight, and am no more worthy to be called thy son !" I rose, eased and strengthened. I despise the superstition of a fanatic, but I love the religion of a man. " The future," said I to myself, " is still before me : there let me

> " On reason build resolve—
> That column of true majesty in man !"

I have difficulties many to encounter," said I ; " but they are not absolutely insuperable : and where is firmness of mind shewn but in exertion ? Mere declamation is bombast rant. Besides, whereever I am, or in whatever situation I may be,

> " 'Tis nought to me
> Since God is ever present, ever felt,
> In the void waste as in the city full ;
> And where he vital breathes, there must be joy."

Saturday Night, Half after Ten.

What luxury of bliss I was enjoying this time yesternight! My ever dearest Clarinda, you have stolen away my soul : but you have refined, you have exalted it; you have given it a stronger sense of virtue, and a stronger relish for piety. Clarinda, first of

your sex! if ever I am the veriest wretch on earth to forget you
—if ever your lovely image is effaced from my soul,

> " May I be lost, no eye to weep my end,
> And find no earth that's base enough to bury me!"

What trifling silliness is the childish fondness of the every-day
children of the world! 'Tis the unmeaning toying of the young-
lings of the fields and forests; but, where sentiment and fancy
unite their sweets, where taste and delicacy refine, where wit adds
the flavour, and good sense gives strength and spirit to all, * *

SYLVANDER.

CX.

TO CLARINDA.

* * * I AM a discontented ghost, a perturbed spirit.
Clarinda, if ever you forget Sylvander, may you be happy, but he
will be miserable.

Oh what a fool I am in love! what an extravagant prodigal
of affection! Why are your sex called the tender sex, when I
never have met with one who can repay me in passion? They
are either not so rich in love as I am, or they are niggards where
I am lavish.

O Thou, whose I am, and whose are all my ways! Thou see'st
me here, the hapless wreck of tides and tempests in my own
bosom: do Thou direct to thyself that ardent love, for which I
have so often sought a return in vain from my fellow-creatures!
If Thy goodness has yet such a gift in store for me as an equal
return of affection from her who, Thou knowest, is dearer to me
than life, do Thou bless and hallow our band of love and friend-
ship; watch over us, in all our outgoings and incomings for good;
and may the tie that unites our hearts be strong and indissoluble
as the thread of man's immortal life!

I am just going to take your blackbird, the sweetest, I am
sure that ever sung, and prune its wings a little.

SYLVANDER.

CXI.

TO CLARINDA.

Tuesday Morning.

I CANNOT go out to-day, my dearest love, without sending you
half a line by way of a sin-offering; but believe me, 'twas the sin
of ignorance. Could you think that I intended to hurt you by
anything I said yesternight? Nature has been too kind to you
for your happiness, your delicacy, your sensibility. Oh why
should such glorious qualifications be the fruitful source of wo'

You have "murdered sleep" to me last night. I went to bed impressed with an idea that you were unhappy; and every start I closed my eyes, busy Fancy painted you in such scenes of romantic misery that I would almost be persuaded you are not well this morning.

> ' If I unwitting have offended,
> Impute it not,"
>   " But while we live
> But one short hour, perhaps, between us two
> Let there be peace."

If Mary is not gone by the time this reaches you, give her my best compliments. She is a charming girl, and highly worthy of the noblest love.

I send you a poem to read till I call on you this night, which will be about nine. I wish I could procure some potent spell, some fairy charm, that would protect from injury, or restore to rest, that bosom chord, " tremblingly alive all o'er," on which hangs your peace of mind. I thought—vainly, I fear, thought—that the devotion of love—love strong as even you can feel, love guarded, invulnerably guarded by all the purity of virtue, and all the pride of honour—I thought such a love might make you happy. Shall I be mistaken? I can no more, for hurry.   SYLVANDER.

CXII.

TO CLARINDA.

Friday Morning, 7 o'clock.

YOUR fears for Mary are truly laughable. I suppose, my love, you and I showed her a scene which, perhaps, made her wish that she had a swain, and one who could love like me; and 'tis a thousand pities that so good a heart as hers should want an aim, an object. I am miserably stupid this morning. Yesterday I dined with a baronet, and sat pretty late over the bottle. And " who hath wo—who hath sorrow? they that tarry long at the wine; they that go to seek mixed wine." Forgive me, likewise, a quotation from my favourite author. Solomon's knowledge of the world is very great. He may be looked on as the " Spectator" or " Adventurer" of his day: and it is, indeed, surprising what a sameness has ever been in human nature. The broken, but strongly characterising hints, that the royal author gives us of the manners of the court of Jerusalem and country of Israel, are in their great outlines the same pictures that London and England, Versailles and France, exhibit some three thousand years later. The loves in the " Song of Songs" are all in the spirit of Lady M. W Montagu, or Madame Ninon de l'Enclos; though, for my part, I dislike both the ancient and modern voluptuaries; and will dare to affirm that such an attachment as mine to Clarinda, and such evenings as she and I have spent, are what these greatly respectable and deeply experienced judges of life and love never dreamed of.

I shall be with you this evening between eight and nine, and shall keep as sober hours as you could wish. I am ever, my dear madam, yours   SYLVANDER.

CXIII.

TO CLARINDA.

MY EVER DEAREST CLARINDA,—I make a numerous dinner-party wait me while I read yours and write this. Do not require that I should cease to love you, to adore you in my soul; 'tis to me impossible: your peace and happiness are to me dearer than my soul. Name the terms on which you wish to see me, to correspond with me, and you have them. I must love, pine, mourn, and adore in secret: this you must not deny me. You will ever be to me

> " Dear as the light that visits those sad eyes,
> Dear as the ruddy drops that warm my heart."

I have not patience to read the Puritanic scrawl. Sophistry! Ye heavens, ye look down with approving eyes on a passion inspired by the purest flame, and guarded by truth, delicacy, and honour; but the half-inch soul of an unfeeling, cold-blooded, pitiful Presbyterian bigot cannot forgive anything above his dungeon-bosom and foggy head.

Farewell! I'll be with you to-morrow evening; and be at rest in your mind. I will be yours in the way you think most to your happiness. I dare not proceed. I love, and will love you; and will, with joyous confidence, approach the throne of the Almighty Judge of men with your dear idea; and will despise the scum of sentiment and the mist of sophistry.   SYLVANDER.

CXIV.

TO CLARINDA.

Wednesday, Midnight.

MADAM,—After a wretched day, I am preparing for a sleepless night. I am going to address myself to the Almighty Witness of my actions—some time, perhaps very soon, my Almighty Judge. I am not going to be the advocate of Passion: be Thou my inspirer and testimony, O God, as I plead the cause of truth!

I have read over your friend's haughty dictatorial letter: you are only answerable to your God in such a matter. Who gave any fellow-creature of yours (a fellow-creature incapable of being your judge, because not your peer) a right to catechise, scold, undervalue, abuse, and insult—wantonly and unhumanly to insult—you thus? I don't wish, not even wish, to deceive you, madam. The Searcher of hearts is my witness how dear you are to me; but though it were possible you could be still dearer to me, I would not even kiss your hand at the expense of your conscience. Away with declamation! let us appeal to the bar of common sense. It is not mouthing everything sacred; it is not vague ranting assertions; it is not assuming—haughtily and insultingly assuming—the dictatorial language of a Roman pontiff, that must dissolve a union like ours. Tell me, madam, are you under the least shadow of an obligation to bestow your love, tenderness, caresses, affections, heart and soul, on Mr M'Lehose—the man who has repeatedly, habitually, and barbarously broken through every tie of duty, nature, or gratitude to you? The laws of your country, indeed, for the most useful reasons of policy and sound government, have made your person inviolate; but are your heart and affections bound to one who gives not the least return of either to you? You cannot do it; it is not in the nature of things that you are bound to do it; the common feelings of humanity forbid it. Have you, then, a heart and affections which are no man's right? You have. It would be highly, ridiculously absurd to suppose the contrary. Tell me, then, in the name of common-sense, can it be wrong, is such a supposition compatible with the plainest ideas of right and wrong, that it is improper to bestow the heart and there affections on another—while that bestowing is not in the smallest degree hurtful to your duty to God, to your children, to yourself, or to society at large.

This is the great test; the consequences—let us see them. In a widowed, forlorn, lonely situation, with a bosom glowing with love and tenderness, yet so delicately situated that you cannot indulge these nobler feelings, ...   SYLVANDER.

CXV.

TO CLARINDA.

"I AM distressed for thee, my brother Jonathan." I have suffered, Clarinda, from your letter. My soul was in arms at the sad perusal. I dreaded that I had acted wrong. If I have wronged you, God forgive me. But, Clarinda, be comforted. Let us raise the tone of our feelings a little higher and bolder. A fellow-creature who leaves us—who spurns us without just cause, though once our bosom friend—up with a little honest pride: let him go. How shall I comfort you, who am the cause of the injury ? Can I wish that I had never seen you—that we had never met ? No, I never will. But, have I thrown you friendless ?—there is almost distraction in the thought. Father of mercies! against Thee often have I sinned : through Thy grace I will endeavour to do so no more. She who Thou knowest is dearer to me than myself—pour Thou the balm of peace into her past wounds, and hedge her about with Thy peculiar care, all her future days and nights. Strengthen her tender, noble mind firmly to suffer and magnanimously to bear. Make me worthy of that friendship —that love she honours me with. May my attachment to her be pure as devotion, and lasting as immortal life! O, Almighty Goodness, hear me! Be to her at all times, particularly in the hour of distress or trial, a friend and comforter, a guide and guard.

> " How are thy servants blest, O Lord,
> How sure is their defence!
> Eternal wisdom is their guide,
> Their help Omnipotence."

Forgive me, Clarinda, the injury I have done you. To-night I shall be with you, as indeed I shall be ill at ease till I see you.

SYLVANDER.

CXVI.

TO CLARINDA.

Two o'clock.

I JUST now received your first letter of yesterday, by the careless negligence of the penny-post. Clarinda, matters are grown very serious with us ; then seriously hear me, and hear me, Heaven—I met you, my dear . . . . . , by far the first of womankind, at least to me ; I esteemed, I loved you at first sight : the longer I am acquainted with you, the more innate amiableness and worth I discover in you. You have suffered a loss, I confess, for my sake : but if the firmest, steadiest, warmest friendship—if every endeavour to be worthy of your friendship—if a love, strong as the ties of nature, and holy as the duties of religion— all these can make anything like a compensation for the ev I have occasioned you, if they be worth your acceptance, or can in the least add to your enjoyments—so help Sylvander, ye Powers above, in his hour of need, as he freely gives these all to Clarinda !

I esteem you, I love you as a friend ; I admire you, I love you as a woman, beyond any one in all the circle of creation ; I know I shall continue to esteem you, to love you, to pray for you—nay, to pray for myself for your sake.

Expect me at eight—and believe me to be ever, my dearest madam, yours most entirely, SYLVANDER.

CXVII.

TO CLARINDA.

WHEN matters, my love, are desperate, we must put on a desperate face—

> "On reason build resolve,
> That column of true majesty in man."—

or, as the same author finely says in another place,

> "Let thy soul spring up,
> And lay strong hold for help on Him that made thee."

I am yours, Clarinda, for life. Never be discouraged at all this. Look forward : in a few weeks I shall be somewhere or other, out of the possibility of seeing you : till then, I shall write you often, but visit you seldom. Your fame, your welfare, your happiness, are dearer to me than any gratification whatever. Be comforted, my love! the present moment is the worst; the lenient hand of time is daily and hourly either lightening the burden, or making us insensible to the weight. None of these friends—I mean Mr —— and the other gentleman—can hurt your worldly support : and of their friendship, in a little time you will learn to be easy, and by and by to be happy without it. A decent means of livelihood in the world, an approving God, a peaceful conscience, and one firm, trusty friend—can anybody that has these be said to be unhappy? These are yours.

To-morrow evening I shall be with you about eight, probably for the last time till I return to Edinburgh. In the meantime, should any of these two unlucky friends question me, whether I am *the man*, I do not think they are entitled to any information. As to their jealousy and spying, I despise them. Adieu, my dearest madam l   SYLVANDER.

CXVIII.

TO MR JAMES CANDLISH.

EDINBURGH, 1788.

MY DEAR FRIEND,—If once I were gone from this scene of hurry and dissipation, I promise myself the pleasure of that correspondence being renewed which has been so long broken. At present I have time for nothing. Dissipation and business engross every moment. I am engaged in assisting an honest Scotch enthusiast,* a friend of mine, who is an engraver, and has taken it into his head to publish a collection of all our songs set to music, of which the words and music are done by Scotsmen. This, you will easily guess, is an undertaking exactly to my taste. I have collected,

* Mr Johnson, publisher of the *Scots Musical Museum.*

begged, borrowed, and stolen, all the songs I could meet with. Pompey's Ghost, words and music, I beg from you immediately, to go into his second number—the first is already published. I shall shew you the first number when I see you in Glasgow, which will be in a fortnight or less. Do be so kind as to send me the song in a day or two—you cannot imagine how much it will oblige me.

Direct to me at Mr W. Cruikshank's, St James's Square, New Town, Edinburgh. R. B.

CXIX.
TO MRS DUNLOP.

EDINBURGH, *February* 12, 1788.

SOME things in your late letters hurt me : not that *you say them*, but that *you mistake me*. Religion, my honoured madam, has not only been all my life my chief dependence, but my dearest enjoyment. I have indeed been the luckless victim of wayward follies ; but, alas! I have ever been "more fool than knave." A mathematician without religion is a probable character ; an irreligious poet is a monster. R. B.

CXX.
TO THE REV. JOHN SKINNER.

EDINBURGH, 14*th February* 1788.

REVEREND AND DEAR SIR,—I have been a cripple now near three months, though I am getting vastly better, and have been very much hurried besides, or else I would have wrote you sooner. I must beg your pardon for the epistle you sent me appearing in the magazine. I had given a copy or two to some of my intimate friends, but did not know of the printing of it till the publication of the magazine. However, as it does great honour to us both, you will forgive it.

The second volume of the songs I mentioned to you in my last is published to-day. I send you a copy, which I beg you will accept as a mark of the veneration I have long had, and shall ever have, for your character, and of the claim I make to your continued acquaintance. Your songs appear in the third volume, with your name in the index ; as I assure you, sir, I have heard your *Tullochgorum*, particularly among our west country folks, given to many different names, and most commonly to the immortal author of *The Minstrel*, who indeed never wrote anything superior to *Gie's a Sang, Montgomery cried.* Your brother has promised me your verses to the Marquis of Huntly's reel, which certainly deserve a place in the collection. My kind host, Mr Cruikshank, of the High School here, and said to be one of the best Latins of this age, begs me to make you his grateful acknowledgments for the entertainment he has got in a Latin publication of yours, that I borrowed for him from your acquaintance and much-respected friend in this place, the Reverend Dr Webster. Mr Cruikshank maintains that you write the best Latin since Buchanan. I leave Edinburgh to-morrow, but shall return in three weeks. Your song you mentioned in your last, to the tune of *Dumbarton Drums*, and the other, which you say was done by a brother in trade of mine, a ploughman, I shall thank you for a copy of each. I am ever, reverend sir, with the most respectful esteem and sincere veneration, yours,   R. B.

CXXI.

TO MR RICHARD BROWN.

EDINBURGH, *February* 15, 1788.

MY DEAR FRIEND,—I received yours with the greatest pleasure. I shall arrive at Glasgow on Monday evening; and beg, if possible, you will meet me on Tuesday: I shall wait you Tuesday all day. I shall be found at Davies's Black Bull Inn. I am hurried, as if hunted by fifty devils, else I should go to Greenock; but if you cannot possibly come, write me, if possible, to Glasgow, on Monday; or direct to me at Mossgiel, by Mauchline; and name a day and place in Ayrshire, within a fortnight from this date, where I may meet you. I only stay a fortnight in Ayrshire, and return to Edinburgh. I am ever, my dearest friend, yours,   R. B.

CXXII.

TO MISS CHALMERS.

EDINBURGH, *Sunday, February.*

TO-MORROW, my dear madam, I leave Edinburgh. I have altered all my plans of future life. A farm that I could live in, I could not find; and, indeed, after the necessary support my brother and the rest of the family required, I could not venture on farming in that style suitable to my feelings. You will condemn me for the next step I have taken: I have entered into the Excise. I stay in the west about three weeks, and then return to Edinburgh for six weeks' instructions; afterwards, for I get employ instantly, I go *où il plait à Dieu—et mon roi*. I have chosen this, my dear friend, after mature deliberation. The question is not, at what door of Fortune's palace shall we enter in, but what doors does she open to us? I was not likely to get anything to do. I wanted *un bût*, which is a dangerous, an unhappy situation. I got this without any hanging on or mortifying solicitation: it is immediate bread; and though poor in comparison with the last eighteen months of my existence, 'tis luxury in comparison of all my preceding life: besides, the commissioners are some of them my acquaintances, and all of them my firm friends.   R. B.

CXXIII.

TO MRS ROSE OF KILRAVOCK.

EDINBURGH, *February* 17, 1788.

MADAM,—You are much indebted to some indispensable business I have had on my hands, otherwise my gratitude threatened such a return for your obliging favour as would have tired your patience. It but poorly expresses my feelings to say, that I am sensible of your kindness. It may be said of hearts such as yours is, and such, I hope, mine is, much more justly than Addison applies it—

" Some souls by instinct to each other turn."

There was something in my reception at Kilravock so different from the cold, obsequious, dancing-school bow of politeness, that it almost got into my head that friendship had occupied her ground without the intermediate march of acquaintance. I wish I could transcribe, or rather transfuse into language, the glow of my heart when I read your letter. My ready fancy, with colours more mellow than life itself, painted the beautiful wild scenery of Kilravock; the venerable grandeur of the castle; the spreading woods; the winding river, gladly leaving his unsightly, heathy source, and lingering with apparent delight as he passes the fairy walk at the bottom of the garden; your late distressful anxieties; your present enjoyments; your dear little angel, the pride of your hopes; my aged friend, venerable in worth and years, whose loyalty and other virtues will strongly entitle her to the support of the Almighty Spirit here, and his peculiar favour in a happier state of existence. You cannot imagine, madam, how much such feelings delight me: they are my dearest proofs of my own immortality. Should I never revisit the north, as probably I never will, nor again see your hospitable mansion, were I, some twenty years hence, to see your little fellow's name making a proper figure in a newspaper paragraph, my heart would bound with pleasure.

I am assisting a friend in a collection of Scottish songs, set to their proper tunes; every air worth preserving is to be included: among others I have given *Morag*, and some few Highland airs which pleased me most, a dress which will be more generally known, though far, far inferior in real merit. As a small mark of my grateful esteem, I beg leave to present you with a copy of the work, as far as it is printed : the Man of Feeling, that first of men,* has promised to transmit it by the first opportunity.

I beg to be remembered most respectfully to my venerable friend, and to your little Highland chieftain.† When you see the "two fair spirits of the hill" at Kildrummie,‡ tell them that I have done myself the honour of setting myself down as one of their admirers for at least twenty years to come—consequently they must look upon me as an acquaintance for the same period ; but, as the apostle Paul says, " this I ask of grace, not of debt." I have the honour to be, madam, &c.   R. B.

CXXIV.

TO CLARINDA.

GLASGOW, *Monday Evening, Nine o'clock.*

THE attraction of love, I find, is in an inverse proportion to the attraction of the Newtonian philosophy. In the system of Sir Isaac, the nearer objects were to one another the stronger was the attractive force. In my system, every milestone that marked my progress from Clarinda awakened a keener pang of attachment to her. How do you feel, my love ? Is your heart ill at ease ? I fear it. God forbid that these persecutors should harass that peace which is more precious to me than my own. Be assured I shall ever think on you, muse on you, and, in my moments of devotion, pray for you. The hour that you are not in my thoughts, " be that hour darkness ; let the shadows of death cover it ; let it not be numbered in the hours of the day !"

> " When I forget the darling theme,
> Be my tongue mute! my fancy paint no more!
> And, dead to joy, forget my heart to beat!"

I have just met with my old friend, the ship-captain (Mr Richard Brown)—guess my pleasure : to meet you could alone have given me more. My brother William, too, the young saddler, has come to Glasgow to meet me ; and here are we three spending the evening.

I arrived here too late to write by post; but I'll wrap half-a-dozen sheets of blank paper together, and send it by the Fly, under the name of a parcel. You will hear from me next post-town. I would write you a longer letter, but for the present circumstances of my friend.

Adieu, my Clarinda ! I am just going to propose your health by way of grace-drink.   SYLVANDER.

* Mr Henry Mackenzie.
† Mrs Rose's mother, and her son Hugh.
‡ Miss Sophia Brodie of Lethin, and Miss Rose of Kilravock.

CXXV.

TO CLARINDA.

KILMARNOCK, *Friday* [Feb. 22].

I WROTE you, my dear madam, the moment I alighted in Glasgow. Since then I have not had opportunity; for in Paisley, where I arrived next day, my worthy, wise friend, Mr Pattison, did not allow me a moment's respite. I was there ten hours; during which time I was introduced to nine men worth six thousands; five men worth ten thousands; his brother, richly worth twenty thousands; and a young weaver, who will have thirty thousands good when his father, who has no more children than the said weaver, and a Whig Kirk, dies. Mr P. was bred a zealous Antiburgher; but during his widowerhood he has found their strictness incompatible with certain compromises he is often obliged to make with those powers of darkness—the devil, the world, and the flesh. * * * His only daughter,—who, " if the beast be to the fore, and the branks bide hale," will have seven thousand pounds when her old father steps into the dark factory-office of eternity with his well-thrummed web of life,—has put him again and again in a commendable fit of indignation by requesting a harpsichord. "Oh, these boarding-schools!" exclaims my prudent friend; " she was a good spinner and sewer till I was advised by her foes and mine to give her a year of Edinburgh!"

After two bottles more, my much-respected friend opened up to me a project—a legitimate child of Wisdom and Good Sense: 'twas no less than a long-thought-on and deeply-matured design, to marry a girl fully as elegant in her form as the famous priestess whom Saul consulted in his last hours, and who had been second maid of honour to his deceased wife. This, you may be sure, I highly applauded; so I hope for a pair of gloves by and by. I spent the two bypast days at Dunlop House, with that worthy family to whom I was deeply indebted early in my poetic career: and in about two hours I shall present your " twa wee sarkies " to the little fellow. My dearest Clarinda, you are ever present with me; and these hours, that drawl by among the fools and rascals of this world, are only supportable in the idea, that they are the forerunners of that happy hour that ushers me to " the mistress of my soul." Next week I shall visit Dumfries, and next again return to Edinburgh. My letters, in these hurrying dissipated hours, will be heavy trash; but you know the writer. God bless you! SYLVANDER.

CXXVI.

TO MR RICHARD BROWN.

MOSSGIEL, 24th February 1788.

MY DEAR SIR,—I arrived here, at my brother's, only yesterday, after fighting my way through Paisley and Kilmarnock against those old powerful foes of mine,—the devil, the world, and the flesh,—so terrible in the fields of dissipation. I have met with few incidents in my life which gave me so much pleasure as meeting you in Glasgow. There is a time of life beyond which we cannot form a tie worth the name of friendship. " Oh youth ! enchanting stage, profusely blest." Life is a fairy scene : almost all that deserves the name of enjoyment or pleasure is only a charming delusion ; and in comes repining age, in all the gravity of hoary wisdom, and wretchedly chases away the bewitching phantom. When I think of life, I resolve to keep a strict look-out in the course of economy, for the sake of worldly convenience and independence of mind ; to cultivate intimacy with a few of the companions of youth, that they may be the friends of age; never to refuse my liquorish humour a handful of the sweetmeats of life, when they come not too dear ; and, for futurity—

> The present moment is our ain,
> The neist we never saw!

How like you my philosophy ? Give my best compliments to Mrs B., and believe me to be, my dear sir, yours most truly, .
                                                                R. B.

———

CXXVII.

TO CLARINDA.

CUMNOCK [Sunday], 2d March 1788.

I HOPE, and am certain, that my generous Clarinda will not think my silence, for now a long week, has been in any degree owing to my forgetfulness. I have been tossed about through the country ever since I wrote you ; and am here, returning from Dumfriesshire, at an inn, the post-office of the place, with just so long time as my horse eats his corn, to write you. I have been hurried with business and dissipation almost equal to the insidious decree of the Persian monarch's mandate, when he forbade asking petition of God or man for forty days. Had the venerable prophet been as throng [busy] as I, he had not broken the decree, at least not thrice a-day.

I am thinking my farming scheme will yet hold. A worthy, intelligent farmer, my father's friend and my own, has been with me on the spot : he thinks the bargain practicable. I am myself on a more serious review of the lands, much better pleased with them. I wont mention this in writing to anybody but you and [Ainslie]. Don't accuse me of being fickle: I have the two plans of life before me, and I wish to adopt the one most likely to procure me independence. I shall be in Edinburgh next week. I long to see you: your image is omnipresent to me; nay, I am convinced I would soon idolatrize it most seriously—so much do absence and memory improve the medium through which one sees the much-loved object. To-night, at the sacred hour of eight, I expect to meet you—at the Throne of Grace. I hope, as I go home to-night, to find a letter from you at the post-office in Mauchline. I have just once seen that dear hand since I left Edinburgh—a letter indeed which much affected me. Tell me, first of womankind! will my warmest attachment, my sincerest friendship, my correspondence—will they be any compensation for the sacrifices you make for my sake? If they will, they are yours. If I settle on the farm I propose, I am just a day and a half's ride from Edinburgh. We will meet—don't you say "perhaps too often!"

Farewell, my fair, my charming poetess! May all good things ever attend you! I am ever, my dearest madam, yours,

SYLVANDER.

CXXVIII.

TO MR WILLIAM CRUIKSHANK.

MAUCHLINE, 3d March 1788.

MY DEAR SIR,—Apologies for not writing are frequently like apologies for not singing—the apology better than the song. I have fought my way severely through the savage hospitality of this country, [the object of all hosts being] to send every guest drunk to bed if they can. . . . .

I should return my thanks for your   hospitality (I leave a blank for the epithet, as I know none can do it justice) to a poor wayfaring bard, who was spent and almost overpowered fighting with prosaic wickednesses in high places; but I am afraid lest you should burn the letter whenever you come to the passage, so I pass over it in silence. I am just returned from visiting Mr Miller's farm. The friend whom I told you I would take with me was highly pleased with the farm; and as he is, without exception, the most intelligent farmer in the country, he has staggered me a good deal. I have the two plans of life before me: I shall balance them to the best of my judgment, and fix on the most eligible. I have written Mr Miller, and shall wait on him when I come to town, which shall be the beginning or middle of next week: I would be in sooner, but my unlucky knee is rather worse and I fear for some time will scarcely stand the fatigue of my Excise instructions. I only mention these ideas to you; and, indeed, except Mr Ainslie, whom I intend writing to to-morrow, I will not write at all to Edinburgh till I return to it. I would send my compliments to Mr Nicol, but he would be hurt if he knew I wrote to anybody, and not to him; so I shall only beg my best, kindest, kindest compliments to my worthy hostess and the sweet little Rosebud.

So soon as I am settled in the routine of life, either as an excise-officer or as a farmer, I propose myself great ·pleasure from a regular correspondence with the only man almost I ever saw who joined the most attentive prudence with the warmest generosity.

I am much interested for that best of men, Mr Wood. I hope he is in better health and spirits than when I saw him last. I am ever, my dearest friend, your obliged, humble servant, R. B.

CXXIX.

TO MR ROBERT AINSLIE.

MAUCHLINE, 3d *March* 1788.

MY DEAR FRIEND—I am just returned from Mr Miller's farm. My old friend whom I took with me was highly pleased with the bargain, and advised me to accept of it. He is the most intelligent, sensible farmer in the county, and his advice has staggered me a good deal. I have the two plans before me; I shall endeavour to balance them to the best of my judgment, and fix on the most eligible. On the whole, if I find Mr Miller in the same favourable disposition as when I saw him last, I shall in all probability turn farmer.

I have been through sore tribulation, and under much buffetting of the Wicked One, since I came to this country. Jean I found banished like a martyr—forlorn, destitute, and friendless. I have reconciled her to her mother. * * *

I shall be in Edinburgh the middle of next week. My farming ideas I shall keep private till I see. I got a letter from Clarinda yesterday, and she tells me she has got no letter of mine but one. Tell her that I·wrote to her from Glasgow, from Kilmarnock, from Mauchline, and yesterday from Cumnock, as I returned from Dumfries. Indeed, she is the only person in Edinburgh I have written to till this day. How are your soul and body putting up? —a little like man and wife, I suppose. Your faithful friend, R. B.

CXXX.

TO THE SAME.

MAUCHLINE, *Between 3d and 8th March* 1788.

MY DEAR SIR,—My life, since I saw you last, has been one continued hurry; that savage hospitality which knocks a man down with strong liquors is the devil. I have a sore warfare in this world—the devil, the world, and the flesh are three formidable foes. The first I generally try to fly from; the second, alas! generally flies from me; but the third is my plague, worse than the ten plagues of Egypt.

I have been looking over several farms in this country; one, in particular, in Nithsdale, pleased me so well, that if my offer to the proprietor is accepted, I shall commence farmer at Whitsunday. If farming do not appear eligible, I shall have recourse to my other shift; but this to a friend.

I set out for Edinburgh on Monday morning; how long I stay there is uncertain, but you will know so soon as I can inform you myself. However, I determine poesy must be laid aside for some time; my mind has been vitiated with idleness, and it will take a good deal of effort to habituate it to the routine of business. I am, my dear sir, yours sincerely, R. B.

CXXXI.

TO CLARINDA.

[*March* 6, 1788.]

I OWN myself guilty, Clarinda: I should have written you last week. But when you recollect, my dearest madam, that yours of this night's post is only the third I have from you, and that this is the fifth or sixth I have sent to you, you will not reproach me, with a good grace, for unkindness. I have always some kind of idea not to sit down to write a letter, except I have time, and possession of my faculties, so as to do some justice to my letter; which at present is rarely my situation. For instance, yesterday I dined at a friend's at some distance: the savage hospitality of this country spent me the most part of the night over the nauseous potion in the bowl. This day—sick—headache—low spirits— miserable—fasting, except for a draught of water or small beer. Now eight o'clock at night; only able to crawl ten minutes' walk into Mauchline, to wait the post, in the pleasurable hope of hearing from the mistress of my soul.

But truce with all this! When I sit down to write to you, all is happiness and peace. A hundred times a day do I figure you before your taper, your book or work laid aside as I get within the room. How happy have I been! and how little of that scantling portion of time, called the life of man, is sacred to happiness, much less transport.

I could moralise to-night like a death's-head.

> " O what is life, that thoughtless wish of all!
> A drop of honey in a draught of gall."

Nothing astonishes me more, when a little sickness clogs the wheels of life, than the thoughtless career we run in the hour of health. " None saith, where is God, my maker, that giveth songs in the night : who teacheth us more knowledge than the beasts of the field, and more understanding than the fowls of the air? "

Give me, my Maker, to remember thee! Give me to act up to the dignity of my nature! Give me to feel " another's wo ; " and continue with me that dear loved friend that feels with mine !

The dignifying and dignified consciousness of an honest man, and the well-grounded trust in approving Heaven, are two most substantial foundations of happiness. * * * *

I could not have written a page to any mortal except yourself. I'll write you by Sunday's post. Adieu! Good-night!

SYLVANDER.

CXXXII.

TO CLARINDA.

MOSSGIEL, *7th March* 1788.

CLARINDA, I have been so stung with your reproach for unkindness,—a sin so unlike me,—a sin I detest more than a breach of the whole Decalogue, fifth, sixth, seventh, and ninth articles excepted,—that I believe I shall not rest in my grave about it, if I die before I see you. You have often allowed me the head to judge, and the heart to feel, the influence of female excellence : was it not blasphemy, then, against your own charms and against my feelings, to suppose that a short fortnight could abate my passion ?

You, my love, may have your cares and anxieties to disturb you ; but they are the usual occurrences of life. Your future views are fixed, and your mind in a settled routine. Could not you, my ever dearest madam, make a little allowance for a man, after long absence, paying a short visit to a country full of friends, relations, and early intimates ? Cannot you guess, my Clarinda, what thoughts, what cares, what anxious forebodings, hopes, and fears, must crowd the breast of the man of keen sensibility, when no less is on the *tapis* than his aim, his employment, his very existence through future life ?

To be overtopped in anything else, I can bear: but in the tests of generous love, I defy all mankind!—not even to the tender, the fond, the loving Clarinda; she whose strength of attachment, whose melting soul, may vie with Eloisa and Sappho; not even she can overpay the affection she owes me!

Now that, not my apology, but my defence, is made, I feel my soul respire more easily. I know you will go along with me in my justification: would to Heaven you could in my adoption, too! I mean the adoption beneath the stars—an adoption where I might revel in the immediate beams of

"She the bright sun of all her sex."

I would not have you, my dear madam, so much hurt at Miss Nimmo's coldness. 'Tis placing yourself below her, an honour she by no means deserves. We ought, when we wish to be economists in happiness—we ought, in the first place, to fix the standard of our own character; and when, on full examination, we know where we stand, and how much ground we occupy, let us contend for it as property! and those who seem to doubt or deny us what is justly ours, let us either pity their prejudices or despise their judgment. I know, my dear, you will say this is self-conceit; but I call it self-knowledge. The one is the overweaning opinion of a fool, who fancies himself to be what he wishes himself to be thought; the other is the honest justice that a man of sense, who has thoroughly examined the subject, owes to himself. Without this standard, this column in our own mind, we are perpetually at the mercy of the petulance, the mistakes, the prejudices, nay, the very weakness and wickedness of our fellow-creatures.

I urge this, my dear, both to conform myself in the doctrine which, I assure you, I sometimes need, and because I know that this causes you often much disquiet. To return to Miss Nimmo. She is most certainly a worthy soul; and equalled by very, very few in goodness of heart. But can she boast more goodness of heart than Clarinda? Not even prejudice will dare to say so: for penetration and decernment, Clarinda sees far beyond her. To wit, Miss Nimmo dare make no pretence: to Clarinda's wit, scarce any of her sex dare make pretence. Personal charms, it would be ridiculous to run the parallel: and for conduct in life Miss Nimmo was never called out, either much to do, or to suffer. Clarinda has been both; and has performed her part, where Miss Nimmo would have sunk at the bare idea.

Away, then, with these disquietudes! Let us pray with the honest weaver of Kilbarchan, "Lord, send us a gude conceit o' oursel!" or, in the words of the auld sang,

"Who does me disdain, I can scorn them again,
And I'll never mind any such foes."

There is an error in the commerce of intimacy. * * *
Happy is our lot, indeed, when we meet with an honest mer-

chant, who is qualified to deal with us on our own terms; but that is a rarity: with almost everybody we must pocket our pearls, less or more, and learn, in the old Scots phrase, " To gie sic like as we get." For this reason we should try to erect a kind of bank or storehouse in our own mind; or, as the Psalmist says, " We should commune with our own hearts and be still." * * *

I wrote you yesternight, which will reach you long before this can. I may write Mr Ainslie before I see him, but I am not sure.

Farewell! and remember   SYLVANDER.

CXXXIII.

TO MR RICHARD BROWN.

MAUCHLINE, 7th March 1788.

I HAVE been out of the country, my dear friend, and have not had an opportunity of writing till now, when I am afraid you will be gone out of the country too. I have been looking at farms, and, after all, perhaps I might settle in the character of a farmer. I have got so vicious a bent to idleness, and have ever been so little a man of business, that it will take no ordinary effort to bring my mind properly into the routine; but you will say a " great effort is worthy of you." I say so myself, and butter up my vanity with all the stimulating compliments I can think of. Men of grave geometrical minds, the sons of " which was to be demonstrated," may cry up reason as much as they please; but I have always found an honest passion, or native instinct, the truest auxiliary in the warfare of this world. Reason almost always comes to me like an unlucky wife to a poor fellow of a husband—just in sufficient time to add her reproaches to his other grievances.   R. B.

CXXXIV.

TO MR ROBERT MUIR.

MOSSGIEL, 7th March 1788.

DEAR SIR,—I have partly changed my ideas, my dear friend, since I saw you. I took old Glenconnor with me to Mr Miller's farm; and he was so pleased with it, that I have wrote an offer to Mr Miller, which, if he accepts, I shall sit down a plain farmer— the happiest of lives when a man can live by it. In this case I shall not stay in Edinburgh above a week. I set out on Monday, and would have come by Kilmarnock, but there are several small sums owing me for my first edition about Galstone and Newmills, and I shall set off so early as to despatch my business and reach

Glasgow by night. When I return, I shall devote a forenoon or two to make some kind of acknowledgment for all the kindness I owe your friendship. Now that I hope to settle with some credit and comfort at home, there was not any friendship or friendly correspondence that promised me more pleasure than yours ; I hope I will not be disappointed. I trust the spring will renew your shattered frame, and make your friends happy. You and I have often agreed that life is no great blessing on the whole. The close of life, indeed, to a reasoning age, is

> " Dark as was chaos, ere the infant sun
> Was rolled together, or had tried his beams
> Athwart the gloom profound."

But an honest man has nothing to fear. If we lie down in the grave, the whole man a piece of broken machinery, to moulder with the clods of the valley, be it so ; at least there is an end of pain, care, woes, and wants : if that part of us called mind does survive the apparent destruction of the man—away with old-wife prejudices and tales ! Every age and every nation has had a different set of stories ; and as the many are always weak, of consequence they have often, perhaps always, been deceived. A man conscious of having acted an honest part among his fellow-creatures—even granting that he may have been the sport at times of passions and instincts—he goes to a great unknown Being, who could have no other end in giving him existence but to make him happy ; who gave him those passions and instincts, and well knows their force.

These, my worthy friend, are my ideas ; and I know they are not far different from yours. It becomes a man of sense to think for himself, particularly in a case where all men are equally interested, and where, indeed, all men are equally in the dark.

Adieu, my dear sir. God send us a cheerful meeting ! R. B.

CXXXV.

TO MRS DUNLOP.

MOSSGIEL, 7th March 1788.

MADAM,—The last paragraph in yours of the 30th February affected me most, so I shall begin my answer where you ended your letter. That I am often a sinner, with any little wit I have, I do confess : but I have taxed my recollection to no purpose to find out when it was employed against you. I hate an ungenerous sarcasm a great deal worse than I do the devil—at least as Milton describes him ; and though I may be rascally enough to be sometimes guilty of it myself, I cannot endure it in others. You, my honoured friend, who cannot appear in any light but you are sure of being respectable—you can afford to pass by an occasion to display your wit, because you may depend for fame on your sense; or, if you choose to be silent, you know you can rely on the gratitude of many and the esteem of all; but God help us who are wits or witlings by profession: if we stand not for fame there, we sink unsupported.

I am highly flattered by the news you tell me of Coila.* I may say to the fair painter who does me so much honour, as Dr Beattie says to Ross, the poet of his Muse Scota, from which, by the by, I took the idea of Coila ('tis a poem of Beattie's in the Scottish dialect, which perhaps you have never seen) :—

> " Ye shake your head, but o' my fegs,
> Ye've set auld Scota on her legs:
> Lang had she lien wi' beffs and flegs,
> Bumbaz'd and dizzie,
> Her fiddle wanted strings and pegs,
> Wae's me. poor hizzie."

R.

CXXXVI.

TO MISS CHALMERS.

EDINBURGH, *March* 14, 1788.

I KNOW, my ever dear friend, that you will be pleased with the news when I tell you I have at last taken the lease of a farm. Yesternight I completed a bargain with Mr Miller of Dalswinton for the farm of Ellisland, on the banks of the Nith, between five and six miles above Dumfries. I begin at Whitsunday to build a house, drive lime, &c.; and Heaven be my help! for it will take a strong effort to bring my mind into the routine of business. I have discharged all the army of my former pursuits, fancies, and pleasures—a motley host!—and have literally and strictly retained only the ideas of a few friends, which I have incorporated into a lifeguard. I trust in Dr Johnson's observation, " Where much is attempted, something is done." Firmness, both in sufferance and exertion, is a character I would wish to be thought to possess; and have always despised the whining yelp of complaint, and the cowardly, feeble resolve.

Poor Miss K. is ailing a good deal this winter, and begged me to remember her to you the first time I wrote to you. Surely woman, amiable woman, is often made in vain. Too delicately formed for the rougher pursuits of ambition; too noble for the dirt of avarice; and even too gentle for the rage of pleasure; formed indeed for, and highly susceptible of, enjoyment and rapture; but that enjoyment, alas! almost wholly at the mercy of the caprice malevolence, stupidity, or wickedness of an animal at all times comparatively unfeeling, and often brutal. R. B.

* A daughter of Mrs Dunlop engaged in painting a sketch of Coila.

CXXXVII.

TO CLARINDA.

Monday, Noon [*17th March*].

I WILL meet you to-morrow, Clarinda, as you appoint. My Excise affair is just concluded, and I have got my order for instructions : so far good. Wednesday night I am engaged to sup among some of the principals of the Excise, so can only make a call for you that evening ; but next day, I stay to dine with one of the Commissioners, so cannot go till Friday morning.

Your hopes, your fears, your cares, my love, are mine ; so don't mind them. I will take you in my hand through the dreary wilds of this world, and scare away the ravening bird or beast that would annoy you. I saw Mary in town to-day, and asked her if she had seen you. I shall certainly bespeak Mr Ainslie, as you desire.

Excuse me, my dearest angel, this hurried scrawl and miserable paper; circumstances make both. Farewell till to-morrow.

SYLVANDER.

CXXXVIII.

TO CLARINDA.

Tuesday Morning [*18th March.*]

I AM just hurrying away to wait on the Great Man, Clarinda ; but I have more respect to my own peace and happiness than to set out without waiting on you ; for my imagination, like a child's favourite bird, will fondly flutter along with this scrawl, till it perch on your bosom. I thank you for all the happiness you bestowed on me yesterday. The walk—delightful ; the evening—rapture. Do not be uneasy to-day, Clarinda ; forgive me. I am in rather better spirits to-day, though I had but an indifferent night. Care, anxiety, sat on my spirits ; and all the cheerfulness of this morning is the fruit of some serious, important ideas that lie, in their realities, beyond "the dark and the narrow house," as Ossian, prince of poets, says. The Father of Mercies be with you, Clarinda ! and every good thing attend you !

SYLVANDER.

CXXXIX.

TO CLARINDA.

Wednesday Morning [*19th March.*]

CLARINDA, will that envious night-cap hinder you from appearing at the window as I pass ? " Who is she that looketh forth as the morning; fair as the sun, clear as the moon, terrible as an army with banners!"

Do not accuse me of fond folly for this line; you know I am a cool lover. I mean by these presents greeting, to let you to wit, that arch-rascal Creech has not done my business yesternight, which has put off my leaving town till Monday morning. To-morrow at eleven I meet with him for the last time; just the hour I should have met far more agreeable company.

You will tell me this evening whether you cannot make our hour of meeting to-morrow one o'clock. I have just now written Creech such a letter, that the very goose-feather in my hand shrunk back from the line, and seemed to say, " I exceedingly fear and quake !" I am forming ideal schemes of véngeance. . . . . . Adieu, and think on   SYLVANDER.

CXL.

TO CLARINDA.

Friday, Nine o'clock, Night [21st March].

I AM just now come in, and have read your letter. The first thing I did was to thank the divine Disposer of events that he has had such happiness in store for me as the connection I have with you. Life, my Clarinda, is a weary, barren path; and woe be to him or her that ventures on it alone! For me, I have my dearest partner of my soul: Clarinda and I will make out our pilgrimage together. Wherever I am, I shall constantly let her know how I go on, what I observe in the world around me, and what adventures I meet with. Will it please you, my love, to get every week, or at least every fortnight, a packet, two or three sheets, full of remarks, nonsense, news, rhymes, and old songs? Will you open, with satisfaction and delight, a letter from a man who loves you, who has loved you, and who will love you to death, through death, and for ever? Oh Clarinda! what do I owe to Heaven for blessing me with such a piece of exalted excellence as you! I call over your idea, as a miser counts over his treasure! Tell me, were you studious to please me last night? I am sure you did it to transport. How rich am I who have such a treasure as you! You know me; you know how to make me happy; and you do it most effectually. God bless you with

" Long life, long youth, long pleasure, and a friend!"

To-morrow night, according to your own direction, I shall watch the window: 'tis the star that guides me to paradise. The great relish to all is, that Honour, that Innocence, that Religion, are the witnesses and guarantees of our happiness. " The Lord God knoweth," and perhaps " Israel he shall know," my love and your merit. Adieu, Clarinda! I am going to remember you in my prayers.   SYLVANDER.

CXLI.

TO MR RICHARD BROWN.

GLASGOW, *26th March* 1788.

I AM monstrously to blame, my dear sir, in not writing to you, and sending you the Directory. I have been getting my tack extended, as I have taken a farm, and I have been racking shop accounts with Mr Creech ; both of which, together with watching, fatigue, and a load of care almost too heavy for my shoulders, have in some degree actually fevered me. I really forgot the Directory yesterday, which vexed me ; but I was convulsed with rage a great part of the day. I have to thank you for the ingenious, friendly, and elegant epistle from your friend Mr Crawford. I shall certainly write to him ; but not now. This is merely a card to you, as I am posting to Dumfriesshire, where many perplexing arrangements await me. I am vexed about the Directory ; but, my dear sir, forgive me : these eight days I have been positively crazed. My compliments to Mrs B. I shall write to you at Grenada. I am ever, my dearest friend, yours, R. B.

CXLII.

TO MR ROBERT CLEGHORN.

MAUCHLINE, *31st March* 1788.

YESTERDAY, my dear sir, as I was riding through a track of melancholy, joyless muirs, between Galloway and Ayrshire, it being Sunday, I turned my thoughts to psalms, and hymns, and spiritual songs ; and your favourite air, *Captain O'Kean*, coming at length into my head, I tried these words to it. You will see that the first part of the tune must be repeated.

> The small birds rejoice in the green leaves returning
> The murmuring streamlet winds clear through the vale ;
> The hawthorn trees blow in the dew of the morning,
> And wild scattered cowslips bedeck the green dale :
> But what can give pleasure, or what can seem fair,
> While the lingering moments are numbered by care ?
> No flowers gaily springing, nor birds sweetly singing,
> Can soothe the sad bosom of joyless despair.

I am tolerably pleased with these verses ; but as I have only a sketch of the tune, I leave it with you to try if they suit the measure of the music.

I am so harassed with care and anxiety about this farming project of mine, that my Muse has degenerated into the veriest prose-wench that ever picked cinders or followed a tinker. When I am fairly got into the routine of business, I shall trouble you with a longer epistle ; perhaps with some queries respecting farming : at present, the world sits such a load on my mind, that it has effaced almost every trace of the poet in me.

My very best compliments and good wishes to Mrs Cleghorn.

R. B.

CXLIII.

TO ———.

MOSSGIEL, *Friday Morning.*

THE language of refusal is to me the most difficult language on earth, and you are the man in the world, excepting one of Right Honourable designation, to whom it gives me the greatest pain to hold such language. My brother has already got money, and shall want nothing in my power to enable him to fulfil his engagement with you; but to be security on so large a scale, even for a brother, is what I dare not do, except I were in such circumstances of life as that the worst that might happen could not greatly injure me.

I never wrote a letter which gave me so much pain in my life, as I know the unhappy consequences: I shall incur the displeasure of a gentleman for whom I have the highest respect, and to whom I am deeply obliged. I am ever, sir, your obliged and very humble servant,   ROBERT BURNS.

CXLIV.

TO MR WILLIAM DUNBAR, EDINBURGH.

MAUCHLINE, *7th April* 1788.

I HAVE not delayed so long to write you, my much respected friend, because I thought no farther of my promise. I have long since given up that kind of formal correspondence, where one sits down irksomely to write a letter, because we think we are in duty bound so to do.

I have been roving over the country, as the farm I have taken is forty miles from this place, hiring servants and preparing matters; but most of all, I am earnestly busy to bring about a revolution in my own mind. As, till within these eighteen months, I never was the wealthy master of ten guineas, my knowledge of business is to learn; add to this, my late scenes of idleness and dissipation have enervated my mind to an alarming degree. Skill in the sober science of life is my most serious and hourly study. I have dropt all conversation and all reading (prose reading) but what tends in some way or other to my serious aim. Except one worthy young fellow, I have not one single correspondent in Edinburgh. You have indeed kindly made me an offer of that kind. The world of wits, and *gens comme il faut* which I lately left, and with whom I never again will intimately mix—from that port, sir, I expect your Gazette : what *les beaux esprits* are saying, what they are doing, and what they are singing. Any sober intelligence from my sequestered walks of life ; any droll original ; any passing remark, important forsooth, because it is mine ; any little poetic effort, however embryoth ; these, my dear sir, are all you have to expect from me. When I talk of poetic efforts, I must have it always understood that I appeal from your wit and taste to your friendship and good-nature. The first would be my favourite tribunal, where I defied censure ; but the last, where I declined justice.

I have scarcely made a single distich since I saw you. When I meet with an old Scots air that has any facetious idea in its name, I have a peculiar pleasure in following out that idea for a verse or two.

I trust that this will find you in better health than I did last time I called for you. A few lines from you, directed to me at Mauchline, were it but to let me know how you are, will set my mind a good deal [at rest.] Now, never shun the idea of writing me, because perhaps you may be out of humour or spirits. I could give you a hundred good consequences attending a dull letter ; one, for example, and the remaining ninety-nine some other time —it will always serve to keep in countenance, my much respected sir, your obliged friend and humble servant,   R. B.

CXLV.

TO MISS CHALMERS.

MAUCHLINE, *7th April* 1788.

I AM indebted to you and Miss Nimmo for letting me know Miss Kennedy. Strange ! how apt we are to indulge prejudices in our judgments of one another ! Even I, who pique myself on my skill in marking characters—because I am too proud of my character as a man to be dazzled in my judgment for glaring wealth, and too proud of my situation as a poor man to be biassed against squalid poverty—I was unacquainted with Miss K.'s very uncommon worth.

I am going on a good deal progressive in *mon grand but*—the sober science of life. I have lately made some sacrifices, for which, were I *vivâ voce* with you to paint the situation and recount the circumstances, you would applaud me.   R. B.

CXLVI.

TO MR JAMES SMITH, AVON PRINTFIELD, LINLITHGOW.

MAUCHLINE, *April* 28, 1788.

BEWARE of your Strasburgh, my good sir! Look on this as the opening of a correspondence, like the opening of a twenty-four gun battery!

There is no understanding a man properly without knowing something of his previous ideas—that is to say, if the man has any ideas; for I know many who, in the animal-muster, pass for men, that are the scanty masters of only one idea on any given subject, and by far the greatest part of your acquaintances and mine can barely boast of ideas, 1·25—1·5—1·75 (or some such fractional matter); so, to let you a little into the secrets of my pericranium, there is, you must know, a certain clean-limbed, handsome, bewitching young hussy of your acquaintance, to whom I have lately and privately given a matrimonial title to my corpus.

'Bode a robe and wear it,
Bode a poke and bear it,"

says the wise old Scots adage! I hate to presage ill-luck; and as my girl has been doubly kinder to me than even the best of women usually are to their partners of our sex, in similar circumstances, I reckon on twelve times a brace of children against I celebrate my twelfth wedding-day. * * *

"Light's heartsome," quo' the wife when she was stealing sheep. You see what a lamp I have hung up to lighten your paths, when you are idle enough to explore the combinations and relations of my ideas. 'Tis now as plain as a pikestaff why a twenty-four gun battery was a metaphor I could readily employ.

Now for business. I intend to present Mrs Burns with a printed shawl, an article of which I daresay you have variety: 'tis my first present to her since I have irrevocably called her mine; and I have a kind of whimsical wish to get the first said present from an old and much-valued friend of hers and mine—a trusty Trojan, whose friendship I count myself possessed of as a liferent lease.

Look on this letter as a "beginning of sorrows;" I will write you till your eyes ache reading nonsense.

Mrs Burns ('tis only her private designation) begs her best compliments to you.   R. B.

———

CXLVII.

TO MRS DUNLOP.

MAUCHLINE. 28*th April* 1788.

MADAM,—Your powers of reprehension must be great indeed,

as I assure you they made my heart ache with penitential pangs, even though I was really not guilty. As I commence farmer at Whitsunday, you will easily guess I must be pretty busy; but that is not all. As I got the offer of the Excise business without solicitation, and as it costs me only six months [weeks?] attendance for instructions to entitle me to a commission—which commission lies by me, and at any future period, on my simple petition, can be resumed—I thought five-and-thirty pounds a-year was no bad *dernier resort* for a poor poet, if fortune in her jade tricks should kick him down from the little eminence to which she has lately helped him up.

For this reason, I am at present attending these instructions, to have them completed before Whitsunday. Still, madam, I prepared with the sincerest pleasure to meet you at the Mount, and came to my brother's on Saturday night, to set out on Sunday; but for some nights preceding I had slept in an apartment where the force of the winds and rains was only mitigated by being sifted through numberless apertures in the windows, walls, &c. In consequence I was on Sunday, Monday, and part of Tuesday, unable to stir out of bed, with all the miserable effects of a violent cold.

You see, madam, the truth of the French maxim, *le vrai n'est pas toujours le vraisemblable*. Your last was so full of expostulation, and was something so like the language of an offended friend, that I began to tremble for a correspondence which I had with grateful pleasure set down as one of the greatest enjoyments of my future life.

Your books have delighted me; Virgil, Dryden, and Tasso, were all equally strangers to me; but of this more at large in my next. R. B.

(VI.*)
TO MR BURNESS, MONTROSE.

LOCHLEA, 21*st June* 1783.

DEAR SIR,—My father received your favour of the 10th current, and as he has been for some months very poorly in health, and is, in his own opinion (and indeed in almost everybody's else), in a dying condition, he has only, with great difficulty, written a few farewell lines to each of his brothers-in-law. For this melancholy reason I now hold the pen for him, to thank you for your kind letter, and to assure you, sir, that it shall not be my fault if my father's correspondence in the north die with him. My brother writes to John Caird, and to him I must refer you for the news of our family.

I shall only trouble you with a few particulars relative to the wretched state of this country. Our markets are exceedingly

* This letter should have been inserted at p. 343.

high—oatmeal, 17d. and 18d. per peck, and not to be got even at that price. We have indeed been pretty well supplied with quantities of white peas from England and elsewhere, but that resource is likely to fail us, and what will become of us then, particularly the very poorest sort, Heaven only knows. This country, till of late, was flourishing incredibly in the manufacture of silk, lawn, and carpet-weaving; and we are still carrying on a good deal in that way, but much reduced from what it was. We had also a fine trade in the shoe way, but now entirely ruined, and hundreds driven to a starving condition on account of it. Farming is also at a very low ebb with us. Our lands, generally speaking, are mountainous and barren; and our landholders, full of ideas of farming gathered from the English and the Lothians, and other rich soils in Scotland, make no allowance for the odds of the quality of land, and consequently stretch us much beyond what in the event we will be found able to pay. We are also much at a loss for want of proper methods in our improvements of farming. Necessity compels us to leave our old schemes, and few of us have opportunities of being well informed in new ones. In short, my dear sir, since the unfortunate beginning of this American war, and its as unfortunate conclusion, this country has been, and still is, decaying very fast. Even in higher life, a couple of our Ayrshire noblemen, and the major part of our knights and squires, are all insolvent. A miserable job of a Douglas, Heron, and Co's bank, which no doubt you have heard of, has undone numbers of them; and imitating English and French, and other foreign luxuries and fopperies, has ruined as many more. There is a great trade of smuggling carried on along our coasts, which, however destructive to the interests of the kingdom at large, certainly enriches this corner of it, but too often at the expense of our morals. However, it enables individuals to make, at least for a time, a splendid appearance; but Fortune, as is usual with her when she is uncommonly lavish of her favours, is generally even with them at the last; and happy were it for numbers of them if she would leave them no worse than when she found them.

My mother sends you a small present of a cheese; 'tis but a very little one, as our last year's stock is sold off. . . .

I shall conclude this long letter with assuring you that I shall be very happy to hear from you, or any of our friends in your country, when opportunity serves.

My father sends you, probably for the last time in this world, his warmest wishes for your welfare and happiness; and my mother and the rest of the family desire to enclose their kind compliments to you, Mrs Burness, and the rest of your family, along with those of, dear sir, your affectionate cousin,   R. B.

CXLVIII.

TO PROFESSOR STEWART.

MAUCHLINE, 3d May 1788.

SIR,—I enclose you one or two more of my bagatelles. If the fervent wishes of honest gratitude have any influence with that great unknown Being who frames the chain of causes and events, prosperity and happiness will attend your visit to the Continent, and return you safe to your native shore.

Wherever I am, allow me, sir, to claim it as my privilege to acquaint you with my progress in my trade of rhymes; as I am sure I could say it with truth, that, next to my little fame, and the having it in my power to make life more comfortable to those whom Nature has made dear to me, I shall ever regard your countenance, your patronage, your friendly good offices, as the most valued consequence of my late success in life.   R. B.

CXLIX.

TO MRS DUNLOP.

MAUCHLINE, 4th May 1788.

MADAM,—Dryden's Virgil has delighted me. I do not know whether the critics will agree with me, but the Georgics are to me by far the best of Virgil. It is indeed a species of writing entirely new to me, and has filled my head with a thousand fancies of emulation: but, alas! when I read the Georgics, and then survey my own powers, 'tis like the idea of a Shetland pony, drawn up by the side of a thorough-bred hunter, to start for the plate. I own I am disappointed in the Æneid. Faultless correctness may please, and does highly please, the lettered critic; but to that awful character I have not the most distant pretensions. I do not know whether I do not hazard my pretensions to be a critic of any kind, when I say that I think Virgil, in many instances, a servile copier of Homer. If I had the Odyssey by me, I could parallel many passages where Virgil has evidently copied, but by no means improved, Homer. Nor can I think there is anything of this owing to the translators; for, from everything I have seen of Dryden, I think him, in genius and fluency of language, Pope's master. I have not perused Tasso enough to form an opinion—in some future letter you shall have my ideas of him; though I am conscious my criticisms must be very inaccurate and imperfect, as there I have ever felt and lamented my want of learning most.

R. B.

CL.

TO MR ROBERT AINSLIE.

MAUCHLINE, *May* 26, 1788.

MY DEAR FRIEND,—I am two kind letters in your debt; but I have been from home, and horridly busy, buying and preparing for my farming business, over and above the plague of my Excise instructions, which this week will finish.

As I flatter my wishes that I foresee many future years' correspondence between us, 'tis foolish to talk of excusing dull epistles: a dull letter may be a very kind one. I have the pleasure to tell you that I have been extremely fortunate in all my buyings and bargainings hitherto—Mrs Burns not excepted; which title I now avow to the world. I am truly pleased with this last affair; it has indeed added to my anxieties for futurity, but it has given a stability to my mind and resolutions unknown before; and the poor girl has the most sacred enthusiasm of attachment to me, and has not a wish but to gratify my every idea of her deportment. I am interrupted.—Farewell! my dear sir.   R. B.

CLI.

TO MRS DUNLOP.

27*th May* 1788.

MADAM,—I have been torturing my philosophy to no purpose, to account for that kind partiality of yours, which has followed me, in my return to the shade of life, with assiduous benevolence. Often did I regret, in the fleeting hours of my late Will-o'-Wisp appearance, that " here I had no continuing city;" and, but for the consolation of a few solid guineas, could almost lament the time that a momentary acquaintance with wealth and splendour put me so much out of conceit with the sworn companions of my road through life—insignificance and poverty.

There are few circumstances relating to the unequal distribution of the good things of this life that give me more vexation (I mean in what I see around me) than the importance the opulent bestow on their trifling family affairs, compared with the very same things on the contracted scale of a cottage. Last afternoon I had the honour to spend an hour or two at a good woman's fireside, where the planks that composed the floor were decorated with a splendid carpet, and the gay table sparkled with silver and china. 'Tis now about term-day, and there has been a revolution among those creatures, who, though in appearance partakers, and equally noble partakers, of the same nature with madame, are from time to time—their nerves, their sinews, their health.

strength, wisdom, experience, genius, time, nay, a good part of their very thoughts—sold for months and years, not only to the necessities, the conveniences, but the caprices of the important few. We talked of the insignificant creatures; nay, notwithstanding their general stupidity and rascality, did some of the poor devils the honour to commend them. But light be the turf upon his breast who taught " Reverence thyself." We looked down on the unpolished wretches, their impertinent wives and clouterly brats, as the lordly bull does on the little dirty ant-hill, whose puny inhabitants he crushes in the carelessness of his ramble, or tosses in the air in the wantonness of his pride.

R. B.

CLII.
TO MRS DUNLOP.
AT MR DUNLOP'S, HADDINGTON.

ELLISLAND, 13th June 1788.

> " Where'er I roam, whatever realms I see,
> My heart, untravell'd, fondly turns to thee;
> Still to my friend it turns with ceaseless pain,
> And drags, at each remove, a lengthen'd chain."
> GOLDSMITH.

THIS is the second day, my honoured friend, that I have been on my farm. A solitary inmate of an old, smoky spence; far from every object I love, or by whom I am beloved; nor any acquaintance older than yesterday, except Jenny Geddes, the old mare I ride on; while uncouth cares and novel plans hourly insult my awkward ignorance and bashful inexperience. There is a foggy atmosphere native to my soul in the hour of care, consequently the dreary objects seem larger than the life. Extreme sensibility, irritated and prejudiced on the gloomy side by a series of misfortunes and disappointments, at that period of my existence when the soul is laying in her cargo of ideas for the voyage of life, is, I believe, the principal cause of this unhappy frame of mind.

> " The valiant, in himself, what can he suffer?
> Or what need he regard his single woes?" &c.

Your surmise, madam, is just; I am indeed a husband. * * *

To jealousy or infidelity I am an equal stranger. My preservative from the first is the most thorough consciousness of her sentiments of honour, and her attachment to me : my antidote against the last is my long and deep-rooted affection for her.

In housewife matters, of aptness to learn and activity to execute, she is eminently mistress; and during my absence in Nithsdale, she is regularly and constantly apprentice to my mother and sisters in their dairy and other rural business.

The Muses must not be offended when I tell them the concerns of my wife and family will, in my mind, always take the *pas;* but I assure them their ladyships will ever come next in place.

You are right that a bachelor state would have insured me more friends; but, from a cause you will easily guess, conscious peace in the enjoyment of my own mind, and unmistrusting confidence in approaching my God, would seldom have been of the number.

I found a once much-loved and still much-loved female, literally and truly cast out to the mercy of the naked elements; but I enabled her to *purchase* a shelter—there is no sporting with a fellow-creature's happiness or misery.

The most placid good-nature and sweetness of disposition; a warm heart, gratefully devoted with all its powers to love me; vigorous health and sprightly cheerfulness, set off to the best advantage by a more than commonly handsome figure; these, I think, in a woman, may make a good wife, though she should never have read a page but the Scriptures of the Old and New Testament, nor have danced in a brighter assembly than a penny pay wedding.   R. B.

CLIII.

TO MR ROBERT AINSLIE.

ELLISLAND, *June* 14, 1788.

THIS is now the third day, my dearest sir, that I have sojourned in these regions; and during these three days you have occupied more of my thoughts than in three weeks preceding: in Ayrshire I have several variations of friendship's compass, here it points invariably to the pole. My farm gives me a good many uncouth cares and anxieties, but I hate the language of complaint. Job, or some one of his friends, says well—" Why should a living man complain ?"

I have lately been much mortified with contemplating an unlucky imperfection in the very framing and construction of my soul; namely, a blundering inaccuracy of her olfactory organs in hitting the scent of craft or design in my fellow-creatures. I do not mean any compliment to my ingenuousness, or to hint that the defect is in consequence of the unsuspicious simplicity of conscious truth and honour: I take it to be, in some way or other, an imperfection in the mental sight; or, metaphor apart, some modification of dulness. In two or three instances lately I have been most shamefully out.

I have all along hitherto, in the warfare of life, been bred to arms among the light-horse—the picket-guards of fancy—a kind of hussars and Highlanders of the brain; but I am firmly resolved to sell out of these giddy battalions, who have no ideas of a battle but fighting the foe, or of a siege but storming the town. Cost what it will, I am determined to buy in among the grave squadrons of heavy-armed thought, or the artillery corps of plodding contrivance.

What books are you reading, or what is the subject of your thoughts, besides the great studies of your profession? You said something about religion in your last. I don't exactly remember what it was, as the letter is in Ayrshire; but I thought it not only prettily said, but nobly thought. You will make a noble fellow if once you were married. I make no reservation of your being well married : you have so much sense and knowledge of human nature, that, though you may not realise perhaps the ideas of romance, yet you will never be ill married.

Were it not for the terrors of my ticklish situation respecting provision for a family of children, I am decidedly of opinion that the step I have taken is vastly for my happiness. As it is, I look to the Excise scheme as a certainty of maintenance. A maintenance!—luxury to what either Mrs Burns or I was born to. Adieu!

R. B.

CLIV.

TO MR ROBERT AINSLIE.

ELLISLAND, 30th June 1788.

MY DEAR SIR—I just now received your brief epistle ; and, to take vengeance on your laziness, I have, you see, taken a long sheet of writing-paper, and have begun at the top of the page, intending to scribble on to the very last corner.

I am vexed at that affair of the * * *, but dare not enlarge on the subject until you send me your direction, as I suppose that will be altered on your late master and friend's death. I am concerned for the old fellow's exit only as I fear it may be to your disadvantage in any respect; for an old man's dying, except he have been a very benevolent character, or in some particular situation of life that the welfare of the poor or the helpless depended on him, I think it an event of the most trifling moment to the world. Man is naturally a kind, benevolent animal, but he is dropped into such a needy situation here in this vexatious world, and has such a hungry, growling, multiplying pack of necessities, appetites, passions, and desires about him, ready to devour him for want of other food, that in fact he must lay aside his cares for others that he may look properly to himself. You have been imposed upon in paying Mr Miers for the profile of a Mr H. I did not mention it in my letter to you, nor did I ever give Mr Miers any such order. I have no objection to lose the money, but I will not have any such profile in my possession.

I desired the carrier to pay you, but as I mentioned only fifteen shillings to him, I will rather enclose you a guinea-note. I have it not, indeed, to spare here, as I am only a sojourner in a strange land in this place; but in a day or two I return to Mauchline, and there I have the bank-notes through the house like salt-permits.

There is a great degree of folly in talking unnecessarily of one's private affairs. I have just now been interrupted by one of my new neighbours, who has made himself absolutely contemptible in my eyes by his silly garrulous pruriency. I know it has been a fault of my own too; but from this moment I abjure it as I would the service of hell! Your poets, spendthrifts, and other fools of that kidney, pretend, forsooth, to crack their jokes on prudence; but 'tis a squalid vagabond glorying in his rags. Still, imprudence respecting money matters is much more pardonable than imprudence respecting character. I have no objection to prefer prodigality to avarice in some few instances: but I appeal to your observation if you have not met, and often met, with the same disingenuousness, the same hollow-hearted insincerity and disintegrative depravity of principle, in the hackneyed victims of profusion, as in the unfeeling children of parsimony. I have every possible reverence for the much-talked-of world beyond the grave, and I wish that which piety believes, and virtue deserves, may be all matter of fact. But in things belonging to, and terminating in this present scene of existence, man has serious and interesting business on hand. Whether a man shall shake hands with welcome in the distinguished elevation of respect, or shrink from contempt in the abject corner of insignificance: whether he shall wanton under the tropic of plenty—at least enjoy himself in the comfortable latitudes of easy convenience—or starve in the arctic circle of dreary poverty; whether he shall rise in the manly consciousness of a self-approving mind, or sink beneath a galling load of regret and remorse—these are alternatives of the last moment.

You see how I preach. You used occasionally to sermonise too; I wish you would in charity favour me with a sheet full in your own way. I admire the close of a letter Lord Bolingbroke writes to Dean Swift:—"Adieu, dear Swift! with all thy faults I love thee entirely; make an effort to love me with all mine!" Humble servant, and all that trumpery, is now such a prostituted business, that honest friendship, in her sincere way, must have recourse to her primitive, simple, farewell!   R. B.

CLV.

TO MR PETER HILL.

MAUCHLINE, 18*th July* 1788.

You injured me, my dear sir, in your construction of the cause of my silence. From Ellisland in Nithsdale to Mauchline in Kyle is forty and five miles. *There*, a house a-building, and farm enclosures and improvements to tend; *here*, a new—not indeed so much a *new* as a *young* wife;—sir, could my dearest brother expect a regular correspondence from me! . . . I am certain that my liberal-minded and much-respected friend would have acquitted me, though I had obeyed to the very letter that famous statute among the irrevocable decrees of the Medes and Persians, not to ask petition, for forty days, of either God or man, save thee O Queen, only!

I am highly obliged to you, my dearest sir, for your kind, your elegant compliments on my becoming one of that most respectable, that truly venerable corps,—they who are, without a metaphor, the fathers of posterity. . . .

Your book came safe, and I am going to trouble you with further commissions. I call it troubling you, because I want only BOOKS—the cheapest way the best; so you may have to hunt for them in the evening auctions. I want Smollett's works, for the sake of his incomparable humour. I have already *Roderick Random* and *Humphrey Clinker. Peregrine Pickle, Launcelot Greaves,* and *Ferdinand Count Fathom,* I still want; but, as I said, the veriest ordinary copies will serve me. I am nice only in the appearance of my poets. I forget the price of *Cowper's Poems,* but I believe I must have them. I saw the other day proposals for a publication entitled *Banks's New and Complete Christian's Family Bible,* printed for C. Cooke, Paternoster Row, London. He promises at least to give in the work, I think it is three hundred and odd engravings, to which he has put the names of the first artists in London. You will know the character of the performance, as some numbers of it are published: and if it is really what it pretends to be, set me down as a subscriber, and send me the published numbers.

Let me hear from you your first leisure minute, and trust me, you shall in future have no reason to complain of my silence The dazzling perplexity of novelty will dissipate and leave me to pursue my course in the quiet path of methodical routine.

R. B.

CLVI.

TO MR GEORGE LOCKHART,

MERCHANT, GLASGOW.

MAUCHLINE, 18*th July* 1788.

MY DEAR SIR,—I am just going for Nithsdale, else I would certainly have transcribed some of my rhyming things for you. The Miss Baillies I have seen in Edinburgh. " Fair and lovely are thy works, Lord God Almighty ! Who would not praise thee for these thy gifts in thy goodness to the sons of men !" It needed not your fine taste to admire them. I declare, one day I had the honour of dining at Mr Baillie's, I was almost in the predicament of the children of Israel, when they could not look on Moses' face for the glory that shone in it when he descended from Mount Sinai.

I did once write a poetic address from the Falls of Bruar to his Grace of Athole when I was in the Highlands. When you return to Scotland let me know, and I will send such of my pieces as pleases myself best. I return to Mauchline in about ten days.

My compliments to Mr Purden. I am in truth, but at present in haste, yours,   R. B.

CLVII.

TO MRS DUNLOP.

MAUCHLINE, *August* 2, 1788.

HONOURED MADAM,—Your kind letter welcomed me yester-night to Ayrshire. I am indeed seriously angry with you at the quantum of your luckpenny; but, vexed and hurt as I was, I could not help laughing very heartily at the noble lord's apology for the missed napkin.

I would write to you from Nithsdale, and give you my direction there, but I have scarce an opportunity of calling at a post-office once in a fortnight. I am six miles from Dumfries, am scarcely ever in it myself, and as yet have little acquaintance in the neigh-bourhood. Besides, I am now very busy on my farm, building a dwelling-house; as at present I am almost an evangelical man in Nithsdale, for I have scarce " where to lay my head."

There are some passages in your last that brought tears in my eyes. " The heart knoweth its own sorrows, and a stranger inter-meddleth not therewith." The repository of these " sorrows of the heart" is a kind of *sanctum sanctorum;* and 'tis only a chosen friend, and that, too, at particular sacred times, who dares enter into them :—

" Heaven oft tears the bosom-chords
That nature finest strung."

You will excuse this quotation for the sake of the author. Instead of entering on this subject farther, I shall transcribe you a few lines I wrote in a hermitage belonging to a gentleman in my Nithsdale neighbourhood (p. 136). They are almost the only favours the Muses have conferred on me in that country. . . .

Since I am in the way of transcribing, the following were the production of yesterday as I jogged through the wild hills of New Cumnock. I intend inserting them, or something like them, in an epistle I am going to write to the gentleman on whose friendship my Excise hopes depend—Mr Graham of Fintry, one of the worthiest and most accomplished gentlemen not only of this country, but, I will dare to say it, of this age. The following are just the first crude thoughts " unhousel'd, unanointed, unaneal'd :"—

> Pity the tuneful Muses' helpless train;
> Weak, timid landsmen on life's stormy main:
> The world were blest, did bliss on them depend;
> Ah, that "the friendly e'er should want a friend!"
> The little Fate bestows they share as soon;
> Unlike sage, proverb'd Wisdom's hard-wrung boon.
> Let Prudence number o'er each sturdy son,
> Who life and wisdom at one race begun;
> Who feel by reason and who give by rule;
> Instinct's a brute and sentiment a fool!
> Who make poor *will do* wait upon *I should ;*
> We own they're prudent, but who owns they're good ?
>
> Ye wise ones, hence! ye hurt the social eye;
> God's image rudely etched on base alloy !
> But come   *   *   *   *

Here the Muse left me. I am astonished at what you tell me of Anthony's writing me. I never received it. Poor fellow ! you vex me much by telling me that he is unfortunate. I shall be in Ayrshire ten days from this date. I have just room for an old Roman farewell.   R. B.

CLVIII.

TO MRS DUNLOP.

MAUCHLINE, *August* 10, 1788.

MY MUCH-HONOURED FRIEND,—Yours of the 24th June is before me. I found it, as well as another valued friend—my wife —waiting to welcome me to Ayrshire : I met both with the sincerest pleasure.

When I write you, madam, I do not sit down to answer every paragraph of yours, by echoing every sentiment, like the faithful Commons of Great Britain in Parliament assembled, answering a speech from the best of kings ! I express myself in the fulness of my heart, and may perhaps be guilty of neglecting some of your kind inquiries ; but not from your very odd reason, that I do not read your letters. All your epistles for several months have cost me nothing except a swelling throb of gratitude, or a deep-felt sentiment of veneration.

I like your way in your churchyard lucubrations. Thoughts that are the spontaneous result of accidental situations, either respecting health, place, or company, have often a strength and always an originality that would in vain be looked for in fancied circumstances and studied paragraphs. For me, I have often thought of keeping a letter in progression by me, to send you when the sheet was written out. Now I talk of sheets, I must tell you my reason for writing to you on paper of this kind is my pruriency of writing to you at large. A page of post is on such a dis-social, narrow-minded scale, that I cannot abide it; and double letters, at least in my miscellaneous reverie manner, are a monstrous tax in a close correspondence.   R. B.

CLIX.

TO MRS DUNLOP.

ELLISLAND, 16th August 1788.

I AM in a fine disposition, my honoured friend, to send you an elegiac epistle, and want only genius to make it quite Shenstonian :—

> " Why droops my heart with fancied woes forlorn?
> Why sinks my soul beneath each wintry sky?"

My increasing cares in this as yet strange country—gloomy conjectures in the dark vista of futurity—consciousness of my own inability for the struggle of the world—my broadened mark to misfortune in a wife and children—I could indulge these reflections till my humour should ferment into the most acid chagrin, that would corrode the very thread of life.

To counterwork these baneful feelings I have sat down to write to you; as I declare upon my soul I always find that the most sovereign balm for my wounded spirit.

I was yesterday at Mr Miller's [at Dalswinton] to dinner, for the first time. My reception was quite to my mind : from the lady of the house quite flattering. She sometimes hits on a couplet or two *impromptu*. She repeated one or two to the admiration of all present. My suffrage as a professional man was expected : I for once went agonizing over the belly of my conscience. Pardon me, ye, my adored household gods, independence of spirit, and integrity of soul! In the course of conversation *Johnson's Musical Museum*, a collection of Scottish songs with the music, was talked of. We got a song on the harpsichord, beginning,

> " Raving winds around her blowing."

The air was much admired : the lady of the house asked me whose were the words. " Mine, madam—they are indeed my very best verses :" she took not the smallest notice of them ! The old Scottish proverb says well, " King's caff is better than ither folk's corn." I was going to make a New-Testament quotation about " casting pearls," but that would be too virulent, for the lady is actually a woman of sense and taste. * * *

After all that has been said on the other side of the question, man is by no means a happy creature. I do not speak of the selected few, favoured by partial Heaven, whose souls are tuned to gladness amid riches, and honours, and prudence, and wisdom. I speak of the neglected many, whose nerves, whose sinews, whose days, are sold to the minions of fortune.

If I thought you had never seen it, I would transcribe for you a stanza of an old Scottish ballad, called *The Life and Age of Man ;* beginning thus :—

> " 'Twas in the sixteen hundredth year
> Of God and fifty-three
> Frae Christ was born, that bought us dear,
> As writings testifie."

I had an old grand-uncle with whom my mother lived a while in her girlish years : the good old man, for such he was, was long blind ere he died, during which time his highest enjoyment was to sit down and cry, while my mother would sing the simple old song of *The Life and Age of Man.*

It is this way of thinking—it is these melancholy truths—that make religion so precious to the poor, miserable children of men. If it is a mere phantom, existing only in the heated imagination of enthusiasm,

> " What truth on earth so precious as the lie ?"

My idle reasonings sometimes make me a little sceptical, but the necessities of my heart always give the cold philosophisings the lie. Who looks for the heart weaned from earth ; the soul affianced to her God ; the correspondence fixed with heaven ; the pious supplication and devout thanksgiving, constant as the vicissitudes of even and morn ; who thinks to meet with these in the court, the palace, in the glare of public life ? No : to find them in their precious importance and divine efficacy, we must search among the obscure recesses of disappointment, affliction, poverty, and distress.

I am sure, dear madam, you are now more than pleased with the length of my letters. I return to Ayrshire middle of next week ; and it quickens my pace to think that there will be a letter from you waiting me there. I must be here again very soon for my harvest.   R. B.

CLX.

TO MR BEUGO, ENGRAVER, EDINBURGH.

ELLISLAND, *9th Sept.* 1788.

MY DEAR SIR,—There is not in Edinburgh above the number of the graces whose letters would have given me so much pleasure as yours of the 3d instant, which only reached me yesternight.

I am here on my farm, busy with my harvest; but for all that most pleasurable part of life called SOCIAL COMMUNICATION, I am here at the very elbow of existence. The only things that are to be found in this country, in any degree of perfection, are stupidity and canting. Prose they only know in graces, prayers, &c., and the value of these they estimate, as they do their plaiding webs— by the ell! As for the Muses, they have as much an idea of a rhinoceros as of a poet. For my old capricious but good-natured hussy of a Muse—

> " By banks of Nith I sat and wept
> When Coila I thought on,
> In midst thereof I hung my harp
> The willow trees upon."

I am generally about half my time in Ayrshire with my " darling Jean ;" and then I, at lucid intervals, throw my horny fist across my be-cobwebbed lyre, much in the same manner as an old wife throws her hand across the spokes of her spinning-wheel.

I will send you the *Fortunate Shepherdess* as soon as I return to Ayrshire, for there I keep it with other precious treasure. I shall send it by a careful hand, as I would not for anything it should be mislaid or lost. I do not wish to serve you from any benevolence, or other grave Christian virtue ; 'tis purely a selfish gratification of my own feelings whenever I think of you.

You do not tell me if you are going to be married. Depend upon it, if you do not make some foolish choice, it will be a very great improvement on the dish of life. I can speak from experience, though my choice was as random as blind-man's buff. . . .

If your better functions would give you leisure to write me, I should be extremely happy ; that is to say, if you neither keep nor look for a regular correspondence. I hate the idea of being obliged to write a letter. I sometimes write a friend twice a week, at other times once a quarter.

I am exceedingly pleased with your fancy in making the author you mention place a map of Iceland instead of his portrait before his works ; 'twas a glorious idea.

Could you conveniently do me one thing ?—whenever you finish any head, I should like to have a proof-copy of it. I might tell you a long story about your fine genius; but as what everybody knows cannot have escaped you, I shall not say one syllable about it.

If you see Mr Nasmyth remember me to him most respectfully, as he both loves and deserves respect; though, if he would pay less respect to the mere carcass of greatness, I should think him much nearer perfection.   R. B.

CLXI.

TO MISS CHALMERS, EDINBURGH.

ELLISLAND, NEAR DUMFRIES, *Sept.* 16, 1788.

WHERE are you? and how are you? and is Lady Mackenzie recovering her health?—for I have had but one solitary letter from you. I will not think you have forgot me, madam; and for my part—

> " When thee, Jerusalem, I forget,
> . Skill part from my right hand!"

" My heart is not of that rock, nor my soul careless as that sea." I do not make my progress among mankind as a bowl does among its fellows—rolling through the crowd without bearing away any mark or impression, except where they hit in hostile collision.

I am here, driven in with my harvest-folks by bad weather; and as you and your sister once did me the honour of interesting yourselves much *à l'égard de moi*, I sit down to beg the continuation of your goodness. I can truly say that, all the exterior of life apart, I never saw two whose esteem flattered the nobler feelings of my soul—I will not say more, but so much, as Lady Mackenzie and Miss Chalmers. When I think of you—hearts the best, minds the noblest of human kind—unfortunate even in the shades of life; —when I think I have met with you, and have lived more of real life with you in eight days than I can do with almost anybody I meet with in eight years—when I think on the improbability of meeting you in this world again—I could sit down and cry like a child! If ever you honoured me with a place in your esteem, I trust I can now plead more desert. I am secure against that crushing grip of iron poverty, which, alas! is less or more fatal to the native worth and purity of, I fear, the noblest souls; and a late important step in my life has kindly taken me out of the way of those ungrateful iniquities, which, however overlooked in fashionable licence, or varnished in fashionable phrase; are indeed but lighter and deeper shades of VILLANY.

Shortly after my last return to Ayrshire, I married " my Jean." This was not in consequence of the attachment of romance, perhaps; but I had a long and much-loved fellow-creature's happiness or misery in my determination, and I durst not trifle with so important a deposit. Nor have I any cause to repent it. If I have not got polite tattle, modish manners, and fashionable dress, I am not sickened and disgusted with the multiform curse of boarding-school affectation; and I have got the handsomest figure, the sweetest temper, the soundest constitution, and the kindest heart in the county. Mrs Burns believes, as firmly as her creed, that I am *le plus bel esprit, et le plus honnête homme* in the universe ; although she scarcely ever in her life, except the Scriptures of the Old and New Testament, and the Psalms of David in metre, spent five minutes together on either prose or verse. I must except also from this last a certain late publication of Scots poems, which she has perused very devoutly, and all the ballads in the country, as she has (Oh, the partial lover! you will cry) the finest "wood-note wild" I ever heard. I am the more particular in this lady's character, as I know she will henceforth have the honour of a share in your best wishes. She is still at Mauchline, as I am building my house ; for this hovel that I shelter in, while occasionally here, is pervious to every blast that blows, and every shower that falls ; and I am only preserved from being chilled to death by being suffocated with smoke. I do not find my farm that pennyworth I was taught to expect ; but I believe in time it may be a saving bargain. You will be pleased to hear that I have laid aside idle *éclat*, and bind every day after my reapers.

To save me from that horrid situation of at any time going down, in a losing bargain of a farm, to misery, I have taken my Excise instructions, and have my commission in my pocket for any emergency of fortune. If I could set all before your view, whatever disrespect you, in common with the world, have for this business, I know you would approve of my idea.

I will make no apology, dear madam, for this egotistic detail ; I know you and your sister will be interested in every circumstance of it. What signify the silly, idle gewgaws of wealth, or the ideal trumpery of greatness! When fellow-partakers of the same nature fear the same God, have the same benevolence of heart, the same nobleness of soul, the same detestation at everything dishonest, and the same scorn at everything unworthy—if they are not in the dependence of absolute beggary, in the name of common sense, are they not EQUALS? And if the bias, the instinctive bias of their souls, run the same way, why may they not be FRIENDS?

When I may have an opportunity of sending this, Heaven only knows. Shenstone says :—" When one is confined idle within doors by bad weather, the best antidote against *ennui* is to read the letters of or write to one's friends ;" in that case, then, if the weather continues thus, I may scrawl you half a quire.

I very lately—namely, since harvest began—wrote a poem, not in imitation, but in the manner of Pope's " Moral Epistles." It is only a short essay, just to try the strength of my Muse's pinion in that way. I will send you a copy of it when once I have heard from you. I have likewise been laying the foundation of some pretty large poetic works: how the superstructure will come on I leave to that great maker and marrer of projects —TIME. Johnson's collection of Scots songs is going on in the third volume ; and, of consequence, finds me a consumpt for a great deal of idle metre. One of the most tolerable things I have done in that way is two stanzas (p. 233) I made to an air a musical gentleman of my acquaintance (Captain Riddell), composed for the anniversary of his wedding-day, which happens on the 7th of November.

I shall give over this letter for shame. If I should be seized with a scribbling fit before this goes away, I shall make it another letter; and then you may allow your patience a week's respite between the two. I have not room for more than the old, kind, hearty farewell!

To make some amends, *mes chères mesdames,* for dragging you on to this second sheet, and to relieve a little the tiresomeness of my unstudied and uncorrectible prose, I shall transcribe you some of my late poetic bagatelles; though I have, these eight or ten months, done very little that way. One day, in a hermitage on the banks of Nith, belonging to a gentleman in my neighbourhood, who is so good as give me a key at pleasure, I wrote as follows, supposing myself the sequestered, venerable inhabitant of the lonely mansion. . . - R. B.

CLXII.

TO MR MORRISON, MAUCHLINE.

ELLISLAND, *September* 22, 1788.

MY DEAR SIR,—Necessity obliges me to go into my new house even before it be plastered. I will inhabit the one end until the other is finished. About three weeks more, I think, will at farthest be my time, beyond which I cannot stay in this present house. If ever you wish to deserve the blessing of him that was ready to perish; if ever you were in a situation that a little kindness would have rescued you from many evils; if ever you hope to find rest in future states of untried being—get these matters of mine ready. My servant will be out in the beginning of next week for the clock. My compliments to Mrs Morrison. I am, after all my tribulation, dear sir, yours, R. B.

CLXIII.

TO MRS DUNLOP OF DUNLOP.

MAUCHLINE, *27th Sept,* 1788.

I HAVE received twins, dear madam, more than once, but scarcely ever with more pleasure than when I received yours of the 12th instant. To make myself understood: I had wrote to Mr Graham, enclosing my poem addressed to him, and the same post which favoured me with yours brought me an answer from him. It was dated the very day he had received mine; and I am quite at a loss to say whether it was most polite or kind.

Your criticisims, my honoured benefactress, are truly the work of a friend. They are not the blasting depredations of a canker-toothed caterpillar critic; nor are they the fair statement of cold impartiality, balancing with unfeeling exactitude the *pro* and *con* of an author's merits: they are the judicious observations of animated friendship, selecting the beauties of the piece. I am just arrived from Nithsdale, and will be here a fortnight. I was on horseback this morning by three o'clock; for between my wife and my farm is just forty-six miles. As I jogged on in the dark, I was taken with a poetic fit as follows (*Lamentation,* p. 136).

You will not send me your poetic rambles, but, you see, I am no niggard of mine. I am sure your impromptus give me double pleasure; what falls from your pen can neither be unentertaining in itself nor indifferent to me.

The one fault you found is just, but I cannot please myself in an emendation.

What a life of solicitude is the life of a parent! You interested me much in your young couple.

I would not take my folio paper for this epistle, and now I repeat it. I am so jaded with my dirty long journey that I was afraid to drawl into the essence of dulness with anything larger than a quarto, and so I must leave out another rhyme of this morning's manufacture.

I will pay the sapientipotent George most cheerfully, to hear from you ere I leave Ayrshire.   R. B.

CLXIV.

TO MR PETER HILL.

MAUCHLINE, *1st October* 1788.

I HAVE been here in this country about three days, and all that time my chief reading has been the *Address to Lochlomond* you were so obliging as to send to me. Were I empannelled one of the author's jury, to determine his criminalty respecting the sin of poesy, my verdict should be "Guilty! A poet of Nature's making!" It is an excellent method for improvement, and what I believe every poet does, to place some favourite classic author, in his own walks of study and composition, before him as a model. Though your author had not mentioned the name, I could have, at half a glance, guessed his model to be Thomson. Will my brother-poet forgive me if I venture to hint that his imitation of that immortal bard is in two or three places rather more servile than such a genius as his required ?—*e. g.*,

> " To soothe the maddening passions all to peace."
> *Address.*
> " To soothe the throbbing passions into peace."
> THOMSON.

I think the *Address* is, in simplicity, harmony, and elegance of versification, fully equal to the *Seasons.* Like Thomson, too, he has looked into nature for himself: you meet with no copied description. One particular criticism I made at first reading : in no one instance has he said too much. He never flags in his progress, but, like a true poet of Nature's making, kindles in his course. His beginning is simple and modest, as if distrustful of the strength of his pinion ; only, I do not altogether like—

> " Truth,
> The soul of every song that's nobly great."

Fiction is the soul of many a song that is nobly great. Perhaps I am wrong: this may be but a prose criticism. Is not the phrase in line 7, page 6, "Great lake," too much vulgarized by every-day language for so sublime a poem ?

> " Great mass of waters, theme for nobler song !"

is perhaps no emendation. His enumeration of a comparison with other lakes is at once harmonious and poetic. Every reader's ideas must sweep the

> " Winding margin of an hundred miles.'

The perspective that follows mountains blue—the imprisoned billows beating in vain—the wooded isles—the digression on the yew-tree—" Benlomond's lofty, cloud-enveloped head," &c., are beautiful. A thunder-storm is a subject which has been often tried, yet our poet in his grand picture has interjected a circumstance, so far as I know, entirely original—

> " The gloom
> Deep seam'd with frequent streaks of moving fire."

In his preface to the storm, " the glens how dark between," is noble Highland landscape ! The " rain ploughing the red mould," too, is beautifully fancied. " Benlomond's lofty, pathless top," is a good expression ; and the surrounding view from it is truly great : the

> " Silver mist
> Beneath the beaming sun,"

is well described ; and here he has contrived to enliven his poem
with a little of that passion which bids fair, I think, to usurp the
modern Muses altogether.   I know not how far this episode is
beauty upon the whole, but the swain's wish to carry " some fain
idea of the vision bright," to entertain her " partial listening ear,'
is a pretty thought.   But in my opinion the most beautiful pas-
sages in the whole poem are the fowls crowding, in wintry frosts,
to Lochlomond's " hospitable flood ;" their wheeling round, their
lighting, mixing, diving, &c., and the glorious description of the
sportsman.   This last is equal to anything in the *Seasons.*   The
idea of " the floating tribes distant seen, far glistering to the
moon,' provoking his eye as he is obliged to leave them, is a
noble ray of poetic genius.   " The howling winds," the " hideous
roar " of " the white cascades," are all in the same style.

I forget that while I am thus holding forth with the heedless
warmth of an enthusiast, I am perhaps tiring you with nonsense.
I must, however, mention that the last verse of the sixteenth
page is one of the most elegant compliments I have ever seen.   I
must likewise notice that beautiful paragraph beginning " The
gleaming lake, &c." I dare not go into the particular beauties of
the last two paragraphs, but they are admirably fine, and truly
Ossianic.

I must beg your pardon for this lengthened scrawl.   I had no
idea of it when I began—I should like to know who the author
is ; but whoever he be, please present him with my grateful
thanks for the entertainment he has afforded me.

A friend of mine desired me to commission for him two books—
Letters on the Religion Essential to Man—a book you sent me be-
fore ; and *The World Unmasked, or, the Philosopher the Greatest.
Cheat.*   Send me them by the first opportunity.   The Bible you
sent me is truly elegant : I only wish it had been in two volumes.

                                                        R. B.

————

CLXV.

TO THE EDITOR OF " THE STAR."

November 8, 1788.

SIR,—Notwithstanding the opprobrious epithets with which
some of our philosophers and gloomy sectarians have branded our
nature—the principal of universal selfishness, the proneness to all
evil, they have given us—still, the detestation in which inhuma-
nity to the distressed, or insolence to the fallen, are held by all
mankind, shows that they are not natives of the human heart.
Even the unhappy partner of our kind who is undone (the bitter
consequence of his follies or his crimes)—who but sympathises

with the miseries of this ruined profligate brother? We forget the injuries, and feel for the man.

I went, last Wednesday, to my parish church, most cordially to join in grateful acknowledgment to the Author of all good for the consequent blessings of the glorious Revolution. To that auspicious event we owe no less than our liberties, civil and religious; to it we are likewise indebted for the present royal family, the ruling features of whose administration have ever been mildness to the subject and tenderness of his rights.

Bred and educated in revolution principles,—the principles of reason and common sense,—it could not be any silly political prejudice which made my heart revolt at the harsh, abusive manner in which the reverend gentleman mentioned the House of Stuart, and which, I am afraid, was too much the language of the day. We may rejoice sufficiently in our deliverance from past evils without cruelly raking up the ashes of those whose misfortune it was, perhaps as much as their crime, to be the authors of those evils; and we may bless God for all his goodness to us as a nation, without at the same time cursing a few ruined, powerless exiles, who only harboured ideas and made attempts that most of us would have done had we been in their situation.

"The bloody and tyrannical House of Stuart" may be said with propriety and justice, when compared with the present royal family, and the sentiments of our days; but is there no allowance to be made for the manners of the times? Were the royal contemporaries of the Stuarts more attentive to their subjects' rights? Might not the epithets of "bloody and tyrannical" be, with at least equal justice, applied to the House of Tudor, of York, or any other of their predecessors.

The simple state of the case, sir, seems to be this:—At that period the science of government, the knowledge of the true relation between king and subject, was, like other sciences and other knowledge, just in its infancy, emerging from dark ages of ignorance and barbarity.

The Stuarts only contended for prerogatives which they knew their predecessors enjoyed, and which they saw their contemporaries enjoying: but these prerogatives were inimical to the happiness of a nation and the rights of subjects.

In this contest between prince and people, the consequence of that light of science which had lately dawned over Europe—the monarch of France, for example, was victorious over the struggling liberties of his people: with us, luckily, the monarch failed, and his unwarrantable pretensions fell a sacrifice to our rights and happiness. Whether it was owing to the wisdom of leading individuals, or to the justling of parties, I cannot pretend to determine; but, likewise, happily for us, the kingly power was shifted into another branch of the family, who, as they owed the throne

solely to the call of a free people, could claim nothing inconsistent
with the covenanted terms which placed them there.

The Stuarts have been condemned and laughed at for the folly
and impracticability of their attempts in 1715 and 1745. That
they failed, I bless God, but cannot join in the ridicule against
them. Who does not know that the abilities or defects of leaders
and commanders are often hidden until put to the touchstone of
exigency; and that there is a caprice of fortune, an omnipotence
in particular accidents and conjectures of circumstances, which
exalt us as heroes, or brand us as madmen, just as they are for or
against us?

Man, Mr Publisher, is a strange, weak, inconsistent being. Who
would believe, sir, that in this our Augustan age of liberality and
refinement, while we seem so justly sensible and jealous of our
rights and liberties, and animated with such indignation against
the very memory of those who would have subverted them—that
a certain people under our national protection should complain,
not against our monarch and a few favourite advisers, but against
our whole legislative body, for similar oppression, and almost in
the very same terms, as our forefathers did of the House of Stuart?
I will not, I cannot, enter into the merits of the case; but I dare-
say the American Congress in 1776 will be allowed to be as able
and as enlightened as the English Convention was in 1688; and
that their posterity will celebrate the centenary of their deliver-
ance from us, as duly and sincerely as we do ours from the oppres-
sive measures of the wrong-headed House of Stuart.

To conclude, sir—let every man who has a tear for the many
miseries incident to humanity feel for a family illustrious as any
in Europe, and unfortunate beyond historic precedent; and let
every Briton (and particularly every Scotsman) who ever looked
with reverential pity on the dotage of a parent, cast a veil over
the fatal mistakes of the kings of his forefathers.   R. B.

CLXVI.

TO MRS DUNLOP, AT MOREHAM MAINS.

MAUCHLINE, 13th November 1788.

MADAM,—I had the very great pleasure of dining at Dunlop
yesterday. Men are said to flatter women because they are weak
—if it be so, poets must be weaker still; for Misses R. and K. and
Miss G. M'K., with their flattering attentions and artful compli-
ments, absolutely turned my head. I own that they did not lard
me over as many a poet does his patron; but they so intoxicated
me with their sly insinuations and delicate inuendos of compli-

ment, that if it had not been for a lucky recollection how much additional weight and lustre your good opinion and friendship must give me in that circle, I had certainly looked upon myself as a person of no small consequence. I dare not say one word how much I was charmed with the Major's friendly welcome, elegant manner, and acute remark, lest I should be thought to balance my orientalisms of applause over against the finest quey* in Ayrshire which he made me a present of to help and adorn my farm-stock. As it was on Hallow-day, I am determined annually as that day returns, to decorate her horns with an ode of gratitude to the family of Dunlop.

So soon as I know of your arrival at Dunlop, I will take the first conveniency to dedicate a day, or perhaps two, to you and friendship, under the guarantee of the Major's hospitality. There will soon be threescore and ten miles of permanent distance between us; and now that your friendship and friendly correspondence is entwisted with the heart-strings of my enjoyment of life, I must indulge myself in a happy day of " the feast of reason and the flow of soul." 　　　R. B.

CLXVII.

TO DR BLACKLOCK.

MAUCHLINE, *November* 15, 1788.

REVEREND AND DEAR SIR,—As I hear nothing of your motions, but that you are or were out of town, I do not know where this may find you, or whether it will find you at all. I wrote you a long letter, dated from the land of matrimony, in June; but either it had not found you, or, what I dread more, it found you or Mrs Blacklock in too precarious a state of health and spirits to take notice of an idle packet.

I have done many little things for Johnson since I had the pleasure of seeing you; and I have finished one piece in the way of Pope's *Moral Epistles;* but from your silence I have everything to fear, so I have only sent you two melancholy things (*Lamentation*, p. 136, and *The Lazy Mist*, p. 233), which I tremble lest they should too well suit the tone of your present feelings.

In a fortnight I move, bag and baggage, to Nithsdale; till then, my direction is at this place; after that period it will be at Ellisland, near Dumfries. It would extremely oblige me were it but half a line, to let me know how you are, and where you are. Can I be indifferent to the fate of a man to whom I owe so much—a man whom I not only esteem but venerate?

My warmest good wishes and most respectful compliments to Mrs Blacklock and Miss Johnson, if she is with you.

* A young heifer.

I cannot conclude without telling you that I am more and more
pleased with the step I took respecting " my Jean." Two things,
from my happy experience, I set down as apophthegms in life,—
A wife's head is immaterial compared with her heart; and,
" Virtue's (for wisdom, what poet pretends to it ?) ways are ways
of pleasantness, and all her paths are peace." Adieu ! R. B.

CLXVIII.

TO MR JAMES JOHNSON, ENGRAVER.

MAUCHLINE, *November* 15, 1788.

MY DEAR SIR,—I have sent you two more songs. If you have
got any tunes, or anything to correct, please send them by return
of the carrier.

I can easily see, my dear friend, that you will very probably
have four volumes. Perhaps you may not find your account lu-
cratively in this business; but you are a patriot for the music of
your country, and I am certain posterity will look on themselves
as highly indebted to your public spirit. Be not in a hurry; let
us go on correctly, and your name shall be immortal.

I am preparing a flaming preface for your third volume. I see
every day new musical publications advertised; but what are
they? Gaudy, painted butterflies of a day, and then vanish for
ever: but your work will outlive the momentary neglects of idle
fashion, and defy the teeth of time.

Have you never a fair goddess that leads you a wild-goose
chase of amorous devotion? Let me know a few of her qualities,
such as whether she be rather black or fair, plump or thin, short
or tall, &c.; and choose your air, and I shall task my Muse to
celebrate her. R. B.

CLXIX.

TO MRS DUNLOP.

ELLISLAND, 17*th December* 1788.

MY DEAR HONOURED FRIEND,—Yours, dated Edinburgh,
which I have just read, makes me very unhappy. " Almost blind
and wholly deaf," are melancholy news of human nature; but
when told of a much-loved and honoured friend, they carry misery
in the sound. Goodness on your part, and gratitude on mine,
began a tie which has gradually entwisted itself among the dear-
est chords of my bosom, and I tremble at the omens of your late
and present ailing habit and shattered health. You miscalculate
matters widely when you forbid my waiting on you, lest it should

hurt my worldly concerns. My small scale of farming is exceedingly more simple and easy than what you have lately seen at Moreham Mains. But, be that as it may, the heart of the man and the fancy of the poet are the two grand considerations for which I live. If miry ridges and dirty dunghills are to engross the best part of the functions of my soul immortal, I had better been a rook or a magpie at once, and then I should not have been plagued with any ideas superior to breaking of clods and picking up grubs; not to mention barn-door cocks or mallards— creatures with which I could almost exchange lives at any time. If you continue so deaf, I am afraid a visit will be no great pleasure to either of us; but if I hear you are got so well again as to be able to relish conversation, look you to it, madam, for I will make my threatening good. I am to be at the New-Year-Day fair of Ayr; and, by all that is sacred in the world, friend, I will come and see you.

Your meeting, which you so well describe, with your old schoolfellow and friend, was truly interesting. Out upon the ways of the world! They spoil these "social offsprings of the heart." Two veterans of the "men of the world" would have met with little more heart-workings than two old hacks worn out on the road. Apropos, is not the Scotch phrase, "auld lang syne," exceedingly expressive? There is an old song and tune which has often thrilled through my soul. You know I am an enthusiast in old Scotch songs. I shall give you the verses on the other sheet, (*Auld Lang Syne*, p. 234), as I suppose Mr Ker will save you the postage.

Light be the turf on the breast of the Heaven-inspired poet who composed this glorious fragment.* There is more of the fire of native genius in it than in half-a-dozen of modern English Bacchanalians! Now I am on my hobby-horse, I cannot help inserting two other old stanzas, which please me mightily (*My Bonnie Mary*, p. 235). R. B.

CLXX.

TO MR JOHN TENNANT.

December 22, 1788.

I YESTERDAY tried my cask of whisky for the first time, and I assure you it does you great credit. It will bear five waters, strong, or six, ordinary toddy. The whisky of this country is a most rascally liquor; and, by consequence, only drunk by the most rascally part of the inhabitants. I am persuaded, if you once get a footing here, you might do a great deal of business in the way

---

* This is a mere attempt at mystification, Burns himself being the author

of consumpt; and should you commence distiller again ,this is
the native barley country. I am ignorant if, in your present way
of dealing, you would think it worth your while to extend your
business so far as this country side. I write you this on the ac-
count of an accident, which I must take the merit of having partly
designed to. A neighbour of mine, a John Currie, miller in Carse-
mill—a man who is, in a word, a "very" good man, even for a
L.500 bargain—he and his wife were in my house the time I
broke open the cask. They keep a country public-house, and sell
a great deal of foreign spirits, but all along thought that whisky
would have degraded their house. They were perfectly astonish-
ed at my whisky, both for its taste and strength ; and by their
desire, I write you to know if you could supply them with liquor
of an equal quality, and what price. Please write me by first
post, and direct to me at Ellisland, near Dumfries. If you could
take a jaunt this way yourself, I have a spare spoon, knife and
fork, very much at your service. My compliments to Mrs Ten
nant and all the good folks in Glenconner and Barquharry.

R. B

CLXXI.

TO MR WILLAIM CRUIKSHANK.

ELLISLAND, [*December*] 1788.

I HAVE not room, my dear friend, to answer all the particulars
of your last kind letter. I shall be in Edinburgh on some business
very soon ; and as I shall be two days, or perhaps three, in town,
we shall discuss matters *vivâ voce*. My knee, I believe, will never
be entirely well; and an unlucky fall this winter has made it still
worse. I well remember the circumstance you allude to respect-
ing Creech's opinion of Mr Nicol ; but as the first gentleman
owes me still about fifty pounds, I dare not meddle in the affair.

It gave me a very heavy heart to read such accounts of the con-
sequence of your quarrel with that puritanic, rotten-hearted,
scoundrel, A———. If, notwithstanding your unprecedented
industry in public, and your irreproachable conduct in private
life, he still has you so much in his power, what ruin may he not
bring on some others I could name ?

Many and happy returns of seasons to you, with your dearest
and worthiest friend, and the lovely little pledge of your happy
union. May the great Author of life, and of every enjoyment
that can render life delightful, make her that comfortable blessing
to you both which you so ardently wish for, and which, allow me
to say, you so well deserve ! Glance over the foregoing verses,
and let me have your blots. Adieu !   R. B.

CLXXII.
TO MRS DUNLOP.

ELLISLAND, *New-Year-Day Morning*, 1789.

THIS, dear madam, is a morning of wishes, and would to God that I came under the apostle James's description !—*the prayer of a righteous man availeth much.* In that case, madam, you should welcome in a year full of blessings : everything that obstructs or disturbs tranquillity and self-enjoyment should be removed, and every pleasure that frail humanity can taste should be yours. I own myself so little a Presbyterian, that I approve set times and seasons of more than ordinary acts of devotion, for breaking in on that habituated routine of life and thought which is so apt to reduce our existence to a kind of instinct, or even sometimes, and with some minds, to a state very little superior to mere machinery.

This day—the first Sunday of May—a breezy, blue-skied noon some time about the beginning, and a hoary morning and calm sunny day about the end of autumn—these, time out of mind, have been with me a kind of holiday.

I believe I owe this to that glorious paper in the "Spectator," *The Vision of Mirza*—a piece that struck my young fancy before I was capable of fixing an idea to a word of three syllables : " On the 5th day of the moon, which, according to the custom of my forefathers, I always *keep holy*, after having washed myself and offered up my morning devotions, I ascended the high hill of Bagdad, in order to pass the rest of the day in meditation and prayer."

We know nothing, or next to nothing, of the substance or structure of our souls, so cannot account for those seeming caprices in them that one should be particularly pleased with this thing, or struck with that, which, on minds of a different cast, makes no extraordinary impression. I have some favourite flowers in spring, among which are the mountain-daisy, the harebell, the foxglove, the wild-brier rose, the budding birch, and the hoary hawthorn, that I view and hang over with particular delight. I never hear the loud, solitary whistle of the curlew in a summer noon, or the wild, mixing cadence of a troop of gray plovers in an autumnal morning, without feeling an elevation of soul like the enthusiasm of devotion or poetry. Tell me, my dear friend, to what can this be owing ? Are we a piece of machinery, which, like the Æolian harp, passive, takes the impression of the passing accident ? Or do these workings argue something within us above the trodden clod ? I own myself partial to such proofs of those awful and important realities—a God that made all things—man's immaterial and immortal nature—and a world of weal or wo beyond death and the grave !   R. B.

CLXXIII.

TO DR MOORE.

ELLISLAND, *4th Jan.* 1789.

SIR,—As often as I think of writing to you, which has been three or four times every week these six months, it gives me something so like the idea of an ordinary-sized statue offering at a conversation with the Rhodian colossus, that my mind misgives me, and the affair always miscarries somewhere between purpose and resolve. I have at last got some business with you, and business letters are written by the style-book. I say my business is with you, sir ; for you never had any with me, except the business that benevolence has in the mansion of poverty.

The character and employment of a poet were formerly my pleasure, but are now my pride. I know that a very great deal of my late *éclat* was owing to the singularity of my situation, and the honest prejudice of Scotsmen ; but still, as I said in the pre- face to my first edition, I do look upon myself as having some pretensions from nature to the poetic character. I have not a doubt but the knack, the aptitude to learn the Muses' trade, is a gift bestowed by Him " who forms the secret bias of the soul ;" but I as firmly believe that *excellence* in the profession is the fruit of industry, labour, attention, and pains—at least I am resolved to try my doctrine by the test of experience. Another appearance from the press I put off to a very distant day—a day that may never arrive ; but poesy I am determined to prosecute with all my vigour. Nature has given very few, if any, of the profession the talents of shining in every species of composition. I shall try (for until trial it is impossible to know) whether she has qualified me to shine in any one. The worst of it is, by the time one has finished a piece, it has been so often viewed and reviewed before the mental eye, that one loses in a good measure the powers of critical discrimination. Here the best criterion I know is a friend, not only of abilities to judge, but with good-nature enough, like a prudent teacher with a young learner, to praise perhaps a little more than is exactly just, lest the thin-skinned animal fall into that most deplorable of all poetic diseases—heart-breaking despon- dency of himself. Dare I, sir, already immensely indebted to your goodness, ask the additional obligation of your being that friend to me ? I enclose you an essay of mine, in a walk of poesy to me entirely new ; I mean the Epistle addressed to R. G., Esquire, or Robert Graham of Fintry, Esq., a gentleman of uncommon worth, to whom I lie under very great obligations. The story of the poem, like most of my poems, is connected with my own story ; and to give you the one I must give you something of the other. I can- not boast of Mr Creech's ingenuous fair-dealing to me. He kept me hanging about Edinburgh from the 7th August 1787 until the 13th April 1788, before he would condescend to give me a statement of affairs ; nor had I got it even then, but for an angry letter I wrote him, which irritated his pride. " I could" not " a tale," but a detail " unfold ;" but what am I that should speak against the Lord's anointed Bailie of Edinburgh ?

I believe I shall in whole (£100 copyright included) clear about £400 some little odds ; and even part of this depends upon what the gentleman has yet to settle with me. I give you this information, because you did me the honour to interest yourself much in my welfare. I give you this information, but I give it to yourself only ; for I am still much in the gentleman's mercy. Perhaps I injure the man in the idea I am sometimes tempted to have of him : God forbid I should ! A little time will try, for in a month I shall go to town to wind up the business, if possible.

To give the rest of my story in brief: I have married " my Jean," and taken a farm. With the first step, I have every day more and more reason to be satisfied ; with the last, it is rather the reverse. I have a younger brother, who supports my aged mother ; another still younger brother, and three sisters in a farm. On my last return from Edinburgh, it cost me about £180 to save them from ruin. Not that I have lost so much : I only interposed between my brother and his impending fate by the loan of so much. I give myself no airs on this, for it was mere selfishness on my part. I was conscious that the wrong scale of the balance was pretty heavily charged, and I thought that throwing a little filial piety and fraternal affection into the scale in my favour, might help to smooth matters at the *grand reckoning*. There is still one thing would make my circumstances quite easy ; I have an Excise-officer's commission, and I live in the midst of a country division. My request to Mr Graham, who is one of the commissioners of Excise, was, if in his power, to procure me that division. If I were very sanguine, I might hope that some of my great patrons might procure me a treasury-warrant for supervisor, surveyor-general, &c.

Thus, secure of a livelihood, " to thee, sweet Poetry, delightful maid," I would consecrate my future days.   R. B.

CLXXIV.

TO MR ROBERT AINSLIE.

ELLISLAND, *January* 6, 1789.

MANY happy returns of the season to you, my dear sir. May you be comparatively happy, up to your comparative worth, among the sons of men ; which wish would, I am sure, make you one of the most blest of the human race.

I do not know if passing a " writer to the signet" be a trial of scientific merit, or a mere business of friends and interest. However it be, let me quote you my two favourite passages, which, though I have repeated them tèn thousand times, still they rouse my manhood, and steel my resolution like inspiration :—

> " On Reason build resolve,
> That column of true majesty in man."—*Young.*

> " Hear, Alfred, hero of the state,
> Thy genius heaven's high will declare;
> The triumph of the truly great,   -
> Is never, never to despair !
> Is never to despair."—*Masque of Alfred.*

I grant you enter the lists of life to struggle for bread, business, notice, and distinction, in common with hundreds. But who are they ? Men like yourself, and of that aggregate body your compeers, seven-tenths of them come short of your advantages, natural and accidental ; while two of those that remain either neglect their parts, as flowers blooming in a desert, or misspend their strength like a bull goring a bramble bush.

But to change the theme : I am still catering for Johnson's publication ; and among others, I have brushed up the following old favourite song a little, with a view to your worship. I have only altered a word here and there ; but if you like the humour of it, we shall think of a stanza or two to add to it.   ___ R. B.

CLXXV.

TO JOHN M'MURDO, ESQ.

ELLISLAND, *9th Jan.* 1789.

SIR,—A poet and a beggar are in so many points of view alike, that one might take them for the same individual character under different designations ; were it not, that though, with a trifling poetic license, poets may be styled beggars, yet the converse of the proposition does not hold, that every beggar is a poet. In one particular, however, they remarkably agree ; if you help either the one or the other to a mug of ale or the picking of a bone, they will very willingly repay you with a song. This occurs to me at present (as I have just despatched a well-lined rib of J. Kilpatrick's Highlander ; a bargain for which I am indebted to you), in the style of our ballad-printers, " Five Excellent New Songs." The enclosed is nearly my newest song, and one that has cost me some pains, though that is but an equivocal mark of its excellence. Two or three others which I have by me shall do themselves the honour to wait on your after-leisure : petitioners for admittance into favour must not harass the condescension of their benefactor.

You see, sir, what it is to patronize a poet. 'Tis like being a magistrate in Pettyborough ; you do them the favour to preside in their council for one year, and your name bears the prefatory stigma of bailie for life.

With not the compliments, but the best wishes, the sincerest prayers of the season for you, that you may see many happy years with Mrs M'Murdo and your family—two blessings, by-the-bye, to which your rank does not entitle you—a loving wife and fine family being almost the only good things of this life to which the farm-house and cottage have an exclusive right—I have the honour to be, sir, your much indebted and very humble servant,

R. BURNS.

CLXXVI.

TO PROFESSOR DUGALD STEWART.

ELLISLAND, 20th Jan. 1789.

SIR,—The enclosed sealed packet I sent to Edinburgh a few lays after I had the happiness of meeting you in Ayrshire, but ,ou were gone for the Continent. I have now added a few more of ly productions, those for which I am indebted to the Nithsdale Muses. The piece inscribed to R. G., Esq., is a copy of verses 1 ent to Mr Graham of Fintry, accompanying a request for his ssistance in a matter to me of very great moment. To that rentleman I am already doubly indebted for deeds of kindness of crious import to my dearest interests, done in a manner grateful) the delicate feelings of sensibility. This poem is a species of composition new to me ; but I do not intend it shall be my last ssay of the kind, as you will see by the *Poet's Progress*. These fragments, if my design succeed, are but a small part of the intended whole. I propose it shall be the work of my utmost exertions, ripened by years : of course I do not wish it much known. The fragment beginning "A little, upright, pert, tart," &c., I have not shewn to man living, till I now send it you. It forms the postulata, the axioms, the definition of a character, which, if it appear at all, shall be placed in a variety of lights. This particular part I send you merely as a sample of my hand at portrait-sketching ; but, lest idle conjecture should pretend to point out the original, please to let it be for your single, sole inspection.

Need 1 make any apology for this trouble to a gentleman who has treated me with such marked benevolence and peculiar kindness ; who has entered into my interests with so much zeal, and on whose critical decisions I can so fully depend ? A poet as I am by trade, these decisions are to me of the last consequence. My late transient acquaintance among some of the mere rank and file of greatness, I resign with ease ; but to the distinguished champions of genius and learning, I shall be ever ambitious of being known. The native genius and accurate discernment in Mr Stewart's critical strictures; the justice (iron justice, for he has no bowels of compassion for a poor poetic sinner) of Dr Gregory's remarks, and the delicacy of Professor Dalzell's taste, I shall ever revere.

I shall be in Edinburgh some time next month. I have the honour to be, sir, your highly obliged and very humble servant,
R. B.

CLXXVII.

TO CAPTAIN RIDDEL.

ELLISLAND, 1789.

SIR,—I wish from my inmost soul it were in my power to give you a more substantial gratification and return for all the goodness to the poet, than transcribing a few of his idle rhymes. However, " an old song," though to a proverb an instance of insignificance, is generally the only coin a poet has to pay with.

If my poems which I have transcribed, and mean still to transcribe, into your book, were equal to the grateful respect and high esteem I bear for the gentleman to whom I present them, they would be the finest poems in the language. As they are, they will at least be a testimony with what sincerity I have the honour to be, sir, your devoted humble servant,   R. B.

CLXXVIII.

TO BISHOP GEDDES.

ELLISLAND, 3d Feb. 1789.

VENERABLE FATHER,—As I am conscious that, wherever I am, you do me the honour to interest yourself in my welfare, it gives me pleasure to inform you that I am here at last, stationary in the serious business of life, and have now not only the retired leisure, but the hearty inclination, to attend to those great and important questions—what I am, where I am, and for what I am destined.

that first concern—the conduct of the man—there was ever but one side on which I was habitually blameable, and there I have secured myself in the way pointed out by nature and nature's God. I was sensible that, to so helpless a creature as a poor poet, a wife and family were encumbrances, which a species of prudence would bid him shun ; but when the alternative was, being at eter-

nal warfare with myself, on account of habitual follies, to give
them no worse name, which no general example, no licentious wit,
no sophistical infidelity, would to me ever justify, I must have
been a fool to have hesitated, and a madman to have made another
choice. Besides, I had in "my Jean" a long and much-loved
fellow-creature's happiness or misery among my hands; and who
could trifle with such a deposit?

In the affair of a livelihood, I think myself tolerably secure. I
have good hopes of my farm; but should they fail, I have an
Excise-commission, which, on my simple petition, will at any time
procure me bread. There is a certain stigma affixed to the cha-
racter of an Excise-officer, but I do not pretend to borrow honour
from my profession; and though the salary be comparatively
small, it is luxury to anything that the first twenty-five years of
my life taught me to expect.

Thus, with a rational aim and method in life, you may easily
guess, my reverend and much-honoured friend, that my character-
istical trade is not forgotten. I am, if possible, more than ever
an enthusiast to the Muses. I am determined to study man and
nature, and in that view incessantly; and to try if the ripening
and corrections of years can enable me to produce something
worth preserving.

You will see in your book—which I beg your pardon for detain-
ing so long—that I have been tuning my lyre on the banks of
Nith. Some large poetic plans that are floating in my imagina-
tion, or partly put in execution, I shall impart to you when I have
the pleasure of meeting with you, which, if you are then in Edin-
burgh, I shall have about the beginning of March.

That acquaintance, worthy sir, with which you were pleased to
honour me, you must still allow me to challenge; for with what-
ever unconcern I give up my transient connection with the merely
great, I cannot lose the patronizing notice of the learned and good
without the bitterest regret.　　　　　　　　　　　R. B.

CLXXIX.

TO MR JAMES BURNES.

ELLISLAND, *9th Feb.* 1789.

MY DEAR SIR,—Why I did not write to you long ago, is what
—even on the rack—I could not answer. If you can in your mind
form an idea of indolence, dissipation, hurry, cares, change of
country, entering on untried scenes of life, all combined, you will
save me the trouble of a blushing apology. It could not be want
of regard for a man for whom I had a high esteem before I knew
him—an esteem which has much increased since I did know him.

and, this caveat entered, I shall plead guilty to any other indict-
ment with which you shall please to charge me.

After I parted from you, for many months my life was one con-
tinued scene of dissipation. Here at last I am become stationary,
and have taken a farm and—a wife.

The farm is beautifully situated on the Nith, a large river that
runs by Dumfries, and falls into the Solway Frith. I have gotten
a lease of my farm as long as I pleased; but how it may turn out
is just a guess, and it is yet to improve and enclose, &c.; however,
I have good hopes of my bargain on the whole.

My wife is "my Jean," with whose story you are partly acquaint-
ed. I found I had a much-loved fellow-creature's happiness or
misery among my hands, and I durst not trifle with so sacred a
deposit. Indeed, I have not any reason to repent the step I have
taken, as I have attached myself to a very good wife, and have
shaken myself loose of a very bad failing.

I have found my book a very profitable business; and with the
profits of it I have begun life pretty decently. Should fortune not
favour me in farming, as I have no great faith in her fickle lady-
ship, I have provided myself in another resource, which, however
some folks may affect to despise it, is still a comfortable shift in
the day of misfortune. In the heyday of my fame, a gentleman,
whose name at least I daresay you know, as his estate lies some-
where near Dundee,—Mr Graham of Fintry, one of the commis-
sioners of Excise,—offered me the commission of an Excise-officer.
I thought it prudent to accept the offer; and accordingly I took
my instructions, and have my commission by me. Whether I
may ever do duty, or be a penny the better for it, is what I do
not know; but I have the comfortable assurance that, come
whatever ill-fate will, I can, on my simple petition to the Excise-
board, get into employ.

We have lost poor uncle Robert this winter. He has long been
very weak, and with very little alteration on him : he expired 3d
January.

His son William has been with me this winter, and goes in May
to be an apprentice to a mason. His other son, the eldest, John,
comes to me, I expect, in summer. They are both remarkably
stout young fellows, and promise to do well. His only daughter,
Fanny, has been with me ever since her father's death, and I
purpose keeping her in my family till she be quite woman-grown,
and fit for better service. She is one of the cleverest girls, and
has one of the most amiable dispositions, I have ever seen.

All friends in this county and Ayrshire are well. Remember
me to all friends in the north. My wife joins me in compliments
to Mrs B. and family. I am ever, my dear cousin, yours sincerely
R. B.

CLXXX.

ISLE, *2d March* 1789.

MY DEAR WILLIAM,—I arrived from Edinburgh only the night before last, so could not answer your epistle sooner. I congratulate you on the prospect of employ; and I am indebted to you for one of the best letters that has been written by any mechanic-lad in Nithsdale, or Annandale, or any dale on either side of the border, this twelvemonth. Not that I would have you always affect the stately stilts of studied composition, but surely writing a handsome letter is an accomplishment worth courting; and, with attention and practice, I can promise you that it will soon be an accomplishment of yours. If my advice can serve you— that is to say, if you can resolve to accustom yourself not only in reviewing your own deportment, manners, &c., but also in carrying your consequent resolutions of amending the faulty parts into practice—my small knowledge and experience of the world is heartily at your service. I intended to have given you a sheetful of counsels, but some business has prevented me. In a word, learn taciturnity; let that be your motto. Though you had the wisdom of Newton, or the wit of Swift, garrulousness would lower you in the eyes of your fellow-creatures. I'll probably write you next week. I am your brother,   ROBERT BURNS.

CLXXXI.

TO CLARINDA.

9th March 1789.

MADAM,—The letter you wrote me to Heron's carried its own answer in its bosom; you forbade me to write you, unless I was willing to plead guilty to a certain indictment that you were pleased to bring against me. As I am convinced of my own innocence, and, though conscious of high imprudence and egregious folly, can lay my hand on my breast and attest the rectitude of my heart, you will pardon me, madam, if I do not carry my complaisance so far as humbly to acquiesce in the name of Villain, merely out of compliment to your opinion, much as I esteem your judgment, and warmly as I regard your worth.

I have already told you, and I again aver it, that at the period of time alluded to, I was not under the smallest moral tie to Mrs Burns; nor did I, nor could I then know, all the powerful circumstances that omnipotent necessity was busy laying wait for me. When you call over the scenes that have passed between us, you will survey the conduct of an honest man, struggling successfully with temptations, the most powerful that ever beset humanity and preserving untainted honour, in situations where the austerest virtue would have forgiven a fall—situations that, I will dare to say, not a single individual of all his kind, even with half his sen. sibility and passion, could have encountered without ruin ; and I leave you to guess, madam, how such a man is likely to digest an accusation of perfidious treachery. ·

Was I to blame, madam, in being the distracted victim of charms which, I affirm it, no man ever approached with impunity ? Had I seen the least glimmering of hope that these charms could ever have been mine ; or even had not iron necessity—— But these are unavailing words.

I would have called on you when I was in town ; indeed I could not have resisted it, but that Mr Ainslie told me that you were determined to avoid your windows while I was in town, lest even a glance of me should occur in the street.

When I shall have regained your good opinion, perhaps I may venture to solicit your friendship ; but, be that as it may, the first of her sex I ever knew shall always be the object of my warmest good wishes.   SYLVANDER.

<hr/>

CLXXXII.

TO MRS DUNLOP.

ELLISLAND, 4th March 1789.

HERE am I, my honoured friend, returned safe from the capital. To a man who has a home, however humble or remote,—if that home is like mine, the scene of domestic comfort,—the bustle of Edinburgh will soon be a business of sickening disgust.

" Vain pomp and glory of this world I hate you."

When I must sculk into a corner, lest the rattling equipage of some gaping blockhead should mangle me in the mire, I am tempted to exclaim, " What merits has he had, or what demerit have I had, in some state of pre-existence, that he is ushered into this state of being with the sceptre of rule and the key of riches in his puny fist, and I am kicked into the world, the sport of folly, or the victim of pride ?" I have read somewhere of a monarch (in Spain I think it was), who was so out of humour with the Ptolemæan system of astronomy, that he said, had he been of the Creator's council, he could have saved him a great deal of labour and absurdity. I will not defend this blasphemous speech ; but often, as I have glided with humble stealth through the pomp of Princes Street, it has suggested itself to me, as an improvement on the present human figure, that a man, in proportion to his own conceit of his consequence in the world, could have pushed out the longitude of his common size, as a snail pushes out his horns, or as we draw out a prospect-glass. This ·trifling alter♦

tion, not to mention the prodigious saving it would be in the tear and wear of the neck and limb sinews of many of His Majesty's liege-subjects, in the way of tossing the head and tiptoe strutting, would evidently turn out a vast advantage, in enabling us at once to adjust the ceremonials in making a bow, or making way to a great man, and that, too, within a second of the precise spherical angle of reverence, or an inch of the particular point of respectful distance, which the important creature itself requires ; as a measuring glance at its towering altitude would determine the affair like instinct.

You are right, madam, in your idea of poor Mylne's poem, which he has addressed to me. The piece has a good deal of merit, but it has one great fault—it is by far too long. Besides, my success has encouraged such a shoal of ill-spawned monsters to crawl into public notice, under the title of Scottish poets, that the very term Scottish poetry borders on the burlesque. When I write to Mr Carfrae, I shall advise him rather to try one of his deceased friend's English pieces. I am prodigiously hurried with my own matters, else I would have requested a perusal of all Mylne's poetic performances, and would have offered his friends my assistance in either selecting or correcting what would be proper for the press. What it is that occupies me so much, and perhaps a little oppresses my present spirits, shall fill up a paragraph in some future letter. In the meantime, allow me to close this epistle with a few lines done by a friend of mine. . . . I give you them, that, as you have seen the original, you may guess whether one or two alterations I have ventured to make in them be any real improvement :—

> " Like the fair plant that from our touch withdraws,
> Shrink, mildly fearful, even from applause,
> Be all a mother's fondest hope can dream,
> And all you are, my charming * * * *, seem.
> Straight as the foxglove, ere her bells disclose,
> Mild as the maiden-blushing hawthorn blows,
> Fair as the fairest of each lovely kind,
> Your form shall be the image of your mind;
> Your manners shall so true your soul express,
> That all shall long to know the worth they guess;
> Congenial hearts shall greet with kindred love,
> And even sick'ning envy must approve."*

R. B.

CLXXXIII.

TO THE REV. P. CARFRAE.

[ELLISLAND, *March* 1789 ?]

REV. SIR,—I do not recollect that I have ever felt a severer pang of shame, than on looking at the date of your obliging letter which accompanied Mr Mylne's poem.

* These beautiful lines, we have reason to believe are the production of the lady to whom this letter is addressed.—CURRIE.

I am much to blame: the honour Mr Mylne has done me,
greatly enhanced in its value by the endearing, though melan-
choly circumstance of its being the last production of his Muse,
deserved a better return.

I-have, as you hint, thought of sending a copy of the poem to
some periodical publication; but, on second thoughts, I am afraid
that, in the present case, it would be an improper step. My suc-
cess—perhaps as much accidental as merited—has brought an in-
undation of nonsense under the name of Scottish poetry. Sub-
scription-bills for Scottish poems have so dunned, and daily do
dun, the public, that the very name is in danger of contempt.
For these reasons, if publishing any of Mr Mylne's poems in a
magazine, &c., be at all prudent, in my opinion it certainly should
not be a Scottish poem. The profits of the labours of a man of
genius are, I hope, as honourable as any profits whatever; and
Mr Mylne's relations are most justly entitled to that honest har-
vest which fate has denied himself to reap. But let the friends of
Mr Mylne's fame (among whom I crave the honour of ranking
myself) always keep in eye his respectability as a man and as a
poet, and take no measure that, before the world knows anything
about him, would risk his name and character being classed with
the fools of the times.

I have, sir, some experience of publishing; and the way in
which I would proceed with Mr Mylne's poems is this:—I will
publish, in two or three English and Scottish public papers any
one of his English poems which should, by private judges, be
thought the most excellent, and mention it at the same time as
one of the productions of a Lothian farmer of respectable charac-
ter, lately deceased; whose poems his friends had it in idea to pub-
lish soon by subscription, for the sake of his numerous family—
not in pity to that family, but in justice to what his friends think
the poetic merits of the deceased; and to secure, in the most
effectual manner, to those tender connections, whose right it is,
the pecuniary reward of those merits.   R. B.

CLXXXIV.

TO MR PETER HILL, BOOKSELLER, EDINBURGH:

[ELLISLAND, *March* 1789?]

MY DEAR HILL,—I shall say nothing to your mad present—
you have so long and often been of important service to me, and
I suppose you mean to go on conferring obligations until I shall
not be able to lift up my face before you.   In the meantime, as
Sir Roger de Coverley, because it happened to be a cold day in
which he made his will, ordered his servants greatcoats for

mourning; so because I have been this week plagued with an in
digestion, I have sent you by the carrier a fine old ewe-milk
cheese.

Indigestion is the devil—nay, 'tis the devil and all. It besets a
.man in every one of his senses. I loose my appetite at the sight
of successful knavery, and sicken to loathing at the noise and non-
sense of self-important folly. When the hollow-hearted wretch
takes me by the hand, the feeling spoils my dinner; the proud
man's wine so offends my palate, that it chokes me in the gullet;
and the *pulvilised*, feathered, pert coxcomb is so disgustful in my
nostril, that my stomach turns.

If ever you have any of these disagreeable sensations, let me
prescribe for you patience and a bit of my cheese. I know that
you are no niggard of your good things among your friends, and
some of them are in much need of a slice. There, in my eye, is
our friend Smellie—a man positively of the first abilities and
greatest strength of mind, as well as one of the best hearts and
keenest wits that I ever met with; when you see him—as alas!
he too is smarting at the pinch of distressful circumstances, aggra-
vated by the sneer of contumelious greatness—a bit of my cheese
alone will not cure him; but if you add a tankard of brown stout,
and superadd a magnum of right Oporto, you will see his sorrows
vanish like the morning mist before the summer sun.

Candlish, the earliest friend, except my only brother, that I
have on earth, and one of the worthiest fellows that ever any man
called by the name of friend, if a luncheon of my best cheese
would help to rid him of some of his superabundant modesty, you
would do well to give it him.

David, with his *Courant*, comes, too, across my recollection, and
I beg you will help him largely from the said ewe-milk cheese, to
enable him to digest those bedaubing paragraphs with which
he is eternally larding the lean characters of certain great men
in a certain great town. I grant you the periods are very
well turned; so, a fresh egg is a very good thing; but when
thrown at a man in a pillory, it does not at all improve his figure,
not to mention the irreparable loss of the egg.

My facetious friend Dunbar I would wish also to be a partaker;
not to digest his spleen, for that he laughs off, but to digest his
last night's wine at the last field-day of the Crochallan corps.

Among our common friends I must not forget one of the dearest
of them—Cunningham. The brutality, insolence, and selfishness
of a world unworthy of having such a fellow as he is in it, I know
sticks in his stomach, and if you can help him to anything that
will make him a little easier on that score, it will be very obliging.

As to honest John Somerville, he is such a contented, happy
man, that I know not what can annoy him, except, perhaps, he
may not have got the better of a parcel of modest anecdotes which

a certain poet gave him one night at supper the last time the said poet was in town.

Though I have mentioned so many men of law, I shall have nothing to do with them professionally : the faculty are beyond my prescription. As to their clients, that is another thing—they have much to digest !

The clergy I pass by : their profundity of erudition and their liberality of sentiment, their total want of pride and their detestation of hypocrisy, are so proverbially notorious, as to place them far, far above either my praise or censure.

I was going to mention a man of worth, whom I have the honour to call friend—the Laird of Craigdarroch,—but I have spoken to the landlord of the King's-Arms Inn here to have at the next county meeting a large ewe-milk cheese on the table, for the benefit of the Dumfriesshire Whigs, to enable them to digest the Duke of Queensberry's late political conduct.

I have just this moment an opportunity of a private hand to Edinburgh, as perhaps you would not digest double postage. So God bless you.   R. B.

CLXXXV.

TO DR MOORE.

ELLISLAND, 23d *March* 1789.

SIR,—The gentleman who will deliver this is a Mr Nielson, a worthy clergyman in my neighbourhood, and a very particular acquaintance of mine. As I have troubled him with this packet, I must turn him over to your goodness, to recompense him for it in a way in which he much needs your assistance, and where you can effectually serve him. Mr Nielson is on his way for France, to wait on his Grace of Queensberry, on some little business of a good deal of importance to him ; and he wishes for your instructions respecting the most eligible mode of travelling, &c., for him when he has crossed the Channel. I should not have dared to take this liberty with you, but that I am told, by those who have the honour of your personal acquaintance, that to be a poor honest Scotchman is a letter of recommendation to you, and that to have it in your power to serve such a character gives you much pleasure.

The enclosed Ode is a compliment to the memory of the late Mrs Oswald of Auchencruive. You probably knew her personally, an honour of which I cannot boast ; but I spent my early years in her neighbourhood, and among her servants and tenants. I know that she was detested with the most heartfelt cordiality. However, in the particular part of her conduct which roused my poetic wrath she was much less blameable. In January last, on my road to Ayrshire, I had put up at Bailie Whigham's, in Sanquhar, the only tolerable inn in the place. The frost was keen, and the grim evening and howling wind were ushering in a night of snow and drift. My horse and I were both much fatigued with the labours of the day; and just as my friend the bailie and I were bidding defiance to the storm, over a smoking bowl, in wheels the funeral pageantry of the late great Mrs Oswald, and poor I am forced to brave all the horrors of the tempestuous night, and jade my horse —my young favourite horse, whom I had just christened Pegasus —twelve miles farther on, through the wildest moors and hills of Ayrshire, to New Cumnock, the next inn. The powers of poesy and prose sink under me when I would describe what I felt. Suffice it to say, that when a good fire at New Cumnock had so far recovered my frozen sinews, I sat down and wrote the enclosed Ode (p. 139).

I was àt Edinburgh lately, and settled finally with Mr Creech; and I must own that at last he has been amicable and fair with me.   R. B.

CLXXXVI.

TO MR PETER HILL.

ELLISLAND, 2d April 1789.

I WILL make no excuse, my dear Bibliopolus, that I have sat down to write you on this vile paper, stained with the sanguinary scores of " thae horse-leeches o' the Excise."

· It is economy, sir—it is that cardinal virtue, prudence; so I beg you will sit down, and either compose or borrow a panegyric. If you are going to borrow, apply to our friend Ramsay for the assistance of the author of the pretty little buttering paragraphs of eulogium on your thrice-honoured and never-enough-to-be-praised MAGISTRACY—how they hunt down a housebreaker with the sanguinary perseverance of a bloodhound— how they outdo a terrier in a badger-hole in unearthing a resetter of stolen goods— how they steal on a thoughtless troop of night-nymphs as a spaniel winds the unsuspecting covey—or how they riot over a ravaged * * as a cat does o'er a plundered mouse-nest—how they new vamp old churches, aiming at appearances of piety, plan squares and colleges, to pass for men of taste and learning, &c., &c., &c.; while Old Edinburgh, like the doting mother of a parcel of wild prodigals, may sing *Hooly and fairly*, or cry *Wae's me that e'er I saw ye!* but still must put her hand in her pocket, and pay whatever scores the young dogs think proper to contract.

I was going to say—but this parenthesis has put me out of breath—that you should get that manufacturer of the tinselled crockery of magistratial reputations, who makes so distinguished and distinguishing a figure in the *Evening Courant*, to compose, or rather to compound, something very clever on my remarkable frugality ; that I write to one of my most esteemed friends on this wretched paper, which was originally intended for the venal fist of some drunken exciseman, to take dirty notes in a miserable vault of an ale-cellar.

O Frugality ! thou mother of ten thousand blessings—thou cook of fat beef and dainty greens ! thou manufacturer of warm Shetland hose and comfortable surtouts ! thou old housewife, darning thy decayed stockings with thy ancient spectacles on thy aged nose—lead me, hand me in thy clutching palsied fist, up those heights and through those thickets hitherto inaccessible and impervious to my anxious, weary feet—not those Parnassian crags, bleak and barren, where the hungry worshippers of fame are, breathless, clambering, hanging between heaven and hell, but those glittering cliffs of Potosi, where the all-sufficient, all-powerful deity, Wealth, holds his immediate court of joys and pleasures ; where the sunny exposure of plenty, and the hot walls of profusion, produce those blissful fruits of luxury, exotics in this world, and natives of paradise 1 Thou withered sibyl, my sage conductress, usher me into thy refulgent, adored presence ! The power, splendid and potent as he now is, was once the puling nursling of thy faithful care and tender arms ! Call me thy son, thy cousin, thy kinsman, or favourite, and adjure the god by the scenes of his infant years no longer to repulse me as a stranger or an alien, but to favour me with his peculiar countenance and protection ! He daily bestows his greatest kindness on the undeserving and the worthless—assure him that I bring ample documents of meritorious demerits ! Pledge yourself for me, that, for the glorious cause of lucre, I will do anything, be anything, but the horse-leech of private oppression, or the vulture of public robbery !

But to descend from heroics—what have you done with my trunk ? Please let me have it by the first carrier.

I want a *Shakspeare :* let me know what plays your used copy of *Bell's Shakspeare* wants. I want likewise an English dictionary —Johnson's, I suppose, is best. In these, and all my *prose* commissions the cheapest is always the best for me. There is a small debt of honour that I owe Mr Robert Cleghorn, in Saughton Mills, my worthy friend and your well-wisher. Please give him, and urge him to take it, the first time you see him, ten shillings worth of anything you have to sell, and place it to my account.

The library scheme that I mentioned to you is already begun under the direction of Captain Riddel and me. There is another in emulation of it going on at Closeburn, under the auspices of Mr Monteath of Closeburn, which will be on a greater scale than ours. I have likewise secured it for you. Captain Riddel gave his infant society a great many of his old books, else I had written you on that subject ; but one of these days, I shall trouble you with a commission for the Monkland Friendly Society. A copy ot *The Spectator, Mirror,* and *Lounger, Man of Feeling, Man of the World, Guthrie's Geographical Grammar,* with some religious pieces, will likely be our first order.

When I grow richer I will write to you on gilt-post, to make amends for this sheet. At present every guinea has a five-guinea errand with, my dear sir, your faithful, poor, but honest friend,

R. B.

CLXXXVII.

TO MRS M'MURDO, DRUMLANRIG.

ELLISLAND, *2d May* 1789.

MADAM,—I have finished the piece which had the happy fortune to be honoured with your approbation; and never did little miss with more sparkling pleasure shew her applauded sampler to partial mamma, than I now send my poem to you and Mr M'Murdo, if he is returned to Drumlanrig. You cannot easily imagine what thin-skinned animals, what sensitive plants, poor poets are. How do we shrink into the imbittered corner of self-abasement when neglected or condemned by those to whom we look up !—and how do we, in erect importance, add another cubit to our stature on being noticed and applauded by those whom we honour and respect ! My late visit to Drumlanrig has, I can tell you, madam, given me a balloon waft up Parnassus, where on my fancied eleva· tion I regard my poetic self with no small degree of complacency. Surely, with all their sins, the rhyming tribe are not ungrateful creatures. I recollect your goodness to your humble guest. I see Mr M'Murdo adding to the politeness of the gentleman the kind· ness of a friend, and my heart swells as it would burst with warm emotions and ardent wishes ! It may be it is not gratitude ; it may be a mixed sensation. That strange, shifting, doubling animal MAN is so generally, at best, but a negative, often a worthless creature, that we cannot see real goodness and native worth without feeling the bosom glow with sympathetic approbation. With every sentiment of grateful respect, I have the honour to be, madam, your obliged and grateful, humble servant, R. B.

CLXXXVIII.

TO MR CUNNINGHAM.

ELLISLAND, *4th May* 1789

MY DEAR SIR,—Your *duty-free* favour of the 26th April 1 received two days ago : I will not say I perused it with pleasure— that is the cold compliment of ceremony—I perused it, sir, with delicious satisfaction; in short, it is such a letter, that not you, nor your friend, but the legislature, by express proviso in their postage-laws, should frank. A letter informed with the soul of friendship is such an honour to human nature, that they should order it free ingress and egress to and from their bags and mails, as an encouragement and mark of distinction to supereminent virtue.

I have just put the last hand to a little poem, which I think will be something to your taste. One morning lately, as I was out pretty early in the fields, sowing some grass seeds, I heard the burst of a shot from a neighbouring plantation, and presently a poor little wounded hare came crippling by me. You will guess my indignation at the inhuman fellow who could shoot a hare at this season, when all of them have young ones. Indeed, there is something in that business of destroying for our sport individuals in the animal creation that do not injure us materially, which I could never reconcile to my ideas of virtue.

Let me know how you like my poem (p. 141). I am doubtful whether it would not be an improvement to keep out the last stanza but one altogether.

Cruikshank is a glorious production of the Author of man. You, he, and the noble Colonel of the Crochallan Fencibles are to me

" Dear as the ruddy drops which warm my heart."

I have got a good mind to make verses on you all, to the tune of " Three guid fellows ayont the glen."   R. B.

CLXXXIX.

TO MR RICHARD BROWN.

MAUCHLINE, 21st May 1789.

MY DEAR FRIEND,—I was in the country by accident, and hearing of your safe arrival, I could not resist the temptation of wishing you joy on your return—wishing you would write to me before you sail again—wishing you would always set me down as your bosom-friend—wishing you long life and prosperity, and that every good thing may attend you—wishing Mrs Brown and your little ones as free of the evils of this world as is consistent with humanity—wishing I had longer time to write to you at present—and, finally, wishing that, if there is to be another state of existence, Mr B., Mrs B., our little ones, and both families, and you and I, in some snug retreat, may make a jovial party to all eternity !

My direction is at Ellisland, near Dumfries. Yours, R. B.

CXC.

TO MR JAMES HAMILTON.

ELLISLAND, 26*th May* 1789.

DEAR SIR,—I would fain offer, my dear sir, a word of sympathy with your misfortunes; but it is a tender string, and I know not how to touch it. It is easy to flourish a set of high-flown sentiments on the subjects that would give great satisfaction to—a breast quite at ease; but as ONE observes who was very seldom mistaken in the theory of life: "The heart knoweth its own sorrows, and a stranger intermeddleth not therewith."

Among some distressful emergencies that I have experienced in life, I ever laid this down as my foundation of comfort: *That he who has lived the life of an honest man has by no means lived in vain !*

With every wish for your welfare and future success, I am, my dear sir, sincerely yours, R. B.

CXCI.

TO WILLIAM CREECH, ESQ.

ELLISLAND, 30*th May* 1789.

SIR,—I had intended to have troubled you with a long letter; but at present the delightful sensations of an omnipotent toothache so engross all my inner man, as to put it out of my power even to write nonsense. However, as in duty bound, I approach my bookseller with an offering in my hand—a few poetic clinches and a song:—to expect any other kind of offering from the rhyming tribe would be to know them much less than you do. I do not pretend that there is much merit in these *morceaux*, but I have two reasons for sending them—*primo*, they are mostly ill-natured, so are in unison with my present feelings, while fifty troops of infernal spirits are driving post from ear to ear along my jawbones; and, *secondly*, they are so short that you cannot leave off in the middle, and so hurt my pride in the idea that you found any work of mine too heavy to get through.

I have a request to beg of you, and I not only beg of you, but conjure you, by all your wishes and by all your hopes, that the Muse will spare the satiric wink in the moment of your foibles ; that she will warble the song of rapture round your hymeneal couch; and that she will shed on your turf the honest tear of elegiac gratitude ! Grant my request as speedily as possible: send me by the very first fly or coach for this place three copies of the last edition of my poems, which place to my account.

Now may the good things of prose, and the good things of verse,
come among thy hands, until they be filled with the *good things
of this life*, prayeth　　　　　　　　　　　　　　　　R. B.

CXCII.
TO MR M'AULAY, OF DUMBARTON.
ELLISLAND, *4th June* 1789.

DEAR SIR,—Though I am not without my fears respecting my
fate at that grand, universal inquest of right and wrong, commonly
called *The Last Day*, yet I trust there is one sin which that arch-
vagabond Satan—who, I understand, is to be king's evidence—
cannot throw in my teeth; I mean ingratitude. There is a certain
pretty large quantum of kindness for which I remain, and from
inability I fear must still remain, your debtor; but though unable
to repay the debt, I assure you, sir, I shall ever warmly remember
the obligation. It gives me the sincerest pleasure to hear by my
old acquaintance, Mr Kennedy, that you are, in immortal Allan's
language, " Hale, and weel, and living ;" and that your charming
family are well, and promising to be an amiable and respectable
addition to the company of performers whom the Great Manager
of the Drama of Man is bringing into action for the succeeding
age.

With respect to my welfare, a subject in which you once warmly
and effectively interested yourself—I am here in my old way, hold-
ing my plough, marking the growth of my corn, or the health of
my dairy, and at times sauntering by the delightful windings of
the Nith—on the margin of which I have built my humble domicile
—praying for seasonable weather, or holding an intrigue with the
Muses, the only gipsies with whom I have now any intercourse. As
I am entered into the holy state of matrimony, I trust my face is
turned completely Zion-ward ; and as it is a rule with all honest
fellows to repeat no grievances, I hope that the little poetic licences
of former days will of course fall under the oblivious influence of
some good-natured statute of celestial prescription. In my family
devotion—which, like a good Presbyterian, I occasionally give to
my household folks—I am extremely fond of the psalm, " Let not
the errors of my youth," &c., and that other, " Lo, children are
God's heritage," &c., in which last Mrs Burns—who, by the by,
has a glorious " wood-note wild" at either old song or psalmody—
joins me with the pathos of Handel's Messiah.　　　　　R. B.

CXCIII.
TO MR ROBERT AINSLIE.
ELLISLAND, *8th June* 1789.

MY DEAR FRIEND,—I am perfectly ashamed of myself when I

look at the date of your last. It is not that I forget the friend of my heart and the companion of my peregrinations, but I have been condemned to drudgery beyond sufferance, though not, thank God, beyond redemption. I have had a collection of poems by a lady put into my hands to prepare them for the press; which horrid task, with sowing corn with my own hand—a parcel of masons, wrights, plasterers, &c., to attend to—roaming on business through Ayrshire—all this was against me, and the very first dreadful article was of itself too much for me.

13th.—I have not had a moment to spare from incessant toil since the 8th. Life, my dear sir, is a serious matter. You know by experience that a man's individual self is a good deal; but, believe me, a wife and family of children, whenever you have the honour to be a husband and a father, will show you that your present and most anxious hours of solitude are spent on trifles. The welfare of those who are very dear to us,—whose only support, hope, and stay we are,—this to a generous mind is another sort of more important object of care than any concerns whatever which centre merely in the individual. On the other hand, let no young, unmarried, wild dog among you make a song of his pretended liberty and freedom from care. If the relations we stand in to king, country, kindred, and friends, be anything but the visionary fancies of dreaming metaphysicians; if religion, virtue, magnanimity, generosity, humanity, and justice be aught but empty sounds; then the man who may be said to live only for others—for the beloved, honourable female, whose tender, faithful embrace endears life, and for the helpless little innocents who are to be the men and women, the worshippers of his God, the subjects of his king, and the support, nay, the very vital existence, of his COUNTRY, in the ensuing age—compare such a man with any fellow whatever, who, whether he bustle and push in business among labourers, clerks, statesmen; or whether he roar and rant, and drink and sing in taverns—a fellow over whose grave no one will breathe a single heigh-ho, except from the cobweb-tie of what is called goodfellowship—who has no view nor aim but what terminates in himself—if there be any grovelling, earthborn wretch of our species, a renegado to common sense, who would fain believe that the noble creature man is no better than a sort of fungus, generated out of nothing, nobody knows how, and soon dissipating in nothing nobody knows where—such a stupid beast, such a crawling reptile, might balance the foregoing unexaggerated comparison, but no one else would have the patience.

Forgive me, my dear sir, for this long silence. *To make you amends* I shall send you soon, and more encouraging still, without any postage, one or two rhymes of my later manufacture.

R. B.

CXCIV

TO MRS DUNLOP.

ELLISLAND, 21*st June* 1789.

DEAR MADAM,—Will you take the effusions, the miserable effusions, of low spirits just as they flow from their bitter spring? I know not of any particular cause for this worst of all my foes besetting me; but for some time my soul has been beclouded with a thickening atmosphere of evil imaginations and gloomy presages.

Monday Evening.

I have just heard Mr Kirkpatrick preach a sermon. He is a man famous for his benevolence, and I revere him; but from such ideas of my Creator, good Lord, deliver me! Religion, my honoured friend, is surely a simple business, as it equally concerns the ignorant and the learned, the poor and the rich. That there is an incomprehensible Great Being, to whom I owe my existence, and that he must be intimately acquainted with the operations and progress of the internal machinery, and consequent outward deportment of this creature which he has made—these are, I think, self-evident propositions. That there is a real and eternal distinction between virtue and vice, and consequently, that I am an accountable creature; that from the seeming nature of the human mind, as well as from the evident imperfection, nay positive injustice, in the administration of affairs, both in the natural and moral worlds, there must be a retributive scene of existence beyond the grave—must, I think, be allowed by every one who will give himself a moment's reflection. I will go farther, and affirm that from the sublimity, excellence, and purity of His doctrine and precepts, unparalleled by all the aggregated wisdom and learning of many preceding ages, though, to *appearance* He himself was the obscurest and most illiterate of our species— therefore Jesus Christ was from God.

Whatever mitigates the woes, or increases the happiness of others, this is my criterion of goodness; and whatever injures society at large, or any individual in it, this is my measure of iniquity.

What think you, madam, of my creed? I trust that I have said nothing that will lessen me in the eye of one whose good opinion I value almost next to the approbation of my own mind.

R. B.

CXCV.

TO MISS WILLIAMS.

ELLISLAND, *August* 1789

MADAM,—Of the many problems in the nature of that wonderful creature, man, this is one of the most extraordinary, that he shall go on from day to day, from week to week, from month to month, or perhaps from year to year, suffering a hundred times more in an hour from the impotent consciousness of neglecting what he ought to do, than the very doing of it would cost him. I am deeply indebted to you, first for an elegant poetic compliment; then for a polite, obliging letter; and, lastly, for your excellent poem on the slave-trade; and yet, wretch that I am! though the debts were debts of honour, and the creditor a lady, I have put off and put off even the very acknowledgment of the obligation, until you must indeed be the very angel I take you for if you can forgive me.

Your poem I have read with the highest pleasure. I have a way whenever I read a book—I mean a book in our own trade, madam, a poetic one—and when it is my own property, that I take a pencil and mark at the ends of verses, or note on margins and odd paper, little criticisms of approbation or disapprobation as I peruse along. I will make no apology for presenting you with a few unconnected thoughts that occurred to me in my repeated perusals of your poem. I want to shew you that I have honesty enough to tell you what I take to be truths, even when they are not quite on the side of approbation; and I do it in the firm faith that you have equal greatness of mind to hear them with pleasure.

I know very little of scientific criticism; so all I can pretend to in that intricate art is merely to note, as I read along, what passages strike me as being uncommonly beautiful, and where the expression seems to be perplexed or faulty.

The poem opens finely. There are none of those idle prefatory lines which one may skip over before one comes to the subject. Verses 9th and 10th in particular—

" Where ocean's unseen bound
Leaves a drear world of waters round"—

are truly beautiful. The simile of the hurricane is likewise fine; and indeed, beautiful as the poem is, almost all the similes rise decidedly above it. From verse 31st to verse 50th is a pretty eulogy on Britain. Verse 36th, "That foul drama deep with wrong," is nobly expressive. Verse 46th, I am afraid, is rather unworthy of the rest; "to dare to feel" is an idea that I do not altogether like. The contrast of valour and mercy, from the 46th verse to the 50th, is admirable.

Either my apprehension is dull, or there is something a little confused in the apostrophe to Mr Pitt. Verse 55th is the antecedent to verses 57th and 58th, but in verse 58th the connection seems ungrammatical:—

" Powers   *   *   *   *
         *   *   *   *   *
With no gradations marked their flight,
But rose at once to glory's height."

Ris'n should be the word instead of rose. Try it in prose. Powers
—their flight marked by no gradations, but [the same powers]
risen at once to the height of glory. Likewise verse 53d, " For
this," is evidently meant to lead on the sense of the verses 59th,
60th, 61st, and 62d ; but let us try how the thread of connection
runs—

> " For this   *   *   *   *
>   *   *   *   *   *
> The deeds of mercy, that embrace
> A distant sphere, an alien race,
> Shall virtue's lips record, and claim
> The fairest honours of thy name."

I beg pardon if I misapprehend the matter, but this appears to
me the only imperfect passage in the poem. The comparison of
the sunbeam is fine.

The compliment to the Duke of Richmond is, I hope, as just as
it is certainly elegant. The thought,

> " Virtue   *   *   *   *
>   *   *   *   *   *
> Sends from her unsullied source,
> The gems of thought their purest force,"

is exceeding beautiful. The idea, from verse 81st to the 85th, that
the " blest decree" is like the beams of morning ushering in the
glorious day of liberty, ought not to pass unnoticed or unapplaud-
ed. From verse 85th to verse 108th, is an animated contrast be-
tween the unfeeling selfishness of the oppressor on the one hand,
and the misery of the captive on the other. Verse 88th might
perhaps be amended thus : " Nor ever *quit* her narrow maze."
We are said to *pass* a bound, but we *quit* a maze. Verse 100th is
exquisitely beautiful—

> " They, whom wasted blessings tire."

Verse 110th is, I doubt, a clashing of metaphors ; " to load a
span" is, I am afraid, an unwarrantable expression. In verse
114th, " Cast the universe in shade," is a fine idea. From the
115th verse to the 142d is a striking description of the wrongs of
the poor African. Verse 120th, " The load of unremitted pain,"
is a remarkable, strong expression. The address to the advocates
for abolishing the slave trade, from verse 143d to verse 208th, is
animated with the true life of genius. The picture of oppres-
sion—

> " While she links her impious chain,
> And calculates the price of pain ;
> Weighs agony in sordid scales,
> And marks if life or death prevails"—

is nobly executed.

What a tender idea is in verse 180th ! Indeed that whole de-
scription of home may vie with Thomson's description of home,
somewhere in the beginning of his *Autumn*. I do not remember

to have seen a stronger expression of misery than is contained in these verses—

> " Condemned, severe extreme, to live
> When all is fled that life can give."

The comparison of our distant joys to distant objects is equally original and striking.

The character and manners of the dealer in the infernal traffic is a well done, though a horrid picture. I am not sure how far introducing the sailor was right; for though the sailor's common characteristic is generosity, yet in this case he is certainly not only an unconcerned witness, but in some degree an efficient agent in the business. Verse 224th is a nervous . . . . expressive—" The heart conclusive anguish breaks." The description of the captive wretch when he arrives in the West Indies is carried on with equal spirit. The thought that the oppressor's sorrow on seeing the slave pine, is like the butcher's regret when his destined lamb dies a natural death, is exceedingly fine.

I am got so much into the cant of criticism, that I begin to be afraid lest I have nothing except the cant of it ; and instead of elucidating my author, am only benighting myself. For this reason, I will not pretend to go through the whole poem. Some few remaining beautiful lines, however, I cannot pass over. Verse 280th is the strongest description of selfishness I ever saw. The comparison in verses 285th and 286th is new and fine ; and the line, " your arms to penury you lend," is excellent.

In verse 317th, " like" should certainly be " as" or " so ;" for instance—

> " His sway the hardened bosom leads
> To cruelty's remorseless deeds:
> As (or, so) the blue lightning when it springs
> With fury on its livid wings,
> Darts on the goal with rapid force,
> Nor heeds that ruin marks its course."

If you insert the word " like" where I have placed " as" you must alter " darts" to " darting," and " heeds" to " heeding," in order to make it grammar. A tempest is a favourite subject with the poets, but I do not remember anything, even in Thomson's *Winter*, superior to your verses from the 347th to the 351st. Indeed, the last simile, beginning with " Fancy may dress," &c., and ending with the 350th verse, is, in my opinion, the most beautiful passage in the poem ; it would do honour to the greatest names that ever graced our profession.

I will not beg your pardon, madam, for these strictures, as my conscience tells me that for once in my life I have acted up to the duties of a Christian, in doing as I would be done by.

I had lately the honour of a letter from Dr Moore, where he tells me that he has sent me some books ; they are not yet come to hand, but I hear they are on the way.

Wishing you all success in your progress in the path of fame,
and that you may equally escape the danger of stumbling through
incautious speed, or losing ground through loitering neglect. I
am, &c.,   R. B.

<hr/>

CXCVI.

TO MR JOHN LOGAN.

ELLISLAND, NEAR DUMFRIES, 7th Aug. 1789.

DEAR SIR,—I intended to have written you long ere now, and
as I told you I had gotten three stanzas and a half on my way in
a poetic epistle to you ; but that old enemy of all *good works*, the
devil, threw me into a prosaic mire, and for the soul of me, I can-
not get out of it.   I dare not write you a long letter, as I am going
to intrude on your time with a long ballad.   I have, as you will
shortly see, finished *The Kirk's Alarm ;* but, now that it is done,
and that I have laughed once or twice at the conceits in some of
the stanzas, I am determined not to let it get into the public ; so
I send you this copy, the first that I have sent to Ayrshire,
except some few of the stanzas which I wrote off in embryo for
Gavin Hamilton, under the express provision and request that you
will only read it to a few of us, and do not on any account give
or permit to be taken any copy of the ballad.   If I could be of
any service to Dr M'Gill I would do it, though it should be at a
much greater expense than irritating a few bigoted priests ; but
I am afraid serving him in his present *embarras* is a task too hard
for me.   I have enemies enow, though I do not wantonly add to
the number.   Still, as I think there is some merit in two or three
of the thoughts, I send it to you as a small, but sincere testimony
how much, and with what respectful esteem, I am, dear sir, your
obliged humble servant,   R. B.

<hr/>

CXCVII.

TO MR [PETER STUART.]

[*September*] 1789.

MY DEAR SIR,—The hurry of a farmer in this particular season,
and the indolence of a poet at all times and seasons, will, I hope,
plead my excuse for neglecting so long to answer your obliging
letter of the 5th of August.

That you have done well in quitting your laborious concern in
* * * I do not doubt ; the weighty reasons you mention were, I
hope, very, and deservedly indeed, weighty ones, and your health
is a matter of the last importance ; but whether the remaining
proprietors of the paper have also done well, is what I much doubt.

The [*Star*], so far as I was a reader, exhibited such a brilliancy of point, such an elegance of paragraph, and such a variety of intelligence, that I can hardly conceive it possible to continue a daily paper in the same degree of excellence : but if there was a man who had abilities equal to the task, that man's assistance the proprietors have lost.

When I received your letter, I was transcribing for [the *Star*] my letter to the magistrates of the Canongate, Edinburgh, begging their permission to place a tombstone over poor Fergusson, and their edict in consequence of my petition ; but now I shall send them ———. Poor Fergusson ! If there be a life beyond the grave, which I trust there is ; and if there be a good God presiding over all nature, which I am sure there is—thou art now enjoying existence in a glorious world, where worth of the heart alone is distinction in the man ; where riches, deprived of all their pleasure-purchasing powers, return to their native sordid matter ; where titles and honours are the disregarded reveries of an idle dream ; and where that heavy virtue, which is the negative consequence of steady dulness, and those thoughtless, though often destructive follies, which are the unavoidable aberrations of frail human nature, will be thrown into equal oblivion as if they had never been !

Adieu, my dear sir ! So soon as your present views and schemes are concentred in an aim, I shall be glad to hear from you, as your welfare and happiness is by no means a subject indifferent to, yours,   R. B.

CXCVIII.
TO MRS DUNLOP.

ELLISLAND, *6th Sept.* 1789.

DEAR MADAM,—I have mentioned in my last my appointment to the Excise, and the birth of little Frank ; who, by the by, I trust will be no discredit to the honourable name of Wallace, as he has a fine manly countenance, and a figure that might do credit to a little fellow two months older ; and likewise an excellent good temper, though when he pleases he has a pipe, only not quite so loud as the horn that his immortal namesake blew as a signal to take out the pin of Stirling Bridge.

I had some time ago an epistle—part poetic and part prosaic—from your poetess, Mrs J. Little, a very ingenious but modest composition. I should have written her as she requested, but for the hurry of this new business. I have heard of her and her compositions in this country, and, I am happy to add, always to the honour of her character. The fact is, I know not well how to write to her. I should sit down to a sheet of paper that I knew not how to stain. I am no dab at fine-drawn letter-writing; and except when prompted by friendship or gratitude, or, which happens extremely rarely, inspired by the Muse (I know not her name) that presides over epistolary writing, I sit down, when necessitated to write, as I would sit down to beat hemp.

Some parts of your letter of the 20th August struck me with the most melancholy concern for the state of your mind at present.

Would I could write you a letter of comfort, I would sit down to it with as much pleasure as I would to write an epic poem of my own composition, that should equal the *Iliad*. Religion, my dear friend, is the true comfort! A strong persuasion in a future state of existence ; a proposition so obviously probable, that, setting revelation aside, every nation and people, so far as investigation has reached, for at least near four thousand years, have, in some mode or other, firmly believed it. In vain would we reason and pretend to doubt. I have myself done so to a very daring pitch ; but when I reflected that I was opposing the most ardent wishes, and the most darling hopes of good men, and flying in the face of all human belief, in all ages, I was shocked at my own conduct.

I know not whether I have ever sent you the following lines, or if you have ever seen them ; but it is one of my favourite quotations, which I keep constantly by me in my progress through life, in the language of the book of Job,

" Against the day of battle and of war."

Spoken of religion :

" 'Tis *this*, my friend, that streaks our morning bright,
'Tis *this* that gilds the horror of our night.
When wealth forsakes us, and when friends are few
When friends are faithless, or when foes pursue;

"'Tis this that wards the blow, or stills the smart,
Disarms affliction, or repels his dart ;
Within the breast bids purest raptures rise,
Bids smiling conscience spread her cloudless skies."

I have been busy with *Zeluco*. The doctor is so obliging as to request my opinion of it ; and I have been revolving in my mind some kind of criticisms on novel-writing, but it is a depth beyond my research. I shall, however, digest my thoughts on the subject as well as I can. *Zeluco* is a most sterling performance.

R. B.

CXCIX.

TO CAPTAIN RIDDEL, CARSE.

ELLISLAND, 16*th Oct.* 1789.

SIR,—Big with the idea of this important day at Friars' Carse, I have watched the elements and skies in the full persuasion that they would announce it to the astonished world by some phenomena of terrific portent. Yesternight until a very late hour did I wait with anxious horror for the appearance of some comet firing half the sky ; or aërial armies of sanguinary Scandinavians darting athwart the startled heavens, rapid as the ragged lightning, and horrid as those convulsions of nature that bury nations.

The elements, however, seem to take the matter very quietly : they did not even usher in this morning with triple suns and a shower of blood, symbolical of the three potent heroes, and the mighty claret-shed of the day.

I have some misgivings that I take too much upon me, when I request you to get your guest, Sir Robert Lawrie, to frank the two enclosed covers for me ; the one of them to Sir William Cunningham of Robertland, Bart. at Kilmarnock—the other, to Mr Allan Masterton, writing-master, Edinburgh. The first has a kindred claim on Sir Robert, as being a brother baronet, and likewise a keen Foxite ; the other is one of the worthiest men in the world, and a man of real genius ; so, allow me to say, he has a fraternal claim on you. I want them franked for to-morrow, as I cannot get them to the post to-night. I shall send a servant again for them in the evening. Wishing that your head may be crowned with laurels to-night, and free from aches to-morrow, I have the honour to be, sir, your deeply indebted, humble servant,

R. B.

CC.

TO FRANCIS GROSE, ESQ., F.S.A.

SIR,—I believe among all our Scots literati you have not met with Professor Dugald Stewart, who fills the moral philosophy chair in the University of Edinburgh. To say that he is a man of the first parts, and, what is more, a man of the first worth, to a gentleman of your general acquaintance, and who so much enjoys the luxury of unencumbered freedom and undisturbed privacy, is not perhaps recommendation enough ; but when I inform you that Mr Stewart's principal characteristic is your favourite feature— *that* sterling independence of mind which, though every man's right, so few men have the courage to claim, and fewer still the magnanimity to support ; when I tell you that, unseduced by splendour and undisgusted by wretchedness, he appreciates the merits of the various actors in the great drama of life, merely as they perform their parts—in short, he is a man after your own heart, and I comply with his earnest request in letting you know that he wishes above all things to meet with you. His house Catrine, is within less than a mile of Sorn Castle, which you proposed visiting ; or if you could transmit him the enclosed, he would, with the greatest pleasure, meet you anywhere in the neighbourhood. I write to Ayrshire to inform Mr Stewart that I have acquitted myself of my promise. Should your time and spirits permit your meeting with Mr Stewart, 'tis well; if not, I I hope you will forgive this liberty, and I have at least an opportunity of assuring you with what truth and respect I am, sir, your great admirer and very humble servant,   R. B.

CCI.

TO MR ROBERT AINSLIE.

ELLISLAND, 1*st Nov.* 1789.

MY DEAR FRIEND,—I had written you long ere now, could I have guessed where to find you, for I am sure you have more good sense than to waste the precious days of vacation-time in the dirt of business and Edinburgh. Wherever you are, God bless you, and lead you not into temptation, but deliver you from evil!

I do not know if I have informed you that I am now appointed to an Excise division, in the middle of which my house and farm lie. In this I was extremely lucky. Without ever having been an expectant, as they call their journeyman excisemen, I was directly planted down to all intents and purposes an officer of Excise, there to flourish and bring forth fruits—worthy of repentance.

I know not how the word exciseman, or, still more opprobrious, gauger, will sound in your ears. I too have seen the day when my auditory nerves would have felt very delicately on this subject; but a wife and children are things which have a wonderful power in blunting these kind of sensations. Fifty pounds a year for life, and a provision for widows and orphans, you will allow is no bad settlement for a *poet*. For the ignominy of the profession, I have the encouragement which I once heard a recruiting sergeant give to a numerous, if not a respectable audience in the streets of Kilmarnock : " Gentleman, for your further and better encouragement, I can assure you that our regiment is the most blackguard corps under the crown, and consequently with us an honest fellow has the surest chance of preferment."

You need not doubt that I find several very unpleasant and disagreeable circumstances in my business ; but I am tired with and disgusted at the language of complaint against the evils of life. Human existence in the most favourable situations does not abound with pleasures, and has its inconveniences and ills : capricious, foolish man mistakes these inconveniences and ills as if they were the peculiar property of his particular situation ; and hence that eternal fickleness, that love of change, which has ruined, and daily does ruin, many a fine fellow, as well as many a blockhead,

and is almost without exception a constant source of disappoint-
ment and misery.

I long to hear from you how you go on—not so much in business
as in life. Are you pretty well satisfied with your own exer-
tions, and tolerably at ease in your internal reflections? 'Tis
much to be a great character as a lawyer, but beyond comparison
more to be a great character as a man. That you may be both
the one and the other is the earnest wish, and that you *will* be
be both is the firm persuasion of, my dear sir, &c., R. B.

CCII.

TO MR RICHARD BROWN.

ELLISLAND, *4th November* 1789.

I HAVE been so hurried, my ever-dear friend, that though I got
both your letters, I have not been able to command an hour to
answer them as I wished; and even now, you are to look on this
as merely confessing debt and craving days. Few things could
have given me so much pleasure as the news that you were once
more safe and sound on *terra firma*, and happy in that place
where happiness is alone to be found—in the fireside circle. May
the benevolent Director of all things peculiarly bless you in all
those endearing connections consequent on the tender and vene-
rable names of husband and father! I have indeed been extremely
lucky in getting an additional income of L.50 a year, while, at the
same time, the appointment will not cost me above L.10 or L.12
per annum of expenses more than I must have inevitably incurred.
The worst circumstance is, that the Excise division which I have
got is so extensive—no less than ten parishes to ride over—and it
abounds, besides, with so much business, that I can scarcely steal
a spare moment. However, labour endears rest, and both toge-
ther are absolutely necessary for the proper enjoyment of human
existence. I cannot meet you anywhere. No less than an order
from the Board of Excise at Edinburgh is necessary, before I can
have so much time as to meet you in Ayrshire. But do you come
and see me. We must have a social day, and perhaps lengthen it
out with half the night, before you go again to sea. You are the
earliest friend I now have on earth, my brothers excepted; and is
not that an endearing circumstance? When you and I first met,
we were at the green period of human life. The twig would
easily take a bent, but would as easily return to its former state.
You and I not only took a mutual bent, but, by the melancholy,
though strong influence of being both of the family of the unfor-
tunate, we were intwined with one another in our growth towards
advanced age; and blasted be the sacrilegious hand that shall

attempt to undo the union ! You and I must have one bumper
to my favourite toast—" May the companions of our youth be the
friends of our old age !" Come and see me one year ; I shall see
you at Port-Glasgow the next, and if we can contrive to have a
gossipping between our two bedfellows, it will be so much addi-
tional pleasure. Mrs Burns joins me in kind compliments to you
and Mrs Brown. Adieu ! I am ever, my dear sir, yours, R. B.

CCIII.

TO ROBERT GRAHAM, ESQ. OF FINTRY.

9th December 1789.

SIR,—I have a good while had a wish to trouble you with a
letter, and had certainly done it long ere now but for a humiliat-
ing something that throws cold water on the resolution, as if one
should say,—" You have found Mr Graham a very powerful and
kind friend indeed, and that interest he is so kindly taking in
your concerns you ought, by everything in your power, to keep
alive and cherish." Now, though, since God has thought proper
to make one powerful and another helpless, the connection of
obliger and obliged is all fair ; and though my being under your
patronage is to me highly honourable, yet, sir, allow me to flatter
myself that as a poet and an honest man you first interested your-
self in my welfare, and principally as such still you permit me to
approach you.

I have found the Excise business go on a great deal smoother
with me than I expected, owing a good deal to the generous
friendship of Mr Mitchel, my collector, and the kind assistance of
Mr Findlater, my supervisor. I dare to be honest, and I fear no
labour. Nor do I find my hurried life greatly inimical to my
correspondence with the Muses. Their visits to me, indeed, and
I believe to most of their acquaintance, like the visits of good
angels, are short and far between ; but I meet them now and then
as I jog through the hills of Nithsdale, just as I used to do on the
banks of Ayr. I take the liberty to enclose you a few bagatelles,
all of them the productions of my leisure thoughts in my Excise
rides.

If you know or have ever seen, Captain Grose, the antiquary,
you will enter into any humour that is in the verses on him
(p. 149). Perhaps you have seen them before, as I sent them to
a London newspaper. Though I daresay you have none of the
Solemn-League-and-Covenant fire which shown so conspicuous in
Lord George Gordon and the Kilmarnock weavers, yet I think you
must have heard of Dr M'Gill, one of the clergymen of Ayr, and
his heretical book. Though he is one of the worthiest, as well as

one of the ablest, of the whole priesthood of the Kirk of Scotland, in every sense of that ambiguous term, yet the poor doctor and his numerous family are in imminent danger of being thrown out to the mercy of the winter winds. The enclosed ballad on that business is, I confess, too local; but I laughed myself at some conceits in it, though I am convinced in my conscience that there are a good many heavy stanzas in it too.

The election ballad (*The Five Carlines*, p. 150), as you will see, alludes to the present canvass in our string of boroughs.* I do not believe there will be such a hard-run match in the whole general election. * * *

I am too little a man to have any political attachments: I am deeply indebted to, and have the warmest veneration for, individuals of both parties; but a man who has it in his power to be the father of a country, and who * * * *, is a character that one cannot speak of with patience.

Sir James Johnston does " what man can do," but yet I doubt his fate. R. B.

CCIV.

TO MRS DUNLOP.

ELLISLAND, 13*th December* 1789.

MANY thanks, my dear madam, for your sheetful of rhymes. Though at present I am below the veriest prose, yet from you everything pleases. I am groaning under the miseries of a diseased nervous-system—a system the state of which is most conducive to our happiness or the most productive of our misery. For now near three weeks I have been so ill with a nervous headache that I have been obliged for a time to give up my Excise-books, being scarce able to lift my head, much less to ride once a week over ten muir parishes. What is man? To-day, in the luxuriance of health, exulting in the enjoyment of existence; in a few days, perhaps in a few hours, loaded with conscious painful being, counting the tardy pace of the lingering moments by the repercussions of anguish, and refusing or denied a comforter. Day follows night, and night comes after day, only to curse him with life which gives him no pleasure; and yet the awful, dark termination of that life is something at which he recoils.

> " Tell us, ye dead; will none of you in pity
> Disclose the secrets * * *
> *What 'tis you are, and we must shortly be?*
> * * * 'tis no matter:
> A little time will make us learned as you are."

Can it be possible, that when I resign this frail, feverish being, I shall still find myself in conscious existence? When the last

* *Maggy*—Dumfries; *Blinking Bess*—Annandale; *Whisky Jean*—Kirkcudbright *Black Joan*—Sanquhar; *Marjory*—Lochmaben.

gasp of agony has announced that I am no more to those that
knew me and the few who loved me; when the cold, stiffened,
unconscious, ghastly corse is resigned into the earth, to be the
prey of unsightly reptiles, and to become in time a trodden clod,
shall I be yet warm in life, seeing and seen, enjoying and enjoyed?
Ye venerable sages and holy flamens, is there probability in your
conjectures, truth in your stories, of another world beyond death;
or are they all alike baseless visions and fabricated fables. If
there is another life, it must be only for the just, the benevolent,
the amiable, and the humane; what a flattering idea, then, is a
world to come! Would to God I as firmly believed it as I ardently
wish it! There I should meet an aged parent, now at rest from
the many buffetings of an evil world, against which he so long
and so bravely struggled. There should I meet the friend, the
disinterested. friend, of my early life; the man who rejoiced to see
me, because he loved me and could serve me. Muir, thy weak-
nesses were the aberrations of human nature, but thy heart glowed
with everything generous, manly, and noble; and if ever emana-
tion from the All-good Being animated a human form, it was thine!
There should I, with speechless agony of rapture, again recognise
my lost, my ever-dear Mary! whose bosom was fraught with truth,
honour, constancy, and love.

My Mary, dear departed shade!
Where is thy place of heavenly rest?
Seest thou thy lover lowly laid?
Hear'st thou the groans that rend his breast?

Jesus Christ, thou amiablest of characters   I trust thou art no
impostor, and that thy revelation of blissful scenes of existence
beyond death and the grave is not one of the many impositions
which time after time have been palmed on credulous mankind.
I trust that in thee " shall all the families of the earth be blessed,"
by being yet connected together in a better world, where every tie
that bound heart to heart in this state of existence shall be, far
beyond our present conceptions, more endearing.

I am a good deal inclined to think with those who maintain
that what are called nervous affections are in fact diseases of the
mind. I cannot reason, I cannot think; and but to you I would
not venture to write anything above an order to a cobbler. You
have felt too much of the ills of life not to sympathize with a
diseased wretch who has impaired more than half of any faculties
he possessed. Your goodness will excuse this distracted scrawl,
which the writer dare scarcely read, and which he would throw
into the fire were he able to write anything better, or indeed any-
thing at all.

Rumour told me something of a son of yours who was returned
from the East or West Indies. If you have gotten news from
James or Anthony, it was cruel in you not to let me know; as I
promise you, on the sincerity of a man who is weary of one world,

and anxious about another, that scarce anything could give me
so much pleasure as to hear of any good thing befalling my
honoured friend.

If you have a minute's leisure, take up your pen in pity to
le pauvre miserable   R. B.

CCV.

TO LADY WINIFRED MAXWELL CONSTABLE.

ELLISLAND, 16*th December* 1789.

MY LADY,—In vain have I from day to day expected to hear
from Mrs Young, as she promised me at Dalswinton that she
would do me the honour to introduce me at Tinwald; and it was
impossible, not from your ladyship's accessibility, but from my
own feelings, that I could go alone. Lately, indeed, Mr Maxwell of
Carruchan, in his usual goodness, offered to accompany me, when
an unlucky indisposition on my part hindered my embracing the
opportunity. To court the notice or the tables of the great, except
where I sometimes have had a little matter to ask of them, or
more often the pleasanter task of witnessing my gratitude to them,
is what I never have done, and I trust never shall do. But with
your ladyship I have the honour to be connected by one of the
strongest and most endearing ties in the whole moral world.
Common sufferers in a cause where even to be unfortunate is
glorious—the cause of heroic loyalty! Though my fathers had
not illustrious honours and vast properties to hazard in the con-
test, though they left their humble cottages only to add so many
units more to the unnoted crowd that followed their leaders, yet
what they could they did, and what they had they lost: with un-
shaken firmness and unconcealed political attachments, they shook
hands with ruin for what they esteemed the cause of their king and
their country. This language and the enclosed verses are for your
ladyship's eye alone. Poets are not very famous for their pru-
dence; but as I can do nothing for a cause which is now nearly
no more, I do not wish to hurt myself. I have the honour to be,
my lady, your ladyship's obliged and obedient humble servant,
                                                                 R. B.

CCVI.

TO PROVOST MAXWELL, OF LOCHMABEN.

ELLISLAND, 20*th December* 1789.

DEAR PROVOST,—As my friend, Mr Graham, goes for your good
town to-morrow, I cannot resist the temptation to send you a few
lines; and as I have nothing to say, I have chosen this sheet of

foolscap, and begun, as you see, at the top of the first page, be-
cause I have ever observed, that when once people have fairly set
out, they know not where to stop.   Now that my first sentence is
concluded, I have nothing to do but to pray Heaven to help me
on to another.   Shall I write you on politics, or religion, two
master-subjects for your sayers of nothing ?   Of the first, I dare-
say by this time you are nearly surfeited ; and for the last, what-
ever they may talk of it who make it a kind of company-concern,
I never could endure it beyond a soliloquy.   I might write you
on farming, on building, on marketing ; but my poor distracted
mind is so torn, so jaded, so racked with the task of making *one
guinea do the business of three*, that I detest, abhor, and swoon at
the very word business, though no less than four letters of my
very short surname are in it.

Well, to make the matter short, I shall betake myself to a sub-
ject ever fruitful of themes—a subject the turtle-feast of the sons
of Satan, and the delicious secret sugar-plum of the babes of grace
—a subject sparkling with all the jewels that wit can find in the
mines of genius, and pregnant with all the stores of learning from
Moses and Confucius to Franklin and Priestley—in short, may
it please your lordship, I intend to write   *   *   *

If at any time you expect a field-day in your town—a day when
dukes, earls, and knights pay their court to weavers, tailors, and
cobblers—I should like to know of it two or three days beforehand.
It is not that I care three skips of a cur-dog for the politics, but I
should like to see such an exhibition of human nature.   If you
meet with that worthy old veteran in religion and good-fellowship,
Mr Jeffrey, or any of his amiable family, I beg you will give them
my best compliments.   R. B.

CCVII.

TO THE COUNTESS OF GLENCAIRN.

ELLISLAND, *December* 1789.

MY LADY,—The honour you have done your poor poet in writ-
ing him so very an obliging letter, and the pleasure the enclosed
beautiful verses have given him, came very seasonably to his aid
amid the cheerless gloom and sinking despondency of diseased
nerves and December weather.   As to forgetting the family of
Glencairn, Heaven is my witness with what sincerity I could use
those old verses, which please me more in their rude simplicity
than the most elegant lines I ever saw—

"If thee, Jerusalem, I forget,
Skill part from my right hand.
My tongue to my mouth's roof let cleave,
If I do thee forget,
Jerusalem, and thee above
My chief joy do not not."

When I am tempted to do anything improper, I dare not, because I look on myself as accountable to your ladyship and family. Now and then, when I have the honour to be called to the tables of the great, if I happen to meet with any mortification from the stately stupidity of self-sufficient squires, or the luxurious insolence of upstart nabobs, I get above the creatures by calling to remembrance that I am patronized by the noble House of Glencairn; and at gala times—such as New-Year's Day, a christening, or the kirn-night, when my punch-bowl is brought from its dusty corner, and filled up in honour of the occasion, I begin with—*The Countess of Glencairn!* My good woman, with the enthusiasm of a grateful heart, next cries—*My Lord!* and so the toast goes on until I end with—*Lady Harriet's little angel!* whose epithalamium I have pledged myself to write.

When I received your ladyship's letter I was just in the act of transcribing for you some verses I have lately composed, and meant to have sent them my first leisure hour, and acquainted you with my late change of life. I mentioned to my lord my fears concerning my farm. Those fears were indeed too true; it is a bargain would have ruined me but for the lucky circumstance of my having an Excise commission.

People may talk as they please of the ignominy of the Excise; L.50 a year will support my wife and children, and keep me independent of the world; and I would much rather have it said that my profession borrowed credit from me, than that I borrowed credit from my profession. Another advantage I have in this business is the knowledge it gives me of the various shades of human character, consequently assisting me vastly in my poetic pursuits. I had the most ardent enthusiasm for the Muses when nobody knew me but myself, and that ardour is by no means cooled now that my Lord Glencairn's goodness has introduced me to all the world. Not that I am in haste for the press. I have no idea of publishing, else I certainly had consulted my noble, generous patron; but after acting the part of an honest man, and supporting my family, my whole wishes and views are directed to poetic pursuits. I am aware that though I were to give performances to the world superior to my former works, still, if they were of the same kind with those, the comparative reception they would meet with would mortify me. I have turned my thoughts on the drama. I do not mean the stately buskin of the tragic Muse. Does not your ladyship think that an Edinburgh theatre would be more amused with affectation, folly, and whim of true Scottish growth, than manners, which by far the greatest part of the audience can only know at second-hand? I have the honour to be your ladyship's ever devoted and grateful humble servant, R. B.

CCVIII.

TO MR GILBERT BURNS.

ELLISLAND, 11th January 1790.

DEAR BROTHER,—I mean to take advantage of the frank, though I have not in my present frame of mind much appetite for exertion in writing. My nerves are in a bad state. I feel that horrid hypochondria pervading every atom of both body and soul. This farm has undone my enjoyment of myself. It is a ruinous affair on all hands. I'll fight it out, and be off with it:

We have got a set of very decent players here just now. I have seen them an evening or two. David Campbell, in Ayr, wrote to me by the manager of the company—a Mr Sutherland, who is a man of apparent worth. On New-Year's-Day evening I gave him the following prologue (*Prologue*, p.153), which he spouted to his audience with applause.

I can no more. If once I was clear of this farm, I should respire more at ease.　　　　　R. B.

CCIX.

TO MR WILLIAM DUNBAR, W.S.

ELLISLAND, 14th January 1790.

SINCE we are here creatures of a day—since "a few summer days, and a few winter nights, and the life of man is at an end"—why, my dear, much-esteemed sir, should you and I let negligent indolence—for I know it is nothing worse—step in between us and bar the enjoyment of a mutual correspondence? We are not shapen out of the common, heavy, methodical clod, the elemental stuff of the plodding selfish race, the sons of Arithmetic and Prudence; our feelings and hearts are not benumbed and poisoned by the cursed influence of riches, which, whatever blessing they may be in other respects, are no friends to the nobler qualities of the heart: in the name of random sensibility, then, let never the moon change on our silence any more. I have had a tract of bad health most part of this winter, else you had heard from me long ere now. Thank Heaven, I am now got so much better as to be able to partake a little in the enjoyments of life.

Our friend Cunningham will perhaps have told you of my going into the Excise. The truth is, I found it a very convenient business to have L.50 per annum, nor have I yet felt any of those mortifying circumstances in it that I was led to fear.

Feb. 2d.—I have not, for sheer hurry of business, been able to spare five minutes to finish my letter. Besides my farm business,

I ride on my Excise matters at least 200 miles every week. I have not by any means given up the Muses. You will see in the third volume of Johnson's *Scots Songs* that I have contributed my mite there.

But, my dear sir, little ones that look up to you for paternal protection are an important charge. I have already two fine, healthy, stout little fellows, and I wish to throw some light upon them. I have a thousand reveries and schemes about them and their future destiny—not that I am a Utopian projector in these things. I am resolved never to breed up a son of mine to any of the learned professions. I know the value of independence ; and since I cannot give my sons an independent fortune, I shall give them an independent line of life. What a chaos of hurry, chance, and changes is this world, when one sits soberly down to reflect on it ! To a father, who himself knows the world, the thought that he shall have sons to usher into it must fill him with dread ; but if he have daughters, the prospect in a thoughtful moment is apt to shock him.

I hope Mrs Fordyce and the two young ladies are well. Do let me forget that they are nieces of yours, and let me say that I never saw a more interesting, sweeter pair of sisters in my life. I am the fool of my feelings and attachments. I often take up a volume of my Spenser to realize you to my imagination, and think over the social scenes we have had together. God grant that there may be another world more congenial to honest fellows beyond this—a world where these rubs and plagues of absence, distance, misfortunes, ill health, &c., shall no more damp hilarity and divide friendship. This, I know, is your throng season ; but half a page will much oblige, my dear sir, yours sincerely,   R. B.

—·——

CCX.

TO MRS DUNLOP.

ELLISLAND, *25th January* 1790.

IT has been owing to unremitting hurry of business that I have not written to you, madam, long ere now. My health is greatly better, and I now begin once more to share in satisfaction and enjoyment with the rest of my fellow-creatures.

Many thanks, my much-esteemed friend, for your kind letters ; but why will you make me run the risk of being contemptible and mercenary in my own eyes ? When I pique myself on my independent spirit, I hope it is neither poetic license nor poetic rant : and I am so flattered with the honour you have done me, in making me your compeer in friendship and friendly correspondence, that

I cannot, without pain and a degree of mortification, be reminded of the real inequality between our situations.

Most sincerely do I rejoice with you, dear madam, in the good news of Anthony. Not only your anxiety about his fate, but my own esteem for such a noble, warm-hearted, manly young fellow, in the little I had of his acquaintance, has interested me deeply in his fortunes.

Falconer, the unfortunate author of the *Shipwreck*, which you so much admire, is no more. After witnessing the dreadful catastrophe he so feelingly describes in his poem, and after weathering many hard gales of fortune, he went to the bottom with the *Aurora* frigate!

I forget what part of Scotland had the honour of giving him birth, but he was the son of obscurity and misfortune. He was one of those daring, adventurous spirits which Scotland, beyond any other country, is remarkable for producing. Little does the fond mother think as she hangs delighted over the sweet little leech at her bosom, where the poor fellow may hereafter wander, and what may be his fate. I remember a stanza in an old Scottish ballad, which, notwithstanding its rude simplicity, speaks feelingly to the heart—

> " Little did my mother think,
> That day she cradled me,
> What land I was to travel in,
> Or what death I should die! ·

Old Scottish songs are, you know, a favourite study and pursuit of mine ; and now I am on that subject, allow me to give you two stanzas of another old simple ballad, which I am sure will please you. The catastrophe of the piece is a poor ruined female lamenting her fate. She concludes with this pathetic wish—

> " O that my father had ne'er on me smiled ;
>   O that my mother had ne'er to me sung !
> O that my cradle had never been rocked ;
>   But that I had died when I was young !
> " O that the grave it were my bed;
>   My blankets were my winding-sheet ;
> The clocks and the worms my bed-fellows a
>   And, oh, sae sound as I should sleep! "

I do not remember in all my reading to have met with anything more truly the language of misery than the exclamation in the last line. Misery is like love; to speak its language truly, the author must have felt it.

I am every day expecting the doctor to give your little godson the small-pox. They are *rife* in the country, and I tremble for his fate. By the way, I cannot help congratulating you on his looks and spirit. Every person who sees him acknowledges him to be the finest, handsomest child he has ever seen. I am myself delighted with the manly swell of his little chest, and a certain miniature dignity in the carriage of his head, and the glance of his fine black eye, which promise the undaunted gallantry of an independent mind.

I thought to have sent you some rhymes, but time forbids. I promise you poetry until you are tired of it next time I have the honour of assuring you how truly I am, &c., R. B.

CCXI.
TO CLARINDA.

[About February 1790.]

I HAVE indeed been ill, madam, this whole winter. An incessant headache, depression of spirits, and all the truly miserable consequences of a deranged nervous system, have made dreadful havoc of my health and peace. Add to all this, a line of life, into which I have lately entered, obliges me to ride upon an average at least two hundred miles every week. However, thank Heaven, I am now greatly better in my health. * * * *

I cannot, will not, enter into extenuatory circumstances, else I could show you how my precipitate, headlong, unthinking conduct, leagued with a conjuncture of unlucky events to thrust me out of a possibility of keeping the path of rectitude; to curse me by an irreconcilable war between my duty and my nearest wishes, and to doom me with a choice only of different species of error and misconduct.

I dare not trust myself farther with this subject. The following song (*My Lovely Nancy*, p. 237) is one of my latest productions, and I send it you as I would do anything else, because it pleases myself. SYLVANDER.

CCXII.
TO MR PETER HILL, BOOKSELLER, EDINBURGH.

ELLISLAND, *2d Feb.* 1790.

No 1 I will not say one word about apologies or excuses for not writing. I am a poor, rascally gauger, condemned to gallop at least 200 miles every week to inspect dirty ponds and yeasty barrels, and where can I find time to write to, or importance to interest anybody? The upbraidings of my conscience, nay, the upbraidings of my wife, have persecuted me on your account these two or three months past. I wish I was a great man, that my correspondence might throw light upon you, to let the world see what you really are; and then I would make your fortune, without putting my hand in my pocket for you, which, like all other great men, I suppose I would avoid as much as possible. What are you doing, and how are you doing? Have you lately seen any of my few friends? What has become of the BOROUGH REFORM, or how is the fate of my poor namesake Mademoiselle Burns decided? Which of their grave lordships can lay his hand on his heart, and say that he has not taken advantage of such frailty? O man! but for thee and thy selfish appetites and dishonest artifices, that beauteous form, and that once innocent and still ingenuous mind, might have shone conspicuous and lovely in the faithful wife and the affectionate mother.

I saw lately in a review some extracts from a new poem, called the *Village Curate;* send it me. I want likewise a cheap copy of *The World.* Mr Armstrong, the young poet, who does me the honour to mention me so kindly in his works, please give him my best thanks for the copy of his book. I shall write him my first leisure hour. I like his poetry much, but I think his style in prose quite astonishing.

What is become of that veteran in genius, wit, and * * * Smellie, and his book? Give him my compliments. Does Mr Graham of Gartmore ever enter your shop now? He is the noblest instance of great talents, great fortune, and great worth that ever I saw in conjunction. Remember me to Mrs Hill; and believe me to be, my dear sir, ever yours,   R. B.

CCXIII.

TO MR WILLIAM NICOL.

ELLISLAND, *Feb.* 9, 1790.

MY DEAR SIR,—That mare of yours is dead. I would freely have given her price to have saved her; she has vexed me beyond description. Indebted as I was to your goodness beyond what I can ever repay, I eagerly grasped at your offer to have the mare with me. That I might at least show my readiness in wishing to be grateful, I took every care of her in my power. She was never crossed for riding above half a score of times by me or in my keeping. I drew her in the plough, one of three, for one poor week. I refused fifty-five shillings for her, which was the highest bode I could squeeze for her. I fed her up, and had her in fine order for Dumfries fair; when, four or five days before the fair, she was seized with an unaccountable disorder in the sinews, or somewhere in the bones of the neck; with a weakness or total want of power in her fillets; and, in short, the whole vertebræ of her spine seemed to be diseased and unhinged; and in eight-and-forty hours, in spite of the two best farriers in the country, she died. The farriers said that she had been quite strained in the fillets beyond cure before you had bought her; and that the poor creature, though she might keep a little flesh, had been jaded and quite worn out with fatigue and oppression. While she was with me she was under my own eye, and I assure you, my much-valued friend, everything was done for her that could be done; and the accident has vexed me to the heart. In fact, I could not pluck up spirits to write to you on account of the unfortunate business.

There is little new in this country. Our theatrical company, of which you must have heard, leave us this week. Their merit and character are indeed very great, both on the stage and in private life: not a worthless creature among them; and their encouragement has been accordingly. Their usual run is from eighteen to twenty-five pounds a night: seldom less than the one, and the house will hold no more than the other. There have been repeated instances of sending away six, and eight, and ten pounds a night for want of room. A new theatre is to be built by sub-scription; the first stone is to be laid on Friday first to come. Three hundred guineas have been raised by thirty subscribers, and thirty more might have been got if wanted. The manager, Mr Sutherland, was introduced to me by a friend from Ayr; and a worthier or cleverer fellow I have rarely met with. Some of our clergy have slipt in by stealth now and then; but they have got up a farce of their own. You must have heard how the Rev. Mr Lawson of Kirkmahoe, seconded by the Rev. Mr Kirkpatrick of Dunscore, and the rest of that faction, have accused, in formal process, the unfortunate and Rev. Mr Heron of Kirkgunzeon, that, in ordaining Mr Nielson to the cure of souls in Kirkbean, he, the said Heron, feloniously and treasonably bound the said Nielson to the confession of faith, *so far as it was agreeable to reason and the word of God!*

Mrs B. begs to be remembered most gratefully to you. Little Bobby and Frank are charmingly well and healthy. I am jaded to death with fatigue. For these two or three months, on an average, I have not ridden less than 200 miles per week. I have done little in the poetic way. I have given Mr Sutherland two *Prologues*, one of which was delivered last week. I have likewise strung four or five barbarous stanzas (p. 155), to the tune of *Chevy Chase*, by way of Elegy on your poor unfortunate mare, beginning (the name she got here was Peg Nicholson).

My best compliments to Mrs Nicol, and little Neddy, and all the family: I hope Ned is a good scholar, and will come out to gather nuts and apples with me next harvest.   R. B.

CCXIV.

TO MR CUNNINGHAM.

ELLISLAND, 13*th February* 1790.

I BEG your pardon, my dear and much-valued friend, for writing to you on this very unfashionable, unsightly sheet.

" My poverty but not my will consents."

But to make amends, since of modish post I have none, except one poor widowed half-sheet of gilt, which lies in my drawer, among my‾plebeian foolscap pages, like the widow of a man of fashion whom that unpolite scoundrel, Necessity, has driven from Burgundy and Pine-apple to a dish of Bohea with the scandal-bearing helpmate of a village priest ; or a glass of whisky-toddy with a ruby-nosed yoke-fellow of a foot-padding exciseman—I make a vow to enclose this sheetful of epistolary fragments in that my only scrap of gilt paper.

I am indeed your unworthy debtor for three friendly letters. I ought to have written to you long ere now ; but it is a literal fact, I have scarcely a spare moment. It is not that I *will not* write to you ; Miss Burnet is not more‾dear to her guardian angel, nor his Grace the Duke of Queensberry to the powers of darkness, than my friend Cunningham to me. It is not that I *cannot* write to you ; should you doubt it, take the following fragment, which was intended for you some time ago, and be convinced that I can *antithesize* sentiment and *circumvolute* periods as well as any coiner of phrase in the regions of philology.

December 1789.

MY DEAR CUNNINGHAM,—Where are you ? And what are you doing ? Can you be that son of levity who takes up a friendship as he takes up a fashion ? or are you, like some other of the worthiest fellows in the world, the victim of indolence, laden with fetters of ever-increasing weight ?

What strange beings we are ? Since we have a portion of conscious existence, equally capable of enjoying pleasure, happiness, and rapture, or of suffering pain, wretchedness, and misery —it is surely worthy of an inquiry, whether there be not such a thing as a science of life ; whether method, economy, and fertility of expedients be not applicable to enjoyment ; and whether there be not a want of dexterity in pleasure which renders our little scantling of happiness still less ; and a profuseness, an intoxication in bliss, which leads to satiety, disgust, and self-abhorrence. There is not a doubt but that health, talents, character, decent competency, respectable friends, are real, substantial blessings ; and yet do we not daily see those who enjoy many or all of these good things, contrive, notwithstanding, to be as unhappy as others to whose lot few of them have fallen ? I believe one great source of this mistake or misconduct is owing to a certain stimulus, with us called ambition, which goads us up the hill of life—not as we ascend other eminences, for the laudable curiosity of viewing an extended landscape—but rather for the dishonest pride of looking down on others of our fellow-creatures seemingly diminutive in humbler stations, &c. &c.

Sunday, 14*th February* 1790

I am now obliged to join

"Night to day, and Sunday to the week."

If there be any truth in the orthodox faith of these churches, I am past redemption, and what is worse, to all eternity. I am deeply read in *Boston's Fourfold State, Marshall on Sanctification, Guthrie's Trial of a Saving Interest*, &c.; but "there is no balm in Gilead, there is no physician there" for me; so I shall e'en turn Arminian, and trust to "sincere though imperfect obedience."

Tuesday, 16*th.*

Luckily for me, I was prevented from the discussion of the knotty point at which I had just made a full stop. All my fears and cares are of this world : if there is another, an honest man has nothing to fear from it. I hate a man that wishes to be a deist; but I fear, every fair, unprejudiced inquirer must in some degree be a sceptic. It is not that there are any very staggering arguments against the immortality of man ; but, like electricity, phlogiston, &c., the subject is so involved in darkness that we want data to go upon. One thing frightens me much : that we are to live for ever seems *too good news to be true*. That we are to enter into a new scene of existence, where, exempt from want and pain, we shall enjoy ourselves and our friends without satiety or separation—how much should I be indebted to any one who could fully assure me that this was certain !

My time is once more expired. I will write to Mr Cleghorn soon. God bless him and all his concerns ! And may all the powers that preside over conviviality and friendship be present with all their kindest influence when the bearer of this, Mr Syme, and you meet ! I wish I could also make one.

Finally, brethren, farewell ! Whatsoever things are lovely, whatsoever things are gentle, whatsoever things are charitable, whatsoever things are kind, think on these things, and think on

R. B.

CCXV.

TO MR PETER HILL.

ELLISLAND, 2*d March* 1790.

AT a late meeting of the Monkland Friendly Society it was resolved to augment their library by the following books, which you are to send us as soon as possible :—*The Mirror, The Lounger Man of Feeling, Man of the World* (these, for my own sake, I wish to have by the first carrier); Knox's *History of the Reformation ;* Rae's *History of the Rebellion in* 1715 ; any good *History of the Rebellion in* 1745 ; *A Display of the Secession Act and Testimony,* by Mr Gibb ; Hervey's *Meditations ;* Beveridge's *Thoughts ;* and another copy of Watson's *Body of Divinity.* This last heavy performance is so much admired by many of our members, that they will not be content with one copy.

I wrote to Mr A. Masterton three or four months ago, to pay some money he owed me into your hands, and lately I wrote to you to the same purpose, but I have heard from neither one nor other of you.

In addition to the books I commissioned in my last, I want very much *An Index to the Excise Laws, or, an Abridgement of all the Statutes now in force Relative to the Excise :* by Jellinger Symons. I want three copies of this book : if it is now to be had, cheap or dear, get it for me. An honest country neighbour of mine wants, too, a Family Bible—the larger the better, but second-handed, for he does not choose to give above ten shillings for the book. I want likewise for myself, as you can pick them up, second-handed or cheap copies of Otway's dramatic works, Ben Jonson's, Dryden's, Congreve's, Wycherley's, Vanbrugh's, Cibber's, or any dramatic works of the more modern Macklin, Garrick, Foote, Colman, or Sheridan. A good copy, too, of Molière in French I much want Any other good dramatic authors in that language I want also ; but comic authors chiefly, though I should wish to have Racine, Corneille, and Voltaire too. I am in no hurry for all or any of these, but if you accidentally meet with them very cheap, get them for me.

And now, to quit the dry walk of business, how do you do, my dear friend ?—and how is Mrs Hill ? I trust, if now and then not so *elegantly* handsome, at least as amiable, and sings as divinely as ever. My good wife, too, has a charming " wood-note wild ;" now, could we four get anyway snugly together in a corner of the New Jerusalem (remember I bespeak your company there), you and I, though we are no singers, &c.———

I am out of all patience with this vile world for one thing. Mankind are by nature benevolent creatures, except in a few scoundrelly instances. I do not think that avarice of the good things we chance to have is born with us ; but we are placed here amid so much nakedness, and hunger, and poverty, and want, that we are under a cursed necessity of studying selfishness in order that we may EXIST! Still, there are in every age a few souls that all the wants and woes of life cannot debase to selfishness, or even to the necessary alloy of caution and prudence. If ever I am in danger of vanity, it is when I contemplate myself on this side of my disposition and character. I am no saint. I have a whole host of follies and sins to answer for; but if I could, and I believe I do it as far as I can, I would wipe away all tears from all eyes. Even the knaves who have injured me, I would oblige them; though, to tell the truth, it would be more out of vengeance, to show them that I was independent of and above them, than out of the over-flowings of my benevolence. Adieu! R. B.

CCXVI.

TO MRS DUNLOP.

ELLISLAND, 10*th April* 1790.

I HAVE just now, my ever-honoured friend, enjoyed a very high luxury, in reading a paper of the *Lounger*. You know my national prejudices. I had often read and admired the *Spectator*, *Adventurer*, *Rambler*, and *World;* but still with a certain regret that they were so thoroughly and entirely English. Alas! have I often said to myself, what are all the boasted advantages which my country reaps from the Union that can counterbalance the annihilation of her independence, and even her very name! I often repeat that couplet of my favourite poet, Goldsmith :—

" States of native liberty possest,
Though very poor may yet be very blest."

Nothing can reconcile me to the common terms English ambassador, English court, &c.; and I am out of all patience to see that equivocal character, Hastings, impeached by " the Commons of England." Tell me, my friend, is this weak prejudice? I believe in my conscience such ideas as " My country; her independence; her honour; the illustrious names that mark the history of my native land," &c.—I believe these, among your *men of the world*—men who, in fact, guide for the most part and govern our world—are looked on as so many modifications of wrong-headedness. They know the use of bawling out such terms, to rouse or lead THE RABBLE; but for their own private use, with almost all the *able statesmen* that ever existed or now exist, when they talk of right and wrong they only mean proper and improper; and their measure of conduct is not what they OUGHT, but what they DARE. For the truth of this I shall not ransack the history of nations. but appeal to one of the ablest judges of men that ever lived—the celebrated Earl of Chesterfield. In fact, a man who could thoroughly control his vices whenever they interfered with his interests, and who could completely put on the appearance of every virtue as often as it suited his purposes, is, on the Stanhopian plan, the *perfect man*—a man to lead nations. But are great abilities, complete without a flaw, and polished without a blemish, the standard of human excellence ? This is certainly the stanch opinion of *men of the world ;* but I call on honour, virtue, and worth to give the Stygian doctrine a loud negative ! However, this must be allowed—that if you abstract from man the idea of an existence beyond the grave, *then* the true measure of human conduct is, *proper and improper.* Virtue and vice, as dispositions of the heart, are in that case of scarcely the same import and value to the world at large as harmony and discord in the modifications of sound ; and a delicate sense of honour, like a nice ear for music, though it may sometimes give the possessor an ecstasy unknown to the coarser organs of the herd, yet, considering the harsh gratings and inharmonic jars in this ill-tuned state of being, it is odds but the individual would be as happy, and certainly would be as much respected by the true judges of society, as it would then stand, without either a good ear or a good heart.

You must know I have just met with the *Mirror* and *Lounger* for the first time, and I am quite in raptures with them ; I should be glad to have your opinion of some of the papers. The one I have just read, *Lounger,* No. 61, has cost me more honest tears than anything I have read of a long time. Mackenzie has been called the Addison of the Scots, and, in my opinion, Addison would not be hurt at the comparison. If he has not Addison's exquisite humour he as certainly outdoes him in the tender and the pathetic. His *Man of Feeling*—but I am not counsel-learned in the laws of criticism—I estimate as the first performance in its kind I ever saw. From what book, moral or even pious, will the susceptible young mind receive impressions more congenial to humanity and kindness, generosity and benevolence—in short, more of all that ennobles the soul to herself, or endears her to others—than from the simple, affecting tale of poor Harley ?

Still, with all my admiration of Mackenzie's writings, I do not know if they are the fittest reading for a young man who is about to set out, as the phrase is, to make his way into life. Do not you think, madam, that among the few favoured of Heaven in the structure of their minds—for such there certainly are—there may be a purity, a tenderness, a dignity, an elegance of soul, which are of no use, nay, in some degree absolutely disqualifying, for the truly important business of making a man's way into life ! If I am not much mistaken, my gallant young friend A—— is very much under these disqualifications ; and for the young females of a family I could mention, well may they excite parental solicitude, for I, a common acquaintance, or, as my vanity will have it, a humble friend, have often trembled for a turn of mind which may render them eminently happy or peculiarly miserable !

I have been manufacturing some verses lately ; but as I have got the most hurried season of Excise business over, I hope to have more leisure to transcribe anything that may shew how much I have the honour to be, madam, yours, &c., R. B.

CCXVII.

TO DR MOORE.

DUMFRIES, EXCISE-OFFICE, 14*th July* 1790.

SIR,—Coming into town this morning to attend my duty in this office, it being collection-day, I met with a gentleman who tells me he is on his way to London; so I take the opportunity of writing to you, as franking is at present under a temporary death. I shall have some snatches of leisure through the day amid our horrid business and bustle, and I shall improve them as well as I can; but let my letter be as stupid as * * * *, as miscellaneous as a newspaper, as short as a hungry grace-before-meat, or as long as a law-paper in the Douglas cause; as ill-spelt as country John's billet-doux, or as unsightly a scrawl as Betty Byre-Mucker's answer to it; I hope, considering circumstances, you will forgive it; and as it will put you to no expense of postage, I shall have the less reflection about it.

I âm sadly ungrateful in not returning my thanks for your most valuable present, *Zeluco*. In fact, you are in some degree blameable for my neglect. You were pleased to express a wish for my opinion of the work, which so flattered me, that nothing less would serve my overweening fancy than a formal criticism on the book. In fact, I have gravely planned a comparative view of you, Fielding, Richardson, and Smollett, in your different qualities and merits as novel-writers. This, I own, betrays my ridiculous vanity, and I may probably never bring the business to bear; but I am fond of the spirit young Elihu shews in the book of Job— "And I said, I will also declare my opinion." I have quite disfigured my copy of the book with my annotations. I never take it up without at the same time taking my pencil, and marking with asterisms, parentheses, &c., wherever I meet with an original thought, a nervous remark on life and manners, a remarkable, well-turned period, or a character sketched with uncommon precision.

Though I should hardly think of fairly writing out my " Comparative View," I shall certainly trouble you with my remarks, such as they are.

I have just received from my gentleman that horrid summons in the book of Revelation—"That time shall be no more!"

The little collection of sonnets have some charming poetry in them. If *indeed* I am indebted to the fair author for the book,* and not, as I rather suspect, to a celebrated author of the other

* This book was the Sonnets of Charlotte Smith.

sex, I should certainly have written to the lady, with my grateful
acknowledgments, and my own ideas of the comparative excellence
of her pieces.   I would do this last, not from any vanity of think-
ing that my remarks could be of much consequence to Mrs Smith,
but merely from my own feelings as an author, doing as I would
be done by.   R. B.

CCXVIII.

TO MR MURDOCH, TEACHER OF FRENCH, LONDON

ELLISLAND, 16th *July* 1790

MY DEAR SIR,—I received a letter from you a long time ago,
but unfortunately, as it was in the time of my peregrinations and
journeyings through Scotland, I mislaid or lost it, and by conse-
quence your direction along with it.   Luckily, my good star
brought me acquainted with Mr Kennedy, who, I understand, is
an acquaintance of yours ; and by his means and mediation I hope
to replace that link which my unfortunate negligence had so
unluckily broke in the chain of our correspondence.   I was the
more vexed at the vile accident, as my brother William, a journey-
man saddler, has been for some time in London, and wished above
all things for your direction, that he might have paid his respects
to his father's friend.

His last address he sent me was, "Wm. Burns, at Mr Barber's,
saddler, No. 181 Strand."   I writ him by Mr Kennedy, but
neglected to ask him for your address ; so, if you find a spare
half minute, please let my brother know by a card where and
when he will find you, and the poor fellow will joyfully wait on
you, as one of the few surviving friends of the man whose name,
and christian name too, he has the honour to bear.

The next letter I write you shall be a long one.   I have much
to tell you of "hairbreadth 'scapes in th' imminent deadly breach,"
with all the eventful history of a life, the early years of which
owed so much to your kind tutorage ; but this at an hour of
leisure.   My kindest compliments to Mrs Murdoch and family.
I am ever, my dear sir, your obliged friend,   R. B.

CCXIX.

TO MR M'MURDO.

ELLISLAND, 2d *August* 1790.

SIR,—Now that you are over with the sirens of Flattery, the
harpics of Corruption, and the furies of Ambition—these infernal
deities that on all sides, and in all parties, preside over the

villanous business of politics—permit a rustic Muse of your acquaintance to do her best to sooth you with a song (*He's gane,* p. 156).

You knew Henderson—I have not flattered his memory. I have the honour to be, sir, your obliged, humble servant,   R. B.

CCXX.

TO MRS DUNLOP.

8th August 1790.

DEAR MADAM,—After a long day's toil, plague, and care, I sit down to write to you. Ask me not why I have delayed it so long? It was owing to hurry, indolence, and fifty other things; in short, to anything but forgetfulness of *la plus aimable de son sexe.* By the by, you are indebted your best courtesy to me for this last compliment, as I pay it from my sincere conviction of its truth —a quality rather rare in compliments of these grinning, bowing, scraping times.

Well, I hope writing to *you* will ease a little my troubled soul. Sorely has it been bruised to-day! A *ci-devant* friend of mine, and an intimate acquaintance of yours, has given my feelings a wound that I perceive will gangrene dangerously ere it cure. H has wounded my pride!   R. B.

CCXXI.

TO MR CUNNINGHAM.

- ELLISLAND, *8th August* 1790.

FORGIVE me, my once dear, and ever dear friend, my seeming negligence. You cannot sit down and fancy the busy life I lead.

I laid down my goose-feather to beat my brains for an apt simile, and had some thoughts of a country grannum at a family christening; a bride on the market-day before her marriage; an orthodox clergyman at a Paisley sacrament; or a tavern-keeper at an election dinner; but the resemblance that hits my fancy best is, that blackguard miscreant, Satan, who, &c., &c., roams about like a roaring lion, seeking, *searching* whom he may devour. However, tossed about as I am, if I choose—and who would not choose?—to bind down with the crampets of attention the brazen foundation of integrity, I may rear up the superstructure of independence, and from its daring turrets bid defiance to the storms of fate   And is not this a " consummation devoutly to be wished?'

" Thy spirit, Independence, let me share;
   Lord of the lion-heart and eagle-eye!
   Thy steps I follow with my bosom bare,
   Nor heed the storm that howls along the sky !"

Are not these noble verses ? They are the introduction of Smollett's *Ode to Independence :* if you have not seen the poem, I will send it to you. How wretched is the man that hangs on by the favours of the great! To shrink from every dignity of man, at the approach of a lordly piece of self-consequence, who, amid all his tinsel glitter and stately hauteur, is but a creature formed as thou art—and perhaps not so well formed as thou art—came into the world a pulling infant as thou didst, and must go out of it as all men must—a naked corse. R. B.

CCXXII.
TO COLLECTOR MITCHELL.

ELLISLAND, *October* 1790.

SIR,—I shall not fail to wait on Captain Riddel to-night. I wish and pray that the goddess of justice herself would appear to-morrow among our hon. gentlemen, merely to give them a word in their ear that mercy to the thief is injustice to the honest man. For my part, I have galloped over my ten parishes these four days, until this moment that I am just alighted, or rather that my poor jackass-skeleton of a horse has let me down; for the miserable creature has been on his knees half a score of times within the last twenty miles, telling me, in his own way—" Behold, am not I thy faithful jade of a horse, on which thou hast ridden these many years ?"

In short, sir, I have broke my horse's wind, and almost broke my own neck, besides some injuries in a part that shall be nameless, owing to a hard-hearted stone of a saddle. I find that every offender has so many great men to espouse his cause, that I shall not be surprised if I am not committed to the stronghold of the law to-morrow for insolence to the dear friends of the gentlemen of the country. I have the honour to be, sir, your obliged and obedient humble R. B.

CCXXIII.
TO CRAUFORD TAIT, ESQ., EDINBURGH.

ELLISLAND, 15*th October* 1790.

DEAR SIR,—Allow me to introduce to your acquaintance the bearer, Mr Wm. Duncan, a friend of mine, whom I have long known and long loved. His father, whose only son he is, has a decent little property in Ayrshire, and has bred the young man to the law, in which department he comes up an adventurer to your good town. I shall give you my friend's character in two words—As to his head, he has talents enough, and more than enough, for common life; as to his heart, when nature had kneaded the kindly clay that composed it, she said—" I can no more."

You, my good sir, were born under kinder stars ; but your fraternal sympathy, I well know, can enter into the feelings of the young man who goes into life with the laudable ambition to *do* something, and to *be* something among his fellow-creatures, but whom the consciousness of friendless obscurity presses to the earth, and wounds to the soul !

Even the fairest of his virtues are against him. That independent spirit, and that ingenuous modesty—qualities inseparable from a noble mind—are, with the million, circumstances not a little disqualifying. What pleasure is in the power of the fortunate and the happy, by their notice and patronage, to brighten the countenance and glad the heart of such depressed youth ! 1 am not so angry with mankind for their deaf economy of the purse : the goods of this world cannot be divided without being lessened—but why be a niggard of that which bestows bliss on a fellow-creature, yet takes nothing from our own means of enjoyment ? We wrap ourselves up in the cloak of our own better fortune, and turn away our eyes, lest the wants and woes of our brother-mortals should disturb the selfish apathy of our souls !

I am the worst hand in the world at asking a favour. That indirect address, that insinuating implication, which, without any positive request, plainly expresses your wish, is a talent not to be acquired at a plough-tail. Tell me, then—for you can—in what periphrasis of language, in what circumvolution of phrase, I shall envelope, yet not conceal, this plain story ?—" My dear Mr Tait, my friend Mr Duncan, whom I have the pleasure of introducing to you, is a young lad of your own profession, and a gentleman of much modesty and great worth. Perhaps it may be in your power to assist him in the, to him, important consideration of getting a place ; but at all events, your notice and acquaintance will be a very great acquisition to him, and I dare pledge myself that he will never disgrace your favour."

You may possibly be surprised, sir, at such a letter from me : 'tis, I own, in the usual way of calculating these matters, more than our acquaintance entitles me to ; but my answer is short. Of all the men at your time of life whom I knew in Edinburgh, you are the most accessible on the side on which I have assailed you. You are very much altered, indeed, from what you were when I knew you, if generosity point the path you will not tread, or humanity call to you in vain.

As to myself—a being to whose interests I believe you are still a well-wisher—1 am here, breathing at all times, thinking sometimes, and rhyming now and then. Every situation has its share of the cares and pains of life, and my situation, I am persuaded, has a full ordinary allowance of its pleasures and enjoyments.

My best compliments to your father and Miss Tait. If you have an opportunity, please remember me in the solemn-league-and-covenant of friendship to Mrs Lewis Hay.* I am a wretch for not writing her; but I am so hackneyed with self-accusation in that way, that my conscience lies in my bosom with scarce the sensibility of an oyster in its shell. Where is Lady M'Kenzie? Wherever she is, God bless her! I likewise beg leave to trouble you with compliments to Mr Wm. Hamilton, Mrs Hamilton, and family, and Mrs Chalmers, when you are in that country. Should you meet with Miss Nimmo, please remember me kindly to her.

R. B.

CCXXIV.

TO FRANCIS GROSE, ESQ.

Among the many witch-stories I have heard relating to Alloway Kirk, I distinctly remember only two or three.

Upon a stormy night, amid whistling squalls of wind and bitter blasts of hail,—in short, on such a night as the devil would choose to take the air in,—a farmer, or farmer's servant, was plodding and plashing homeward with his plough-irons on his shoulder, having been getting some repairs on them at a neighbouring smithy. His way lay by the Kirk of Alloway; and being rather on the anxious look-out in approaching a place so well known to be a favourite haunt of the devil, and the devil's friend's and emissaries, he was struck aghast by discovering through the horrors of the storm and stormy night, a light, which, on his nearer approach, plainly showed itself to proceed from the haunted edifice. Whether he had been fortified from above on his devout supplication, as is customary with people when they suspect the immediate presence of Satan, or whether, according to another custom, he had got courageously drunk at the smithy, I will not pretend to determine; but so it was, that he ventured to go up to, nay, into the very kirk. As luck would have it, his temerity came of unpunished.

The members of the infernal junto were all out on some midnight business or other, and he saw nothing but a kind of kettle or caldron, depending from the roof, over the fire, simmering some heads of unchristened children, limbs of executed malefactors, &c., for the business of the night. It was in for a penny, in for a pound, with the honest ploughman: so without ceremony he unhooked the caldron from off the fire, and pouring out the horrible ingredients, inverted it on his head, and carried it fairly home,

---

* Formerly Miss Margaret Chalmers.

where it remained long in the family, a living evidence of the truth of the story.

Another story, which I can prove to be equally authentic, was as follows :—

On a market-day in the town of Ayr, a farmer from Carrick, and consequently whose way lay by the very gate of Alloway Kirkyard, in order to cross the river Doon at the old Bridge, which is about two or three hundred yards farther on than the said gate, had been detained by his business, till by the time he reached Alloway it was the wizard hour, between night and morning.

Though he was terrified with a blaze streaming from the kirk, yet as it is a well-known fact, that to turn back on these occasions is running by far the greatest risk of mischief, he prudently advanced on his road. When he had reached the gate of the kirkyard, he was surprised and entertained, through the ribs and arches of an old Gothic window, which still faces the highway, to see a dance of witches merrily footing it round their old sooty blackguard master, who was keeping them all alive with the power of his bagpipe. The farmer, stopping his horse to observe them a little, could plainly descry the faces of many old women of his acquaintance and neighbourhood. How the gentleman was dressed, tradition does not say, but that the ladies were all in their smocks : and one of them happening, unluckily, to have a smock which was considerably too short to answer all the purpose of that piece of dress, our farmer was so tickled, that he involuntarily burst out, with a loud laugh, " Weel luppen, Maggy wi' the short sark !" and recollecting himself, instantly spurred his horse to the top of his speed. I need not mention the universally-known fact, that no diabolical power can pursue you beyond the middle of a running stream. Lucky it was for the poor farmer that the river Doon was so near, for notwithstanding the speed of his horse, which was a good one, against he reached the middle of the arch of the bridge, and consequently the middle of the stream, the pursuing, vengeful hags were so close at his heels, that one of them actually sprang to seize him : but it was too late ; nothing was on her side of the stream but the horse's tail, which immediately gave way, at her infernal grip, as if blasted by a stroke of lightning ; but the farmer was beyond her reach. However, the unsightly, tail-less, condition of the vigorous steed was, to the last hour of the noble creature's life, an awful warning to the Carrick farmers not to stay too late in Ayr markets.

The last relation I shall give, though equally true, is not so well identified as the two former with regard to the scene ; but as the best authorities give it for Alloway, I shall relate it.

On a summer's evening, about the time Nature puts on her sables to mourn the expiry of the cheerful day, a shepherd-boy, belonging to a farmer in the immediate neighbourhood of Alloway Kirk, had just folded his charge, and was returning home. As he passed the kirk, in the adjoining field, he fell in with a crew of men and women, who were busy pulling stems of the plant rag-wort. He observed that as each person pulled a ragwort, he or she got astride of it, and called out, " Up horsie !" on which the ragwort flew off, like Pegasus, through the air with its rider. The foolish boy likewise pulled his ragwort, and cried with the rest, " Up horsie !" and, strange to tell, away he flew with the company. The first stage at which the cavalcade stopt was a merchant's wine-cellar in Bordeaux, where, without saying by your leave, they quaffed away at the best the cellar could afford, until the morning—foe to the imps and works of darkness—threatened to throw light on the matter, and frightened them from their carousals.

The poor shepherd lad, being equally a stranger to the scene and the liquor, heedlessly got himself drunk ; and when the rest took horse, he fell asleep, and was found so next day by some of the people belonging to the merchant. Somebody that understood Scotch, asking him what he was, he said such-a-one's herd in Alloway ; and by some means or other getting home again, he lived long to tell the world the wondrous tale.

R. B.

CCXXV.

TO MRS DUNLOP.

ELLISLAND, *November* 1790.

" As cold waters to a thirsty soul, so is good news from a far country."

Fate has long owed me a letter of good news from you, in return for the many tidings of sorrow which I have received. In this instance I most cordially obey the apostle : " Rejoice with them that do rejoice'—for me to *sing* for joy is no new thing ; but *to preach* for joy, as I have done in the commencement of this epistle, is a pitch of extravagant rapture to which I never rose before.

I read your letter—I literally jumped for joy. How could such a mercurial creature as a poet lumpishly keep his seat on the re-ceipt of the best news from his best friend ? I seized my gilt-headed Wangee rod, an instrument indispensably necessary, in my left hand, in the moment of inspiration and rapture ; and stride, stride—quick and quicker—out skipt I among the broomy banks of Nith to muse over my joy by retail. To keep within the bounds of prose was impossible. Mrs Little's is a more elegant, but not a more sincere compliment to the sweet little fellow, than I, ex-tempore almost, poured out to him in the following verses (p. 163).

I am much flattered by your approbation of my *Tam o' Shanter*, which you express in your former letter, though, by the by, you load me in that said letter with accusations heavy and many, to all which I plead, *not guilty !* Your book is, I hear, on the road to reach me. As to printing of poetry, when you prepare it for the press, you have only to spell it right, and place the capital letters properly—as to the punctuation, the printers do that themselves.

I have a copy of *Tam o' Shanter* ready to send you by the first opportunity—it is too heavy to send by post.

I heard of Mr Corbet lately. He, in consequence of your recommendation, is most zealous to serve me. Please favour me soon with an account of your good folks ; if Mrs H. is recovering, and the young gentleman doing well. R. B.

CCXXVI.

TO WILLIAM DUNBAR, W.S.

ELLISLAND, 17*th January* 1791.

I AM not gone to Elysium, most noble colonel, but am still here in this sublunary world, serving my God by propagating his image, and honouring my king by begetting him loyal subjects.

Many happy returns of the season await my friend. May the thorns of care never beset his path ! May peace be an inmate of his bosom, and rapture a frequent visitor of his soul ! May the bloodhounds of misfortune never track his steps, nor the screech-owl of sorrow alarm his dwelling ! May enjoyment tell thy hours, and pleasure number thy days, thou friend of the bard ! " Blessed be he that blesseth thee, and cursed be he that curseth thee ! ! !"

As a further proof that I am still in the land of existence, I send you a poem, the latest I have composed. I have a particular reason for wishing you only to show it to select friends, should you think it worthy a friend's perusal ; but if, at your first leisure hour, you will favour me with your opinion of, and strictures on, the performance, it will be an additional obligation on, dear sir, your deeply-indebted humble servant, R. B.

CCXXVII.

TO MR PETER HILL.

ELLISLAND, 17*th January* 1791.

TAKE these two guineas, and place them over against that account of yours, which has gagged my mouth these five or six months ! I can as little write good things as apologies to the man I owe money to. Oh the supreme curse of making three guineas do the business of five ! Not all the labours of Hercules ; not all the Hebrews' three centuries of Egyptian bondage, were such an insuperable business, such a desperate task !! Poverty ! thou half-sister of death, thou cousin-german of destruction !—where shall I find force of execration equal to the amplitude of thy demerits? Oppressed by thee, the venerable ancient, grown hoary in the practice of every virtue, laden with years and wretchedness, implores a little, little aid to support his existence, from a stony-hearted son of Mammon, whose sun of prosperity never knew a cloud, and is by him denied and insulted. Oppressed by thee, the man of sentiment, whose heart glows with independence, and melts with sensibility, inly pines under the neglect, or writhes, in bitterness of soul, under the contumely of arrogant, unfeeling wealth. Oppressed by thee, the son of genius, whose ill-starred ambition plants him at the tables of the fashionable and polite, must see, in suffering silence, his remark neglected, and his person despised, while shallow greatness, in his idiot attempts at wit, shall meet with countenance and applause. Nor is it only the family of worth that have reason to complain of thee—the children of folly and vice, though in common with thee the offspring of evil, smart equally under thy rod. Owing to thee, the man of unfortunate disposition and neglected education is condemned as a fool for his dissipation, despised and shunned as a needy wretch when his follies as usual bring him to want; and when his un principled necessities drive him to dishonest practices, he is ab horred as a miscreant, and perishes by the justice of his country But far otherwise is the lot of the man of family and fortune *His* early follies and extravagance are spirit and fire ;· *his* conse-quent wants are the embarrassments of an honest fellow; and when, to remedy the matter, he has gained a legal commission to plunder distant provinces, or massacre peaceful nations, he returns, perhaps, laden with the spoils of rapine and murder ; lives wicked and re-spected, and dies a scoundrel and a lord.

Well, divines may say of it what they please, but execration is to the mind what phlebotomy is to the body—the vital sluices of both are wonderfully relieved by their respective evacuations.

R. B.

CCXXVIII.

TO MR CUNNINGHAM.

ELLISLAND, 23d January 1791.

MANY happy returns of the season to you, my dear friend ! As many of the good things of this life as is consistent with the usual mixture of good and evil in the cup of being !

I have just finished a poem—*Tam o' Shanter*—which you will receive enclosed. It is my first essay in the way of tales.

I have these several months been hammering at an elegy on the amiable and accomplished Miss Burnet. I have got, and can get, no farther than the following fragment (p. 164), on which please give me your strictures. In all kinds of poetic composition I set great store by your opinion ; but in sentimental verses, in the poetry of the heart, no Roman Catholic ever set more value on the infallibility of the Holy Father than I do on yours.

I mean the introductory couplets as text verses.

Let me hear from you soon. Adieu l R. B.

CCXXIX.
TO THE REV. ARCHIBALD ALISON.

ELLISLAND, 14th Feb 1791

SIR,—You must by this time have set me down as one of the most ungrateful of men. You did me the honour to present me with a book which does honour to science and the intellectual powers of man, and I have not even so much as acknowledged the receipt of it. The fact is, you yourself are to blame for it. Flattered as I was by your telling me that you wished to have my opinion of the work, the old spiritual enemy of mankind, who knows well that vanity is one of the sins that most easily beset me, put it into my head to ponder over the performance with the look-out of a critic, and to draw up forsooth a deep-learned digest of strictures on a composition, of which, in fact, until I read the book, I did not even know the first principles. I own, sir, that at first - glance several of your propositions startled me as paradoxical. That the martial clangour of a trumpet had something in it vastly more grand, heroic, and sublime, than the twingle-twangle of a Jew's harp—that the delicate flexure of a rose-twig, when the half-blown flower is heavy with the tears of the dawn, was infinitely more beautiful and elegant than the upright stub of a burdock—and that from something innate and independent of all associations of ideas—these I had set down as irrefragable, orthodox truths, until perusing your book shook my faith. In short, sir, except Euclid's *Elements of Geometry*, which I made a shift to unravel by my father's fireside in the winter evenings of the first season I held the plough, I never read a book which gave me such a quantum of information, and added so much to my stock of ideas, as your *Essays on the Principles of Taste*. One thing, sir, you must forgive my mentioning as an uncommon merit in the work—I mean the language. To clothe abstract philosophy in elegance of style sounds something like a contradiction in terms ; but you have convinced me that they are quite compatible.

I enclose you some poetic bagatelles of my late composition. The one in print is my first essay in the way of telling a tale. I am, sir, &c. R. B.

CCLXXXIX.
TO MR THOMSON.

June 1793.

WHEN I tell you, my dear sir, that a friend of mine, in whom I am much interested, has fallen a sacrifice to these accursed times, you will easily allow that it might unhinge me for doing any good among ballads. My own loss, as to pecuniary matters, is trifling; but the total ruin of a much-loved friend is a loss indeed. Pardon my seeming inattention to your last commands.

I cannot alter the disputed lines in *The Mill, Mill O!* What you think a defect, I esteem as a positive beauty; so you see how doctors differ. I shall now, with as much alacrity as I can muster, go on with your commands.

You know Fraser, the hautboy-player in Edinburgh—he is here instructing a band of music for a fencible corps quartered in this county. Among many of his airs that please me, there is one, well known as a reel, by the name of *The Quaker's Wife;* and which I remember, a grand-aunt of mine used to sing by the name of *Liggeram Cosh, my Bonnie Wee Lass.* Mr Fraser plays it slow, and with an expression that quite charms me. I became such an enthusiast about it, that I made a song for it, which I here subjoin, and enclose Fraser's set of the tune. If they hit your fancy, they are at your service; if not, return me the tune, and I will put it in *Johnson's Museum.* I think the song is not in my worst manner (*Blythe*, &c., p. 267). I should wish to hear how this pleases you.   R. B.

CCXC.
TO MR THOMSON.

25th June 1793.

HAVE you ever, my dear sir, felt your bosom ready to burst with indignation, on reading of those mighty villains who divide kingdom against kingdom, desolate provinces, and lay nations waste, out of the wantonness of ambition, or often from still more ignoble passions? In a mood of this kind to-day I recollected the air of *Logan Water*, and it occurred to me that its querulous melody probably had its origin from the plaintive indignation of some swelling, suffering heart, fired at the tyrannic strides of some public destroyer, and overwhelmed with private distress, the consequence of a country's ruin. If I have done anything at all like justice to my feelings, the following song (p. 268), composed in three-quarters of an hour's meditation in my elbow-chair, ought to have some merit.   R. B.

they have passed that bourne where all other kindness ceases to be of avail. Whether, after all, either the one or the other be of any real service to the dead, is, I fear, very problematical, but I am sure they are highly gratifying to the living : and as a very orthodox text, I forget where, in Scripture says,—" whatsoever is not of faith is sin ;" so say I, whatsoever is not detrimental to society, and is of positive enjoyment, is of God, the giver of all good things, and ought to be received and enjoyed by His creatures with thankful delight. As almost all my religious tenets originate from my heart, I am wonderfully pleased with the idea that I can still keep up a tender intercourse with the dearly-beloved friend, or still more dearly-beloved sweetheart, who is gone to the world of spirits.

The ballad on Queen Mary was begun while I was busy with *Percy's Reliques of English Poetry*. By the way, how much is every honest heart, which has a tincture of Caledonian prejudice, obliged to you for your glorious story of Buchanan and Targe ! 'Twas an unequivocal proof of your loyal gallantry of soul giving Targe the victory. I should have been mortified to the ground if you had not.

I have just read over once more of many times your *Zeluco*. I marked with my pencil as I went along every passage that pleased me particularly above the rest, and one or two which, with humble deference, I am disposed to think unequal to the merits of the book. I have sometimes thought to transcribe these marked passages, or at least so much of them as to point where they are, and send them to you. Original strokes that strongly depict the human heart, is your and Fielding's province beyond any other novelist I have ever perused. Richardson, indeed, might perhaps be excepted ; but unhappily his *dramatis personæ* are beings of another world ; and, however they may captivate the inexperienced, romantic fancy of a boy or a girl, they will ever, in proportion as we have made human nature our study, dissatisfy our riper years.

As to my private concerns—I am going on, a mighty tax-gatherer, and have lately had the interest to get myself ranked on the list of Excise as a supervisor. I am not yet employed as such, but in a few years I shall fall into the file of supervisorship by seniority. I have had an immense loss in the death of the Earl of Glencairn, the patron from whom all my fame and fortune took its rise. Independent of my grateful attachment to him, which was indeed so strong that it pervaded my very soul, and was entwined with the thread of my existence ; so soon as the prince's friends had got in,—and every dog you know has his day,—my getting forward in the Excise would have been an easier business than otherwise it will be. Though this was a consummation devoutly to be wished, yet I can live and rhyme as I am ;

and as to my boys, poor little fellows! if I cannot place them on as high an elevation in life as I could wish, I shall, if I am favoured so much by the Disposer of events as to see that period, fix them on as broad and independent a basis as possible. Among the many wise adages which have been treasured up by our Scottish ancestors, this is one of the best—*Better be the head o' the commonalty than the tail o' the gentry.*

But I am got on a subject, which, however interesting to me, is of no manner of consequence to you: so I shall give you a short poem on the other page, and close this with assuring you how sincerely I have the honour to be, yours, &c.   R. B.

CCXXXII.

TO THE REV. G. BAIRD.

ELLISLAND, *February* 1791.

REVEREND SIR,—Why did you, my dear sir, write to me in such a hesitating style on the business of poor Bruce? Don't I know, and have I not felt, the many ills, the peculiar ills, that poetic flesh is heir to? You shall have your choice of all the unpublished poems I have; and had your letter had my direction so as to have reached me sooner, it only came to my hand this moment, I should have directly put you out of suspense on the subject. I only ask that some prefatory advertisement in the book, as well as the subscription-bills, may bear that the publication is solely for the benefit of Bruce's mother. I would not put it in the power of ignorance to surmise, or malice to insinuate, that I clubbed a share in the work from mercenary motives. Nor need you give me credit for any remarkable generosity in my part of the business. I have such a host of peccadilloes, failings, follies, and backslidings—anybody but myself might perhaps give some of them a worse appellation—that by way of some balance, however trifling, in the account, I am fain to do any good that occurs in my very limited power to a fellow-creature, just for the selfish purpose of clearing a little the vista of retrospection.   R. B.

CCXXXIII.

TO MR CUNNINGHAM.

ELLISLAND, 12*th March* 1791.

IF the foregoing piece be worth your strictures, let me have them. For my own part, a thing that I have just composed always appears through a double portion of that partial medium in which an author will ever view his own works. I believe, in general, novelty has something in it that inebriates the fancy, and not unfrequently dissipates and fumes away like other intoxication, and leaves the poor patient, as usual, with an aching heart. A striking instance of this might be adduced in the revolution of many a hymeneal honeymoon. But lest I sink into·stupid prose, and so sacrilegiously intrude on the office of my parish priest, I shall fill up the page in my own way, and give you another song of my late composition, which will appear perhaps in Johnson's work, as well as the former.

You must know a beautiful Jacobite air—" *There'll never be peace till Jamie comes hame*" (p. 244). When political combustion ceases to be the object of princes and patriots, it then, you know, becomes the lawful prey of historians and poets.

If you like the air, and if the stanzas hit your fancy, you can not imagine, my dear friend, how much you would oblige me, if, by the charms of your delightful voice, you would give my honest effusion to " the memory of joys that are past" to the few friends whom you indulge in that pleasure. But I have scribbled on till I hear the clock has intimated the near approach of

> " That hour, o' night's black arch the keystane."

So, good-night to you! Sound be your sleep, and delectable your dreams! Apropos, how do you like this thought in a ballad I have just now on the tapis?

> " I look to the west when I gae to rest,
> That happy my dreams and my slumbers may be;
> Far, far in the west is he I loe best,
> The lad that is dear to my baby and me!"

Good-night once more, and God bless you!   R. B.

CCXXXIV.

TO MR ALEXANDER DALZELL,

FACTOR, FINDLASTON.

ELLISLAND, 19*th March* 1791.

MY DEAR SIR,—I have taken the liberty to frank this letter to you, as it encloses an idle poem of mine, which I send you; and you may perhaps pay dear enough for it if you read it through. Not that this is my own opinion; but the author, by the time he has composed and corrected his work, has quite pored away all his powers of critical discrimination.

I can easily guess, from my own heart, what you have felt on a late most melancholy event. God knows what I have suffered at the loss of my best friend, my first and dearest patron and benefactor—the man to whom I owe all that I am and have! I am gone into mourning for him, and with more sincerity of grief than I fear some will, who, by nature's ties, ought to feel on the occasion.

I will be exceedingly obliged to you, indeed, to let me know the news of the noble family, how the poor mother and the two sisters support their loss. I had a packet of poetic bagatelles ready to send to Lady Betty when I saw the fatal tidings in the newspaper. I see; by the same channel, that the honoured REMAINS of my noble patron are designed to be brought to the family burial-place. Dare I trouble you to let me know privately before the day of interment, that I may cross the .country, and steal among the crowd, to pay a tear to the last sight of my ever-revered benefactor ? It will oblige me beyond expression.   R. B.

CCXXXV.
TO LADY E. CUNNINGHAM.

My LADY,—I would, as usual, have availed myself of the privilege your goodness has allowed me, of sending you. anything I compose in my poetical way ; but as I had resolved, so soon as the shock of my irreparable loss would allow me, to pay a tribute to my late benefactor, I determined to make that the first piece I should do myself the honour of sending you. Had the wing of my fancy been equal to the ardour of my heart, the enclosed (p. 166), had been much more worthy your perusal : as it is, I beg leave to lay it at your ladyship's feet. As all the world knows my obligations to the late Earl of Glencairn, I would wish to shew, as openly, that my heart glows, and shall ever glow, with the most grateful sense and remembrance of his lordship's goodness. The sables I did myself the honour to wear to his lordship's memory were not the "mockery of wo." Nor shall my gratitude perish with me! If among my children I shall have a.son that has a heart, he shall hand it down to his child as a family honour and a family debt, that my dearest existence I owe to the noble house of Glencairn !

I was about to say, my lady, that if you think the poem may venture to see the light, I would, in some way or other, give it to the world.   R. B.

CCXXXVI.
TO MRS DUNLOP.

ELLISLAND, *7th April* 1791.

WHEN I tell you, madam, that by a fall, not from my horse, but with my horse, I have been a cripple some time, and that this is the first day my arm and hand have been able to serve me in writing, you will allow that it is too good an apology for my seemingly ungrateful silence. I am now getting better, and am able to rhyme a little, which implies some tolerable ease, as I cannot think that the most poetic genius is able to compose on the rack.

I do not remember if ever I mentioned to you my having an idea of composing an elegy on the late Miss Burnet of Monboddo. I had the honour of being pretty well acquainted with her, and have seldom felt so much at the loss of an acquaintance, as when I heard that so amiable and accomplished a piece of God's work was no more. I have, as yet, gone no further than the following fragment, of which please let me have your opinion. You know that elegy is a subject so much exhausted, that any new idea on the business is not to be expected : 'tis well if we can place an old idea in a new light. How far I have succeeded as to this last, you will judge from what follows : * * *

I have proceeded no farther.

Your kind letter, with your kind *remembrance* of your godson, came safe. This last, madam, is scarcely what my pride can bear. As to the little fellow,* he is, partiality apart, the finest boy I have for a long time seen. He is now seventeen months old, has the small-pox and measles over, has cut several teeth, and never had a grain of doctors' drugs in his bowels.

I am truly happy to hear that the "little floweret" is bloom-ing so fresh and fair, and that the "mother plant" is rather re-covering her drooping head. I have written thus far with a good deal of difficulty. When I get a little abler, you shall hear further from, madam, yours, R. B.

CCXXXVII.

TO MRS DUNLOP.

ELLISLAND, 11*th April* 1791.

I AM once more able, my honoured friend, to return you, with my own hand, thanks for the many instances of your friendship, and particularly for your kind anxiety in this last disaster that my evil genius had in store for me. However life is chequered—joy and sorrow—for on Saturday morning last, Mrs Burns made me a present of a fine boy ; rather stouter, but not so handsome as your godson was at his time of life. Indeed, I look on your little namesake to be my *chef d'œuvre* in that species of manufac-ture, as I look on *Tam o' Shanter* to be my standard performance in the poetical line. 'Tis true, both the one and the other dis-cover a spice of roguish waggery that might perhaps be as well spared ; but then, they also shew, in my opinion, a force of genius, and a finishing polish, that I despair of ever excelling. Mrs Burns is getting stout again, and laid as lustily about her to-day

* Francis Wallace Burns, the poet's second son.

at breakfast as a reaper from the corn-ridge. That is the peculiar privilege and blessing of our hale, sprightly damsels, that are bred among the *hay and heather*. We cannot hope for that highly-polished mind, that charming delicacy of soul, which is found among the female world in the more elevated stations of life, and which is certainly by far the most bewitching charm in the famous cestus of Venus. It is indeed such an inestimable treasure, that where it can be had in its native heavenly purity, unstained by some one or other of the many shades of affectation, and un-alloyed by some one or other of the many species of caprice, I de-clare I should think it cheaply purchased at the expense of every other earthly good ! But as this angelic creature is, I am afraid, extremely rare in any station and rank of life, and totally denied to such an humble one as mine, we meaner mortals, must put up with the next rank of female excellence,—as fine a figure and face we can produce as any rank of life whatever ; rustic, native grace ; unaffected modesty and unsullied purity ; nature's mother-wit, and the rudiments of taste ; a simplicity of soul, unsuspicious of, because unacquainted with, the crooked ways of a selfish, in-terested, disingenuous world ; and the dearest charm of all the rest—a yielding sweetness of disposition, and a generous warmth of heart, grateful for love on our part, and ardently glowing with a more than equal return : these, with a healthy frame, a sound, vigorous constitution, which your higher ranks can scarcely ever hope to enjoy, are the charms of lovely women in my humble walk of life.

This is the greatest effort my broken arm has yet made. Do let me hear, by first post, how *cher petit Monsieur** comes on with his small-pox. May Almighty goodness preserve and restore him !   R. B.

CCXXXVIII.

TO A. F. TYTLER, ESQ.

ELLISLAND, *April* 1791.

SIR,—Nothing less than the unfortunate accident I have met with could have prevented my grateful acknowledgments for your letter. His own favourite poem, and that an essay in the walk of the Muses entirely new to him, where consequently his hopes and fears were on the most anxious alarm for his success in the attempt—to have that poem so much applauded by one of the first judges, was the most delicious vibration that ever thrilled along the heart-strings of a poor poet. However, Providence, to keep up the proper proportion of evil with the good, which it seems

* The grandchild of Mrs Dunlop.

is necessary in this sublunary state, thought proper to check my exultation by a very serious misfortune. A day or two after I received your letter, my horse came down with me and broke my right arm. As this is the first service my arm has done me since its disaster, I find myself unable to do more than just, in general terms, thank you for this additional instance of your patronage and friendship. As to the faults you detected in the piece, they are truly there. One of them, the hit at the lawyer and priest, I shall cut out : as to the falling off in the catastrophe, for the reason you justly adduce, it cannot easily be remedied. Your approbation, sir, has given me such additional spirits to persevere in this species of poetic composition, that I am already revolving two or three stories in my fancy. If I can bring these floating ideas to bear any kind of embodied form, it will give me an additional opportunity of assuring you how much I have the honour to be, &c.   R. B.

CCXXXIX.

TO LADY W. M. CONSTABLE.

ELLISLAND, 11*th April* 1791.

My LADY,—Nothing less than the unlucky accident of having lately broken my right arm could have prevented me, the moment I received your ladyship's elegant present by Mrs Miller, from returning you my warmest and most grateful acknowledgments. I assure your ladyship I shall set it apart—the symbols of religion shall only be more sacred. In the moment of poetic composition the box shall be my inspiring genius. When I would breathe the comprehensive wish of benevolence for the happiness of others, I shall recollect your ladyship ; when I would interest my fancy in the distresses incident to humanity, I shall remember the unfortunate Mary.   R. B.

CCXL.

TO MR CUNNINGHAM.

11*th June* 1791.

LET me interest you, my dear Cunningham, in behalf of the gentleman who waits on you with this. He is a Mr Clarke of Moffat, principal schoolmaster there, and is at present suffering severely under the persecution of one or two powerful individuals of his employers. He is accused of harshness to boys that were placed under his care. God help the teacher, if a man of sensibility and genius—and such is my friend Clarke—when a booby father presents him with his booby son, and insists on lighting up

the rays of science in a fellow's head whose skull is impervious
and inaccessible by any other way than a positive fracture with
a cudgel—a fellow whom, in fact, it savours of impiety to attempt
making a scholar of, as he has been marked a blockhead in the
book of fate at the Almighty fiat of his Creator.

The patrons of Moffat School are the ministers, magistrates, and
town-council of Edinburgh; and as the business comes now before
them, let me beg my dearest friend to do everything in his power
to serve the interests of a man of genius and worth, and a man
whom I particularly respect and esteem. You know some good
fellows among the magistracy and council; but particularly you
have much to say with a reverend gentleman to whom you have
the honour of being very nearly related, and whom this country
and age have had the honour to produce. I need not name the
historian of Charles V. I tell him, through the medium of his
nephew's influence, that Mr Clarke is a gentleman who will not
disgrace even his patronage: I know the merits of the cause
thoroughly, and say it, that my friend is falling a sacrifice to
prejudiced ignorance, and . . . .

God help the children of dependence! Hated and persecuted
by their enemies, and too often, alas! almost unexceptionably,
received by their friends with disrespect and reproach, under the
thin disguise of cold civility and humiliating advice. Oh to be a
sturdy savage, stalking in the pride of his independence, amid the
solitary wilds of his deserts, rather than in civilised life helplessly
to tremble for a subsistence, precarious as the caprice of a fellow-
creature! Every man has his virtues, and no man is without his
failings; and curse on that privileged plain-dealing of friendship
which, in the hour of my calamity, cannot reach forth the helping-
hand without at the same time pointing out those failings, and
apportioning them their share in procuring my present distress.
My friends—for such the world calls ye, and such ye think your-
selves to be—pass by my virtues if you please, but do also spare
my follies. The first will witness in my breast for themselves, and
the last will give pain enough to the ingenuous mind without you.
And since deviating more or less from the paths of propriety and
rectitude must be incident to human nature, do thou, Fortune,
put it in my power, always from myself and of myself, to bear the
the consequence of those errors! I do not want to be independ-
ent that I may sin, but I want to be independent in my sinning.

To return in this rambling letter to the subject I set out with,
let me recommend my friend Mr Clarke to your acquaintance and
good offices. His worth entitles him to the one, and his gratitude
will merit the other. I long much to hear from you. Adieu!

R. B.

CCXLI.

TO MR THOMAS SLOAN.

ELLISLAND, 1st *Sept.* 1791.

MY DEAR SLOAN,—Suspense is worse than disappointment for that reason I hurry to tell you that I just now learn that Mr Ballantine does not choose to interfere more in the business. I am truly sorry for it, but cannot help it.

You blame me for not writing you sooner ; but you will please to recollect that you omitted one little necessary piece of information—your address.

However, you know equally well my hurried life, indolent temper, and strength of attachment. It must be a longer period than the longest life " in the world's hale and undegenerate days," that will make me forget so dear a friend as Mr Sloan. I am prodigal enough at times, but I will not part with such a treasure as that. I can easily enter into the *embarrass* of your present situation. You know my favourite quotation from Young—

" On Reason build RESOLVE !
That column of true majesty in man."

And that other favourite one from Thomson's *Alfred*—

" What proves the hero truly GREAT,
Is, never, never to despair."

Or, shall I quote you an author of your acquaintance ?

" Whether DOING, SUFFERING, or FORBEARING,
You may do miracles by—PERSEVERING."

I have nothing new to tell you. The few friends we have are going on in the old way. I sold my crop on this day se'en-night, and sold it very well. A guinea an acre, on an average, above value. But such a scene of drunkenness was hardly ever seen in this country. After the roup was over, about thirty people engaged in a battle, every man for his own hand, and fought it out for three hours. Nor was the scene much better in the house. You will easily guess how I enjoyed the scene, as I was no farther over than you used to see me.

Mrs B. and family have been in Ayrshire these many weeks. Farewell ! and God bless you, my dear friend ! R. B.

CCXLII.

TO THE EARL OF BUCHAN.

ELLISLAND, *September* 1790

MY LORD,—Language sinks under the ardour of my feelings when I would thank your lordship for the honour you have done me in inviting me to make one at the coronation of the bust of Thomson. In my first enthusiasm in reading the card you did me the honour to write me, I overlooked every obstacle, and determined to go; but I fear it will not be in my power. A week or two's absence, in the very middle of my harvest, is what I much doubt I dare not venture on. I once already made a pilgrimage *up* the whole course of the Tweed, and fondly would I take the same delightful journey *down* the windings of that delightful stream.

Your lordship hints at an ode for the occasion; but who would write after Collins? I read over his verses to the memory of Thomson, and despaired. I got indeed to the length of three or four stanzas, in the way of address to the shade of the bard, on crowning his bust. ·I shall trouble your lordship with the subjoined copy of them (p. 168), which, I am afraid, will be but too convincing a proof how unequal I am to the task. However, it affords me an opportunity of approaching your lordship, and declaring how sincerely and gratefully I have the honour to be, &c.

R. B.

CCXLIII.
TO COLONEL FULLARTON, OF FULLARTON.

ELLISLAND, *October* 3, 1791.

SIR,—I have just this minute got the frank, and next minute must send it to post; else I purposed to have sent you two or three other bagatelles that might have amused a vacant hour, about as well as *Six Excellent New Songs,* or the *Aberdeen Prognostications for the Year to come.* I shall probably trouble you soon with another packet. About the gloomy month of November, when the people of England hang and drown themselves, anything generally is better than one's own thoughts.

Fond as I may be of my own productions, it is not for their sake that I am so anxious to send you them. I am ambitious, covetously ambitious, of being known to a gentleman whom I am proud to call my countryman—a gentleman, who was a foreign ambassador as soon as he was a man, and a leader of armies as soon as he was a soldier, and that with an *éclat* unknown to the usual minions of a court—men who, with all the adventitious advantages of princely connections and princely fortunes, must yet, like the caterpillar, labour a whole lifetime before they reach the wished-for height, there to roost a stupid chrysalis, and doze out the remaining glimmering existence of old age.

If the gentleman that accompanied you when you did me the honour of calling on me, is with you, I beg to be respectfully remembered to him. I have the honour to be your highly obliged and most devoted humble servant,   R. B.

CCXLIV
TO MISS DAVIES.

MADAM,—I understand my very worthy neighbour, Mr Riddel, has informed you that I have made you the subject of some verses. There is something so provoking in the idea of being the burden of a ballad, that I do not think Job or Moses, though such patterns of patience and meekness, could have resisted the curiosity to know what that ballad was ; so my worthy friend has done me a mischief, which I daresay he never intended, and reduced me to the unfortunate alternative of leaving your curiosity ungratified, or else disgusting you with foolish verses, the unfinished production of a random moment, and never meant to have met your ear. I have heard or read somewhere of a gentleman who had some genius, much eccentricity, and very considerable dexterity with his pencil. In the accidental group of life into which one is thrown, wherever this gentleman met with a character in a more than ordinary degree congenial to his heart, he used to steal a sketch of the face : merely, he said, as a *nota bene*, to point out the agreeable recollection to his memory. What this gentleman's pencil was to him, my Muse is to me; and the verses I do myself the honour to send you are a *memento* exactly of the same kind that he indulged in.

It may be more owing to the fastidiousness of my caprice than the delicacy of my taste, but I am so often tired, disgusted, and hurt with the insipidity, affectation, and pride of mankind, that when I meet with a person " after my own heart," I positively feel what an orthodox Protestant would call a species of idolatry, which acts on my fancy like inspiration ; and I can no more desist rhyming on the impulse, than an Æolian harp can refuse its tones to the streaming air. A distich or two would be the consequence, though the object which hit my fancy were gray-bearded age ; but where my theme is youth and beauty,—a young lady whose personal charms, wit, and sentiment, are equally striking and unaffected,—though I had lived threescore years a married man, and threescore years before I was a married man, my imagination would hallow the very idea : and I am truly sorry that the enclosed stanzas (*Lovely Davies*, p. 244) have done such poor justice to such a subject. R. B.

CCXLV.
TO MISS DAVIES.

IT is impossible, madam, that the generous warmth and angelic purity of your youthful mind can have any idea of that moral

disease under which I unhappily must rank as the chief of sinners
—-I mean a torpitude of the moral powers, that may be called a
lethargy of conscience. In vain Remorse rears her horrent crest,
and rouses all her snakes : beneath the deadly fixed eye and leaden
hand of Indolence, their wildest ire is charmed into the torpor of
the bat, slumbering out the rigours of winter in the chink of a
ruinéd wall. Nothing less, madam, could have made me so long
neglect your obliging commands. Indeed, I had one apology—
the bagatelle was not worth presenting. Besides, so strongly am
I interested in Miss Davies' fate and welfare in the serious busi-
ness of life, amid its chances and changes, that to make her the
subject of a silly ballad is downright mockery of these ardent feel-
ings ; 'tis like an impertinent jest to a dying friend.

Why this disparity between our wishes and our powers ? Why
is the most generous wish to make others blest impotent and
ineffectual as the idle breeze that crosses the pathless desert ?
In my walks of life I have met with a few people to whom how
gladly would I have said—" Go ! be happy ! I know that your
hearts have been wounded by the scorn of the proud, whom acci-
dent has placed above you—or, worse still, in whose hands are
perhaps placed many of the comforts of your life. But there !
ascend that rock, Independence, and look justly down on their
littleness of soul. Make the worthless tremble under your indig-
nation, and the foolish sink before your contempt ; and largely
impart that happiness to others which, I am certain, will give
yourselves so much pleasure to bestow."

Why, dear madam, must I wake from this delightful reverie,
and find it all a dream ? Why, amid my generous enthusiasm,
must I find myself poor and powerless, incapable of wiping one
tear from the eye of Pity, or of adding one comfort to the friend
I love ! Out upon the world ! say I, that its affairs are adminis-
tered so ill ! They talk of reform ; what a reform would I make
among the sons, and even the daughters, of men ! Down imme-
diately should go fools from the high places where misbegotten
chance has perked them up, and through life should they skulk,
ever haunted by their native insignificance, as the body marches
accompanied by its shadow. As for a much more formidable
class,—the knaves,—I am at a loss what to do with them. Had I a
world, there should not be a knave in it.

But the hand that could give I would liberally fill ; and I would
pour delight on the heart that could kindly forgive, and gener-
ously love.

Still, the inequalities of life are, among men, comparatively
tolerable ; but there is a delicacy, a tenderness, accompanying
every view in which we can place lovely woman, that are grated
and shocked at the rude, capricious distinctions of Fortune.
Woman is the blood-royal of life. Let there be slight degrees of

precedency among them—but let them be ALL sacred. Whether this last sentiment be right or wrong, I am not accountable; it is an original component feature of my mind.   R. B.

CCXLVI.
TO CHARLES SHARPE, ESQ. OF HODDAM:
ENCLOSING A BALLAD.

IT is true, sir, you are a gentleman of rank and fortune, and I am a poor fellow—you are a feather in the cap of Society, and I am a very hobnail in his shoes; yet I have the honour to belong to the same family with you, and on that score I now address you. You will perhaps suspect that I am going to claim affinity with the ancient and honourable house of Kirkpatrick. No, no, sir; I cannot indeed be properly said to belong to any house, or even any province or kingdom; as my mother, who for many years was with a marching regiment, gave me into this bad world, aboard the packet-boat, somewhere between Donaghadee and Portpatrick. By our common family,—I mean sir, the family of the Muses,—I am a fiddler and a poet; and you, I am told, play an exquisite violin, and have a standard taste in the *belles lettres*. The other day, a brother catgut gave me a charming Scots air of your composition. If I was pleased with the tune, I was in raptures with the title you have given it; and, taking up the idea, I have spun it into the three stanzas enclosed. Will you allow me, sir, to present you them, as the dearest offering that a misbegotten son of poverty and rhyme has to give! I have a longing to take you by the hand and unburden my heart, by saying—" Sir, I honour you as a man who supports the dignity of human nature, amid an age when frivolity and avarice have, between them, debased us below the brutes that perish!" But, alas, sir! to me you are unapproachable. It is true the Muses baptised me in Castalian streams; but the thoughtless gipsies forgot to give me a name. As the sex have served many a good fellow, the Nine have given me a great deal of pleasure; but, bewitching jades! they have beggared me. Would they but spare me a little of their cast-linen! were it only to put it in my power to say that I have a shirt on my back! But the idle wenches, like Solomon's lilies, " they toil not, neither do they spin;" so I must e'en continue to tie my remnant of a cravat, like the hangman's rope, round my naked throat, and coax my galligaskins to keep together their many-coloured fragments. As to the affair of shoes, I have given that up. My pilgrimages in my ballad-trade from town to town, and on your stony-hearted turnpikes too, are what not even the hide of Job's behemoth could bear. The coat on my back is no more: I shall not speak evil of the dead. It would be equally unhandsome and ungrateful to find fault with my old surtout, which so kindly supplies and conceals the want of that coat. My hat, indeed, is a great favourite, and though I got it literally for an old song, I would not exchange it for the best beaver in Britain. I was during several years a kind of fac-totum servant to a country clergyman, where I picked up a good many scraps of learning, particularly in some branches of the mathematics. Whenever 1 feel inclined to rest myself on my way, I take my seat under a hedge, laying my poetic wallet on the one side, and my fiddle-case on the other, and placing my hat between my legs, I can by means of its brim, or rather brims, go through the whole doctrine of the conic sections.

However, sir, don't let me mislead you, as if I would interest your pity. Fortune has so much forsaken me, that she has taught me to live without her; and, amid all my rags and poverty, I am as independent, and much more happy, than a monarch of the world. According to the hackneyed metaphor, I value the several actors in the great drama of life simply as they act their parts. I can look on a worthless fellow of a duke with unqualified contempt, and can regard an honest scavenger with sincere respect. As you, sir, go through your *rôle* with such distinguished merit, permit me to make one in the chorus of universal applause, and assure you that, with the highest respect. I have the honour to be, &c.   **R. B.**

CCXLVII.

TO SIR JOHN SINCLAIR.

1791.

SIR,—The following circumstance has, I believe, been omitted in the statistical account transmitted to you of the parish of Dunscore, in Nithsdale. I beg leave to send it to you because it is new, and may be useful. How far it is deserving of a place in your patriotic publication you are the best judge.

To store the minds of the lower classes with useful knowledge is certainly of very great importance, both to them as individuals and to society at large. Giving them a turn for reading and reflection, is giving them a source of innocent and laudable amusement, and, besides, raises them to a more dignified degree in the scale of rationality. Impressed with this idea, a gentleman in this parish, Robert Riddel, Esq. of Glenriddel, set on foot a species of circulating library, on a plan so simple as to be practicable in any corner of the country; and so useful as to deserve the notice of every country gentleman who thinks the improvement of that part of his own species, whom chance has thrown into the humble walks of the peasant and the artisan, a matter worthy of his attention.

Mr Riddel got a number of his own tenants and farming neighbours to form themselves into a society for the purpose of having a library among themselves. They entered into a legal engagement to abide by it for three years; with a saving-clause or two, in case of removal to a distance or of death. Each member at his entry paid five shillings; and at each of their meetings, which were held every fourth Saturday, sixpence more. With their entry-money, and the credit which they took on the faith of their future funds, they laid in a tolerable stock of books at the commencement. What authors they were to purchase was always decided by the majority. At every meeting, all the books, under certain fines and forfeitures, by way of penalty, were to be produced; and the members had their choice of the volumes in rotation. He whose name stood for that night first on the list had his choice of what volume he pleased in the whole collection; the second had his choice after the first; the third after the second; and so on to the last. At next meeting, he who had been first on the list at the preceding meeting was last at this; he who had been second was first; and so on through the whole three years. At the expiration of the engagement, the books were sold by auction, but only among the members themselves; and each man had his share of the common stock, in money or in books, as he chose to be a purchaser or not.

At the breaking up of this little society, which was formed under Mr Riddel's patronage, what with benefactions of books from him, and what with their own purchases, they had collected together upwards of one hundred and fifty volumes. It will easily be guessed that a good deal of trash would be bought. Among the books, however, of this little library, were—*Blair's Sermons, Robertson's History of Scotland, Hume's History of the Stuarts, The Spectator, Idler, Adventurer, Mirror, Lounger, Observer, Man of Feeling, Man of the World, Chrysal, Don Quixote, Joseph Andrews,* &c. A peasant who can read, and enjoy such books, is certainly a much superior being to his neighbour who perhaps stalks beside his team, very little removed, except in shape, from the brutes he drives.

Wishing your patriotic exertions their so much merited success, I am, sir, your humble servant,　　　　　A PEASANT

CCXLVIII.

TO MRS DUNLOP.

ELLISLAND, 17th December 1791.

MANY thanks to you, madam, for your good news respecting the little floweret and the mother-plant. I hope my poetic prayers have been heard, and will be answered up to the warmest sincerity of their fullest extent; and thèn Mrs Henri will find her little darling the representative of his late parent, in everything but his abridged existence.

I have just finished the following song (*Song of Death*, p. 245), which, to a lady, the descendant of Wallace, and many heroes of his truly illustrious line—and herself the mother of several soldiers —needs neither preface nor apology.

The circumstance that gave rise to the foregoing verses was— Looking over with a musical friend M'Donald's collection of Highland airs, I was struck with one—an Isle of Skye tune—entitled *Oran an Aoig*, or *the Song of Death*, to the measure of which I have adapted my stanzas. I have of late composed two or three other little pieces, which, ere yon full-orbed moon, whose broad impudent face now stares at old Mother Earth all night, shall have shrunk into a modest crescent, just peeping forth at dewy-dawn, I shall find an hour to transcribe for you. *A Dieu je vous commende.* R. B.

CCXLIX.
TO MR AINSLIE.

MY DEAR AINSLIE,—Can you minister to a mind diseased? Can you, amid the horrors of penitence, regret, remorse, headache, nausea, and all the rest of the hounds of hell that beset a poor wretch who has been guilty of the sin of drunkenness—can you speak peace to a troubled soul?

Misérable perdu that I am! I have tried everything that used to amuse me, but in vain. Here must I sit, a monument of the vengeance laid up in store for the wicked, slowly counting every chick of the clock as it slowly, slowly numbers over these lazy scoundrels of hours, who, * * * *, are ranked up before me, every one following his neighbour, and every one with a burden of anguish on his back, to pour on my devoted head—and there is none to pity me. My wife scolds me, my business torments me, and my sins come staring me in the face, every one telling a more bitter tale than his fellow. * * I began *Elibanks and Elibraes*, but the stanzas fell unenjoyed and unfinished from my listless tongue. At last I luckily thought of reading over an old letter of yours that lay by me in my book-case, and I felt something, for the first time since I opened my eyes, of pleasurable existence ——Well—I begin to breathe a little since I began to write to you. How are you, and what are you doing? How goes law? Apropos, for connection's sake, do not address to me supervisor, for that is an honour I cannot pretend to. I am on the list, as we call it, for a supervisor, and will be called out by-and-by to act as one; but at present I am a simple gauger, though t'other day I got an appointment to an excise division of L.25 per annum better than the rest. My present income, down money, is L.70 per annum.

I have one or two good fellows here whom you would be glad to know. R. B.

CCL.

TO CLARINDA.

I HAVE received both your last letters, madam, and ought, and would have answered the first long ago. But on what subject shall I write you? How can you expect a correspondent should write you when you declare that you mean to preserve his letters with a view, sooner or later, to expose them on the pillory of derision and the rack of criticism? This is gagging me completely as to speaking the sentiments of my bosom; else, madam, I could perhaps too truly

" Join grief with grief, and echo sighs to thine!"

I have perused your most beautiful, but most pathetic poem—do not ask me how often or with what emotions. You know that " I dare to *sin*, but not to *lie*." Your verses wring the confession from my inmost soul, that—I will say it, expose it if you please—that I have, more than once in my life, been the victim of a condemning conjuncture of circumstances; and that to me you must be ever

" Dear as the light that visits those sad eyes.

I have just, since I had yours, composed the following stanzas. Let me know your opinion of them (*Sweet Sensibility*, p. 169).

I have one other piece in your taste; but I have just a snatch of time. SYLVANDER.

CCLI.

TO CLARINDA

LEADHILLS, *Thursday, Noon* [*Dec.* 11, 1791].

[After transcribing the *Lament of Mary Queen of Scots,* he adds] —Such, my dearest Clarinda, were the words of the amiable but unfortunate Mary. Misfortune seems to take a peculiar pleasure in darting her arrows against " honest men and bonny lasses." Of this you are too, too just a proof; but may your future fate be a bright exception to the remark. In the words of Hamlet—

" Adieu, adieu, adieu! Remember me."

SYLVANDER.

CCLII.

TO CLARINDA.

DUMFRIES [15*th Dec.* 1791].

I HAVE some merit, my ever dearest of women, in attracting and securing the heart of Clarinda. In her I met with the most accomplished of all womankind, the first of all God's works; and yet I, even I, had the good-fortune to appear amiable in her sight. By the by, this is the sixth letter that I have written you since I left you; and if you were an ordinary being, as you are a creature very extraordinary,—an instance of what God Almighty in the plenitude of his power and the fulness of his goodness can make,— I would never forgive you for not answering my letters.

I have sent your hair, a part of the parcel you gave me, with a measure, to Mr Bruce the jeweller in Princes Street, to get a ring done for me. I have likewise sent in the verses *On Sensibility.* altered to

" Sensibility how charming,
Dearest Nancy, thou canst tell," &c.

to the editor of the *Scots Songs,* of which you have three volumes, to set to a most beautiful air—out of compliment to the first of women, my ever-beloved, my ever-sacred Clarinda. I shall probably write you to-morrow. In the meantime, from a man who is literally drunk, accept and forgive l   R. B.

CCLIII.

TO CLARINDA.

DUMFRIES, 27*th December* 1791.

I HAVE yours, my ever-dearest madam, this moment. I have just ten minutes before the post goes, and these I shall employ in sending you some songs (*As Fond Kiss*, p. 246, and *Behold the Hour*, p. 274) I have just been composing to different tunes for the *Collection of Songs,* of which you have three volumes, and of which you shall have the fourth.   SYLVANDER.

CCLIV.

TO MR WILLIAM SMELLIE, PRINTER.

DUMFRIES, 22*d January* 1792.

I SIT down, my dear sir, to introduce a young lady to you, and a lady in the first ranks of fashion too. What a task! to you—who care no more for the herd of animals called young ladies, than you do for the herd of animals called young gentlemen. To you—who despise and detest the groupings and combinations of Fashion, as an idiot painter that seems industrious to place staring fools and unprincipled knaves in the foreground of his picture, while men of sense and honesty are too often thrown in the dimmest shades. Mrs Riddel, who will take this letter to town with her, and send it to you, is a character that, even in your own way, as a naturalist and a philosopher, would be an acquisition to your acquaintance. The lady, too, is a votary to the Muses; and as I think myself somewhat of a judge in my own trade, I assure you that her verses, always correct, and often elegant, are much beyond the common run of the *lady-poetesses* of the day. She is a great admirer of your book ; and hearing me say that I was acquainted with you, she begged to be known to you, as she is just going to pay her first visit to our Caledonian capital. I told her that her best way was to desire her near relation, and your intimate friend, Craigdarroch, to have you at his house while she was there ; and lest you might think of a lively West Indian girl of eighteen, as girls of eighteen too often deserve to be thought of, I should take care to remove that prejudice. To be impartial, however, in appreciating the lady's merits, she has one unlucky failing,—a failing which you will easily discover, as she seems rather pleased with indulging in it,—and a failing that you will easily pardon, as it is a sin which very much besets yourself,—where she dislikes or despises, she is apt to make no more a secret of it than where she esteems and respects.

I will not present you with the unmeaning *compliments of the season*, but I will send you my warmest wishes and most ardent prayers, that FORTUNE may never throw your SUBSISTENCE to the mercy of a KNAVE, or set your CHARACTER on the judgment of a FOOL ; but that, upright and erect, you may walk to an honest grave, where men of letters shall say—" Here lies a man who did honour to science ;" and men of worth shall say—" Here lies a man who did honour to human nature." R. B.

CCLV.
TO MR WILLIAM NICOL.
20th February 1792.

O THOU, wisest among the wise, meridian blaze of prudence, full-moon of discretion, and chief of many counsellors ! How infinitely is thy puddle-headed, rattle-headed, wrong-headed, round-headed slave indebted to thy supereminent goodness, that from the luminous path of thy own right-lined rectitude, thou lookest benignly down on an erring wretch, of whom the zig-zag wanderings defy all the powers of calculation, from the simple copu-

lation of units up to the hidden mysteries of fluxions! May one
feeble ray of that light of wisdom which darts from thy sensorium,
straight as the arrow of heaven, and bright as the meteor of in-
spiration, may it be my portion, so that I may be less unworthy
of the face and favour of that father of proverbs and master of
maxims,—that antipode of folly and magnet among the sages,—
the wise and witty Willie Nicol! Amen! Amen! Yea, so
be it!

For me! I am a beast, a reptile, and know nothing! From
the cave of my ignorance, amid the fogs of my dulness, and pes-
tilential fumes of my political heresies, I look up to thee, as doth
a toad through the iron-barred lucerne of a pestiferous dungeon,
to the cloudless glory of a summer sun! Sorely sighing in bit-
terness of soul, I say, when shall my name be the quotation of
the wise, and my countenance be the delight of the godly, like
the illustrious lord of Laggan's many hills? As for him, his
works are perfect. Never did the pen of calumny blur the fair
page of his reputation, nor the bolt of hatred fly at his dwelling.

Thou mirror of purity, when shall the elfin lamp of my glim-
merous understanding, purged from sensual appetites and gross
desires, shine like the constellation of thy intellectual powers!
As for thee, thy thoughts are pure, and thy lips are holy. Never
did the unhallowed breath of the powers of darkness and the
pleasures of darkness pollute the sacred flame of thy sky-de-
scended and heaven-bound desires ; never did the vapours of im-
purity stain the unclouded serene of thy cerulean imagination.
O that like thine were the tenor of my life, like thine the tenor of
my conversation!—then should no friend fear for my strength, no
enemy rejoice in my weakness! Then should I lie down and rise
up, and none to make me afraid. May thy pity and thy prayer
be exercised for, O thou lamp of wisdom and mirror of morality!
thy devoted slave,   R. B.

CCLVI.

TO MR SAMUEL CLARKE, EDINBURGH.

16th July 1792.

MR BURNS begs leave to present his most respectful compli-
ments to Mr Clarke. Mr B. some time ago did himself the honour
of writing Mr C. respecting coming out to the country, to give a
little musical instruction in a highly respectable family, where
Mr C. may have his own terms, and may be as happy as indolence,
the devil, and the gout will permit him. Mr B. knows well how
Mr C. is engaged with another family ; but cannot Mr C. find
two or three weeks to spare to each of them? Mr B. is deeply
impressed with, and awfully conscious of, the high importance of

Mr C.'s time, whether in the winged moments of symphonious exhibition, at the keys of harmony, while listening seraphs cease their own less delightful strains ; or, in the drowsy arms of slumberous repose, in the arms of his dearly-beloved elbow-chair, where the frowsy but potent power of indolence circumfuses her vapours round, and sheds her dews on the head of her darling son. But half a line conveying half a meaning from Mr C would make Mr B. the happiest of mortals

---

CCLVII.
TO MRS DUNLOP.

ANNAN WATER-FOOT, 22d *August* 1792.

Do not blame me for it, madam—my own conscience, hackneyed and weather-beaten as it is, in watching and reproving my vagaries, follies, indolence, &c., has continued to punish me sufficiently.

, Do you think it possible, my dear and honoured friend, that I could be so lost to gratitude for many favours, to esteem for much worth, and to the honest, kind, pleasurable tie of, now old acquaintance,—and I hope and am sure of progressive, increasing friendship,—as for a single day, not to think of you—to ask the Fates what they are doing and about to do with my much-loved friend and her wide-scattered connections, and to beg of them to be as kind to you and yours as they possibly can ?

Apropos !—though how it is apropos I have not leisure to explain—do you know that I am almost in love with an acquaintance of yours ? Almost ! said I—I am in love, souse over head and ears, deep as the most unfathomable abyss of the boundless ocean —but the word love, owing to the *intermingledoms* of the good and the bad, the pure and the impure, in this world, being rather an equivocal term for expressing one's sentiments and sensations, I must do justice to the sacred purity of my attachment. Know then, that the heart-struck awe, the distant, humble approach, the delight we should have in gazing upon and listening to a messenger of Heaven, appearing in all the unspotted purity of his celestial home, among the coarse, polluted, far inferior sons of men, to deliver to them tidings that make their hearts swim in joy, and their imaginations soar in transport—such, so delighting and so pure, were the emotions of my soul on meeting the other day with Miss Lesley Baillie, your neighbour at Mayfield. Mr B. with his two daughters, accompanied by Mr H. of G., passing through Dumfries a few days ago, on their way to England, did me the honour of calling on me ; on which I took my horse— though, I could ill spare the time — and accompanied them fourteen or fifteen miles, and dined and spent the day with them. 'Twas about nine, I think, when I left them, and riding home, I composed the following ballad, of which you will probably think you have a dear bargain, as it will cost you another groat of postage. You must know that there is an old ballad beginning with—

> " My bonnie Lizzie Baillie,
> I'll rowe thee in my plaidie," &c.

So I parodied it as follows (*Bonnie Lesley*, p. 248), which is literally the first copy, " unanointed, unannealed," as Hamlet says.

So much for ballads. I regret that you are gone to the east country, as I am to be in Ayrshire in about a fortnight. This world of ours, notwithstanding it has many good things in it, yet it has ever had this curse—that two or three people, who would be the happier the oftener they met together, are, almost without exception, always so placed as never to meet but once or twice a year, which, considering the few years of a man's life, is a very great " evil under the sun," which I do not recollect that Solomon has mentioned in his catalogue of the miseries of man. I hope and believe that there is a state of existence beyond the grave, where the worthy of this life will renew their former intimacies, with this endearing addition—that " we meet to part no more."

> " Tell us, ye dead,
> Will none of you in pity disclose the secret,
> What 'tis you are, and we must shortly be?"

A thousand times have I made this apostrophe to the departed sons of men, but not one of them has ever thought fit to answer the question. " O that some courteous ghost would blab it out !" But it cannot be : you and I, my friend, must make the experiment by ourselves, and for ourselves. However, I am so convinced that an unshaken faith in the doctrines of religion is not only necessary, by making us better men, but also by making us happier men, that I should take every care that your little godson, and every little creature that shall call me father, shall be taught them.

So ends this heterogeneous letter, written at this wild place of the world, in the intervals of my labour of discharging a vessel of rum from Antigua. R. B.

CCLVIII.

TO MR CUNNINGHAM.

DUMFRIES, 10*th September* 1792.

No! I will not attempt an apology. Amid all my hurry of business, grinding the faces of the publican and the sinner on the merciless wheels of the Excise ; making ballads, and then drinking and singing them ; and, over and above all, the correcting the press-work of two different publications; still, still I might have stolen five minutes to dedicate to one of the first of my friends and fellow-creatures. I might have done, as I do at present, snatched an hour near "witching-time of night," and scrawled a page or two. I might have congratulated my friend on his marriage; or I might have thanked the Caledonian archers for the honour they have done me (though, to do myself justice, I intended to have done both in rhyme, else I had done both long ere now). Well, then, here is to your good health!—for you must know, I have set a nipperkin of toddy by me, just by way of spell, to keep away the meikle horned deil or any of his subaltern imps, who may be on their nightly rounds.

But what shall I write to you?—" The voice said, Cry;" and I said, "What shall I cry?" O thou spirit! whatever thou art, or wherever thou makest thyself visible!—Be thou a bogle by the eerie side of an auld thorn, in the dreary glen through which the herd-callan maun bicker in his gloamin rout frae the fauld! Be thou a brownie, set, at dead of night, to thy task by the blazing ingle, or in the solitary barn, where the repercussions of thy iron flail half affright thyself, as thou performest the work of twenty of the sons of men, ere the cock-crowing summon thee to thy ample cog of substantial brose. Be thou a kelpie, haunting the ford or ferry in the starless night, mixing thy laughing yell with the howling of the storm and the roaring of the flood, as thou viewest the perils and miseries of man on the foundering horse, or in the tumbling boat! Or, lastly, be thou a ghost, paying thy nocturnal visits to the hoary ruins of decayed grandeur; or performing thy mystic rites in the shadow of the time-worn church, while the moon looks without a cloud on the silent, ghastly dwellings of the dead around thee; or, taking thy stand by the bedside of the villain or the murderer, portraying on his dreaming fancy pictures dreadful as the horrors of unveiled hell, and terrible as the wrath of incensed Deity! Come, thou spirit, but not in these horrid forms: come with the milder, gentle, easy inspirations which thou breathest round the wig of a prating advocate, or the *tête-à-tête* of a tea-sipping gossip, while their tongues run at the light-horse gallop of clish-maclaver for ever and ever—come and assist a poor fellow who is quite jaded in the attempt to share half an idea among half a hundred words; to fill up four quarto pages, while he has not got one single sentence of recollection, information, or remark, worth putting pen to paper for. * * * *

Apropos, how do you like—I mean, *really* like—the married life? Ah, my friend! matrimony is quite a different thing from what your love-sick youths and sighing girls take it to be! But marriage, we are told, is appointed by God, and I shall never quarrel with any of His institutions. I am a husband of older standing than you, and shall give you *my* ideas of the conjugal

state. (*En passant;* you know I am no Latinist; is not *conjugal* de-
rived from *jugum,* a yoke ?) Well, then, the scale of good wifeship
I divide into ten parts:—Good-nature, four ; Good Sense, two;
Wit, one ; Personal Charms—namely, a sweet face, eloquent eyes,
fine limbs, graceful carriage (I would add a fine waist too, but
that is soon spoilt, you know),—all these, one. As for the other
qualities belonging to or attending on a wife, such as Fortune,
Connections, Education (I mean education extraordinary), family
blood, &c., divide the two remaining degrees among them as you
please ; only, remember that all these minor properties must be
expressed by *fractions,* for there is not any one of them, in the
aforesaid scale, entitled to the dignity of an *integer.*

As for the rest of my fancies and reveries—how I lately met
with Miss Lesley Baillie, the most beautiful, elegant woman in
the world—how I accompanied her and her father's family fifteen
miles on their journey out of pure devotion, to admire the loveli-
ness of the works of God, in such an unequalled display of them—
how, in galloping home at night, I made a ballad on her, of which
these two stanzas make a part:—

> "Thou, bonnie Lesley, art a queen,
> Thy subjects we before thee;
> Thou, bonnie Lesley, art divine,
> The hearts o' men adore thee.
>
> The very deil he couldna scatho
> Whatever wad belang thee !
> He d look into thy bonnie face,
> And say, 'I canna wrang thee.'"

Behold all these things are written in the chronicles of my imagi-
nation, and shall be read by thee, my dear friend, and by thy be-
loved spouse, my other dear friend, at a more convenient season.

Now, to thee, and to thy before-designed *bosom*-companion, be
given the precious things brought forth by the sun, and the pre-
cious things brought forth by the moon, and the benignest in-
fluences of the stars, and the living streams which flow from the
fountains of life, and by the tree of life, for ever and ever
Amen ! R. B.

CCLIX.

TO MR THOMSON.

DUMFRIES, 16*th Sept.* 1792.

SIR,—I have just this moment got your letter. As the request
you make to me will positively add to my enjoyments in comply
ing with it, I shall enter into your undertaking with all the small
portion of abilities I have, strained to their utmost exertion by
the impulse of enthusiasm. Only, don't hurry me—" Deil tak the
hindmost " is by no means the *cri de guerre* of my Muse. Will

you, as I am inferior to none of you in enthusiastic attachment
to the poetry and music of old Caledonia, and, since you request
it, have cheerfully promised my mite of assistance—will you let
me have a list of your airs, with the first line of the printed verses
you intend for them, that I may have an opportunity of suggest-
ing any alteration that may occur to me? You know 'tis in the
way of my trade; still leaving you, gentlemen, the undoubted
right of publishers to approve or reject, at your pleasure, for your
own publication. Apropos, if you are for English verses, there is,
on my part, an end of the matter. Whether in the simplicity of
the ballad, or the pathos of the song, I can only hope to please
myself in being allowed at least a sprinkling of our native tongue.
English verses, particularly the works of Scotsmen that have
merit, are certainly very eligible. *Tweedside! Ah! the poor
shepherd's mournful fate! Ah! Chloris, could* I *now but sit*, &c.,
you cannot mend; but such insipid stuff as *To Fanny fair could* 1
impart, &c., usually set to *The Mill, Mill, O!* is a disgrace to the
collections in which it has already appeared, and would doubly
disgrace a collection that will have the very superior merit of
yours. But more of this in the further prosecution of the busi-
ness, if I am called on for my strictures and amendments—I say
amendments, for I will not alter except where I myself, at least,
think that I amend.

As to any remuneration, you may think my songs either above
or below price; for they shall absolutely be the one or the other.
In the honest enthusiasm with which I embark in your undertak-
ing, to talk of money, wages, fee, hire, &c., would be downright
prostitution of soul! A proof of each of the songs that I compose
or amend I shall receive as a favour. In the rustic phrase of the
season, " Gude speed the wark !" I am, sir, your very humble
servant,   R. BURNS.

CCLX.

TO MRS DUNLOP.

DUMFRIES, *24th September* 1792.

I HAVE this moment, my dear madam, yours of the 23d. All
your other kind reproaches, your news, &c., are out of my head,
when I read and think on Mrs Henri's situation. A heart-
wounded, helpless young woman—in a strange foreign land, and
that land convulsed with every horror that can harrow the human
feelings—sick—looking, longing for a comforter, but finding none
—a mother's feelings too—but it is too much: He who wounded
—He only can—may He heal!

I wish the farmer great joy of his new acquisition to his family.
* * * I cannot say that I give him joy of his life as a farmer

'Tis as a farmer paying a dear, unconscionable rent—a *horrid life*
As to a laird farming his own property, sowing his own corn in
hope and reaping it, in spite of brittle weather, in gladness;
knowing that none can say unto him, " What dost thou ?"—fatten-
ing his herds, shearing his flocks, rejoicing at Christmas, and
begetting sons and daughters, until he be the venerated, gray-
haired leader of a little tribe—'tis a heavenly life ! but it is very
bitter to reap the fruits that another must eat.

Well, your kind wishes will be gratified as to seeing me when
I make my Ayrshire visit. I cannot leave Mrs B. until her nine
months' race is run, which may, perhaps be in three or four weeks.
She, too, seems determined to make me the patriarchal leader of
a band. However, if heaven will be so obliging as to let me have
them in the proportion of three boys to one girl, I shall be so
much the more pleased. I hope, if I am spared with them, to
show a set of boys that will do honour to my cares and name ; but
I am not equal to the task of rearing girls. Besides, I am too
poor—a girl should always have a fortune. Apropos—your
little godson is thriving charmingly, but is a very tiger. He,
though two years younger, has completely mastered his brother.
Robert is indeed the mildest, gentlest creature I ever saw. He
has a most surprising memory, and is quite the pride of his
schoolmaster.

You know how readily we get into prattle upon a subject dear to
our heart—you can excuse it. God bless you and yours! R. B.

CCLXI.

TO MR THOMSON.

My dear Sir,—Let me tell you that you are too fastidious in
your ideas of songs and ballads. I own that your criticisms are
just. The songs you specify in your list have, all but one, the
faults you remark in them; but who shall mend the matter ?
Who shall rise up and say, " Go to! I will make a better ?" For
instance, on reading over *The Lea-Rig*, I immediately set about
trying my hand on it, and, after all, I could make nothing more
of it than the following (p. 259), which is poor enough.

Your observation as to the aptitude of Dr Percy's ballad to the
air, *Nannie O!* is just. It is besides, perhaps, the most beautiful
ballad in the English language. But let me remark to you, that
in the sentiment and style of our Scottish airs there is a pastoral
simplicity, a something that one may call the Doric style and
dialect of vocal music, to which a dash of our native tongue and
manners is particularly—nay, peculiarly apposite. For this reason,
and, upon my honour, for this reason alone, I am of opinion—but,

as I told you before, my opinion is yours, freely yours, to approve or reject, as you please—that my ballad of *Nannie, O!* might perhaps do for one set of verses to the tune. Now don't let it enter into your head that you are under any necessity of taking my verses. I have long ago made up my mind as to my own reputation in the business of authorship, and have nothing to be pleased or offended at in your adoption or rejection of my verses. Though you should reject one-half of what I give you, I shall be pleased with your adopting the other half, and shall continue to serve you with the same assiduity.

In the printed copy of *My Nannie, O!* the name of the river is horridly prosaic. I will alter it—

" Behind yon hills where Lugar flows."

Girvan is the name of the river that suits the idea of the stanza best, but Lugar is the most agreeable modulation of syllables.

I will soon give you a great many more remarks on this business ; but I have just now an opportunity of conveying you this scrawl, free of postage, an expense that it is ill able to pay ; so, with my best compliments to honest Allan, Gude be wi' ye, &c.

Friday Night.

· *Saturday Morning.*

As I find I have still an hour to spare this morning before my conveyance goes away, I will give you *Nannie O!* at length.

Your remarks on *Ewe-bughts, Marion,* are just ; still it has obtained a place among our more classical Scottish songs ; and what with many beauties in its composition, and more prejudices in its favour, you will not find it easy to supplant it.

In my very early years, when I was thinking of going to the West Indies, I took the following farewell of a dear girl. It is quite trifling, and has nothing of the merits of *Ewe-bughts ;* but it will fill up this page. You must know that all my earlier love-songs were the breathings of ardent passion ; and though it might have been easy in after-times to have given them a polish, yet that polish to me, whose they were, and who perhaps alone cared for them, would have defaced the legend of my heart, which was so faithfully inscribed on them. Their uncouth simplicity was, as they say of wines, their race.

Gala Water and *Auld Rob Morris,* I think, will most probably be the next subject of my musings. However, even on my verses, speak out your criticisms with equal frankness. My wish is, not to stand aloof, the uncomplying bigot of *opiniâtreté,* but cordially to join issue with you in the furtherance of the work. R. B.

CCLXII.

TO MRS DUNLOP.

DUMFRIES, *October* 1792.

I HAD been from home, and did not receive your letter until my return the other day. What shall I say to comfort you, my much-valued, much-afflicted friend? I can but grieve with you; consolation I have none to offer, except that which religion holds out to the children of affliction,—(*children of affliction !*—how just the expression!),—and, like every other family, they have matters among them which they hear, see, and feel in a serious, all-important manner, of which the world has not, nor cares to have, any idea. The world looks indifferently on, makes the passing remark, and proceeds to the next novel occurrence.

Alas, madam! who would wish for many years? What is it but to drag existence until our joys gradually expire, and leave us in a night of misery—like the gloom which blots out the stars, one by one, from the face of night, and leaves us without a ray of comfort in the howling waste!

I am interrupted, and must leave off. You shall soon hear from me again.   R. B.

CCLXIII.

TO MR THOMSON.

November 8, 1792.

IF you mean, my dear sir, that all the songs in your collection shall be poetry of the first merit, I am afraid you will find more difficulty in the undertaking than you are aware of. There is a peculiar rhythmus in many of our airs, and a necessity of adapting syllables to the emphasis, or what I would call the feature-notes of the tune, that cramp the poet, and lay him under almost insuperable difficulties. For instance, in the air, *My Wife's a Wanton Wee Thing*, if a few lines smooth and pretty can be adapted to it, it is all you can expect. The following (p. 258) were made extempore to it; and though, on further study, I might give you something more profound, yet it might not suit the light-horse gallop of the air so well as this random clink.

I have just been looking over the *Collier's Bonnie Dochter*; and if the following rhapsody (*Bonnie Lesley*, p. 248), which I composed the other day on a charming Ayrshire girl, Miss Lesley Baillie of Mayfield, as she passed through this place to England, will suit your taste better than the *Collier Lassie*, fall on, and welcome.

I have hitherto deferred the sublimer, more pathetic airs, until more leisure, as they will take, and deserve, a greater effort,

However, they are all put into your hands, as clay into the hands of the potter, to make one vessel to honour, and another to dishonour. Farewell, &c. R. B.

CCLXIV.

TO MR THOMSON.

14th November 1792.

MY DEAR SIR,—I agree with you that the song, *Katharine Ogie*, is very poor stuff, and unworthy, altogether unworthy, of so beautiful an air. I tried to mend it, but the awkward sound, Ogie, recurring so often in the rhyme, spoils every attempt at introducing sentiment into the piece. The foregoing song (*Highland Mary*, p. 258) pleases myself; I think it is in my happiest manner; you will see at first glance that it suits the air. The subject of the song is one of the most interesting passages of my youthful days, and I own that I should be much flattered to see the verses set to an air which would insure celebrity. Perhaps, after all, 'tis the still glowing prejudice of my heart that throws a borrowed lustre over the merits of the composition.

I have partly taken your idea of *Auld Rob Morris*. I have adopted the two first verses, and am going on with the song on a new plan, which promises pretty well. I take up one or another, just as the bee of the moment buzzes in my bonnet-lug; and do you, *sans cérémonie*, make what use you choose of the productions. Adieu, &c. R. B.

CCLXV.

TO MISS FONTENELLE.

MADAM,—In such a bad world as ours, those who add to the scanty sum of our pleasures are positively our benefactors. To you, madam, on our humble Dumfries boards, I have been more indebted for entertainment than ever I was in prouder theatres. Your charms as a woman would insure applause to the most indifferent actress, and your theatrical talents would insure admiration to the plainest figure. This, madam, is not the unmeaning or insidious compliment of the frivolous or interested; I pay it from the same honest impulse that the sublime of nature excites my admiration, or her beauties give me delight.

Will the foregoing lines (p. 170) be of any service to you in your approaching benefit night? If they will, I shall be prouder of my Muse than ever. They are nearly extempore: I know they have no great merit; but though they should add but little to the entertainment of the evening, they give me the happiness of an opportunity to declare how much I have the honour to be, &c., R. B.

CCLXVI.

TO MRS RIDDEL.

I **AM** thinking to send my *Address* to some periodical publica-tion, but it has not got your sanction; so pray look over it.

As to the Tuesday's play, let me beg of you, my dear madam, to give us *The Wonder, a Woman keeps a Secret!* to which please add *The Spoilt Child*—you will highly oblige me by so doing.

Ah, what an enviable creature you are! There now, this gloomy blue-devil day, you are going to a party of choice spirits—

> " To play the shapes
> Of frolic fancy, and incessant form
> Those rapid pictures, an assembled train
> Of fleet ideas, never joined before,
> Where lively *Wit* excites to gay surprise;
> Or folly-painting *Humour*, grave himself,
> Calls laughter forth, deep shaking every nerve."

But as you rejoice with them that do rejoice, do also remember to weep with them that weep, and pity your melancholy friend,

R. B.

CCLXVII.

TO ——

MADAM,—You were so very good as to promise me to honour my friend with your presence on his benefit night. That night is fixed for Friday first; the play a most interesting one—*The Way to Keep Him.* I have the pleasure to know Mr G. well. His merit as an actor is generally acknowledged. He has genius and worth which would do honour to patronage: he is a poor and modest man; claims which, from their very *silence*, have the more forcible power on the generous heart. Alas, for pity! that from the indolence of those who have the good things of this life in their gift, too often does brazen-fronted importunity snatch that boon, the rightful due of retiring, humble want! Of all the qualities we assign to the Author and Director of Nature, by far the most enviable is, to be able "to wipe away all tears from all eyes." O what insignificant, sordid wretches are they, however chance may have loaded them with wealth, who go to their graves, to their magnificent *mausoleums*, with hardly the consciousness of having made one poor honest heart happy.

But I crave your pardon, madam; I came to beg not to preach.

R. B.

CCLXVIII.

TO MRS RIDDEL.

I WILL wait on you my ever-valued friend, but whether in the morning I am not sure. Sunday closes a period of our provoking revenue business, and may probably keep me employed with my pen until noon. Fine employment for a poet's pen! There is a species of the human genius that I call the *gin-horse class*—what enviable dogs they are! Round, and round, and round they go. Mundell's ox, that drives his cotton-mill, is their exact prototype —without an idea or wish beyond their circle—fat, sleek, stupid, patient, quiet, and contented; while here I sit, altogether November-berish, a melange of fretfulness and melancholy; not enough of the one to rouse me to passion, nor of the other to repose me in torpor; my soul flouncing and fluttering round her tenement, like a wild-finch, caught amid the horrors of winter, and newly thrust into a cage. Well, I am persuaded that it was of me the Hebrew sage prophesied, when he foretold—" And, behold, on whatsoever this man doth set his heart, it shall not prosper!" If my. resentment is awaked, it is sure to be where it dare not squeak.

Pray that wisdom and bless be more frequent visitors of

R. B.

CCLXIX.

TO MR THOMSON.

DUMFRIES, 1st Dec. 1792.

YOUR alterations of *My Nannie, O!* are perfectly right. So are those of *My Wife's a Winsome Wee Thing.* Your alteration of the second stanza is a positive improvement. Now, my dear sir, with the freedom which characterises our correspondence, I must not, cannot alter *Bonnie Lesley.* You are right; the word "Alexander" makes the line a little uncouth, but I think the thought is pretty. Of Alexander, beyond all other heroes, it may be said, in the sublime language of Scripture, that "he went forth conquering and to conquer."

> " For nature made her what she is,
> And never made anither."

This is, in my opinion, more poetical than "Ne'er made sic anither." However, it is immaterial; make it either way. "Caledonie," I agree with you, is not so good a word as could be wished, though it is sanctioned in three or four instances by Allan Ramsay; but 1 cannot help it. In short, that species of stanza is the most difficult that I have ever tried.

The *Lea-Rig* is as follows (p. 259).

I am interrupted. Yours, &c., · R. B.

CCLXX.
TO MISS MARY PEACOCK.

Dec. 6, 1792.

DEAR MADAM,—I have written so often to you and have got no answer that I had resolved never to lift a pen to you again; but this eventful day, *the Sixth of December*, recalls to my memory such a scene! * * when I remember a far-distant person!— but no more of this until I learn from you a proper address, and why my letters have lain by you unanswered, as this is the third I have sent you. The opportunities will be all gone, now, I fear, of sending over the book I mentioned in my last. Do not write me for a week, as I shall not be at home, but as soon after that as possible.

> "Ance mair I hail thee, thou gloomy December,
> Ance mair I hail thee wi' sorrow and care; .
> Dire was the parting thou bids me remember,
> Parting wi' Nancy, oh, ne'er to meet mair!"

Yours, R. B.

CCLXXI.
TO CAPTAIN JOHNSTONE.

DUMFRIES, *Nov.* 13, 1792.

SIR,—I have just read your prospectus of the *Edinburgh Gazetteer.* If you go on in your paper with the same spirit, it will, beyond all comparison, be the first composition of the kind in Europe. I beg leave to insert my name as a subscriber, and if you have already published any papers, please send me them from the beginning. Point out your own way of settling payments in this place, or I shall settle with you through the medium of my friend, Peter Hill, bookseller in Edinburgh.

Go on, sir! Lay bare with undaunted heart and steady hand that horrid mass of corruption called politics and state-craft. Dare to draw in their native colours those—

> "Calm-thinking villains whom no faith can fire,"

whatever be the shibboleth of their pretended party.

The address to me at Dumfries will find, sir, your very humble servant, ROBERT BURNS.

CCLXXII.
TO MRS DUNLOP.

DUMFRIES, *6th December* 1792

I SHALL be in Ayrshire, I think, next week; and, if at all

possible, I shall certainly, my much-esteemed friend, have the pleasure of visiting at Dunlop House.

Alas, madam, how seldom do we meet in this world, that we have reason to congratulate ourselves on accessions of happiness! I have not passed half the ordinary term of an old man's life, and yet I scarcely look over the obituary of a newspaper that I do not see some names that I have known, and which I and other acquaintances little thought to meet with there so soon. Every other instance of the mortality of our kind makes us cast an anxious look into the dreadful abyss of uncertainty, and shudder with apprehension for our own fate. But of how different an importance are the lives of different individuals! Nay, of what importance is one period of the same life more than another? A few years ago I could have lain down in the dust, " careless of the voice of the morning;" and now not a few, and these most helpless individuals, would, on losing me and my exertions, lose both their "staff and shield." By the way, these helpless ones have lately got an addition—Mrs B. having given me a fine girl since I wrote you. There is a charming passage in Thomson's *Edward and Eleanora* :—

> " The valiant, *in himself*, what can he suffer?
> Or what need he regard his *single* woes?"—&c.

As I am got in the way of quotations, I shall give you another from the same piece, peculiarly—alas! too peculiarly—apposite, my dear madam, to your present frame of mind :—

> " Who so unworthy but may proudly deck him
> With his fair-weather virtue, that exults
> Glad o'er the summer main! The tempest comes,
> The rough winds rage aloud; when from the helm
> This virtue shrinks, and in a corner lies
> Lamenting. Heavens! if privileged from trial,
> How cheap a thing were virtue!"

I do not remember to have heard you mention Thomson's dramas. I pick up favourite quotations, and store them in my mind as ready armour, offensive or defensive, amid the struggle of this turbulant existence. Of these is one, a very favourite one, from his *Alfred* :—

> " Attach thee firmly to the virtuous deeds
> And offices of life; to life itself,
> With all its vain and transient joys, sit loose."

Probably I have quoted some of these to you formerly, as indeed, when I write from the heart, I am apt to be guilty of such repetitions. The compass of the heart, in the musical style of expression, is much more bounded than that of the imagination, so the notes of the former are extremely apt to run into one another; but in return for the paucity of its compass, its few notes are much more sweet. I must still give you another quotation, which I am almost sure I have given you before, but I can-

not resist the temptation.   The subject is religion : speaking of
its importance to mankind, the author says—

"'Tis this, my friend, that streaks our morning bright," &c.

I see you are in for double postage, so I shall e'en scribble out
t'other sheet.   We in this country here have many alarms of the
reforming, or rather the republican spirit of your part of the king-
dom.   Indeed we are a good deal in commotion ourselves.   For
me, I am a placeman, you know ; a very humble one indeed
Heaven knows, but still so much as to gag me.   What my priv te
sentiments are you will find out without an interpreter.

I have taken up the subject, and the other day, for a pretty
actress's benefit night, I wrote an Address, which I will give on the
other page, called *The Rights of Woman*.

I shall have the honour of receiving your criticisms in person
at Dunlop.   R. B.

CCLXXIII.

TO R. GRAHAM, ESQ., FINTRY.

December 1792

SIR,—I have been surprised, confounded, and distracted by Mr
Mitchell, the collector, telling me that he has received an order
from your Board to inquire into my political conduct, and blam-
ing me as a person disaffected to government.

Sir, you are a husband and a father ; you know what you
would feel to see the much-loved wife of your bosom, and your
helpless, prattling little ones turned adrift into the world, degraded
and disgraced from a situation in which they had been respect-
able and respected, and left almost without the necessary support of
a miserable existence.   Alas ! sir, must I think that such soon will
be my lot ! and from the dark insinuations of wicked, groundless
envy too !   I believe, sir, I may aver it, and in the sight of Omni-
science, that I would not tell a deliberate falsehood, no, not though
even worse horrors, if worse can be, than those I have mentioned,
hung over my head ; and I say, that the allegation, whatever
villain has made it, is a lie !   To the British Constitution, on re-
volution principles, next after my God, I am most devoutly at-
tached.   You, sir, have been much and generously my friend—
Heaven knows how warmly I have felt the obligation, and how
gratefully I have thanked you.   Fortune, sir, has made you power-
ful, and me impotent—has given you patronage, and me depend-
ence.   I would not, for my single self, call on your humanity ; were
such my insular, unconnected situation, I would despise the tear
that now swells in my eye—I could brave misfortune, I could face
ruin, for at the worst " Death's thousand doors stand open ;" but,

the tender concerns that I have mentioned, the claims and ties that I see at this moment, and feel around me, how they unnerve courage and wither resolution! To your patronage, as a man of some genius, you have allowed me a claim ; and your esteem, as an honest man, I know is my due. To these, sir, permit me to appeal ; by these may I adjure you to save me from that misery which threatens to overwhelm me, and which—with my latest breath I will say it—I have not deserved.   R. B.

CCLXXIV.
TO MRS DUNLOP.

DUMFRIES, 31st December 1792.

DEAR MADAM,—A hurry of business, thrown in heaps by my absence, has, until now, prevented my returning my grateful acknowledgments to the good family of Dunlop, and you in particular, for that hospitable kindness which rendered the four days I spent under that genial roof four of the pleasantest I ever enjoyed. Alas, my dearest friend! how few and fleeting are those things we call pleasures. On my road to Ayrshire I spent a night with a friend whom I much valued—a man whose days promised to be many ; and on Saturday last we laid him in the dust!

Jan. 2d, 1793.

I have just received yours of the 30th, and feel much for your situation. However, I heartily rejoice in your prospect of recovery from that vile jaundice. As to myself, I am better, though not quite free of my complaint. You must not think, as you seem to insinuate, that in my way of life I want exercise. Of that I have enough ; but occasional hard drinking is fatal to me. Against this I have again and again bent my resolution, and have greatly succeeded. Taverns I have totally abandoned : it is the private parties in the family way, among the hard-drinking gentlemen of this country, that do me the mischief ; but even this I have more than half given over.

Mr Corbet can be of little service to me at present ; at least I should be shy of applying. I cannot possibly be settled as a supervisor for several years. I must wait the rotation of the list ; and there are twenty names before mine. I might, indeed, get a job of officiating where a settled supervisor was ill or aged ; but that hauls me from my family, as I could not remove them on such an uncertainty. Besides, some envious, malicious fellow has raised a little demur on my political principles, and I wish to let that matter settle before I offer myself too much in the eye of my supervisors. I have set, henceforth, a seal on my lips as to these unlucky politics ; but to you I must breathe my sentiments. In this, as in

everything else, I shall shew the undisguised emotions of my soul.
War I deprecate : misery and ruin to thousands are in the blast
that announces the destructive demon. * * * *   R. B.

CCLXXV.

TO THE SAME.

5th January 1793.

You see my hurried life, madam; I can only command starts
of time; however, I am glad of one thing—since I finished the
other sheet the political blast that threatened my welfare is over-
blown. I have corresponded with Commissioner Grabam—for the
Board had made me the subject of their animadversions ; and now
I have the pleasure of informing you that all is set to rights in
that quarter.

Alas! how little do the wantonly or idly officious think what
mischief they do by their malicious insinuations, indirect imperti-
nence, or thoughtless blabbings. What a difference there is in
intrinsic worth, candour, benevolence, generosity, kindness—in all
the charities and all the virtues—between one class of human
beings and another. For instance, the amiable circle I so lately
mixed with in the hospitable hall of Dunlop,—their generous hearts,
their uncontaminated dignified minds, their informed and polished
understandings,—what a contrast when compared—if such com-
paring were not downright sacrilege—with the soul of the mis-
creant who can deliberately plot the destruction of an honest man
that never offended him, and with a grin of satisfaction see the
unfortunate being, his faithful wife, and prattling innocents,
turned over to beggary and ruin.

Your cup, my dear madam, arrived safe. I had two worthy
fellows dining with me the other day, when I with great forma-
lity produced my whigmaleerie cup, and told them that it had
been a family-piece among the descendants of William Wallace.
This roused such an enthusiasm that they insisted on bumpering
the punch round in it ; and by and by never did your great ances-
tor lay a *suthron* more completely to rest than for a time did your
cup my two friends. Apropos, this is the season of wishing. May
God bless you, my dear friend, and bless me, the humblest and
sincerest of your friends, by granting you yet many returns of the
season ! May all good things attend you and yours, wherever
they are scattered over the earth !   . R. B.

CCLXXVI.
TO MR THOMSON.

26th January 1793.

I APPROVE greatly, my dear sir, of your plans. Dr Beattie's
Essay will of itself be a treasure. On my part I mean to draw up
an appendix to the Doctor's Essay, containing my stock of anec-
dotes, &c., of our Scots songs. All the late Mr Tytler's anecdotes
I have by me, taken dòwn in the course of my acquaintance with
him from his own mouth. I am such an enthusiast, that in the
course of my several peregrinations through Scotland I made a
pilgrimage to the individual spot from which every song took its
rise—*Lochaber* and the *Braes of Ballenden* excepted. So far as
the locality, either from the title of the air or the tenor of the
song, could be ascertained, I have paid my devotions at the par-
ticular shrine of every Scots Muse.

I do not doubt but you might make a very valuable collection
of Jacobite songs; but would it give no offence? In the mean-
time, do not you think that some of them, particularly *The Sow's
Tail to Geordie,* as an air, with other words, might be well worth
a place in your collection of lively songs?

If it were possible to procure songs of merit, it would be proper
to have one set of Scots words to every air, and that the set of
words to which the notes ought to be set. There is a *naïveté*, a
pastoral simplicity, in a slight intermixture of Scots words and
phraseology, which is more in unison—at least to my taste, and
I will add, to every genuine Caledonian taste—with the simple
pathos or rustic sprightliness of our native music, than any Eng-
lish verses whatever.

The very name of Peter Pindar is an acquisition to your work.
His *Gregory* is beautiful. I have tried to give you a set of stanzas
in Scots on the same subject, which are at your service. Not that
I intend to enter the lists with Peter; that would be presumption
indeed. My song, though much inferior in poetic merit, has, I
think, more of the ballad simplicity in it (p. 263).   R. B.

CCLXXVII.
TO CLARINDA.

I SUPPOSE, my dear madam, that by your neglecting to inform
me of your arrival in Europe,—a circumstance that could not be
indifferent to me, as indeed no occurrence relating to you can,—
you meant to leave me to guess and gather that a correspondence
I once had the honour and felicity to enjoy is to be no more

Alas! what heavy-laden sounds are these—" No more!"   The
wretch who has never tasted pleasure has never known wo; what
drives the soul to madness is the recollection of joys that are " no
more!" But this is not language to the world—they do not under-
stand it.   But come, ye few—the children of Feeling and Senti-
ment!—ye whose trembling bosom-chords ache to unutterable
anguish as recollection gushes on the heart!—ye who are capable
of an attachment keen as the arrow of Death, and strong as the
vigour of immortal being—come! and your ears shall drink a
tale——But, hush! I must not, cannot tell it; agony is in the re-
collection, and frenzy in the recital!

But, madam, to leave the paths that lead to madness, I congra-
tulate your friends on your return; and I hope that the precious
health, which Miss P. tells me is so much injured, is restored or
restoring.   There is a fatality attends Miss Peacock's correspond-
ence and mine.   Two of my letters, it seems, she never received;
and her last came while I was in Ayrshire, was unfortunately
mislaid, and only found about ten days or a fortnight ago, on
removing a desk of drawers.

I present you a book—may I hope you will accept of it.   I
daresay you will have brought your books with you.   The fourth
volume of the *Scots Songs* is published; I will presume to send
it you.   Shall I hear from you?   But first hear me.   No cold
language—no prudential documents: I despise advice and scorn
control.   If you are not to write such language, such sentiments
as you know I shall wish, shall delight to receive, I conjure you,
by wounded pride, by ruined peace, by frantic, disappointed pas-
sion, by all the many ills that constitute that sum of human woes,
a broken heart!!!—to me be silent for ever.   *   *   *   *   R. B.

CCLXXVIII.

TO MR CUNNINGHAM.

3d March 1793.

SINCE I wrote to you the last lugubrious sheet, I have not had
time to write you farther.   When I say that I had not time, that,
as usual, means that the three demons—Indolence, Business, and
Ennui—have so completely shared my hours among them as not to
leave me a five minutes' fragment to take up a pen in.

Thank Heaven, I feel my spirits buoying upwards with the
renovating year.   Now I shall in good earnest take up Thomson's
songs.   I daresay he thinks I have used him unkindly; and, I
must own, with too much appearance of truth.   Apropos, do
you know the much-admired old Highland air called *The Sutor's
Dochter?*   It is a first-rate favourite of mine, and I have written
what I reckon one of my best songs to it.   I will send it to you as

it was sung, with great applause, in some fashionable circles,. by Major Robertson of Lude, who was here with his corps.

There is one commission that I must trouble you with. I lately lost a valuable seal, a present from a departed friend, which vexes me much. I have gotten one of your Highland pebbles, which I fancy would make a very decent one, and I want to cut my armorial bearing on it : will you be so obliging as inquire what will be the expense of such a business ? I do not know that my name is matriculated, as the heralds call it, at all, but I have invented arms for myself; so, you know, I shall be chief of the name, and, by courtesy of Scotland, will likewise be entitled to supporters. These, however, I do not intend having on my seal. I am a bit of a herald, and shall give you, *secundum artem*, my arms. On a field, azure, a holly-bush, seeded, proper, in base ; a shepherd's pipe and crook, saltier-wise, also proper, in chief. On a wreath of the colours, a woodlark perching on a sprig of bay-tree, proper, for crest. Two mottoes : round the top of the crest, *Wood-notes wild ;* at the bottom of the shield, in the usual place, *Better a wee bush than nae bield.* By the shepherd's pipe and crook I do not mean the nonsense of painters of Arcadia, but a *stock and horn,* and a *club,* such as you see at the head of Allan Ramsay, in Allan's quarto edition of the *Gentle Shepherd.* By the by, do you know Allan ? He must be a man of very great genius. Why is he not more known ? Has he no patrons ?—or do " Poverty's cold wind and crushing rain beat keen and heavy" on him ? I once, and but once, got a glance of that noble edition of the noblest pastoral in the world ; and dear as it was—I mean dear as to my pocket—I would have bought it, but I was told that it was printed and engraved for subscribers only. He is the *only* artist who has hit *genuine* pastoral *costume.* What, my dear Cunningham, is there in riches that they narrow and harden the heart so ? I think, that were I as rich as the sun, I should be as generous as the day ; but as I have no reason to imagine my soul a nobler one than any other man's, I must conclude that wealth imparts a bird-lime quality to the possessor, at which the man in his native poverty would have revolted. What has led me to this is the idea of such merit as Mr Allan possesses, and such riches as a nabob or government contractor possesses, and why they do not form a mutual league. Let wealth shelter and cherish unprotected merit, and the gratitude and celebrity of that merit will richly repay it. R. B.

CCLXXIX.

TO MR THOMSON.

20th March 1793.

MY DEAR SIR,—The song prefixed (*Mary Morison*) is one of my juvenile works. I leave it in your hands. I do not think it very remarkable, either for its merits or demerits. It is impossible—at least I feel it so in my stinted powers—to be always original, entertaining, and witty.

What is become of the list, &c., of your songs? I shall be out of all temper with you by and by. I have always looked on myself as the prince of indolent correspondents, and valued myself accordingly : and I will not, cannot, bear rivalship from you nor anybody else. R. B.

CCLXXX.

TO MISS BENSON.

DUMFRIES, 21st March 1793.

MADAM,—Among many things for which I envy those hale, long-lived old fellows before the Flood, is this, in particular —that when they met with anybody after their own heart, they had a charming long prospect of many, many happy meetings with them in after-life.

Now, in this short, stormy winter-day of our fleeting existence, when you, now and then, in the chapter of accidents, meet an individual whose acquaintance is a real acquisition, there are all the probabilities against you that you shall never meet with that valued character more. On the other hand, brief as this miserable being is, it is none of the least of the miseries belonging to it, that if there is any miscreant whom you hate, or creature whom you despise, the ill run of the chances shall be so against you, that in the overtakings, turnings, and jostlings of life, pop, at some unlucky corner, eternally comes the wretch upon you, and will not allow your indignation or contempt a moment's repose. As I am a sturdy believer in the powers of darkness, I take these to be the doings of that old author of mischief, the Devil. It is well known that he has some kind of short-hand way of taking down our thoughts; and I make no doubt that he is perfectly acquainted with my sentiments respecting Miss Benson : how much I admired her abilities and valued her worth, and how very fortunate I thought myself in her acquaintance. For this last reason, my dear madam, I must entertain no hopes of the very great pleasure of meeting with you again.

Miss Hamilton tells me that she is sending a packet to you,

and I beg leave to send you the enclosed sonnet; though, to tell you the real truth, the sonnet is a mere pretence, that I may have the opportunity of declaring with how much respectful esteem I have the honour to be, &c.   R. B.

CCLXXXI.
TO THE HON. THE PROVOST, BAILIES, AND TOWN-COUNCIL OF DUMFRIES.

GENTLEMEN,—The literary taste and liberal spirit of your good town has so ably filled the various departments of your schools, as to make it a very great object for a parent to have his children educated in them. Still to me, a stranger, to give my young ones that education I wish, at the high school-fees which a stranger pays, will bear hard upon me.

Some years ago, your good town did me the honour of making me an honorary burgess. Will you allow me to request that this mark of distinction may extend so far as to put me on the footing of a real freeman of the town in the schools?

If you are so very kind as to grant my request, it will certainly be a constant incentive to me to strain every nerve where I can officially serve you, and will, if possible, increase that grateful respect with which I have the honour to be, gentlemen, &c.
R. B.

CCLXXXII.
TO PATRICK MILLER, ESQ., OF DALSWINTON.

DUMFRIES, *April* 1793.

SIR,—My Poems being inst come out in another edition, will you do me the honour to accept of a copy?—a mark of my gratitude to you, as a gentleman to whose goodness I have been much indebted; of my respect for you, as a patriot who, in a venal, sliding age, stands forth the champion of the liberties of my country; and of my veneration for you, as a man whose benevolence of heart does honour to human nature.

There *was* a time, sir, when I was your dependent: this language *then* would have been like the vile incense of flattery—I could not have used it. Now that that connection is at an end, do me the honour to accept of this *honest* tribute of respect from, sir, your much indebted humble servant,   R. B.

CCLXXXIII.
TO JOHN M'MURDO, ESQ., DRUMLANRIG.

DUMFRIES. 1793.

WILL Mr M'Murdo do me the favour to accept of these volumes?
—a trifling but sincere mark of the very high respect I bear for his
worth as a man, his manners as a gentleman, and his kindness as
a friend. However inferior now, or afterwards, I may rank as a
poet, one honest virtue to which few poets can pretend, I trust I
shall ever claim as mine—to no man, whatever his station in life,
or his power to serve me, have I ever paid a compliment at the
expense of TRUTH. THE AUTHOR.

CCLXXXIV
TO THE EARL OF GLENCAIRN.

MY LORD,—When you cast your eye on the name at the bottom
of this letter, and on the title-page of the book I do myself the
honour to send your lordship, a more pleasurable feeling than my
vanity tells me that it must be a name not entirely unknown to
you. The generous patronage of your late illustrious brother
found me in the lowest obscurity. He introduced my rustic Muse
to the partiality of my country ; and to him I owe all. My sense
of his goodness, and the anguish of my soul at losing my truly
noble protector and friend, I have endeavoured to express in a
poem to his memory, which I have now published. This edition
is just from the press ; and in my gratitude to the dead, and my
respect for the living (fame belies you, my lord, if you possess not
the same dignity of man, which was your noble brother's charac-
teristic feature), I had destined a copy for the Earl of Glencairn.
I learnt just now that you are in town : allow me to present it
you.

I know, my lord, such is the vile, venal contagion which per-
vades the world of letters, that professions of respect from an
author, particularly from a poet to a lord, are more than suspi-
cious. I claim my by-past conduct, and my feelings at this mo-
ment, as exceptions to the too just conclusion. Exalted as are the
honours of your lordship's name, and unnoted as is the obscurity
of mine, with the uprightness of an honest man, I come before your
lordship, with an offering—however humble, 'tis all I have to give
—of my grateful respect ; and to beg of you, my lord,—'tis all I
have to ask of you,—that you will do me the honour to accept of
it. I have the honour to be, R. B.

CCLXXXV.

TO MR THOMSON.

7th April 1793.

THANK you, my dear sir, for your packet. You cannot imagine how much this business of composing for your publication has added to my enjoyments. What with my early attachment to ballads, your book, &c., ballad-making is now as completely my hobby-horse as ever fortification was Uncle Toby's; so I'll e'en canter it away till I come to the limit of my race (God grant that I may take the right side of the winning-post!), and then cheerfully looking back on the honest folks with whom I have been happy, I shall say or sing, *Sae Merry as we a' hae been !* and raising my last looks to the whole human race, the last words of the voice of Coila shall be, *Good-night, and joy be wi' you a' !* So much for my last words; now for a few present remarks, as they have occurred at random, on looking over your list.

The first lines of *The Last Time I came o'er the Moor,* and several other lines in it, are beautiful; but, in my opinion—pardon me, revered shade of Ramsay !—the song is unworthy of the divine air. I shall try to make or mend. *For ever, Fortune, wilt thou prove,* is a charming song; but *Logan Burn and Logan Braes,* is sweetly susceptible of rural imagery. I'll try that likewise, and if I succeed, the other song may class among the English ones. I remember the two last lines of a verse in some of the old songs of *Logan Water*—for I know a good many different ones—which I think pretty :—

> "Now my dear lad maun face his faes,
> Far, far frae me and Logan braes."

My Patie is a Lover gay, is unequal. " His mind is never muddy," is a muddy expression indeed.

> " Then I'll resign and marry Pate,
> And syne my cockernony."—

This is surely far unworthy of Ramsay, or your book. My song, *Rigs of Barley,* to the same tune, does not altogether please me ; but if I can mend it, and thrash a few loose sentiments out of it, I will submit it to your consideration. *The Lass o' Patie's Mill,* is one of Ramsay's best songs ; but there is one loose sentiment in it, which my much-valued friend Mr Erskine will take into his critical consideration. In Sir John Sinclair's statistical volumes are two claims—one, I think, from Aberdeenshire, and the other from Ayrshire—for the honour of this song. The following anecdote, which I had from the present Sir William Cunningham of Robertland, who had it of the late John, Earl of Loudon, I can, on such authorities, believe :—

Allan Ramsay was residing at Loudon Castle with the then Earl, father to Earl John; and one forenoon, riding or walking out together, his lordship and Allan passed a sweet, romantic spot on Irvine Water, still called Patie's Mill, where a bonnie lass was "tedding hay, bareheaded, on the green." My lord observed to Allan that it would be a fine theme for a song. Ramsay took the hint, and, lingering behind, he composed the first sketch of it, which he produced at dinner.

One Day I heard Mary say, is a fine song; but, for consistency's sake, alter the name Adonis. Were there ever such banns published as a purpose of marriage between Adonis and Mary! I agree with you that my song, *There's nought but Care on every Hand*, is much superior to *Puirtith Cauld*. The original song, *The Mill, Mill O!* though excellent, is, on account of delicacy, inadmissible; still I like the title, and think a Scottish song would suit the notes best; and let your chosen song, which is very pretty follow as an English set. *The Banks of the Dee* is, you know, literally *Langolee*, to slow time. The song is well enough, but has some false imagery in it: for instance,

" And sweetly the nightingale sang from the tree."

In the first place, the nightingale sings in a low bush, but never from a tree; and, in the second place, there never was a nightingale seen or heard on the banks of the Dee, or on the banks of any other river in Scotland. Exotic rural imagery is always comparatively flat. If I could hit on another stanza, equal to "The small birds rejoice," &c., I do myself honestly avow that I think it a superior song. *John Anderson, my Jo*—the song to this tune in *Johnson's Museum* is my composition, and I think it not my worst; if it suit you, take it, and welcome. Your collection of sentimental and pathetic songs is, in my opinion, very complete; but not so your comic ones. Where are *Tullochgorum, Lumps o' Puddin, Tibbie Fowler*, and several others, which, in my humble judgment, are well worthy of preservation? There is also one sentimental song of mine in the *Museum*, which never was known out of the immediate neighbourhood, until I got it taken down from a country girl's singing. It is called *Cragieburn Wood*, and, in the opinion of Mr Clarke, is one of the sweetest Scottish songs. He is quite an enthusiast about it; and I would take his taste in Scottish music against the taste of most connoisseurs.

You are quite right in inserting the last five in your list, though they are certainly Irish. *Shepherds, I have lost my Love!* is to me a heavenly air—what would you think of a set of Scottish verses to it? I have made one to it, a good while ago, which I think * * *, but in its original state it is not quite a lady's song. I enclose an altered, not amended, copy for you, if you choose of set the tune to it; and let the Irish verses follow.

Mr Erskine's songs aro all pretty, but his *Lone Vale* is divine.
Yours, &c.
Let me know just how you like these random hints.   R. B.

CCLXXXVI.

TO JOHN FRANCIS ERSKINE, ESQ., OF MAR.

DUMFRIES, 13*th April* 1793.

SIR,—Degenerate as human nature is said to be,—and, in many instances, worthless and unprincipled it is,—still there are bright examples to the contrary ; examples that, even in the eyes of superior beings, must shed a lustre on the name of man.

Such an example have I now before me, when you, sir, came forward to patronize and befriend a distant obscure stranger, merely because poverty had made him helpless, and his British hardihood of mind had provoked the arbitrary wantonness of power. My much esteemed friend, Mr Riddle of Glenriddel, has just read me a paragraph of a letter he had from you. Accept, sir, of the silent throb of gratitude ; for words would but mock the emotions of my soul.

You have been misinformed as to my final dismission from the Excise ; I am still in the service. Indeed, but for the exertions of a gentleman who must be known to you, Mr Graham of Fintry, —a gentleman who has ever been my warm and generous friend, —I had, without so much as a hearing, or the slightest previous intimation, been turned adrift with my helpless family to all the horrors of want. Had I had any other resource, probably I might have saved them the trouble of a dismission ; but the little money I gained by my publication is, almost every guinea, embarked to save from ruin an only brother, who, though one of the worthiest, is by no means one of the most fortunate of men.

In my defence to their accusations I said, that whatever might be my sentiments of republics, ancient or modern, as to Britain I abjured the idea—that a CONSTITUTION which, in its original principles, experience had proved to be every way fitted for our happiness in society, it would be insanity to sacrifice to an untried visionary theory ; that, in consideration of my being situated in a department, however humble, immediately in the hands of people in power, I had forborne taking any active part, either personally or as an author, in the present business of REFORM ; but that, where I must declare my sentiments, I would say there existed a system of corruption between the executive power and the representative part of the legislature, which boded no good to our glorious CONSTITUTION, and which every patriotic Briton must wish to see amended. Some such sentiments as these I stated in

a letter to my generous patron, Mr Graham, which he laid before
the Board at large, where, it seems, my last remark gave great
offence ; and one of our supervisors-general, a Mr Corbet, was
instructed to inquire on the spot, and to document me—that my
business was to act, *not to think ;* and that, whatever might be
men or measures, it was for me to be *silent* and *obedient.*

Mr Corbet was likewise my steady friend ; so between Mr
Graham and him I have been partly forgiven : only I understand
that all hopes of my getting officially forward are blasted.

Now, sir, to the business in which I would more immediately
interest you. The partiality of my COUNTRYMEN·has brought
me forward as a man of genius, and has given me a character to
support. In the POET I have avowed manly and independent
sentiments, which I trust will be found in the MAN. Reasons of
no less weight than the support of a wife and family, have pointed
out as the eligible, and, situated as I was, the only eligible line of
life for me, my present occupation. Still my honest fame is my
dearest concern ; and a thousand times have I trembled at the
idea of those *degrading* epithets that malice or misrepresentation
may affix to my name. I have often, in blasting anticipation,
listened to some future hackney scribbler, with the heavy malice
of savage stupidity, exulting in his hireling paragraphs—" BURNS,
notwithstanding the *fanfaronade* of independence to be found in
his works, and after having been held forth to public view and to
public estimation as a man of some genius, yet, quite destitute of
resources within himself to support his borrowed dignity, he
dwindled into a paltry exciseman, and slunk out the rest of his
insignificant existence in the meanest of pursuits, and among the
vilest of mankind."

In your illustrious hands, sir, permit me to lodge my disavowal
and defiance of these slanderous falsehoods. BURNS was a poor
man from birth, and an exciseman by necessity ; but—*I will* say
it—the sterling of his honest worth no poverty could debase, and
his independent British mind oppression might bend, but could
not subdue. Have not I, to me, a more precious stake in my
country's welfare than the richest dukedom in it ? I have a large
family of children, and the prospect of many more. I have three
sons, who, I see already, have brought into the world souls ill
qualified to inhabit the bodies of SLAVES. Can I look tamely on,
and see any machination to wrest from them the birthright of my
boys—the little independent BRITONS, in whose veins runs my
own blood ? No ! I will not, should my heart's blood stream
around my attempt to defend it !

Does any man tell me, that my full efforts can be of no service,
and that it does not belong to my humble station to meddle with
the concern of a nation?

I can tell him that it is on such individuals as I that a nation has to rest, both for the hand of support and the eye of intelligence. The uninformed MOB may swell a nation's bulk ; and the titled, tinsel, courtly throng may be its feathered ornament ; but the number of those who are elevated enough in life to reason and to reflect, yet low enough to keep clear of the venal contagion of a court—these are a nation's strength !

I know not how to apologize for the impertinent length of this epistle; but one small request I must ask of you farther—When you have honoured this letter with a perusal, please to commit it to the flames. BURNS, in whose behalf you have so generously interested yourself, I have here, in his native colours, drawn *as he is ;* but should any of the people in whose hands is the very bread he eats get the least knowledge of the picture, *it would ruin the poor BARD for ever.*

My poems having just come out in another edition, I beg leave to present you with a copy, as a small mark of that high esteem and ardent gratitude with which I have the honour to be, sir, your deeply-indebted, and ever-devoted humble servant,   R. B.

CCLXXXVII.

TO MR THOMSON.

April 1793.

I HAVE yours, my dear sir, this moment. I shall answer it and your former letter, in my desultory way of saying whatever comes uppermost.

The business of many of our tunes wanting at the beginning what fiddlers call a starting-note, is often a rub to us poor rhymers.

"There's braw, braw lads on Yarrow braes,
That wander through the blooming heather."

you may alter to

"Braw, braw lads on Yarrow braes,
Ye wander," &c.

My song, *Here awa, there awa,* as amended by Mr Erskine, I entirely approve of, and return you.

Give me leave to criticise your taste in the only thing in which it is, in my opinion, reprehensible. You know I ought to know something of my own trade. Of pathos, sentiment, and point you are a complete judge; but there is a quality more necessary than either in a song, and which is the very essence of a ballad—I mean simplicity. Now, if I mistake not, this last feature you are a little apt to sacrifice to the foregoing.

Ramsay, as every other poet, has not been always equally happy in his pieces; still I cannot approve of taking such liberties with an author as Mr Walker proposes doing with *The Last Time I came o'er the Moor.* Let a poet, if he chooses, take up the idea of another, and work it into a piece of his own ; but to mangle the works of the poor bard whose tuneful tongue is now mute for ever in the dark and narrow house—'twould be sacrilege ! I grant that Mr Walker's version is an improvement ; but I know Mr Walker well, and esteem him much ; let him mend the song, as the Highlander mended his gun—he gave it a new stock, a new lock, and a new barrel.

I do not by this object to leaving out improper stanzas, where that can be done without spoiling the whole. One stanza in *The Lass o' Patie's Mill* must be left out : the song will be nothing worse for it. I am not sure if we can take the same liberty with *Corn-rigs are Bonnie.* Perhaps it might want the last stanza, and be the better for it. *Cauld Kail in Aberdeen* you must leave with me yet awhile. I have vowed to have a song to that air on the lady whom I attempted to celebrate in the verses *Puirtith Cauld and Restless Love.* At any rate, my other song, *Green grow the Rashes,* will never suit. That song is current in Scotland under the old title, and to the merry old tune of that name, which of course would mar the progress of your song to celebrity. Your book will be the standard of Scots songs for the future : let this idea ever keep your judgment on the alarm.

I send a song on a celebrated toast in this country to suit *Bonnie Dundee.* I send you also a ballad to *The Mill, Mill O !*

The Last Time I came o'er the Moor, I would fain attempt to make a Scots song for, and let Ramsay's be the English set. You shall hear from me soon. When you go to London on this business can you come by Dumfries ? I have still several MS. Scots airs by me, which I have picked up mostly from the singing of country lasses. They please me vastly ; but your learned *lugs* (ears) would perhaps be displeased with the very feature for which I like them. I call them simple ; you would pronounce them silly. Do you know a fine air called *Jackie Hume's Lament ?* I have a song of considerable merit to that air. I'll enclose you both the song and tune, as I had them ready to send to *Johnson's Museum.* I send you likewise, to me, a beautiful little air, which I had taken down from *viva voce.* Adieu.   R. B.

CCLXXXVIII.
TO MR ROBERT AINSLIE,
ST JAMES'S STREET, EDINBURGH.
April 26, 1793.

I AM out of humour, my dear Ainslie, and this is the reason why I take up the pen to *you* : 'tis the nearest way (*probatum est*) to recover my spirits again.

I received your last, and was much entertained with it; but I will not at this time, nor at any other time, answer it. Answer a letter!—I never could answer a letter in my life. I have written many a letter in return for letters I have received; but then, they were original matter—spurt-away! zig here, zag there; as if the devil, that my grannie (an old woman *indeed!*) often told me, rode on Will-o'-Wisp, or, in her more classic phrase, SPUNKIE, were looking over my elbow. A happy thought that idea has engendered in my head! SPUNKIE, thou shalt henceforth be my Symbol, Signature, and Tutelary Genius! Like thee, hap-step-and-loup, here-awa-there-awa, higglety-pigglety, pell-mell, hither-and-yont, ram-stam, happy-go-lucky, up tails-a'-by-the-light-o'-the-moon—has been, is, and shall be, my progress through the mosses and moors of this vile, bleak, barren wilderness of a life of ours.

Come, then, my guardian spirit! like thee, may I*skip away, amusing myself by and at my own light; and if any opaque-souled lubber of mankind complain that my elfine, lambent, glimmerous wanderings have misled his stupid steps over precipices or into bogs, let the thick-headed blunderbuss recollect that he is not SPUNKIE:—that

> " SPUNKIE's wanderings could not copied be;
> Amid these perils none durst walk but he."

I feel vastly better. I give you joy. . . . I have no doubt but scholarcraft may be caught by friction. How else can you account for it, that born blockheads, by mere dint of *handling* books, grow so wise that even they themselves are equally convinced of and surprised at their own parts? I once carried this philosophy to that degree, that in a knot of country folks who had a library amongst them, and who, to the honour of their good sense, made me factotum in the business; one of our members, a little, wise-looking, squat, upright, jabbering body of a tailor, I advised him, instead of turning over the leaves, *to bind the book on his back.* Johnnie took the hint, and as our meetings were every fourth Saturday, and Pricklouse having a good Scots mile to walk in coming, and of course another in returning, Bodkin was sure to lay his hand on some heavy quarto or ponderous folio, with, and under which, wrapt up in his gray plaid, he grew wise as he grew weary, all the way home. He carried this so far, that an old musty Hebrew concordance, which we had in a present from a neighbouring priest, by mere dint of applying it, as doctors do a blistering plaster, between his shoulders, Stitch, in a dozen pilgrimages, acquired as much *rational* theology as the said priest had done by forty years' perusal of the pages.

Tell me, and tell me truly, what you think of this theory. Yours,

SPUNKIE.

CCXXX.
TO MRS GRAHAM OF FINTRY.

ELLISLAND, *February* 1791.

MADAM,—Whether it is that the story of our Mary Queen of Scots has a peculiar effect on the feelings of a poet, or whether I have in the enclosed ballad (p. 165) succeeded beyond my usual poetic success, I know not, but it has pleased me beyond any effort of my Muse for a good while past; on that account I enclose it particularly to you. It is true the purity of my motives may be suspected. I am already deeply indebted to Mr Graham's goodness; and what, *in the usual ways of men,* is of infinitely greater importance, Mr G. can do me service of the utmost importance in time to come. I was born a poor dog; and however I may occasionally pick a better bone than I used to do, I know I must live and die poor: but I will indulge the flattering faith that my poetry will considerably outlive my poverty; and without any fustian affectation of spirit, I can promise and affirm that it must be no ordinary craving of the latter shall ever make me do anything injurious to the honest fame of the former. Whatever may be my failings—for failings are a part of human nature—may they ever be those of a generous heart and an independent mind! It is no fault of mine that I was born to dependence, nor is it Mr Graham's chiefest praise that he can command influence: but it is his merit to bestow, not only with the kindness of a brother, but with the politeness of a gentleman, and I trust it shall be mine to receive with thankfulness, and remember with undiminished gratitude.　　　　　　　　　　　　R. B.

CCXXXI.
TO DR MOORE.

ELLISLAND, 28*th February* 1791.

I DO not know, sir, whether you are a subscriber to *Grose's Antiquities of Scotland.* If you are, the enclosed poem will not be altogether new to you. Captain Grose did me the favour to send me a dozen copies of the proof-sheet, of which this is one. Should you have read the piece before, still this will answer the principal end I have in view—it will give me another opportunity of thanking you for all your goodness to the rustic bard, and also of shewing you that the abilities you have been pleased to commend and patronise are still employed in the way you wish.

The *Elegy on Captain Henderson* is a tribute to the memory of a man I loved much. Poets have in this the same advantage as Roman Catholics; they can be of service to their friends after

CCXCI.

TO MR THOMSON.

2d July 1793.

MY DEAR SIR,—I have just finished the following ballad (p. 269), and, as I do think it in my best style, I send it you. Mr Clarke, who wrote down the air from Mrs Burns's " wood-note wild," is very fond of it, and has given it a celebrity by teaching it to some young ladies of the first fashion here. If you do not like the air enough to give it a place in your collection, please return it. The song you may keep, as I remember it.

I have some thoughts of inserting in your index, or in my notes, the names of the fair ones, the themes of my songs. I do not mean the name at full, but dashes or asterisms, so as ingenuity may find them out.

The heroine of the foregoing is Miss M'Murdo, daughter to Mr M'Murdo of Drumlanrig, one of your subscribers. I have not painted her in the rank which she holds in life, but in the dress and character of a cottager.   R. B.

CCXCII.

TO MR THOMSON.

July 1793.

I ASSURE you, my dear sir, that you truly hurt me with your pecuniary parcel. It degrades me in my own eyes. However, to return it would savour of affectation ; but as to any more traffic of that debtor and creditor kind, I swear, by that HONOUR which crowns the upright statue of ROBERT BURNS'S INTEGRITY—on the least motion of it, I will indignantly spurn the bypast trans- action, and from that moment commence entire stranger to you! BURNS'S character for generosity of sentiment and independence of mind will, I trust, long outlive any of his wants which the cold, unfeeling ore can supply ; at least I will take care that such a character he shall deserve.

Thank you for my copy of your publication. Never did my eyes behold in any musical work such elegance and correctness. Your preface, too, is admirably written ; only your partiality to me has made you say too much : however, it will bind me down to double every effort in the future progress of the work. The following are a few remarks on the songs in the list you sent me. I never copy what I write to you, so I may be often tautological, or perhaps contradictory.

The Flowers o' the Forest is charming as a poem, and should be,

CCXXX.
TO MRS GRAHAM OF FINTRY.

ELLISLAND, *February* 1791.

MADAM,—Whether it is that the story of our Mary Queen of Scots has a peculiar effect on the feelings of a poet, or whether I have in the enclosed ballad (p. 165) succeeded beyond my usual poetic success, I know not, but it has pleased me beyond any effort of my Muse for a good while past; on that account I enclose it particularly to you. It is true the purity of my motives may be suspected. I am already deeply indebted to Mr Graham's goodness ; and what, *in the usual ways of men,* is of infinitely greater importance, Mr G. can do me service of the utmost importance in time to come. I was born a poor dog ; and however I may occasionally pick a better bone than I used to do, I know I must live and die poor : but I will indulge the flattering faith that my poetry will considerably outlive my poverty ; and without any fustian affectation of spirit, I can promise and affirm that it must be no ordinary craving of the latter shall ever make me do anything injurious to the honest fame of the former. Whatever may be my failings—for failings are a part of human nature—may they ever be those of a generous heart and an independent mind ! It is no fault of mine that I was born to dependence, nor is it Mr Graham's chiefest praise that he can command influence : but it is his merit to bestow, not only with the kindness of a brother, but with the politeness of a gentleman, and I trust it shall be mine to receive with thankfulness, and remember with undiminished gratitude.   R. B.

CCXXXI.
TO DR MOORE.

ELLISLAND, 28*th February* 1791.

I DO not know, sir, whether you are a subscriber to *Grose's Antiquities of Scotland.* If you are, the enclosed poem will not be altogether new to you. Captain Grose did me the favour to send me a dozen copies of the proof-sheet, of which this is one. Should you have read the piece before, still this will answer the principal end I have in view—it will give me another opportunity of thanking you for all your goodness to the rustic bard, and also of shewing you that the abilities you have been pleased to commend and patronise are still employed in the way you wish. The *Elegy on Captain Henderson* is a tribute to the memory of a man I loved much. Poets have in this the same advantage as Roman Catholics; they can be of service to their friends after

CCXCI.

TO MR THOMSON.

2d July 1793.

MY DEAR SIR,—I have just finished the following ballad (p. 269), and, as I do think it in my best style, I send it you. Mr Clarke, who wrote down the air from Mrs Burns's " wood-note wild," is very fond of it, and has given it a celebrity by teaching it to some young ladies of the first fashion here. If you do not like the air enough to give it a place in your collection, please return it. The song you may keep, as I remember it.

I have some thoughts of inserting in your index, or in my notes, the names of the fair ones, the themes of my songs. I do not mean the name at full, but dashes or asterisms, so as ingenuity may find them out.

The heroine of the foregoing is Miss M'Murdo, daughter to Mr M'Murdo of Drumlanrig, one of your subscribers. I have not painted her in the rank which she holds in life, but in the dress and character of a cottager.   R. B.

CCXCII.

TO MR THOMSON.

July 1793.

I ASSURE you, my dear sir, that you truly hurt me with your pecuniary parcel. It degrades me in my own eyes. However, to return it would savour cf affectation; but as to any more traffic of that debtor and creditor kind, I swear, by that HONOUR which crowns the upright statue of ROBERT BURNS'S INTEGRITY—on the least motion of it, I will indignantly spurn the bypast trans- action, and from that moment commence entire stranger to you! BURNS'S character for generosity of sentiment and independence of mind will, I trust, long outlive any of his wants which the cold, unfeeling ore can supply; at least I will take care that such a character he shall deserve.

Thank you for my copy of your publication. Never did my eyes behold in any musical work such elegance and correctness. Your preface, too, is admirably written; only your partiality to me has made you say too much: however, it will bind me down to double every effort in the future progress of the work. The following are a few remarks on the songs in the list you sent me. I never copy what I write to you, so I may be often tautological, or perhaps contradictory.

The Flowers o' the Forest is charming as a poem, and should be, and must be, set to the notes; but, though out of your rule, the three stanzas beginning,

" I hae seen the smiling o' fortune beguiling,"

are worthy of a place, were it but to immortalise the author of them, who is an old lady of my acquaintance, and at this moment living in Edinburgh. She is a Mrs Cockburn, I forget of what place, but from Roxburghshire. What a charming apostrophe is—

" O fickle fortune, why this cruel sporting,
Why, why torment us, poor sons of a day !"

The old ballad, *I wish I were where Helen lies*, is silly, to contemptibility. My alteration of it, in *Johnson*, is not much better. Mr Pinkerton, in his, what he calls, ancient ballads—many of them notorious, though beautiful enough, forgeries—has the best set. It is full of his own interpolations—but no matter.

In my next I will suggest to your consideration a few songs which may have escaped your hurried notice. In the meantime, allow me to congratulate you now as a brother of the quill. You have committed your character and fame, which will now be tried, for ages to come, by the illustrious jury of the SONS AND DAUGHTERS OF TASTE—all whom poesy can please, or music charm.

Being a bard of nature, I have some pretensions to second-sight; and I am warranted by the spirit to foretell and affirm, that your great-grandchild will hold up your volumes, and say, with honest pride—" This so-much-admired selection was the work of my ancestor !"   R. B

CCXCIII.

TO MISS CRAIK.

DUMFRIES, *August* 1793.

MADAM,—Some rather unlocked-for accidents have prevented my doing myself the honour of a second visit to Arbigland, as I was so hospitably invited, and so positively meant to have done. However, I still hope to have that pleasure before the busy months of harvest begin. •

I enclose you two of my late pieces, as some kind of return for the pleasure I have received in perusing a certain MS. volume of poems in the possession of Captain Riddel. To repay one with an *old song* is a proverb whose force you, madam, I know, will not allow. What is said of illustrious descent is, I believe, equally true of a talent for poetry—none ever despised it who had pretensions to it. The fates and characters of the rhyming tribe often employ my thoughts when I am disposed to be melancholy. There is not, among all the martyrologies that ever were penned,

so rueful a narrative as the lives of the poets. In the compara·
tive view of wretches, the criterion is not what they are doomed
to suffer, but how they are formed to bear. Take a being of our
kind, give him a stronger imagination and a more delicate sensi·
bility, which between them will ever engender a more ungovern-
able set of passions than are the usual lot of man ; implant in him
an irresistible impulse to some idle vagary, such as arranging
wild-flowers in fantastical nosegays, tracing the grasshopper to
his haunt by his chirping song, watching the frisks of the little
minnows in the sunny pool, or hunting after the intrigues of but-
terflies—in short, send him adrift after some pursuit which shall
eternally mislead him from the paths of lucre, and yet curse him
with a keener relish than any man living for the pleasures that
lucre can purchase ; lastly, fill up the measure of his woes by
bestowing on him a spurning sense of his own dignity—and you
have created a wight nearly as miserable as a poet. To you,
madam, I need not recount the fairy pleasures the Muse bestows,
to counterbalance this catalogue of evils. Bewitching poetry is
like bewitching woman. She has in all ages been accused of mis-
leading mankind from the councils of wisdom and the paths of
prudence, involving them in difficulties, baiting them with po-
verty, branding them with infamy, and plunging them in the
whirling vortex of ruin ; yet where is the man but must own
that all our happiness on earth is not worthy the name—that
even the holy hermit's solitary prospect of paradisiacal bliss is but
the glitter of a northern sun rising over a frozen region—com-
pared with the many pleasures, the nameless raptures, that we
owe to the lovely queen of the heart of man !   R. B.

CCXCIV.

TO MR THOMSON.

August 1793.

You may readily trust, my dear sir, that any exertion in my
power is heartily at your service. But one thing I must hint to
you—the very name of Peter Pindar is of great service to your
publication ; so get a verse from him now and then, though I have
no objection, as well as I can, to bear the burden of the business.

Is *Whistle, and I'll come to you, my Lad*, one of your airs ? I
admire it much, and yesterday I set the following verses to it,
(p. 271). Urbani, whom I have met with here, begged them of
me, as he admires the air much ; but as I understand that he looks
with rather an evil eye on your work, I did not choose to comply.
However, if the song does not suit your taste, I may possibly send
it him. He is, *entre nous*, a narrow, contracted creature but he
sings so delightfully, that whatever he introduces at your concert

must have immediate celebrity. The set of the air which I had in my eye is in *Johnson's Museum*. Another favourite air of mine is *The Mucking o' Geordie's Byre*. When sung slow with expression, I have wished that it had had better poetry: that I have endeavoured to supply as follows (p. 272).

Mr Clarke begs you to give Miss Phillis a corner in your book, as she is a particular flame of his. She is a Miss Phillis M'Murdo, sister to "Bonnie Jean." They are both pupils of his. You shall hear from me the very first grist I get from my rhyming-mill.

R. B.

CCXCV.

TO MR THOMSON.

[28*th*] *August* 1793.

THAT tune, *Cauld Kail*, is such a favourite of yours, that I once more roved out yesterday for a gloamin-shot (twilight) at the Muses; when the Muse that presides o'er the shores of Nith, or rather my old inspiring dearest Nymph, Coila, whispered me the following (*Come let me*, p. 273). I have two reasons for thinking that it was my early, sweet, simple inspirer that was by my elbow, " smooth gliding without step," and pouring the song on my glowing fancy. In the first place, since I left Coila's native haunts, not a fragment of a poet has arisen to cheer her solitary musings, by catching inspiration from her, so I more than suspect that she has followed me hither, or at least makes me occasional visits; secondly, the last stanza of this song I send you is the very words that Coila taught me many years ago, and which I set to an old Scots reel in *Johnson's Museum*.

If you think the above will suit your idea of your favourite air, I shall be highly pleased. *The last Time I came o'er the Moor*, I cannot meddle with as to mending it; and the musical world have been so long accustomed to Ramsay's words, that a different song, though positively superior, would not be so well received. I am not fond of choruses to songs, so I have not made one for the foregoing. R. B.

CCXCVI.

TO MR THOMSON.

Sept. 1793.

YOU know that my pretensions to musical taste are merely a few of nature's instincts, untaught and untutored by art. For this reason many musical compositions, particularly where much of the merit lies in counterpoint, however they may transport and

ravish the ears of you connoisseurs, affect my simple lug no other-
wise than merely as melodious din.   On the other hand, by way
of amends, I am delighted with many little melodies, which the
learned musician despises as silly and insipid.   I do not know
whether the old air, *Hey, tuttie taitie*, may rank among this
number ; but well I know that, with Fraser's hautboy, it has
often filled my eyes with tears.   There is a tradition which I have
met with in many places in Scotland, that it was Robert Bruce's
march at the battle of Bannockburn.   This thought, in my yester-
night's evening walk, warmed me to a pitch of enthusiasm on the
theme of liberty and independence, which I threw into a kind of
Scottish ode (p. 273), fitted to the air, that one might suppose to
be the gallant royal Scot's address to his heroic followers on that
eventful morning.

So may God ever defend the cause of truth and liberty, as He
did that day !   Amen.

P.S.—I showed the air to Urbani, who was highly pleased with
it, and begged me to make soft verses for it ; but I had no idea of
giving myself any trouble on the subject, till the accidental recol-
lection of that glorious struggle for freedom, associated with the
glowing ideas of some other struggles of the same nature, *not quite
so ancient*, roused my rhyming mania.   Clarke's set of the tune,
with his bass, you will find in the *Museum*, though I am afraid
that the air is not what will entitle it to a place in your elegant
selection.   R. B.

CCXCVII.

TO MR THOMSON.

[*Sept.* 1793.]

I DARESAY, my dear sir, that you will begin to think my corre-
spondence is persecution.   No matter, I can't help it : a ballad is
my hobby-horse, which, though otherwise a simple sort of harm-
less idiotical beast enough, has yet this blessed headstrong pro-
perty, that when once it has fairly made off with a hapless wight,
it gets so enamoured with the tinkle-gingle, tinkle-gingle of its
own bells, that it is sure to run poor Pilgarlick, the bedlam jockey,
quite beyond any useful point or post in the common race of men.

The following song (*Behold the Hour*, p. 274) I have composed
for *Oran Gaoil*, the Highland air that you tell me in your last you
have resolved to give a place to in your book.   I have this moment
finished the song, so you have it glowing from the mint.   If it
suit you, well !—if not, 'tis also well !   R. B.

CCXCVIII.

TO MR THOMSON.

Sept. 1793.

I HAVE received your list, my dear sir, and here go my obser-vations on it.

Down the Burn, Davie—I have this moment tried an alteration, leaving out the last half of the third stanza, and the first half of the last stanza ; thus (p. 274).

Through the Wood, Laddie—I am decidedly of opinion that both in this, and *There'll never be Peace till Jamie comes Hame*, the second or high part of the tune being a repetition of the first part an octave higher, is only for instrumental music, and would be much better omitted in singing.

Cowden-knowes—Remember in your index, that the song in pure English to this tune, beginning—

" When summer comes, the swains on Tweed,"

is the production of Crawford. Robert was his Christian name.

Laddie be near me, must lie by me for some time. I do not know the air ; and until I am complete master of a tune, in my own singing (such as it is), I can never compose for it. My way is—I consider the poetic sentiment correspondent to my idea of the musical expression ; then choose my theme ; begin one stanza : when that is composed, which is generally the most difficult part of the business, I walk out, sit down now and then, look out for objects in nature around me that are in unison and harmony with the cogitations of my fancy, and workings of my bosom ; humming every now and then the air with the verses I have framed. When I feel my Muse beginning to jade, I retire to the solitary fireside of my study, and there commit my effusions to paper ; swinging at intervals on the hind-legs of my elbow-chair, by way of calling forth my own critical strictures as my pen goes on. Seriously, this, at home, is almost invariably my way.

What egotism !

Gill Morice I am for leaving out. It is a plaguy length ; the air itself is never sung ; and its place can well be supplied by one or two songs for fine airs that are not in your list—for in-stance, *Craigieburn Wood*, and *Roy's Wife*. The first, beside its intrinsic merit, has novelty ; and the last has high merit, as well as great celebrity. I have the original words of a song for the last air, in the handwriting of the lady who composed it ; and they are superior to any edition of the song which the public has yet seen.

Highland Laddie—The old set will please a mere Scotch ear best ; and the new one an Italianized one. There is a third, and what Oswald calls the old *Highland Laddie*, which pleases me

more than either of them. It is sometimes called *Ginglin Johnnie*
—it being the air of an old humorous tawdry song of that name.
You will find it in the *Museum—I hae been at Crookieden*, &c. I
would advise you, in this musical quandary, to offer up your
prayers to the Muses for inspiring direction; and in the mean-
time, waiting for this direction, bestow a libation to Bacchus;
and there is not a doubt but you will hit on a judicious choice.
Probatum est.

Auld Sir Simon I must beg you to leave out, and put in its place
The Quaker's Wife.

Blithe hae I been o'er the Hill is one of the finest songs ever I
made in my life, and, besides, is composed on a young lady, posi-
tively the most beautiful, lovely woman in the world. As I pur-
pose giving you the names and designations of all my heroines, to
appear in some future edition of your work, perhaps half a cen-
tury hence, you must certainly include *The Bonniest Lass in a' the
Warld* in your collection.

Dainty Davie I have heard sung nineteen thousand nine hun-
dred and ninety-nine times, and always with the chorus to the
low part of the tune; and nothing has surprised me so much as
your opinion on this subject. If it will not suit as I proposed,
we will lay two of the stanzas together, and then make the chorus
follow.

Fee him, Father—I enclose you Fraser's set of this tune when
he plays it slow; in fact, he makes it the language of despair. I
shall here give you two stanzas, in that style, merely to try if it
will be any improvement. Were it possible, in singing, to give it
half the pathos which Fraser gives it in playing, it would make
an admirably pathetic song. I do not give these verses (p. 274)
for any merit they have. I composed them at the time in which
" Patie Allan's mither died—that was about the back o' midnight,"
and by the lee-side of a bowl of punch, which had overset every
mortal in company except the hautboys and the Muse.

Jockie and Jenny I would discard, and in its place would put
There's nae Luck about the House, which has a very pleasant air,
and which is positively the finest love-ballad in that style in the
Scottish, or perhaps in any other language. *When she came ben
she bobbit*, as an air, is more beautiful than either, and in the
andante way would unite with a charming sentimental ballad.

Saw ye my Father? is one of my greatest favourites. The
evening before last, I wandered out, and began a tender song, in
what I think is its native style. I must premise, that the old way,
and the way to give most effect, is to have no starting-note, as the
fiddlers call it, but to burst at once into the pathos. Every country
girl sings *Saw ye my Father?* &c.

My song is but just begun (*Where are*, &c., p. 274); and I
should like, before I proceed, to know your opinion of it. I have

sprinkled it with the Scottish dialect, but it may be easily turned into correct English.

Todlin Hame—Urbani mentioned an idea of his, which has long been mine, that this air is highly susceptible of pathos : accordingly, you will soon hear him at your concert try it to a song of mine in the *Museum, Ye Banks and Braes o' bonnie Doon.* One song more, and I have done—*Auld Lang Syne.* The air is but mediocre ; but the following song (p. 234)—the old song of the olden times, and which has never been in print, nor even in manuscript, until I took it down from an old man's singing—is enough to recommend any air.*

Now, I suppose, I have tried your patience fairly. You must after all is over, have a number of ballads, properly so called *Gill Morice, Tranent Muir, Macpherson's Farewell, Battle of Sheriff-muir,* or, *We ran and they ran* (I know the author of this charming ballad, and his history), *Hardiknute, Barbara Allan* (I can furnish a finer set of this tune than any that has yet appeared); and besides, do you know that I really have the old tune to which *The Cherry and the Slae* was sung, and which is mentioned as a well known air in *Scotland's Complaint*—a book published before poor Mary's days ? It was then called, *The Banks o' Helicon* — an old poem, which Pinkerton has brought to light. You will see all this in Tytler's *History of Scottish Music.* The tune, to a learned ear, may have no great merit ; but it is a great curiosity. I have a good many original things of this kind.

R. B

CCXCIX.

TO JOHN M'MURDO, ESQ.

DUMFRIES, December 1793.

SIR,—It is said that we take the greatest liberties with our greatest friends, and I pay myself a very high compliment in the manner in which I am going to apply the remark. I have owed you money longer than ever I owed it to any man. Here is Ker's account, and here is six guineas ; and now, I don't owe a shilling to man—or woman either. But for these dirty, dog-eared little pages, I had done myself the honour to have waited on you long ago. Independent of the obligations your hospitality has laid me under, the consciousness of your superiority in the rank of man and gentleman, of itself was fully as much as I could ever make head against ; but to owe you money, too, was more than I could face.

I think I once mentioned something of a collection of Scots songs I have for some years been making—I send you a perusal

---

* This is only an attempt at mystification, Burns himself being the author.

of what I have got together. I could not conveniently spare them above five or six days, and five or six glances of them will probably more than suffice you. A very few of them are my own. When you are tired of them, please leave them with Mr Clint, of the King's Arms. There is not another copy of the collection in the world; and I should be sorry that any unfortunate negligence should deprive me of what has cost me a good deal of pains.

R. B.

CCC.

TO CAPTAIN ——.

DUMFRIES, 5th December 1793.

SIR,—Heated as I was with wine yesternight, I was perhaps rather seemingly impertinent in my anxious wish to be honoured with your acquaintance. You will forgive it—it was the impulse of heartfelt respect. "He is the father of the Scottish county reform, and is a man who does honour to the business, at the same time that the business does honour to him," said my worthy friend Glenriddel to somebody by me, who was talking of your coming to this country with your corps. "Then," I said, "I have a woman's longing to take him by the hand, and say to him,—'Sir, I honour you as a man to whom the interests of humanity are dear, and as a patriot to whom the rights of your country are sacred.'"

In times like these, sir, when our commoners are barely able, by the glimmering of their own twilight understandings, to scrawl a frank, and when lords are what gentlemen would be ashamed to be, to whom shall a sinking country call for help? To the independent country gentleman. To him who has too deep a stake in his country not to be in earnest for her welfare; and who, in the honest pride of man, can view with equal contempt the insolence of office and the allurements of corruption.

I mentioned to you a Scots ode or song (Bruce's Address) I had lately composed, and which, I think, has some merit. Allow me to enclose it. When I fall in with you at the theatre, I shall be glad to have your opinion of it. Accept of it, sir, as a very humble but most sincere tribute of respect from a man who, dear as he prizes poetic fame, yet holds dearer an independent mind. I have the honour to be, &c.,

R. B.

CCCI.

TO THE EARL OF BUCHAN.

DUMFRIES, 12th January 1794.

MY LORD,—Will your lordship allow me to present you with

the enclosed little composition of mine (*Bruce's Address*), as a
small tribute of gratitude for the acquaintance with which you
have been pleased to honour me ? Independent of my enthusiasm
as a Scotsman, I have rarely met with anything in history which
interests my feelings as a man, equal with the story of Bannock-
burn. On the one hand, a cruel but able usurper leading on the
finest army in Europe to extinguish the last spark of freedom
among a greatly-daring and greatly-injured people ; on the other
hand, the desperate relics of a gallant nation devoting themselves
to rescue their bleeding country, or perish with her.

Liberty ! thou art a prize truly and indeed invaluable, for never
canst thou be too dearly bought !

If my little ode has the honour of your lordship's approbation,
it will gratify my highest ambition. I have the honour to be, &c.,
                                                    R. B.

_____

CCCII.

TO CAPTAIN MILLER, DALSWINTON.

DEAR SIR,—The following ode (*Bruce's Address*), is on a sub-
ject which I know you by no means regard with indifference. O
Liberty,

" Thou mak'st the gloomy face of nature gay,
Giv'st beauty to the sun, and pleasure to the day."

It does me so much good to meet with a man whose honest bosom
glows with the generous enthusiasm, the heroic daring of liberty,
that I could not forbear sending you a composition of my own on
the subject, which I really think is in my best manner. I have
the honour to be, dear sir, &c.,   R. B.

_____

CCCIII.

TO MRS RIDDEL.

DEAR MADAM,—I meant to have called on you yesternight,
but as I edged up to your box-door, the first object which greeted
my view was one of those lobster-coated puppies, sitting like ano-
ther dragon, guarding the Hesperian fruit. On the conditions
and capitulations you so obligingly offer, I shall certainly make
my weather beaten rustic phiz a part of your box-furniture on
Tuesday, when we may arrange the business of the visit.

Among the profusion of idle compliments which insidious craft
or unmeaning folly incessantly offer at your shrine—a shrine,
how far exalted above such adoration !—permit me, were it but for
rarity's sake, to pay you the honest tribute of a warm heart and

an independent mind; and to assure you that I am, thou most amiable and most accomplished of thy sex, with the most respectful esteem and fervent regard, thine, &c., R. B.

CCCIV.

TO MR STEPHEN CLARKE, JUN., DUMFRIES.

Sunday morning.

DEAR SIR,—I was, I know, drunk last night, but I am sober this morning. From the expressions Capt. —— made use of to me, had I had nobody's welfare to care for but my own, we should certainly have come, according to the manners of the world, to the necessity of murdering one another about the business. The words were such as, generally, I believe, end in a brace of pistols; but I am still pleased to think that I did not ruin the peace and welfare of a wife and family of children in a drunken squabble. Further, you know that the report of certain political opinions being mine, has already once before brought me to the brink of destruction. I dread lest last night's business may be misrepresented in the same way. You, I beg, will take care to prevent it. I tax your wish for Mrs Burns's welfare with the task of waiting, as soon as possible, on every gentleman who was present, and state this to him, and, as you please, show him this letter. What, after all, was the obnoxious toast? " May our success in the present war be equal to the justice of our cause"—a toast that the most outrageous frenzy of loyalty cannot object to. I request and beg that this morning you will wait on the parties present at the foolish dispute. I shall only add, that I am truly sorry that a man who stood so high in my estimation as Mr —— should use me in the manner in which I conceive he has done. R. B.

CCCV.

TO MRS RIDDEL.

MADAM,—I daresay that this is the first epistle you ever received from this nether world. The time and manner of my leaving your earth I do not exactly know, as I took my departure in the heat of a fever of intoxication, contracted at your too hospitable mansion; but, on my arrival here, I was fairly tried, and sentenced to endure the purgatorial tortures of this infernal confine for the space of ninety-nine years, eleven months, and twenty-nine days, and all on account of the impropriety of my conduct yesternight under your roof. Here am I, laid on a bed of pitiless furze, with my aching head reclined on a pillow of ever-piercing

thorn, while an infernal tormenter, wrinkled, and old, and cruel—
his name, I think, is *Recollection*—with a whip of scorpions, forbids
peace or rest to approach me, and keeps anguish eternally awake.
Still, madam, if I could in any measure be reinstated in the good
opinion of the fair circle whom my conduct last night so much
injured, I think it would be an alleviation to my torments. For
this reason, I trouble you with this letter. To the men of the
company I will make no apology. Your husband, who insisted on
my drinking more than I chose, has no right to blame me; and
the other gentlemen were partakers of my guilt. But to you,
madam, I have much to apologise. Your good opinion I valued
as one of the greatest acquisitions I had made on earth, and I
was truly a beast to forfeit it. There was a Miss I——, too, a
woman of fine sense, gentle and unassuming manners—do make,
on my part, a miserable wretch's best apology to her. A Mrs
G——, a charming woman, did me the honour to be prejudiced
in my favour; this makes me hope that I have not outraged her
beyond all forgiveness. To all the other ladies, please present my
humblest contrition for my conduct, and my petition for their
gracious pardon. O all ye powers of decency and decorum! whisper
to them that my errors, though great, were involuntary—that an
intoxicated man is the vilest of beasts—that it was not in my
nature to be brutal to any one—that to be rude to a woman, when
in my senses, was impossible with me—but——

    ＊   ＊   ＊   ＊   ＊

Regret! Remorse! Shame! ye three hell-hounds that ever dog
my steps and bay at my heels, spare me! spare me!

Forgive the offences, and pity the misery of, madam, your
humble slave,   R. B.

CCCVI.

TO MRS RIDDEL.

MADAM,—I return your commonplace-book. I have perused it
with much pleasure, and would have continued my criticisms, but
as it seems the critic has forfeited your esteem, his strictures must
lose their value.

If it is true that "offences come only from the heart," before
you I am guiltless. To admire, esteem, and prize you, as the
most accomplished of women, and the first of friends—if these are
crimes, I am the most offending thing alive.

In a face where I used to meet the kind complacency of friendly
confidence, *now* to find cold neglect and contemptuous scorn, is a
wrench that my heart can ill bear. It is, however, some kind of
miserable good-luck, that while *de haut-en-bas* rigour may depress
an unoffending wretch to the ground, it has a tendency to rouse a

stubborn something in his bosom, which, though it cannot heal the wounds of his soul, is at least an opiate to blunt their poignancy.

With the profoundest respect for your abilities ; the most sincere esteem and ardent regard for your gentle heart and amiable manners ; and the most fervent wish and prayer for your welfare, peace, and bliss—I have the honour to be, madam, your most devoted humble servant, R. B.

CCCVII.

TO THE SAME.

I HAVE this moment got the song from Syme, and I am sorry to see that he has spoilt it a good deal. It shall be a lesson to me how I lend him anything again.

I have sent you *Werter*, truly happy to have any, the smallest, opportunity of obliging you.

'Tis true, madam, I saw you once since I was at Woodley; and that once froze the very life-blood of my heart. Your reception of me was such that a wretch meeting the eye of his judge, about to pronounce sentence of death on him, could only have envied my feelings and situation. But I hate the theme, and nevei more shall write or speak on it.

One thing I shall proudly say, that I can pay Mrs R. a highei tribute of esteem, and appreciate her amiable worth more truly than any man whom I have seen approach her. R. B.

CCCVIII.

TO MR ALEXANDER CUNNINGHAM.

25th February 1794.

CANST thou minister to a mind diseased ? Canst thou speak peace and rest to a soul tost on a sea of troubles, without one friendly star to guide her course, and dreading that the next surge may overwhelm her ? Canst thou give to a frame, trembling alive as the tortures of suspense, the stability and hardihood of the rock that braves the blast ? If thou canst not do the least of these, why wouldst thou disturb me in my miseries with thy inquiries after me ?

For these two months I have not been able to lift a pen. My constitution and frame were, *ab origine*, blasted with a deep, incurable taint of hypochondria, which poisons my existence. Ol late, a number of domestic vexations, and some pecuniary share

in the ruin of these wretched times,—losses which, though trifling,
were yet what I could ill bear,—have so irritated me, that my
feelings at times could only be envied by a reprobate spirit listen-
ing to the sentence that dooms it to perdition,

Are you deep in the language of consolation? I have exhausted
in reflection every topic of comfort. *A heart at ease* would have
been charmed with my sentiments and reasonings; but as to
myself, I was like Judas Iscariot preaching the gospel: he might
melt and mould the hearts of those around him, but his own kept
its native incorrigibility.

Still, there are two great pillars that bear us up amid the wreck
of misfortune and misery. The ONE is composed of the different
modifications of a certain noble, stubborn something in man,
known by the names of Courage, Fortitude, Magnanimity. The
OTHER is made up of those feelings and sentiments which, how-
ever the sceptic may deny them, or the enthusiast disfigure them,
are yet, I am convinced, original and component parts of the
human soul; those *senses of the mind*—if I may be allowed the
expression—which connect us with, and link us to those awful
obscure realities—an all-powerful and equally beneficent God,
and a world to come, beyond death and the grave. The first gives
the nerve of combat, while a ray of hope beams on the field; the
last pours the balm of comfort into the wounds which time can
never cure.

I do not remember, my dear Cunningham, that you and I ever
talked on the subject of religion at all. I know some who laugh
at it as the trick of the crafty FEW to lead the undiscerning
MANY; or, at most, as an uncertain obscurity which mankind
can never know anything of, and with which they are fools if they
give themselves much to do. Nor would I quarrel with a man
for his irreligion any more than I would for his want of a musical
ear. I would regret that he was shut out from what, to me and to
others, were such superlative sources of enjoyment. It is in this
point of view, and for this reason, that I will deeply imbue the
mind of every child of mine with religion. If my son should
happen to be a man of feeling, sentiment, and taste, I shall thus
add largely to his enjoyments. Let me flatter myself that this
sweet little fellow, who is just now running about my desk, will
be a man of a melting, ardent, glowing heart; and an imagination
delighted with the painter, and wrapt with the poet. Let me
figure him wandering out in a sweet evening, to inhale the balmy
gales, and enjoy the growing luxuriance of the spring; himself
the while in the blooming youth of life. He looks abroad on all
nature, and through nature up to nature's God. His soul, by
swift, delighting degrees, is wrapt above this sublunary sphere,
until he can be silent no longer, and bursts out into the glorious
enthusiasm of Thomson—

"These, as they change, Almighty Father, these
Are but the varied God. The rolling year
Is full of thee;"

and so on, in all the spirit and ardour of that charming hymn. These are no ideal pleasures—they are real delights; and I ask, what of the delights among the sons of men are superior, not to say equal, to them? And they have this precious, vast addition, that conscious Virtue stamps them for her own, and lays hold on them to bring herself into the presence of a witnessing, judging, and approving God. R. B.

CCCIX.
TO MR JAMES JOHNSON.

DUMFRIES, *February* 1794.

MY DEAR SIR,—I send you, by my friend Mr Wallace forty-one songs for your fifth volume. Mr Clarke has also a good many, if he have not, with his usual indolence, *cast them at the cocks.* I have still a good parcel amongst my hands in scraps and fragments; so that I hope we will make shift with our last volume.

You should have heard from me long ago; but over and above some vexatious share in the pecuniary losses of these accursed times, I have all this winter been plagued with low spirits and blue devils; so that *I have almost hung my harp on the willow-trees.*

In the meantime, at your leisure, give a copy of the *Museum* to my worthy friend, Mr Peter Hill, bookseller, to bind for me, interleaved with blank leaves, exactly as he did the Laird of Glenriddel's, that I may insert every anecdote I can learn, together with my own criticisms and remarks on the songs. A copy of this kind I shall leave with you, the editor, to publish at some after-period, by way of making the *Museum* a book famous to the end of time, and you renowned for ever.

I have got a Highland dirk, for which I have great veneration, as it once was the dirk of Lord Balmerino. It fell into bad hands, who stripped it of the silver-mounting, as well as the knife and fork. I have some thoughts of sending it to your care, to get it mounted anew. Our friend Clarke owes me an account, somewhere about one pound, which would go a good way in paying the expense. I remember you once settled an account in this way before, and as you still have money-matters to settle with him, you might accommodate us both. . . . My best compliments to your worthy old father and your better-half. Yours, R. B.

CCCX.

TO MISS ———.

DUMFRIES, *May or June* 1794 ?

MADAM,—Nothing short of a kind of absolute necessity could have made me trouble you with this letter. Except my ardent and just esteem for your sense, taste, and worth, every sentiment arising in my breast, as I put pen to paper to you, is painful. The scenes I have passed with the friend of my soul, and his amiable connections ! the wrench at my heart to think that he is gone, for ever gone, from me, never more to meet in the wander-ings of a weary world ! and the cutting reflection of all, that I had most unfortunately, though most undeservedly, lost the confi-dence of that soul of worth, ere it took its flight !—these, madam, are sensations of no ordinary anguish. However you also may be offended with some *imputed* improprieties of mine ; sensibility you know I possess, and sincerity none will deny me.

To oppose those prejudices which have been raised against me, is not the business of this letter. Indeed, it is a warfare I know not how to wage. The powers of positive vice I can in some degree calculate, and against direct malevolence I can be on my guard ; but who can estimate the fatuity of giddy caprice, or ward off the unthinking mischief of precipitate folly ?.

I have a favour to request of you, madam, and of your sister, Mrs Riddell, through your means. You know that, at the wish of my late friend, I made a collection of all my trifles in verse which I had ever written. They are many of them local, some of them puerile and silly, and all of them unfit for the public eye. As I have some little fame at stake,—a fame that I trust may live when the hate of those " who watch for my halting," and the con-tumelious sneer of those whom accident has made my superiors, will, with themselves, be gone to the regions of oblivion,—I am uneasy now for the fate of those manuscripts. Will Mrs Riddel have the goodness to destroy them, or return them to me ? As a pledge of friendship they were bestowed ; and that circumstance, indeed, was all their merit. Most unhappily for me, that merit they no longer possess ; and I hope that Mrs Riddel's goodness, which I well know, and ever will revere, will not refuse this favour to a man whom she once held in some degree of estimation.

With the sincerest esteem, I have the honour to be, madam, &c.,

R. B.

CCCXI.

TO MR THOMSON.

May 1794.

MY DEAR SIR,—I return you the plates, with which I am highly pleased ; I would humbly propose, instead of the younker knitting stockings, to put a stock and horn into his hands. A friend of mine, who is positively the ablest judge on the subject I have ever met with, and though an unknown, is yet a superior artist with the burin, is quite charmed with Allan's manner. I got him a peep of the *Gentle Shepherd ;* and he pronounces Allan a most original artist of great excellence.

For my part, I look on Mr Allan's choosing my favourite poem for his subject, to be one of the highest compliments I have ever received.

I am quite vexed at Pleyel's being cooped up in France, as it will put an entire stop to our work. Now, and for six or seven months, I shall be quite in song, as you shall see by and by. I know you value a composition because it is made by one of the great ones as little as I do. However, I got an air, pretty enough, composed by Lady Elizabeth Heron of Heron, which she calls *The Banks of Cree.* Cree is a beautiful romantic stream ; and as her ladyship is a particular friend of mine, I have written the following song to it (p. 282). R. B.

CCCXII.

TO DAVID M'CULLOCH, ESQ.

DUMFRIES, 21st *June* 1794.

MY DEAR SIR,—My long-projected journey through your country is at last fixed ; and on Wednesday next, if you have nothing of more importance to do, take a saunter down to Gatehouse about two or three o'clock ; I shall be happy to take a draught of M'Kune's best with you. Collector Syme will be at Glen's about that time, and will meet us about dish-of-tea hour. Syme goes also to Kerrochtree ; and let me remind you of your kind promise to accompany me there. I will need all the friends I can muster, for I am indeed ill at ease when I approach your honourables and right honourables. Yours sincerely, R. B.

CCCXIII.

TO MRS DUNLOP.

CASTLE-DOUGLAS, 25th *June* 1794.

HERE, in a solitary inn, in a solitary village, am I set by myself, to amuse my brooding fancy as I may. Solitary confinement, you know, is Howard's favourite idea of reclaiming sinners ; so let me consider by what fatality it happens that I have so long been so exceeding sinful as to neglect the correspondence of the most valued friend I have on earth. To tell you that I have been in poor health will not be excuse enough, though it is true. I am afraid that I am about to suffer for the follies of my youth. My medical friends threaten me with a flying gout; but I trust they are mistaken.

I am just going to trouble your critical patience with the first sketch of a stanza I have been framing as I passed along the road. The subject is Liberty: you know, my honoured friend, how dear the theme is to me. I design it as an irregular ode for General Washington's birthday. After having mentioned the degeneracy of other kingdoms, I come to Scotland thus (*Thee, Caledonia*, p. 175).

You will probably have another scrawl from me in a stage or two.   R. B.

CCCXIV.

TO CLARINDA.

BEFORE you ask me why I have not written you, first let me be informed by you, *how* I shall write you? " In friendship," you say; and I have many a time taken up my pen to try an epistle of " friendship" to you, but it will not do; 'tis like Jove grasping a pop-gun after having wielded his thunder. When I take up the pen, recollection ruins me. Ah, my ever dearest Clarinda! What a host of Memory's tenderest offspring crowd on my fancy at that sound! But I must not indulge that subject · you have forbid it.

I am extremely happy to learn that your precious health is re-established, and that you are once more fit to enjoy that satisfaction in existence which health alone can give us. My old friend Ainslie has indeed been kind to you. Tell him that I envy him the power of serving you. I had a letter from him awhile ago, but it was so dry, so distant, so like a card to one of his clients, that I could scarce bear to read it, and have not yet answered it. He is a good, honest fellow, and *can* write a friendly letter, which would do equal honour to his head and his heart, as a whole sheaf of his letters which I have by me will witness; and though Fame does not blow her trumpet at my approach *now* as she did *then*, when he first honoured me with his friendship, yet I am as proud as ever; and when I am laid in my grave, I wish to be stretched at my full length, that I may occupy every inch of ground I have a right to.

You would laugh were you to see me where I am just now. Would that you were here to laugh with me, though I am afraid that crying would be our first employment! Here am I set, a solitary hermit, in the solitary room of a solitary inn, with a solitary bottle of wine by me, as grave and as stupid as an owl, but, like that owl, still faithful to my old song; in confirmation of which, my dear Mrs Mac, here is your good health! May the hand-waled benisons o' Heaven bless your bonny face. Amen.

You must know, my dearest madam, that these now many years, wherever I am, in whatever company, when a married lady is called as a toast, I constantly give you; but as your name has never passed my lips, even to my most intimate friend, I give you by the name of Mrs Mac. This is so well known among my acquaintances, that when any married lady is called for, the toast-master will say, "Oh, we need not ask him who it is: here's Mrs Mac!" I have also, among my convivial friends, set on foot a round of toasts, which I call a round of Arcadian Shepherdesses —that is, a round of favourite ladies, under female names cele-brated in ancient song; and then you are my Clarinda. So, my lovely Clarinda, I devote this glass of wine to a most ardent wish for you happiness.

> In vain would Prudence, with decorous sneer,
> Point out a censuring world, and bid me fear
> Above that world on wings of love I rise,
> I know its worst, and can that worst despise.
>
> " Wronged, injured, shunned, unpitied, unredrest;
> The mocked quotation of the scorner's jest"—
> Let Prudence' direst bodements on me fall,
> Clarinda, rich reward! o'erpays them all.

I have been rhyming a little of late, but I do not know if they are worth postage.

Tell me what you think of the following monody. * * *

The subject of the foregoing is a woman of fashion in this country, with whom at one period I was well acquainted. By some scandalous conduct to me, and two or three other gentlemen here as well as me, she steered so far to the north of my good opinion, that I have made her the theme of several ill-natured things. The following epigram (*Monody*, p. 172) struck me the other day as I passed her carriage. * * * SYLVANDER.

CCCXV.

TO MR THOMSON.

July 1794.

Is there no news yet of Pleyel? Or is your work to be at a dead stop until the allies set our modern Orpheus at liberty from the savage thraldom of democrat discords? Alas the day! And wo is me! That auspicious period, pregnant with the happiness of millions * * * seems by no means near.

I have presented a copy of your songs to the daughter of a much-valued and much-honoured friend of mine, Mr Graham of

Fintry. I wrote on the blank side of the title-page the follow-
ing address to the young lady (p. 175).   R. B.

CCCXVI.

TO MR THOMSON.

30th August 1794.

THE last evening, as I was straying out, and thinking of *O'er
the Hills and far away,* I spun the following stanza (p. 282) for it;
but whether my spinning will deserve to be laid up in store like
the precious thread of the silkworm, or brushed away like the
vile manufacture of the spider, I leave, my dear sir, to your
usual candid criticism. I was pleased with several lines in it at
first, but I own that now it appears rather a flimsy business.

This is just a hasty sketch until I see whether it be worth a
critique. We have many sailor-songs, but as far as I at present
recollect, they are mostly the effusions of the jovial sailor, not the
wailings of his love-lorn mistress. I must here make one sweet
exception—*Sweet Annie frae the Sea-beach came.*

I give you leave to abuse this song, but do it in the spirit of
Christian meekness.   R. B.

CCCXVII.

TO MR THOMSON.

Sept. 1794.

I SHALL withdraw my *On the Seas and far away* altogether: it
is unequal, and unworthy the work. Making a poem is like be-
getting a son; you cannot know whether you have a wise man or
a fool until you produce him to the world to try him.

For that reason, I send you the offspring of my brain, abor-
tions and all; and, as such, pray look over them, and forgive
them, and burn them. I am flattered at your adopting *Ca' the
Yowes to the Knowes,* as it was owing to me that ever it saw the
light. About seven years ago, I was well acquainted with a
worthy little fellow of a clergyman, a Mr Clunie, who sang it
charmingly; and, at my request, Mr Clarke took it down from his
singing. When I gave it to Johnson, I added some stanzas to the
song, and mended others; but still it will not do for you. In a
solitary stroll which I took to-day, I tried my hand on a few pas-
toral lines, following up the idea of the chorus, which I would pre-
serve. Here it is, with all its crudities and imperfections on its
head (p. 283).

I shall give you my opinion of your other newly-adopted songs
my first scribbling fit.   R. B.

CCCXVIII.

TO MR THOMSON.

Sept. **1794.**

Do you know an Irish song called *Onagh's Waterfall?* Our friend Cunningham sings it delightfully. The air is charming, and I have often regretted the want of decent verses to it. It is too much, at least for my humble rustic Muse, to expect that every effort of hers shall have merit; still, I think that it is better to have mediocre verses to a favourite air than none at all. On this principle I have all along proceeded in the *Scots Musical Museum;* and as that publication is at its last volume, I intend the following song (p. 284), to the air above mentioned, for that work.

If it does not suit you as an editor, you may be pleased to have verses to it that you can sing in the company of ladies.

Not to compare small things with great, my taste in music is like the mighty Frederick of Prussia's taste in painting. We are told that he frequently admired what the connoisseurs decried, and always, without any hypocrisy, confessed his admiration. I am sensible that my taste in music must be inelegant and vulgar, because people of undisputed and cultivated taste can find no merit in my favourite tunes. Still, because I am cheaply pleased, is that any reason why I should deny myself that pleasure? Many of our strathspeys, ancient and modern, give me most exquisite enjoyment, where you and other judges would probably be showing disgust. For instance, I am just now making verses for *Rothemurchie's Rant,* an air which puts me in raptures; and, in fact, unless I be pleased with the tune, I never can make verses to it. Here I have Clarke on my side, who is a judge that I will pit against any of you. *Rothemurchie,* he says, " is an air both original and beautiful;" and on his recommendation I have taken the first part of the tune for a chorus, and the fourth or last part for the song. I am but two stanzas deep in the work, and possibly you may think, and justly, that the poetry is as little worth your attention as the music.

I have begun anew, *Let me in this ae Night.* Do you think that we ought to retain the old chorus? I think we must retain both the old chorus and the first stanza of the old song. I do not altogether like the third line of the first stanza, but cannot alter it to please myself. I am just three stanzas deep in it. Would you have the *denouement* to be successful or otherwise?—should she " let him in" or not?

Did you not once propose *The Sow's Tail to Geordie* as an air for your work? I am quite delighted with it; but I acknowledge that is no mark of its real excellence. I once set about verses for it, which I meant to be in the alternate way of a lover and his

mistress chanting together. I have not the pleasure of knowing
Mrs Thomson's Christian name, and yours, I am afraid, is rather
burlesque for sentiment, else I had meant to have made you [two]
the hero and heroine of the little piece.

How do you like the following epigram, which I wrote the other
day on a lovely young girl's recovery from a fever ? Dr Maxwell
was the physician who seemingly saved her from the grave ; and
to him I address the following (p. 178).   R. B.

                            CCCXIX.

                       TO MR THOMSON.

                                             19th October 1794.
My dear Friend,—By this morning's post I have your list,
and, in general, I highly approve of it. I shall, at more leisure,
give you a critique on the whole. Clarke goes to your town by
to-day's fly, and I wish you would call on him, and take his opi-
nion in general : you know his taste is a standard. He will return
here again in a week or two, so please do not miss asking for him.
One thing I hope he will do, which would give me high satisfac-
tion—persuade you to adopt my favourite, *Craigieburn Wood*, in
your selection : it is as great a favourite of his as of mine. The
lady on whom it was made is one of the finest women in Scotland ;
and, in fact (*entre nous*), is in a manner to me what Sterne's Eliza
was to him—a mistress, or friend, or what you will, in the guile-
less simplicity of Platonic love. (Now, don't put any of your
squinting constructions on this, or have any clishmaclaver about
it among our acquaintances.) I assure you, that to my lovely
friend you are indebted for many of your best songs of mine. Do
you think that the sober, gin-horse routine of existence could in-
spire a man with life, and love, and joy—could fire him with en-
thusiasm, or melt him with pathos, equal to the genius of your
book ? No—no! Whenever I want to be more than ordinary in
song—to be in some degree equal to your diviner airs—do you
imagine I fast and pray for the celestial emanation? *Tout au
contraire!* I have a glorious recipe ; the very one that for his
own use was invented by the divinity of healing and poetry, when
erst he piped to the flocks of Admetus. I put myself in a regimen
of admiring a fine woman ; and, in proportion to the adorability
of her charms, in proportion you are delighted with my verses.
The lightning of her eye is the godhead of Parnassus, and the
witchery of her smile the divinity of Helicon!

To descend to the business with which I began : If you like my
idea of *When she cam ben she bobbit*, the following stanzas of mine
(p. 285), altered a little from what they were formerly, when set
to another air, may perhaps do instead of worse stanzas.

Now for a few miscellaneous remarks. *The Posie* (in the *Museum*) is my composition; the air was taken down from Mrs Burns's voice. It is well known in the west country, but the old words are trash. By the by, take a look at the tune again, and tell me if you do not think it is the original from which *Roslin Castle* is composed. The second part, in particular, for the first two or three bars, is exactly the old air. *Strathallan's Lament* is mine; the music is by our right trusty and deservedly well-beloved Allan Masterton. *Donocht-Head* is not mine; I would give ten pounds it were. It appeared first in the *Edinburgh Herald*, and came to the editor of that paper with the Newcastle post-mark on it. *Whistle o'er the Lave o't* is mine; the music said to be by a John Bruce, a celebrated violin-player in Dumfries about the beginning of this century. This I know—Bruce, who was an honest man, though a red-wud Highlandman, constantly claimed it; and by the old musical people here is believed to be the author of it.

Andrew and his Cutty Gun.—The song to which this is set in the *Museum* is mine, and was composed on Miss Euphemia Murray, of Lintrose, commonly and deservedly called The Flower of Strathmore.

How long and dreary is the Night!—I met with some such words in a collection of songs somewhere, which I altered and enlarged; and to please you, and to suit your favourite air, I have taken a stride or two across my room, and have arranged it anew, as you will find on the other page (p. 285).

Tell me how you like this. I differ from your idea of the expression of the tune. There is, to me, a great deal of tenderness in it. You cannot, in my opinion, dispense with a bass to your addenda airs. A lady of my acquaintance, a noted performer, plays *Nae luck about the House*, and sings it at the same time so charmingly, that I shall never bear to see any of her songs sent into the world as naked as Mr What-d'ye-call-um has done in his London collection.

These English songs gravel me to death. I have not that command of the language that I have of my native tongue. In fact, I think my ideas are more barren in English than in Scotch. I have been at *Duncan Gray*, to dress it in English, but all I can do is deplorably stupid. For instance (*Let not Woman*, p. 286).

Since the above, I have been out in the country taking a dinner with a friend, where I met with the lady whom I mentioned in the second page in this odds-and-ends of a letter. As usual, I got into song; and, returning home, I composed the following (*The Lover's*, &c., p. 286).

If you honour my verses by setting the air to them, I will vamp up the old song, and make it English enough to be understood.

I enclose you a musical curiosity, an East Indian air, which you would swear was a Scottish one. I know the authenticity of it,

as the gentleman who brought it over is a particular acquaintance
of mine. Do preserve me the copy I send you, as it is the only one
I have. Clarke has set a bass to it, and I intend putting it into
the *Musical Museum*. Here follow the verses I intend for it
(*The Auld Man*, p. 287).

I would be obliged to you if you would procure me a sight of
Ritson's collection of English songs which you mention in your
letter. I will thank you for another information, and that as
speedily as you please : whether this miserable, drawling, hotch-
potch epistle has not completely tired you of my correspondence.

R. B.

CCCXX.

TO MR PETER HILL, EDINBURGH.

DUMFRIES, October 1794.

MY DEAR HILL,—By a carrier of yesterday, Henry Osborn by
name, I sent you a kippered* salmon, which I trust you will duly
receive, and which I also trust will give you many a toothful of
satisfaction. If you have the confidence to say that there is any-
thing of the kind in all your great city superior to this in true
kipper relish and flavour, I will be revenged by—not sending you
another next season. In return, the first party of friends that
dine with you—provided that your fellow-travellers and my
trusty and well-beloved veterans in intimacy, Messrs Ramsay and
Cameron, be of the party—about that time in the afternoon when
a relish or devil becomes grateful, give them two or three slices
of the kipper, and drink a bumper to your friends in Dumfries.
Moreover, by last Saturday's fly I sent you a hare, which I hope
came, and carriage-free, safe to your hospitable mansion and
social table. So much for business.

My best good-wishes to Mrs Hill ; and believe me to be, ever
yours,   R. BURNS.

CCCXXI.

TO MR THOMSON,

November 1794.

MANY thanks to you, my dear sir, for your present ; it is a
book of the utmost importance to me. I have yesterday begun my
anecdotes, &c., for your work. I intend drawing them up in the
form of a letter to you, which will save me from the tedious, dull
business of systematic arrangement. Indeed, as all I have to say
consists of unconnected remarks, anecdotes, scraps of old songs,
&c., it would be impossible to give the work a beginning, a middle

* Dried and cured.

and an end, which the critics insist to be absolutely necessary in a work. In my last, I told you my objections to the song you had selected for *My Lodging is on the cold Ground*. On my visit the other day to my fair Chloris—that is the poetic name of the lovely goddess of my inspiration—she suggested an idea, which I, on my return from the visit, wrought into the following song (p. 287).

How do you like the simplicity and tenderness of this pastoral ? I think it pretty well.

I like you for entering so candidly and so kindly into the story of "*ma chere amie.*" I assure you, I was never more in earnest in my life, than in the account of that affair which I sent you in my last. Conjugal love is a passion which I deeply feel and highly venerate ; but, somehow, it does not make such a figure in poesy as that other species of the passion—

"Where Love is liberty and Nature law."

Musically speaking, the first is an instrument of which the gamut is scanty and confined, but the tones inexpressibly sweet, while the last has powers equal to all the intellectual modulations of the human soul. Still, I am a very poet in my enthusiasm of the passion. The welfare and happiness of the beloved object is the first and inviolate sentiment that pervades my soul ; and whatever pleasures I might wish for, or whatever might be the raptures they would give me, yet if they interfere with that first principle, it is having these pleasures at a dishonest price ; and justice forbids, and generosity disdains, the purchase ! . . . .

Despairing of my own powers to give you variety enough in English songs, I have been turning over old collections to pick out songs, of which the measure is something similar to what I want ; and, with a little alteration, so as to suit the rhythm of the air exactly, to give you them for your work. Where the songs have hitherto been but little noticed, nor have ever been set to music, I think the shift a fair one. A song which, under the same first verse, you will find in Ramsay's *Tea-Table Miscellany*, I have cut down for an English dress to your *Dainty Davie*, as follows (p. 288).

You may think meanly of this, but take a look at the bombast original, and you will be surprised that I have made so much of it. I have finished my song to *Rothemurchie's Rant* (p. 288), and you have Clarke to consult as to the set of the air for singing.

This piece has at least the merit of being a regular pastoral the vernal morn, the summer noon, the autumnal evening, and the winter night, are regularly rounded. If you like it, well ; if not, I will insert it in the *Museum*.

I am out of temper that you should set so sweet, so tender an air as *Deil tak' the Wars* to the foolish old verses. You talk of the silliness of *Saw ye My Father ?* The odds is gold to brass ! Besides, the old song, though now pretty well modernized into the

Scottish language, is originally, and in the early editions, a bung-
ling low imitation of the Scottish manner, by that genius, Tom
D'Urfey, so has no pretension to be a Scottish production.
There is a pretty English song by Sheridan, in the *Duenna*, to
this air, which is out of sight superior to D'Urfey's. It begins—
    " When sable night each drooping plant restoring."
The air, if I understand the expression of it properly, is the
very native language of simplicity, tenderness, and love. I have
again gone over my song to the tune as follows (p. 286).

There is another air, *The Caledonian Hunt's Delight*, to which
I wrote a song that you will find in Johnson, *Ye Banks and Braes
o' Bonnie Doon ;* this air, I think, might find a place among your
hundred, as Lear says of his knights. Do you know the history
of the air ? It is curious enough. A good many years ago, Mr
James Miller, writer in your good town, a gentleman whom pos-
sibly you know, was in company with our friend Clarke ; and
talking of Scottish music, Miller expressed an ardent ambition
to be able to compose a Scots air. Mr Clarke, partly by way of
joke, told him to keep to the black keys of the harpsichord, and
preserve some kind of rhythm, and he would infallibly compose a
Scots air. Certain it is that, in a few days, Mr Miller produced
the rudiments of an air, which Mr Clarke, with some touches and
corrections, fashioned into the tune in question. Ritson, you
know, has the same story of the black keys ; but this account
which I have just given you, Mr Clarke informed me of several
years ago. Now, to show you how difficult it is to trace the origin
of our airs, I have heard it repeatedly asserted that this was an
Irish air : nay, I met with an Irish gentleman who affirmed that
he heard it in Ireland among the old women ; while, on the other
hand, a lady of fashion, no less than a countess, informed me
that the first person who introduced the air into this country
was a baronet's lady of her acquaintance, who took down the
notes from an itinerant piper in the Isle of Man. How difficult,
then, to ascertain the truth respecting our poesy and music ! I
myself have lately seen a couple of ballads sung through the
streets of Dumfries, with my name at the head of them as the
author, though it was the first time I had ever seen them.

I thank you for admitting *Craigieburn Wood*, and I shall take
care to furnish you with a new chorus. In fact, the chorus was
not my work, but a part of some old verses to the air. If I can
catch myself in a more than ordinarily propitious moment, I shall
write a new *Craigieburn Wood* altogether. My heart is much in
the theme.

I am ashamed, my dear fellow, to make the request—'tis dun-
ning your generosity ; but in a moment when I had forgotten
whether I was rich or poor, I promised Chloris a copy of your
songs. It rings my honest pride to write you this ; but an un-

gracious request is doubly so by a tedious apology. To make you some amends, as soon as I have extracted the necessary informa-mation out of them, I will return you Ritson's volumes.

The lady is not a little proud that she is to make so distinguished a figure in your collection, and I am not a little proud that I have it in my power to please her so much. Lucky it is for your patience that my paper is done, for when I am in a scribbling humour, I know not when to give over. R. B.

CCCXXII.

TO MR THOMSON.

19th November 1794.

You see, my dear sir, what a punctual correspondent I am , though, indeed, you may thank yourself for the *tedium* of my letters, as you have so flattered me on my horsemanship with my favourite hobby, and have praised the grace of his ambling so much, that I am scarcely ever off his back. For instance, this morning, though a keen-blowing frost, in my walk before break-fast, I finished my duet, which you were pleased to praise so much. Whether I have uniformly succeeded, I will not say ; but here it is for you, though it is not an hour old (*Philly and Willy*, p. 289). Tell me honestly how you like it, and point out whatever you think faulty.

I am much pleased with your idea of singing our songs in alter-nate stanzas, and regret that you did not hint it to me sooner. In those that remain, I shall have it in my eye. I remember your objections to the name Philly, but it is the common abbrevia-tion of Phillis. Sally, the only other name that suits, has, to my ear, a vulgarity about it which unfits it for anything except bur-lesque. The legion of Scottish poetasters of the day, whom your brother-editor, Mr Ritson, ranks with me as my coevals, have always mistaken vulgarity for simplicity ; whereas, simplicity is as much *eloignée* from vulgarity on the one hand, as from affected point and puerile conceit on the other.

I agree with you as to the air *Craigieburn Wood*, that a chorus would in some degree spoil the effect, and shall certainly have none in my projected song to it. It is not, however, a case in point with *Rothemurchie ;* there, as in *Roy's Wife of Aldivalloch*, a chorus goes, to my taste, well enough. As to the chorus going first, that is the case with *Roy's Wife*, as well as *Rothemurchie.* In fact, in the first part of both tunes the rhythm is so peculiar and irregular, and on that irregularity depends so much of their beauty, that we must e'en take them with all their wildness, and humour the verse accordingly. Leaving out the starting note in

both tunes has, I think, an effect that no regularity could counter
balance the want of.

> Try   { O Roy's wife of Aldivalloch.
>   { O lassie wi' the lint-white locks.
> and
> compare with { Roy's wife of Aldivalloch.
>   { Lassie wi' the lint-white locks.

Does not the tameness of the prefixed syllable strike you ? In the
last case, with the true furor of genius, you strike at once into the
wild originality of the air ; whereas in the first insipid method, it
is like the grating screw of the pins before the fiddle is brought
into tune. This is my taste ; if I am wrong, I beg pardon of the
cognoscenti.

   The Caledonian Hunt is so charming, that it would make any
subject in a song go down ; but pathos is certainly its native
tongue. Scottish bacchanalians we certainly want, though the
few we have are excellent. For instance, *Todlin Hame* is, for wit
and humour, an unparalleled composition ; and *Andrew and his
Cutty Gun* is the work of a master. By the way, are you not quite
vexed to think that those men of genius—for such they certainly
were—who composed our fine Scottish lyrics, should be unknown ?
It has given me many a heartache. Apropos to bacchanalian
songs in Scottish, I composed one yesterday for an air I like
much—*Lumps o' Pudding* (p. 290).

   If you do not relish this air, I will send it to Johnson.

   Since yesterday's penmanship, I have framed a couple of English
stanzas, by way of an English song to *Roy's Wife* (p. 290). You
will allow me, that in this instance my English corresponds in
sentiment with the Scottish.

   Well ! I think this, to be done in two or three turns across my
room, and with two or three pinches of Irish Blackguard, is not
so far amiss. You see I am determined to have my quantum of
applause from somebody.

   Tell my friend Allan—for I am sure that we only want the
trifling circumstance of being known to one another, to be the
best friends on earth—that I much suspect he has, in his plates,
mistaken the figure of the stock and horn. I have at last gotten
one, but it is a very rude instrument. It is composed of three
parts : the stock, which is the hinder thigh-bone of a sheep, such
as you see in a mutton ham ; the horn, which is a common High-
land cow's horn, cut off at the smaller end until the aperture be
large enough to admit the stock to be pushed up through the horn
until it be held by the thicker end of the thigh-bone ; and lastly,
an oaten reed, exactly cut and notched like that which you see
every shepherd-boy have when the corn-stems are green and full-
grown. The reed is not made fast in the bone, but is held by the
lips, and plays loose in the smaller end of the stock ; while the
stock, with the horn hanging on its larger end, is held by the
hands in playing. The stock has six or seven ventages on the

upper side, and one back-ventage, like the common flute. This of mine was made by a man from the Braes of Athole, and is exactly what the shepherds wont to use in that country.

However, either it is not quite properly bored in the holes or else we have not the art of blowing it rightly; for we can make little of it. If Mr Allan chooses, I will send him a sight of mine, as I look on myself to be a kind of brother-brush with him. "Pride in poets is nae sin;" and I will say it, that I look on Mr Allan and Mr Burns to be the only genuine and real painters of Scottish costume in the world.   R. B.

CCCXXIII.

TO PETER MILLER, JUN., ESQ.

DUMFRIES, *Nov.* 1794.

DEAR SIR,—Your offer is indeed truly generous, and most sincerely do I thank you for it; but in my present situation I find that I dare not accept it. You well know my political sentiments; and were I an insular individual, unconnected with a wife and a family of children, with the most fervid enthusiasm I would have volunteered my services: I then could and would have despised all consequences that might have ensued.

My prospect in the Excise is something; at least, it is—encumbered as I am with the welfare, the very existence, of near half-a-score of helpless individuals—what I dare not sport with.

In the meantime, they are most welcome to my Ode; only, let them insert it as a thing they have met with by accident, and unknown to me. Nay, if Mr Perry, whose honour, after your character of him, I cannot doubt, if he will give me an address and channel by which anything will come safe from those spies with which he may be certain that his correspondence is beset, I will now and then send him any bagatelle that I may write. In the present hurry of Europe, nothing but news and politics will be regarded; but against the days of peace, which Heaven send soon, my little assistance may perhaps fill up an idle column of a newspaper. I have long had it in my head to try my hand in the way of little prose essays, which I propose sending into the world through the medium of some newspaper; and should these be worth his while, to these Mr Perry shall be welcome: and all my reward shall be—his treating me with his paper, which, by the by, to anybody who has the least relish for wit, is a high treat indeed. With the most grateful esteem, I am ever, dear sir,

R. B.

CCCXXIV.

TO MRS DUNLOP,

IN LONDON.

DUMFRIES, *20th December* 1794

I HAVE been prodigiously disappointed in this London journey of yours. In the first place, when your last to me reached Dum‑fries, I was in the country, and did not return until too late to answer your letter ; in the next place, I thought you would cer‑tainly take this route ; and now I know not what has become of you, or whether this may reach you at all. God grant that it may find you and yours in prospering health and good spirits! Do let me hear from you the soonest possible.

As I hope to get a frank from my friend Captain Miller, I shall, every leisure hour, take up the pen, and gossip away whatever comes first—prose or poetry, sermon or song. In this last article I have abounded of late. I have often mentioned to you a superb publication of Scottish Songs, which is making its appear‑ance in your great metropolis, and where I have the honour to preside over the Scottish verse, as no less a personage than Peter Pindar does over the English.

December 29th.

Since I began this letter, I have been appointed to act in the capacity of supervisor here ; and I assure you, what with the load of business, and what with that business being new to me, I could scarcely have commanded ten minutes to have spoken to you had you been in town, much less to have written you an epistle. This appointment is only temporary, and during the illness of the present incumbent; but I look forward to an early period when I shall be appointed in full form—a consummation devoutly to be wished! My political sins seem to be forgiven me.

This is the season (New‑Year's Day is now my date) of wish‑ing : and mine are most fervently offered up for you! May life to you be a positive blessing while it lasts, for your own sake ; and that it may yet be greatly prolonged, is my wish for my own sake, and for the sake of the rest of your friends! What a transient business is life! Very lately, I was a boy; but t'other day I was a young man; and I already begin to feel the rigid fibre and stiffen‑ing joints of old age coming fast o'er my frame. With all my follies of youth, and, I fear, a few vices of manhood, still I con‑gratulate myself on having had, in early days, religion strongly impressed on my mind. I have nothing to say to any one as to which sect he belongs to, or what creed he believes ; but I look on the man who is firmly persuaded of Infinite Wisdom and Goodness superintending and directing every circumstance that can happen in his lot—I felicitate such a man as having a solid foundation for

his mental enjoyment—a firm prop and sure stay in the hour of
difficulty, trouble, and distress—and a never-failing anchor of hope
when he looks beyond the grave.

12th January [1795].

You will have seen our worthy and ingenious friend, the doctor
[Dr Moore], long ere this. I hope he is well, and beg to be re-
membered to him. I have just been reading over again, I daresay
for the hundred and fiftieth time, his *View of Society and Manners ;*
and still I read it with delight. His humour is perfectly original
—it is neither the humour of Addison, nor Swift, nor Sterne, nor
of anybody but Dr Moore. By the by, you have deprived me of
Zeluco ; remember that when you are disposed to rake up the sins
of my neglect from among the ashes of my laziness.

He has paid me a pretty compliment by quoting me in his last
publication. R. B.

CCCXXV.

[In the neighbourhood of Dumfries lived a farmer whom Burns fre-
quently visited. The farmer fell in love, and asked Burns to assist him
in framing a proper letter to the lady. Burns furnished him with the two
following drafts of a love-letter The farmer was successful in his
suit.]

MADAM,—What excuse to make for the liberty I am going to
assume in this letter, I am utterly at a loss. If the most unfeigned
respect for your accomplished worth—if the most ardent attach-
ment—if sincerity and truth—if these, on my part, will in any
degree weigh with you, my apology is these, and these alone.
Little as I have had the pleasure of your acquaintance, it has
been enough to convince me what enviable happiness must be his
whom you shall honour with your particular regard, and more
than enough to convince me how unworthy I am to offer myself
a candidate for that partiality. In this kind of trembling hope,
madam, I intend very soon doing myself the honour of waiting
on you, persuaded that, however little Miss G—— may be dispos-
ed to attend to the suit of a lover as unworthy of her as I am, she
is still too good to despise an honest man, whose only fault is lov-
ing her too much for his own peace. I have the honour to be,
madam, your most devoted humble servant.

DEAR MADAM,—The passion of love had need to be productive
of much delight ; as where it takes thorough possession of the man,
it almost unfits him for anything else. The lover who is certain
of an equal return of affection is surely the happiest of men ; but
he who is a prey to the horrors of anxiety and dreaded disappoint-
ment is a being whose situation is by no means enviable. Of this,

my present experience gives me sufficient proof. To me, amuse-
ment seems impertinent, and business intrusion, while you alone
engross every faculty of my mind. May I request you to drop
me a line, to inform me when I may wait on you; for pity's sake,
do; and let me have it soon. In the meantime, allow me, in all
the artless sincerity of truth, to assure you that I truly am, my
dearest madam, your ardent lover, and devoted humble servant.

CCCXXVI.

[The following note was written on behalf of a friend who complained
to Burns of the irregular delivery of the newspaper. From prudential
motives, it was never sent.]

TO THE EDITOR OF THE "MORNING CHRONICLE."*

SIR,—You will see, by your subscribers' list, that I have been
about nine months of that number.

I am sorry to inform you, that in that time seven or eight of
your papers either have never been sent me, or else have never
reached me. To be deprived of any one number of the first news-
paper in Great Britain for information, ability, and independence
is what I can ill brook and bear; but to be deprived of that most
admirable oration of the Marquis of Lansdowne, when he made
the great though ineffectual attempt (in the language of the poet,
I fear too true) "to save a SINKING STATE"—this was a loss that
I neither can nor will forgive you. That paper, sir, never reached
me; but I demand it of you. I am a BRITON, and must be
interested in the cause of LIBERTY; I am a MAN, and the RIGHTS
OF HUMAN NATURE cannot be indifferent to me. However, do
not let me mislead you—I am not a man in that situation of life
which, as your subscriber, can be of any consequence to you in
the eyes of those to whom SITUATION OF LIFE ALONE is the
criterion of MAN. I am but a plain tradesman in this distant,
obscure country-town; but that humble domicile in which I shel-
ter my wife and children is the CASTELLUM of a BRITON; and
that scanty, hard-earned income which supports them is as truly
my property as the most magnificent fortune of the most PUIS-
SANT MEMBER of your HOUSE OF NOBLES.

These sir, are my sentiments, and to them I subscribe my
name; and were I a man of ability and consequence enough to
address the PUBLIC, with that name should they appear. I am,
&c.

CCCXXVII.

TO MR THOMSON.

January 1795.

I FEAR for my songs; however, a few may please, yet originality is a coy feature in composition, and in a multiplicity of efforts in the same style, disappears altogether. For these three thousand years, we poetic folks have been describing the spring, for instance; and as the spring continues the same, there must soon be a sameness in the imagery, &c., of these said rhyming folks. . . . .

A great critic (Aikin) on songs says, that love and wine are the exclusive themes for song-writing. The following is on neither subject, and consequently is no song, but will be allowed, I think, to be two or three pretty good prose thoughts inverted into rhyme (p. 291).

Jan. 15*th.*—The foregoing has lain by me this fortnight, for want of a spare moment. The supervisor of excise here being ill, I have been acting for him, and I assure you I have hardly five minutes to myself to thank you for your elegant present of Pindar. The typography is admirable, and worthy of the truly original bard.

I do not give you the foregoing song for your book, but merely by way of *vive la bagatelle;* for the piece is not really poetry.

R. B.

CCCXXVIII.

TO MRS RIDDEL.

MR BURNS'S compliments to Mrs Riddel—is much obliged to her for her polite attention in sending him the book. Owing to Mr B. at present acting as supervisor of Excise, a department that occupies his every hour of the day, he has not that time to spare which is necessary for any belles-lettres pursuit; but as he will in a week or two again return to his wonted leisure, he will then pay that attention to Mrs R.'s beautiful song, *To thee, loved Nith,* which it so well deserves. When *Anacharsis's Travels* come to hand, which Mrs Riddel mentioned as her gift to the public library, Mr B. will feel honoured by the indulgence of a perusal of them before presentation. It is a book he has never yet seen, and the regulations of the library allow too little leisure for deliberate reading.

Friday evening.

P.S.—Mr Burns will be much obliged to Mrs Riddel, if she will favour him with a perusal of any of her poetical pieces which he may not have seen.

CCCXXIX.

TO MR THOMSON.

ECCLEFECHAN, *7th February* 1795.

MY DEAR THOMSON,—You cannot have any idea of the predi· cament in which I write to you. In the course of my duty as supervisor—in which capacity I have acted of late—I came yester· night to this unfortunate, wicked little village. I have gone for· ward, but snows of ten feet deep have impeded my progress; I have tried to *gae back the gait* I *cam again,* but the same obstacle has shut me up within insuperable bars. To add to my misfor· tune, since dinner, a scraper has been torturing catgut, in sounds that would have insulted the dying agonies of a sow under the hands of a butcher, and thinks himself, on that very account, ex· ceeding good company. In fact, I have been in a dilemma, either to get drunk, to forget these miseries; or to hang myself, to get rid of them. Like a prudent man—a character congenial to my every thought, word, and deed—I, of two evils, have chosen the least, and am very drunk, at your service!

I wrote you yesterday from Dumfries. I had not time then to tell you all I wanted to say, and at present I have not capacity.

Do you know an air—I am sure you must know it—*We'll gang nae mair to yon Town?* I think, in slowish time, it would make an excellent song. I am highly delighted with it; and if you should think it worthy of your attention, I have a fair dame in my eye, to whom I would consecrate it. Try it with this doggrel (p. 299)—until I give you a better.

As I am just going to bed, I wish you a good-night. R. B.

P.S.—As I am likely to be storm-staid here to-morrow, if I am in the humour, you shall have a long letter from me.

CCCXXX.

TO MR HERON OF HERON.

SIR,—I enclose you some copies of a couple of political ballads, one of which, I believe, you have never seen. Would to Heaven I could make you master of as many votes in the Stewartry—but—

> Who does the utmost that he can,
> Does well, acts nobly—angels could no more.

In order to bring my humble efforts to bear with more effect on the foe, I have privately printed a good many copies of both ballads, and have sent them among friends all about the country.

To pillory on Parnassus the rank reprobation of character, the utter dereliction of all principle, in a profligate junto, which has

not only outraged virtue, but violated common decency, spurning
even hypocrisy as paltry iniquity below their daring—to unmask
their flagitiousness to the broadest day—to deliver such over to
their merited fate—is surely not merely innocent, but laudable;
is not only propriety, but virtue.   You have already, as your
auxiliary, the sober detestation of mankind on the heads of your
opponents; and I swear by the lyre of Thalia, to muster on your
side all the votaries of honest laughter, and fair, candid ridicule.

I am extremely obliged to you for your kind mention of my
interests in a letter which Mr Syme shewed me.   At present, my
situation in life must be in a great measure stationary, at least for
two or three years.   The statement is this—I am on the super-
visors' list, and as we come on there by precedency, in two or three
years I shall be at the head of that list, and be appointed *of course.*
Then, a FRIEND might be of service to me in getting me into a
place of the kingdom which I would like.   A supervisor's income
varies from about a hundred and twenty to two hundred a year;
but the business is an incessant drudgery, and would be nearly a
complete bar to every species of literary pursuit.   The moment I
am appointed supervisor, in the common routine, I may be nomi-
nated on the collector's list; and this is always a business purely
of political patronage.   A collectorship varies much, from better
than two hundred a year to near a thousand.   They also come
forward by precedency on the list; and have, besides a handsome
income, a life of complete leisure.   A life of literary leisure, with
a decent competency, is the summit of my wishes.   It would be
the prudish affectation of silly pride in me to say that I do not
need, or would not be indebted to, a political friend; at the same
time, sir, I by no means lay my affairs before you thus, to hook
my dependent situation on your benevolence.   If, in my progress
of life, an opening should occur where the good offices of a gentle-
man of your public character and political consequence might
bring me forward, I shall petition your goodness with the same
frankness as I now do myself the honour to subscribe myself,

R. B.

CCCXXXI.

TO JOHN SYME, ESQ.

You know that, among other high dignities, you have the
honour to be my supreme court of critical judicature, from which
there is no appeal.   I enclose you a song (*O wat ye*, p. 299) which
I composed since I saw you, and I am going to give you the history
of it.   Do you know that among much that I admire in the char-
acters and manners of those great folks whom I have now the
honour to call my acquaintances,—the Oswald family,—there is

nothing charms me more than Mr Oswald's unconcealable attach
ment to that incomparable woman ? · Did you ever, my dear Syme,
meet with a man who owed more to the Divine Giver of all good
things than Mr O. ?   A fine fortune, a pleasing exterior, self-
evident amiable dispositions, and an ingenuous, upright mind,
and that informed, too, much beyond the usual run of young
fellows of his rank and fortune : and to all this, such a woman !—
but of her I must say nothing at all, in despair of saying anything
adequate.   In my song, I have endeavoured to do justice to what
would be his feelings, on seeing, in the scene I have drawn, the
habitation of his Lucy.   As I am a good deal pleased with my
performance, I, in my first fervour, thought of sending it to Mrs
Oswald, but, on second thoughts, perhaps what I offer as the
honest incense of genuine respect, might, from the well-known
character of poverty and poetry, be construed into some modi-
fication or other of that servility which my soul abhors.   Do let
me know some convenient moment, ere the worthy family leave
the town, that I, *with propriety*, may wait on them.   In the circle
of the fashionable herd, those who come either to show their own
consequence, or to borrow consequence from the visit—in such a
mob I will not appear ; mine is a different errand.   Yours,

                                                ROBᵀ. BURNS.

CCCXXXII.

TO MR THOMSON.

May 1795.

WELL ! this is not amiss (p. 302).   You see how I answer your
orders—your tailor could not be more punctual.   I am just now
in a high fit for poetising, provided that the strait-jacket of criti-
cism don't cure me.   If you can, in a post or two, administer a
little of the intoxicating potion of your applause, it will raise your
humble servant's frenzy to any height you want.   I am at this
moment " holding high converse" with the Muses, and have not
a word to throw away on such a prosaic dog as you are.   R. B.

CCCXXXIII.

TO MR THOMSON.

May 1795.

TEN thousand thanks for your elegant present—though I am
ashamed of the value of it being bestowed on a man who has not,
by any means, merited such an instance of kindness.   I have
shown it to two or three judges of the first abilities here, and they
all agree with me in classing it as a first-rate production.   My

phiz is sae kenspeckle, that the very joiner's apprentice, whom Mrs Burns employed to break up the parcel (I was out of town that day), knew it at once. My most grateful compliments to Allan, who has honoured my rustic Muse so much with his masterly pencil. One strange coincidence is, that the little one who is making the felonious attempt on the cat's tail, is the most striking likeness of an ill-deedie, wee, rumble-gairie urchin of mine, whom, from that propensity to witty wickedness, and manfu' mischief, which, even at twa days auld, I foresaw would form the striking features of his disposition, I named Willie Nicol, after a certain friend of mine, who is one of the masters of a grammar-school in a city which shall be nameless. Several people think that Allan's likeness of me is more striking than Nasmyth's, for which I sat to him half-a-dozen times. However, there is an artist of considerable merit just now in this town, who has hit the most remarkable likeness of what I am at this moment, that I think ever was taken of anybody. It is a small miniature, and as it will be in your town getting itself be-crystallized, &c., I have some thoughts of suggesting to you to prefix a vignette taken from it to my song, *Contented wi' Little and Canty wi' Mair*, in order that the portrait of my face and the picture of my mind may go down the stream of time together.

Give the enclosed epigram to my much-valued friend Cunningham, and tell him, that on Wednesday I go to visit a friend of his, to whom his friendly partiality in speaking of me in a manner introduced me—I mean a well-known military and literary character, Colonel Dirom.

You do not tell me how you liked my two last songs. Are they condemned ?

R. B.

CCCXXXIV.

TO MRS DUNLOP.

15th December 1795.

MY DEAR FRIEND,—As I am in a complete Decemberish humour, gloomy, sullen, stupid, as even the Deity of Dullness herself could wish, I shall not drawl out a heavy letter with a number of heavier apologies for my late silence. Only one I shall mention, because I know you will sympathize in it : these four months, a sweet little girl, my youngest child, has been so ill, that every day, a week or less threatened to terminate her existence. There had much need be many pleasures annexed to the states of husband and father, for they have many peculiar cares. I cannot describe to you the anxious, sleepless hours these ties frequently give me. I see a train of helpless little folks—me and my exertions all their stay ; and on what a brittle thread does the life of man hang ! If I am nipt off at the command of fate, even in all the vigour of manhood, as I am—such things happen every day—what would become of my little flock? 'Tis here that I envy your people of fortune. A father on his death-bed, taking an everlasting leave of his children, has indeed woe enough ; but the man of competent fortune leaves his sons and daughters independency and friends while I—— But I shall run distracted if I think any longer on the subject

24th December.

We have had a brilliant theatre here this season; only, as all other business does, it experiences a stagnation of trade from the epidemical complaint of the country—*want of cash*. I mentioned our theatre merely to lug in an occasional Address, which I wrote for the benefit of one of the actresses, which is as follows (p. 180).

25th, Christmas Morning.

This, my much-loved friend, is a morning of wishes; accept mine—so Heaven hear me as they are sincere!—that blessings may attend your steps, and affliction know you not! In the charming words of my favourite author, The " Man of Feeling"— " May the Great Spirit bear up the weight of thy gray hairs, and blunt the arrow that brings them rest !"

Now that I talk of authors, how do you like Cowper? Is not the *Task* a glorious poem ! The religion of the *Task*, bating a few scraps of Calvinistic divinity, is the religion of God and Nature —the religion that exalts, that ennobles man. Were not you to send me your *Zeluco*, in return for mine? Tell me how you like my marks and notes through the book. I would not give a farthing for a book unless I were at liberty to blot it with my criticisms.

I have lately collected, for a friend's perusal, all my letters—I mean those which I first sketched, in a rough draught, and afterwards wrote out fair. On looking over some old musty papers, which from time to time I had parcelled by as trash that was scarce worth preserving, and which yet, at the same time, I did not care to destroy, I discovered many of these rude sketches, and have written, and am writing them out, in a bound MS. for my friend's library. As I wrote always to you the rapsody of the moment, I cannot find a single scroll to you, except one, about the commencement of our acquaintance. If there were any possible conveyance, I would send you a perusal of my book.   R. B.

———

CCCXXXV.

TO MRS RIDDEL.

DUMFRIES, 20th January 1796.

I CANNOT express my gratitude to you for allowing me a longer perusal of *Anacharsis*. In fact, I never met with a book that bewitched me so much ; and I, as a member of the library, must warmly feel the obligation you have laid us under. Indeed, to me the obligation is stronger than to any other individual of our society ; as *Anacharsis* is an indispensible desideratum to a son of the Muses.

The health you wished me in your morning's card is, I think, flown from me for ever. I have not been able to leave my bed to-day till about an hour ago. These wickedly unlucky advertise-ments I lent (I did wrong) to a friend, and I am ill able to go in quest of him.

The Muses have not quite forsaken me. The following de-tached stanzas I intend to interweave in some disastrous tale of a shepherd. R. B.

CCCXXXVI.

TO MRS DUNLOP.

DUMFRIES, 31*st January* 1796.

THESE many months you have been two packets in my debt— what sin of ignorance I have committed against so highly valued a friend, I am utterly at a loss to guess. Alas! madam, ill can I afford, at this time, to be deprived of any of the small remnant of my pleasures. I have lately drunk deep of the cup of affliction. The autumn robbed me of my only daughter and darling child, and that at a distance, too, and so rapidly, as to put it out of my power to pay the last duties to her. I had scarcely begun to re-cover from that shock, when I became myself the victim of a most severe rheumatic fever, and long the die spun doubtful ; until, after many weeks of a sick-bed, it seems to have turned up life, and I am beginning to crawl across my room, and once indeed have been before my own door in the street.

> When pleasure fascinates the mental sight,
> Affliction purifies the visual ray,
> Religion hails the drear, the untried night,
> And shuts, for ever shuts! life's doubtful day.

R. B.

CCCXXXVII.

TO MR THOMSON.

February 1796.

MANY thanks, my dear sir, for your handsome, elegant present to Mrs Burns, and for my remaining volume of P. Pindar. Peter is a delightful fellow, and a first favourite of mine. I am much pleased with your idea of publishing a collection of our songs in

octavo, with etchings. I am extremely willing to lend every as-
sistance in my power. The Irish airs I shall cheerfully under-
take the task of finding verses for.

I have already, you know, equipt three with words, and the
other day I strung up a kind of rhapsody to another Hibernian
melody which I admire much (*Hey for a Lass*, p. 306).

If this will do, you have now four of my Irish engagement. In
my by-past songs I dislike one thing—the name Chloris; I meant
it as the fictitious name of a certain lady; but, on second thoughts,
it is a high incongruity to have a Greek appellation to a Scottish
pastoral ballad. Of this, and some things else, in my next: I
have more amendments to propose. What you once mentioned of
" flaxen locks" is just; they cannot enter into an elegant descrip-
tion of beauty. Of this also again—God bless you!   R. B.

CCCXXXVIII.

TO MR THOMSON.

April 1796.

ALAS! my dear Thomson, I fear it will be some time ere I tune
my lyre again! " By Babel streams I have sat and wept" almost
ever since I wrote you last. I have only known existence by the
pressure of the heavy hand of sickness, and have counted time by
the repercussions of pain! Rheumatism, cold, and fever, have
formed to me a terrible combination. I close my eyes in misery,
and open them without hope. I look on the vernal day, and say,
with poor Fergusson—

> " Say, wherefore has an all-indulgent Heaven
> Light to the comfortless and wretched given?"

This will be delivered to you by a Mrs Hyslop, landlady of the
Globe Tavern here, which for these many years has been my
howff, and where our friend Clarke and I have had many a merry
squeeze. I mention this, because she will be a very proper hand
to bring that seal you talk of. I am highly delighted with Mr
Allan's etchings. *Woo'd an' married an' a'*, is admirable! The
grouping is beyond all praise. The expression of the figures
conformable to the story in the ballad, is absolutely faultless per-
fection. I next admire *Turnimspike*. What I like least is *Jenny
said to Jocky*. Besides the female being in her appearance quite
a virago, if you take her stooping into the account, she is at least
two inches taller than her lover. Poor Cleghorn! I sincerely
sympathise with him. Happy I am to think that he has a well-
grounded hope of health and enjoyment in this world. Farewell.

R. B.

CCCXXXIX.

TO MR THOMSON.

[*May* 17, 1796.]

MY DEAR SIR,—I once mentioned to you an air which I have long admired—*Here's a health to them that's awa, hiney*, but I forget if you took any notice of it. I have just been trying to suit it with verses, and I beg leave to recommend the air to your attention once more. I have only begun it (p. 307).

This will be delivered by a Mr Lewars, a young fellow of uncommon merit; indeed, by far the cleverest fellow I have met with in this part of the world. His only fault is D-m-cratic heresy. As he will be a day or two in town, you will have leisure, if you choose, to write me by him; and if you have a spare half hour to spend with him, I shall place your kindness to my account. I have no copies of the songs I have sent you, and I have taken a fancy to review them all, and possibly may mend some of them: so, when you have complete leisure, I will thank you for either the originals or copies. I had rather be the author of five well-written songs than of ten otherwise. I have great hopes that the genial influence of the approaching summer will set me to rights, but as yet I cannot boast of returning health. I have now reason to believe that my complaint is a flying gout—a sad business!

Do let me know how Cleghorn is, and remember me to him.

This should have been delivered to you a month ago, but my friend's trunk miscarried, and was not recovered till he came here again. I am still very poorly, but should like much to hear from you. R. B.

CCCXL.

TO MRS RIDDEL.

DUMFRIES, 4*th June* 1796.

I AM in such miserable health, as to be utterly incapable of shewing my loyalty in any way. Racked as I am with rheumatisms, I meet every face with a greeting, like that of Balak to Balaam—" Come, curse me, Jacob; and come, defy me, Israel!" So say I : Come, curse me, that east wind; and come, defy me the north! Would you have me in such circumstances copy you out a love-song?

I may perhaps see you on Saturday, but I will not be at the ball. Why should I ?—" Man delights not me, nor woman either!" Can you supply me with the song, *Let us all be unhappy together* ?—do, if you can, and oblige *le pauvre misérable*, R. B.

CCCXLI.
TO MR JAMES CLARKE.
SCHOOLMASTER, FORFAR.

DUMFRIES, *26th June* 1796.

My DEAR CLARKE,—Still, still the victim of affliction! Were you to see the emaciated figure who now holds the pen to you, you would not know your old friend. Whether I shall ever get about again, is only known to Him, the Great Unknown, whose creature I am. Alas, Clarke! I begin to fear the worst. As to my individual self, I am tranquil, and would despise myself if I were not; but Burns's poor widow, and half-a-dozen of his dear little ones—helpless orphans!—there I am weak as a woman's tear. Enough of this! 'Tis half of my disease.

I duly received your last, enclosing the (pound) note. It came extremely in time, and I am much obliged by your punctuality. Again I must request you to do me the same kindness. Be so very good as, *by return of post*, to enclose me another note. I trust you can do it without inconvenience, and it will seriously oblige me. If I must go, I shall leave a few friends behind me, whom I shall regret while consciousness remains. I know I shall live in their remembrance. Adieu, dear Clarke. That I shall ever see you again is, I am afraid, highly improbable. R. B.

CCCXLII.
TO MR JAMES JOHNSON, EDINBURGH.

DUMFRIES, *4th July* 1796.

How are you, my dear friend, and how comes on your fifth volume? You may probably think that for some time past I have neglected you and your work; but, alas! the hand of pain and sorrow, and care, has these many months lain heavy on me. Personal and domestic affliction have almost entirely banished that alacrity and life with which I used to woo the rural Muse of Scotia.

You are a good, worthy, honest fellow, and have a good right to live in this world—because you deserve it. Many a merry meeting this publication has given us, and possibly it may give us more, though, alas! I fear it. This protracting, slow, consuming illness which hangs over me, will, I doubt much, my ever-dear friend, arrest my sun before he has well reached his middle career, and will turn over the poet to far more important concerns than studying the brilliancy of wit or the pathos of sentiment. However, *hope* is the cordial of the human heart, and I endeavour to cherish it as well as I can.

Let me hear from you as soon as convenient. Your work is a great one ; and now that it is finished, I see, if we were to begin again, two or three things that might be mended ; yet I will venture to prophesy, that to future ages your publication will be the text-book and standard of Scottish song and music.

I am ashamed to ask another favour of you, because you have been so very good already ; but my wife has a very particular friend of hers, a young lady who sings well, to whom she wishes to present the *Scots Musical Museum.* If you have a spare copy, will you be so obliging as to send it by the very first *fly*, as I am anxious to have it soon ? Yours ever, R. B.

CCXLIII.

TO MR GEORGE THOMSON.

Brow, *4th July.*

My dear Sir,—I received your songs ; but my health is so precarious, nay, dangerously situated, that as a last effort I am here at sea-bathing quarters. Besides my inveterate rheumatism, my appetite is quite gone, and I am so emaciated as to be scarce able to support myself on my own legs. Alas! is this a time for me to woo the Muses ? However, I am still anxiously willing to serve your work, and, if possible, shall try. I would not like to see another employed, unless you could lay your hand upon a poet whose productions would be equal to the rest. You will see my remarks and alterations on the margin of each song. My address is still Dumfries. Farewell, and God bless you !

R. Burns.

CCCXLIV.

TO MR CUNNINGHAM.

Brow, *Sea-bathing Quarters, 7th July* 1796.

My dear Cunningham,—I received yours here this moment, and am indeed highly flattered with the approbation of the literary circle you mention—a literary circle inferior to none in the two kingdoms. Alas! my friend, I fear the voice of the bard will soon be heard among you no more. For these eight or ten months, I have been ailing, sometimes bedfast, and sometimes not ; but these last three months I have been tortured with an excruciating rheumatism, which has reduced me to nearly the last stage. You actually would not know me if you saw me. Pale, emaciated, and so feeble as occasionally to need help from my chair—my spirits fled! fled!—but I can no more on the subject ; only the medical folks tell me that my last and only chance is bathing, and country quarters, and riding. The worst of the

matter is this : when an exciseman is off duty, his salary is re-
duced to L.35 instead of L.50.   What way, in the name of thrift,
shall I maintain myself, and keep a horse in country quarters,
with a wife and five children at home, on L.35 ?   I mention this,
because I had intended to beg your utmost interest, and that of
all the friends you can muster, to move our commissioners of
Excise to grant me the full salary ; I daresay you know them all
personally.   If they do not grant it me, I must lay my account
with an exit truly *en poëte*—if I die not of disease, I must perish
with hunger.

I have sent you one of the songs ; the other my memory does
not serve me with, and I have no copy here ; but I shall be at
home soon, when I will send it you.   Apropos to being at home
Mrs Burns threatens in a week or two to add one more to my
paternal charge, which, if of the right gender, I intend shall be
introduced to the world by the respectable designation of *Alexander
Cunningham Burns*.   My last was *James Glencairn*, so you can
have no objection to the company of nobility.   Farewell !   R. B.

CCCXLV.
TO MR GILBERT BURNS.

Sunday, 10th July 1796.

DEAR BROTHER,—It will be no very pleasing news to you to
be told that I am dangerously ill, and not likely to get better
An inveterate rheumatism has reduced me to such a state of de-
bility, and my appetite is so totally gone, that I can scarcely
stand on my legs.   I have been a week at sea-bathing, and I will
continue there, or in a friend's house in the country, all the sum-
mer.   God keep my wife and children ; if I am taken from their
head, they will be poor indeed.   I have contracted one or two
serious debts, partly from my illness these many months, partly
from too much thoughtlessness as to expense when I came to
town, that will cut in too much on the little I leave them in your
hands.   Remember me to my mother.   Yours,   R. B.

CCCXLVI.
TO MRS DUNLOP.

BROW, *12th July* 1796

MADAM,—I have written you so often, without receiving any
answer, that I would not trouble you again, but for the circum-
stances in which I am.   An illness which has long hung about
me, in all probability will speedily send me beyond that *bourn
whence no traveller returns*.   Your friendship, with which, for many
years you honoured me, was a friendship dearest to my soul.
Your conversation, and especially your correspondence, were at

once highly entertaining and instructive. With what pleasure did I use to break up the seal! The remembrance yet adds one pulse more to my poor palpitating heart. Farewell!!! R. B.

CCCXLVII.

TO MR JAMES BURNES,

WRITER, MONTROSE.

DUMFRIES, 12th July.

MY DEAR COUSIN,—When you offered me money assistance, little did I think I should want it so soon. A rascal of a haberdasher, to whom I owe a considerable bill, taking it into his head that I am dying, has commenced a process against me, and will infallibly put my emaciated body into jail.* Will you be so good as to accommodate me, and that by return of post, with ten pounds? Oh, James! did you know the pride of my heart, you would feel doubly for me! Alas! I am not used to beg. The worst of it is, my health was coming about finely. You know, and my physician assured me, that melancholy and low spirits are half my disease—guess, then, my horrors since this business began. If I had it settled, I would be, I think, quite well in a manner. How shall I use the language to you—oh, do not disappoint me! but strong necessity's command.

I have been thinking over and over my brother's affairs, and I fear I must cut him up; but on this I will correspond at another time, particularly as I shall [require] your advice.

Forgive me for once more mentioning by return of post—save me from the horrors of a jail!

My compliments to my friend James, and to all the rest. I do not know what I have written. The subject is so horrible, I dare not look it over again. Farewell! R. B.

CCCXLVIII.

TO MR THOMSON.

BROW, on the Solway Frith, 12th July 1796.

AFTER all my boasted independence, necessity compels me to implore you for five pounds. A cruel scoundrel of a haberdasher, to whom I owe an account, taking into his head that I am dying, has commenced a process, and will infallibly put me into jail. Do, for God's sake, send me that sum, and that by return of post. Forgive me this earnestness; but the horrors of a jail have made me half distracted. I do not ask all this gratuitously; for, upon

* There is no reason to suppose Burns was threatened with being put in jail; he was only written to by a lawyer for payment of an old debt, and, in his excitable state, he took this view of the application.

returning health, I hereby promise and engage to furnish you
with five pounds' worth of the neatest song-genius you have seen.
I tried my hand on *Rothemurchie* this morning.   The measure is
so difficult, that it is impossible to infuse much genius into the
lines ; they are on the other side (p. 308).   Forgive, forgive me !
R. B.

CCCXLIX.
TO JAMES GRACIE, ESQ.
BROW, *Wednesday morning,* [*13th July.*]

MY DEAR SIR—It would [be] doing high injustice to this place
not to acknowledge that my rheumatisms have derived great bene-
fits from it already ; but alas ! my loss of appetite still continues.
I shall not need your kind offer *this week,* and I return to town
the beginning of next week, it not being a tide-week.   I am de-
taining a man in a burning hurry.   So, God bless you !   R. B.

CCCL.
TO MRS BURNS.
BROW, *Thursday.*

MY DEAREST LOVE,—I delayed writing until I could tell you
what effect sea-bathing was likely to produce.   It would be injustice
to deny that it has eased my pains, and I think has strengthened
me ; but my appetite is still extremely bad.   No flesh nor fish can
I swallow ; porridge and milk are the only thing I can taste.   I
am very happy to hear, by Miss Jess Lewars, that you are all
well.   My very best and kindest compliments to her, and to all
the children.   I will see you on Sunday.   Your affectionate hus-
band,   R. B.

CCCLI.
TO MR JAMES ARMOUR, MAUCHLINE.*
DUMFRIES, *18th July* 1796.

MY DEAR SIR,—Do, for Heaven's sake, send Mrs Armour
here immediately.   My wife is hourly expecting to be put to bed.
What a situation for her to be in, poor girl, without a friend !   I
returned from sea-bathing quarters to-day, and my medical friends
would almost persuade me that I am better ; but I think and feel
that my strength is so gone, that the disorder will prove fatal to
me.   Your son-in-law,   R. B.

* Supposed to be the last letter or composition written by Burns: he died on the
21st.

BURNS' AUTOBIOGRAPHY.

TO DR MOORE.

MAUCHLINE, 2d August 1787.

SIR,—For some months past I have been rambling over the country, but I am now confined with some lingering complaints, originating, as I take it, in the stomach. To divert my spirits a little in this miserable fog of *ennui*, I have taken a whim to give you a history of myself. My name has made some little noise in this country—you have done me the honour to interest yourself very warmly in my behalf; and I think a faithful account of what character of a man I am, and how I came by that character, may perhaps amuse you in an idle moment. I will give you an honest narrative, though I know it will be often at my own expense; for I assure you, sir, I have, like Solomon, whose character, excepting in the trifling affair of *wisdom*, I sometimes think I resemble—I have, I say, like him, *turned my eyes to behold madness and folly*, and, like him, too frequently shaken hands with their intoxicating friendship. * * * After you have perused these pages, should you think them trifling and impertinent, I only beg leave to tell you that the poor author wrote them under some twitching qualms of conscience, arising from suspicion that he was doing what he ought not to do—a predicament he has more than once been in before.

*　　*　　*　　*　　*　　*　　*

I have not the most distant pretensions to assume that character which the pye-coated guardians of escutcheons call a gentleman. When at Edinburgh last winter, I got acquainted in the Herald's Office; and looking through that granary of honours, I there found almost every name in the kingdom; but for me,

> "My ancient but ignoble blood
> Has crept through scoundrels ever since the flood."

Gules, Purpure, Argent, &c., quite disowned me.

My father was of the north of Scotland, the son of a farmer, and was thrown by early misfortunes on the world at large, where, after many years' wanderings and sojournings, he picked up a pretty large quantity of observation and experience, to which 1 am indebted for most of my little pretensions to wisdom. I have met with few who understood *men, their manners, and their ways,* equal to him ; but stubborn, ungainly integrity, and headlong ungovernable irascibility, are disqualifying circumstances ; consequently I was born a very poor man's son. For the first six or seven years of my life, my father was gardener to a worthy gentleman of small estate in the neighbourhood of Ayr. Had he continued in that station, I must have marched off to be one of the little underlings about a farmhouse ; but it was his dearest wish and prayer to have it in his power to keep his children under his own eye till they could discern between good and evil ; so, with the assistance of his generous master, my father ventured on a small farm on his estate. At those years I was by no means a favourite with anybody. I was a good deal noted for a retentive memory, a stubborn sturdy something in my disposition, and an enthusiastic idiot piety. I say *idiot* piety, because I was then but a child. Though it cost the schoolmaster some thrashings, I made an excellent English scholar, and by the time I was ten or eleven years of age, I was a critic in substantives, verbs, and particles. In my infant and boyish days, too, I owed much to an old woman who resided in the family, remarkable for her ignorance, credulity, and superstition. She had, I suppose, the largest collection in the country of tales and songs concerning devils, ghosts, fairies, brownies, witches, warlocks, spunkies, kelpies, elf-candles, dead-lights, wraiths, apparitions, cantraips, giants, enchanted towers, dragons, and other trumpery. This cultivated the latent seeds of poetry, but had so strong an effect on my imagination, that to this hour, in my nocturnal rambles, I sometimes keep a sharp look-out in suspicious places ; and though nobody can be more sceptical than I am in such matters, yet it often takes an effort of philosophy to shake off these idle terrors. The earliest composition that I recollect taking pleasure in was *The Vision of Mirza,* and a hymn of Addison's beginning, " How are thy servants blest, O Lord !" I particularly remember one stanza, which was music to my boyish ear :—

> " For though on dreadful whirls we hung
> High on the broken wave."

I met with these pieces in *Mason's English Collection,* one of my school-books. The two first books I ever read in private, and which gave me more pleasure than any two books I ever read since, were, *The Life of Hannibal,* and *The History of Sir William Wallace.* Hannibal gave my young ideas such a turn, that I used to strut in raptures up and down after the recruiting drum and bagpipe, and wish myself tall enough to be a soldier ; while the story of Wallace poured a Scottish prejudice into my veins, which will boil along there till the floodgates of life shut in eternal rest.

Polemical divinity about this time was putting the country half mad; and I, ambitious of shining in conversation parties on Sundays, between sermons, at funerals, &c., used, a few years afterwards, to puzzle Calvinism with so much heat and indiscretion, that I raised a hue and cry of heresy against me, which has not ceased to this hour.

My vicinity to Ayr was of some advantage to me. My social disposition, when not checked by some modification of spirited pride, was, like our Catechism definition of infinitude, *without bounds or limits*. I formed several connections with other younkers who possessed superior advantages—the *youngling* actors, who were busy in the rehearsal of parts in which they were shortly to appear on the stage of life, where, alas! I was destined to drudge behind the scenes. It is not commonly at this green age that our young gentry have a just sense of the immense distance between them and their ragged playfellows. It takes a few dashes into the world to give the young great man that proper, decent, unnoticing disregard for the poor, insignificant, stupid devils, the mechanics and peasantry around him, who were perhaps born in the same village. My young superiors never insulted the *clouterly* appearance of my plough-boy carcase, the two extremes of which were often exposed to all the inclemencies of all the seasons. They would give me stray volumes of books: among them, even then, I could pick up some observations; and one, whose heart I am sure not even the *Munny Begum* scenes have tainted, helped me to a little French. Parting with these my young friends and benefactors, as they occasionally went off for the East or West Indies, was often to me a sore affliction; but I was soon called to more serious evils. My father's generous master died; the farm proved a ruinous bargain; and to clench the misfortune, we fell into the hands of a factor, who sat for the picture I have drawn of one in my tale of "Twa Dogs." My father was advanced in life when he married; I was the eldest of seven children; and he, worn out by early hardships, was unfit for labour. My father's spirit was soon irritated, but not easily broken. There was a freedom in his lease in two years more; and to weather these two years, we retrenched our expenses. We lived very poorly. I was a dexterous ploughman for my age; and the next eldest to me was a brother (Gilbert) who could drive the plough very well, and help me to thrash the corn. A novel-writer might perhaps have viewed these scenes with some satisfaction, but so did not I; my indignation yet boils at the recollection of the scoundrel factor's insolent threatening letters, which used to set us all in tears.

This kind of life—the cheerless gloom of a hermit, with the unceasing moil of a galley-slave—brought me to my sixteenth year; a little before which period I first committed the sin of rhyme. You know our country custom of coupling a man and woman together as partners in the labours of harvest. In my fifteenth autumn, my partner was a bewitching creature, a year younger than myself. My scarcity of English denies me the power of doing her justice in that language; but you know the Scottish idiom—she was a *bonnie, sweet, sonsie lass.* In short, she altogether, unwittingly to herself, initiated me in that delicious passion which, in spite of acid disappointment, gin-horse prudence, and book-worm philosophy, I hold to be the first of human joys, our dearest blessing here below! How she caught the contagion I cannot tell: you medical people talk much of infection from breathing the same air, the touch, &c., but I never expressly said I loved her. Indeed, I did not know myself why I liked so much to loiter behind with her when returning in the evening from our labours; why the tones of her voice made my heartstrings thrill like an Æolian harp; and particularly why my pulse beat such a furious ratan when I looked and fingered over her little hand to pick out the cruel nettle-stings and thistles. Among her other love-inspiring qualities, she sang sweetly.; and it was her favourite reel to which I attempted to give an embodied vehicle in rhyme. I was not so presumptuous as to imagine that I could make verses like printed ones, composed by men who had Greek and Latin; but my girl sang a song which was said to be composed by a small country laird's son on one of his father's maids with whom he was in love, and I saw no reason why I might not rhyme as well as he; for excepting that he could smear sheep, and cast peats, his father living in the moorlands, he had no more scholar-craft than myself.

Thus with me began love and poetry, which at times have been my only, and till within the last twelve months, have been my highest enjoyment. My father struggled on till he reached the freedom in his lease, when he entered on a large farm, about ten miles farther in the country. The nature of the bargain he made was such as to throw a little ready money into his hands at the commencement of his lease; otherwise the affair would have been impracticable. For four years we lived comfortably here; but a difference commencing between him and his landlord as to terms, after three years' tossing and whirling in the vortex of litigation, my father was just saved from the horrors of a jail by a consumption, which, after two years' promises, kindly stepped in, and carried him away to *where the wicked cease from troubling, and the weary are at rest.*

It is during thet ime that we lived on this farm that my little story is most eventful. I was, at the beginning of this period, perhaps the most ungainly, awkward boy in the parish—no *solitaire* was less acquainted with the ways of the world. What I knew of ancient story was gathered from *Salmon's and Guthrie's Geográghical Grammars;* and the ideas I had formed of modern

manners, of literature and criticism, I got from the *Spectator.*
These, with *Pope's Works,* some plays of *Shakspeare, Tull and
Dickson on Agriculture, the Pantheon, Locke's Essay on the Human
Understanding, Stackhouse's History of the Bible, Justice's British
Gardener's Directory, Bayle's Lectures, Allan Ramsay's Works,
Taylor's Scripture Doctrine of Original Sin, A Select Collection of
English Songs,* and *Hervey's Meditations,* had formed the whole of
my reading. The collection of songs was my *vade mecum.* I
pored over them driving my cart, or walking to labour, song by
song, verse by verse—carefully noting the true, tender, or sublime,
from affectation and fustian. I am convinced I owe to this prac-
tice much of my critic craft, such as it is.

In my seventeenth year, to give my manners a brush, I went
to a country dancing-school. My father had an unaccountable
antipathy against these meetings, and my going was, what to this
moment I repent, in opposition to his wishes. My father, as I
said before, was subject to strong passions; from that instance of
disobedience in me he took a sort of dislike to me, which I believe
was one cause of the dissipation which marked my succeeding
years. I say dissipation, comparatively with the strictness, and
sobriety and regularity of Presbyterian country life; for though
the Will-o'-Wisp meteors of thoughtless whim were almost the
sole lights of my path, yet early-ingrained piety and virtue kept
me for several years afterwards within the line of innocence.
The great misfortune of my life was to want an aim. I had felt
early some stirrings of ambition, but they were the blind gropings
of Homer's Cyclops round the walls of his cave. I saw my
father's situation entailed on me perpetual labour. The only two
openings by which I could enter the temple of fortune was, the
gate of niggardly economy, or the path of little chicaning bargain-
making. The first is so contracted an aperture, I never could
squeeze myself into it; the last I always hated—there was con-
tamination in the very entrance! Thus, abandoned of aim or
view in life, with a strong appetite for sociability, as well from
native hilarity as from a pride of observation and remark; a
constitutional melancholy or hypochondriasm that made me fly to
solitude; add to these incentives to social life my reputation for
bookish knowledge, a certain wild logical talent, and a strength
of thought, something like the rudiments of good sense, and it
will not seem surprising that I was generally a welcome guest
where I visited, or any great wonder that always where two or
three met together, there was I among them. But far beyond all
other impulses of my heart, was *un penchant à l'adorable moitié
du genre humain.* My heart was completely tinder, and was
eternally lighted up by some goddess or other; and as in every
other warfare in this world, my fortune was various, sometimes I
was received with favour, and sometimes I was mortified with a

repulse. At the plough, scythe, or reap-hook, I feared no compe-
titor, and thus I set absolute want at defiance ; and as I never
cared farther for my labours than while I was in actual exercise,
I spent the evenings in the way after my own heart. A country
lad seldom carries on a love adventure without an assisting con-
fidant. I possessed a curiosity, zeal, and intrepid dexterity that
recommended me as a proper second on these occasions ; and I
daresay I felt as much pleasure in being in the secret of half the
loves of the parish of Torbolton, as ever did statesman in knowing
the intrigues of half the courts of Europe. The very goose feather
in my hand seems to know instinctively the well-worn path of my
imagination, the favourite theme of my song, and is with difficulty
restrained from giving you a couple of paragraphs on the love ad-
ventures of my compeers, the humble inmates of the farmhouse
and cottage ; but the grave sons of science, ambition, or avarice
baptise these things by the name of follies. To the sons and
daughters of labour and poverty they are matters of the most
serious nature ; to them the ardent hope, the stolen interview, the
tender farewell, are the greatest and most delicious parts of their
enjoyments.

Another circumstance in my life which made some alteration
in my mind and manners was, that I spent my nineteenth summer
on a smuggling coast, a good distance from home, at a noted
school, to learn mensuration, surveying, dialling, &c., in which I
made a pretty good progress. But I made a greater progress in
the knowledge of mankind. The contraband trade was at that
time very successful, and it sometimes happened to me to fall in
with those who carried it on. Scenes of swaggering riot and
roaring dissipation were till this time new to me ; but I was no
enemy to social life. Here, though I learnt to fill my glass, and
to mix without fear in a drunken squabble, yet I went on with a
high hand with my geometry, till the sun entered Virgo, a month
which is always a carnival in my bosom, when a charming *fillette*
who lived next door to the school, overset my trigonometry, and
set me off at a tangent from the sphere of my studies. I, however,
struggled on with my *sines* and *co-sines* for a few days more ; but
stepping into the garden one charming noon to take the sun's
altitude, there I met my angel,

> " Like Proserpine gathering flowers,
> Herself a fairer flower."

It was in vain to think of doing any more good at school. The
remaining week I stayed, I did nothing but craze the faculties of
my soul about her, or steal out to meet her ; and the two last
nights of my stay in the country, had sleep been a mortal sin, the
image of this modest and innocent girl had kept me guiltless.

I returned home very considerably improved. My reading was
enlarged with the very important addition of Thomson's and

Shenstone's works. I had seen human nature in a new phasis; and I engaged several of my schoolfellows to keep up a literary correspondence with me. This improved me in composition. I had met with a collection of letters by the wits of Queen Anne's reign, and I poured over them most devoutly : I kept copies of any of my own letters that pleased me ; and a comparison between them and the composition of most of my correspondents flattered my vanity. I carried this whim so far, that though I had not three farthings' worth of business in the world, yet almost every post brought me as many letters as if I had been a broad plodding son of day-book and ledger.

My life flowed on much in the same course till my twenty-third year. *Vive l'amour, et vive la bagatelle*, were my sole principles of action. The addition of two more authors to my library gave me great pleasure ; Sterne and M'Kenzie—*Tristram Shandy* and *The Man of Feeling*—were my bosom favourites. Poesy was still a darling walk for my mind, but it was only indulged in according to the humour of the hour. I had usually half-a-dozen or more pieces on hand ; I took up one or other, as it suited the momentary tone of the mind, and dismissed the work as it bordered on fatigue. My passions, when once lighted up, raged like so many devils, till they got vent in rhyme ; and then the conning over my verses, like a spell, soothed all into quite ! None of the rhymes of those days are in print, except *Winter, a dirge*, the eldest of my printed pieces ; *The Death of Poor Mailie, John Barleycorn*, and songs first, second, and third. Song second was the ebullition of that passion which ended the forementioned school-business.

My twenty-third year was to me an important era. Partly through whim, and partly that I wished to set about doing something in life, I joined a flax-dresser in a neighbouring town (Irvine) to learn his trade. This was an unlucky affair, and, to finish the whole, as we were giving a welcome carousal to the New-Year, the shop took fire and burnt to ashes, and I was left like a true poet, not worth a sixpence.

I was obliged to give up this scheme. The clouds of misfortune were gathering thick round my father's head ; and, what was worst of all, he was visibly far gone in a consumption ; and, to crown my distresses, a *belle fille* whom I adored, and who had pledged her soul to meet me in the field of matrimony, jilted me, with peculiar circumstances of mortification. The finishing evil that brought up the rear of this infernal file, was my constitutional melancholy being increased to such a degree, that for three months I was in a state of mind scarcely to be envied by the hopeless wretches who have got their mittimus—*Depart from me, ye accursed !*

From this adventure I learned something of a town life ; but the principal thing which gave my mind a turn, was a friendship I formed with a young fellow, a very noble character, but a hapless son of misfortune. He was the son of a simple mechanic; but a great man in the neighbourhood taking him under his patronage, gave him a genteel education, with a view of bettering his situation in life. The patron dying just as he was ready to launch out into the world, the poor fellow in despair went to sea, where, after a variety of good and ill fortune, a little before I was acquainted with him, he had been sent on shore by an American privateer on the wild coast of Connaught, stripped of everything. I cannot quit this poor fellow's story without adding that he is at this time master of a large West Indiaman belonging to the Thames.

His mind was fraught with independence, magnanimity, and every manly virtue. I loved and admired him to a degree of enthusiasm, and of course strove to imitate him. In some measure I succeeded. I had pride before, but he taught it to flow in proper channels. His knowledge of the world was vastly superior to mine, and I was all attention to learn. He was the only man I ever saw who was a greater fool than myself where woman was the presiding star; but he spoke of illicit love with the levity of a sailor, which hitherto I had regarded with horror. Here his friendship did me a mischief; and the consequence was, that soon after I resumed the plough, I wrote the *Poet's Welcome*. My reading only increased, while in this town, by two stray volumes of *Pamela*, and one of *Ferdinand Count Fathom*, which gave me some idea of novels. Rhyme, except some religious pieces that are in print, I had given up; but meeting with *Fergusson's Scottish Poems*, I strung anew my wildly-sounding lyre with emulating vigour. When my father died, his all went among the hounds that prowl in the kennel of justice; but we made a shift to collect a little money in the family amongst us, with which, to keep us together, my brother and I took a neighbouring farm. My brother wanted my hairbrained imagination, as well as my social and amorous madness; but in good sense, and every sober qualification, he was far my superior.

I entered on this farm with a full resolution, *Come, go to, I will be wise!* I read farming books—I calculated crops—I attended markets, and, in short, in spite of *the devil, and the world, and the flesh*, I believe I should have been a wise man; but the first year, from unfortunately buying bad seed, the second, from a late harvest, we lost half our crops. This overset all my wisdom, and I returned, *like the dog to his vomit, and the sow that was washed, to her wallowing in the mire.*

I now began to be known in the neighbourhood as a maker of rhymes. The first of my poetic offspring that saw the light was a burlesque lamentation on a quarrel between two reverend Calvinists, both of them *dramatis personæ* in my *Holy Fair.*

I had a notion myself that the piece had some merit; but to prevent the worst, I gave a copy of it to a friend who was very fond of such things, and told him that I could not guess who was the author of it, but that I thought it pretty clever. With a certain description of the clergy, as well as laity, it met with a roar of applause. *Holy Willie's Prayer* next made its appearance, and alarmed the kirk-session so much, that they held several meetings to look over their spiritual artillery, if haply any of it might be pointed against profane rhymers. Unluckily for me, my wanderings led me on another side, within point-blank shot of their heaviest metal. This is the unfortunate story that gave rise to my printed poem, *The Lament*. This was a most melancholy affair, which I cannot yet bear to reflect on, and had very nearly given me one or two of the principal qualifications for a place among those who have lost the chart and mistaken the reckoning of rationality. I gave up my part of the farm to my brother—in truth it was only nominally mine—and made what little preparation was in my power for Jamaica. But before leaving my native country for ever, I resolved to publish my poems. I weighed my productions as impartially as was in my power : I thought they had merit; and it was a delicious idea that I should be called a clever fellow, even though it should never reach my ears—a poor negro-driver; or, perhaps, a victim to that inhospitable clime, and gone to the world of spirits. I can truly say that *pauvre inconnu* as I then was, I had pretty nearly as high an idea of myself and of my works as I have at this moment, when the public has decided in their favour. It never was my opinion that the mistakes and blunders, both in a rational and religious point of view, of which we see thousands daily guilty, are owing to their ignorance of themselves. To know myself had been all along my constant study. I weighed myself alone—I balanced myself with others—I watched every means of information, to see how much ground I occupied as a man and as a poet—I studied assiduously Nature's design in my formation—where the lights and shades in my character were intended. I was pretty confident my poems would meet with some applause; but, at the worst, the roar of the Atlantic would deafen the voice of censure, and the novelty of West Indian scenes make me forget neglect. I threw off six hundred copies, of which I had got subscriptions for about three hundred and fifty. My vanity was highly gratified by the reception I met with from the public; and besides, I pocketed, all expenses deducted, nearly twenty pounds. This sum came very seasonably, as I was thinking of indenting myself, for want of money, to procure my passage. As soon as I was master of nine guineas, the price of wafting me to the torrid zone, I took a steerage passage in the first ship that was to sail from the Clyde; for

" Hungry ruin had me in the wind."

I had been for some days skulking from covert to covert, under all the terrors of a jail : as some ill-advised people had uncoupled the merciless pack of the law at my heels. I had taken the last farewell of my friends ; my chest was on the road to Greenock ; I had composed the last song I should ever measure in Caledonia—*The Gloomy Night is Gathering Fast*—when a letter from Dr Blacklock to a friend of mine overthrew all my schemes, by opening new prospects to my poetic ambition. The doctor belonged to a set of critics for whose applause I had not dared to hope. His opinion that I would meet with encouragement in Edinburgh for a second edition, fired me so much, that away I posted for that city, without a single acquaintance, or a single letter of introduction. The baneful star that had so long shed its blasting influence in my zenith, for once made a revolution to the nadir ; and a kind Providence placed me under the patronage of one of the noblest of men—the Earl of Glencairn. *Oublie moi, Grand Dieu, si jamais je l'oublie !*

I need relate no farther. At Edinburgh I was in a new world ; I mingled among many classes of men, but all of them new to me, and I was all attention to *catch* the characters and *the manners living as they rise.* Whether I have profited, time will show. . .

Made in the USA
Las Vegas, NV
15 September 2021